*Wilton* **Inspiration for Every Celebration!**

Dear Friend,

A first birthday party is an event parents remember forever. It's a day that brings the whole family together to celebrate. Of course, a cake is at the center of all the fun. Watching the birthday boy or girl dive into their very own cake is the highlight of the day. You'll be looking at those pictures and sharing the memories for years.

To create the perfect first birthday celebration, start with the 2010 Wilton Yearbook. Our special section, *First Birthday Bash!*, is filled with irresistible decorating ideas that put a fun new spin on favorite toddler themes. Our cover cake, "Birthday on the Bounty", shows what the excitement is all about. This thrilling pirate ship sails through waves of fondant with a jolly crew, a colorful parrot, and a Happy Birthday greeting flying from the mainsail! It's part of a complete party scene with matching cupcakes, cereal treats and a treasure chest smash cake for the little one. Every treat works together to set the tone for a fantastic celebration.

There are many more first birthday surprises in store, from Noah's Ark to a jungle journey. Your guests will love our "bathday party" too, with flocks of rubber ducky cupcakes and a bubbly birthday cake with a giant stand-up duck on top. Find more amazing cake ideas at our website, www.wilton.com. It's the best place on the Internet to find inspiration for your party. You can even post photos and share memories of your family's first birthday bash.

The 2010 Yearbook is also filled with birthday and holiday fun for all ages. We've created 2 incredible multi-level cakes on our 3-Tier Party Stand—a delightful miniature golf course with twisting fairway ramps connecting the tiers and a whirling waterslide with candy boats riding through the cascades. Cakes like these are sure to get the conversation started at any party. This year, we're also dressing up brownies for your seasonal celebrations. Using our new Brownie Pops mold, it's easy to decorate melting witches, festive reindeer and Easter bunnies that stand up on everyone's plate.

With our largest collection of signature wedding cakes in history, plus an expanded product section and Decorating Guide, there is more than ever to discover in this 2010 Yearbook. Be sure to keep it handy as you plan a year full of outstanding celebrations and special moments with your family.

Marvin Oakes

Marvin Oakes
President
Wilton Enterprises

Wilton CAKE DECORATING

Wish Upon a Star! .... p. 24

The characters every kid wants to be seen with are here! Action-packed Transformers treats, featuring Optimus Prime in a blaze of color. Enchanting Tinker Bell, hosting the party at her candy teapot treehouse. Topping the bill, it's Hannah Montana, with a star-sparkled cake and cookies in electric colors—it's a "Happy Birthday" hit!

Big Time Birthdays! .... p. 4

Celebrate the big day in an unforgetable way! Find exciting all-ages designs like the colossal cupcake stack, bright with dazzling fondant decorations. Plus, party themes kids love—pirates, pink ponies, brownie space aliens and ballerinas. What more could anyone wish for?

Exceptional Events .... p. 64

Celebrate your proudest moments with decorated desserts you'll be proud to serve. Delightful theme designs pull it all together, including baby feet and rubber duckies for the shower, candy caps and diplomas for the grad.

Savor Every Season .... p. 38

What a year you'll have! From Halloween tricks and treats around a creepy color flow haunted house cake to a candy basket of bright spring flowers, we'll help you capture the color and fun with exciting desserts month after month.

Big Time Birthdays!

This party doesn't need noisemakers. Your cake will do the shouting—along with all of your guests. Wait until they see our miniature golf course, built on the 3-Tier Party Stand, with cookie golfers playing on fairway ramps which connect each tier. You can rock your little guy's world with rocking horse cakes and cereal treats, plus cookie-topped trucks and airplanes. For girls, look for pink ponies, bold bug brownies and a magical princess Wonder Mold cake. Here, it's a birthday blast for any age, with a gathering of gift cakes exploding with colorful fondant ribbons and balloons. When you gear your goodies toward your birthday star, the fun begins!

Can't Contain Our Excitement!

Pans: 6, 8 x 2 in. Square, p. 157

Tips: 1, 3, p. 136

Colors:* Lemon Yellow, Royal Blue, Leaf Green, Orange, Rose, Violet, Red-Red, Christmas Red, p. 148

Fondant: White Ready-To-Use Rolled Fondant (192 oz.), Gum-Tex, p. 149; Brush Set, Easy-Glide Fondant Smoother, p.151; Fondant Ribbon Cutter/Embosser Set, p. 152; 20 in. Rolling Pin, Roll & Cut Mat, Happy Birthday Fondant Imprint Mat, p. 150

Recipe: Buttercream Icing, p. 118

Also: 101 Cookie Cutters (letters), p. 203; White Candy Melts, p. 196; 8 in. Lollipop Sticks, p. 200; Piping Gel, p. 145; Red Colored Sugar, p. 146; 9 in. Crystal-Clear Twist Legs, 6 in. Crystal-Clear Cake Plate, p. 239; Wooden Dowel Rods, p. 240; Cake Boards, Fanci-Foil Wrap, p. 241; scissors, ruler, cornstarch, curling ribbon (blue, violet, green, yellow), toothpicks, 16 in. square foamcore board (½ in. thick), knife

2-3 days in advance: Make fondant bow loops, name, balloons, streamers (p. 123).

Bake and cool four 6 in. 2-layer base cakes (bake two 1½ in. high layers for each 3 in. high cake), one 8 in. 2-layer main cake (bake 2 in. high layers for a 4 in. high cake) and one 8 in. 1-layer lid cake (1 in. high). Set on cut-to-fit cake boards and prepare for rolled fondant. Tint 20 oz. each rose and dark violet, 22 oz. each green and blue, 2 oz. red. Cover base cakes with tinted fondant (p. 119). Roll out some yellow, green, blue and red fondant for ribbons. Cut 3 strips 1 x 8 in. long for each cake. Brush with damp brush and attach. Roll out 36 oz. of white fondant. Cover main cake; smooth. Roll out an additional 36 oz. and imprint using Happy Birthday mat (p. 150). Cut a 10½ in. square and cover lid cake. Cut four 8 x 4 in. strips and attach to sides of main cake. Use tip 1 and tinted icing to fill in imprinted designs. Position base cakes on foil-covered foamcore board. Use lid cake to lightly mark where main cake will sit; insert dowel rod supports (p. 116). Position main cake. Attach 3 bow loops to top of base cakes. Attach lid cake to round plate. Build bow on lid cake. Trim 6 loop ends to a "V." Arrange in a circle; attach with melted candy. Attach 3 center loops.

At party: Assemble cakes. Line up lid cake and mark feet positions of round plate on main cake top; insert Twist Legs. Insert balloons, streamers and name, trimming sticks as needed. Position lid cake on legs. Serves 78.

*Combine Violet with Rose for violet shown. Combine Red-Red with Christmas Red for red shown.

Eye-Popping Presents

Cookie: Round Comfort-Grip Cutter, p. 202; Square Cut-Outs, p. 153; Cookie Sheet, Cooling Grid, p. 159

Tips: 3, 6, p. 136

Colors: Leaf Green, Lemon Yellow, Rose, Sky Blue, Orange, Black, p. 148

Recipes: Color Flow Icing, Roll-Out Cookies, p. 118

Also: Color Flow Mix, p. 145; Parchment Triangles, p. 138

Prepare and roll out dough. For each treat, cut 1 round and 1 medium square cookie; trim ⅛ in. off square sides for angled shape. Bake and cool. Using full-strength icing, outline rounds with tip 6, squares with tip 3; let set. Using thinned icing in cut parchment bag, flow in rounds and background area for presents; immediately pipe dots or stripes on presents. Let all dry. With full-strength icing, attach present to round cookie; pipe tip 6 bead bows with dot knots. Each serves 1.

Gift-Wrapped Goodies

Pan: Standard Muffin, p. 159

Recipe: Buttercream Icing, p. 118

Also: Celebration Standard Baking Cups, Party Icing Decorations, p. 177; Flowerful Medley Sprinkles, p. 146; Spatula, p. 140

Bake and cool cupcakes. Spatula ice tops. Position confetti sprinkles and icing decoration. Each serves 1.

Packages in Pastel

Pan: 9 x 13 x 2 in. Sheet, p. 157

Tip: 2, p. 136

Colors: Royal Blue, Leaf Green, Lemon Yellow, Rose, Violet, p. 148

Recipe: Buttercream Icing, p. 118

Fondant: White Ready-To-Use Rolled Fondant (6 oz. per treat), p. 149; Cutter/Embosser, p. 152; Square Cut-Outs, p. 153; 20 in. Rolling Pin, Roll & Cut Mat, p. 150

Also: Disposable Decorating Bags, p. 138; Cake Boards, Fanci-Foil Wrap, p. 241; Decorator Brush Set, p. 199; craft knife, ruler

Bake and cool sheet cake. For each treat, cut 1 medium and 1 large square for middle and top tier using Cut-Outs; trim to 1 in. high. For bottom tier, use knife to cut a 3¼ in. square; trim to 1½ in. high. Prepare tiers for rolled fondant (p. 119). Tint portions of fondant blue, green, yellow, rose and violet; reserve 1 portion white. Roll out ⅛ in. thick. Cut pieces to cover treats: 1¾ x 14 in. for bottom tier, 1¼ x 9 in. for middle tier, 1¼ x 6 in. for top tier. Cover tiers with fondant, smooth and trim off excess.

For ribbons on cake sides, roll out fondant ⅛ in. thick and cut strips ¼ to ½ in. wide; stack cakes and attach with damp brush. For bow loops roll ½ in. balls and shape into teardrops for knot, roll a ¼ in. ball. For streamers, cut ¼ x 1 in. strips. Attach with damp brush. With tip 2, pipe swirls, dots and stripes on tiers. Each serves 1.

◀ Sizzling Swirls

Pan: 8 x 2 in. Square, p. 157

Tips: 2, 6, 10, p. 136

Candy: White and Light Cocoa Candy Melts, p. 196; Primary, Garden Candy Color Sets, p. 199; Dessert Accents Candy Mold, p. 197; 10-Pack Candy Mold Set, p. 198

Recipe: Chocolate Buttercream Icing, p. 118

Also: Flowerful Medley Sprinkles, p. 144; Hot Colors Twist Candles, p. 185; Parchment Triangles, p. 138, Cake Board, Fanci-Foil Wrap, p. 241

In advance: Make candy trims. Tint portions of melted white candy pink, yellow, green and orange using candy colors. Mold 2-tone letters in Alphabet Mold Set using layering method (p. 130); fill cavities ¼ deep with melted pink candy, chill until firm and fill remainder of mold with melted cocoa candy. Chill until firm. Mold 4 swirls in each color using Dessert Accents Mold. Chill until firm; unmold.

Bake and cool 2-layer 8 in. square. Ice cake smooth. Attach candy swirls and confetti sprinkles to cake sides with tip 2 dots of icing. Pipe tip 6 bead top and tip 10 bead bottom borders. Position letters. Pipe tip 10 dots for candle holders; insert candles. Serves 20.

▶ Cupcake Stack

Pans: Dimensions Large Cupcake, p. 166; Jumbo, Standard, Mini Muffin, p. 159
Tips: 2, 12, p. 136
Colors:* Orange, Rose, Leaf Green, Lemon Yellow, Violet, p. 148
Fondant: White Ready-To-Use Rolled Fondant (10 oz.), p. 149; Brush Set, p. 151; Fondant Ribbon Cutter/Embosser Set, p. 152; 9 in. Rolling Pin, Roll & Cut Mat, p. 150
Recipes: Buttercream Icing, p. 118
Also: Assorted Celebration Candles, p. 183; Dowel Rod, p. 240; ruler, knife, cornstarch

Bake and cool 1 of each size cake and muffin; trim off crowns. Bake and cool 2 additional swirl tops for tiers 2 and 3 using Dimensions pan; use only ½ cup cake batter for tier 2 then ⅓ cup for tier 3. Trim off pointed tops; trim sides to match diameters of Jumbo and Standard muffins. Ice bottoms smooth in assorted colors. Tint 2 oz. fondant in each color. Roll out 1/16 in. thick. For bottom tier, cut 17 wavy strips, 3½ in. long, using Cutter/Embosser fitted with 2 wavy wheels and ¼ in. spacer. Brush backs with damp brush and attach, about 1 in. apart. Cut 17 plain strips, 3½ in. long, using cutter fitted with 2 straight wheels and ¼ in. spacer. Attach over wavy strips. For 2nd tier, cut 12 circles using wide end of tip 12; attach. Use icing to pipe tip 2 swirls. For 3rd tier, cut 12 zigzag strips, 1½ in. long, using cutter fitted with 2 zigzag wheels and no spacer; attach about ½ in. apart. For top tier, cut 10 dots using small end of tip 12; attach. Ice tops fluffy for bottom 3 tiers. Assemble bottom tiers. Insert wooden dowel rod into stacked cakes (p. 116). Ice Mini Muffin top and position on tower. Position candle. Serves 15.

*Combine Violet with Rose for violet shown. Combine Leaf Green with Lemon Yellow for green shown.

▲ Dazzling Dessert Duo

Pans: 10 x 2 in. Round, p. 157; Cookie Sheet, Cooling Grid, p. 159
Tip: 1M, p. 137
Colors:* Rose, Violet, Lemon Yellow, Leaf Green, Royal Blue, Orange, p. 148
Fondant: White Ready-To-Use Rolled Fondant (66 oz.), p. 149; Star Cut-Outs, p. 153; 20 in. Rolling Pin, Roll & Cut Mat, p. 150; Brush Set, Easy-Glide Fondant Smoother, p. 151
Recipe: Buttercream Icing, p. 118
Also: Smiley Stars Chunky Candles (2 pks.), p. 178; 12 in. Silver Cake Base, p. 241; Pastel Round Silicone Baking Cups, p. 174; Pink, Yellow, Blue, Orange, Green Colored Sugars, Flowerful Medley Sprinkles, p. 146; Piping Gel, p. 145; 101 Cookie Cutters, p. 203

In advance: Tint 16 oz. fondant violet. Roll out ⅛ in. thick and cover Cake Base (p. 123).

Bake and cool 2-layer round cake and 7 cupcakes in silicone cups supported by cookie sheet. Cover cupcakes with tip 1M swirl; top with confetti sprinkles. Tint 36 oz. fondant rose, 12 oz. yellow and divide 2 oz. for orange, blue and green. Prepare for rolled fondant and cover cake (p. 119); smooth with Fondant Smoother. Position cake on prepared base. Roll ¾ in. yellow balls and attach for bottom border with Piping Gel. Roll out remaining tinted fondant ⅛ in. thick. Cut letters using alphabet cutters from set and stars using medium Cut-Out. Brush with Piping Gel and sprinkle with matching sugars. Attach to cake with damp brush. Position cupcakes and insert candles. Cake serves 28; each cupcake serves 1.

*Combine Violet with Rose for violet shown. Combine Leaf Green with Lemon Yellow for green shown.

▲ Flight of Fancy

Pans: 12 x 2 in. Round, p. 157; Non-Stick Cookie Sheet, p. 159

Tips: 1, 2, 2A, p. 136

Colors:* Sky Blue, Lemon Yellow, Golden Yellow, Red-Red, Brown, Copper (for light skin tone shown), Black, p. 148

Fondant: Primary & Neon Colors Fondant Multi Packs, White Ready-To-Use Rolled Fondant (5 oz.), p. 149; Brush Set, p. 151; Oval & People Cut-Outs, p. 153; 9 in. Rolling Pin, Roll & Cut Mat, p. 150

Candy: White Candy Melts (2 pks.), p. 196; Primary & Garden Candy Color Sets, p. 199; Dessert Shells Candy Mold, p. 197; Dancing Daisies Lollipop Mold, p. 199

Recipes: Buttercream, Royal Icings, p. 118

Also: Parchment Triangles, Cake Dividing Set, p. 138; Piping Gel, Meringue Powder, p. 145; Hidden Pillars, p. 237; Wooden & Plastic Dowel Rods, p. 240; 14 in. Silver Cake Base, p. 241; candy sticks, candy-coated chocolates, sour cherry balls, hot glue gun, glue stick, knife, ruler, cornstarch, waxed paper, toothpicks

In advance: Make fondant passengers (p. 123). **Also:** Prepare spinning center support (p. 123). **And:** Prepare candy planes. Melt candy and tint 3 oz. each red, orange, yellow and blue. Use Dessert Shells mold to make 1 shell in each color (p. 130). Use Daisies mold to make 1 propeller in each color. Tape lollipop opening closed; fill cavity ⅛ in. deep. Tap to eliminate bubbles; chill until firm. Use largest oval Cut-Out to mold 2 ovals in each color for wings. Set Cut-Out on cookie sheet and fill ⅛ in. deep, tap, chill until firm. Use warm knife to trim ½ in. off each oval. Attach wings to top edge of shell with melted candy. Chill until firm.

Bake and cool 2-layer cake; ice smooth. Use clean plastic dowel rod to cut a center hole; remove cake. Dip end of candy-filled 9 in. plastic dowel rod in melted candy; re-insert in hole and hold straight until rod attaches to base. Chill until firm. Use Cake Dividing Wheel to divide cake into 10ths; use Garland Marker to mark 1¼ in. deep garlands around cake. Cut candy sticks to height of cake and attach at divisions. Attach candy-coated chocolates for garland and bottom border. Use melted candy to attach sour cherry to top of each candy stick. Place striped pole with arms upside down on a waxed paper-covered surface. Use melted candy to attach planes to arms; hold level until set. Slide striped pole over 9 in. dowel rod in cake. Using melted candy in cut parchment bag, attach propellers to front of planes; attach candy to center. Attach 2 people inside each plane with melted candy. Attach fondant ball to top of pole.

At party: Slide center support over attached 9 in. plastic dowel rod. Serves 40.

*Combine Lemon Yellow with Golden Yellow for yellow shown. Combine Brown with Red-Red for dark brown shown.

▲ Water Whirled

Pans: 6, 8, 10 x 2 in. Round, p. 157

Tips: 1, 2, 2A, 19, p. 136-137

Colors:* Sky Blue, Lemon Yellow, Golden Yellow, Brown, Red-Red, Black, Copper (for light skin tone shown), p. 148

Fondant: White Ready-To-Use Rolled Fondant (24 oz.), Primary & Neon Colors Fondant Multi Packs, p. 149; Brush Set, p. 151; People Cut-Outs, p. 153; 20 in. Rolling Pin, Roll & Cut Mat, p. 150

Candy: White Candy Melts (2 pks.), p. 196; Primary & Garden Candy Color Sets, p. 199; Dessert Shells Candy Mold, p. 197

Recipes: Buttercream, Royal Icings, p. 118

Also: 2010 Pattern Book (Wave, Sign), p. 132; Cakes 'N More

3-Tier Party Stand, p. 236; Jumbo Confetti Sprinkles, p. 146; 8 in. Cookie Treat Sticks, p. 205; Piping Gel, Meringue Powder, p. 145; 12 in. Cake Circles, 13 x 19 in. Cake Board, Fanci-Foil Wrap, p. 241; tape, scissors, knife, ruler, waxed paper, card stock, fine tip marker, cornstarch

In advance: Make candy shell boats (p. 130). Melt candy and tint portions red, orange and yellow. Use Dessert Shells mold to make 2 or 3 shells (8 needed), in each color. **Also:** Make sign and prepare cake stand. Use pattern to cut out paper sign. Cut card stock ¼ in. larger on all sides; tape paper sign to cardstock. Print name with marker. Tape Cookie Sticks to back. Use royal icing dots to attach Jumbo Confetti around edge of sign and around edges of cake stand. **And:** Make fondant passengers (p. 123) and attach 2 in each boat.

Bake and cool 2-layer cakes (trim to 3 in. high). Prepare slides and bottom pool. Cut 13 x 19 in. cake board into 3 slides, 3½ in. wide, 7, 8½ and 12½ in. long; shape curves. Cover slides and 12 in. cake circle with foil. Use buttercream to ice cakes, slides and pool smooth; attach confetti around pool using royal icing. Pipe tip 19 C-motion bottom borders on cakes. For waves, tint 18 oz. fondant blue; roll out ⅛ in. thick and cut using pattern. Attach around cake tops, leaving 3¾ in. openings where slides will go. Attach to sides of slides and on top of pool. Attach boats on slides with melted candy. Let set. Tint piping gel blue for water; brush onto cake tops, slides and pool. **At party:** Position slides and remaining boats; insert sign. Serves 60.

*Combine Lemon Yellow with Golden Yellow for yellow shown. Combine Brown with Red-Red for brown shown.

▶ Dancing for Joy!

Pan: Ballerina Bear, p. 161
Tips: 3, 5, 16, 17, 21, 127D, p. 136-137
Colors: Violet, Black, Rose, p. 148
Recipes: Buttercream, Chocolate Buttercream, Royal Icings, p. 118
Also: 2010 Pattern Book (Crown), p. 132; Meringue Powder, p. 145; Cake Boards, Fanci-Foil Wrap, p. 241; toothpicks, knife, craft knife, cornstarch

In advance: Make crown. Using pattern, cut out crown from Cake Board. Decorate with royal icing. Use tip 5 to pipe in teardrops (pat smooth with finger dipped in cornstarch). Cover with tip 16 stars. Pipe tip 5 balls at points. Let dry.

Bake and cool cake. Trim off muzzle. Ice sides and background areas smooth; lightly ice ruffle area. Use tip 5 to pipe eye (pat smooth). Use tip 3 to pipe outline mouth and to outline all details. Cover bodice, shoes, arms, legs and face with tip 16 stars; overpipe nose and cheeks. Pipe tip 127D ruffles; overpipe 5 outline at waist. Pipe tip 17 S-motion curls; position crown then add more curls. Pipe tip 21 shell bottom border. Serves 12.

*Combine Violet with Rose for violet shown. Add Black to chocolate buttercream for hair and facial features.

◀ Her Crowning Glory

Pan: Crown, p. 161
Tips: 3, 7, 14, p. 136-137
Color: Rose, p. 148
Recipes: Snow-White Buttercream, Color Flow Icings, p. 118
Also: 2010 Pattern Book (Crown Band, Crown Loops in 5 sizes, Curlicues in 3 sizes), p. 132; White Pearl Dust, Brush Set, p. 151; Color Flow Mix, p. 145; Cake Boards, p. 241; Parchment Triangles, p. 138; waxed paper, cornstarch, non-stick pan spray, facial tissue

Two days in advance: Make color flow pieces for crown. Copy band and loop patterns and tape to cake boards; cover with waxed paper. For easy release, spray with pan spray, then wipe with facial tissue to remove excess spray. Outline using tip 3 and full-strength color flow; fill in with thinned color flow (p. 130). Repeat for additional pieces as indicated on patterns; make extras to allow for breakage. Let dry. **Also:** Make curlicues. Tape patterns to board and cover with waxed paper. Pipe curlicues using tip 14 and full-strength color flow. Repeat for 2 smaller sizes; make extras to allow for breakage, let dry. **And:** Make puddle dots (p. 122). Using thinned color flow icing in cut parchment bag, pipe 75 small dots (¼ in. diameter) and 14 large dots (½ in. diameter) on waxed paper-covered board. Make extras to allow for breakage; let dry. Brush color flow dots and crown pieces with white Pearl Dust.

Bake and cool cake; ice smooth. Position bottom crown band on cake, then center two B loops, then add an A loop on each side. For top layer, position E-loop in center then a D loop on each side and then two C loops. Position top crown band on top of points. Attach curlicues with icing, placing largest on center loop, then medium and small on side loops. Attach puddle dots with icing. Pipe tip 7 bead bottom border. Serves 12.

◀ **Light on Her Feet**

Pans: Cookie Sheet, Cooling Grid, p. 159

Tips: 2, 3, p. 136

Color: Rose, p. 148

Recipes: Color Flow Icing, Roll-Out Cookies, p. 118

Also: 2010 Pattern Book (Ballet Slipper), p. 132; Color Flow Mix, p. 145; Oval Cut-Outs, p. 153; Parchment Triangles, p. 138; ¼ in. wide ribbon (8 in. per pair), toothpicks, cornstarch

Prepare and roll out dough. Use largest Cut-Out to cut 2 cookies per treat. Bake and cool. Trace pattern on cookie with toothpick. Use tip 2 and full-strength pink icing to outline center slipper area; let set. Use thinned icing in cut parchment bag to flow in white center. Flow in rose top and sides; let set. Use tip 3 and full-strength rose icing to outline and fill in bows (pat smooth with finger dipped in cornstarch). Pipe tip 3 dot knot. Tie ribbon into bow and attach to cookies with tip 3 dots of full-strength icing; let set. Each treat serves 1.

▼ **Angel-In-Training**

Pans: 8-Cavity Silicone Round Brownie Pops Mold, p. 170; Cookie Sheet, Cooling Grid, p. 159

Tips: 1, 2, 3, p. 136

Colors:* Rose, Copper (for skin tone shown), Black, Red-Red, Brown, p. 148

Fondant: White Ready-To-Use Rolled Fondant (3 oz. per treat), Gum-Tex, p. 149; Heart Cut-Outs, p. 153; White Pearl Dust, Brush Set, p. 151; 9 in. Rolling Pin, Roll & Cut Mat, p. 150

Recipe: favorite brownie recipe or mix

Also: White Ready-To-Use Decorator Icing, p. 145; Cake Boards, p. 241; black shoestring licorice, cornstarch, toothpicks, knife

In advance: Make wings. Combine 1 oz. fondant with ⅛ teaspoon Gum-Tex for each treat. Roll out ⅛ in. thick and cut 2 wings using medium Cut-Outs; let dry on cornstarch-dusted board. Brush with Pearl Dust.

Bake and cool brownies in silicone mold supported by cookie sheet. Tint portion of icing rose and thin to pouring consistency following package directions. Cover brownies with thinned icing (p. 130); let dry. For each treat, tint 1 oz. fondant each rose and light copper. Make and attach the following pieces with damp brush. For upper body, shape a 1 x ¾ in. diameter log. For waistband, roll out fondant ¹⁄₁₆ in. thick and cut a ¼ in. strip. For sleeves, roll two ½ in. balls, shape into teardrops. Imprint pleat lines with toothpick. For arms, roll ¾ x ¼ in. diameter logs; flatten end for hand and cut slits for fingers with knife. For head, roll a 1 in. ball. For nose, roll a ¹⁄₁₆ in. ball. With full-strength icing, pipe tip 2 dot eyes, tip 1 outline mouth. Pipe tip 3 pull-out hair. Attach wings with dots of icing. For antennae, cut licorice into 1½ in. pieces; attach tiny balls of fondant to ends with icing and insert in head. Each serves 1.

*Combine Brown with Red-Red for brown shown.

▲ **Working on Your Wishes**

Pans: Classic Wonder Mold, p. 160; Mini Ball, p. 165

Tips: 1A, 3, 10, p. 136

Colors: Royal Blue, Rose, Black, Lemon Yellow, Copper (for skin tone shown), p. 148

Fondant: White Ready-To-Use Rolled Fondant (48 oz.), Gum-Tex, p. 149; Star Cut-Outs, p. 153; 9 in. Rolling Pin, Roll & Cut Mat, p. 150; White Pearl Dust, Brush Set, Easy-Glide Fondant Smoother, p. 151

Candy: White Candy Melts (1 pk.), p. 196; Primary Candy Color Set, p. 199; 11¾ in. Lollipop Sticks, p. 200

Recipe: Buttercream Icing, p. 118

Also: 2010 Pattern Book (Tiara), p. 132; Cake Board, Fanci-Foil Wrap, p. 241; Heart Comfort-Grip Cutter, p. 202; Yellow Colored Sugars, White Sparkling Sugar, p. 146; cornstarch

In advance: Make fondant wings, upper body and tiara (p. 123). **Also:** Make candy head (p. 123).

Bake and cool Wonder Mold cake. Prepare and cover with reserved blue fondant (p. 119); smooth with Fondant Smoother. Insert stick in cake top; position upper body. Attach head to upper body, securing with melted candy.

Using reserved copper fondant, roll ¾ x 3½ in. logs for arms. Flatten end and indent fingers with knife. Attach inside sleeves with melted candy; let set. Roll out blue fondant ⅛ in. thick; cut a ¼ x 8 in. strip and attach for waistband with damp brush. Tint 5 oz. fondant yellow; mix with ¼ teaspoon Gum-Tex. Roll out ⅛ in. thick and cut a 5 x 1½ in. strip to cover top of head for hair placement. Attach with damp brush. Cut star for wand using medium Cut-Out; attach to 4 in. lollipop stick with melted candy. Make yellow curliques (p. 123) for hair, wrapping strips around lollipop stick. Attach to head with damp brush, working from bottom to top. Before all hair is placed, attach tiara with damp brush. Tint 5 oz. fondant light blue and roll 12 ropes, 8 x ¼ in. diameter. Attach to hem with damp brush, in loops 2 x 1¼ in. wide, with a 2 in. tail extending to right. Roll out fondant ⅛ in. thick and cut 12 smallest stars using Cut-Out and 12 dots using small end of tip 1A. Attach stars ¼ in. above loops and attach dots at loop points. Cut 7 dots using small end of tip 10 and attach for necklace. Using tip 3 and icing, pipe swirls on wings; sprinkle with Sparkling Sugar. Insert wings into back of cake. Serves 12.

◄ The Princess' Pony

Pans: Party Pony, p. 161; 18 x 3 in. Half Round, p. 158
Tips: 2, 3, 4, 6, 16, 18, 102, 126, 129, 225, p. 136-137
Colors: Rose, Violet, p. 148
Recipes: Buttercream, Royal, Color Flow Icings, p. 118
Also: 2010 Pattern Book (Oval), p. 132; White Pearl Dust, Brush
    Set, p. 151; Cake Dividing Set, p. 138; Flower Nail No. 7, p. 140;
    Pink Celebration Candles, p. 183; Color Flow Mix, Meringue
    Powder, p. 145; Dowel Rods, p. 240; Cake Boards, Fanci-Foil
    Wrap, p. 241; 20 in. diameter plywood or foamcore board
    (½ in. thick), waxed paper, cornstarch, toothpicks, ruler, tape

Several days in advance: Make plaques for cake sides. Use
pattern to make 10 ovals; tape to board and cover with waxed
paper. Outline with tip 2 and full-strength color flow; fill in with
thinned color flow. Let dry. Using royal icing, fill 10 tip 102 roses
with tip 6 bases; let dry. Pipe 140 small drop flowers with tip
225 and 30 medium with tip 129; add tip 2 dot centers. Make
extras to allow for breakage; let dry. Attach center rose plus
3 medium and 10 small drop flowers to each oval using royal
icing dots. Let dry. Brush all with Pearl Dust (p. 122).

Bake and cool Pony cake plus 2-layer base cake (bake four
2 in. high Half-Rounds to make 4 in. high round). Ice base
cake smooth and prepare for Stacked Construction (p. 116).
For Pony cake, use tip 3 to outline all features. Pipe in ear,
eye, pupil, nostril and bridle (pat smooth with finger dipped
in cornstarch). Cover with tip 16 stars and tip 18 pull-out star
mane. For round cake, pipe tip 16 shell bottom border; cover
with tip 126 ruffle. Use Cake Dividing Set to divide cake sides
into 10ths; attach prepared ovals at marks, about ½ in. down
from top edge. Mark midpoint between ovals at top edge; use
tip 4 to pipe 2 double drop strings, each 2½ in. wide, 1½ in. and
1 in. deep. Attach small drop flower at midpoint; pipe tip 4 dots
over ends. Position Pony cake. Pipe tip 3 message. Position
small drop flowers, about 1 in. apart, around edge. Pipe tip 18
rosettes on cake top; insert candles. Serves 122.

*Combine Violet with Rose for violet shown.

◀ Pegasus Party Cake

Pans: Rocking Horse, p. 163; 18 x 3 in. Half Round, p. 158

Tips: 3, 12, 16, 18, p. 136-137

Colors:* Sky Blue, Rose, Lemon Yellow, Leaf Green, Violet, Orange, p. 148

Fondant: White Ready-To-Use Rolled Fondant (12 oz.), Gum-Tex, p. 149; Brush Set, Flower Former Set, p. 151; Leaf and Flower Cut-Outs, p. 153; 9 in. Rolling Pin, Roll & Cut Mat, p. 150

Recipe: Buttercream, Royal Icings, p. 118

Also: 2010 Pattern Book (Wings), p. 132; White Candy Melts (2 pks.), p. 196; Candy Melting Plate, p. 199; Piping Gel, p. 145; White Cake Sparkles, Pink, Orange, Yellow, Lavender and Light Green Colored Sugars, p. 146; 13 x 19 in. Cake Boards, Fanci-Foil Wrap, p. 241; Meringue Powder, p. 145; Dowel Rods, p. 240; knife, scissors, tape, ruler, toothpicks, cornstarch, tea strainer, foamcore board 12 x 20 in. (¼ in. thick)

In advance: Make candy plaque and decorate with royal icing (p. 130). **Also:** Add 1 teaspoon Gum-Tex to 12 oz. white fondant. Make fondant flowers and leaves (p. 123). **And:** Make fondant wings. Roll out ⅛ in. thick. Using patterns, cut out wings; let dry on cornstarch-dusted surface. Press Cake Sparkles through tea strainer for finer texture. Use Piping Gel and tip 3 to outline wings and feather details. Immediately sprinkle on Cake Sparkles. Let dry.

Bake and cool 1-layer cake (trim to 2 in. high). Position on wrapped board 1 in. larger than cake on all sides (p. 112). Ice cake smooth. Use toothpicks to mark rainbow stripes ½ in. wide. Cover with tip 16 stars. Pipe tip 12 ball clouds around cake sides. Attach flowers and leaves with icing. Cut dowel rods 1 in. higher than cake. Insert into cake where candy plaque will rest above cake surface. Using melted candy, attach candy plaque to dowel rods; attach wings to back, then front of plaque. Pipe tip 3 name. Serves 55.

*Combine Violet with Rose for lighter violet shown.

▲ Bug-Eyed Brownies

Pans: 8-Cavity Silicone Round Brownie Pops Mold, p. 170; Cookie Sheet, Cooling Grid, p. 159

Candy: White Candy Melts (2 oz. for each treat), p. 196; Primary, Garden Candy Color Sets, p. 199

Recipe: Favorite brownie recipe or mix

Also: Parchment Triangles, p. 138; regular and mini candy-coated chocolates, malted milk balls, black shoestring licorice, waxed paper, mini marshmallows

Bake and cool brownies in silicone mold, supported by cookie sheet, filling cavities halfway. Tint portions of melted white candy yellow and pink. Cover with melted candy (p. 130); chill until firm. Attach malted milk ball head, ¼ in. from bottom, with melted candy; support with marshmallows and let set. Tint small portions of melted white candy green, orange and black. Using melted candy in cut parchment bags, pipe swirls, outline mouth and dot eyes and pupils; let set. With melted candy, attach regular chocolates for feet; cut ½ in. pieces of licorice for antennae and attach mini chocolate. Let set. Attach antennae with melted candy. Each serves 1.

◀ Joy Buzzer!

Pans: Oval Set (7.75 x 5.5 in. used), p. 156; Animal Crackers, p. 164

Tips: 6, 12, 19, p. 136-137

Colors:* Lemon Yellow, Rose, Violet, Leaf Green, Orange, Black, p. 148

Fondant: White Ready-To-Use Rolled Fondant (30 oz.), Gum-Tex, p. 149; Brush Set, p. 151; 20 in. Rolling Pin, Roll & Cut Mat, p. 150

Recipes: Buttercream Icing, p. 118

Also: 2010 Pattern Book (Wings, Upper and Lower Inserts), p. 132; Piping Gel, p. 145; 4 in. Lollipop Sticks, p. 200; Cake Boards, Fanci-Foil Wrap, p. 241; 15 x 18 in. plywood or foamcore board (¼ in. thick), waxed paper, ruler, knife, cornstarch

2-3 days in advance: Make antennas (p. 124). **Also:** Prepare base board. Use cake pans and wing patterns to trace shape. Cut to fit and cover with Fanci-Foil (p. 112).

Bake and cool 1-layer cakes. Trim ears off Animal Crackers cake. Tint fondant as follows: 1 oz. orange, 2 oz. violet, 8 oz. light rose, 16 oz. dark rose; roll out ⅛ in. thick as needed. Use pattern to cut dark rose double wings; reverse pattern and cut another. Brush backs with piping gel and position on board. Use patterns to cut light rose Upper and Lower Inserts; reverse patterns and cut another set. Brush with damp brush and attach to wings. Cut 24 violet circles using wide end of tip 12; brush with damp brush and attach. Position head. Outline and pipe in tip 12 eyes (flatten slightly with finger dipped in cornstarch). Add tip 6 dot pupils and outline mouth. Cover head with tip 19 stars; overpipe cheeks for dimension. Overpipe mouth with tip 6. Roll orange fondant cone nose 1½ in. high; attach. Position oval cake body. Cover with tip 19 stars, alternating colors for 1 in. wide stripes. Insert antennas. Serves 16.

*Combine Violet with Rose for violet shown. Combine Leaf Green with Lemon Yellow for light and dark green shown.

◄ UFO Friends

Pans: 8-Cavity Silicone Round Brownie Pops Mold, p. 170; Cookie Sheet, Cooling Grid, p. 159

Tips: 1, 2, 3, 6, 9, p. 136

Colors:* Leaf Green, Violet, Orange, Lemon Yellow, Rose, Black, p. 148

Candy: White Candy Melts (3 pks. for 20 treats), p. 196; Garden Candy Color Set, p. 199

Recipes: Buttercream Icing, Roll-Out Cookies, p. 118, favorite brownie recipe or mix

Also: 23-Count Standard Cupcakes 'N More Dessert Stand, p. 173; Round Comfort-Grip Cutter, p. 202; Flowerful Medley Sprinkles, p. 146; Parchment Triangles, Disposable Decorating Bags, p. 138; spice drops, knife, ruler, cornstarch, waxed paper

In advance: Make cookie bases. Prepare and roll out dough. Use cutter to cut 20 rounds. Bake and cool. Tint 1 package Candy Melts gray using black candy color. Cover cookies (p. 130); chill until firm.

Bake and cool brownie pops in silicone mold, supported by cookie sheet. Cover with melted candy (p. 130). Repeat 2 more times to totally hide brownie. Using melted candy in cut parchment bag, attach pops to center of cookies. Pipe tip 3 bead borders. Attach confetti sprinkles around cookie edge. Cut bottom half off spice drops; attach rounded top to pop. Let set. Pipe aliens with buttercream. Use tip 9 to pipe 1¼ in. round head (smooth with finger dipped in cornstarch). Pull out tip 6 arms, tip 3 hand and fingers, tip 2 hair. Pipe tip 3 dot eyes, tip 1 dot pupils and zigzag mouth, tip 2 dot cheeks. Position on stand at party. Each serves 1.

*Combine Violet with Rose for violet shown. Combine Leaf Green with Lemon Yellow for green shown.

HAPPY BIRTHDAY

ANTHONY

▲ Party Payload

Pans: Firetruck, p. 162; Cookie Sheet, Cooling Grid, p. 159

Tips: 2, 3, 5, 16, 18, p. 136-137

Colors:* Royal Blue, Christmas Red, Red-Red, Lemon Yellow, Golden Yellow, Black, Violet, Rose, Leaf Green, Orange, p. 148

Recipes: Buttercream, Royal Icings, Roll-Out Cookies, p. 118

Also: 2010 Pattern Book (Tiered Cake, Wheel, Hubcap, Dump Truck), p. 132; Meringue Powder, p. 145; Parchment Triangles, p. 138; Cake Board, Fanci-Foil Wrap, p. 241; Plastic Dowel Rods, p. 240; knife, cornstarch, toothpick, waxed paper, ruler

In advance: Make cookies. Prepare and roll out dough. Using patterns, cut 4 wheels and 1 tiered cake; bake and cool cookies. Ice tiered cake smooth with royal icing. Pipe tip 5 zigzag icing drips on each layer (smooth with finger dipped in cornstarch). Pipe tip 2 message. Sandwich 2 cookies together with icing to make each wheel. Cover wheels with thinned royal icing (p. 130); let set. On wheel, using pattern, outline hubcap with tip 2 and full-strength royal icing; let set. Flow in with thinned royal icing; let set. Cut 2 in. dowel rod sections and attach 1 to top half on back of each cookie with royal icing; let set. **Also:** Make puddle dot (p. 122) lug nuts and axle, ¼ in. diameter, on waxed paper using thinned royal icing. Let set.

Bake and cool cake; cut off bell area on top. Ice cake top smooth in buttercream to level; mark pattern with toothpick. Ice sides and background areas smooth. Outline pattern areas with tip 3. Pipe in headlight, window and fender areas with tip 3 (smooth with finger). Cover truck with tip 16 stars. Overpipe bed area. Overpipe tip 16 outlines on bed. Pipe tip 18 shell bottom border. Using tip 2 and full-strength royal icing, attach lug nuts and axles to wheels. Position wheels and tiered cake. Cake serves 12; each cookie serves 1.

*Combine Christmas Red with Red-Red for red shown. Combine Lemon Yellow with Golden Yellow for yellow shown. Combine Violet with Rose for violet shown.

◄ Kid on Cloud 9

Pans: 3-Pc. Paisley Set (12.75 x 9 in. used), p. 156; Cookie Sheet, Cooling Grid, p. 159

Tips: 4, 5, 18, p. 136-137

Colors:* Leaf Green, Lemon Yellow, Christmas Red, Violet, Rose, Sky Blue, Black, p. 148

Recipes: Buttercream Icing, Roll-Out Cookies, p. 118

Also: 2010 Pattern Book (Propeller, Windows, Wing, Upper and Lower Tail, Large and Small Clouds), p. 132; Blue Colored Sugar, p. 146; 4 in. Lollipop Sticks, p. 200; Cake Boards, Fanci-Foil Wrap, p. 241; large spice drop, knife, waxed paper, tape, toothpicks

In advance: Make cookies. Prepare and roll out dough. Use patterns to cut propeller, wing, tail sections and clouds. Bake and cool.

Bake and cool 1-layer cake. Ice area for windows smooth. Let set then use patterns to mark window edges. Cover plane, wing and tail section cookies with tip 18 stars. Add tip 5 dots. Position wing and lower tail section at a 30° angle, supporting each cookie with 2 Lollipop Sticks, cut to fit. Insert 2 Lollipop Sticks into cake side at an angle where upper tail section will sit, leaving 2 in. extended. Attach cookie to stick using icing. Ice propeller and cloud cookies smooth; let set. Cut 2 Lollipop Sticks to 3 in. long; insert into cake side where propeller will sit, leaving 1 in. extended. Attach propeller using icing. Pipe tip 5 outlines at edge and ¼ in. inside edge; attach spice drop to center. Pipe tip 4 outline on clouds; immediately sprinkle with colored sugar, shaking off excess. Pipe tip 4 message, tip 5 name. Cake serves 14; each cookie serves 1.

*Combine Leaf Green with Lemon Yellow for green shown. Combine Violet with Rose for violet shown.

▲ Candy Copter

Pans: Mini Ball, p. 165; Cookie Sheet, Cooling Grid, p. 159

Candy: Red, White, Blue Candy Melts (1 pk. each), p. 196; Garden Candy Color Set (Black used), p. 199

Also: 2010 Pattern Book (Propeller, Bolt, Fin), p. 132; Parchment Triangles, p. 138; Round Cut-Outs, p. 153; sugar ice cream cone, waxed paper, candy for filling

Tape patterns for 2 propellers, 1 bolt and 3 fins to cookie sheet; smooth and tape waxed paper over cookie sheet. Tint about ¼ cup melted white candy gray using black candy color; melt small amount of red candy. Pipe over patterns using melted candy in cut parchment bags. For base, place largest round Cut-Out on cookie sheet; fill ³⁄₁₆ in. deep with melted blue candy. Chill until firm.

Make two ⅛ in. thick candy shells (p. 130) using melted red candy and Mini Ball pan. Chill until firm. Using melted candy in cut parchment bag, pipe front and side windows onto top half; let set. Attach bottom half to base. Position top half. Trim ¾ in. off wide end of ice cream cone. Cover with melted candy (p. 130); let set, then attach to back of bottom half. Attach 1 upright and 2 side fins; attach 2 propellers and bolt. Fill with candy or other treats. Each serves 1.

◀ Buccaneer Tiers

Pans: 6, 10 x 2 in. Square, p. 157

Tips: 1, 1A, 2A, 3, 9, 12, p. 136-137

Colors:* Royal Blue, Red-Red, Christmas Red, Lemon Yellow, Leaf Green, Orange, Violet, Rose, Black, Copper (for skin tone shown), p. 148

Fondant: White Ready-To-Use Rolled Fondant (140 oz.), p. 149; Brush Set, Easy-Glide Fondant Smoother, p. 151; 20 in. Rolling Pin, Roll & Cut Mat, p. 150

Recipes: Buttercream Icing, p. 118

Also: 2010 Pattern Book (Hat), p. 132; Piping Gel, p. 145; White Candy Melts (1 pk.), p. 196; 2 in. Globe Pillar Sets (2 pks.), 2½ in. Globe Pillar Set, p. 238; Decorator Preferred 6 in. Square Plate, p. 237; Cake Boards, Fanci-Foil Wrap, p. 241; 14 in. square plywood or foamcore board (½ in. thick), scissors, tape, knife, ruler, pastry brush, graham cracker crumbs, wrapped candy coins, assorted rock candy

In advance: Tint fondant as follows: 1 oz. gray, 2 oz. green, 3 oz. orange, 3 oz. yellow, 4 oz. red, 6 oz. black, 12 oz. light copper. Make pirates (p. 124). **Also:** Cover base board with 36 oz. ivory fondant (p. 123).

Bake and cool 2-layer cakes (bake 1½ in. high layers for 3 in. high cakes). Prepare for Globe Pillar Construction (p. 117). Tint 54 oz. light blue and 20 oz. medium blue. Prepare and cover both cakes with light blue fondant (p. 119). Cut 5 pillars to 7 in. long. Use 6 in. plate to mark feet positions on 10 in. cake, then insert 4 pillars. Insert last pillar in center of 6 in. cake. Roll out medium blue fondant ⅛ in. thick. Cut a strip 2¼ x 24 in. long; cut random waves 1¼ to 2¼ in. deep on top edge. Brush back with damp brush and attach around sides of 6 in. cake. Repeat for 10 in. cake using two 20 in. long strips. Brush cake tops and base board with piping gel; cover with graham cracker "sand." Slide pirates onto pillars. Attach candy around border with dots of icing.

At party: Assemble cakes. Serves 42.

*Combine Red-Red with Christmas Red for red shown. Combine Violet with Rose for violet shown.

▶ Galloping Goodies

Cookie: 101 Cookie Cutters, p. 203; Cookie Sheet, Cooling Grid, p. 159; 6 in. Cookie Treat Sticks, p. 205

Tips: 1, 3, p. 136

Colors:* Brown, Red-Red, Black, Golden Yellow, Royal Blue, p. 148

Recipes: Color Flow Icing, Roll-Out Cookies, p. 118

Also: Color Flow Mix, p. 145; Parchment Triangles, p. 138; Cake Board, p. 241; waxed paper, yellow and blue curling ribbon, ruler, scissors, cellophane tape, knife

In advance: Make cookies. Prepare and roll out dough. Cut head using stocking cutter from set. Trim off cuff overhang and ½ in. from top of stocking. Bake and cool. Outline cookie with tip 3 and full-strength icing; let set. Flow in with thinned icing in cut parchment bag. Let set overnight.

Decorate with full-strength icing. Pipe tip 1 dot nostril and outline mouth; tip 3 dot eye and pupil, outline bridle, pull-out ear and s-curve hair. Pipe in inside ear with tip 3. Cut a 7 in. piece of ribbon and attach to cookie stick with tape in a spiral design. Attach cookies to sticks with full-strength icing. Let dry. Each serves 1.

*Combine Brown with Red-Red for brown shown.

◄ Toddler Tex

Pans: Rocking Horse, p. 163; Cookie Sheet, Cooling Grid, p. 159
Tips: 3, 4, 5, 13, 16, 18, 363, p. 136-137
Colors:* Lemon Yellow, Golden Yellow, Brown, Christmas Red, Copper (for skin tone shown), Black, Kelly Green, Royal Blue, p. 148
Fondant: White Ready-To-Use Rolled Fondant (11 oz.), Gum-Tex, p. 149; 9 in. Rolling Pin, Roll & Cut Mat, p. 150; Brush Set, p. 151
Recipes: Buttercream, Royal Icings, Roll-Out Cookies, p. 118
Also: 2010 Pattern Book (Cowboy, Left Arm, Message Oval), p. 132; White Candy Melts, p. 196; Cake Boards, Fanci-Foil Wrap, p. 241; Meringue Powder, p. 145; cornstarch, knife, ruler

2 days in advance: Make message oval. Tint 5 oz. fondant blue and mix with ½ teaspoon Gum-Tex. Roll out ⅛ in. thick and cut oval using pattern; let dry on cornstarch-dusted board. **Also:** Make rope. Tint 6 oz. fondant yellow and mix with ½ teaspoon Gum-Tex; roll two ⅛ in. diameter ropes and twist together. Attach rope to edge of oval, leaving 4 in. at bottom. Cut 2 in. from end to attach to bottom of hand. Let dry. **And:** Make cookies. Prepare and roll out dough. Cut cowboy and left arm using patterns. Also cut 2 each 2 x 5 in. supports for oval and 2¼ x 5 in. supports for cowboy. Bake and cool. Position cowboy and arm cookies on waxed paper and decorate with royal icing. Outline cookies with tip 3; pipe in face, hands, hat band. Cover pants, boots and hat with tip 16 stars. Cover shirt with tip 13 stars. Pipe in tip 3 scarf (pat smooth with finger dipped in cornstarch). Pipe in tip 3 mouth, pull-out hair and outline eyes. Pipe tip 4 outline ears and dot nose.

Bake and cool cake; position on foil-wrapped board. Ice background and rocker areas smooth. Outline horse, saddle and bridle with tip 3. Pipe in hooves, eye, saddle, bridle and ear with tip 5. Cover horse with tip 16 stars; pipe tip 3 dot nostril and outline mouth. Pipe tip 18 pull-out tail and mane. Pipe tip 363 shell cactus at bottom of cake. Attach supports to cookies with melted candy; let set. Position cowboy on cake. For reins, tint a 1 in. ball of fondant blue; roll out ⅛ in. thick and cut a ¼ x 7 in. strip. Position on cake. Attach 2 in. rope piece to hand with melted candy; pipe tip 5 fingers over rope and reins. Print tip 4 message. Position message oval. Serves 12.

*Combine Brown with Christmas Red for dark brown shown. Combine Golden Yellow with Lemon Yellow for yellow shown.

▶ Rocking Their World

Pan: Rocking Horse, p. 163
Tips: 6, 12, 18, p. 136-137
Colors: Lemon Yellow, Red-Red, p. 148
Recipes: Buttercream, Chocolate Buttercream Icings, p. 118; favorite crisped rice cereal treats (2 recipes)
Also: Cake Boards, Fanci-Foil Wrap, p. 241; Spatula, p. 140; regular and mini candy-coated chocolates, waxed paper, scissors, tape, knife, cornstarch

In advance: Using pan as a pattern, prepare same-size cake board; wrap with foil (p. 112).

Prepare cereal treats mixture and press into lightly greased pan. Release immediately onto waxed paper-covered board. Position on prepared cake board; use knife to trim cereal as needed. Ice saddle and rocker base smooth. Pipe tip 12 outline on saddle (pat smooth with finger dipped in cornstarch). Using tip 6, pipe number; pipe outline bridle (pat smooth). Use icing dots to attach mini candies to saddle and bridle; attach regular-size candies for eye and on rocker. Outline and pipe in hooves with tip 6 (smooth). Pipe tip 18 pull-out star mane and tail. Serves 12.

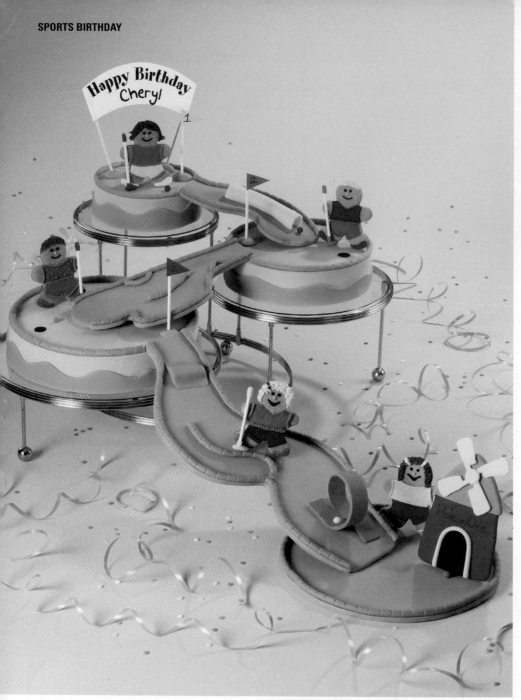

◀ Par-Tee on the Green!

Pans: 6, 8, 10 x 2 in. Round, p. 157; Cookie Sheet, Cooling Grid, p. 159

Tips: 2, 3, p. 136

Colors:* Kelly Green, Royal Blue, Red-Red, Lemon Yellow, Orange, Brown, Black, Copper (for skin tone shown), p. 148

Fondant: White Ready-To-Use Rolled Fondant (57 oz.), Gum-Tex, Fine Tip Primary Colors FoodWriter Edible Color Markers, p. 149; Easy-Glide Fondant Smoother, Brush Set, p. 151; Cutter/Embosser, p. 152; 20 in. Rolling Pin, Roll & Cut Mat, p. 150

Recipes: Buttercream, Royal Icings, p. 118

Also: 2010 Pattern Book (Windmill, Sign, Flag, Easel; Small, Medium, Large Fairway Ramps), p. 132; Cakes 'N More 3-Tier Party Stand, p. 236; Gingerbread Boy Metal Cutter, p. 204; Meringue Powder, Piping Gel, p. 145; 8 in. Lollipop Sticks, p. 200; Plastic Dowel Rods, p. 240; Cake Circles, Cake Boards, Fanci-Foil Wrap, p. 241; construction paper (flags), scissors, ruler, tape, craft knife, waxed paper, cornstarch, 2½ in. diameter cylinder, cardstock

2-3 days in advance: Make golfers. Prepare cookie dough and tint copper for skin tone shown. Roll out and cut 5 golfers using Gingerbread Boy Cutter. Use pattern to cut 10 easels. Bake and cool cookies. Tint fondant as follows: 2 oz. red, 2 oz. blue, 6 oz. orange, 2 oz. yellow, 1 oz. black. Add ½ teaspoon Gum-Tex to orange and yellow fondant. Roll out ⅛ in. thick as needed. Decorate golfers using royal icing. Outline and pipe in pants and shirts with tip 3 (pat smooth with finger dipped in cornstarch). Pipe dot, outline and zigzag trims on clothes. Using tip 2, pipe dot eyes and nose; outline mouth. Pipe tip 3 outline, pull-out dot and C-motion hair; dot and bead barrettes. When dry, attach easels to backs with royal icing; let dry. **Also:** Make golf course details (p. 124) and fairway ramps. **And:** Make birthday sign. Use pattern to cut out sign. Use FoodWriters to print message. Tape 2 lollipop sticks to back.

Bake and cool 1-layer cakes. Ice smooth in light green. Using reserved dark green fondant; roll out ⅛ in. thick. Cut a 1¾ x 19 in. long strip. Use knife to cut wavy top edge for hills from 1 to 1½ in. high. Attach around 6 in. cake. Repeat using two 13 in. strips for 8 in. cake, two 16 in. strips for 10 in. cake. Use leftover fondant to shape a 1½ x 2 in. wide speed bump; attach to large ramp. Using reserved light brown fondant, roll ¼ in. diameter logs; attach to cake tops, leaving open spaces where ramps will rest. Imprint brick lines ½ in. apart. Roll out small amount of black fondant ¹⁄₁₆ in. thick. Use wide end of tip 3 to cut 2 circles for holes.

At party: Assemble cakes on cake stand. Position ramps and windmill. Insert sign. Position golfers, trimming easels if needed. Attach tunnel, loop, flags, balls and holes with icing. Serves 30.

*Combine Brown with Red-Red for brown hair shown.

▶ Brownie Trophy Treats

Pans: 8-Cavity Silicone Round Brownie Pops Mold, Silicone Bite-Size Brownie Squares Mold, p. 170; Cookie Sheet, Cooling Grid, p. 159

Also: Yellow (2 pks. makes 10-12 treats), Light Cocoa (1 pk. makes 10-12 treats) Candy Melts, p. 196; Parchment Triangles, p. 138; waxed paper, mini marshmallows, toothpicks, knife

Bake and cool brownies in silicone molds supported by cookie sheet. Make 1 pop and 1 bite-size square for each treat; set aside 3 yellow Candy Melts for each treat. Set brownie squares on cooling rack set over drip pan; cover with melted light cocoa candy (p. 130). Chill until set then add 2nd layer; chill. Seal bottoms with candy. Chill until set then repeat if needed. Cover brownie pops as above using yellow candy. Insert toothpicks into mini marshmallows. Dip in melted yellow candy to cover. Chill until set then dip for 2nd layer; chill. Assemble using melted candy. Attach yellow Candy Melts disk to coated square; add marshmallow then brownie pop, narrow end down. Trim 2 yellow candies for handles; attach. Chill until set. Using melted candy in cut parchment bag, pipe bead borders, scroll decorations and number. Each serves 1.

▶ He's a Goal-Getter

Pans: Star, p. 165; Cookie Sheet, Cooling Grid, p. 159

Tips: 2, 3, 6, 16, 18, p. 136-137

Colors: Christmas Red, Lemon Yellow, Copper (for skin tone shown), Royal Blue, Black, Brown, p. 148

Recipes: Buttercream, Royal Icings, Roll-Out Cookies, p. 118

Also: 2010 Pattern Book (Head, Body, Shoes), p. 132; Hand Cookie Cutter, p. 203; Soccer Ball Icing Decorations, p. 180; Meringue Powder, p. 145; 4 in. Lollipop Sticks, p. 200; Cake Boards, Fanci-Foil Wrap, p. 241; marshmallows, scissors, tape, ruler, toothpicks, knife, waxed paper, cornstarch

In advance: Make cookies. Prepare and roll out dough. Using patterns, cut out head and 2 shoes (flip pattern for 2nd shoe). Use cookie cutter to cut 2 hands; flip 1 before baking. Cut six 1 x 2 in. rectangles for cookie supports. Bake and cool. **Also:** Decorate cookies using royal icing. Outline all cookies with tip 3. Cover hands and shoes with tip 16 stars. For head, use tip 3 to outline and fill in mouth and tongue (pat smooth with finger dipped in cornstarch). Pipe tip 6 dot eyes; pat smooth. Cover face and ears with tip 16 stars; overpipe nose and cheeks for dimension. Pipe tip 18 pull-out stars for hair and shoe spikes. Pipe tip 2 outline shoe laces. Let dry.

Bake and cool cake. Position on wrapped board cut 1 in. larger than cake on all sides. Ice sides and background areas smooth. Use pattern to mark body details with toothpicks. Outline details with tip 3; cover with tip 16 stars. Pipe tip 2 name and tip 3 number. Pipe tip 18 pull-out star grass bottom border. Position icing decorations. Use melted candy to attach cookie supports to back of head (use 2), hands and shoes; position on star points. Cake serves 12; each cookie serves 1.

◀ He's a Heads-Up Player!

Pans: 14 x 2 in. Square, p. 157; Helmet, p. 165

Tips: 4, 7, 10, 16, 233, p. 136-137

Colors: Kelly Green, Golden Yellow, Red-Red, Black, Royal Blue, p. 148

Recipe: Buttercream Icing, p. 118

Also: Football Icing Decorations (2 pks.), p. 180; Cake Board, Fanci-Foil Wrap, p. 241; Dowel Rods, p. 240; toothpicks, 16 in. square foamcore board (¼ in. thick), ruler

Bake and cool 1-layer square and helmet cakes. Ice sides and background areas of helmet smooth. Cover helmet with tip 16 stars. Pipe in face mask with tips 7 and 4. Ice square cake smooth; position on wrapped board cut 1 in. wider then cake on all sides. Mark yard lines 2 in. apart. Position helmet cake. Pipe tip 7 yard lines. Pipe tip 233 pull-out grass bottom border. Attach icing decorations with dots of icing. Print tip 10 name and tip 7 initials. Serves 44.

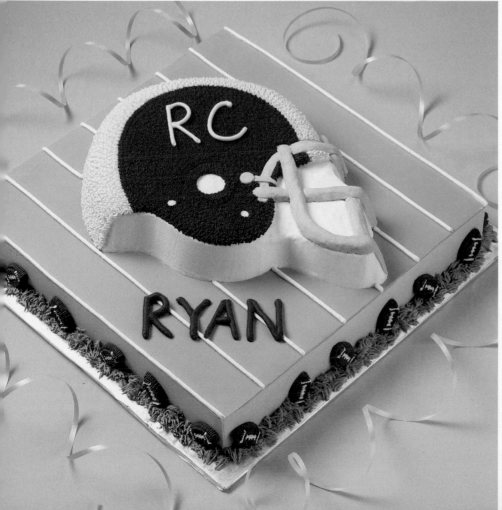

◄ Fudgy Fish

Pans: 8-Cavity Silicone Round Brownie Pops Mold, p. 170; Cookie Sheet, Cooling Grid, p. 159

Tip: 3, p. 136

Recipes: Buttercream Icing, p. 118; favorite brownie recipe or mix

Also: 2010 Pattern Book (Top, Side, Tail Fins), p. 132; Yellow, Orange Candy Melts (1 pk. makes 7 treats), p. 196; Black Tube Decorating Icing, Coupler Ring Set, p. 144; 9 in. Rolling Pin, p. 150; white candy-coated chocolates, spice drops, granulated sugar, scissors, waxed paper

Bake and cool brownies in silicone mold supported by cookie sheet. Place on cooling grid and cover with melted candy (p. 130); chill until firm. Repeat. For fins, roll out spice drops on waxed paper sprinkled with sugar. Cut fins using patterns. Roll out spice drops and cut 2 V-shaped lips. Attach candy-coated chocolate eyes, lips and fins with melted candy; let set. Pipe tip 3 dot pupils with icing. Each serves 1.

► Wake Up Cups

Pans: 8-Cavity Silicone Round Brownie Pops Mold, p. 170; Non-Stick Cookie Sheet, Cooling Grid, p, 167

Candy: White, Orange and Yellow Candy Melts, p. 196; Garden Candy Color Set, p. 199

Also: Round Cut-Outs, p. 153; Parchment Triangles, p. 138; Spatula, p. 140; knife, waxed paper

In advance: Make candy saucers. Tint a portion of melted candy pink using candy color. Place largest Cut-Out on cookie sheet and fill ³⁄₁₆ in. deep with melted candy. Tap to remove air bubbles and chill until firm. Reserve remaining pink candy. Repeat for each color. **Also:** Make handles. On waxed paper, using melted candy in cut parchment bag, pipe a ¾ in. "U" shape. Chill until firm. Turn over and overpipe; let set. Repeat for each color.

Bake and cool brownie pops in silicone mold, supported by cookie sheet. Trim ¼ in. off narrow end. Cover brownies with melted candy (p. 130); chill until firm. Repeat if needed. Using spatula, ice wide end smooth with melted candy. Let set. Pipe dots on cups in assorted colors. Attach handles and saucers to cups with dots of melted candy. Each serves 1.

◄ Cupcake Bouquet

Pan: Mini Muffin, p. 159

Tip: 21, p. 137

Candy: White Candy Melts, p. 196; Garden, Primary Candy Color Sets, Decorator Brush Set, p. 199

Recipe: Buttercream Icing, p. 118

Also: White Mini Baking Cups, p. 186; 8 in. Cookie Treat Sticks, p. 205; Yellow, Orange, Pink, Blue, Green Colored Sugar, p. 146; Cake Release, p. 154; 8 x 2 in. round craft block, white curling ribbon, 2 in. and ½ in. wide satin ribbon (30 in.), straight pins

In advance: Make candy cups. Tint melted candy yellow, pink, green, blue and orange using candy colors. Place baking cups in pan; make candy shells in cups (p. 130). Chill until firm; peel off paper.

Bake and cool mini muffins without cups in pan prepared with Cake Release. Make small hole through bottom of candy cup, insert cookie stick positioning halfway to top edge. Attach stick with melted candy; let set. Slide mini muffin inside candy cup onto stick. With buttercream, pipe tip 21 swirl top. Sprinkle with colored sugar. Wrap 2 in. and ½ in. wide ribbons around craft block, securing with pins. Insert sticks into craft block. Cut curling ribbon into 18 in. lengths, curl and position around sticks. Each serves 1.

◀ Sand Castle Mini Cake

Pan: 9 x 13 x 2 in. Sheet, p. 157
Tip: 3, p. 136
Color: Brown, p. 148
Candy: Red, Yellow, Peanut Butter Candy Melts, p. 196; Cordial Cups Candy Mold, p. 197
Recipe: Buttercream Icing, p. 118
Also: 2010 Pattern Book (Shovel Handle, Doorway, Window), p. 132; Square Cut-Outs, p. 153; 8 in. Cake Board, Fanci-Foil Wrap, p. 241; Disposable Decorating Bags, p. 138; granulated brown sugar, spice drops, pretzel sticks, waxed paper, ruler, knife

In advance: Make candy pail, shovel handle, doorway and window (p. 124). **Also:** Make turrets. Shape spice drops for turret tops. Dip spice drops and pretzel sticks in melted peanut butter candy; sprinkle with brown sugar and let set on waxed paper. Attach spice drops to pretzels with melted candy; let set.

Bake and cool cake using firm-textured batter such as pound cake. For each treat, cut out 1 top tier and 1 middle tier using medium and large Cut-Outs; trim to 1 in. high. For bottom tier, cut a 3¼ in. square; trim to 1½ in. high. Ice lightly, stack and cover with brown sugar. Attach doorway, window and turrets with melted candy; let set. Pipe top of pail with melted candy; attach handle and sprinkle with sugar; let set. Ice foil-wrapped board smooth; sprinkle with sugar. Position cake and pail. Each serves 1.

*Combine Brown with Red-Red for brown shown.

▶ Candy Cache

Pans: Mini, Standard Muffin, Cooling Grid, p. 159
Candy: White Candy Melts (3 oz needed for each set), p. 196; Primary and Garden Candy Color Sets, Decorator Brush Set, p. 199
Recipe: Favorite crisped rice cereal treats
Also: White Mini and Standard Baking Cups, p. 174; Parchment Triangles, p. 138; cherry sour balls, candy-coated chocolates

In advance: Make ⅛ in. thick candy shells in baking cups (p. 130). You will need 1 mini and 1 standard shell for each treat. Chill until firm, then carefully peel baking cup off candy shell. Level top edge with knife or place on warming plate if necessary.

Prepare cereal treats. Shape into small (2 x 1¼ in. high) and large (3¼ x 1 in. high) mounds for icing tops. Cover with melted white candy (p. 130). Attach cherry sour to top of small mound and mini candy cup to top of large mound. Let set. Using melted candy in cut parchment bag, pipe swirls; let set. Fill cups with chocolates and stack. Each serves 1.

◀ Petal-Perfect Cupcakes

Pans: Jumbo Muffin, Cookie Sheet, Cooling Grid, p. 159
Tip: 3, 8, p. 136
Colors: Orange, Rose, p. 148
Recipes: Buttercream, Color Flow Icings, Roll-Out Cookies, p. 118
Also: Stackable! Flower Cookie Cutter Set, p. 204; Yellow Candy Melts, p. 196; White Jumbo Baking Cups, p. 174; Color Flow Mix, p. 145; White Pearl Dust, Brush Set, p. 151; Parchment Triangles, p. 138; Cake Boards, p. 241; cornstarch, waxed paper

In advance: Make cookies. Prepare and roll out dough. Cut 6 petals for each flower using petal cutter from set. Bake and cool cookies. Using tip 3, outline with full-strength and fill-in with thinned color flow icing (p. 130). Let dry 24 hours. **Also:** Brush cookie petals and yellow Candy Melts wafers (1 for each flower) with Pearl Dust.

Bake and cool cupcakes, filling baking cups only ⅓ full with batter. Ice even with top of baking cup. Pipe 6 tip 8 dots around outer edge of cupcake; position petals. Attach yellow candy center with a tip 8 dot. Each serves 1.

◀ Friendly Frog Cookies

Cookie: Stackable! Teddy Bear Cutter Set, p. 204; Heart Cut-Outs, p. 153; Cookie Sheet, Cooling Grid, p. 159

Tips: 4, 5, 10, 12, p. 136-137

Colors:* Leaf Green, Lemon Yellow, Black, p. 148

Recipes: Royal Icing, Roll-Out Cookies, p. 118

Also: Cake Boards, p. 241; Meringue Powder, p. 145; Disposable Decorating Bags, p. 138; waxed paper, cornstarch

Prepare and roll out dough. Cut 1 teddy bear face and 2 medium heart cookies for each treat. Bake and cool. Cover cookies with thinned royal icing (p. 130); let dry on waxed paper-covered boards. Attach face to 2 hearts with tip 12 and full-strength royal icing. Pipe tip 10 ball eyes (flatten and smooth with finger dipped in cornstarch). Pipe tip 5 outline eyelids, tip 4 dot pupils and outline mouth. Pipe tip 12 front legs. Let dry. Each serves 1.

*Combine Leaf Green with Lemon Yellow for green shown.

▶ Fun-Filled Balloon

Pans: Cookie Sheet, Cooling Grid, p. 159

Tips: 3, 8, p. 136

Colors: Christmas Red, Brown, Copper (for skin tone shown), p. 148

Candy: Yellow Candy Melts, p. 196; Cordial Cups Candy Mold, p. 197; 4 in. Lollipop Sticks, p. 200

Recipes: Royal Icing, Roll-Out Cookies, p. 118; favorite crisped rice cereal treats

Also: Round Cut-Outs, p. 153; White Ready-To-Use Rolled Fondant (1 oz. per treat), p. 149; Decorator Brush Set, p. 199; Meringue Powder, p. 145; Fine Tip Primary Colors FoodWriter Edible Color Markers, p. 149; Parchment Triangles, p. 138; knife

In advance: Make candy basket. Mold a ⅛ in. thick candy shell (p. 130) in Cordial Cups Mold; chill until firm.

Prepare and roll out dough. Cut cookies using largest round Cut-Out. Bake and cool. Using royal icing, pipe tip 8 stripes on cookie. Prepare cereal treats and fill basket. Insert lollipop sticks. Cover top of basket using melted candy in cut parchment bag. Tint fondant copper. Roll a ¾ in. ball for head and ¼ in. balls for hands. Flatten hands and imprint fingers with knife. Shape small ball nose and ears; attach with damp brush. Draw eyes and mouth with black FoodWriter. Pipe tip 3 pull-out hair. Attach head and hands to basket and cookie to sticks with melted candy; chill until firm. Each serves 1.

◀ Chocolate Chimps

Pans: Mini Ball, p. 165; Non-Stick Large Cookie/Jelly Roll, p. 167

Tips: 2, 3, p. 136

Colors: Brown, Black, Rose, Royal Blue, Leaf Green, p. 148

Recipes: Buttercream Icing, p. 118; favorite brownie recipe or mix

Also: 101 Cookie Cutters, p. 203; Light Cocoa Candy Melts, p. 196; 4 in. Lollipop Sticks, p. 200; Disposable Decorating Bags, p. 138; cone-shaped corn snacks, cornstarch

In advance: Make ears. Place smallest round cutter from set on non-stick pan. Fill ⅛ in. deep with melted candy. Chill until firm.

Bake and cool brownies, filling Mini Ball Pan cavities ½ full. Trim to level. Using tip 3, pipe in muzzle, pipe dot eyes, pupils, nose (pat all smooth with finger dipped in cornstarch). Add tip 3 outline mouth. For hats, trim bottom of corn snack for even edge; ice smooth. Cut lollipop stick to 3 in.; insert in brownie and position hat. Pipe tip 2 dots and pull-out fringe. Pipe in inner ear with tip 3, ⅜ in. from edge (pat smooth). Position heads on ears, attaching with melted candy. Each serves 1.

◀ Visitors from Venus

Pans: Cookie Sheet, Cooling Grid, p. 159
Tips: 1A, 2, p. 136
Colors: Leaf Green, Lemon Yellow, Black, p. 148
Candy: White Candy Melts, p. 196; Primary and Garden Candy Color Sets, p. 199; 6 in. Lollipop Sticks, p. 200
Recipes: Buttercream (stiff consistency) Icing, p. 118
Also: Silly Feet! Silicone Baking Cups, p. 174; Meringue Powder, p. 145; Parchment Triangles, p. 138; Cake Boards, p. 241; pretzel sticks, spice drops, mini candy-coated chocolates, hollow center hard candies, waxed paper

In advance: Pipe candy features on waxed paper-covered board using melted, tinted candy in cut parchment bags. Pipe ¾ in. diamond-shaped ears and ⅝ in. long hands; chill until firm. Carefully turn over and overpipe backs; chill until firm. Pipe pull-out hair strands; chill until firm. **Also:** Make arms. Dip pretzel stick in melted candy; set on waxed paper and chill until firm. Attach hands using melted candy. **And:** Make antennas. Cut lollipop sticks to 3¼ in. long. Roll spice drop into ball; insert stick.

Bake and cool cupcakes in silicone cups supported by cookie sheet. Cover tops and build up icing mound with tip 1A; smooth with spatula. Insert arms and antenna. Position hair, ears and hollow center eye. Attach mini candy-coated chocolate to center with icing. Pipe tip 2 zigzag mouth. Each serves 1.

*Combine Leaf Green with Lemon Yellow for green shown.

▶ Can't-Miss Treats!

Pans: 9 x 13 x 2 in. Sheet, p. 157; Cookie Sheet, Cooling Grid, p. 159
Colors: Kelly Green, Royal Blue, Black, p. 148
Fondant: White Ready-To-Use Rolled Fondant (1½ oz. per treat), Brush Set, p. 149; 9 in. Rolling Pin, Roll & Cut Mat, p. 150
Candy: Sports Large Lollipop Mold, p. 198; White, Red, Orange, Light Cocoa and Peanut Butter Candy Melts, p. 196; Garden Candy Color Set, p. 199; 6 in. Lollipop Sticks, p. 200
Recipes: Favorite crisped rice cereal treats
Also: Circle Metal Cutter, p. 204; Parchment Triangles, p. 138; Cake Boards, p. 241; knife, ruler, waxed paper, tape, non-stick vegetable pan spray

In advance: Make candy heads in lollipop mold. Tape over openings for sticks. Mold basketball and baseball using piping method (p. 130); chill until firm. Unmold. Pipe on seams and facial features with melted candy; let set. **Also:** Use melted candy to attach one 5 in. stick across back for arms; attach two 4 in. sticks about 1 in. apart below 5 in. stick for legs. Let set.

Prepare cereal treats recipe and press into prepared pan, 1 in. deep; cool. Unmold onto waxed paper-covered board; cut into 3 in. squares. Cover with melted candy (p. 130); let set. Use circle cutter to mark basketball center court; pipe details using melted red candy in cut parchment bag. Tint portions of fondant black, blue and green; reserve some white. For each hand, roll a ⅜ in. ball; flatten, shape and cut fingers. For each shoe, roll a ⅝ in. ball; flatten bottom and shape. For hat, roll a 1 in. ball; flatten bottom and shape. Score seam lines with knife. Roll a small portion to ¹⁄₁₆ in. thick for brim. Cut a 1¼ in. wide oval and attach hat bottom using damp brush, leaving ⅜ in. extended for brim. Attach tiny ball for top button. For grass, roll out fondant ¹⁄₁₆ in. thick. Cut 2 strips, 1¼ x 12 in. long. Cut V-slits for blades of grass. Attach around treat at 2 different heights using damp brush. To insert figures, mark where legs will go; use knife tip to cut small holes through candy. Slide shoes onto legs and push sticks into treats. Slide hands onto sticks and attach with melted candy. Attach hat with melted candy. Each serves 1.

*Add Light Cocoa to Orange for orange candy shown. Add Peanut Butter to White for tan candy shown. Add Black candy color to Light Cocoa candy for black candy shown.

WiSH UPON a star!

It's an "A-list" birthday party with all their favorite celebrities! Transformers start the action with a bold cake starring Optimus Prime and a colorful birthday greeting written in flames. Tinker Bell is here too, sending best wishes from her candy teapot treehouse, which appears as both a charming cake topper and an enchanting candy-filled centerpiece. Here, Hannah Montana rocks the house with chart-topping treats like a cupcake and cookie tower and a dazzling star cake with her name up in lights.

Today's Big Star!

Pans: *Hannah Montana,* (includes Facemaker) p. 188; Cookie Sheet, Cooling Grid, p. 159

Tips: 3, 4, 5, 10, 13, 14, 15, 16, 21, p. 136-137

Colors: *Hannah Montana* Icing Color Set (purple, blue, pink, bright pink), p. 188; Violet, Orange, Rose, Black Icing Colors, p. 148

Recipes: Buttercream, Color Flow Icings, Roll-Out Cookies, p. 118

Also: Nesting Stars Metal Cookie Cutters, p. 204; Disposable Decorating Bags, Parchment Triangles, p. 138; Cake Board, Fanci-Foil Wrap, p. 241; Color Flow Mix, p. 145; 6 x 1 in. high craft foam circle, cornstarch, scissors, tape

In advance: Make cookies. Prepare and roll out dough; cut cookies using 2 largest star cutters. Bake and cool. Outline with tip 3 and full-strength color flow, flow in with thinned color flow. Let dry. Using full-strength color flow, pipe graduated stars using tips 13, 14, 15 and 16 beginning with tip 13 at the centers; let dry. **Also:** Wrap craft circle with foil.

Bake and cool cake; position on foil-wrapped board, cut to fit. Decorate in buttercream. Outline star with tip 5 in bright pink, then purple and blue (smooth with finger dipped in cornstarch). Outline names with tip 4 in black (smooth). Pipe in initials with tip 10, remaining letters with tip 5 (smooth all). Cover center star with tip 16 stars in pink. Pipe tip 21 star bottom border in pink. Position facemaker. Place cake on craft foam, position cookies. Cake serves 12, each cookie serves 1.

Hannah's Brownies

Pan: 9 x 13 x 2 in. Sheet, p. 157

Tip: 3, p. 136

Colors: *Hannah Montana* Icing Color Set (pink, purple), p. 188

Recipes: Buttercream Icing, p. 118; favorite brownie recipe or mix

Also: *Hannah Montana* Icing Decorations, p. 188; Star Comfort-Grip Cutter, p. 202; Star Plastic Nesting Cutter Set, p. 203; Decorator Brush Set, p. 199; Pink, Purple Cake Sparkles, p. 146; tea strainer, spoon

Bake and cool brownies. Cut stars using Comfort-Grip Cutter (1 cake makes 6 stars). Ice smooth. Use spoon to press Cake Sparkles through tea strainer for finer texture. Set smallest plastic star cutter on brownie. Spoon in Cake Sparkles; use brush to spread evenly. Remove cutter. Pipe tip 3 dots around edge. Position icing decorations. Each serves 1.

Backstage Pass

Pans: Cookie Sheet, Cooling Grid, p. 159

Tips: 2, 3, p. 136

Colors: *Hannah Montana* Icing Color Set (bright pink, purple), p. 188; Black, p. 148

Recipes: Color Flow Icing, Roll-Out Cookies, p. 118

Also: Color Flow Mix, p. 145; *Hannah Montana* Icing Decorations, Treat Bags, p. 188; Parchment Triangles, p. 138; ruler, knife

Prepare and roll out dough. Cut 3 x 4 in. rectangles; bake and cool cookies. Outline with tip 3 and full-strength color flow, flow in with thinned color flow. Let dry. Pipe dot message and attach icing decorations with tip 2 and full-strength color flow. Let dry. Place cookies in treat bags. Each serves 1.

Hannah's Dazzling Display

Pans: 10 x 3 in. Round, p. 158; Standard Muffin, Cooling Grid, p. 159

Tips: 1, 3, p. 136

Colors: *Hannah Montana* Icing Color Set (pink, bright pink, purple), p. 188; Black, p. 148

Fondant: White Ready-To-Use Rolled Fondant (48 oz.), Gum-Tex, p. 149; Brush Set, White Pearl Dust, p. 151; 20 in. Rolling Pin, Roll & Cut Mat, p. 150

Recipes: Buttercream, Royal Icings, p. 118

Also: *Hannah Montana* Party Toppers (4 pks.), Candle, Standard Baking Cups, p. 188; 23 Count Standard Cupcakes 'N More Dessert Stand, p. 173; Nesting Stars Metal Cutter Set, p. 204; Lavender Colored Sugar, p. 146; Meringue Powder, p. 145; waxed paper, cellophane tape

At least 2 days in advance: Make fondant base ring. Combine 24 oz. fondant with 3 teaspoons Gum-Tex; tint black. Fold a 32 in. sheet of waxed paper in half lengthwise and wrap around side of 10 x 3 in. round pan; tape seam together but do not tape to pan. Roll out fondant ⅛ in. thick; cut a 32 x 3 in. strip. Wrap fondant around sides of prepared pan and smooth seam with fingers. For fondant stars, tint 8 oz. rose, 8 oz. violet; roll out ⅛ in. thick. Cut 7 violet stars with smallest cutter and 7 rose stars with second smallest cutter. Brush with Pearl Dust and attach to fondant ring with damp brush. With royal icing and tips 1 and 3, pipe graduated-size dots; let set. After ring has completely dried, carefully slide off pan and remove waxed paper.

Bake and cool 22 cupcakes. Ice smooth with buttercream and sprinkle with lavender sugar. Position cupcake stand in base ring and cupcakes on stand. Position toppers and candle. Each serves 1.

©Disney

▶ Transformers 360°

Pans: 8 x 2 in. Round, p. 157; Cooling Grid, p. 159

Tips: 1, 1A, 2, 2A, 12, p. 136-137

Colors:* Black, Christmas Red, Red-Red, Sky Blue, Royal Blue, p. 148

Fondant: White Ready-To-Use Rolled Fondant (48 oz.), p. 149; 20 in. Rolling Pin, Roll & Cut Mat, p. 150; Brush Set, Easy-Glide Fondant Smoother, p. 151; Alphabet/Number Cut-Outs, p. 153

Recipe: Buttercream Icing, p. 118

Also: 2010 Pattern Book (*Transformers* Autobot shield), p. 132; *Transformers* Cake Decoration, p. 189; Cake Board, Fanci-Foil Wrap, p. 241; toothpick

Bake and cool 2-layer cake. Prepare for rolled fondant (p. 119). Tint 24 oz. fondant royal blue; cover cake and smooth with Fondant Smoother. Tint 5 oz. fondant each red and sky blue. Roll out ⅛ in. thick and use pattern to cut 4 shields in each color. Attach shields to cake sides, ½ in. apart, with damp brush. Mark pattern details with toothpick. Outline and pipe in details with tip 2. Cut red letters for name and attach with damp brush. Tint 12 oz. fondant black. Roll a ⅝ x 26 in. log and attach for bottom border with damp brush. Roll out remaining black ⅛ in. thick; cut 30 wheel circles using wide end of tip 2A. Roll out white fondant 1/16 in. thick. Cut 30 inner circles using narrow end of tip 1A; make another mark for center circle with tip 12. Attach white circles to wheels with damp brush. Pipe tip 1 center circle; edge with tip 1 dots. Attach wheels to bottom border with damp brush. Position cake decoration. Serves 20.

*Combine Red-Red with Christmas Red for red shown.

▼ Take your Place with *Transformers*

Pans: Cookie Sheet, Cooling Grid, p. 159
Tips: 1, 5, p. 136
Colors:* Orange, Golden Yellow, Violet, Rose, Black, p. 148
Recipes: Color Flow Icing, Roll-Out Cookies, p. 118
Also: 2010 Pattern Book (Flame), p. 132; *Transformers* Icing Decorations, p. 189; Color Flow Mix, p. 145; toothpicks, knife, ruler

Prepare and roll out dough; cut 5¼ x 2¼ in. rectangles. Bake and cool cookies. Cover with color flow icing (p. 130); let dry. Mark flame pattern with toothpick. Using thinned color flow and tip 1, pipe in flames and attach icing decoration. Let dry. Print name with tip 5 and full-strength color flow icing. Let dry. Each serves 1.

*Combine Violet with Rose for violet shown. Combine Orange with Golden Yellow for orange shown.

▼ *Transformers* Take Their Stand

Pans: Standard Muffin, Cookie Sheet, Cooling Grid, p. 159
Tips: 2, 3, p. 136
Colors:* Sky Blue, Royal Blue, Red-Red, Christmas Red, p. 148
Recipes: Buttercream, Color Flow Icings, Roll-Out Cookies, p. 118
Also: 2010 Pattern Book (*Transformers* Autobot shield), p. 132; *Transformers* Cake Decoration, Party Toppers (2 pks.), Standard Baking Cups, p. 189; 13 Count Standard Cupcakes 'N More Dessert Stand, p. 173; Color Flow Mix, p. 145; Blue Colored Sugar, p. 146; knife, toothpicks

In advance: Make cookies. Prepare and roll out dough. Use pattern to cut 12 Transformers Autobot shields; cut 1¼ x 2¼ in. triangle easel backs, making 2 for each cookie. Bake and cool cookies. Outline cookies with tip 3 and full-strength color flow; flow in thinned color flow. Let dry. Mark pattern on cookie with toothpick. Use tip 2 to outline and flow in design with color flow; let dry. Attach easels to back using full strength color flow; let dry.

Bake and cool cupcakes. Ice with buttercream; sprinkle with blue sugar. Position on Dessert Stand. Position party toppers and cake decoration on top. Each serves 1.

*Combine Red-Red with Christmas Red for red shown. Combine Sky Blue with Royal Blue for darker blue shown.

▲ Fired Up for a Birthday!

Pan: *Transformers*, p. 189
Tips: 3, 16, p. 136
Colors: *Transformers* Icing Color Set (blue, dark blue, gray, black), p. 189; Red-Red, Black (additional needed for base board), p. 148
Fondant: White Ready-To-Use Rolled Fondant (96 oz.), p. 149; Brush Set, Easy-Glide Fondant Smoother, p. 151; 20 in. Rolling Pin, Roll & Cut Mat, p. 150
Recipes: Buttercream Icing, p. 118; Chocolate Fondant (2 recipes), Thinned Fondant Adhesive, p. 119
Also: 2010 Pattern Book (Flames), p. 132; Dark Cocoa Candy Melts, p. 196; 101 Cookie Cutters, p. 203; Piping Gel, p.145; 13 x 19 in. Cake Board, Fanci-Foil Wrap, p. 241; 18 x 31 in. foamcore board (¼ in. thick), tape, ruler, knife, toothpicks, cornstarch

2-3 days in advance: Prepare base board. Prepare 2 recipes chocolate fondant. Knead in 24 oz. additional fondant and tint black. Cover foamcore board with black fondant (p. 123); smooth with Fondant Smoother. Using additional white fondant, tint 4 oz. blue, 20 oz. red. Roll out blue ⅛ in. thick. Use cutters from set to cut out message; let dry on cornstarch-dusted surface. Roll out red ⅛ in. thick, cut a 12 x 18 in. rectangle. Lift and position on board where flames will go. Use pattern to mark flames; use knife to cut and remove excess. Reroll remaining red fondant; cut individual flames. Brush backs with damp brush and attach. Let dry overnight.

Bake and cool cake. Ice background areas smooth. Use tip 3 to outline details. Pipe in eyes with tip 3 (smooth with finger dipped in cornstarch). Cover cake with tip 16 stars. Position cake on prepared board. Attach message using thinned fondant adhesive. Serves 12.

◄ *Dora* Eyes the Butterflies!

Pans: *Dora the Explorer*, p. 194; Cookie Sheet, Cooling Grid, p. 159

Tips: 3, 16, p. 136-137

Colors:* *Dora the Explorer* Icing Color Set (red, pink, brown, *Dora* skin tone), p. 194; Lemon Yellow, Golden Yellow, Violet, Rose, Royal Blue, Orange, Teal, Kelly Green, Black, p. 148

Fondant: White Ready-To-Use Rolled Fondant (20 oz.), p. 149; Brush Set, White & Orchid Pink Pearl Dust, p. 151; 20 in. Rolling Pin, Roll & Cut Mat, p. 150

Recipes: Buttercream, Color Flow Icings, Roll-Out Cookies, p. 118

Also: Butterfly Plastic Cutter, p. 203; Color Flow Mix, p. 145; Cake Boards, 10 in. Cake Circle, Fanci-Foil Wrap, p. 241; scissors, tape, toothpicks, knife, ruler, cornstarch

In advance: Make cookies. Prepare and roll out dough. Cut cookies using Butterfly Cutter; bake and cool. Use tip 3 to outline outer edge and details with full-strength color flow; fill in with thinned color flow (p. 130). Let dry 24 hours.

Bake and cool cake. Use knife to trim off shirt, backpack, socks and tops of shoes. Ice cake sides, background areas, whites of eyes and body from waist down smooth. Pipe details using tip 3. Outline face, hair, arms, bracelet, eyes, mouth and nose. Fill in irises, pupils, mouth, tongue and bracelet (pat smooth with finger dipped in cornstarch). Add dot highlights to eyes. Cover face, hair and arms with tip 16 stars. For dress and shoes, tint fondant as follows: 10 oz. hot pink, 4 oz. yellow, 2 oz. violet, 1 oz. green, 1 oz. light pink; reserve 2 oz. white. Roll out ⅛ in. thick as needed. Using inside of pan as mold, shape fondant shoes; position on cake. Cover feet with tip 16 stars. Cut 2 triangles and a small circle to make ¾ in. wide bows; attach.

Cut a strip ¾ x 3¼ in. for bodice top, 4 strips ¼ x 3¼ in. for stripes and 2 straps ½ x ¾ in. Position on cake, trimming as needed to fit. Roll 4 logs 4 in. long, tapering from ¼ to ¾ in. diameter. Attach on skirt area of cake, wide end down, to create dimension. For skirt, roll out fondant ⅛ in. thick and cut a half-circle using 10 in. Cake Circle as a guide. Gradually taper in sides and top to 5 in. at waist. Attach over logs, shaping for full skirt effect. Cut 3 strips ¼ x 15 in.; use damp brush to attach over skirt for trim. Cut 25 diamonds ¼ x ⅝ in.; attach to skirt using damp brush. Brush diamonds with white Pearl Dust (p. 122); brush skirt around diamonds with pink Pearl Dust. Pipe tip 16 shell bottom border. Position cookies. Cake serves 12; each cookie serves 1.

*Combine Lemon Yellow with Golden Yellow for yellow shown. Combine Violet with Rose for violet shown. Combine Dora Red with Rose for hot pink shown.

► *Dora* Sees the Rainbow

Pan: Standard Muffin, p. 159

Tip: 1, p. 136

Recipe: Buttercream Icing, p. 118

Also: *Dora the Explorer* Icing Decorations, Standard Baking Cups, p. 194; Lemon Yellow, Leaf Green, Royal Blue, Violet, Pink Tube Decorating Gel, p. 144; White Cake Sparkles, p. 146

Bake and cool cupcakes; ice smooth. Using Decorating Gels, pipe lines for rainbow, about ½ in. wide. Sprinkle Cake Sparkles on rainbow. Position Icing Decoration. Pipe tip 1 outline starbursts. Each serves 1.

▶ Go, Diego, Go!

Pans: *Go, Diego, Go!*, p. 194; Cookie Sheet, Cooling Grid, p. 159
Tips: 1, 3, 4, 6, 16, 233, p. 136-137
Colors:* *Go, Diego, Go!* Icing Color Set (brown, black, blue, *Diego* skin tone), p. 194; Royal Blue, Leaf Green, Kelly Green, Lemon Yellow, Golden Yellow, Orange, Terra Cotta, p. 148
Recipes: Buttercream Icing, Roll-Out Cookies, p. 118
Also: 101 Cookie Cutters, p. 203; Football Icing Decorations (2 pks.), p. 180; Flowerful Medley Sprinkles, p. 146; Cake Boards, Fanci-Foil Wrap, p. 241; knife, cornstarch, toothpicks

In advance: Make football cookie. Prepare and roll out dough. Cut football using cutter from set. Bake and cool.

Bake and cool cake. Use knife to trim off vest, level arm with watch and straighten other arm. Ice cake sides and background areas smooth. Outline facial features with tip 3, remainder of cake with tip 4. Fill in and pat smooth (with finger dipped in cornstarch) the following: mouth and tongue; accents and soles of shoes; chest patch; insides of pant legs and sleeve; eye, iris and pupil. Add tip 1 dot highlights to pupils. Cover remainder of *Diego* with tip 16 stars. Ice football cookie smooth. Use tip 6 to outline and pipe in stripes (pat smooth). Pipe tip 3 outline laces. Attach cookie to cake with icing. Use tip 4 to outline hand and sleeve; fill in with tip 16 stars. Pipe tip 233 pull-out grass bottom border. Position icing decorations. Sprinkle confetti from Flowerful Medley assortment on background. Serves 12.

*Combine Leaf Green with Lemon Yellow for lighter green shown.

◀ Good Sport *Diego*

Pans: Cookie Sheet, Cooling Grid, p. 159
Tips: 2, 3, p. 136
Colors:* Brown, Black, Terra Cotta, Orange, Red-Red, p. 148
Recipes: Color Flow Icing, Roll-Out Cookies, p. 118
Also: 2010 Pattern Book (Soccer Ball), p. 132; *Go, Diego, Go!* Icing Decorations, p. 194; 101 Cookie Cutters, p. 203; Color Flow Mix, p. 145; cornstarch, toothpick

In advance: Make cookies. Prepare and roll out dough. Cut cookies using medium round and football cutters from set; bake and cool. Using full-strength color flow, outline cookies with tip 2. Flow in with thinned color flow (p. 130); let dry.

Decorate using full-strength color flow and tip 3. Pipe lines on baseball and basketball. Outline and pipe in football stripes (pat smooth with finger dipped in cornstarch). Use pattern to mark soccer ball design; outline and fill in (pat large areas smooth). Attach icing decorations with icing dots. Each serves 1.

*Combine Terra Cotta with Orange for orange shown. Combine Brown with Red-Red for brown shown.

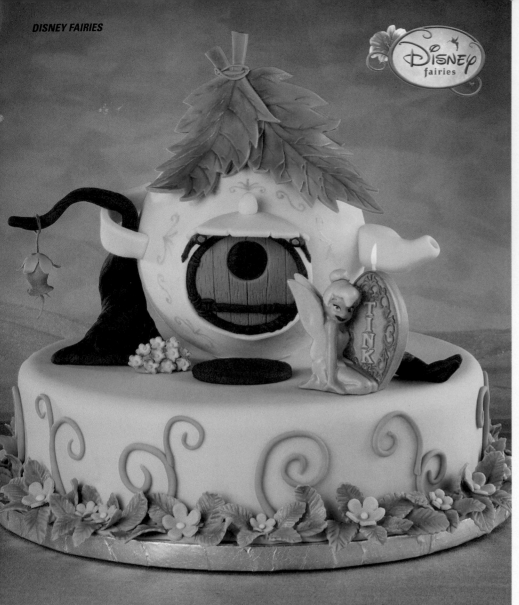

◀ *Tinker Bell's* Teapot Townhouse

Pans: 12 x 2 in. Round, p. 157; Sports Ball, p. 165

Tip: 2A, p. 136

Colors:* Kelly Green, Rose, Brown, Red-Red, Black, Violet, Lemon Yellow, p. 148

Fondant/Gum Paste: White Ready-To-Use Rolled Fondant (120 oz.), Gum-Tex, p. 149; Gold & White Pearl Dust, Brush Set, Easy-Glide Fondant Smoother, 10-Pc. Fondant/Gum Paste Tool Set, Flower Former Set, p. 151; Floral Collection Flower Making Set, p. 153; 20 in. Rolling Pin, Roll & Cut Mat, p. 150

Recipe: Buttercream Icing, p. 118, Thinned Fondant Adhesive, p. 119

Also: 2010 Pattern Book (Large, Small Leaves), p. 132; *Disney Fairies* Candle, p. 193; White Candy Melts (5 pks.), p. 196; 101 Cookie Cutters, p. 203; 14 in. Silver Cake Base, Cake Circles, p. 241; Plastic Dowel Rods, p. 240; tea strainer, non-toxic pastel chalk (green, yellow, pink, ivory), 26 gauge florist wire (4 in.), cotton balls, lemon extract, knife, ruler, waxed paper, cornstarch

Several days in advance: Make large teapot (p. 124). **Also:** Make flowers and leaves, hanging flower and branch (p. 124).

Bake and cool 2-layer cake (bake two 1½ in. high layers for a 3 in. high cake). Prepare for Stacked Construction (p. 116) and rolled fondant (p. 119). Tint 36 oz. fondant light green. Cover cake with rolled fondant; smooth with Fondant Smoother. Cut a Cake Circle to 3 in. diameter for under teapot; cover with green fondant. Tint 6 oz. fondant dark green. Roll ¼ in. diameter logs. Using damp brush, attach to cake sides in various scroll patterns. Arrange and attach leaves and flowers around base using thinned fondant adhesive. Position teapot on cake. Attach tree branch to teapot using melted candy. Marbleize reserved dark and medium brown fondant (p. 123). Use 1 oz. to shape fallen branch behind candle; attach using damp brush. Roll out 1 oz. ¼ in. thick. Cut a circle using medium round cutter from 101 Cutters Set. Attach to cake for door mat. Use remaining brown mixture to shape tree trunk; position on cake and smooth top to attach to branch. Use veining tool to imprint wood grain on all pieces. Place small log of green fondant on cake near tree; attach forget-me-nots. Wrap wire stem of hanging flower around tree branch. Position candle. Serves 40.

*Combine Violet with Rose for violet shown. Combine Brown with Red-Red and Black for medium and dark brown fondant. Combine Brown with Red-Red for light brown.

▶ Take Tea with *Tinker Bell*

Pan: Mini Ball, p. 165

Tip: 3, p. 136

Colors:* Kelly Green, Rose, Brown, Red-Red, Black, p. 148

Fondant/Gum Paste: White Ready-To-Use Rolled Fondant (24 oz.), p. 149; 20 in. Rolling Pin, Roll & Cut Mat, p. 150; White & Gold Pearl Dust, Brush Set, 10-Pc. Fondant/Gum Paste Tool Set, Easy-Glide Fondant Smoother, Flower Former Set, p. 151; Floral Collection Flower Making Set, p. 153

Candy: Garden Goodies Lollipop Mold 2-Pack, p. 198; White, Yellow Candy Melts, p. 196; Garden Candy Color Set, p. 199

Also: 2010 Pattern Book (Large, Small Leaves), p. 132; 101 Cookie Cutters, p. 203; Piping Gel, p. 145; 6 in. Cake Circle, Fanci-Foil Wrap, p. 241; *Disney Fairies* Party Toppers, p. 193; fine tip brush, non-toxic pastel chalk (green, yellow, ivory), tea strainer, lemon extract, knife, ruler, cornstarch, tape, scissors

Prepare base. Tint 8 oz. fondant green; roll out ⅛ in. thick. Cover cake circle (p. 123); add ½ teaspoon Gum-Tex to remaining green fondant. Roll out ⅛ in. thick. Use patterns to cut 1 large and 3 small leaves for lid. Vein leaves using veining tool from set on thin foam. Let dry in large Flower Former dusted with cornstarch. Make candy flowers for inside teapot. Tint portion of melted white candy pink. Use candy mold, piping method (p. 130) and melted candy in cut parchment bags to make 45 separate flowers with yellow centers. Make fondant flowers. Tint small amount of fondant rose; roll out ⅛ in. thick. Use forget-me-not cutter from Flower Making Set to cut 5 flowers. Place flowers on thin foam; cup using ball tool from set. Use damp brush to attach small balls of green fondant for centers; let dry. Make small teapot (p.125). Roll out remaining brown ⅛ in. thick for doorstep; cut a circle using smallest round cutter from set. Use knife to imprint grain lines and attach to board. Arrange fondant flowers on small mound of fondant; attach topper at other side. Fill teapot with prepared candies. Position lid.

*Combine Brown with Red-Red and Black for medium and dark brown shown. Combine Brown with Red-Red for light brown shown.

◄ *Ariel's* **Cameo Cake**

Pans: *Disney Princess*, p. 193; Cooling Grid, p. 159

Tips: 2, 3, 16, 363, p. 136-137

Colors:*Disney Princess* Icing Color Set (red, teal, *Ariel* skin tone), p. 193; Royal Blue, Rose, Violet, Leaf Green, Lemon Yellow, Black, p. 148

Fondant/Gum Paste: White Ready-To-Use Rolled Fondant (58 oz.), Gum-Tex, p. 149; 10-Pc. Fondant/Gum Paste Tool Set, Flower Forming Cups, Easy-Glide Fondant Smoother, p. 151; 9 in. Rolling Pin, Roll & Cut Mat, p. 150; Floral Collection Flower Making Set, Flower Cut-Outs, p. 153

Recipes: Buttercream Icing, p. 118; Thinned Fondant Adhesive, p. 119

Also: Candy Melting Plate, Decorator Brush Set, p. 199; Piping Gel, p. 145, Cake Board, Fanci-Foil Wrap, p. 241; 20 x 16 in. plywood or foamcore board (½ in. thick), cotton balls

In advance: Make Fondant Border Accents (p. 125). **Also:** Prepare base board. Tint 40 oz. fondant violet. Cut foamcore into 19½ x 16 in. wide oval and cover with fondant (p. 123).

Bake and cool cake. Ice sides smooth to match base board. Use tip 3 to outline hair, eyebrows, eyes, nose, mouth, body and swimsuit top. Outline pupils using tip 2. Use tip 3 to pipe in lips, pupils, whites of eyes and irises. (smooth with decorating brush dipped in cornstarch). Add tip 2 dot eye highlights. Outline flower with tip 3 and cover with tip 16 stars. Pipe tip 3 petal lines and dot flower center. Cover remaining areas with tip 16 stars. Pipe pull-out eyelashes with tip 2. Position cake on base board. Pipe tip 363 shell bottom border. For vine on base board, tint 3 oz. fondant green; roll out ⅛ in. thick. Cut three ¼ in. wide x 18 in. long strips. Attach approximately 1 in. from board edge using damp brush. Attach bow. Roll out reserved rose fondant ⅛ in. thick and cut two 1 x 7 in. long streamers. Attach with damp brush; support with cotton balls until dry. Attach remaining accents with Thinned Fondant Adhesive. Remove cotton balls before serving. Serves 12.

*Combine Royal Blue with Teal for aqua shown. Combine Violet with Rose for violet shown. Combine Rose with Lemon Yellow for rose shown on lips.

▶ *Ariel's* **Ocean Hearts**

Pans: Cookie Sheet, Cooling Grid, p. 159

Tip: 2, p. 136

Colors:* *Disney Princess* Icing Color Set (teal), p. 193; Rose, Violet, p. 148

Fondant: White Ready-To-Use Rolled Fondant, p 149; Floral Garland Cutter/Ejector Set, p. 153; 9 in. Rolling Pin, Roll & Cut Mat, p. 150, Brush Set, p. 151

Recipes: Royal Icing, Roll-Out Cookies, p. 118

Also: *Disney Princess* Party Toppers, p. 193; 101 Cookie Cutters, p. 203; Meringue Powder, p. 145; Cake Board, p. 241; White Candy Melts, p. 196; Parchment Triangles, p. 138; ruler, toothpick, cornstarch

Prepare and roll out cookie dough. For each treat cut 1 medium round and 1 medium heart using cutters from set. Cut ½ in. off bottom of heart cookie. Bake and cool. Tint portions of fondant rose and teal; reserve some white. Roll out rose ¹⁄₁₆ in. thick. Using ejector, make an assortment of 8 flowers using the 2 flower shapes. Pipe tip 2 dot centers using royal icing. Let dry on cornstarch-dusted cake board. For shells, marbleize white with teal fondant (p. 123). Shape into teardrops; mark ridges with toothpick and let dry.

Using tip 2 and full-strength royal icing, outline heart cookie. Flow in using thinned royal icing. let dry. Roll out rose fondant ⅛ in. thick. Cut ¼ in. wide x 10 in. long strip and shape into simple bow and streamers (p. 123). Roll small amount of fondant into a ball. Attach to center of bow with damp brush; let dry. Ice round cookie smooth. Attach heart cookie to back edge of round cookie using melted candy. Hold in place till set. Attach flowers, shells and bow to heart cookie using royal icing. Position topper. Each serves 1.

*Combine Violet with Rose for violet shown.

©Disney

▼ *Elmo's* Snack Shuttle

Pans: Mini Ball, p. 165; Cookie Sheet, Cooling Grid, p. 159

Color: Black, p. 148

Fondant: White Ready-To-Use Rolled Fondant, p. 149; Brush Set, p. 151; Star Cut-Outs, p. 153; 9 in. Rolling Pin, Roll & Cut Mat, p. 150

Candy: White Candy Melts (1 pk. makes 3-4 treats), p. 196; Garden Candy Color Set, p. 199

Recipe: Roll-Out Cookies, p. 118

Also: *Elmo* Icing Decorations, p. 195; Yellow Colored Sugar, p. 146; mini candy-coated chocolates, orange spice drops, warming tray, spoon, scissors, toothpick, granulated sugar, ruler, waxed paper

In advance: Tint melted white candy gray using black candy color. Make two ³⁄₁₆ in. thick candy shells (p. 130) for each treat. Rub bottom half over warming tray or warm cookie sheet to flatten just enough to stand without tipping. **Also:** Make cookie stars. Prepare and roll out dough. Using medium Cut-Out, cut 6 cookies for each spaceship. Sprinkle with colored sugar. Bake and cool cookies. **And:** Make raised arm. Roll a fondant log ³⁄₁₆ x ½ in. long for arm. Shape a ½ in. flattened teardrop for hand; cut slits for fingers. Let dry 24 hours. **And:** Make fondant stars. Roll out fondant ⅛ in. thick. Cut stars using smallest cut-out. Let dry.

Attach hand to arm with melted candy. Roll a ⅛ in. diameter log; use damp brush to attach around arm for cuff. For exhaust pipe, dip a spice drop in melted gray candy; let set on waxed paper. For flame, using scissors, cut 4 slits, ½ in. deep; cut each section into 3rds; dip in granulated sugar to keep sections separated. Using melted candy, connect wide ends of flame and pipe; let set then attach pipe to bottom half of shell, trimming if necessary to follow curve. Attach mini candies, about ½ in. apart. Tint 1 oz. fondant gray; roll out ⅛ in. thick. Cut a strip ⅜ x 11 in.; attach around edge of top half of shell using melted candy. Attach *Elmo* using melted candy. For collar, roll a ⅛ x 2½ in. log of white fondant. For fingers on ship, roll a ¼ x ½ in. log; use toothpick to shape fingers. Use melted candy to attach collar, fingers and raised arm. Position cookies inside; position top half of shell. Each serves 1.

SESAME STREET
™/© 2009 *Sesame Workshop*

▲ Blast Off *Elmo*!

Pans: *Elmo*, p. 195; 18 x 3 in. Half-Round, p. 158; Cookie Sheet, Cooling Grid, p. 159

Tips: 3, 5, 16, p. 136-137

Colors:* Black, No-Taste Red, Lemon Yellow, Royal Blue, Christmas Red, Violet, Rose, Orange, p. 148

Fondant: White Ready-To-Use Rolled Fondant (82 oz.), p. 149; 20 in. Rolling Pin, Roll & Cut Mat, p. 150; Easy-Glide Fondant Smoother, p. 151; Star Cut-Outs, p. 153

Recipes: Buttercream, Color Flow Icings, Roll-Out Cookies, p. 118

Also: 2010 Pattern Book (*Elmo's* Arm and Hand, Exhaust Pipe, Exhaust Flames, Small, Medium and Large Ovals), p. 132; Cake Boards, Fanci-Foil Wrap, p. 241; 101 Cookie Cutters, p. 203; Color Flow Mix, Piping Gel, p. 145; Red Colored Sugar, p. 146; 20 x 24 in. plywood or foamcore board (½ in. thick), ruler, knife

In advance: Make cookies. Prepare and roll out dough. Using star cookie cutters from 101 Cutter Set, cut 1 medium and 6 small cookies. Using large round cutter, cut circle, then move up 1½ in. to cut moon. Using pattern, cut exhaust flames shape. Bake and cool cookies. Outline with tip 3 and full-strength color flow; flow in with thinned color flow. Let set. With full-strength color flow, pipe tip 3 dot eyes, pupils and mouth on medium star. Let set. **Also:** Cut fondant stars. Roll out fondant ⅛ in. thick; cut stars using smallest cut-out. Let dry.

Bake and cool *Elmo* cake and two half-round cakes 2 in. high. Decorate Elmo with buttercream. Pipe in mouth, nose, eyes and pupils with tip 3 (smooth with finger dipped in cornstarch); add tip 3 smile lines. Cover face with tip 16 stars. Cut 2 in. off straight edge of each half-round; ice edges together for spaceship. Decorate fondant spaceship and Elmo features (p. 125). Position cookies. Serves 34.

*Combine Violet with Rose for violet shown. Combine Christmas Red and No-Taste Red for red used for fondant letters.

◀ *Sesame Street* Starlet!

Pans: *Abby Cadabby*, p. 195; Cookie Sheet, Cooling Grid, p. 159

Tips: 1s, 2, 3, 12, 13, 16, 21, p. 136-137

Colors: *Abby Cadabby* Icing Color Set (pink, yellow, purple, blue), p. 195; Rose, Black, p. 148

Fondant: White Ready-To-Use Rolled Fondant (114 oz.), p. 149; Brush Set, Easy-Glide Fondant Smoother, p. 151; 20 in. Rolling Pin, Roll & Cut Mat, p. 150

Recipes: Buttercream, Color Flow Icings, Roll-Out Cookies, p. 118

Also: 2010 Pattern Book (Large Star), p. 132; Nesting Stars Metal Cutter Set, p. 204; Color Flow Mix, Piping Gel, p. 145; Cake Boards, Fanci-Foil Wrap, p. 241; 22 x 22 in. foamcore boards (¼ in. thick, 2 needed), tape, knife, scissors, ruler, waxed paper, toothpicks, cornstarch

2-3 days in advance: Make cookies. Prepare and roll out dough. Cut stars using 2 smallest cutters from set. Bake and cool cookies. Using purple color flow, outline cookies with tip 3 and full-strength icing; flow in with thinned icing (p. 130). Let dry 24 hours. Using pink color flow, outline cookies ⅛ in. from edge with tip 3 and full-strength icing; flow in with thinned icing. Immediately pipe tip 1s dots and outline stars with full-strength white color flow; let dry. **Also:** Prepare large star base board using double-thick foamcore. Increase pattern to 22 in. wide. Cut foamcore star; prepare for rolled fondant (p. 123). Tint 60 oz. fondant pink and 54 oz. fondant violet. Roll out pink ⅛ in. thick. Cover base board and smooth with Fondant Smoother. Roll out violet fondant ⅛ in. thick. Cut out fondant star ¾ in. smaller than pattern on all sides. Brush back with damp brush and attach to base. Pipe tip 2 dot and outline stars with full-strength white color flow.

Bake and cool cake. Ice sides and background areas smooth. Using tip 3, outline and pipe in whites of eyes, eyelashes and eyelids (pat smooth with finger dipped in cornstarch). Use tip 3 to overpipe iris then pupil (pat smooth); add dot highlights. Use tip 3 to outline and fill in barrettes and mouth (pat smooth). Pipe tip 3 bead heart tongue. Outline wand with tip 3; fill in with tip 12 (pat smooth). Outline *Abby* and dress with tip 3; cover with tip 16 stars. Pipe tip 16 pull-out star hair and tip 3 pull-out string pompom on wand. Pipe tip 21 shell bottom border. Position *Abby* cake on prepared base. Position star cookies. Cake serves 12; each cookie serves 1.

▶ Starring *Abby Cadabby!*

Pans: Mini Star, p. 225; Cookie Sheet, Cooling Grid, p. 159

Candy: White Candy Melts, p. 196; Garden Candy Color Set, p. 199

Also: Heart Cut-Outs, p. 153; *Abby Cadabby* Icing Decorations, p. 195; Pink Colored Sugar, p. 146; Parchment Triangles, p. 138; spoon, warming tray

Prepare and roll out cookie dough. Cut 5-6 hearts for each treat using medium Cut-Out. Sprinkle with pink sugar; bake and cool. Mold two ¼ in. thick candy shells (p. 130) for each treat in Mini Star Pan using melted white candy tinted pink. Smooth top edges by sliding across warm cookie sheet or warming tray. Using a finely-cut parchment bag with melted candy, pipe line and dot stars on top half. Attach icing decoration with dot of melted candy. Fill bottom half with cookies and assemble box. Each serves 1.

TM/© 2009 *Sesame Workshop*

◄ **High Climb to Fight Crime!**

Pan: *Spider-Man*, p. 190
Tips: 3, 14, p. 136-137
Colors: *Spider-Man* Icing Color Set (blue, red, black), p. 190; Golden Yellow, p. 148
Fondant/Gum Paste: White Ready-To-Use Rolled Fondant (72 oz.), p. 149; 10-Pc. Fondant/Gum Paste Tool Set, Easy-Glide Fondant Smoother, Brush Set, p. 151; 20 in. Rolling Pin, Roll & Cut Mat, p. 150
Recipe: Buttercream Icing, p. 118
Also: Piping Gel, p. 145; 101 Cookie Cutters, p. 203; Cake Boards, Fanci-Foil Wrap, p. 241; 16 x 22 in. plywood or foamcore board (½ in. thick), ruler, non-toxic pastel chalk, tea strainer, cornstarch, ruler, knife, toothpicks, tape, scissors

In advance: Make base board. Tint 68 oz. fondant light blue. Prepare and cover foamcore board with rolled fondant (p. 123). Using small veining tool from set, mark random lines for wall cracks and opening. Starting at bottom, mark 1 x 2 in. wide bricks. Use tea strainer to grate blue chalk; brush mixture over marks for definition. **Also:** Make letters. Tint about 4 oz. fondant yellow. Roll out ⅛ in. thick. Cut message using alphabet cutters from set. Let dry on cornstarch-dusted surface.

Bake and cool cake. Position on foil-wrapped, cut-to-fit cake board (p. 112). Ice cake sides and background areas smooth. Use tip 3 to outline and pipe in eyes and spider (pat smooth with finger dipped in cornstarch). Use tip 3 to outline all details. Cover with tip 14 stars. Position cake on fondant-covered board. Pipe tip 3 bead bottom border. Attach letters using damp brush. Serves 12.

► **Web Wonder Cupcakes**

Pans: Standard Muffin, Cooling Grid, p. 159
Tip: 3, p. 136
Color: Golden Yellow, p. 148
Recipe: Buttercream Icing, p. 118
Also: *Spider-Man* Standard Baking Cups, Icing Decorations, p. 190

Bake and cool cupcakes; ice smooth. Divide top of cupcake into 6ths. Using tip 3, pipe straight then curved outlines from division marks to form web. Position icing decorations. Each serves 1.

▶ Well Done, SpongeBob!

Pans: *SpongeBob SquarePants*™, p. 191; 9 x 2 in. Round, p. 157; Soccer Ball, p. 165

Colors:* Golden Yellow, Lemon Yellow, Brown, Leaf Green, Royal Blue, Red-Red, Black, Orange, p. 148

Fondant: White Ready-To-Use Rolled Fondant (72 oz.), p. 149; Brush Set, Easy-Glide Fondant Smoother, p. 151; 20 in. Rolling Pin, Roll & Cut Mat, p. 150

Candy: Yellow (2 pks.), White (1 pk.) Candy Melts, p. 196; Primary and Garden Candy Color Sets, p. 199

Recipe: Buttercream Icing, p. 118

Also: Parchment Triangles, p. 138; Wooden & Plastic Dowel Rods, p. 240; 10 in. Silver Cake Base, Fanci-Foil Wrap, 10 in. Cake Circles, p. 241; mini marshmallows, knife, ruler, scissors, tape

In advance: Make *SpongeBob* candy plaque (p. 130).

Bake and cool 1 soccer ball (trim flat side for a 3½ in. high cake) and two 9 in. rounds (trim each to 1½ in. high). Place each cake on cake circle cut to same size and prepare for Stacked Construction (p. 116) and rolled fondant (p. 119). Tint fondant as follows: 28 oz. light brown (bun), 14 oz. dark brown (burger), 5 oz. medium brown (pants), 9 oz. green (lettuce), 8 oz. yellow (cheese), 3 oz. golden yellow (legs), 3 oz. black, ½ oz. each of blue, red, tan (seeds); reserve 1 oz. white. Make sandwich (p. 125). Roll out medium brown fondant ¹⁄₁₆ in. thick; cut a 7 x 1¼ in. strip for pants. Use melted candy to attach around candy plaque, trimming as needed. Cut 6 very thin strips 1 in. long and attach for belt. Insert candy plaque into cake top. Roll 2 fondant logs ¾ x 1½ in. and flatten slightly for pant legs; roll 2 logs ¼ x 2 in. and curve for legs. Attach legs to pant legs with melted candy. Roll out white fondant 1 in. thick; cut 2 strips ¾ x 2½ in. and wrap around legs for socks. Attach ⅛ in. wide red and blue stripes using damp brush. Shape 1 in. long shoes and push onto legs. Use melted candy to attach pant legs and back of shoes in position on cake. Shape teardrop sesame seeds and attach to bun with damp brush. Serves 36.

*Combine Brown with Red-Red and Orange for light brown bun. Combine Brown with Red-Red, Orange and Black for brown pants. Combine Brown with Black and Red-Red for brown burger. Combine Golden Yellow with Lemon Yellow for yellow cheese.

◀ Snackin' with SpongeBob

Pans: Standard Muffin, Mini Muffin, Cooling Grid, p. 159

Tips: 2, 2A, 6, 12, 104, p. 136-137

Colors:* Brown, Lemon Yellow, Red-Red, Orange, Leaf Green, p. 148

Recipe: Buttercream Icing, p. 118

Also: *SpongeBob SquarePants*™ Baking Cups, Icing Decorations, p. 191; Disposable Decorating Bags, p. 138; cornstarch

Bake and cool standard cupcakes in baking cups, mini cupcakes without. Turn mini cupcake narrow end up and position at center of standard cupcake. Outline bottom of bun, then patty with tip 12. Pipe in tip 6 cheese triangles, tip 104 ruffled lettuce. Build up round top of bun with tip 2A (pat smooth with finger dipped in cornstarch). Pipe tip 2 bead sesame seeds. Position icing decoration. Each serves 1.

*Combine Brown with Red-Red and Orange for bun color. Combine Brown with Red-Red for burger.

▶ Growing Up with *WALL•E*

Pans: *Disney/Pixar WALL•E,* p. 192; 9 x 13 x 2 in. Sheet, p. 157; Non-Stick Cookie Sheet, p. 167

Tips: 1, 3, p. 136

Colors:* *Disney/Pixar WALL•E* Icing Color Set (red, black, yellow), p. 192; Leaf Green, Royal Blue, Brown, p. 148

Fondant: White Ready-To-Use Rolled Fondant (80 oz.), Gum-Tex, p. 149; Brush Set, Flower Former Set, Easy-Glide Fondant Smoother, p. 151; Leaf Cut-Outs, p. 153; 20 in. Rolling Pin, Roll & Cut Mat, p. 150

Candy: Yellow (2 pks.), White (1 pk.) Candy Melts, p. 196; Primary & Garden Candy Color Sets, p. 199; 6 in. Lollipop Sticks, p. 200

Recipe: Buttercream Icing, p. 118

Also: 2010 Pattern Book (Boot), p. 132; 101 Cookie Cutters, p. 203; Yellow Colored Sugar, p. 146; Piping Gel, p. 145; Disposable Decorating Bags, Parchment Triangles, p. 138; Wooden & Plastic Dowel Rods, p. 240; Cake Boards, Fanci-Foil Wrap, p. 241; 9 x 12 in. plywood or foamcore board (½ in. thick), black non-toxic pastel chalk, tea strainer, knife, craft knife, ruler, waxed paper, cornstarch

Several days in advance: Make fondant boot, leaves and vine (p. 125). **Also:** Make candy name. Place letter cutters from set on cookie sheet; fill ¼ in. deep with melted candy. Chill until firm. Using melted candy, attach lollipop sticks to back; allow 3 in. of stick to extend at bottom. Brush front with piping gel; dip into colored sugar. **And:** Make *WALL•E* candy plaque (p. 130). **And:** Cover base board with rolled fondant (p. 123).

Bake and cool 2-layer sheet cake (bake 2 layers 1½ in. high for a 3 in. high cake). Cut into 8 cubes, 3 x 3 x 3 in. Place each cake on a cut-to-fit cake board; lightly ice. Cover cubes with fondant using Blended Fondant method (p. 125). **At party:** Position candy plaque by sliding plastic dowel rods over wooden dowel rods to base of top cubes. Insert candy name, trimming sticks if needed. Each cube serves 1.

*Combine Brown with Red-Red for brown boot shown.

WALL•E

◀ *WALL•E* Welcome

Pans: 9 x 13 x 2 in. Sheet, p. 157; Cookie Sheet, Cooling Grid, p. 159

Candy: White, Red, Yellow, Blue Candy Melts (1 pk. each makes 12-14 treats), p. 196; Garden Candy Color Set, p. 199

Also: *Disney/Pixar WALL•E* Party Toppers, p. 192; Parchment Triangles, p. 138

Bake and cool 1-layer cake using firm batter such as pound cake. Cut into 1¾ in. squares 1 in. high. Tint melted white candy light and dark gray using black candy color. Place cakes on cooling grid positioned over cookie sheet. Pour light gray candy on cake. While candy is still wet, use melted candy in cut parchment bags to pipe blue, yellow, red and dark gray over cakes. Tap cake on cooling grid so colors will blend together. Chill until firm. Position party toppers on top of cakes. Each serves 1.

◀ Spin-Out Cookies

Cookie: 101 Cookie Cutters, p. 203; Cookie Sheet, Cooling Grid p. 159

Tips: 3, 8, p. 136

Color: Black, p. 148

Recipes: Buttercream Icing, Roll-Out Cookies, p. 118

Also: Flower Cut-Outs, p. 153; *Disney/Pixar Cars* Party Toppers, p. 192

Prepare and roll out cookie dough. For each treat, cut one flower using large Cut-Out and 1 circle using largest round cutter from set. Trim off one petal on flower to create flat bottom edge. Bake and cool. Ice circle cookie smooth; add tip 3 outline tire tracks. For smoke cloud, build up tip 8 beads on flower cookie. With tip 3, print name and add motion lines. Attach flower cookie and topper to circle cookie with icing. Secure with additional icing if necessary. Each serves 1.

▼ Once Around the Oval

Pans: *Disney/Pixar Cars*, p. 192; Oval Set (16.5 x 12.38 in. used), p. 156

Tips: 3, 5, p. 136

Color: Black, p. 148

Fondant: White Ready-To-Use Rolled Fondant (42 oz.), Gum-Tex, p. 149; 20 in. Rolling Pin, Roll & Cut Mat, p. 150; Fondant Ribbon Cutter/Embosser Set, p. 152; Square Cut-Outs, p. 153; Easy-Glide Fondant Smoother, p. 151

Candy: Red (3 pks.), White (1 pk.), Dark Cocoa (1 pk.) Candy Melts, p. 196; Primary and Garden Candy Color Sets, p. 199; 6 in. Lollipop Sticks, p. 200

Recipe: Buttercream Icing, p. 118

Also: 2010 Pattern Book (Smoke), p. 132; Piping Gel, p. 145; Parchment Triangles, p. 138; Cake Boards, Fanci-Foil Wrap, p. 241; Plastic Dowel Rods, p. 240; 14 x 19 in. plywood or foamcore board (½ in. thick), ruler, toothpicks, scissors, tape, knife, waxed paper, cornstarch

In advance: Make *Cars* candy plaque (p. 130). **Also:** Prepare base board. Using pan as a guide, cut base 1 in. larger than pan on all sides. Cover with 38 oz. rolled fondant tinted gray (p. 123). Reserve remaining fondant. **And:** Make smoke. Add ½ teaspoon Gum-Tex to 4 oz. white fondant. Roll out ⅛ in. thick. Cut smoke using pattern. Let dry on waxed paper-covered board dusted with cornstarch.

Bake and cool 1-layer oval cake. Ice smooth, using white for sides, light gray for top. Position on prepared board. Tint remaining gray fondant black. Roll out 4 oz. ¹⁄₁₆ in. thick. Using smallest Cut-Out, cut squares. Attach with dots of icing to form checkerboard pattern, starting at top edge of cake. Pipe tip 3 bead bottom border. Pipe tip 3 motion lines on top, varying from ½ to 1 in. apart. Attach Lollipop Stick to back of smoke using melted candy, allowing 2 in. to extend at bottom to insert into cake. Pipe tip 5 message with icing. Position smoke and car. Serves 34.

Savor Every Season

Don't let holidays come and go without making great memories. Here are the treat ideas that help you look forward to each season's celebrations, and give your family wonderful moments to look back on. Greet Christmas with the Decked-Out Tree Tower, a 3-tier centerpiece with hanging fondant ornaments and holly leaves at every level. Show off the first flowers of spring, with fresh tulip cookie pops sprouting from a cake covered with lush blades of piped grass. For Halloween, set the bats flying around our color flow castle cake. Surround the grounds with tombstone cupcakes, candy and marshmallow mansions and a goblet of glowing truffles.

WICKED REMEDY

INSTANT RELIEF
FOR ANY AGE

Halloween Homebodies

Pans: 6, 8, 10 x 2 in. Round, p. 157; Standard Muffin, p. 159; Halloween Non-Stick Cookie Shapes Pan, p. 210

Tips: 2, 3, 5, p. 136

Colors:* Orange, Black, Violet, Rose, p. 148

Fondant: White Ready-To-Use Rolled Fondant (96 oz.), p. 149; Brush Set, Easy-Glide Fondant Smoother, p. 151; 20 in. Rolling Pin, Roll & Cut Mat, p. 150

Recipes: Buttercream, Color Flow Icings, p. 118; Chocolate Fondant, p. 119

Also: 2010 Pattern Book (Haunted House, Fence, Bats/Crows/Scrolls), p. 132; White, Midnight Black and Dark Cocoa Candy Melts, p. 208; Haunted Manor Standard Baking Cups, p. 207; 6-Mix Halloween Pumpkin Sprinkles, p. 209; Color Flow Mix, Piping Gel, p. 145; Parchment Triangles, p. 138; 4 in. Lollipop Sticks, p. 200; Cake Circles, Cake Board, Fanci-Foil Wrap, p. 241; Dowel Rods, p. 240; drawing compass, craft knife, scissors, waxed paper, non-stick cooking spray, toothpicks, tape, tissue, cornstarch, ruler

At least 2 days in advance: Make color flow house. Tape pattern to a cake board and cover with waxed paper. For easy release, spray lightly with non-stick cooking spray, wipe with tissue leaving minimal residue. Outline all areas using tip 2 and full-strength color flow. Flow in using thinned color flow in cut parchment bag. Let dry. Cover top 2 in. of 2 Lollipop Sticks with full-strength color flow. Attach sticks to back of house leaving 2 in. extended at bottom. Let dry. **Also:** Mold 12 candy tombstones in cookie pan. Use painting method (p. 130) to add black details; let set. Fill cavities half full; chill until firm and unmold. **And:** Cover base board. Prepare Chocolate Fondant and tint black. Cut 3 cake circles to 11 in. diameter and tape together. Cover with fondant rolled 1/8 in. thick (p. 123). Reserve remaining black fondant.

Bake and cool 1-layer 6 in. cake, 2-layer 8 in. cake (trim each layer to 1½ in. for a 3 in. high cake) and 2-layer 10 in. cake (4 in. high). Tint 54 oz. fondant orange. Prepare cakes for Stacked Construction (p. 116) and cover with rolled fondant (p. 119). Stack cakes. Using patterns and toothpick, mark fence around 8 in. cake and bats/crows/scrolls around 10 in.

cake. Using tip 3 and buttercream, outline fence; outline and fill in bats and crows (pat smooth with finger dipped in cornstarch). Pipe tip 3 violet scrolls. Pipe tip 5 bead bottom borders on all cakes. Bake and cool cupcakes; ice smooth and add sprinkles. Attach tombstones with icing. Position around cake. Insert house in cake top. Cake serves 54; each cupcake serves 1.

*Combine Violet with Rose for violet shown.

Bat Attitude

Cookie: Bat Comfort-Grip Cutter, p. 209; Cookie Sheet, Cooling Grid, p. 159

Tips: 2, 3, p. 136

Colors:* Orange, Black, Violet, Lemon Yellow, Golden Yellow, p. 148

Recipes: Royal Icing, Roll-Out Cookies, p. 118

Also: Black Sparkle Gel, p. 144; Round Cut-Outs, p. 153; Brush Set, p. 151; Meringue Powder, p. 145; chocolate chips

In advance: Make cookies. Prepare and roll out dough. Use medium Round Cut-Out to cut heads and Bat cutter to cut bodies. Bake and cool cookies. Attach heads using royal icing. Using tip 2, pipe orange outlines and mouth. Using tip 3 pipe dot eyes, pupils and nose, pipe pull out fangs. Attach chocolate chip ears with icing dots. Let dry. Pipe a thin layer of Sparkle Gel on body and head; brush into tight areas. Let dry. Each serves 1.

*Combine Lemon Yellow with Golden Yellow for yellow shown.

Rocky Road Residence

Candy: White, Light Cocoa Candy Melts (1 pk. White, 2 pks. Light Cocoa makes approx. 6 treats), p. 196; Haunted Halloween Pretzel Mold, p. 208; Primary & Garden Color Sets, p. 199

Also: Jumbo Ghost Sprinkles, p. 209; Haunted Manor Treat Bags, p. 207; Fine Tip Primary Colors FoodWriters Edible Color Markers, p. 149; Parchment Triangles, p. 138; 6 in. Cake Circles, p. 241; marshmallows, chopped walnuts, waxed paper

In advance: Tint melted white candy orange and gray using candy colors (use black to make gray). Tint portion of melted cocoa candy black. Mold castles without pretzels using piping method (p. 130); chill until firm.

Stir 1½ cups marshmallows and ½ cup chopped walnuts into 1 pk. melted cocoa candy. Spoon onto waxed paper-covered Cake Circles, making ovals approx. 3½ x 3 x 1¼ in. high. Let set 5-10 minutes; attach castle at center with melted candy. Draw facial features on ghost sprinkles with black FoodWriter. Attach to ovals and castle with melted candy; let set. Place treats in bags. Each serves 1.

Ghoulish Goblet

Pan: Mini Wonder Mold, p. 160

Candy: Light Cocoa, Spooky Green, Orange, White Candy Melts, p. 196; Creepy Tombstone Mold, p. 208; Dipping Set, p. 199

Recipes: Truffles, Spooky Popcorn, p. 118

Also: Parchment Triangles, p. 138; Plastic Dowel Rods, p. 240; Cake Boards, p. 241; Haunted Manor Party Bags, p. 207; waxed paper, knife, wooden spoon, ruler

In advance: Prepare truffles. Follow recipe directions to make approx. 24 to 30 truffles, ¾ in. diameter. Dip in melted green candy; let set on waxed paper-covered board. **Also:** Prepare popcorn.

Using melted cocoa candy, make candy shell (p. 130) goblet cup and base in Mini Wonder Mold. For base, fill mold only 1¼ in. deep. Chill until firm. For stem, cut a dowel rod 2 in. long. Spread a small amount of melted cocoa candy on a waxed paper-covered board. Stand dowel rod upright in candy; chill until firm. Fill dowel rod with melted cocoa candy; tap to remove air bubbles and chill until firm. Remove dowel rod from board and push out candy stem using handle end of dipping spoon. Trim off excess candy. Mold skull in tombstone mold; chill until firm and unmold. Attach stem to cup and base with melted candy; let set. Using melted orange candy in cut parchment bag, pipe scrolls; let set. Fill with truffles. Fill party bags with popcorn.

◀ Pumpkinfolk Party

Pans: Iridescents! Jack-O-Lantern, p. 206; Cookie Sheet, Cooling Grid, p. 159

Tips: 2A, 3, 5, 16, 44, 349, 352, 366, p. 136-137

Colors:* Orange, Leaf Green, Black, Red-Red, p. 148

Recipes: Buttercream Icing, Roll-Out Cookies, p. 118

Also: Pumpkin 4-Pc. Nesting Cutter Set, p. 210; Orange Cookie Icing, 206; Cake Boards, Fanci-Foil Wrap, p. 241; foamcore board (¼ in. thick), spatula, scissors, cellophane tape, craft knife, toothpicks, cornstarch

In advance: Make cookies. Prepare and roll out dough. Cut pumpkins: 1 with 2nd smallest cutter, 2 with 2nd largest cutter and 2 with largest cutter. Bake and cool cookies. Outline all cookies with Cookie Icing. Heat bottle according to directions. Flow in icing to cover. Let dry. Using buttercream, pipe tip 5 dot eyes, tip 3 outline stems, dot nose, cheeks and pupils, outline or outline and fill-in mouths and bead tongue. Add tip 44 teeth. Pipe leaves using tip 349 on small cookie, tip 352 on larger cookies.

Bake and cool cake. Lightly ice mouth area smooth. Using tip 3, outline pumpkin rib lines. Cover with tip 16 stars. Pipe tip 2A dot eyes (flatten and smooth with finger dipped in cornstarch). Pipe tip 5 dot pupils. Overpipe nose and cheeks with tip 16 stars. Pipe tip 3 outlines for stem; add tip 366 leaves. Position cookies. Cake serves 12; each cookie serves 1.

*Combine Orange with Red-Red for orange shown on cake.

▶ We're Wary of Werewolves!

Pan: Teddy Bear, p. 163

Tip: 14, p. 136

Colors:* Violet, Rose, Leaf Green, Lemon Yellow, Golden Yellow, Black, p. 148

Fondant: White Ready-To-Use Rolled Fondant (24 oz.), p. 149; 9 in. Rolling Pin, Roll & Cut Mat, p. 150; Brush Set, p. 151

Recipe: Chocolate Buttercream Icing, p. 118

Also: 2010 Pattern Book (Shirt, Pants, Mouth, Eye), p. 132; Cake Board, Fanci-Foil Wrap, p. 241; scissors, tape, knife, toothpicks

Bake and cool cake. Trim ears for pointed shape. Ice smooth inner ears and areas where fondant will go. Tint fondant as follows: 8 oz. violet, 8 oz. green, 4 oz. black, 2 oz. yellow; reserve 2 oz. white. Roll out fondant ⅛ in. thick. Using patterns and knife, cut shirt, pants, mouth, teeth, eyes, pupils and eyebrows (reverse pattern for opposite eye). Position on cake. Shape a 1 in. fondant oval; attach for nose. Cover werewolf with tip 14 pull-out star fur. Shape ¾ in. high fondant cones for claws; attach. Serves 12.

*Combine Violet with Rose for violet shown. Combine Leaf Green with Lemon Yellow for green shown. Combine Lemon Yellow with Golden Yellow for yellow shown.

◀ Playing Jacks

Pans: 8-Cavity Silicone Round Brownie Pops Mold, p. 170; Cookie Sheet, Cooling Grid, p. 159

Tips: 2, 3, p. 136

Recipe: favorite brownie recipe or mix

Also: Orange Cookie Icing, Black, White Tube Decorating Icings, p. 206; Coupler Ring Set, p. 144; 6 in. Cookie Treat Sticks, p. 205; green mini spice drops, cornstarch, knife

Bake and cool brownies in silicone mold supported by cookie sheet. Push cookie stick into center. Place on cooling grid over drip pan. Cover with heated orange cookie icing; let set. Poke hole in center of spice drop with a cookie stick then slide onto pumpkin for stem. Use Tube Icings fitted with coupler and tip 3 to outline and fill in mouth and whites of eyes (pat smooth with finger dipped in cornstarch). Pipe tip 2 dot pupils and outline eyebrows. Pipe tip 3 dot nose using room temperature orange icing. Each serves 1.

▶ Halloween High Stepper

Pan: Lady Bug, p. 164

Tips: 1A, 3, 6, 12, 16, p. 136-137

Colors:* Leaf Green, Lemon Yellow, Black, p. 148

Recipe: Buttercream Icing, p. 118

Also: White Ready-To-Use Rolled Fondant (6 oz.), p. 149; Midnight Black Candy Melts, p. 208; Cake Circles, Fanci-Foil Wrap, p. 241; 16 x 24 in. foamcore board (¼ in. thick), pretzel rods, knife, cornstarch, ruler

In advance: Make legs and shoes. For shorter legs, cut pretzel rods to 2½ in. and 6½ in. long (4 each). For longer legs, cut pretzel rods to 4½ in. and 6½ in. long (4 each). Tint fondant black. Roll 8 each ¾ in. balls for leg joints; reserve remaining black fondant. Assemble shorter legs, inserting 1 of each size pretzel in leg joints at a 45° angle; secure with melted candy. Repeat for longer legs, assembling at slightly less than a 90° angle. Let dry.

Bake and cool cake. Pipe tip 1A ball eyes (flatten and smooth with finger dipped in cornstarch). Pipe tip 12 dot nose and pupils (smooth with finger dipped in cornstarch). Pipe tip 3 outline mouth; cover cake with tip 16 pull-out stars. Overpipe mouth and pull out teeth with tip 6. Make shoes using remaining black fondant. Roll ¾ in. diameter logs; cut into 1½ in. pieces (8 needed). Shape into oval shoes. Insert long end of legs into shoes; secure with melted candy. Position and insert legs into cake. Serves 12.

*Combine Leaf Green with Lemon Yellow for green shown.

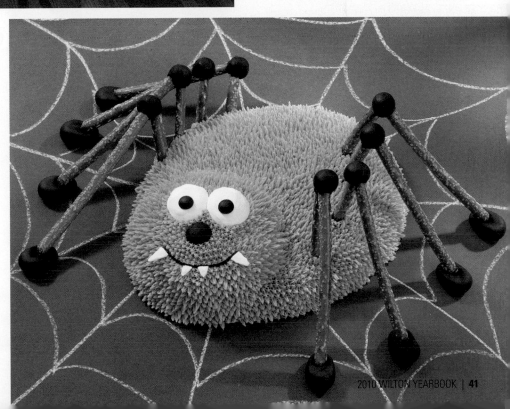

◄ The Witch Waltz

Pans: Ballerina Bear, p. 161; Cookie Sheet, Cooling Grid, p. 159
Tips: 3, 6, 9, 16, 18, 45, 127D, p. 136-137
Colors:* Black, Orange, Leaf Green, Lemon Yellow, Golden Yellow, Violet, Rose, p. 148
Recipes: Buttercream Icing, Roll-Out Cookies, p. 118
Also: 2010 Pattern Book (Hat, Eye, Mouth), p. 132; Cake Boards, Fanci-Foil Wrap, p. 241; Bell Metal Cutter, p. 204; 6 in. Cookie Treat Sticks, p. 205; White Candy Melts, p. 196; pretzel rod, knife, cornstarch, toothpick, scissors

In advance: Make cookies. Prepare and roll out dough. Use pattern and knife to cut hat; use bell cutter to cut broom top. Bake and cool cookies. Attach hat cookie to cookie stick with melted candy, leaving 3 in. extended at bottom. Attach broom top cookie to pretzel with melted candy; let set.

Bake and cool cake. Trim off top of bow, muzzle, laces and sides of legs to shape. Ice cake sides and background areas smooth. Ice face and skirt areas smooth. Use toothpick to mark all details. Use patterns to mark eyes and mouth. Use tip 3 to outline details; fill in eyes, pupils, mouth, empty hand and add bead tongue (smooth with finger dipped in cornstarch). Pipe tip 45 stripe on hat and at waist. Cover top of dress, face, arms, slippers and cookie hat with tip 16 stars; overpipe nose and cheeks with tip 16 stars. Pipe tip 9 outline striped socks (smooth with finger). Insert cookie hat. Pipe tip 18 pull-out star hair. Pipe tip 127D ruffles for hat brim and skirt. Add tip 6 outline hat buckle. Position pretzel broom; cover with tip 18 bristles. Build up fingers over pretzel with tip 9 lines. Outline with tip 3 and cover with tip 18 stars. Pipe tip 9 ball bottom border. Serves 12.

*Combine Leaf Green with Lemon Yellow for green shown. Combine Violet with Rose for light violet shown. Combine Lemon Yellow with Golden Yellow for yellow shown.

► Happy Tabby

Pans: 6 x 2 in. Round, p. 157; 8 x 2 in. Heart, p. 218; Cookie Sheet, Cooling Grid, p. 159
Tips: 1A, 3, 12, 21, p. 136-137
Colors: Black, Orange, p. 148
Recipes: Buttercream, Chocolate Buttercream Icings, Roll-Out Cookies, p. 118
Also: 2010 Pattern Book (Ears, Front Leg, Back Foot, Tail), p. 132; Light Cocoa Candy Melts, p. 196; 6 in. Cookie Treat Sticks, p. 205; Cake Boards, Fanci-Foil Wrap, p. 241; knife, cornstarch

In advance: Make cookies. Prepare and roll out dough. Use patterns to cut ear, front leg and 2 back feet; reverse patterns and repeat. Cut 1 tail. Bake and cool cookies. Trim 2 cookie sticks to 4 in. Attach stick to back of each ear with melted candy, leaving 2½ in. extending at bottom. Let set.

Bake and cool 2 in. high round and 1 in. high heart cake. Position cakes on foil-covered board. Position tail and insert ears. Sandwich matching back feet cookies with icing and position. Pipe in tip 1A eyes (flatten and smooth with finger dipped in cornstarch). Pipe tip 12 dot nose and pupils (pat smooth). Use tip 3 to outline and pipe in mouth and inner ears (pat smooth). Cover all with tip 21 stars. Position front legs. Cover with tip 21 stars. Overpipe tip 3 outline mouth and whiskers. Cakes serve 12; each cookie serves 1.

◀ She's Melting!

Pans: 8-Cavity Silicone Round Brownie Pops Mold, p. 170; Non-Stick Cookie Sheet, Cooling Grid, p. 167

Colors:* Moss Green, Lemon Yellow, Golden Yellow, Violet, Rose, Orange, p. 148

Fondant: White Ready-To-Use Rolled Fondant (approx. 2 oz. per treat), Fine Tip Primary Colors FoodWriter Edible Color Markers, p. 149; 9 in. Rolling Pin, Roll & Cut Mat, p. 150

Recipe: Favorite brownie recipe or mix

Also: Dark Cocoa Candy Melts, p. 196; Parchment Triangles, p. 138; pretzel sticks, mini-size chocolate nougat candy, cone-shaped corn snacks, knife, ruler, cornstarch, waxed paper

In advance: Prepare bodies. Bake and cool brownies in silicone mold supported by cookie sheet, filling cavities ⅔ full. Cover with melted candy (p. 130), allowing excess to puddle around bottom for melting effect. Chill until firm. **Also:** Prepare witch hats and heads (p. 125).

Cut nougat candy into ¾ x ⅜ in. diameter logs for arms; attach with melted candy. Flatten a ½ in. fondant ball for hands; cut slits for fingers and shape. Attach to arms with melted candy. For broom bristles, shape a 1 x 1¼ in. fondant triangle; trim ¼ in. off point and mark lines with knife. Attach bristles to pretzel stick and pretzel stick to hand using melted candy. Attach head and had with melted candy. Each serves 1.

*Combine Moss Green with Lemon Yellow for green shown. Combine Lemon Yellow with Golden Yellow for yellow shown. Combine Violet with Rose for violet shown.

▶ Creeping on Cat Feet

Pans: Halloween Non-Stick Cookie Shapes Pan, p. 210; Standard Muffin, p. 159

Tip: 1A, p. 136

Candy: Light Cocoa (1 pk. makes 4 treats), Yellow and Orange Candy Melts, p. 196; Decorator Brush Set, p. 199

Recipe: Chocolate Mousse, p. 118

Also: White Standard Baking Cups, p. 186; Parchment Triangles, p. 138; Cake Boards, p. 241; mini-size chocolate nougat candy, waxed paper, knife, ruler

In advance: Make candy pieces. Use melted candy in cut parchment bag to pipe 2½ in. long curled tails on waxed paper-covered board; chill until firm. Turn over and overpipe reverse side; let set. Use painting method (p. 130) to mold cat heads in cookie pan, filling cavities ½ full. Chill until firm; unmold. Pipe pupils with melted candy. Make candy shells in baking cups (p. 130); chill until firm. Carefully peel off paper. If necessary, even top edge using knife or warming tray. For feet, cut nougat ⅞ in. high; attach to bottom of candy shell using melted candy. Prepare mousse and fill cups using tip 1A. Attach head to candy shell with melted candy; insert tail. Refrigerate until serving time (at least 3 hours). Each serves 1.

◀ Spell Chick

Pans: 6-Cavity Silicone Mini Jack-O-Lantern, p. 206; Non-Stick Cookie Sheet, Cooling Grid, p. 167

Tips: 2, 6, 8, 46, p. 136-137

Colors: Leaf Green, Black, Violet, Orange, p. 148

Recipe: Buttercream Icing, p. 118

Also: Midnight Black Candy Melts (1 pk. makes 10-12 hats), p. 208; Circle Metal Cutter, p. 204; black shoestring licorice, sugar ice cream cone, knife, ruler

In advance: Make hats. Place Circle Cutter on non-stick pan; fill ⅛ in. deep with melted black candy. Chill until firm. Cut sugar cone to 2¼ in. long. Cover with melted candy (p. 130); let set. Attach cone to center of candy circle using melted candy; let set.

Bake and cool mini cakes; ice smooth. Pipe tip 8 dot eyes. Pipe tip 2 dot pupils, outline mouth, outline and pipe-in tooth. Pipe tip 6 pull-out dot nose. Pipe tip 46 outline hat band and tip 2 buckle. Cut 2¾ in. long pieces of licorice for hair. Attach hair and hat using dots of icing. Each serves 1.

◄ Brownie Bride

Pans: 8-Cavity Silicone Round Brownie Pops Mold, p. 170; Non-Stick Cookie Sheet, Cooling Grid, p. 167

Candy:* White, Midnight Black, Spooky Green Candy Melts, p. 208; 4 in. Lollipop Sticks, p. 200

Recipe: Favorite brownie recipe or mix

Also: Parchment Triangles, p. 138; Angled Spatula, p. 140; Cake Board, p. 241; scissors, ruler, toothpicks, waxed paper, knife

Bake and cool 2 brownies for each treat in silicone mold supported by cookie sheet. For bodies, ice flat side of brownie with melted white candy; for heads, ice flat side with melted green candy; let set. Cover brownies with white or green candy (p. 130); let set.

For head, mark hair area with toothpick, 1 in. down from flat side; score a curved line on front and back. Pipe outline mouth, dot eyes, neck bolts, pupils and nose; let set. Pipe zigzag hair highlights in white; let set. Place head on waxed paper, flat side down. Pipe in remaining hair with melted gray candy; let set. Pipe hands on cookie sheet using melted green candy in cut parchment bag; let set. For arms, cut 2 lollipop sticks to 3 in.; bend on an angle, leaving 1¾ in. to insert in treat. Attach hands with melted candy and let set. Using knife, cut a small hole in rounded tops of brownies. To assemble, cut lollipop stick to 3 in. long; insert into rounded top of body. Position head over stick; secure with melted candy. Insert arms. Each serves 1.

*Combine melted White candy with Midnight Black for gray shown.

► Invasion of the Body Snackers

Cookie: Non-Stick Halloween Cookie Shapes Pan, p. 210; Non-Stick Cookie Sheet, p. 167; 6 in. Cookie Treat Sticks, p. 205

Tip: 2A, p. 137

Color: Orange, p. 148

Recipes: Buttercream Icing, p. 118; favorite crisped rice cereal treats

Also: White, Midnight Black, Spooky Green Candy Melts, p. 208; Silly-Feet! Silicone Baking Cups, p.174; Parchment Triangles, p. 138, scissors, ruler

In advance: Using piping method (p. 130), mold candy heads in cookie pan cavities, filling ⅓ full. Chill until firm. Pipe hands on cookie sheet using melted green candy in cut parchment bag. Chill until firm. For each treat, cut 1 cookie stick to 3 in.; attach to back of head with melted candy leaving 1½ in. extending.

Fill silicone cups with cereal treats mixture. Round tops and ice smooth. For arms, cut 2 sticks to 3 in long; bend at a 90° angle, leaving 1 in. to insert straight down in treat. Insert head and arms. Using tip 2A, coat sticks with icing (p. 123). Attach hands to arms with melted candy; let set. Each serves 1.

*Combine melted White candy with Midnight Black for gray shown.

◄ The Perfect Party Plot

Pan: 11 x 15 x 2 in. Sheet, p. 157

Color: Kelly Green, p. 148

Candy: Mummies Pretzel Mold, Creepy Tombstone Candy Mold, White, Midnight Black Candy Melts, p. 208; Primary and Garden Candy Color Sets, Decorator Brush Set, p. 199

Recipe: Favorite brownie recipe or mix (double or triple recipe as needed)

Also: Smiling Pumpkins Icing Decorations (2 pks.), p. 207; Cake Boards, Fanci-Foil Wrap, p. 241; Parchment Triangles, p. 138; shredded coconut, knife, spoon, waxed paper, ruler, toothpicks, zip-close plastic bag

In advance: Make candies. Tint portions of white candy orange, yellow and violet using candy colors. Lighten portions of black candy with white for shades of gray. Using painting method (p. 130), mold 4 tombstones; mold 3 mummies without pretzels. Mold 1 mummy head only. Pipe 2 hands on waxed paper using melted candy in cut parchment bag; chill until firm, then overpipe back for strength. **Also:** Tint coconut (p. 123).

Bake and cool brownies, about 1½ in. thick. Mark 4 graves, each 2 x 4¾ in. Scoop out 3, about ¾ in. deep, and scatter crumbled brownie "dirt" around graves and over 4th grave. Position candy mummies, head, hands and tombstones. Attach icing decorations around sides with melted candy. Scatter tinted coconut grass. Serves 27.

Candy Corn Cheesecake

Pan: Checkerboard Cake Set, p. 167
Colors:* Orange, Lemon Yellow, Golden Yellow, p. 148
Recipe: Favorite no-bake cheesecake mix (2)
Also: 9 in. Angled Spatula, p.140; Disposable Decorating Bags, p. 138

Prepare 2 mixes of cheesecake batter following package directions. Prepare 1 crust and place in bottom of pan following package directions. Position Batter Dividing Ring in pan. Fill center ring with batter to ¼ in. from top of ring, level with top edge of pan. Tint remainder of batter yellow. Fill outer ring with batter. Tint remaining yellow batter orange and fill middle ring. Smooth each section with spatula dipped in warm water. Carefully remove ring and smooth again with spatula if needed. Refrigerate following package or recipe directions. Serves 12.

*Combine Lemon Yellow with Golden Yellow for bright yellow shown.

▼ Keeping Mum

Pan: Teddy Bear, p. 163
Tips: 2A, 4, 45, p. 136-137
Colors: Black, Lemon Yellow, p. 148
Recipe: Buttercream Icing, p. 118
Also: Cake Boards, Fanci-Foil Wrap, p. 241; knife, tape, scissors

Bake and cool cake. Trim off ears and level muzzle area. Spatula ice face area smooth. Pipe and overpipe tip 45 bands to cover cake. Pipe tip 2A dot eyes. Add tip 4 dot pupils. Serves 12.

▲ Boneyard Boss

Cookie: Cookie Sheet, Cooling Grid, p. 159; Hand, Foot, Dog Bone Plastic Cookie Cutters, p. 203; White Cookie Icing (2), p. 202
Tip: 3, p. 136
Recipe: Roll-Out Cookies, p. 118
Also: 2010 Pattern Book (Skull, Pelvis, Spine), p. 132; Light Cocoa Candy Melts (1 pk.), p. 196; Smiling Pumpkins Icing Decorations, Boo! Scary! Party Bags, p. 207; Disposable Decorating Bags, 15 in. Parchment Triangles, p. 138; 3 in. Grecian Pillars, 8 in. Decorator Preferred Smooth Edge Plates (2), p. 237; assorted candy, 3 x 8 in. diameter craft foam circle, ½ in. thick wooden dowel rods (two 36 in. lengths), pruning shears, black construction paper, 1⅜ in. wide black ribbon (3 yds.), ⅝ in. wide white ribbon (4½ yds.), glue gun, double-stick tape, waxed paper, scissors, ruler, craft knife

In advance: Prepare frame for upper body and dowel rods for lower legs and feet (p. 125).
Also: Make cookies. Prepare and roll out dough. Use patterns to cut skull, pelvis and 3 spine sections. Use cookie cutters to cut 2 feet (reverse one), 2 hands (reverse one), 8 bones. Bake and cool cookies. Cover with Candy Melts (p. 130); let set. Using a small amount of Cookie Icing in disposable bag fitted with tip 3, outline bones, spine sections, pelvis and skull, including facial features as shown on pattern. Pipe fingers and toes, outline and fill in hands and feet. Let set about 30 minutes. Heat Cookie Icing in bottle following bottle directions. Flow onto remaining cookies to cover. Let set.

Assemble upper body. Chill all cookies in freezer for at least 30 minutes for easier assembly. Working on flat, waxed paper-covered surface, use melted candy to attach chilled cookies to frame. Hold each cookie in position until set. Let set completely. Using craft foam base as a pattern, cut a construction paper circle; set aside. Cover sides of base with 3 rows of black ribbon; use hot glue to secure. Use double-stick tape to secure base to plate; position on plate and pillars. Use craft knife to cut small slits in ribbon where rods for lower legs will go, about 1 in. from top edge. Push 2 rods into base at an angle; secure with hot glue, holding until set. Use hot glue to attach 2 angled rods for feet; hold until set. Use double-stick tape to attach paper circle to top; cut small center hole. Push upper body into base. Using melted candy, attach chilled cookies over lower leg and feet dowel rods, holding each until set. Attach upper leg bones to top and icing decorations to sides of base. Surround base with candy-filled party bags. Each cookie and treat serves 1.

◄ It's Santa Season!

Pan: Oval Pan Set (13.5 x 9.8 in. used), p. 156
Colors:* Christmas Red, Red-Red, Brown, Creamy Peach (for skin tone shown), p. 148
Fondant: White Ready-To-Use Rolled Fondant (86 oz.), Gum-Tex, p. 149; Rolling Pin, Roll & Cut Mat, p. 150; Easy-Glide Fondant Smoother, p. 151;
Recipe: Buttercream Icing, p. 118
Also: 2010 Pattern Book (Face, Beard Edge, Ears, Hat, Hat Brim and Pompom), p. 132; Cake Boards, Fanci-Foil Wrap, p. 241; 4 in. Lollipop Sticks, p. 200; Decorator Brush Set, p. 199; knife, cornstarch

2 days in advance: Make fondant hat and ears. Add 2 teaspoons Gum-Tex to 25 oz. fondant. Tint 15 oz. red and 2 oz. light peach; reserve 8 oz. white. Roll out colors ⅛ in. thick. Using patterns and knife, cut hat, brim, pompom and ears. Let all dry on cornstarch-dusted cake board. Reserve remaining red fondant.

Prepare 1-layer oval cake for rolled fondant (p. 119). Tint 36 oz. fondant light peach. Roll out fondant ⅛ in. thick and cover cake; smooth with Fondant Smoother. Roll out approximately 24 oz. white fondant and cover wide end of cake, ending about 10 in. from bottom edge. Trim with knife using beard edge pattern; smooth with Fondant Smoother. For eyes, tint 1 oz. fondant brown; roll two ½ in. diameter balls, flatten and attach with damp brush. For mouth and nose, use reserved red fondant. Roll ¼ x 1 ½ in. long log for mouth and a 1½ in. x 1 in. oval for nose; attach pieces. Using white fondant, roll two ¼ x 8 in. long ropes for mustache and a ¼ x 20 in. long rope for beard; attach. Attach hat pieces with dots of icing. Trim two lollipop sticks to 3 in. and insert on each side of head, extending 1 in. Attach ears to sticks with icing. Serves 15.

*Combine Christmas Red with Red-Red for red shown. Combine Brown with Red-Red for brown shown.

► Holiday Head Honchos

Pans: 8-Cavity Silicone Round Brownie Pops Mold, p. 170; Cookie Sheet, Cooling Grid, p. 159
Also: White, Green, Dark Cocoa Candy Melts, p. 196; Primary Candy Color Set, p. 199; Parchment Triangles, p. 138; Cake Boards, p. 241; sugar ice cream cones, waxed paper, knife, ruler

Bake and cool brownie pops in silicone mold supported by cookie sheet. Unmold; trim bottoms if necessary for flat surface. Cover with melted candy (p. 130); let set then repeat. Using melted candy in cut parchment bag, cover bottoms to seal. Let set on waxed paper-covered board. Cut cones to 2 in. high. Set on cooling grid and cover with melted candy (p. 130); let set on waxed paper-covered board. Assemble and decorate using melted candy in cut parchment bags. Attach hats to heads. Pipe Santa's swirl beard, mustache, both hat brims and pompoms. Pipe dot eyes and fill-in mouths. Pipe Santa's dot nose, Elf's dot cheeks, pull-out nose and ears. Each serves 1.

▶ Silly Santa

Pan: 6-Cavity Mini Snowman and Stocking, p. 212
Tips: 3, 5, 44, p. 136-137
Colors:* Christmas Red, Red-Red, Black, Creamy Peach, Golden Yellow, Lemon Yellow, p. 148
Recipe: Buttercream Icing, p. 118
Also: Red Candy Melts, p. 196; 4 in. Lollipop Sticks, p. 200; Angled Spatula, p. 140; spice drops, mini marshmallows, sugar ice cream cones, knife, ruler, cornstarch

Bake and cool cakes in snowman cavities. Trim off details (bottom will become Santa's head). Ice face and body smooth. Trim cone to 3 in. high for hat. Ice smooth; push into position. Using tip 3, pipe outline eyes; dot nose, outline and fill in mouth (pat smooth with finger dipped in cornstarch). Pipe tip 44 outline belt and tip 5 outline belt buckle. Dip 2 mini marshmallows in melted red candy; let set. Flatten spice drops slightly and cut to shape gloves and shoes. Trim lollipop stick to 3 in. long; push through body to hold arms. Slide mini marshmallows and gloves onto stick. Using tip 5, attach shoes; pipe zigzag cuffs around shoes and gloves. Pipe tip 5 pull-out mustache and swirls for beard, hair, hat brim and pompom. Each serves 1.

*Combine Red-Red with Christmas Red for red shown.

▶ Festive Face Cupcakes

Pans: Standard Muffin, Cookie Sheet, Cooling Grid, p. 159
Tips: 1, 2, 6, 12, p. 136
Colors: No-Taste Red, Copper, Brown, p. 148
Recipes: Buttercream, Royal Icings, Roll-Out Cookies, p. 118
Also: Snowflake Wishes Standard Baking Cups, p. 213; Oval Cut-Outs, p. 153; 4 in. Lollipop Sticks, p. 200; Meringue Powder, p. 145; Cake Board, p. 241; waxed paper, cornstarch

In advance: Make Santa face cookies. Prepare and roll out dough; cut cookies using small oval Cut-Out. Bake and cool. Decorate cookies on waxed paper-covered board using royal icing. Ice smooth; let set. Outline and pipe in tip 6 hat and ears (pat smooth with finger dipped in cornstarch). Pipe tip 1 dot eyes, nose and outline mouth. Pipe tip 2 swirl beard and hat trim. Let dry. Attach cookies to sticks with dots of icing; let dry.

Ice cupcakes smooth in buttercream; use spatula to create rounded top. Insert cookie in cupcake. Pipe tip 12 outline arms, tip 6 dots gloves. Add tip 2 swirl cuffs. Pipe tip 6 dot border. Each serves 1.

◀ Claus Cookies

Cookie: 18-Pc. Holiday Cutter Set, p. 216; Cookie Sheet, Cooling Grid, p. 159
Tips: 1, 3, 8, p. 136
Colors:* Red-Red, Christmas Red, Brown, Creamy Peach, Leaf Green, Lemon Yellow, p. 148
Recipes: Royal Icing, Roll-Out Cookies, p. 118
Also: Oval Cut-Outs, p. 153; Red Candy Melts, p. 196; Meringue Powder, p. 145; Angled Spatula, p. 140; Disposable Decorating Bags, p. 138; Cake Boards, p. 241; red licorice twists, large spice drops, waxed paper, scissors, granulated sugar, knife, cornstarch

In advance: Make cookies. Prepare and roll out dough. For each Santa, cut 1 head using largest oval Cut-Out and 1 body using bell cutter from set (cut clapper off bell). Bake and cool cookies.

Decorate cookies on waxed paper covered board using royal icing. Ice oval cookie smooth in light peach. Pipe tip 8 hat with tail extending about ½ in. beyond cookie (smooth with finger dipped in cornstarch). Add tip 3 C-motion beard, zigzag hat brim, swirl pompom and outline ears. Pipe tip 1 dot eyes and nose, outline mouth; let dry. Ice bell cookie smooth in red. Pipe tip 3 ball trim and tip 1 outline buttons; let dry. Cut licorice into 1½ in. sections for arms, 1¾ in. sections for legs. Attach to back of body with melted candy. Flatten spice drops slightly between waxed paper. Cut 1 in. semi-circles for shoes; shape mittens from ¾ in. ovals. Attach with melted candy. Trim mittens with tip 3 zigzags; let dry. Attach head to body with melted candy; let set. Each serves 1.

*Combine Red-Red with Christmas Red for red shown. Combine Brown with Red-Red for brown shown. Combine Creamy Peach with Ivory for skin tone shown. Combine Leaf Green with Lemon Yellow for green shown.

▲ Deer-licious Brownies

Pans: 8-Cavity Silicone Round Brownie Pops Mold, p. 170; Cookie Sheet, Cooling Grid, p. 159
Candy: Light Cocoa, Red, White Candy Melts, p. 196; Garden Candy Color Set, p. 199; Christmas Candy Making Kit MEGA PACK, p. 214
Recipe: Favorite brownie recipe or mix
Also: Parchment Triangles, p. 138; chocolate nougat candies, knife

In advance: Mold candy reindeer heads using piping method (p. 130). For black, tint portion of light cocoa candy using black candy color. For tan antlers, add a small amount of light cocoa candy to white. Fill cavities ¾ full. Chill until firm.

Bake and cool brownie pop bodies in silicone mold supported by cookie sheet. Trim bottoms flat if needed. Cover with melted candy (p. 130); chill until firm. Roll nougat candies to shape legs (if necessary, soften by placing wrapped candies in microwave for about 5 seconds). Attach legs, then head, using melted candy. Position reindeer. Each serves 1.

▼ Santa's Deer Friend

Pans: 6-Cavity Mini Stocking and Snowman, p. 212; Cooling Grid, p. 159
Tips: 3, 8, 12, 16, p. 136-137
Colors:* Brown, Red-Red, Black, p. 148
Recipe: Buttercream Icing, p. 118
Also: Light Cocoa Candy Melts, p. 196; Disposable Decorating Bags, p. 138; large pretzel twists, candy-coated chocolates, waxed paper, serrated knife

In advance: Make antlers (p. 125).

Bake and cool mini stocking cake. Turn cuff end down and ice smooth for collar. Pipe tip 3 dot eye and outline mouth. Pipe tip 8 dot nose. Cover reindeer with tip 16 stars. Add tip 12 pull-out ear. Pipe in inner ear with tip 3. Attach yellow candy-coated chocolates to collar with dots of icing. Insert antlers. Each serves 1.

*Combine Brown with Red-Red for brown shown.

▼ Sleigh Pal Cookies

Pans: Cookie Sheet, Cooling Grid, p. 159
Tips: 1, 2, 3, 5, p. 136
Colors: Brown, Red-Red, p. 148
Recipes: Color Flow Icing, Roll-Out Cookies, p. 118
Also: 2010 Pattern Book (Antlers, Ears), p. 132; 9-Pc. Holiday Cutter Set, p. 216; Snowflake Wishes Party Bags, p. 213; Color Flow Mix, p. 145; Cake Boards, p. 241; Disposable Decorating Bags, p. 138; waxed paper, cornstarch, knife

In advance: Make cookies. Prepare and roll out dough. Cut heads using bell cutter; cut off clapper. Bake and cool cookies. Outline cookies with tip 3 and full-strength color flow; flow in with thinned color flow in cut bag. Let dry overnight.

Tape antlers and ears patterns to cake board; cover with waxed paper. Position cookies. Using full-strength color flow and tip 5, pipe antlers and ears against cookie; let dry. Pipe in inside ears with tip 3. Pipe tip 5 dot hair and nose, tip 2 dot eyes and outline mouth. Outline accent on nose with tip 1. Let dry. Carefully remove waxed paper and overpipe antlers and ears on back side; let dry. Each serves 1.

▶ Heading Up the Sleigh

Pans: Guitar, p. 165; Cookie Sheet, Cooling Grid, p. 159
Tips: 2A, 4, 12, 18, p. 136-137
Colors:* Brown, Christmas Red, Red-Red, Black, p. 148
Candy: Light Cocoa, White Candy Melts (14 oz. each), p. 196; Primary Candy Color Set, p. 199
Recipe: Buttercream Icing, Roll-Out Cookies, p. 118
Also: 2010 Pattern Book (Antlers), p. 132; Oval Cut-Outs, p. 153; Cake Boards, Fanci-Foil Wrap. p. 241; knife

In advance: Make cookies. Prepare and roll out dough. Cut 3 antler cookies using pattern and knife; reverse pattern and cut 3 more. For ears, cut 4 oval using largest Cut-Out. Trim off ¼ in. from one narrow end of each oval. Bake and cool cookies.

Bake and cool guitar cake; cut off neck. Stack and ice together 3 cookies for each antlers; stack and ice together 2 oval cookies for each ear. Ice top and sides of antlers smooth. Combine melted white and cocoa candy; tint with orange candy color to match icing color. Cover antlers with melted candy (p. 130); chill until firm. Position ears against cake, attaching with icing. Ice inside of ears smooth. Using tip 12, pipe in nose and add dot eyes. Pipe tip 4 string mouth and string highlight on nose. Cover head and ears with tip 18 stars. Position antlers against cake. Pipe tip 2A balls on top of head. Cake serves 10; each cookie serves 1.

*Combine Brown with Christmas Red for brown shown. Combine Brown, Christmas Red and Black for dark brown shown. Combine Christmas Red with Red-Red for red shown.

▲ Hoofs on the Roofs

Pans: Long Loaf, p. 159; Non-Stick Large Cookie/Jelly Roll, Cooling Grid, p. 167

Tips: 1, 3, p. 136

Colors: Royal Blue, White-White, p. 148

Fondant/Gum Paste: White Ready-To-Use Rolled Fondant (96 oz.), p. 149; Star Power Fondant Imprint Mat, 20 in. Rolling Pin, Roll & Cut Mat, p. 150; Easy-Glide Fondant Smoother, Brush Set, 10 Pc. Fondant/Gum Paste Tool Set, p. 151

Candy: White, Green, Red, Light Cocoa Candy Melts, p. 196; Garden Candy Color Set, p. 199; Santa & Reindeer Pretzel Mold, p. 214; 6 in. Lollipop Sticks, p. 200

Recipe: Buttercream Icing, p. 118

Also: Cake Boards, Fanci-Foil Wrap, p. 241; 18 Pc. Holiday Metal Cutter Set, p. 216; White Sparkle Gel, p. 144; Spatula, p. 140; Parchment Triangles, p. 138; ⅛ in. wide red ribbon (1 yd.), waxed paper, ruler, knife, fine tip artist brush, aluminum foil

In advance: Mold candy sleigh, reindeer and Santa. (p. 130).

Prepare 3 in. high cake for rolled fondant (p. 119). Tint 72 oz. fondant light blue. Cover cake; smooth with Fondant Smoother. For cake sides, roll out remaining blue fondant ⅛ in. thick. Imprint star design following instructions on Imprint Mat package. Cut strips to fit cake sides; attach with damp brush. Add a small amount of White-White to piping gel. Using tip 1, outline stars, then use decorating brush to fill in area. Using full-strength White-White and fine tip brush, fill in swirls; repeat 2-3 times if needed. Using buttercream, pipe tip 3 beads on side seams.

Position candy sleigh on cake top. Insert front row of 3 reindeer lollipops. Using dots of melted candy, attach 15 in. ribbons from reindeer to inside of sleigh; start with reindeer farthest from sleigh and leave some slack in the ribbon between reindeer. Insert back row of reindeer and repeat. Attach Santa in sleigh with melted candy. For clouds, roll white fondant balls ½ to 1 in. diameter. Shape together 3-5 balls and cover with a thin sheet of fondant. Sculpt fondant to shape with veining tool. Position clouds at bottom border. Serves 18.

◀ Snow-Capped Chap

Pans: Soccer Ball, p. 165; Iridescents! Tree, p. 212

Tips: 1M, 2A, 5, 16 p. 136-137

Colors:* Violet, Black, Orange, Rose, p. 148

Recipe: Buttercream Icing, p. 118

Also: Cake Boards, Fanci-Foil Wrap, p. 241; Cooling Grid, p. 159; knife, cornstarch, ruler

Bake and cool cakes. For tree, trim off bottom section, leaving top 3 sections for hat. Trim off ½ in. from tree branch tips on each side to form triangle. Ice tree to level and smooth in buttercream. For soccer ball, trim 2 in. off one end. Ice flat ends of cakes and position end-to-end on foil-wrapped, double thick board, cut to fit. Ice ball cake smooth for head. Pipe tip 5 oval eyes and string mouth. Pipe tip 2A pull-out nose and dot cheeks (pat eyes, cheeks and nose smooth using finger dipped in cornstarch). Cover hat with 1 in. wide stripes of violet and white tip 16 stars. Pipe tip 1M swirl brim and pompom. Serves 20.

*Combine Violet with Rose for violet shown.

▲ Snowflakes Shine

Cookie: Snowflakes Nesting Cutter Set, p. 216; Cookie Sheet, Cooling Grid, p. 159

Tips: 2, 3, p. 136

Color: Royal Blue, p. 148

Recipes: Royal Icing, Roll-Out Cookies, p. 118

Also: White Sparkle Gel, p. 144; Meringue Powder, p. 145

In advance: Make cookies. Prepare and roll out dough. Cut snowflakes using largest and second smallest cutter from set. Bake and cool.

Using royal icing, outline outer edge of large cookies with tip 3, small cookies with tip 2. Fill in centers with Sparkle Gel; let set. Pipe tip 2 outline veins and dot centers. Attach cookies with dots of icing. Each serves 1.

◀ The Coolest Friends

Pans: 8-Cavity Silicone Round Brownie Pops Mold, p. 170; Cookie Sheet, Cooling Grid, p. 159

Tips: 2, 3, 5, p. 136

Colors: Sky Blue, Red-Red, Kelly Green, p. 148

Recipe: Buttercream Icing, p. 118; favorite brownie mix or recipe

Also: Snowman Icing Decorations, p. 213; White Cookie Icing, p. 202; knife; cornstarch, ruler

Bake and cool brownies in silicone mold supported by cookie sheet. Trim to 1¼ in. high with knife. Cover with heated Cookie Icing (p. 130). Let set. Attach icing decorations with buttercream. Pipe tip 5 outline scarf with tip 2 pull-out fringe. Pipe in tip 5 coat (pat smooth with finger dipped in cornstarch). Pipe in tip 3 bow tie, dot knot and buttons. Each serves 1.

▶ Snowman Summit

Pans: 6, 10 x 3 in. Round, p. 158

Tips: 6, 7, 8, p. 136

Colors:* Royal Blue, Black, Red-Red, Christmas Red, Violet, Rose, Leaf Green, Orange, p. 148

Fondant: White Ready-To-Use Rolled Fondant (108 oz.), Gum-Tex, p. 149; White Pearl Dust, Brush Set, Easy-Glide Fondant Smoother, p. 151; 20 in. Rolling Pin, Roll & Cut Mat, p. 150; Round, Star Cut-Outs, p. 153

Recipes: Buttercream Icing, p. 118; Thinned Fondant Adhesive, Chocolate Fondant, p. 119

Also: Dark Cocoa Candy Melts, p. 196; Piping Gel, p. 145; White Sparkling Sugar, p. 146; 11¾ in. Lollipop Sticks, p. 200; Circle Metal Cutter (3 in.), p. 204; Parchment Triangles, p. 138; Dowel Rods, p. 240; 12 in. Round Silver Cake Base, Cake Circles, p. 241; knife, ruler, cornstarch, waxed paper

In advance: Prepare Chocolate Fondant and tint black. Roll out ⅛ in. thick and cover base board (p. 123). Reserve remaining black fondant. **Also:** Make and assemble snowmen (p. 125). **And:** Prepare stars. Roll out white fondant ⅛ in. thick. Cut 45 stars using smallest Cut-Out. Brush with Piping Gel and sprinkle with Sparkling Sugar. Let dry on cornstarch-dusted surface.

Bake and cool 2-layer cakes (trim layers to 2½ in. for 5 in. high tiers). Prepare for Stacked Construction (p. 116) and cover with 60 oz. tinted rolled fondant (p. 119). Roll out white fondant ⅛ in. thick for snow drifts. For 6 in. cake, cut a 20 x 2 in. strip; use knife to cut random waves into top edge. Roll up strip then unroll around base of cake, attaching with damp brush; smooth. For 10 in. cake, cut a 20 x 2 in. and a 12 x 2 in. strip and repeat as above. For scrolls, roll white fondant into ⅛ in. diameter ropes in various lengths. Use piping gel in cut parchment bag to pipe scroll designs onto snow drifts; attach ropes over designs, trimming as needed. Pipe a line of piping gel over ropes; use brush to spread to coat evenly. Sprinkle with Sparkling Sugar. Position cakes on prepared base. Attach stars to cake sides using piping gel. Insert snowmen, trimming sticks as needed. For bottom snowman, use tip of knife to cut a small hole in base board to hold stick. Serves 40.

*Combine Red-Red with Christmas Red for red shown. Combine Violet with Rose for violet shown.

◀ Snow Peeks

Pan: Non-Stick Cookie Sheet, p. 167

Candy: White Candy Melts, p. 196; Primary and Garden Candy Color Sets, p. 199; Christmas Candy Kit for Pretzels, Christmas Candy Making Kit MEGA PACK, p. 214

Also: Letters & Numbers Gum Paste & Fondant Mold Set, p. 153; 101 Cookie Cutters, p. 203; White Nonpareils Sprinkles, p. 146; Parchment Triangles, p. 138; Fanci-Foil Wrap, p. 241; pretzel rods, 6 x 4 x 2 in. high craft foam block, 1½ yards ribbon (2 in. wide), glue gun, knife, ruler, scissors, plastic wrap

In advance: Mold candy. Using Piping Method, make snowmen pretzels using mold from Pretzel Kit and candy tinted various colors. Using Layering Method, make snowflake lollipops and letters using molds and white and blue tinted candy. Make 6 hills. Set large and medium round cutters on non-stick pan. Fill ¼ in. deep with melted candy; chill until firm. Unmold and let come to room temperature. Use a warm knife to cut a straight bottom edge for heights from 1½ to 2¼ in. Using melted candy in cut parchment bag, pipe on random swirls; immediately sprinkle on nonpareils. Let set.

Wrap craft block with foil. Wrap ribbon around edge and secure in back with hot glue. Attach candy letters using melted candy. Attach hills across front and back with melted candy. Wrap bottom end of pretzels with plastic wrap. Insert pretzels and lollipops in center. Each serves 1.

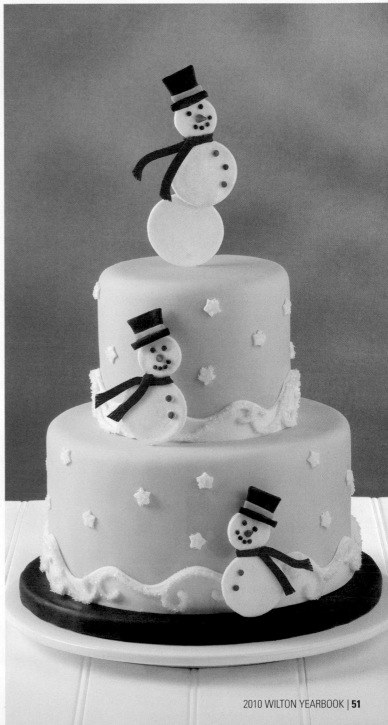

◄ All The Tree's Treasures

Cookie: Tree Comfort-Grip Cutter, p. 216; Cookie Sheet, Cooling Grid, p. 159
Tip: 3, p. 136
Colors:* Kelly Green, Violet, Rose, p. 148
Candy: White, Yellow, Red Candy Melts, p. 196; Garden Candy Color Set, p. 199; Stars Candy Mold, p. 226; Gift Truffles Classic Candy Mold, p. 197
Recipes: Royal Icing, Roll-Out Cookies, p. 118
Also: White, Silver, Gold Pearl Dust, Brush Set, p. 151; 6 in. Cake Circles, p. 241; Meringue Powder, p. 145; Parchment Triangles, p. 138; waxed paper, knife, ruler

In advance: Make cookies. Prepare and roll out dough. For each treat, make 1 full tree, 1 half-tree easel support (cut tree in half vertically before baking) and 1 circle using 6 in. Cake Circle as a pattern. Bake and cool cookies. **Also:** Ice full tree cookies. Outline trees using tip 3 and full-strength royal icing; fill in with thinned icing. Let dry. **And:** Make dot ornaments. Using thinned royal icing, pipe tip 3 dots, ⅜ in. diameter, on waxed paper-covered board. Make 11 for each tree. Let dry; brush with Pearl Dust. **And:** Mold candies (p. 130). Tint portion of melted white candy gray using black candy color. For each treat, make 1 star and 10-15 gifts; use painting or piping method for bow and ribbons. Chill until firm. Brush bow and ribbons with Pearl Dust.

Assemble treats. Attach half-tree support to back of full tree using melted candy; let set. Attach star and ornaments using royal icing; let set. Spatula ice round cookie. Stand tree in center and position candy gifts. Each serves 1.

*Combine Violet with Rose for violet shown.

► The Sock Exchange

Pans: 6-Cavity Silicone Mini Stocking/Boy/Tree Mold, p. 212; Cookie Sheet, Cooling Grid, p. 159
Tip: 12, p. 136
Colors*: Kelly Green, Violet, Rose, Christmas Red, Red-Red, p. 148
Fondant: White Ready-To-Use Rolled Fondant (2 oz. for 3-5 treats), p. 149; Silver, Gold Pearl Dust, Brush Set, p. 151; Cutter/Embosser, p. 152; 9 in. Rolling Pin, Roll & Cut Mat, p. 150
Recipe: Buttercream Icing, p. 118
Also: White Sparkling Sugar, p. 146; lemon extract, knife

Bake and cool stocking cakes in silicone mold supported by cookie sheet. Ice cakes smooth; let set. Using tip 12, build up cuff; sprinkle immediately with Sparkling Sugar. Roll out fondant ⅛ in. thick. Cut dots for red stocking using large opening of tip 12. Cut stripes for violet stocking in random widths with knife. Cut ½ in. squares for green stocking using wavy-edge wheel of Cutter/Embosser. Attach fondant decorations with dots of icing; trim squares with knife as needed. Paint fondant pieces with mixture of Pearl Dust and lemon extract; let dry. Each serves 1.

*Combine Violet with Rose for violet shown. Combine Christmas Red with Red-Red for red shown.

◄ Brownie Blast!

Pans: 12-Cavity Silicone Petite Snowflake Mold, p. 212; Cookie Sheet, Cooling Grid, p. 159
Candy: Snowflake Large Lollipop Mold, White Candy Melts, p. 214
Recipe: Favorite brownie recipe or mix
Also: Parchment Triangles, p. 138; pastry brush

In advance: Make candy snowflakes. Using melted candy in cut parchment bag, pipe in only center snowflake designs of candy mold. Chill until firm. Overpipe for strength; chill until firm. Repeat as needed.

Bake and cool brownies in silicone mold supported by cookie sheet. Attach snowflakes with melted candy. Each serves 1.

◀ Lights in the Forest

Pans: 8-Cavity Silicone Round Brownie Pops Mold, p. 170; Mini Muffin, Cookie Sheet, Cooling Grid, p. 160

Candy: Green, Yellow, White Candy Melts, p. 196; Stars Candy Mold, p. 226

Recipe: Favorite brownie recipe or mix

Also: Flowerful Medley Sprinkles, p. 146; Parchment Triangles, p. 138; Cake Boards, p. 241; small chocolate nougat candies, knife, waxed paper

In advance: Mold candy pieces (p. 130). Mold stars in candy mold, filling only ⅓ full. Lighten portion of melted green candy with a small portion of melted white candy. Mold circle bases in Mini Muffin pan, filling cavities ⅛ in. deep. Chill until firm;.

Bake and cool brownie pops in silicone mold supported by cookie sheet. Cover with melted candy (p. 130); chill until firm. Using melted candy in cut parchment bag, cover bottoms to seal; let set on waxed paper-covered board. Assemble using melted candy, allowing candy to set between each step. Attach nougat candy to bottom for trunk; attach trunk to circle base. Attach confetti sprinkle lights and candy star. Each serves 1.

▶ Decked-Out Tree Tower

Pans: 6, 8, 10 x 2 in. Round, p. 157

Tips: 2, 3, p. 136

Colors:* Kelly Green, Moss Green, Buttercup Yellow, Brown, Black, p. 148

Fondant: White Ready-To-Use Rolled Fondant (77 oz.), Gum-Tex, p. 149; Green, Gold and Silver Pearl Dust, Brush Set, 10-Pc. Fondant/Gum Paste Tool Set, Easy-Glide Fondant Smoother, Fondant Shaping Foam, Flower Former Set, p. 151; 20 in. Rolling Pin, Roll & Cut Mat, p. 150

Recipes: Buttercream, Royal Icings, p. 118; Thinned Fondant Adhesive, p. 119

Also: 2010 Pattern Book (Star Topper), p. 132; Meringue Powder, Piping Gel, Clear Vanilla Extract, p. 145; Red Colored Sugar, p. 146; Cake Dividing Set, p. 138; 3-Pc. Holiday Metal Cutter Set, 6 Pc. Christmas Mini Metal Cutter Set, p. 216; 6, 8 and 10 in. (2) Decorator Preferred Smooth Edge Plates, Hidden Pillars (3 pks.), p. 237; 6 in. Lollipop Sticks, p. 200; Cake Circles, p. 241; ⅛ in. wide ribbon (5 yds.), knife, scissors, waxed paper, ruler, cornstarch, 4, 6 and 8 in. diameter craft foam circles (2 in. high)

2-3 days in advance: Prepare fondant for trims. Add 3 teaspoons Gum-Tex to 30 oz. fondant. Tint as follows: 12 oz. green, 8 oz. gold and 8 oz. silver (use a small amount of Black); reserve 2 oz. white. **Also:** Make star topper and ornaments; attach ornaments to plates (p. 125). **And:** Make leaves and berries (p. 126).

Bake and cool 1-layer cakes. Prepare and cover with 48 oz. light green fondant (p. 119). Prepare for Push-In Pillar Construction (p. 116); use 6 in. and 8 in. plates to mark positions for pillars on 8 in. and 10 in. cakes. Trim 8 hidden pillars to 5½ in. high for top 2 tiers; trim 4 pillars to 3½ in. high for bottom tier. **At party:** Assemble cakes and attach leaves and berries to cakes using thinned fondant adhesive. Insert star topper. Serves 30.

*Combine Kelly Green with Moss Green for green leaves. Combine Buttercup Yellow with Brown for gold ornaments.

▼ Ski Scene

Cookie: Christmas Cookie Tree Cutter Kit, p. 214; Christmas Tree Comfort-Grip Cutter, 18-Pc. Holiday Cutter Set, p. 216; Cookie Sheet, Cooling Grid, p. 159

Tips: 1, 2, 3, 4, 5, 12, 15, 16, 17, p. 136-137

Colors:* Kelly Green, Christmas Red, Royal Blue, Rose, Violet, Lemon Yellow, Orange, Brown, Black, Copper, p. 148

Fondant: White Ready-To-Use Rolled Fondant (86 oz.), Gum-Tex, p. 149; Brush Set, p. 151; 20 in. Rolling Pin, Roll & Cut Mat, p. 150

Recipes: Royal Icing, Roll-Out Cookies (4 recipes), p. 118; Thinned Fondant Adhesive, p. 119

Also: 2010 Pattern Book (Upper, Lower Slopes), p. 132; 3-Tier Pillar Cake Stand, p. 235; Jumbo Confetti and Jumbo Rainbow Nonpareils Sprinkles, Flowerful Medley and Rainbow Nonpareils Sprinkles, p. 146; 4 in. Lollipop Sticks, p. 200; Cake Boards, Cake Circles, Fanci-Foil Wrap, p. 241; Meringue Powder, p. 145; waxed paper, knife, ruler, cornstarch, scissors, tape

In advance: Make cookies for stacked trees. Prepare and roll out dough; cut using cutters from Cookie Tree Set. For large tree, cut 2 cookies using each size cutter. For each medium tree, cut 2 cookies using each of 6 smallest cutters and 1 cookie using 7th smallest cutter. Bake and cool cookies. **Also:** Make cookies for other features. Prepare and roll out dough. Using cutters from 18 Pc. Set, cut 7 gingerbread boys, 2 snowmen and 4 trees. Cut 9 more trees to make 18 easel back supports; trim off tree trunks and cut trees in half vertically. Using Tree Comfort-Grip Cutter, cut 4 trees. Using pattern and knife, cut Upper Ski Slope; reverse pattern and cut Lower Ski Slope. Bake and cool all cookies. **And:** Prepare fondant skis, ski poles and scarf ends. (p. 126)

Assemble and decorate stacked trees using royal icing. Beginning with largest cookies and working up, build trees following package directions. Pipe tip 17 pull-out stars for branches. Sprinkle with Jumbo Nonpareils. Attach Jumbo Confetti with icing dots. Pipe tip 5 pull-out snow. Let dry.

Decorate standing cookies using royal icing. Cover larger trees with tip 16 pull-out stars, smaller trees with tip 15 pull-out stars. Sprinkle with nonpareils; attach confetti. Let dry. Use tip 5 to outline and fill in snowmen (pat smooth with finger dipped in cornstarch). Pipe hat and scarf with tip 4. Pipe tip 3 hat band and pull-out dot nose. Pipe tip 2 dot eyes, mouth and buttons. Let dry. Decorate skiers in assorted colors. Use tip 5 to outline and fill in faces, jackets and pants (pat smooth). Using tip 2, pipe dot eyes and nose, outline or dot mouth, C-motion ears on boys; dot cheeks on girls; pipe hair using curls, outlines and pull-out dots. Use tip 4 to pipe shoes. Attach ski poles to hands; pipe tip 3 gloves and tip 2 fingers over stick. Pipe earmuffs and hats with tip 3; add tip 1 outline and zigzag trims to hats and jackets. For neck portion of scarf, roll out reserved fondant 1/16 in. thick. Cut a 1/4 x 2 in. strip; attach using damp brush. Attach matching scarf ends using fondant adhesive. Let dry. Attach easel backs using royal icing; let dry.

Prepare ski slopes. Use pattern to cut upper and lower ski slopes from cake boards; cover with foil (p. 112). Using royal icing, attach ski slope cookies. Spatula ice to cover; build up outside edges using tip 12 then swirl with spatula. Let dry.

Prepare cake stand. Roll out remaining white fondant 1/8 in. thick. To cover 10 in. plate, roll a 17 in. circle. Place a 12 in. cake circle in center as your guide; use knife to cut random snow "drifts" from 1 to 2½ in. long. Transfer fondant to cover 10 in. plate, allowing fondant to drape down over sides. Repeat using 14 in. cake circle to cover 12 in. plate and 16 in. cake circle to cover 14 in. plate rolling fondant 5 in. larger then cake circles.

Assemble at party: Position stacked cookie trees on cake stand. Attach ski slopes with icing. Attach skis, then skiers, trimming easel backs as needed. Position standing trees and snowmen. Each cookie serves 1.

*Combine Violet with Rose for violet shown.

◄ North Pole Climbers

Pans: Standard Muffin, p. 159; 17.25 x 11.5 x 1 in. Non-Stick Large Cookie/Jelly Roll, Cooling Grid, p. 167

Candy: White, Light Cocoa, Green, Red, Orange, Blue Candy Melts, p. 196; Santa Claus Candy Cane Mold, Frosty Friends Candy Cane Mold, p. 214

Recipe: Favorite crisped rice cereal treats

Also: Round Comfort-Grip Cutter, p. 202; Decorator Brush Set, p. 199 or Parchment Triangles, p 138; Jumbo Confetti Sprinkles, p. 146; candy canes, white card stock, black fine-tip marker

In advance: Make candy cane candies. For skin tone shown, tint a small portion of melted white candy with melted orange candy. Mold candies on candy canes using painting or piping method (p. 130). Chill until firm. To make base, place round cutter on jelly roll pan and fill ¼ in. deep with melted cocoa candy. Chill until firm.

Prepare cereal treats mixture and press while still warm into muffin pan cavities to shape; immediately unmold. Make hole in top with end of candy cane. Cover treats with melted candy (p. 130); chill until firm. Attach treats to bases and confetti to treats with melted candy. Insert candy canes. Print names on card stock with marker; attach to candy cane with melted candy. Each serves 1.

► Toy Shop Trooper

Pans: 6-Cavity Silicone Mini Stocking/Boy/Tree Mold, p. 212; Cookie Sheet, Cooling Grid, p. 160

Tips: 1, 2, 3, p. 136

Colors:* Golden Yellow, Lemon Yellow, Red-Red, Christmas Red, Black, Royal Blue, Brown, Copper (for skin tone shown), p. 148

Candy: Dark Cocoa Candy Melts*, p. 196; Garden Candy Color Set, p. 199; Cordial Cups Candy Mold, p. 197

Recipes: Sugar Cookies, Royal Icing, p 118

Also: Parchment Triangles, p. 138; Circle Metal Cutter, p. 204; Meringue Powder, p. 145; Cake Board, p. 241; waxed paper

In advance: Make candy hat. Tint melted candy black using candy color. Mold solid hat in Cordial Cups Mold (p. 130); chill until firm. Place hat on waxed paper-covered board; pipe brim using melted candy in cut parchment bag; chill until firm.

Prepare cookie recipe and press into boy molds ½ in. deep. Bake and cool cookies in silicone mold supported by cookie sheet. For base, roll out dough ¼ in. thick and cut using circle cutter. Decorate soldier using royal icing. Ice face, hands and clothing smooth. Pipe tip 2 string belt, shirt collar, cuffs, shoulder pads; dot nose, eyes and buttons. Pipe tip 1 string mouth, button detail; pull-out dot epaulets. Attach soldier to round cookie with melted candy; attach hat to head. Pipe tip 3 pull-out string hair, hat band and fleur-de-lis. Each serves 1.

*Combine Golden Yellow with Lemon Yellow for yellow shown. Combine Red-Red with Christmas Red for red shown. Combine Brown with Red-Red for brown shown.

◄ Let's Raise the Roof!

Cookie: Gingerbread House Comfort-Grip Cutter, 6-Pc. Holiday Mini Cutter Set, p. 216; Cookie Sheet, Cooling Grid, p. 159

Tips: 1, 2, 3, 4, p. 136

Colors: Red-Red, Kelly Green, p. 148

Recipes: Royal Icing, Grandma's Gingerbread, p. 118

Also: 6 in. Cake Circles, Cake Board, Silver Fanci-Foil Wrap, p. 241; Flowerful Medley Sprinkles, Jumbo Confetti Sprinkles, p. 146; Meringue Powder, p. 145; Small Angled Spatula, p. 140; 9 in. Rolling Pin, p. 150; spice drops, red pinwheel candies, mini candy canes, sugared jelly ropes, striped rectangle hard candies, spice drops, granulated sugar, scissors, ruler, serrated knife, cornstarch

Prepare gingerbread dough and roll out ⅛ in. thick. For house front and back, cut 2 cookies with Comfort-Grip cutter. Trim off chimney. Cut 2 side walls, each 2 x 2½ in. high and 2 roof panels, each 3½ x 2⅞ in. high. Bake and cool all pieces. If pieces expand during baking, measure when cool and trim to original size using serrated knife. Cut approximately 18-24 gingerbread boys using cutter from set; bake and cool. Assemble and decorate house (p. 126). Decorate gingerbread boys with tip 1 facial features and tip 2 clothing; let dry. Fill house with boys. Each cookie serves 1.

◀ A Ravishing Rose!

Pan: 9 x 13 x 2 in. Sheet, p. 157; Cookie Sheet, Cooling Grid, p. 159
Also: Large Icing Roses, p. 147; 101 Cookie Cutters, p. 203; Pink Colored Sugar, p. 146; White Candy Melts (1 pk. makes 14 treats), p. 196; Cake Boards, p. 241; Brush Set, p. 151; Parchment Triangles, p. 138; waxed paper, knife

Bake and cool cake; trim to 1½ in. high. Cut treats with a knife using smallest round cutter from set as a guide. Ice bottoms with melted candy; place on waxed paper-covered board and chill until firm. Cover treats with melted candy (p. 130); chill until firm. Fill a shallow bowl with pink sugar. Using melted candy in cut parchment bag, pipe line around bottom edge of treat. Place treat in bowl and coat edge with sugar. Brush off excess sugar. Repeat for top edge, then center. Attach rose with melted candy. Each serves 1.

▶ Valentine Brownie Points

Pan: 9 x 13 x 2 in. Sheet, p. 157
Tip: 3, p. 136
Recipe: Favorite brownie recipe or mix
Also: Heart Comfort-Grip Cutter, p. 220; Valentine Candy Making MEGA PACK, p. 219; Light Cocoa Candy Melts, p. 219; Brownie Fudge Icing, p. 169; Pink, White Cookie Icing, p. 220; Parchment Triangles, p. 138

In advance: Make candy hearts. Using heart lollipop mold from set, mold hearts without lollipop sticks. Tap to settle; chill until firm.

Bake and cool brownies. Cut out hearts using cutter. Ice tops smooth with Fudge Icing. Using Cookie Icing in parchment bag fitted with tip 3, pipe lines, swirls and letters. Attach candy heart with icing. Each serves 1.

◀ Nonpareil Valentines

Pans: Petite Heart, p. 218; Cookie Sheet, Cooling Grid, p. 159
Also: White Candy Melts (1 pk. covers 12-14 hearts), p. 196; Valentine Nonpareils, p. 219; Cake Boards, p. 241; waxed paper, shallow bowl, spoon

Bake and cool heart cakes. Decorate 3-4 at a time. Cover with melted candy (p. 130). Let set briefly, then place in bowl of nonpareils. Spoon nonpareils over top to cover; transfer to waxed paper-covered board. Chill until firm. Each serves 1.

◀ Lip-Smacking Snack

Pans: 6-Pc. Nesting Hearts Cutter Set, p. 220; Cookie Sheet, Cooling Grid, p. 159
Tip: 4, p. 136
Color: Rose, p. 148
Candy: Red Candy Melts, Kissy Lips Candy Mold, p. 219; Decorator Brush Set, p. 199
Recipes: Color Flow Icing, Roll-Out Cookies, p. 118
Also: Pink Cake Sparkles, p. 219; Color Flow Mix, p. 145; Cake Boards, p. 241; Disposable Decorating Bags, p. 138; tea strainer, spoon, waxed paper

In advance: Make candies. Mold red lips in candy mold, filling cavities just ¾ full. Tap to settle; chill until firm. **Also:** Make cookies. Prepare and roll out dough. Cut cookies using largest heart cutter from set. Bake and cool. Cover with thinned icing (p. 130). Let dry 24 hours on waxed paper-covered board.

Push Cake Sparkles through tea strainer for a finer texture. Using full-strength icing, pipe tip 4 message; immediately sprinkle on Cake Sparkles. Let set, then brush off excess. Attach candy lips with icing. Each serves 1.

▶ Got a Crush on You Cupcakes

Pans: Standard Muffin, Cookie Sheet, Cooling Grid, p. 159
Recipes: Buttercream Icing, Roll-Out Cookies, p. 118
Also: 6-Pc. Nesting Hearts Cutter Set, p. 220; Red, Pink Colored Sugars, p. 219; Sweetheart Bandana Standard Baking Cups, p. 219

In advance: Make cookies. Prepare and roll out dough. For each treat, cut 2 hearts using 2 smallest cutters from set. Sprinkle with sugar; bake and cool. Layer cookies with icing.

Bake and cool cupcakes; ice tops. Insert cookies, mounding icing to support back if needed. Each serves 1.

▶ Butterfly Kiss Cookies

Cookie: 6-Pc. Nesting Hearts Cutter Set, p. 220; Cookie Sheet, Cooling Grid, p. 159
Tip: 1, p. 136
Colors: Red-Red, Rose, Burgundy, Black, p. 148
Recipes: Color Flow Icing, Roll-Out Cookies, p. 118
Also: 2010 Pattern Book (Swirls, Butterfly), p. 132; Sweetheart Bandana Treat Bags, p. 219; Color Flow Mix, p. 145; Cake Boards, p. 241; toothpicks, waxed paper

In advance: Make cookies. Prepare and roll out dough. For each treat, cut 1 large heart using 2nd largest cutter from set and 1 small heart using 2nd smallest cutter from set. Bake and cool. Cover with thinned icing (p. 130). Let dry 24 hours on waxed paper-covered board.

Use patterns to mark designs on cookies. Use tip 1 and full-strength color flow to pipe dot swirls and outline butterfly. Attach small cookie to large using icing. Each serves 1.

◀ Sweet & Tart Hearts

Cookie: 6-Cavity Silicone Ruffled Heart Mold, p. 218; Cookie Sheet, p. 159
Candy: White, Light Cocoa Candy Melts, p. 219; Decorator Brush Set, p. 199
Also: Piping Gel, p. 145; Pink and White Sparkling Sugars, p. 146; fresh blueberries and raspberries

Mold ³⁄₁₆ in. thick candy shells (p. 130) in silicone mold supported by cookie sheet. Chill until firm. Brush top edges of heart molds with Piping Gel and dip into Sparkling Sugars. Fill with fruit. Each serves 1.

◀ Cheep Thrills!

Pans: 3-Pc. Paisley Set (12.75 x 9 x 2 in. used), p. 156
Tip: Any standard tip, p. 136-137
Colors:* Lemon Yellow, Golden Yellow, Orange, Brown, Red-Red, Black, Leaf Green, p. 148
Fondant/Gum Paste: White Ready-To-Use Rolled Fondant (38 oz.), Gum-Tex, p.149; Brush Set, 10-Pc. Fondant/Gum Paste Tool Set, Easy-Glide Fondant Smoother, p. 151; 20 in. Rolling Pin, Roll & Cut Mat, p. 150
Recipes: Buttercream Icing, p. 118; Thinned Fondant Adhesive, p. 119
Also: 6 in. Lollipop Sticks, p. 200; Cake Boards, p. 241; shredded coconut, zip-close plastic bag, jelly beans, ruler, knife, waxed paper, cornstarch

In advance: Make beak and feet (p.126).

Bake and cool 1-layer cake. Prepare for rolled fondant. Tint ¼ oz. fondant black, 36 oz. yellow. Roll out ⅛ in. thick as needed. Cover cake with rolled fondant (p. 119), smoothing with Fondant Smoother. For wing, shape 4 oz. fondant into flattened teardrop, 3 x 4½ in. long. Use veining tool to make indentations for feathers. Attach using damp brush. Cut black eye using wide end of tip; attach. Insert beak and legs. Sprinkle around cake with tinted coconut (p. 123). Position jelly beans. Serves 14.

*Combine Lemon Yellow with Golden Yellow for yellow shown. Combine Brown with Red-Red for brown shown.

▶ Easter Enthusiast

Pans: Teddy Bear, p. 163; Cookie Sheet, Cooling Grid, p. 159
Tips: 1A, 5, 12, 18, p. 136-137
Colors:* Sky Blue, Violet, Rose, Leaf Green, Lemon Yellow, Black, p. 148
Recipes: Buttercream Icing, Roll-Out Cookies, p. 118
Also: 2010 Pattern Book (Ear, Hand, Foot, Bow Tie, Knot), p. 132; 6 in. Cookie Treat Sticks, p. 205; White Candy Melts, p. 222; knife, cornstarch, toothpicks

In advance: Make cookies. Prepare and roll out dough. Using patterns, cut 2 ears, 2 hands and 2 feet (reverse patterns for 2nd of each); cut 1 bow tie and 1 knot. Bake and cool. Cut Cookie Sticks to 4½ in.; attach to backs of hands and ears using melted candy, leaving 2-2½ in. extended.

Bake and cool cake. Trim off ears and level face. Lightly ice pants area and mark stripes with toothpick. Pipe tip 1A puffy cheeks (pat smooth with finger dipped in cornstarch). Use tip 5 to outline and fill in nose and mouth (pat smooth). Use tip 12 to pipe dot eyes (pat smooth). Cover head, shirt, suspenders and striped pants with tip 18 stars. Ice inside ears, soles of feet and toes smooth. Position and insert hands and ears; attach feet with icing. Cover cookies with tip 18 stars. Pipe tip 12 dot buttons (pat smooth). Pipe tip 5 dot buttonholes. Cake serves 12; each cookie serves 1.

*Combine Violet with Rose for violet shown. Combine Leaf Green with Lemon Yellow for green shown.

◄ Pecking Order

Pans: 12-Cavity Silicone Petite Easter Egg Mold, p. 221; Cookie Sheet, p. 159
Tip: 7, p. 136
Colors: Sky Blue, Rose, Orange, Black, p. 148
Fondant/Gum Paste: White Ready-To-Use Rolled Fondant (2½ oz. per treat), p. 149; Brush Set, 10-Pc. Fondant/Gum Paste Tool Set, p. 151; 9 in. Rolling Pin, Roll & Cut Mat, p. 150
Recipe: Buttercream Icing, p. 118
Also: Black string licorice, scissors, ruler, knife

Bake and cool mini cakes in silicone mold supported by cookie sheet. Prepare for rolled fondant (p. 119), icing smooth in buttercream and covering egg design. For 2 treats, tint fondant as follows: 2 oz. blue, 2 oz. pink, ½ oz. orange, ¼ oz. black. Roll out pink and blue ⅛ in. thick. Cover mini cakes; smooth and trim away excess. For each wing and tail, begin with a ¾ in. ball of fondant. Shape into flattened teardrop; use small end of veining tool to score feathers. Attach using damp brush. For beak, use fingers to shape an orange cone, ⅜ in. tall; attach. Roll cut black fondant ⅛ in. thick. Cut eyes using narrow end of tip 7; attach. For 2 feet, begin with a ½ in. ball of fondant. Cut ball in half and shape each portion into a flattened oval. Use veining tool to indent toes. Cut 1 in. lengths of licorice. Push on feet and insert other end into cake. Each serves 1.

► They're All Ears for Easter!

Pans: 8-Cavity Silicone Round Brownie Pops Mold, p. 170; Cookie Sheet, Cooling Grid, p. 159
Candy: White (1 pk. makes 5-6 treats), Light Cocoa Candy Melts, p. 196; Garden Candy Color Set, p. 199; 4 in. Lollipop Sticks, p. 200
Also: 2010 Pattern Book (Ears), p. 132; Parchment Triangles, p. 138; Cake Board, p. 241; waxed paper

In advance: Make ears using melted candy in cut parchment bags. Copy pattern and tape to board; cover with waxed paper. Pipe white ears; chill until firm. Tint portion of melted white candy pink. Overpipe pink inner ears; chill until firm. Cut lollipop sticks to 3 in; attach to back of ears with melted candy. Let set.

Bake and cool brownies in silicone mold supported by cookie sheet. Cover with melted candy (p. 130). Let set then repeat. Chill until firm. Decorate using melted candy in cut parchment bags. Pipe outline mouth, dot eyes, nose and cheeks. Insert ears into head. Each serves 1.

◄ Holiday Headliners

Pans: 6-Cavity Bunny Non-Stick Mini Cake, p. 221; Cookie Sheet, Cooling Grid, p. 159
Candy: White (1 pk. makes 4 treats), Light Cocoa Candy Melts, p.196; Garden Candy Color Set, p. 199
Also: White Ready-To-Use Rolled Fondant (1 oz. for each treat), p. 149; Parchment Triangles, p. 138; ruler

Bake and cool mini cakes. Use a 1 x ½ in. log of fondant to make teardrop-shaped feet. Cover cakes and feet with melted candy (p. 130). Chill until firm. Tint portion of melted white candy pink. Using melted candy in cut parchment bags, pipe brown dot eyes and pink dot nose, outline whiskers and pipe-in inner ears. Attach feet with white melted candy. Each serves 1.

◀ Flower Fun!

Pans: Mini Daisy, p. 160; Standard Muffin, p. 159
Candy: White Candy Melts (1 pk. makes 18-20 flowers), p. 196; Primary, Garden Candy Color Sets, p. 199
Recipe: Buttercream Icing, p. 118
Also: White Standard Baking Cups, p. 186; Parchment Triangles, p. 138

In advance: Mold flowers. Divide Candy Melts in 4ths. Tint portions violet, pink, yellow and orange using candy colors. Using melted candy in cut parchment bags, fill center of daisy cavity; chill until firm. Pipe in petal sections with melted candy ¼ in. deep; chill until firm; unmold.

Bake and cool cupcakes; ice tops. Position flower. Each serves 1.

▶ Sweet Sprout Brownies

Pans: 24-Cavity Silicone Bite-Size Brownie Squares Mold, p. 170; Cookie Sheet, Cooling Grid, p. 159
Color: Leaf Green, p. 148
Fondant: White Ready-To-Use Rolled Fondant (1 oz. per treat), p. 149; Cutter/Embosser, p. 152; Flower Former Set, Fondant Shaping Foam, Brush Set, p. 151; Leaf Cut-Outs, p. 153; 9 in. Rolling Pin, Roll & Cut Mat, p. 150
Recipes: Buttercream Icing, p. 118; favorite brownie recipe or mix
Also: Icing Daisies, Pansies, Posies, p. 147; White Candy Melts (1 pk. covers 12-14 treats), p. 196; Garden Candy Color Set, p. 199; 4 in. Lollipop Sticks, p. 200; scissors, cornstarch, ruler, knife

In advance: Make leaves. Tint 1 oz. fondant green for each treat; roll out ¹⁄₁₆ in. thick. Cut leaves using smallest Cut-Out; reserve remaining fondant for grass. Set leaves on thin shaping foam and score veins using smooth wheel of Cutter/Embosser. Let dry in small Flower Former dusted with cornstarch.

Bake and cool brownies. Tint melted candy green. Cover brownies (p. 130). Chill until firm. Roll out reserved green fondant ¹⁄₁₆ in. thick. Cut 2 strips, 5¼ x 1 in., for each treat. Use scissors to cut thin V-shaped slits, ½ in. deep, for blades of grass. Attach strip around brownie using damp brush; repeat with 2nd strip. Separate and curve blades. Use melted candy to attach flower and leaf to Lollipop Stick; let set. Insert into brownie. Each serves 1.

◀ Spring in a Basket

Candy: White, Light Cocoa, Blue & Yellow Candy Melts, p. 196; Garden Candy Color Set, p. 199; Dessert Shells Candy Mold, p. 197; Fuzzy Bunny Lollipop Mold, p. 222
Also: 2010 Pattern Book (Basket Handle), p. 132; Cake Boards, p. 241; Parchment Triangles, p. 138; Pastel Jordan Almonds, p. 244; jelly spearmint leaves, waxed paper, tape, knife, scissors, granulated sugar

In advance: Mold flowers. Tint portions of melted candy violet, green and pink. Use piping method (p. 130) to make flower trio in Fuzzy Bunny mold, without sticks. Chill until firm. **Also:** Make candy shells (p. 130); chill until firm. **And:** Make candy handles. Copy pattern and tape to board; cover with waxed paper. Using melted candy in cut parchment bag, pipe over pattern; chill until firm. Carefully peel off waxed paper and turn over. Pipe back side for strength; chill until firm.

Attach handles using melted candy (do not lift baskets by handle!). Insert almonds or molded candies. For leaves, use scissors to cut spearmint leaves into 3rds lengthwise; roll cut edges in sugar. Position in baskets. Each serves 1.

◄ Nesting 1-2-3!

Pan: Standard Muffin, p. 159
Candy: Light Cocoa, Yellow and Blue Candy Melts, p. 196; Hoppy Easter Lollipop Mold, p. 222
Recipe: Buttercream Icing, p. 118
Also: Assorted Pastel Standard Baking Cups, p. 186; Chocolate Jimmies, p. 146; Parchment Triangles, p. 138

In advance: Mold bluebirds without lollipop sticks using piping method (p. 130). Chill until firm; unmold.

Bake and cool cupcakes. Ice tops and immediately roll edges in Chocolate Jimmies. Position candies on cupcakes, supporting backs with additional icing if needed. Each serves 1.

► Spring Awakening

Pans: 6 x 2 in. Square, p. 157; Cookie Sheet, Cooling Grid, p. 159
Tip: 3, p. 136
Colors:* Leaf Green, Lemon Yellow, Golden Yellow, Violet, Rose, p. 148
Candy: White Candy Melts (2 pks.), p. 196; Primary & Garden Candy Color Sets, p. 199; 11¾ in. Lollipop Sticks, p. 200
Recipes: Buttercream, Color Flow Icings, Roll-Out Cookies, p. 118
Also: 3-Pc. Easter Cutter Set (Tulip), p. 223; Color Flow Mix, Piping Gel, p. 145; Parchment Triangles, p. 138; Cake Boards, Fanci-Foil Wrap, p. 241; tape, scissors, ruler, knife

1 day in advance: Make cookies. Prepare and roll out dough. Cut tulips using cutter from set; cut off stems. Bake and cool. Use tip 3 to outline cookies with full-strength color flow icing; flow in with thinned color flow. Let dry 24 hours. Attach Lollipop Sticks to backs using melted candy. Let set. **Also:** Make blades of grass. Melt candy and tint green, combining green with some yellow candy color. Using cut parchment bag, pipe individual tapered blades of grass on waxed paper-covered boards. Make 283 blades 1¼ in. long for cake top; make 456 blades 5¼ in. long for around cake. Make extras to allow for breakage. Chill until firm. **And:** Prepare base board. Cut 2 cake boards 7½ in. square. Tape together and wrap with foil (p. 112).

Bake and cool 2-layer cake. Ice smooth. Position on board or serving plate. Insert short blades of grass into cake to cover top. Chill cake and long blades of grass. Use melted candy to attach long blades of grass around cake, 26 per side and 4 rows deep. Work one side of cake at a time, chilling cake and grass as needed so melted candy will set up quicker. Insert cookies into cake, trimming sticks as needed. Cake serves 12; each cookie serves 1.

*Combine Lemon Yellow with Golden Yellow for yellow shown. Combine Violet with Rose for violet shown.

◄ Petals Are Poppin'

Pans: Round Cookie Treat, p. 205; 6-Cavity Non-Stick Flower, p. 221; Cookie Sheet, Cooling Grid, p. 159
Candy: White Candy Melts (2 pks. makes 10-12 treats), p. 196; Garden, Primary Candy Color Sets, p. 199
Recipe: Roll-Out Cookies, p. 118
Also: Parchment Triangles, p. 138; Cake Boards, p. 241; 8 in. Cookie Treat Sticks, p. 205; ¼ in. wide satin ribbon (11 in. per treat), waxed paper

In advance: Make flowers. Tint portions of melted candy blue, pink and yellow using candy colors. Using melted candy in cut parchment bags, mold flower centers in non-stick pan; chill until firm. Mold petals ¼ in. deep; chill until firm.

Prepare dough. Press into pan with cookie sticks; bake and cool. Cover cookies with melted candy (p. 130); let set. Attach flowers with melted candy; let set. Tie ribbon bow around stick. Each serves 1.

◄ Holiday All-Stars

Cookie: 6-Pc. Nesting Stars Plastic Cutter Set, p. 225; Round Comfort-Grip Cutter, p. 202; Cookie Sheet, Cooling Grid, p. 159
Colors: Red-Red, Royal Blue, p.148
Candy: Light Cocoa (2 pks.), White Candy Melts (1 pk.), p. 196; 11¾ in. Lollipop Sticks, p. 200
Recipes: Buttercream, Royal Icings, Roll-Out Cookies, p. 118
Also: Red, White, Blue Sparkle Gel, p. 225; Red, Blue Colored Sugars, p. 226; Piping Gel, p. 145; Brush Set, p. 151; Cake Boards, Fanci-Foil Wrap, p. 241; curling ribbon, 2 x 8 in. diameter craft foam circle, 2 in. wide ribbon (25 in. long), glue gun, glue stick, scissors, granulated sugar

In advance: Make cookies. Prepare and roll out dough. Cut 16 circles using Comfort-Grip cutter; cut out centers of 8 cookies using smallest star cutter from set. Cut 20 stars using same cutter. Bake and cool. **Also:** Decorate cookies. Brush tops of small star cookies with Piping Gel; sprinkle half with red, half with blue Colored Sugar. Place star-center and solid round cookies on cooling grid set over cookie sheet. Cover all with melted light cocoa candy (p. 130). Chill until firm. **And:** Prepare base. Hot glue craft foam circle on same size cake circle and wrap with foil. Attach 2 in. wide ribbon around outside, securing with glue stick.

Using melted candy, attach Lollipop Sticks to backs of solid round cookies; chill until firm. Ice tops with red, white or blue buttercream; position star-center cookies on top. Sprinkle open star centers with red, white or blue sugar. Pipe swirls on star-center cookies using red, white and blue Sparkle Gel. Let set. Attach small star cookies around base using melted candy. Insert cookies. Cut and curl 16 ribbons, 18 in. long, and tie 2 to each cookie. Curl additional pieces to cover base as needed, attaching with dots of glue. Each serves 1.

◄ Patriotic Pinwheel Cake

Pan: Star, p. 225
Tips: 13, 16, 21, p. 137
Colors:* Christmas Red, Red-Red, Royal Blue, p. 148
Recipe: Buttercream Icing, p. 118
Also: 2010 Pattern Book (Star Point Section), p. 132; Cake Board, Fanci-Foil Wrap, p. 241; toothpick

Bake and cool cake. Ice sides smooth and lightly ice top. Mark pattern in each star point section with toothpick. Cover with tip 16 stars. In solid blue areas, overpipe tip 13 white stars. Pipe tip 21 star bottom border. Serves 12.

*Combine Christmas Red with Red-Red for red shown.

◄ Standing Up for Freedom

Pans: Standard Muffin, Cookie Sheet, Cooling Grid, p. 159
Colors: Royal Blue, Red-Red, p. 148
Recipes: Buttercream Icing, Roll-Out Cookies, p. 118
Also: 6-Pc. Nesting Stars Plastic Cutter Set, p. 225; Patriotic Stars Standard Baking Cups, p. 226; White Sparkling Sugar, p. 146

In advance: Make cookies. Prepare and roll out dough. Cut star cookies using smallest cutter from set; bake and cool. Ice cookies smooth.

Bake and cool cupcakes. Ice tops and sprinkle with Sparkling Sugar. Position star cookies on cupcakes; support with additional icing if needed. Each serves 1.

► Stars and Stripes Forever!

Pans: Mini Star Pan, p. 225; Cookie Sheet, Cooling Grid, p. 159
Color: Royal Blue, p. 148
Cookie: 6-Pc. Nesting Stars Cutter Set, p. 225; White, Red Cookie Icing, p. 225
Recipe: Roll-Out Cookies, p. 118
Also: Blue Colored Sugar, p. 226; Disposable Decorating Bags, p. 138

In advance: Make cookies. Prepare and roll out dough. Cut stars using smallest cutter from set. Sprinkle with colored sugar; bake and cool.

Bake and cool cakes. Heat white Cookie Icing following package directions; cover cake with white icing (p. 130). Tint portion of cookie icing blue and place in a disposable decorating bag. While icing is still wet, pipe stripes with red and blue icing. Position cookie. Each serves 1.

◄ Star-Making Brownies

Pan: 11 x 7 x 1.5 in. Non-Stick Biscuit/Brownie, p. 167
Recipe: Favorite brownie recipe or mix
Also: Comfort-Grip Star Cutter, p. 202; Star Cut-Outs, p. 153; Brownie Fudge Icing, p. 169; Blue, Red Colored Sugars, White Sparkling Sugar, White Nonpareils, p. 146; Patriotic Nonpareils, p. 226; Decorator Brush Set, p. 199; small spoon, toothpick

Bake and cool brownies. Cut stars using Comfort-Grip Cutter. Ice tops smooth with Fudge Icing. For star center design, position medium Cut-Out on brownie; cover area with nonpareils using spoon. Brush into points and remove cutter. For flag design, mark stripes and star field with toothpick. Cover stripes and blue field areas with sugars. Position white nonpareils on blue field. Each serves 1.

Exceptional Events

These are the moments you live for! Whether a baby's on the way, your grand-daughter's being confirmed or your son is graduating with honors you want a cake that will capture the moment for all time. Like our graduation tower, embossed with colorful comets, separated by diploma pillars and topped with stars to mark the year. Or baby steps for the shower—a running theme for cakes, cookies and cupcakes with fun footprints that really make an impression. For showers, check the bathtime design here, decked out with 3-D duckies from top to bottom, swimming sweetly over fondant waves and bubbles.

Bathtime Buddies

Pans: 6, 10 x 2 in. Square, p. 157
Tips: 1A, 2A, 10, 12, p. 136
Colors: Sky Blue, Lemon Yellow, Orange, Black, White-White, p. 148
Fondant: White Ready-To-Use Rolled Fondant (140 oz.), p. 149; Brush Set, Easy-Glide Fondant Smoother, p. 151; Leaf Cut-Outs, p. 153; 20 in. Rolling Pin, Roll & Cut Mat, p. 150
Also: Rubber Ducky Candy Mold, p. 199; Piping Gel, p. 145; 2 in. (2 sets) and 2½ in. Globe Pillar Sets, p. 238; Decorator Preferred 6 in. Square Plate, p. 237; Cake Boards, Fanci-Foil Wrap, p. 241; 12½ x 12½ in. plywood or foamcore board (½ in. thick), knife, scissors, ruler, tape, cornstarch

In advance: Tint fondant as follows: 1 oz. black, 2 oz. orange, 18 oz. light blue, 30 oz. medium blue, 30 oz. yellow. Make 1 large, 4 medium and 12 small ducks (p. 126). **Also:** Use 24 oz. medium blue to cover base board (p. 123). Reserve remaining fondant.

Bake and cool 2-layer cakes (make two 1½ in. high cakes for each 3 in. high tier). Prepare for Globe Pillar Set Construction

(p. 117) and cover with white fondant; smooth with Fondant Smoother. Position bottom tier on prepared board. Cut 4 pillars to 7 in. long and insert into bottom tier. Slide on medium ducks; position feet. Cut 1 pillar to 7½ in. long and insert into top tier. Slide on large duck. Roll out light blue fondant ⅛ in. thick. Cut a strip 2¼ x 18 in. long; use knife to cut waves up to ¾ in. deep across top edge. Attach around base of top tier using damp brush. Cut 2 strips 2¼ x 20 in. long; cut waves as above and attach around bottom tier. Cut medium blue strips ¼ in. wide; attach over waves, about ½ in. apart, trimming to fit. Use tip 12 to cut dots; attach with damp brush. Attach small ducks around bottom tier.

At party: Position top tier. Serves 42.

Candy Cup Bassinets

Candy: Mini Baby Icons Candy Mold, p. 245; Dessert Shells Classic Candy Mold, p. 197; White, Blue, Yellow Candy Melts, p. 196; Garden Candy Color Set, p. 199
Colors:* Violet, Rose, p. 148
Fondant: White Ready-To-Use Rolled Fondant, Gum-Tex, p. 149; White Pearl Dust,

Brush Set, p. 151; 9 in. Rolling Pin, Roll & Cut Mat, p. 150
Also: Parchment Triangles, p. 138; knife, ruler, cornstarch

In advance: Mold candies (p. 130). Tint portions of melted candy pink and green using candy colors; mold about 15 candies (3 oz. total) for each treat in Mini Icons Mold. Chill until firm; unmold. **Also:** Make candy shells using white candy (about 2½ oz. per shell) in Dessert Shells Mold. Make 2 shells for each treat. Chill until firm; unmold. **And:** Make fondant bows. Mix ¼ teaspoon Gum-Tex into 3 oz. fondant (enough for 18 treats); tint violet. Roll out ⅛ in. thick. Cut a 4 x ¼ in. strip. Fold ends to center to form loops; brush with damp brush and pinch slightly. Let dry on sides on cornstarch-dusted surface. Cut a 1 x ¼ in. strip. Wrap around bow center for knot; secure in back using damp brush. Cut a 2½ x ¼ in. strip. Fold in half for V-shaped streamers; use knife to make V-cut on ends. Brush with damp brush and attach to back of bow. Let dry then brush with Pearl Dust.

Assemble cradle. Mark ½ in. section on bottom of candy shell. Use hot knife to cut away section. Attach shell upright to bottom shell using melted candy; hold until set. Attach fondant bow using melted candy; hold until set. Fill with assorted mini candies. Each serves 1.

*Combine Violet with Rose for violet shown.

A Bear for Baby

Cookie: Baby Cutter Set, p. 244; Cookie Sheet, Cooling Grid, p. 159
Tips: 1, 1s, 2, 4, 6, p. 136
Colors: Copper (for skin tone shown), Rose, Black, Kelly Green, Lemon Yellow, p. 148
Recipes: Royal Icing, Roll-Out Cookies, p. 118
Also: Mini Baby Icons Candy Mold, Light Cocoa Candy Melts, p. 196; Parchment Triangles, p. 138; Meringue Powder, p. 145; knife, cornstarch

In advance: Make cookies. Prepare and roll out dough. Cut baby using bear cutter from set; use knife to cut off ears. Bake and cool cookies. **Also:** Ice cookies. Tint royal icing light copper. Outline using tip 2 and full-strength icing; pipe in with thinned icing in cut parchment bag. Let dry 24 hours. **And:** Mold candy bears (p. 130). Pipe tip 1s bow ties with royal icing after unmolding. Let dry.

Use tip 4 to outline and pipe in diaper area with icing (pat smooth with finger dipped in cornstarch). Pipe tip 4 feet and tip 1 dot toes. Position candy bear. Pipe tip 6 pull-out arms and hands. Add tip 1 pull-out dot fingers, outline mouth and dot eyes, cheeks and nose (flatten slightly). Pipe tip 2 outline ears. Each serves 1.

◀ Toddler Teddy

Pan: Teddy Bear, p. 245
Tips: 4, 7, 16, 17, p. 136-137
Colors: Lemon Yellow, Black, p. 148
Recipes: Buttercream, Chocolate Buttercream Icings, p. 118
Also: Cake Boards, Fanci-Foil Wrap, p. 241; scissors, tape, cornstarch

Bake and cool cake. Ice inside ears, paws and feet smooth (lighten portion of chocolate with white buttercream). Using tip 4, pipe outline mouth; outline and pipe in eyes and nose (smooth with finger dipped in cornstarch). Using tip 7, outline and pipe in banded trims of outfit (smooth with finger). Cover outfit with tip 16 stars; pipe tip 7 initial. Cover bear with tip 17 stars. Serves 12.

◀ Cookie Onesies!

Pans: Cookie Sheet, Cooling Grid, p. 159
Tips: 1, 2, p. 136
Colors: Rose, Royal Blue, Kelly Green, Lemon Yellow, p. 148
Recipes: Color Flow Icing, Roll-Out Cookies, p. 118
Also: Baby Cookie Cutter Set, p. 244; Color Flow Mix, p. 145; Parchment Triangles, p. 138

Prepare and roll out cookie dough. Cut using onesie cutter from set. Bake and cool cookies. Pipe tip 2 outlines using full-strength color flow icing; fill in with thinned icing in cut parchment bag. Let dry. Add tip 1 outline edging, initial and dot trims. Each serves 1.

▲ Strolling in Style

Pan: Oval Pan Set (13.5 x 9.8 in. used), p. 156

Tips: 2, 3, p. 136

Colors:* Royal Blue, Delphinium Blue, Leaf Green, Juniper Green, Brown, Red-Red, Black, p. 148

Fondant: White Ready-To-Use Rolled Fondant (60 oz.), Gum-Tex, p. 149; Brush Set, Easy-Glide Fondant Smoother, p. 151; 20 in. Rolling Pin, Roll & Cut Mat, p. 150

Recipes: Buttercream Icing, p. 118; Chocolate Fondant, p. 119

Also: 2010 Pattern Book (Carriage), p. 132; Dark Cocoa Candy Melts, p. 196; Disposable Decorating Bags, p. 138; Piping Gel, p. 145; Cake Boards, Fanci-Foil Wrap, p. 241; cornstarch, knife, ruler, scissors, tape

In advance: Prepare base board. Prepare Chocolate Fondant and tint darker by adding a small amount of black color; reserve 3 oz. for carriage. Cut board ¾ in. larger than pan on all sides. Cover base board with rolled chocolate fondant (p. 123). **Also:** Make carriage. Add 1 teaspoon Gum-Tex to reserved fondant. Roll out ⅛ in. thick. Use pattern to cut out carriage. Let dry on cornstarch-dusted surface.

Bake and cool 1-layer cake. Tint 36 oz. fondant blue. Prepare cake and cover with rolled fondant (p. 119); reserve remaining blue fondant. Position cake on prepared board. Decorate sides with tip 2 dot swirls in assorted colors. Roll blue fondant into ¼ in. diameter balls; attach for bottom border using damp brush. Attach carriage to cake top using damp brush. Add tip 3 buttercream message. Serves 15.

*Combine Royal Blue with Delphinium Blue for blue shown. Combine Leaf Green with Juniper Green for green shown. Combine Brown with Red-Red for light brown shown.

▲ Baby Carriage Brownies

Pans: 9 x 13 x 2 in. Sheet, p. 157; Cooling Grid, p. 159

Tip: 2, p. 136

Colors:* Royal Blue, Juniper Green, Leaf Green, p. 148

Candy: Light Cocoa Candy Melts, p. 196; Dessert Accents, Mint Discs Candy Molds, p. 197

Recipes: Buttercream Icing, p. 118; favorite brownie mix or recipe

Also: Baby Cookie Cutter Set, p, 244; Cake Board, p. 241; Parchment Triangles, Disposable Decorating Bags, p. 138; waxed paper

In advance: Mold 2 candy wheels for each treat in Mint Discs Mold and handle in double scroll cavity of Dessert Accents Mold (use larger scroll). Chill until firm; unmold. Overpipe scrolls on back side. Chill until firm.

Bake and cool brownies in sheet pan. Cut out carriage shapes using cutter. Coat back of carriages in melted candy; let set on waxed paper. Cover carriages with melted candy (p. 130); let set. Trim off excess candy if needed. Attach wheels and handle with melted candy; let set. In buttercream, pipe tip 2 dots for wheel axles and on carriage hood in scroll design. Each serves 1.

*Combine Juniper Green with Leaf Green for green shown.

▲ Bow-tie Bear Cookies

Cookie: 101 Cookie Cutters, p. 203; Baby Cookie Cutter Set, p. 244; Cookie Sheet, Cooling Grid, p. 159

Tips: 1, 2, 3, 8, p. 136

Colors:* Royal Blue, Leaf Green, Juniper Green, Brown, Red-Red, Black, p. 148

Recipes: Roll-Out Cookies, Color Flow Icing, p. 118

Also: Color Flow Mix, p. 145; Disposable Decorating Bags, p. 138; cornstarch

In advance: Make cookies. Prepare and roll out dough. Cut rounds using largest circle cutter from 101 Cutter Set; cut bears using cutter from Baby Set. Bake and cool cookies. **Also:** Tint color flow and reserve a small amount of each color for details. Outline all cookies with tip 3 and full-strength color flow; flow in with thinned icing and let dry.

Decorate bears with full-strength color flow. Pipe tip 8 pull-out dot muzzle, tip 2 dot eyes and nose, tip 1 outline mouth. Pipe tip 3 outline and fill-in bow tie (pat smooth with finger dipped in cornstarch). Attach bears to round cookies with icing dots. Pipe tip 3 dots using reserved full-strength color flow. Each serves 1.

*Combine Brown with Red-Red for brown shown. Combine Leaf Green with Juniper Green for green shown.

Show your love for baby and the earth with Eco-Occasions Bear Invitations (p. 242). Crafted in recycled paper with cute die-cut teddy bear shape and easy fill-in party information format.

▲ Pitter Patter Pretzels

Candy: Baby Pretzel Mold, p. 245; White, Blue Candy Melts, p. 196; Garden Candy Color Set, p. 199
Also: Parchment Triangles, p. 138; pretzel rods

Tint portions of melted white candy pink using candy color. Use Piping Method (p. 130) and Pretzel Mold to make treats. Chill until firm; unmold. Each serves 1.

▲ Baby's Kicking Cake

Pan: 3-Pc. Paisley Set (12.75 x 9 in. used), p. 156
Tips: 3, 5, p. 136
Colors: Rose, Royal Blue, Kelly Green, Lemon Yellow, p. 148
Recipes: Buttercream, Color Flow Icings, p. 118
Also: 2010 Pattern Book (Foot, Toes), p. 132; Color Flow Mix, p. 145; Cake Boards, Fanci-Foil Wrap, p. 241; Parchment Triangles, p. 138; waxed paper, scissors, tape

Two days in advance: Make color flow feet and toes. Make 2 copies of patterns. Reverse 1 right foot for left foot. Tape patterns to boards and cover with waxed paper. Outline with tip 3 and full-strength color flow. Fill in with thinned color flow. Let dry completely.

Bake two 1-layer cakes; cool 1 top side down, 1 top side up. Ice cakes smooth in buttercream. Pipe tip 5 ball borders in assorted colors. Position color flow pieces.†† Serves 28.

††Buttercream icing will break down color flow. Position color flow pieces on a piece of parchment paper or waxed paper cut to fit, on sugar cubes or on mini marshmallows.

▲ Crib Cuddler Cupcakes

Pan: Standard Muffin, p. 159
Tip: 1, p. 136
Colors: Rose, Sky Blue, Lemon Yellow, Copper (for skin tone shown), Black, p. 148
Recipes: Buttercream, Royal Icings, p. 118
Also: White Ready-To-Use Rolled Fondant (24 oz. makes about 10-12), p. 149; Brush Set, p. 151; Circle Metal Cutter, p. 204; Baby Feet Standard Baking Cups, p. 243; Meringue Powder, p. 145; scissors, knife, ruler, cornstarch

In advance: For each cupcake, tint fondant as follows: 1 oz. in blanket color, 1 oz. in light copper; reserve 1 oz. white. **Also:** Shape fondant head, hands and feet. For head, roll a 1 in. ball of fondant with ⅛ in. balls for nose and ears; flatten ears. For feet, roll a ½ x ¾ in. log and flatten; roll tiny balls for toes. For hands, roll ¼ x ⅜ in. logs, flatten to shape and indent fingers with edge of knife. Attach pieces using a damp brush. Pipe tip 1 dot eyes and outline mouth with royal icing. Let dry on cornstarch-dusted surface.

Bake and cool cupcakes. Ice smooth with buttercream, building up a small mound in center for baby's tummy. Roll out white fondant ⅛ in. thick. Using cutter, cut 1 circle for each cupcake; attach to cover top of iced cupcake (trim if necessary). Roll out and cut fondant blanket using circle cutter; reroll gently to increase size by ½ in. Trim off top ½ in.; fold back top edge about ¼ in. Position blanket on cupcake (trim if necessary). Fold up bottom where feet will go; tuck in feet, head and hands, attaching with damp brush. Each serves 1.

▲ Baby Steps Cookies

Pans: Cookie Sheet, Cooling Grid, p. 159
Tip: 2, p. 136
Colors: Royal Blue, Rose, p. 148
Recipes: Color Flow Icing, Roll-Out Cookies, p. 118
Also: Color Flow Mix, p. 145; Foot Plastic Cutter, p. 205; Parchment Triangles, p. 138; knife

Prepare and roll out cookie dough. For each pair, cut 2 feet using foot cutter, reversing 1. Bake and cool cookies. Use tip 2 and full-strength color flow to outline base of foot (about ¼ in. from edge) and toes. Let set. Fill in using thinned color flow. Let dry. Each serves 1.

The pitter-patter of little feet brings smiles to all your guests! Begin with Baby Feet Invitations (p. 242) that are easy to print on your home computer. At the party, place a Baby Feet Party Bag (p. 243 and shown at top) filled with White Gum Drops or Baby Feet Favor Candy (p. 244) at each guest's place setting.

◄ Moonbeam Dreams

Candy: Stars Candy Mold, Garden Candy Color Set, p. 199; 2-Pk. Baby Candy Mold, p. 198; White, Yellow, Light Cocoa, Blue Candy Melts, p. 196

Also: Parchment Triangles, p. 138; Cake Board, p. 241; waxed paper, mini marshmallows, scissors, toothpicks

In advance: Mold candy moon and stars. For stars, using cut parchment bag, pipe melted yellow candy to make star points, about ¼ in. from center of mold cavity. Tap to spread evenly;

chill until firm. Unmold using toothpick. Mold moon using 2-pack mold (p. 130); Tint portion of white candy pink using candy color. Pipe facial features, hat stripes and pompom using melted candy in cut parchment bags; let each stripe set before piping the next.

For clouds, mix ¼ cup of mini marshmallows with 3 oz. of melted white candy. Gently stir to cover marshmallows and pour on a waxed paper covered board. Use spoon to shape; chill until firm. Attach moon and stars with melted candy; let set. Each serves 1.

▶ Sandman in the Moon

Cookie: Round Cookie Treat Pan, Cooling Grid, 8 in. Cookie Treat Sticks, p. 205

Tips: 1, 4, 6, p. 136

Colors: Golden Yellow, Royal Blue, Leaf Green, Violet, Rose, Brown, p. 148

Recipes: Royal Icing, Roll-Out Cookies, p. 118

Also: Yellow Candy Melts, p. 196; Baby 2-Pack Candy Mold Set, p. 198; Meringue Powder, p. 145; ⅛ in. wide picot ribbon (8 in. per treat), scissors, ruler, cornstarch

In advance: Make cookies. Prepare dough and press into pan cavities. Insert sticks. Bake and cool. **Also:** Make stars using melted candy and candy mold, filling ¼ in. deep (p. 130).

Ice cookie smooth. Using tip 6, outline and fill in moon. Pipe tip 4 hat stripes (pat smooth). Pipe tip 1 outline eye, nose, mouth and dot cheek on moon; pipe dot eyes and outline mouth on star. Tie ribbon into bow. Attach bow and star with icing. Let set. Each serves 1.

* Combine Violet with Rose for violet shown.

◄ Lunar Lullabyes

Pans: 3-Pc. Diamond Set (10.25 x 7.4 x 2 in. and 15 x 11 x 2 in. used), p. 156

Tip: 1, p. 136

Colors: Royal Blue, Lemon Yellow, White-White, Copper (for skin tone shown), p. 148

Fondant: White Ready-To-Use Rolled Fondant (160 oz.), Fine Tip Primary Colors FoodWriter Edible Color Markers, Gum-Tex, p. 149; Star Power Fondant Imprint Mat, 20 in. Rolling Pin, Roll & Cut Mat, p. 150; Yellow, Leaf Green, Orchid Pink, Lilac Purple Pearl Dust, Color Tray, Brush Set, Easy-Glide Fondant Smoother, p. 151; Star Cut-Outs, p. 153

Recipes: Buttercream Icing, p. 118; Thinned Fondant Adhesive, p. 119

Also: Yellow Cake Sparkles, p. 146; Piping Gel, p. 145; 6 in. Lollipop Sticks, p. 200; Wooden Dowel Rods, p. 240; Cake Boards, Fanci-Foil Wrap, p. 241; fine tip artist brush, tea strainer, 5 in. diameter bowl, 17 x 13 in. foamcore board (½ in. thick), scissors, ruler, knife, spoon, cornstarch

In advance: Make baby topper (p. 126). **Also:** Prepare base board. Using larger pan as a guide, cut foamcore board 1 in. wider than pan on all sides. Roll out fondant ⅛ in. thick. Cover board with rolled fondant (p. 123).

Bake and cool 2-layer cakes using diamond pans (top tier is 4 in. high; trim bottom cake layers 1½ in. high for a 3 in. high tier). Prepare for Stacked Construction (p. 116) and rolled fondant (p. 119). Tint 108 oz. fondant blue. Roll out half ⅛ in. thick and cover cakes. Roll out remaining half ⅛ in. thick. Place on Imprint Mat and roll over once to imprint design. Cut a 24 x 4 in. strip; attach around top tier using damp brush. Cut two 18 x 3 in. strips; attach around bottom tier; trim to fit. Paint fine lines using artist brush and White-White color. Prepare assorted gel colors by mixing 2-3 tablespoons Piping Gel with ⅛ teaspoon Pearl Dust and a few drops of White-White. Fill in stars using tip 1 and gel. Position cakes on board. Roll wide fondant balls ½ to 1 in. diameter. shape together 3-5 balls and cover with a thin sheet of fondant. Sculpt fondant to shape with brush handle. Roll out small amount of fondant ⅛ in. thick. Cut 40 stars using smallest Cut-Out. Attach to clouds. Brush on gel colors. Insert topper. Position additional fondant cloud and stars; brush on gel. Serves 32.

▶ Shining in the Spirit

Pan: Cross, p. 221

Tip: 4, p. 136

Fondant: White Ready-To-Use Rolled Fondant (90 oz.), Gum-Tex, p. 149; Brush Set, White Pearl Dust, 10-Pc. Fondant/Gum Paste Tool Set, Easy-Glide Fondant Smoother, Fondant Shaping Foam, Flower Forming Cups, p. 151; Graceful Vines Fondant Imprint Mat, 20 in. Rolling Pin, 9 in. Rolling Pin, Roll & Cut Mat, p. 150; Daisy Cut-Outs, p. 153

Recipe: Buttercream Icing, p. 118

Also: White Sparkling Sugar, p. 146; Piping Gel, p. 145; Cake Board, Fanci-Foil Wrap, p. 241; 15 x 18 in. plywood or foamcore board (¼ in. thick), tape, scissors, knife, cornstarch

In advance: Make 14 fondant daisies (p. 126) using medium Cut-Out. **Also:** Prepare base board. Using pan as a pattern, cut plywood or foamcore 1½ in. wider than pan on all sides. Roll out fondant ⅛ in. thick and imprint design following instructions on Imprint Mat package. Cover board with rolled fondant (p. 123). Brush outer 2 in. with Pearl Dust.

Bake and cool cake. Prepare and cover with rolled fondant. Use brush to cover flat areas of cake top with Pearl Dust. Position cake on prepared board. Using buttercream icing, pipe tip 4 bead bottom border. Attach daisies across top with dots of icing. Serves 12.

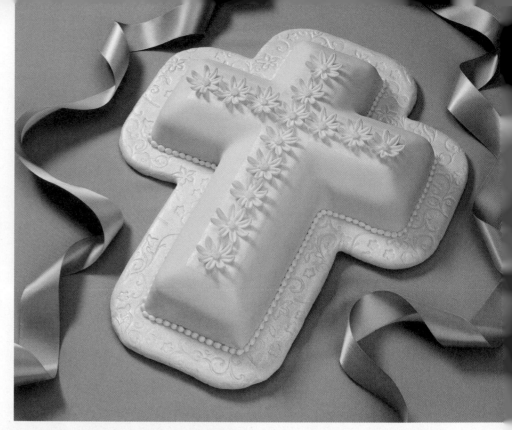

◀ Christening Carriage

Pans: Baby Buggy, p. 163; Oval Pan Set (16.5 x 12.38 x 2 in. pan used for base board pattern), p. 156; Cookie Sheet, Cooling Grid, p. 159

Tips: 3, 12, 16, 131, p. 136-137

Color: Kelly Green, p. 148

Fondant: White Ready-To-Use Rolled Fondant (48 oz.), p.149; 20 in.Rolling Pin, Roll & Cut Mat, p. 150; Easy-Glide Fondant Smoother, Brush Set, p. 151

Recipes: Buttercream, Royal Icings, Roll-Out Cookies, p. 118

Also: Meringue Powder, Piping Gel, p. 145; Round Comfort-Grip Cutter, p. 202; Disposable Decorating Bags, p. 138; Plastic Dowel Rods, p. 240; Cake Circle, Fanci-Foil Wrap, p. 241; ⅞ in. wide white ribbon (18 in.), 20 x 15½ in. plywood or foamcore board (¼ in. thick), waxed paper, scissors, ruler, knife

In advance: Make flowers. Using royal icing, pipe 13 tip 131 drop flowers with tip 3 dot centers. Make extras to allow for breakage; let dry. **Also:** Make wheels. Prepare and roll out dough; cut 2 wheels with round cutter. Bake and cool. Cover cookies with thinned royal icing (p. 130). Using full-strength royal icing, outline with tip 12; add tip 3 scrolls and dot center. Attach drop flower. Cut plastic dowel rods to 10 in. long. Attach wheels over bottom 2 in. of rod with royal icing; let dry. **And:** Prepare base board. Using largest oval pan as a guide, cut foamcore or plywood board 1½ in. larger than pan on all sides. Tint 48 oz. fondant, roll out ⅛ in. thick and cover board (p. 123). Roll 2 x ¼ in. diameter fondant logs; attach around edge of board for scallop trim. Roll out fondant ⅛ in. thick. Cut circles using wide end of tip 3; roll into balls and attach to points with dots of icing.

Bake and cool buggy cake. Trim off void area, portion of wheels and level bottom of cake as needed. Ice handle and inner hood areas smooth. Position cake on prepared board. Outline buggy with tip 3; pipe tip 12 swirl on handle; attach drop flower. Cover buggy with tip 16 stars. Insert legs with wheels. Attach drop flowers around top of legs with dots of icing. Tie a ribbon bow and attach. Serves 12.

◀ A Glorious Ascent

Pans: 8, 10, 12 x 3 in. Round, p. 158

Tips: 2, 3, 5, 349, p. 136-137

Colors: Rose (for Girl), Royal Blue (for Boy), Kelly Green, p. 148

Fondant/Gum Paste: White Ready-To-Use Rolled Fondant (108 oz.), Ready-To-Use Gum Paste (3 pks.), p. 149; White Pearl Dust, Brush Set, Easy-Glide Fondant Smoother, p. 151; Floral Collection Flower Making Set, p. 153; 20 in. Rolling Pin, Roll & Cut Mat, p. 150

Topper: Communion Girl (or Boy), p. 224

Recipes: Buttercream, Royal Icings, p. 118; Thinned Fondant Adhesive, p. 119

Also: 2010 Pattern Book (Stair Side, Step, Top Step; Large and Small Railing, Side and Center Arch) p. 132; 3-Tier Pillar Cake Stand, p. 235; 101 Cookie Cutters, p. 203; Meringue Powder, Clear Vanilla Extract, p. 145; Cake Dividing Set, p. 138; Cake Boards, Circles, p. 241; Cake Spikes, p. 240; 4 in., 8 in. Lollipop Sticks, p. 200; ⅝ in. wide ribbon (8 ft. in pink or blue), knife, craft knife, ruler, scissors, waxed paper, cornstarch, double-stick tape

About 1 week in advance: Make stairs, arches and railings (p. 126). **Also:** Make 120 tip 2 puddle dots (p. 122), ¼ in. diameter on waxed paper-covered board. **And:** Make 9 floral arrangements (p. 126).

Bake and cool 1-layer cakes to tort (3 in. high). Prepare and cover with rolled fondant (p. 123). Using Cake Dividing Set, divide 8 in. cake into 10ths, 10 in. cake into 12ths. Mark 14 divisions 2¾ in. apart on 12 in. cake. Using buttercream, pipe tip 3 triple drop strings (¾ in., 1 in. and 1½ in. deep) between all division points, except leave one division on the 8 and 10 in. cake for stair placement. Attach a puddle dot at each point. Use pattern and toothpick to mark positions of railing supports. Insert a 4 in. Lollipop Stick at each mark, allowing 1 in. to extend above cake top. Use fondant adhesive to pipe a tip 3 dot on top of each stick; carefully attach railings.

For stair runners, roll out reserved rose (or blue) fondant ⅛ in. thick. Cut 2 strips 1½ x 12 in. Brush back with damp brush and attach over 1 staircase. Repeat for 2nd staircase. For platform, cut 2 circles using large and medium round cutters from 101 Cutter Set. Center medium circle over large circle; attach to 8 in. tier ¾ in. from front edge to allow room for arches and bouquets. Paint runners and platform with a mixture of vanilla and Pearl Dust. Position cakes on plates from stand. Attach ribbon at bottom of each tier, securing with double-stick tape. Pipe tip 5 bead bottom borders.

At party: Arrange plates on stand. Position arches, topper, bouquets and stairs. Serves 88.

◄ The Quinceañera's Court

Pans: 10, 12 x 3 in. Round, p. 158; Classic, Mini Wonder Molds, p. 160

Tips: 2, 3, 7, p. 136

Color: Rose, p. 148

Fondant: White Ready-To-Use Rolled Fondant (160 oz.), p. 149; Floral Collection Flower Making Set, p. 153; 20 in. Rolling Pin, Roll & Cut Mat, p. 150; Easy-Glide Fondant Smoother, Brush Set, p. 151

Recipe: Buttercream Icing, p. 118; Thinned Fondant Adhesive, p. 119

Also: 3-Tier Pillar Cake Stand, p. 235; Cake Dividing Set, p. 138; Teen Doll Pick, Mini Doll Pick Set (3 sets), p. 160; Wooden Dowel Rods, p. 240; Cake Boards, p. 241; cornstarch, knife, 26-gauge white florist wire, ruler

In advance: Make flowers. Tint 8 oz. fondant rose. Roll out rose and white fondant ⅛ in. thick and cut 66 rose pansies, 12 white pansies and 375 rose forget-me-nots and 80 white apple blossoms using cutters from set. Reserve remaining fondant. Place flowers on thick foam and cup using modeling stick from set. Add tip 2 dot centers to forget-me-nots and apple blossoms, tip 3 dot centers to pansies; let dry on cornstarch-dusted board.

Bake and cool round cakes, 3 in. high, Wonder Mold cake and 11 Mini Wonder Mold cakes. Tint 68 oz. fondant rose; knead in reserved rose fondant. Prepare cakes for rolled fondant (p. 119) and cover cakes; smooth with Fondant Smoother. Roll out white and rose fondant 1/16 in. thick. For Quinceañera's bodice, cut a 2½ x 4 in. strip and attach with damp brush; for attendants' bodices, cut 1 x 1½ in. strips and attach. Cut 4 x ¼ in. waistband for Quinceañera, 1 x ¼ in. waistband for attendants; attach. Attach 34 forget-me-nots to each attendant, 75 apple blossoms to Quinceañera. Pipe tip 2 dots on edge and front of Quinceañera's bodice. Secure hands on 6 attendants and Quinceañera girl together with wire. Attach white pansies over wire with thinned fondant adhesive. Divide 10 in. cake in 10ths and 12 in. cake in 12ths. Make fondant swags (p. 126); attach to cakes with damp brush at division points. Attach 3 rose pansies between each swag with thinned fondant adhesive. Position round cakes on stand plates; pipe tip 7 bead bottom borders on round cakes.

At party: Assemble stand; position attendants and Quinceañera girl. Mini cakes each serve 1; remaining cakes serve 80.

▲ Fulfilling the Commitment

Pans: 16 x 2 in. Square, p. 157

Tips: 3, 6, p. 136

Color: Royal Blue, p. 148

Fondant: White Ready-To-Use Rolled Fondant (208 oz.), Gum-Tex, p. 149; White Pearl Dust, Brush Set, Easy-Glide Fondant Smoother, p. 151; 20 in. Rolling Pin, Roll & Cut Mat, p. 150

Recipe: Buttercream, Royal Icings, p. 118; Thinned Fondant Adhesive, p. 119

Also: 2010 Pattern Book (Star of David), p. 132; Piping Gel, Meringue Powder, p. 145; Cake Boards, Fanci-Foil Wrap, p. 241; 19 in. square plywood or foamcore board (½ in. thick), 8 x ½ in. diameter dowel rods (5), solid shortening, lemon extract, knife, ruler, cornstarch, toothpicks

In advance: Make fondant drape (p. 126). Tint 72 oz. fondant dark blue. Use 12 oz. for drape; reserve remainder for base board. **Also:** Prepare base board and cover with reserved fondant

(p. 123). **And:** Make fondant star. Mix 4 oz. fondant with ¼ teaspoon Gum-Tex. Roll out ³⁄₁₆ in. thick. Use pattern to cut star; make extras to allow for breakage. Let dry on cornstarch-dusted board. Paint with Pearl Dust mixed with lemon extract; let dry. Using royal icing, pipe tip 3 outlines. Let dry.

Bake and cool 2-layer cake (bake 2 layers 1½ in. high for a 3 in. high cake). Prepare and cover with 96 oz. fondant tinted medium blue (p. 119). Position on prepared base board. Roll out 24 oz. white fondant ⅛ in. thick. Cut a 13 in. square; attach to cake top using damp brush. Attach drape halves with thinned fondant adhesive; position star on drape with small fondant balls supporting side points. For bottom border, roll 12 oz. white fondant into 4 logs 36 in. long, ¼ in. diameter. Twist two lengths together to form rope (p. 121). Attach to sides, trimming ends as necessary. Repeat. Pipe tip 6 message. Serves 80.

◀ Salute the Students

Pans: 6, 10 x 2 in. Round, p. 157
Colors:* Lemon Yellow, Golden Yellow, Red-Red, Christmas Red, Black, p. 148
Fondant: White Ready-To-Use Rolled Fondant (140 oz.), Gum-Tex, p. 149; Brush Set, Gold, Yellow, Ruby Red, Sapphire Blue and Leaf Green Pearl Dust, Easy-Glide Fondant Smoother, p. 151; Alphabet/Number Cut-Outs, p. 153; Star Power Fondant Imprint Mat, 20 in. Rolling Pin, Roll & Cut Mat, p. 150
Recipes: Buttercream Icing, p. 118; Thinned Fondant Adhesive, p. 119
Also: A-B-C and 1-2-3 50-Pc. Cutter Set, Star Plastic Nesting Cutter Set, p. 203; Piping Gel, p. 145; 11¾ in. Lollipop Sticks, p. 200; 8 in. Decorator Preferred Smooth Edge Plate, 9 in. Bakers Best Disposable Pillars with Rings, p. 237; 12 in. Round Silver Cake Base, Cake Circles, Boards, p. 241; lemon extract, knife, ruler, fine tip brush, cornstarch, waxed paper, curling ribbon, scissors

2-3 days in advance: Prepare fondant stars. Add ½ teaspoon Gum-Tex to 6 oz. white fondant. Roll out ⅛ in. thick. Using Nesting Stars, cut 4 stars using 3rd smallest cutter and 1 star using largest cutter. Position on waxed paper-covered board dusted with cornstarch. Let dry. Mix gold Pearl Dust with lemon extract (p. 122). Paint over small stars and around edge of large star. When dry, use thinned fondant adhesive to attach Lollipop Sticks and curling ribbon to backs. **Also:** Add red fondant pieces. Tint 16 oz. fondant red. Cover 8 in. plate with rolled fondant (p. 123). Add ½ teaspoon Gum-Tex to remaining 6 oz. of red; roll out ⅛ in. thick. Cut numbers using small plastic cutters; cut message using alphabet Cut-Outs (reserve excess for simple bows). Attach to stars using damp brush; let dry. Make Simple Bows (p. 123). Reserve remaining red fondant. **And:** Cover Cake Base with 16 oz. rolled fondant tinted black (p. 123).

Bake and cool 2-layer cakes. Prepare and cover with rolled fondant tinted a pale yellow (p. 119). Prepare for Push-In Pillar Construction (p. 116). Roll out 48 oz. white fondant ⅛ in. thick. Cut a 19 x 5 in. strip; place diagonally across Imprint Mat and roll over once to transfer design. Trim to match height of cake. Brush cake sides with water; attach fondant strip, smoothing gently with hands. Repeat using 24 x 5 in. and 8 x 5 in. strips to cover sides of 10 in. cake; reserve remaining fondant. Paint design with Pearl Dust and lemon extract (p. 122), using assorted colors for stars, gold for streamers and backgrounds behind larger stars. Position pillars in 10 in. cake. Roll out white fondant, ¼ in. thick. Cut 4 strips, 3 x 3½ in. Brush straight section of pillars with piping gel and wrap strips around to create wider pillar. Roll out fondant and cut ⅛ in. thick, 5 in. square. Wrap whole pillar to create diploma. Roll out reserved red fondant ⅛ in. thick. Cut 4 strips, 4 x ¼ in. and attach around diplomas using damp brush. Attach bows with fondant adhesive. **At party:** Position 6 in. cake. Insert stars. Serves 40.

*Combine Lemon Yellow with Golden Yellow for yellow shown. Combine Red-Red with Christmas Red for red shown.

▶ The Best and Brightest!

Pans: 3-Pc. Diamond Set, p. 156; Mini Wonder Mold, p. 160
Tip: 18, p. 136
Colors:* Christmas Red, Red-Red, Royal Blue, Violet, Rose, Black, Leaf Green, Golden Yellow, p. 148
Fondant: White Ready-To-Use Rolled Fondant (72 oz.), Gum-Tex, p. 149; 20 in. Rolling Pin, Guide Rings, Roll & Cut Mat, p. 150; Brush Set, Easy-Glide Fondant Smoother, p. 151
Candy: White (2), Light Cocoa Candy Melts, p. 196; Garden, Primary Candy Color Sets, p. 199; Graduation Lollipop Mold, p. 227
Recipe: Buttercream Icing, p. 118; Thinned Fondant Adhesive, p. 119
Also: Parchment Triangles, p. 138; Dowel Rods, p. 240; Piping Gel, p. 145; Cake Boards, Fanci-Foil Wrap, p. 241; 25 x 20 in. plywood or foamcore board (½ in. thick), knife, ruler, cornstarch

In advance: Make mortarboard. Tint 7 oz. fondant black. Mix ½ teaspoon of Gum-Tex with 3 oz. black fondant; roll out 3/16 in. thick. Cut a 4 in. square with knife. Let dry on cornstarch-dusted board. **Also:** Mold candies. Tint portions of melted white candy green, violet, blue, red and yellow using candy colors. Mold 16 diplomas and 12 caps using piping method (p. 130). Chill until firm; unmold. **And:** Prepare base board. Cut plywood or foamcore board 1 in. larger on all sides than largest diamond pan. Tint 48 oz. fondant yellow; cover board with fondant (p. 123).

Bake and cool 2-layer diamond cakes and mini Wonder Mold Cake. Trim mini Wonder Mold to 2½ in. and prepare for rolled fondant (p. 119). Cover with reserved black fondant. Ice diamond cakes smooth; prepare for Stacked Construction (p. 116). Position cakes on base board. Pipe tip 18 shell top and bottom borders. Attach candies to cake sides with dots of icing. Attach mortarboard to cap with thinned fondant adhesive. Position cap. Tint 2 oz. fondant green; roll out ⅛ in. thick. For cord, cut a 2½ x ¼ in. strip. For tassel, cut a 1 x 2 in strip; cut ⅛ in. wide x ¾ in. deep slits for fringe. Roll tassel into a log; attach to cord with damp brush. Cut a ¼ in. wide strip; wrap around top of tassel. Attach cord to cap. Roll a ⅜ in. ball of black fondant; flatten to form button. Attach with damp brush. Serves 75.

*Combine Christmas Red with Red-Red for red shown. Combine Violet with Rose for violet shown.

▶ Grads Grab Success!

Pans: 8-Cavity Silicone Round Brownie Pops Mold, p. 170; Non-Stick Cookie Sheet, Cooling Grid, p. 167

Colors: * Brown, Red-Red, Copper (for skin-tone shown), Golden Yellow, Ivory, Lemon Yellow, p. 148

Recipe: Favorite brownie mix or recipe

Fondant: White Ready-To-Use Rolled Fondant (2½ oz. for each treat.), Fine Tip Neon Colors FoodWriter Edible Color Markers, p. 149; Square Cut-Outs, p. 153; Brush Set, p. 151; 9 in. Rolling Pin, Roll & Cut Mat, p. 150

Also: White, Light Cocoa Candy Melts, p. 196; Parchment Triangles, p. 138, knife

In advance: Make candy mortarboards. Position medium square Cut-Out on cookie sheet; fill ⅛ in. thick with melted candy in cut parchment bag. Chill until firm.

Bake and cool brownies in silicone pan supported by cookie sheet. Unmold, swipe bottom with candy, let set. Repeat as needed. Cover with melted candy (p. 130); let set. Tint 2 oz. fondant light copper for heads and hands, 1 oz. for white arms and caps using a small amount of Golden Yellow and Ivory, 1 oz. brown with Red-Red for brown arms, caps and hair, 1 oz. yellow for tassels, strings and hair . Make and attach fondant features and decorations (p. 126). Draw eyes and mouth with black FoodWriter. Each serves 1.

▼ A Tip of the Cap

Pans: 8-Cavity Silicone Round Brownie Pops Mold, p. 170; Non-Stick Cookie Sheet, Cooling Grid, p. 167

Fondant: Primary Colors Fondant Multi Pack, p. 149; Square Cut-Outs, p. 153; 9 in. Rolling Pin, Roll & Cut Mat, p. 150; Brush Set, p. 151

Recipe: favorite brownie mix or recipe

Also: Light Cocoa Candy Melts (1 pk. makes 5-7 treats), p. 196; Parchment Triangles, p. 138; embroidery scissors, knife, cornstarch, waxed paper

In advance: Make candy mortarboards. Place medium square Cut-Out on cookie sheet. Fill ³⁄₁₆ in. deep with melted candy. Chill until firm; unmold. Repeat as needed. For buttons, pipe ¼ in. dots of candy on waxed paper. Chill until firm; peel off paper.

Bake and cool brownies in silicone mold supported by cookie sheet. Unmold and trim to 1¼ in. high. Seal bottoms with melted candy; chill until firm. Cover brownies with melted candy (p. 130); let set. Attach mortarboard with melted candy; let set. For tassels, roll out colored fondant ¹⁄₁₆ in. thick. Cut a 1¼ x 1½ in. wide strip for each tassel needed. Cut 1 in. deep x ⅛ in. wide slits for fringe; brush uncut edge with water and roll up to form tassel. For cord, cut ⅛ in. wide x ¾ in. long strip and attach to mortarboard with damp brush; attach tassel. Attach button to top with melted candy; let set. Each serves 1.

▲ Star Student Cookies

Cookie: 101 Cookie Cutters, p. 203; Cookie Sheet, Cooling Grid, p. 159

Tip: 3, p. 136

Color: Violet, p. 148

Recipes: Color Flow Icing, Roll-Out Cookies, p. 118

Also: Yellow Colored Sugar, p. 146; Congrats Party Bags, p. 227; Parchment Triangles, p. 138; Color Flow Mix, p. 145

Prepare dough; roll out and cut cookies using largest star and number cutters from set. Sprinkle stars with yellow sugar. Bake and cool. Using tip 3, outline numbers with full-strength color flow icing; let set. Flow in with thinned color flow; let set. Attach numbers to stars with dots of icing; let set. Place cookies in bags. Each serves 1.

Perfect Harmony

On this day, you'll state your vows, hear the toasts and dance to "your song". Your cake will be there through it all, expressing your style while complementing the themes and colors of the day. Choose a vision of romance, like the pure white cascades of "Floral Frost", shown here, or the sparkling fondant bubble tiers of "An Uplifting Love". Celebrate your exciting new life with the eye-opening colors of our flower towers on "The Future's Wide Open". Or capture the honeymoon thrills with our "Beach Bound" cakes—trunks packed with fondant accessories for the trip of a lifetime. For showers, the wedding day or your 50th anniversary, look here for a cake to set the perfect tone.

Floral Frost

Pans: 8, 10, 12 x 2 in. Round, p. 157
Tips: 2, 4, p. 136
Fondant/Gum Paste: White Ready-To-Use Rolled Fondant (108 oz.), Ready-To-Use Gum Paste (3 pks.), p. 149; Easy-Glide Fondant Smoother, Flower Former Set, 10-Pc. Fondant/Gum Paste Tool Set, White Pearl Dust, Brush Set, p. 151; Floral Collection Flower Making Set, Stepsaving Rose Bouquets Flower Cutter Set, p. 153; 20 in. Rolling Pin, Roll & Cut Mat, p. 148
Recipes: Buttercream, Royal Icings, p.118; Gum Paste Adhesive, p. 119
Also: Heart Plastic Nesting Cutter Set, p. 203; 3-Tier Pillar Cake Stand, p. 235; Cake Spikes, p. 240; Meringue Powder, p. 145; Candy Melting Plate, p. 199; Cake Circles, p. 241; white cloth-covered wire (6 in. each: 24 of 22-gauge, 21 of 24-gauge, 18 of 26-gauge); white florist tape, craft blocks, bubble wrap, waxed paper, plastic wrap, tape, cornstarch, knife, scissors

At least 1 week in advance: Make gum paste roses and stephanotis (p. 122), blossoms (p.127) and leaves (p. 122).

Make 24 roses on 22-gauge wires using largest rose cutter and 18 leaves on 26-gauge wires using rose leaf cutter. Make 21 stephanotis on 24-gauge wires using calyx cutter. Also make 308 small blossoms and 196 medium blossoms using apple blossom and pansy cutters. Make extras to allow for breakage and let dry. **Also:** Make draped hearts (p. 127).

Bake and cool 2-layer cakes. Prepare and cover with rolled fondant (p. 119); smooth with Fondant Smoother. Position cakes on tier stand plates. Remove plastic wrap from fondant logs used for setting up draped hearts and attach at base of each cake with icing dots. Assemble 3 bouquets with florist tape using 8 roses, 7 stephanotis and 6 leaves for each. Insert into flower spikes filled with fondant. Insert in cakes.

At reception: Assemble cakes on stand. Attach draped hearts around 12 in. cake with dots of royal icing. With tip 4 dots, attach additional small blossoms in garland shape, 1½ in. deep, starting 2 in. from top edge of cake. Attach a medium blossom below each garland point. Add a tip 2 dot above each small blossom in garland. Repeat with 10 in. then 8 in. cakes. Serves 94.**

**The top tier is often saved for the first anniversary. The number of servings given does not include the top tier.

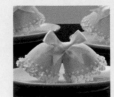

Tolling for Two

Pans: 8-Cavity Silicone Round Brownie Pops Mold, p. 170; Cookie Sheet, Cooling Grid, p. 159
Tips: 2, 225, p. 136-137
Recipe: Royal Icing, p. 118

Also: White Candy Melts (1 pk. covers 3 sets of bells), p. 196; Meringue Powder, p. 145; ⅝ in. wide white satin ribbon (10 in. per treat), waxed paper, sissors, ruler

In advance: Make flowers. Using royal icing, make 28 tip 225 drop flowers for each pair of bells; add tip 2 dot centers. Make extras to allow for breakage and let dry.

Bake and cool bells using your favorite brownie recipe or firm-textured cake batter such as pound cake; unmold. Ice bottom of treats with melted candy; let set. Cover treats with melted candy (p. 130); let set. Cover treats again if desired. Using royal icing, attach flowers and add dots with tip 2. Attach tops together with melted candy; let set. Tie ribbon bow and attach with dots of icing. Each treat serves 1.

Shimmering pearl-look bands and bunches of fresh flowers provide color and texture on this perfect style for weddings or anniversaries.

◀ Dripping with Pearls

Pans: 6 x 3 in. Round, p. 158; Petal Pan Set (15 in. used), p. 156
Tips: 4, 5, p. 136
Fondant: White Ready-To-Use Rolled Fondant (36 oz.), p. 149; 20 in. Rolling Pin, Roll & Cut Mat, p. 150; White Pearl Dust, Easy-Glide Fondant Smoother, Brush Set, p. 151
Recipes: Buttercream, Royal Icings, p. 118
Also: 16 in. Round Silver Cake Base, Cake Circles, p. 241; Meringue Powder, Piping Gel, p. 145; Cake Spikes, Wooden Dowel Rods, Crystal-Look Bowl, p. 240; Cake Dividing Set, Parchment Triangles, p. 138; waxed paper, plastic ruler, fresh flowers, knife

In advance: Make 530 puddle dots (p. 122), ⅜ in. diameter, on waxed paper-covered board using thinned royal icing and tip 4. Make extras to allow for breakage and let dry overnight.
Also: Make fondant strips. Roll out fondant ⅛ in. thick. Using knife, cut ⅜ in. wide strips in the following lengths: For 6 in. cake, cut six each 3½ in. and 2 in. and twelve 2¾ in. long; for 15 in. petal, cut eight 3 in. and sixteen each 1¾ and 2¼ in. long. Attach puddle dots to all strips with dots of icing. Brush strips and remaining puddle dots with Pearl Dust. Let dry on waxed paper-covered board. **And:** Prepare base board. Cover with 24 oz. of fondant (p. 123) and set aside.

Bake and cool 2-layer petal and round cakes (bake two 6 in. cakes 2½ in. high for a 5 in. high cake). Ice cakes smooth and prepare for Stacked Construction (p. 116). Divide 6 in. cake into 6ths and attach a 3½ in. strip at each division point with tip 4 dots of icing. Attach a 2¾ in. strip, on each side of 3½ in. strip, ½ in. apart. In each open section, attach a 2 in. strip. For 15 in. petal cake, attach a 3 in. fondant strip at center of each petal; attach a 2¼ in. strip on each side of the 3 in. strip, ⅜ in. apart. Attach a 1¾ in. strip next to each 2¼ in. strip, ⅜ in. apart. Pipe tip 5 bead bottom borders. Attach remaining puddle dots around edge of base board with tip 4 dots of icing.

At reception: Insert flower spikes with flowers. Position bowl on cake and arrange fresh flowers. Serves 64*.

*Our joy will be complete
if you can share
in the marriage celebration
of our daughter*

*Susane Marie
to
Jordan Jake Allman*

*on Saturday, the eighth of August
Two thousand twelve
at 2214 River Way
Little Falls, Virginia*

Mr. and Mrs. Frank Waters

Since ancient times, pearls have been a symbol of bridal perfection and are the perfect wedding decoration. The String of Pearls Pocket Invitation Kit (p. 229) makes a beautiful statement, and sets the tone for your wedding celebration.

◄ Sterling Silver Memories

Pans: 11 x 15 x 2 in. Sheet, p. 157; Cooling Grid, p. 159
Tip: 3, p. 136
Fondant: White Ready-To-Use Rolled Fondant (24 oz. for 12-14 treats.), p. 149; Round Cut-Outs, p. 153; Floral Fantasy Fondant Imprint Mat, 20 in. Rolling Pin, Roll & Cut Mat, p. 150; Brush Set, Silver Pearl Dust, p. 151
Candy: White Candy Melts, p. 196; Garden Candy Color Set, p. 199; 10-Pack Candy Mold Set, p. 198
Recipe: Royal Icing, p. 118
Also: White Ready-To-Use Decorator Icing (each 1 lb. container covers 7-8 mini cakes), Clear Vanilla Extract, Meringue Powder, p. 145; waxed paper, knife, ruler

In advance: Make numbers. Tint melted white candy gray using black color. Using numbers mold from set, fill cavities halfway with melted candy; chill until firm. Brush numbers with Pearl Dust.

Bake and cool 1-layer sheet cake using firm-textured batter such as pound cake. Trim cake to 1½ in. high. Use largest Cut-Out to cut round cakes. Place cakes on cooling grid over sheet pan; cover with heated Ready-To-Use Decorator Icing (p. 130). Let set. For cake sides, roll out fondant ⅛ in. thick. Imprint floral design following instructions on Imprint Mat package. Cut strips 2 x 6½ in. long; attach around cakes with dots of icing. Paint imprinted areas with Pearl Dust/vanilla mixture; let dry. Place cakes on waxed paper squares and pipe tip 3 bead bottom borders with royal icing; let dry. Attach numbers to cakes with dots of icing. Each serves 1.

► A Formal Invitation

Pan: 10 x 2 in. Square, p. 157
Tips: 2, 3, p. 136
Color: Black, p. 148
Fondant/Gum Paste: White Ready-To-Use Rolled Fondant (48 oz.), p. 149; White Pearl Dust, Brush Set, 10 Pc. Fondant/Gum Paste Tool Set, Easy-Glide Fondant Smoother, p. 151; 20 in. Rolling Pin, Roll & Cut Mat, p. 150
Recipe: Buttercream Icing, p. 118
Also: Piping Gel, Clear Vanilla Extract, p. 145; Cake Boards, Fanci-Foil Wrap, p. 241; ruler

In advance: Prepare base board (p. 123) using double-thick cake board cut to 12 in. square. Tint 20 oz. of fondant black and cover board.

Prepare 1-layer cake for rolled fondant (p. 119). Cover cake and smooth with Fondant Smoother. For ribbon, roll out fondant ⅛ in. thick and cut a 1¼ x 12 in. long strip. Cut bottom end of strip diagonally. Quilt all edges using serrated quilting wheel from set. Starting at back side of cake, 1¼ in. from left edge, attach strip with damp brush. Cut two strips ⅛ x 14 in. long and attach ¼ in. from each side of ribbon with damp brush. Paint ribbon and strips with mixture of Pearl Dust and vanilla.

For monogram background, roll out fondant ¼ in. thick; cut a 1¾ x 2 in. rectangle. Attach to ribbon with damp brush. Cut and attach ⅛ in. wide strips to rectangle edges with damp brush. Paint edges with Pearl Dust/vanilla mixture. Write tip 2 initial and tip 3 message. Pipe tip 3 bead bottom border. Serves 15.

A monogram is an elegant visual reminder of your new status as Mr. and Mrs. from this moment on. Coordinate the vision of your cake and your invitations with our stunning Monogram Ribbon Invitations (p.229).

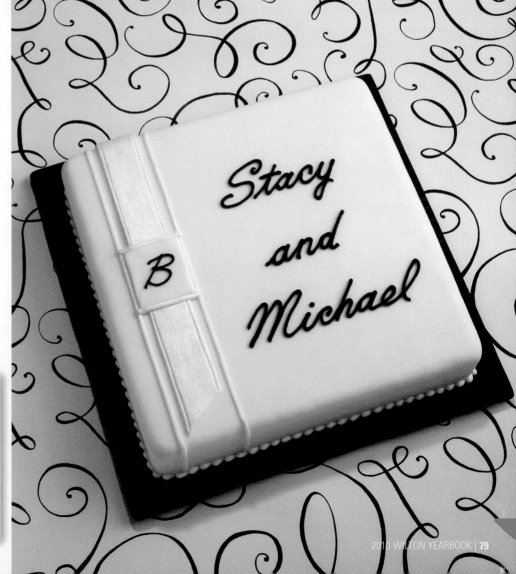

▶ Words Ring True

Pan: 12 x 2 in. Heart, p. 218

Colors:* Violet, Rose, p. 148

Fondant: White Ready-To-Use Rolled Fondant (108 oz.), p. 149; Brush Set, Easy-Glide Fondant Smoother, Cutter/Embosser, p. 151; 20 in. Rolling Pin, Roll & Cut Mat, p. 150

Topper: Two Rings, p. 234

Recipes: Buttercream Icing, p. 118; Thinned Fondant Adhesive, p. 119

Also: Candy Melting Plate, p. 199; Piping Gel, p. 145; 16 in. Cake Circles, Fanci-Foil Wrap, p. 241; ruler, scissors, cornstarch, tape

In advance: Prepare base board. Tint 60 oz. fondant violet. Cut 2 cake circles 1½ in. on all sides larger than pan. Cover with rolled fondant (p. 123). **Also:** Make 40 ribbon roses (p. 122). Let dry; reserve remaining fondant.

Bake and cool 2-layer cake (bake two 1½ in. layers for a 3 in. high cake). Prepare cake and cover with white fondant (p. 119); smooth with Fondant Smoother. Reserve remaining fondant. Roll out reserved violet fondant ⅛ in. thick. Cut 21 strips, 1 x 3 in. high; use wavy wheel of Cutter/Embosser to imprint lines about ¼ in. from side edges. Attach strips with damp brush to cake sides, 1 in. apart. Center first strip over heart point and even with top edge. Continue to left and right, trimming bottoms and last strips to fit.

Position cake on prepared base. Attach ribbon roses to base with fondant adhesive. Roll 63 white fondant balls, ³⁄₁₆ in. diameter. Attach 3 to each strip using Piping Gel. Roll remaining violet fondant into a ³⁄₁₆ in. diameter rope. Allowing room for topper, cut and shape letters on cake top; attach using damp brush. Position topper at reception. Serves 34.

*Combine Violet with Rose for violet shown.

Spell out your feelings for everyone to see. The shower designs shown on these 2 pages begin a fun dialogue with your guests while the cool blue and white tiers here speak volumes at the wedding.

◀ A Future of Promise

Pans: 8, 10, 12, 14 x 2 in. Square, p. 157

Tips: 1, 2, 5, p. 136

Colors:* Sky Blue, Teal, p. 148

Fondant: White Ready-To-Use Rolled Fondant (360 oz.), p. 149; Crinkle Shapes Cut-Outs, p. 153; 20 in. Rolling Pin, Roll & Cut Mat, p. 150; Easy-Glide Fondant Smoother, Brush Set, p. 151

Ornament: I DO Cake Pick, p. 235

Recipe: Buttercream Icing, p. 118

Also: Cake Boards, Fanci-Foil Wrap, p. 241; Plastic Dowel Rods, p. 240; Piping Gel, p. 145; ruler, knife, 18 in. square plywood or foamcore board (½ in. thick)

In advance: Prepare base board. Tint 72 oz. of fondant blue and cover board (p. 123).

Prepare 2-layer cakes for Stacked Construction (p. 116). Prepare for rolled fondant (p. 119); cover and smooth with Fondant Smoother. For side ribbons, tint 36 oz. of fondant to match base board; roll out ⅛ in. thick. Cut two 1½ in. wide strips for each tier in the following lengths: For 8 in. tier, 16 in. long; for 10 in. tier, 20 in. long; for 12 in. tier, 24 in. long; for 14 in. tier, 28 in. long. Brush tier side centers in ribbon areas with damp brush. To position ribbons without stretching fondant, roll up each strip and slowly unroll, pressing lightly to attach as you go. Start at center of one side and continue with the second strip, aligning the ends. Pipe tip 1 scroll and horizontal C-scroll designs with dots above and below side ribbons. Roll out remaining blue fondant ⅛ in. thick. To cover ribbon seams, cut 8 squares using crinkle Cut-Out; attach in diamond position with damp brush. Pipe tip 1 scallops and dots on squares. Assemble cakes on base board. Pipe message with tip 2. Pipe tip 5 bead bottom borders.

At reception: Position ornament.† Serves 220.**

*Combine Sky Blue with Teal for blue shown.

**The top tier is often saved for the first anniversary. The number of servings given does not include the top tier.

†Always place a separator plate, or cake board cut to fit, on the cake where you position any figurine or topper. This protects both the cake and your keepsake. For extra stability, secure topper to the plate with double-stick tape.

▶ Good Answer!

Pans: Standard Muffin, Non-Stick Cookie Pan, Cooling Grid, p. 159
Color: Rose, p. 148
Fondant: White Ready-To-Use Rolled Fondant (8 oz.), Gum-Tex, p. 149; White, Orchid Pink, Silver Pearl Dust, Brush Set, p. 151; Rolling Pin, Roll & Cut Mat, p. 150
Candy: White Candy Melts (2 pks.), p. 196; Garden Candy Color Set, p. 199; Girl Power Candy Mold, p. 198
Recipe: Buttercream Icing, p. 118
Also: 2010 Pattern Book ("Yes" Heart), p. 132; Pink Colored Sugar, p. 146; White Standard Baking Cups, p. 186; 13 Count Cupcakes 'N More Dessert Stand, p. 173; Clear Vanilla Extract, p. 145; Circle Metal Cookie Cutter, p. 204; Cake Board, p. 241; Parchment Triangles, p. 138; waxed paper, cornstarch, knife.

Two days in advance: Make fondant heart plaque. (p. 127) **Also:** Mold candy base for plaque and rings. For base, place circle cutter on cookie pan and fill ¼ in. deep with melted candy. Tap pan to level candy. Refrigerate until firm; unmold. For rings, tint a portion of melted white candy gray using black color. Fill diamond area of mold with white candy and band area with gray, filling cavities ¾ full. Chill until firm. Paint diamond and band using separate mixtures of White and Silver Pearl Dust with vanilla.

Attach letters to heart with melted candy. Position flat edge of heart on back edge of candy base; attach with melted candy in cut parchment bag. Support if needed until set; refrigerate until firm. Reinforce back of heart with melted candy; let set.

Ice cupcakes smooth; sprinkle with pink sugar. Position cupcakes on stand. Insert rings. Attach heart plaque and base to stand with melted candy; let set. Immediately position top cupcake to weigh down base. Each cupcake serves 1.

◀ Engaging Silhouettes

Pan: 11 x 15 x 2 in. Sheet, p. 157
Tips: 2, 6, p. 136
Colors:* Black, Rose, Orange, p. 148
Fondant/Gum Paste: White Ready-To-Use Rolled Fondant (112 oz.), Ready-To-Use Gum Paste (1 pk.), p. 149; 20 in. Rolling Pin, Roll & Cut Mat, p. 150; Easy-Glide Fondant Smoother, p. 151
Recipe: Buttercream Icing, p. 118
Also: 2010 Pattern Book (Engagement Couple), p. 132; 13 x 19 in. Cake Boards (2), Fanci-Foil Wrap, p. 241; White Sparkle Gel, p. 144; Piping Gel, p. 145; craft knife, tape, cornstarch

Two days in advance: Make couple. Tint gum paste black and roll out ⅟₁₆ in. thick. Position pattern and cut with knife. Cut an extra couple to allow for breakage; let dry on cake board dusted with cornstarch. **Also:** Tint 30 oz. fondant black. Cover two cake boards (13 x 17 in.) with fondant (p. 123).

Tint 60 oz. fondant bright pink, 12 oz. light pink. Prepare 1-layer cake for rolled fondant (p. 119); cover with bright pink and smooth with Fondant Smoother. Roll out light pink ⅛ in. thick. Cut an 11 x 7 in. rectangle and position on cake. Position couple. Pipe tip 6 bead bottom border. With tip 2, print message, and pipe sparkle lines around ring. Pipe in diamond with white Sparkle Gel. Serves 27.

*Combine Rose with Orange for bright and light pink shown.

Every girl's dream is to show off a sparkling diamond engagement ring. Clever Bended Knee Invitations (p. 229), created in silhouette, showcase this moment perfectly. Great for shower and bachelorette events.

Warm up the anniversary gathering or wedding reception with a dash of fresh peach. It's the ideal color to complement your table linens or floral arrangements.

◄ Peach Pair

Pans: 8, 14 x 2 in. Square, p. 157

Tip: 5, p. 136

Colors:* Rose, Creamy Peach, p. 148

Fondant: White Ready-To-Use Rolled Fondant (144 oz.), Gum-Tex, p. 149; Floral Fantasy Fondant Imprint Mat, 20 in. Rolling Pin, Roll & Cut Mat, p. 150; White Pearl Dust, Brush Set, Easy-Glide Fondant Smoother, p. 151

Recipe: Buttercream Icing, p. 118

Also: Dowel Rods, Flower Display Cups, p. 240; Clear Vanilla Extract, Piping Gel, p. 145; Cake Boards, Fanci Foil Wrap, p. 241; 18 in. square plywood or foamcore board (½ in. thick), fresh flowers, knife, cornstarch, ruler

2 days in advance: Make bow loops. Combine ½ teaspoon Gum-Tex with 4 oz. fondant. Roll out fondant ⅛ in. thick. Cut 14 strips 5 x ⅜ in. wide. Attach ends with damp brush; let dry on sides on cornstarch-dusted surface. **Also:** Prepare base board. Roll out 68 oz. white fondant ⅛ in. thick. Place on Imprint Mat and roll over once to imprint design. Cover base board (p. 123).

Tint 72 oz. fondant peach. Prepare 2-layer 8 in. cake (bake two 1½ in. high layers for a 3 in. high cake) and 1-layer 14 in. cake (2 in. high) for Stacked Construction (p. 116); position dowel rods to support 8 in. cake near back right corner of 14 in. cake, 1¼ in. from edge. Prepare cakes for rolled fondant and cover with peach fondant (p. 119); smooth with Fondant Smoother. Position cakes on base board. Mix Pearl Dust with a small amount of vanilla; paint on base board imprint areas. For ribbons, roll out reserved white fondant ⅛ in. thick. Cut two ⅜ x 18 in. strips for 14 in. cake and two ⅜ x 12 in. strips for 8 in. cake. Attach 1½ in. from edges with damp brush. Pipe tip 5 bead bottom borders.

At reception: Insert small ball of fondant and position fresh flowers following Display Cups directions; insert cups where ribbon strips meet. Attach bow loops with dots of icing. Serves 49.**

*Combine Creamy Peach with Rose for peach shown.

▶ Contemporary Curves

Pans: 3-Pc. Paisley Set, p. 156

Tips: 2, 4, 5, 7, 10, 12, 101, 102, 103, 104, 124, 225, 352, p. 136-137

Colors: Creamy Peach, Pink, Moss Green, Lemon Yellow, p. 148

Fondant: White Ready-To-Use Rolled Fondant (48 oz.), p. 149; Brush Set, Easy-Glide Fondant Smoother, p. 151; 20 in. Rolling Pin, Roll & Cut Mat, p. 150

Topper: Double Hearts Cake Pick, p. 235

Recipes: Buttercream, Royal Icings, p. 118

Also: Piping Gel, Meringue Powder, p. 145; Flower Nail No. 7, p. 140; Cake Spikes, Dowel Rods, p. 240; Cake Boards, Fanci-Foil Wrap, p. 241; 15 x 21 in. plywood or foamcore board (½ in. thick), green cloth-covered wire (6 in. lengths: 12 of 20-gauge, 70 of 24-gauge), florist tape, craft block, waxed paper, drinking straws, scissors, ruler

Several days in advance: Make royal icing roses (p. 121) and attach to wires (p. 122). Let dry. **Also:** Using royal icing, make 40 tip 352 leaves on wires (p. 122) and 100 tip 225 drop flowers with tip 2 dot centers. Let dry. **And:** Prepare base board. Cut out board shape 1 in. larger on all sides than largest pan. Cover with rolled fondant (p. 123).

Bake and cool 2-layer cakes (bake two 1½ in. high layers for 3 in. high cakes). Prepare for Stacked Construction (p. 116). Ice smooth. Attach drop flowers to cake sides with icing dots. Pipe tip 4 bead bottom borders. Prepare rose sprays. For top tier, gather 4 tip 101, 1 tip 103 and 2 tip 104 roses with 6 leaves; secure with florist tape. Gather 2 tip 124, 1 tip 103 and 2 tip 101 roses with 6 leaves; secure with florist tape. Tape 2 groups together and arrange in Flower Spike, securing with extra fondant if needed. Repeat for 2 additional sprays, increasing number of flowers and size for each tier.

At reception: Insert flower spikes. Cut drinking straws to 3 in.; insert cake pick into straws, then insert into cake top. Serves 94.**

▼ Their Official Initials

Pans: 6, 8 x 2 in. Round, p. 157; Hexagon Set (15 x 2 in. used), p. 156

Tips: 1, 2, 2A, 4, p. 136

Colors:* Brown, Black, Red-Red, Ivory, p. 148

Fondant: White Ready-To-Use Rolled Fondant (210 oz.), Gum-Tex, p. 149; White Pearl Dust (2 pks.), Brush Set, Easy-Glide Fondant Smoother, p. 151; 20 in. Rolling Pin, Roll & Cut Mat, p. 150

Recipes: Buttercream, Royal Icings, p. 118; Thinned Fondant Adhesive, p. 119

Also: Cake Circles, Cake Boards, Fanci-Foil Wrap, p. 241; Wooden Dowel Rods, p. 240; 4 in. Lollipop Sticks, p. 200; Piping Gel, Meringue Powder, p. 145; 18 in. square plywood or foamcore board (½ in. thick), ¼ in. wide brown ribbon (7 yds.), waxed paper, cornstarch, knife, ruler, scissors, paper, double-stick tape

Several days in advance: Make last name initial. Draw letter, about 5 in. tall, and tape pattern to cake board; cover with waxed paper and dust with cornstarch. Tint 60 oz. fondant brown to match ribbon. Add 1 teaspoon Gum-Tex to 8 oz. brown fondant (reserve remaining fondant). Roll a ⅜ in. diameter rope and position over pattern; let dry at least 48 hours. Use fondant adhesive to attach 2 (or more, depending on letter) lollipop sticks to back of letter, allowing 2 in. at bottom to insert into cake. Make an extra to allow

for breakage and let dry. **Also:** Prepare hexagon base board. Cut plywood or foamcore 1½ in. wider on all sides of hexagon pan. Cover with brown fondant (p. 123); reserve remaining fondant.

Bake and cool 2-layer round cakes. For hexagon cake, bake and cool 3 layers 2 in. high; trim 1 layer to 1 in. high to make a 5 in. high cake. Prepare cakes for Stacked Construction (p. 116). Tint 150 oz. fondant ivory; cover cakes and smooth with Fondant Smoother. Brush cake tops with Pearl Dust. Stack cakes on base board; pipe tip 4 bead bottom borders in buttercream. Cut 12 ribbons 4¼ in. long. Attach to hexagon cake sides with royal icing dots. Cut 2 ribbons to circle each round cake; attach about ¼ in. apart. Pipe monogram on each side of hexagon cake using tips 1 and 2. Make tassels. Tint reserve brown fondant a darker shade. Roll out fondant 1/16 in. thick. For each tassel, cut a 2 x 5 in. strip; cut 1¾ in. long slits for fringe, ⅛ in. apart. Brush plain edge with damp brush and roll; separate fringe ends slightly. Roll ⅝ in. ball of fondant and attach to top using damp brush. Attach tassels to cake sides using fondant adhesive. Roll out fondant ⅛ in. thick; cut out 6 circles using small opening of tip 2A. Attach to cake corners.

At reception: Insert letter. Serves 94.**

*Combine Brown with Black and Red-Red for brown shown.

**The top tier is often saved for the first anniversary. The number of servings given does not include the top tier.

Letter-perfect for a wedding or anniversary party, this monogram design links brown fondant tassels and initials with cocoa-colored ribbon accents.

▲ Cookie Commemoration

Cookie: 4-Pc. Wedding Metal Cutter Set, p. 204; Cookie Sheet, Cooling Grid, p. 159

Tips: 1, 1s, 2, 3, p. 136

Recipes: Royal Icing, Roll-Out Cookies, p. 118

Also: White Sparkling Sugar, p. 146; White Pearl Dust, Brush Set, p. 151; Meringue Powder, Clear Vanilla Extract, p. 145; Cake Boards, p. 241; Parchment Triangles, p. 138; waxed paper

One day in advance: Make cookies. Roll out dough and cut shapes using cutters; bake and cool. Outline cookies with tip 2. Flow in using thinned icing in cut parchment bag. Let dry overnight.

Decorate cookies as follows and let dry. For cake, pipe tip 1 double drop strings, ½ in. wide with bottom ½ in. deep. Pipe tip 2 dots and bead bottom border. For hearts, pipe tip 3 initials. Lightly brush edges of cookie with thinned royal icing; immediately sprinkle edges with Sparkling Sugar. For dress, outline waistband and overpipe top edge of bodice with tip 3. Pipe tip 1s dots at hem in a scallop pattern. When dry, paint detail areas on all cookies using Pearl Dust mixed with vanilla. Each serves 1.

◄ An Uplifting Love

Pans: 6, 10, 14 x 2 in. Round, 18 x 3 in. Half Round, p. 158
Tips: 3, 7, 9, p. 136
Fondant: White Ready-To-Use Rolled Fondant (72 oz.), p. 149; Brush Set, p. 151
Topper: First Kiss, p. 234
Recipe: Buttercream Icing, p. 118; Thinned Fondant Adhesive, p. 119
Also: White Sparkling Sugar (4), p. 146; Piping Gel, p. 145; 8, 12, 16 in. Decorator Preferred Smooth Edge Plates, p. 237; 9 in. Twist Legs (3 pks.), p. 239; 11¾ in. Lollipop Sticks (7 pks.), p. 200; Cake Circles, Silver Fanci-Foil Wrap, p. 241; 20 in. plywood or foamcore circle (½ in. thick), scissors, ruler, 10 in. square craft block

Two weeks in advance: Make bubble sticks. You will need 28 for 10 in. cake, 40 for 14 in. cake, 54 for 18 in. cake. Cut lollipop sticks in various lengths no shorter than 10 in.; leave some full-length sticks. Roll approximately 885 fondant balls, ½ to ¾ in. diameter. Insert 7 to 8 balls on each stick, leaving 4 in. extended. Attach with thinned fondant adhesive. Let dry 2-4 hours. Brush balls with thin coat of Piping Gel and cover with Sparkling Sugar. Let dry.

Bake and cool 2-layer cakes (bake 4 half-rounds to create 18 x 4 in. base cake); using firm-textured batter such as pound cake. Ice smooth in buttercream. Prepare cakes for Push-In Pillar Construction (p. 116). Mark cakes in 3 ¼ in. sections. Pipe tip 9 drop strings, 1½ in. deep at each division; overpipe twice with tip 7, then tip 3 strings. Pipe tip 7 drop strings, 1 in. deep at each division; overpipe with tip 3 drop string. Pipe a tip 9 ball at each division point. Pipe tip 7 bead bottom border on all cakes.

At reception: Assemble cakes. Insert bubble sticks 1 in. apart and ⅝ in. from edge on each cake. Position topper.†
Serves 262.**

Only one favor can match our tiered cake's bubbly personality! Wrap up Peppermint Pearls (p. 233) with our Martini Glass Favor Kit (p. 232). Just fill the tulle circles with candy, tie with the satin ribbons and place in the glass near every guest's plate.

◀ Ruffles and Roses

Pans: Oval Pan Set, p. 156

Tips: 104, 127D, p. 137

Color: Ivory, p. 148

Topper: Two Rings, p. 234

Recipes: Buttercream, Royal Icings, p. 118

Also: Flower Nail No. 7, p. 140; Cake Boards, Fanci-Foil Wrap, p. 241; 12 and 16 in. Disposable Decorating Bags, p. 138; Meringue Powder, p. 145; Dowel Rods, p. 240; waxed paper, 20 x 16 in. foamcore or plywood board (½ in. thick), ½ in. wide white ribbon (2 yards), double stick tape, knife, scissors

In advance: Make 120 tip 104 ribbon roses (p. 121) in royal icing. Make extras to allow for breakage and let dry. **Also:** Prepare oval base board. Cut foamcore or plywood 1½ in. wider on all sides of the largest pan. Cover in Fanci Foil.

Prepare 2-layer cakes for Stacked Construction (p. 116). Ice smooth in buttercream. Pipe tip 127D ruffle top and bottom borders. Attach ribbon roses between top and bottom ruffles with dots of icing.

At reception: Position topper.† Attach ribbon to base boards. Serves 141.**

**The top tier is often saved for the first anniversary. The number of servings given does not include the top tier.

†Always place a separator plate, or cake board cut to fit, on the cake where you position any figurine or topper. This protects both the cake and your keepsake. For extra stability, secure topper to the plate with double-stick tape.

▶ A World in White

Pans: 6 x 3, 10 x 2 in. Round, p. 158

Tip: 2, p. 136

Fondant/Gum Paste: White Ready-To-Use Rolled Fondant (90 oz.), p. 149; 20 in. Rolling Pin, Roll & Cut Mat, p. 150; Leaf Cut-Outs, p. 153; 10-Pc. Fondant/Gum Paste Tool Set, Fondant Shaping Foam, Easy-Glide Fondant Smoother, Brush Set, p. 151

Topper: First Kiss, p. 234

Recipe: Buttercream Icing, p. 118

Also: Cake Boards, p. 241; Plastic Dowel Rods, p. 240; cornstarch, ruler, pedestal cake stand (12 in. diameter), knife

Bake and cool 2-layer 10 in. cake (4 in. high) and 6 in. cake (bake two 2½ in. high layers for a 5 in. high cake). Prepare for Stacked Construction (p. 116) and rolled fondant (p. 119). Cover cakes with fondant and smooth with Fondant Smoother. On 6 in. cake, using knife to imprint lines 1½ in. apart at a 45° angle. Using tip 2 and buttercream icing, outline imprinted lines and pipe dots where lines intersect. For 10 in. cake, roll a ½ in. diameter log of fondant; attach around bottom border with damp brush.

For leaves, roll out fondant ⅛ in. thick. Cut leaves using largest Cut-Out. Work in small batches to prevent drying. Set on thin foam and score veins using small veining tool. Heavily vein leaves to create feather effect. This will increase leaf size by approximately ¼ to ½ in. around. Beginning at bottom of cake, attach leaves with damp brush, positioning so that leaves hang over edge of cake plate. Repeat, overlapping leaves until cake is completely covered.

At reception: Position topper.† Serves 38.**

This gently flowing cake will be ideal served at the engagement celebration or the bridal shower. With the softly-pleated detail of our First Kiss topper (p. 234) and a luxurious blanket of fondant leaves, it's the picture of romantic bliss.

◄ **Cordial Reception**

Candy: Light Cocoa Candy Melts, p. 196; Cordial Cups Candy Mold, p. 197; Decorator Brush Set, p. 199
Tip: 32, p. 137
Recipe: Mocha Mousse, p. 118
Also: Letters & Numbers Fondant & Gum Paste Mold Set, p. 153; Parchment Triangles, p. 138

Mold cordial cups using Candy Shells method (p. 130); refrigerate until firm and unmold. Mold candy letters using piping method (p. 130), filling first level only. Chill until firm. Prepare mousse and fill cups with tip 32 swirl; chill until serving. Position letter. Each serves 1.

► Setting the Gold Standard

Pans: 6, 8 x 2 in. Round, p. 157; Petal Set (15 x 2 in.), p. 156
Tips: 3, 5, p. 136
Color: Ivory, p. 148
Fondant/Gum Paste: White Ready-To-Use Fondant (72 oz.), Ready-To-Use Gum Paste, p. 149; Gold Pearl Dust, Brush Set, 10-Pc. Fondant/Gum Paste Tool Set, Easy-Glide Fondant Smoother, Flower Former Set, p. 151; Floral Collection Flower Making Set, Stepsaving Rose Bouquets Flower Cutter Set, p. 153; Rolling Pin, Roll & Cut Mat, Graceful Vines Fondant Imprint Mat, p. 150
Topper: Gold 50th Anniversary Cake Pick, p. 235
Recipes: Buttercream, Chocolate Buttercream, Royal Icings, p. 118; Gum Paste Adhesive, p. 119
Also: 2010 Pattern Book (Scallop, Side Diamond), p. 132; Meringue Powder, Piping Gel, p. 145; Cake Spikes, Dowel Rods, p. 240; 16 in. Round Silver Cake Base, Cake Boards, Cake Circles, p. 241; Candy Melting Plate, p. 199; white cloth-covered florist wire (6 in. each: 15 of 22-gauge, 12 of 24-gauge, 13 of 26-gauge), white florist tape, two drinking straws, craft block, lemon extract, waxed paper, cornstarch, toothpicks, knife

One week in advance: Make gum paste flowers. Make 8 rounded blossoms (p. 127). Make 15 roses, 12 stephanotis and 13 leaves on wires (p. 122). **Also:** Make 125 puddle dots (p. 122), ¼ in. diameter, using tip 3. Let dry completely. Paint dots gold using Pearl Dust mixed with lemon extract; let dry. **And:** Prepare base board (p. 123). Cover Cake Base with 24 oz. fondant.

Ice 2-layer cakes smooth with chocolate buttercream. Prepare for Stacked Construction (p. 116). Tint 48 oz. fondant ivory. Prepare and position overlays for round cakes. (p. 127) Cut fondant for top of petal cake using lip of pan as a guide; position on cake, trimming edges if needed to fit. For side diamonds, roll out remaining ivory fondant ³⁄₁₆ in. thick. Place on imprint mat and roll over once to imprint design. Use pattern to cut 8 diamonds. Attach to cake sides using dots of icing; position top points at petal indentations. Attach blossoms where side points meet. Stack tiers on prepared base. Pipe tip 5 bead bottom borders. Arrange bouquet of roses, stephanotis and leaves, securing with florist tape. Trim wire ends as needed and insert into flower spike, securing with extra fondant if needed. Insert spike into cake top. Trim straws to 8 in. and slide onto ends of 50th pick; insert into cake above bouquet. Serves 80.

Who can resist rich, romantic chocolate? Begin your wedding celebration surrounded by shades of this delightful confection using our Chocolate Daisy Invitation Kit (p. 229).

It's a groom's cake that looks so tempting, he may not want to share. Three chocolate-iced tiers are accented with dark fondant ribbing, separated by our Tailored Tiers Display Set and topped with a broad chocolate fondant bow. Of course, chocolate is always welcome at any event, so consider this for anniversaries as well.

◀ Choc Full of Excitement!

Pans: 6, 10, 14 x 2 in. Round, p. 157
Colors:* Brown, Red-Red, Black, Ivory, p. 148
Fondant: White Ready-To-Use Rolled Fondant (60 oz.), Gum-Tex, p. 149; Brush Set, Easy-Glide Fondant Smoother, Cutter/Embosser, p. 151; 20 in. Rolling Pin, Roll & Cut Mat, p.150
Recipes: Chocolate Buttercream Icing, p. 118; Chocolate Fondant, p. 119
Also: Dark Cocoa Candy Melts (3 pks.), p. 196; Tailored Tiers Cake Display Set, p. 238; 16 in. Round Silver Cake Base, Cake Boards, Cake Circles, p. 241; Dowel Rods, p. 240; Piping Gel, p. 145; ruler, waxed paper, cornstarch, knife

3 days in advance: Tint 8 oz. fondant ivory; reserve. Prepare 2 recipes chocolate fondant. Tint 8 oz. to match chocolate buttercream icing; knead in Gum-Tex and make bow (p. 127). Tint remaining chocolate fondant black; roll out ⅛ in. thick. Cover silver base and all 4 plates from Tailored Tiers set with rolled fondant (p. 123); cover 6 in. and one 8 in. plate prong side up, 12 in. and other 8 in. plate prong side down. Reserve remaining fondant. **Also:** Remove fabric from foam separators and lightly coat foam sides with piping gel. Roll out ivory fondant ⅛ in. thick; cut one strip each 2 x 14 in. and 2 x 23 in. Cover sides of separators and smooth. Let all pieces dry.

Bake and cool cakes. Prepare for Tailored Tiers Construction (p. 117). Ice smooth in Chocolate Buttercream. Roll out reserved black fondant ⅛ in. thick. Cut into ¼ in. wide strips that match height of cakes. Attach to cake sides, ¼ in. apart, using dots of icing. Assemble tiers at reception. Position bow on top. Serves 116.**

*Combine Brown with Red-Red for brown bow shown.

**The top tier is often saved for the first anniversary. The number of servings given does not include the top tier.

▶ Diamond Dreams

Pans: 3-Pc. Diamond Set, p. 156
Tip: 2, p. 136
Color: Kelly Green, p. 148
Fondant: White Ready-To-Use Rolled Fondant (180 oz.), p. 149; Graceful Vines Fondant Imprint Mat, 20 in. Rolling Pin, Roll & Cut Mat, p. 150; Easy-Glide Fondant Smoother, Brush Set, p. 151
Topper: First Kiss, p. 234
Recipes: Buttercream, Chocolate Buttercream, p. 118; Chocolate Fondant, p. 119
Also: Dark Cocoa Candy Melts (1 pk.), p. 196; Piping Gel, p. 145; Cake Boards, Fanci-Foil Wrap, p. 241; Dowel Rods, p. 240; 22 x 17 in. plywood or foamcore board (½ in. thick), ruler, knife

In advance: Prepare base board. Cut plywood or foamcore board 1 in. wider on all sides than largest diamond pan. Prepare Chocolate Fondant. Cover base board (p. 123).

Prepare 2-layer cakes for Stacked Construction (p. 116). Tint 108 oz. fondant light green. Prepare and cover cakes with rolled fondant (p. 119); smooth with Fondant Smoother. Roll out remaining white fondant ⅛ in. thick. Place on Imprint Mat and roll over once to imprint design. Cut a 3 x 24 in. strip for small cake, two 3 x 18 in. strips for medium cake and two 3 x 24 in. strips for large cake. Attach strips to cake sides with damp brush; lightly press seams together. For easier handling and to prevent stretching design, after cutting strips, roll up starting at one end; transfer to cake and unroll in place. Using chocolate buttercream, fill in imprint areas with tip 2. Position topper.† Serves 107.**

†Always place a separator plate, or cake board cut to fit, on the cake where you position any figurine or topper. This protects both the cake and your keepsake. For extra stability, secure topper to the plate with double-stick tape.

Red stands for regal and romantic on these intricately-decorated tiers. Find fascinating detail at every corner, including scrolled fondant circles, 2-tone teardrops and our Fillable Pillars with twists of ruby ribbon.

◀ Crimson Lace

Pans: 6, 10, 14 x 2 in. Square, p. 157
Tip: 1, p. 136
Colors:* Red-Red, Christmas Red, p. 148
Fondant/Gum Paste: White Ready-To-Use Rolled Fondant (48 oz.), Ready-To-Use Gum Paste, Gum-Tex, p. 149; 10-Pc. Fondant/Gum Paste Tool Set, Brush Set, p. 151; Round Cut-Outs, Floral Collection Flower Making Set, p. 153; 20 in. Rolling Pin, Roll & Cut Mat, p. 150
Recipes: Buttercream, Royal Icings, p. 118
Also: 2010 Pattern Book (Scrolled Flower, Cutting Guides for bottom border appliqués), p. 132; 8, 12 in. (2 each) and 16 in. (1) Decorator Preferred Square Plates, 4, 6 in. Fillable Pillars, p. 237; Cake Boards, p. 241; Meringue Powder, p. 145; 8 x 3 in. craft foam square, craft foam block, 3 in. wide white ribbon (24 in.), ⅝ in. wide red ribbon (6 ft.), 4 in. high containers for drying hanging circles, cornstarch, 20-gauge florist wire (18 pieces, 5 in. long), tea strainer, red non-toxic pastel chalk, glue stick, wire cutters, toothpicks, ruler, knife, cornstarch

One week in advance: Make rose topper (p. 127). **Several days in advance:** Make fondant flowers. Tint 8 oz. fondant red, add ½ teaspoon gum-tex and roll out ⅛ in. thick. Cut 530 forget-me-nots and 200 apple blossoms using cutters from Floral Collection Set. Place flowers on thick foam and cup centers using rounded end of modeling stick from set. Using royal icing, pipe tip 1 dot centers on all flowers; let dry. **Also:** Make teardrops. Use remaining red fondant and 4 oz. white fondant. Roll out each ⅛ in. thick. Using rose petal cutters from set, cut 60 each large red, large white and small white teardrops. Attach small white teardrops to red teardrops with damp brush; Pipe red scroll design on large white teardrops using tip 1 and royal icing. Let all dry on cornstarch-dusted board. **And:** Make 84 Top Border Circles and 60 Hanging Plate Circles (p. 127). **And:** Prepare base riser. Attach white ribbon to sides of 8 x 3 in. craft foam square using glue stick.

Remove hanging circles from plates. Prepare 2-layer cakes for Separator Plate and Pillar Construction (p. 116); ice smooth in buttercream. Make bottom border circles. Roll out white fondant ⅛ in. thick. Using largest Cut-Out, cut 8 circles for 6 in. cake, 16 for 10 in. cake and 24 for 14 in. cake. Using Cutting Guide for each bottom border appliqués each cake size, trim off bottom sections of circles using large Cut-Out. Mark center of each cake side. Attach pair of circles to each side of center mark about ¼ in. apart. For 10 and 14 in. cakes, add additional pairs of circles, about ¼ in. apart. Mark Scrolled Flower pattern on bottom border circles with toothpick. Cover pattern using tip 1 and royal icing; add tip 1 dots. Attach an apple blossom at top of each piped pattern. Attach Top Border Circles with dots of icing, positioning top half above cake edge; use 4 per side on 6 in. cake, 7 per side on 10 in. cake, 10 per side on 14 in. cake. Attach a large white teardrop between each circle.

At reception: Assemble cakes. Position 14 in. cake on base riser. Fill pillars with lengths of twisted ribbon (7 in. lengths for 4 in. pillars, 11 in. lengths for 6 in. pillars) and position remaining cakes. Reattach hanging circles to separator plates with royal icing; attach apple blossoms where circles meet. Remove rose topper from cake circle and position on cake top. Serves 148.**

*Combine Red-Red with Christmas Red for red shown.

▶ Jeweled Cupcakes

Pans: Standard Muffin, p. 159
Recipes: Buttercream Icing, p. 118
Also: Large Icing Roses (2 pkgs.), Sugar Pearls, Ruby Pearlized Sugar, p. 147; White Standard Baking Cups, p. 186

Bake and cool cupcakes; ice smooth. Decorate by adding Sugar Pearls or by rolling edge in Pearlized Sugar. Position roses. Each serves 1.

◀ Poised in Pearls

Pans: 6, 10 x 2 in. Round, p. 157

Tip: 5, p. 136

Fondant/Gum Paste: White Ready-To-Use Rolled Fondant (72 oz.), Brush Set, p. 149; White Pearl Dust, Easy-Glide Fondant Smoother, p. 151; Rolling Pin, Roll & Cut Mat, p. 150

Recipe: Buttercream Icing, p. 118

Also: Clear Vanilla Extract, p. 145; Cake Spikes, Dowel Rods, p. 240; White Candy Melts (1 pk.), p. 196; Cake Circles, p. 241; fresh flowers, embroidery needle, dental floss, scissors, pedestal cake stand (12 in. diameter)

Two days in advance: Make pearls. Roll 117 fondant balls, ½ in. diameter. Let dry overnight. Using needle and dental floss, string together 6 strands using 12, 18, 19 (make 2 strands), 22 and 27 balls. Tie knots to join ends of each strand; trim off excess thread. Mix Pearl Dust with a small amount of vanilla; paint on pearls. Let dry overnight on waxed paper-covered board.

Prepare 2-layer cakes for Stacked Construction (p. 116). Prepare cakes for rolled fondant (p. 119); cover cakes and smooth with Fondant Smoother. Position cakes on stand. Attach pearls to cakes with melted candy as follows: 12 and 18 pearl strand at base of 10 in. cake, 22 and one 19 pearl strand on top of 10 in. cake, 27 and 2nd 19 pearl strand on top of 6 in. cake; let set.

At reception: Insert flower spikes with fresh flowers. Serves 38.**

▶ A Joyous Union

Pans: 8, 12, 16 x 2 in. Square, p. 157

Color: Rose, p. 148

Fondant: White Ready-To-Use Rolled Fondant (276 oz.), p. 149; 20 in. Rolling Pin, Roll & Cut Mat, p. 150; Easy-Glide Fondant Smoother, Brush Set, p. 151

Topper: Two Rings, p. 234

Recipes: Buttercream Icing, p. 118; Thinned Fondant Adhesive, p. 119

Also: 4, 6 in. Fillable Pillars, 10, 14 in. Decorator Preferred Square Plates, p. 237; Dowel Rods, p. 240; Fanci-Foil Wrap, White Pearl Beading (6 pks.), p. 241; Piping Gel, p. 145; ⅝ in. wide black satin ribbon (10 ½ yds.), 18 in. square plywood or foamcore board (½ in. thick), ruler, toothpick

In advance: Tint 48 oz. fondant rose. Prepare and cover base board with fondant (p. 123).

Bake and cool 2-layer cakes and prepare for Separator Plate and Pillar Construction (p. 116). Prepare cakes for rolled fondant (p. 119); cover cakes and smooth with Fondant Smoother. Attach ribbon to base board and top and bottom cake borders with Fondant Adhesive. For placement of center strand of pearl beading, mark cake sides 2 in. from bottom with toothpick. Attach beading, cut to fit, around cakes at markings with Fondant Adhesive. Repeat, attaching a strand above and below center strand. Attach separator plate on 12 and 16 in. cakes with icing. Attach pearl beading around plate with adhesive. Fill pillars with remaining pearl beading.

At reception: Assemble cakes. Position ornament.† Serves 200.**

**The top tier is often saved for the first anniversary. The number of servings given does not include the top tier.

†Always place a separator plate, or cake board cut to fit, on the cake where you position any figurine or topper. This protects both the cake and your keepsake. For extra stability, secure topper to the plate with double-stick tape.

Rings are presented in the perfect setting for showers, the wedding day or a milestone anniversary. The glittering ring topper is accessorized with pearl beading on cake sides and in our Fillable Pillars (p.237).

These wide-awake fondant blossoms in eye-popping pastels have just the excitement your shower or wedding needs! Add to the fun by pairing this cake with colorful table accents including napkin ring cookies, individual flower cakes and a topiary centerpiece.

A flower for everyone at the shower! It's an easy favor your guests will love. Use our Funny Flower and Leaf Cut-Outs (p. 153) to trace patterns on construction paper, cut blossoms and leaves, then tape to florist wire. Fill bottles from the Love Potion Favor Kit (p. 232) with Pastel Pearls (p. 233) and plant your flower.

◄ The Future's Wide Open!

Pans: 6, 10, 14 x 3 in. Round, p. 157

Tips: 2, 4, p. 136

Colors: * Royal Blue, Orange, Leaf Green, Lemon Yellow, Rose, Violet, White-White, p. 148

Fondant/Gum Paste: White Ready-To-Use Rolled Fondant (24 oz.), Gum-Tex, p.149; Button Flower and Rose Leaf Fondant Cut & Press Sets, p. 152; 9 in. Rolling Pin, Roll & Cut Mat, p. 150; Brush Set, Flower Forming Cups, p. 151; Heart Cut-Outs, p. 153

Recipe: Buttercream Icing, p. 118

Also: Round Floating Tiers Cake Stand, p. 236; 8 in. Lollipop Sticks, p. 200; White, Green Candy Melts, p. 196; Cake Boards, p. 241; lemon extract, cornstarch, waxed paper

Two days in advance: Make flowers. Add 1 tablespoon Gum-Tex to 24 oz. fondant. Tint 4 oz. portions light pink, light violet and light orange. Tint 3 oz. portions dark pink, dark violet and dark orange. Tint a 2 oz. portion green and 1 oz. yellow. Roll out fondant ⅛ in. thick. Following Cut & Press directions (p. 152), make 9 pink, 9 violet and 10 orange 2-tone flowers, 28 yellow centers and 52 medium leaves. Let flowers dry in cornstarch-dusted Forming Cups. Dry centers and leaves on cornstarch-dusted cake boards. **Also:** Prepare stems. Cut 26 sticks to 6½ in. and 1 stick to 5½ in. Gently curve two 6½ in. sticks by bending slightly against table edge. Mix green, yellow and white-white colors with lemon extract. Brush all cut lollipop sticks and one 8 in. stick with mixture and let dry on waxed paper-covered board.

Bake and cool 3 in. high round cakes. Ice smooth. Pipe tip 4 bead top and bottom borders on all cakes. Imprint cake sides with smallest heart Cut-Out. Outline imprints with tip 2. Assemble flowers. Lighten melted green candy with white candy; attach flowers to stems. Let set. Insert flowers in 10 and 14 in. cakes, positioning 2½ in. apart and 1 in. from edge. Attach 2 leaves to each stem with melted candy; let set. For top tier, insert 1 uncut flower stem in center, 2 curved stems on either side and 5½ in. stem in front. Attach 1 leaf to each stem with melted candy; let set. Serves 116.**

*Combine Leaf Green with Lemon Yellow for green shown. Combine Violet with Rose for violet shown. Combine Royal Blue with Violet for blue cake shade shown.

**The top tier is often saved for the first anniversary. The number of servings given does not include the top tier.

Pick a pink, playful daisy to inform your guests of a special event for the couple. Our Pink Gerber Daisy Invitations (p. 229) get you started!

▼ Napkin Ring Cookies

Cookie: Flower Plastic Cutter, p. 203; Cookie Sheet, Cooling Grid, p. 159
Tips: 3, 5, p. 136
Colors: Lemon Yellow, Orange, p. 148
Recipes: Color Flow Icing, Roll-Out Cookies, p. 118
Also: Color Flow Mix, p. 145; White Candy Melts, p. 196; Yellow Colored Sugar, p. 146; Parchment Triangles, p. 136; napkin rings, cloth napkins

Prepare and roll out dough. Cut cookies using flower cutter; bake and cool. Outline petals with tip 3 and full-strength color flow. Flow in with thinned color flow in cut parchment bag; let dry. Using full-strength color flow, pipe tip 5 inner petal outlines and dot flower center; sprinkle center with yellow sugar. Attach cookies to napkin rings with melted candy; let set.

At reception: Insert napkin. Each serves 1.

For petits fours instructions, see p. 127.

▲ Tie-the-Knot Topiary

Cookie: Comfort Grip Cookie Press, p. 217; Cookie Sheet, Cooling Grid, p. 159
Tip: 6, p. 136
Color: Rose, p. 148
Recipes: Royal Icing, Spritz Cookies, p. 118
Also: White Ready-To-Use Rolled Fondant (48 oz.), p. 149; White Candy Melts, p. 196; Plastic Dowel Rod, p. 240; Meringue Powder, p. 145; white tulle (7 yds.), self-sealing plastic wrap, 8 in. craft foam ball, 2¼ x 2¼ x 4 in. high craft foam rectangle, ⅝ in. diameter wooden dowel rod (19 in. long), glue gun, ⅞ in. wide white satin ribbon (20 in.), 26-gauge white florist wire (14 pieces, 6 in. long), yellow candy-coated chocolates, 6 x 4¾ in. high white metal pail, jelly spearmint leaves

In advance: Make topiary stand and ball (p. 127).

Press 60 cookies using cookie press with flower disk; bake and cool. Pipe petals with tip 6; attach yellow candy-coated chocolates for centers with tip 6 dots of icing. Attach cookies to wrapped ball with melted candy; let set. Cut spearmint leaves horizontally in thirds; trim ¼ in. off bottoms. Attach leaves between flowers with melted candy; let set.

Make 14 tulle puffs using 18 x 6 in. wide pieces of tulle. Starting on short end, gather and fold in half, securing with wire. Insert wires into fondant in pail. Tie a ribbon bow around dowel rod; secure with melted candy or glue gun. Each cookie serves 1.

◄ Sunbeam Blossoms

Pan: 9 x 13 x 2 in. Sheet, p. 157
Colors: Leaf Green, Lemon Yellow, Creamy Peach, Rose, p. 148
Fondant/Gum Paste: White Ready-To-Use Rolled Fondant (24 oz.) makes 6-8 mini cakes), Gum-Tex, p. 149; Daisy and Leaf Cut-Outs, p. 153; Flower Forming Cups, Fondant Shaping Foam, 10-Pc. Fondant/Gum Paste Tool Set, Brush Set, Easy-Glide Fondant Smoother, p. 151; 9 in. Rolling Pin, Roll & Cut Mat, p. 150
Recipes: Buttercream Icing, p. 118; Thinned Fondant Adhesive, p. 119
Also: Yellow Colored Sugar, p. 146; 6 in. Lollipop Sticks, p. 200; scissors, plastic ruler, cornstarch

In advance: Make flowers and leaves (p. 127). Trim lollipop sticks to 5 in. and attach flower and leaf with thinned fondant adhesive; let dry.

Bake 1½ in. high sheet cake using firm-textured batter such as pound cake. Cut into 2 in. squares. Prepare cakes for rolled fondant (p. 119). Tint fondant green; cover cakes and smooth with Fondant Smoother. For grass, roll out fondant ⅛ in. thick. Cut 2 x 8 in. strip for top layer; cut triangle-shaped blades on edge with scissors. Brush strips with water and attach to cake sides. Repeat for bottom layer, using a 1 x 8 in. strip. Insert flower. Each serves 1.

When the wedding day rush is over, bride and groom can focus on the fun of their honeymoon. These cakes are a great way to get them started—at the shower or on the big day! His and Hers carry-on cakes are topped by candy compartments and lid, filled with fondant travel essentials. At right, fluffy iced tiers are ringed by tropical fondant flowers.

▲ Beach Bound

Pans: 9 x 13 x 2 in. Sheet, p. 157; Medium Non-Stick Cookie Sheet, p. 167

Tips: 1, 1A, 2, 5, p. 136

Colors:* Brown, Ivory, Copper, Royal Blue, Rose, Black, Golden Yellow, p. 148

Fondant/Gum Paste: White Ready-To-Use Rolled Fondant (288 oz.—120 oz. for each cake, 48 oz. for accessories), Neon Color Fondant Multi Pack, Fine Tip Primary Colors FoodWriter Edible Color Markers, Gum-Tex, p. 149; Brush Set, White and Silver Pearl Dust, 10-Pc. Fondant/Gum Paste Tool Set, Easy-Glide Fondant Smoother, Fondant Shaping Foam, p. 151; Cutter/Embosser, p. 152; Flower Cut-Outs, p. 153; Graceful Vines Fondant Imprint Mat, 20 in. Rolling Pin, Roll & Cut Mat, p. 150

Candy: Light Cocoa (16 pks.), Dark Cocoa (2 pks.) Candy Melts, p. 196; Candy Melting Plate, p. 199; 6 in. Lollipop Sticks, p. 200

Topper: Our Day, p. 234

Recipes: Buttercream, Royal Icings, p. 118; Chocolate Fondant, Thinned Fondant Adhesive, p. 119; favorite crisped rice cereal treats (1 in. thick)

Also: 2010 Pattern Book (Flip-Flops, Nameplate), p. 132; 101 Cookie Cutters, p. 203; Make-Any-Message Letter Press Set, p. 142; Piping Gel, Meringue Powder, p. 145; Wooden and Plastic Dowel Rods, p. 240; Cake Boards, p. 241; Tapered Spatula, p. 140; Veil and Tiara (available at www.wilton.com); Graceful Toasting Glasses, p. 228; White Pearl Beading, p. 241; ruler, knife, craft knife, waxed paper, paper towels, cornstarch

At least 1 week in advance: Prepare trunk lids, accessory trays, support rods and accessories (p. 127-128). Let fondant pieces dry on cornstarch-dusted surface.

Bake and cool a 2-layer sheet cake for each trunk. Prepare for Stacked Construction (p. 116). Position accessory tray on top. Assemble trunk (p. 127). For each trunk, tint 48 oz. fondant tan. Roll out 1⁄8 in. thick. For each trunk, cut 2 panels 6¼ x 13¼ in. and 2 panels 6¼ x 9½ in.; attach to trunk sides. Roll out reserved Chocolate Fondant 1⁄8 in. thick. For each trunk, cut 1 in. wide strips as follows: two each 9½ in. and 13½ in. long and eight 5½ in. long. Attach to side edges using a damp brush. Imprint stitching lines using ridged wheel of Cutter/Embosser. Roll out remaining Chocolate Fondant 1⁄8 in. thick. Use pattern to cut 2 nameplates. Imprint "His" and "Hers" using Letter Press. Use ridged wheel of Cutter/Embosser to imprint edge. Attach to trunk front using damp brush. Attach lid and support rods using melted candy. Arrange accessories in trunks. Position veil, tiara, pearl beading and topper. Each cake serves 66.

*Combine Brown with Ivory for tan shown.

▼ Headed for a Honeymoon!

Pans: 6, 10 x 3 in. Round, p. 158

Tip: 1, p. 136

Colors:* Rose, Lemon Yellow, Violet, Orange, Royal Blue, Brown, Red-Red, Leaf Green, Copper, p. 148

Fondant/Gum Paste: White Ready-To-Use Rolled Fondant (14 oz.), Fine Tip Primary Colors FoodWriters Edible Color Markers, Gum-Tex, p. 149; 10-Piece Fondant/Gum Paste Tool Set, Flower Former Set, Fondant Shaping Foam, Brush Set, p. 151; 9 in. Rolling Pin, Roll & Cut Mat, p. 150; Flower, Leaf Cut-Outs, p. 153

Recipes: Buttercream Icing, p. 118; Thinned Fondant Adhesive, p. 119

Also: 2010 Pattern Book (Veil, Tiara, Dress, Shirt Collar), p. 132; 101 Cookie Cutters, p. 203; Yellow Colored Sugar, p. 146; Piping Gel, p. 145; Cake Boards, p. 241; 6 in. Lollipop Sticks, p. 200; Dowel Rods, p. 240; knife, waxed paper, cornstarch, toothpicks, 12 in. cake plate

Two days in advance: Make fondant couple (p. 128). Make flowers. Tint 2 oz. fondant each in violet, orange, rose, green and yellow; add ¼ teaspoon Gum-Tex to all except yellow. Roll out all colors ⅛ in. thick. **Also:** Cut 20 flowers each in violet, orange and rose using medium Cut-Out. Shape flowers on thick foam with large ball tool; let dry on small Flower Formers dusted with cornstarch. Cut 3 flowers in rose using small Cut-Out. Place on foam and cup with small ball tool; let dry in small flower formers. Cut 80 leaves using small Cut-Out. Score veins with veining tool and let dry in small flower formers. For flower centers, roll yellow fondant into ¼ in. balls and attach to medium flowers with damp brush. Roll smaller balls and attach to small flowers. Let all dry. Brush centers with Piping Gel and attach yellow sugar. **And:** Attach crown with veil and small flowers to bride. Cut lollipop sticks to 5 in. and attach to back of bride and groom with fondant adhesive; allow 2½ in. to extend at bottom for insertion in cake. Let dry.

Prepare 1-layer 6 and 10 in. cakes 3 in. high for Stacked Construction (p. 116). Position on 12 in. cake plate. Ice fluffy with spatula. Attach medium flowers and leaves with dots of icing.

At reception: Insert bride and groom. Serves 30.**

*Combine Violet with Rose for violet shown. Combine Brown with Red-Red for brown shown.

**The top tier is often saved for the first anniversary. The number of servings given does not include the top tier.

First Birthday Bash!

You've been waiting all year to dress baby up for the celebration. From shirt to socks, it all goes together—coordinated colors in the perfect theme. Your party treats can be just as perfectly matched! In this special section, we'll show you party scenes and themes that fit your one-year-old to a tee. We start with this "1 Great Day" celebration, as pastel cakes, cookies and candies feature the lucky number (find the instructions on page 110). Elsewhere, the baby will discover pink palaces and pirate ships, sail away on Noah's ark or simply splash away with a flock of rubber duckies. We'll help you create a party for the ages—for an age you'll always treasure.

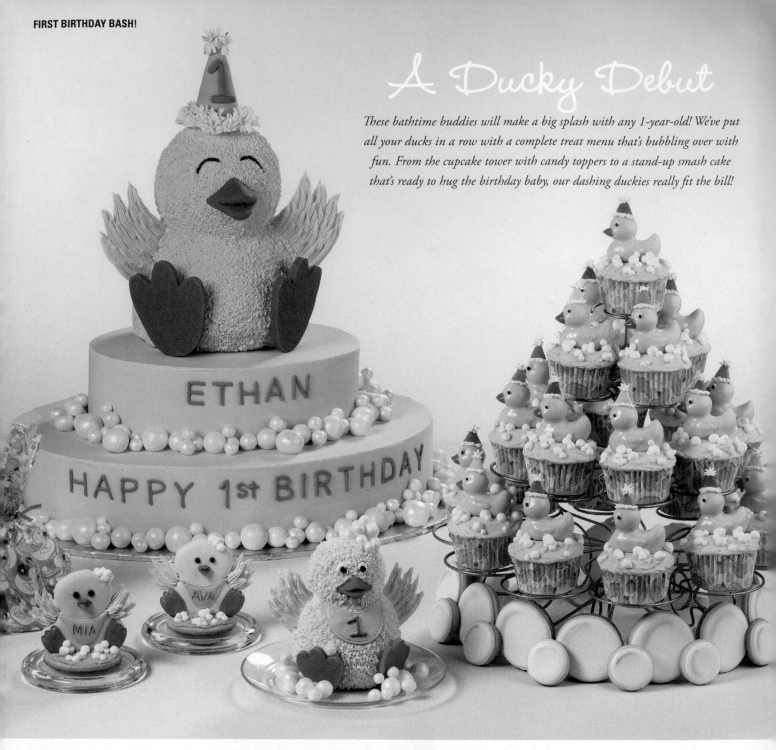

A Ducky Debut

These bathtime buddies will make a big splash with any 1-year-old! We've put all your ducks in a row with a complete treat menu that's bubbling over with fun. From the cupcake tower with candy toppers to a stand-up smash cake that's ready to hug the birthday baby, our dashing duckies really fit the bill!

▲ Happy Bathday!

Pans: Oval Pan Set (10.75 x 7.8 in., 16.5 x 12.38 in. used), p. 156; Stand-Up Cuddly Bear Set, p. 164

Tips: 3, 5, 16, 18, p. 136-137

Colors: Sky Blue, Lemon Yellow, Orange, Leaf Green, Violet, Brown, p. 148

Fondant: White Ready-To-Use Rolled Fondant (72 oz.), Gum-Tex, p. 149; White Pearl Dust, Brush Set, p. 151; 9 in. Rolling Pin, Roll & Cut Mat, p. 150

Recipes: Buttercream, Royal Icings, p. 118

Also: 2010 Pattern Book (Large Wings, Feet), p. 132; White Candy Melts, p. 196; 4 in. Lollipop Sticks, p. 200; Plastic Dowel Rods, p. 240; Cake Circles, Cake Boards, Fanci-Foil Wrap, p. 241; Meringue Powder, p. 145; sugar ice cream cone, plastic bag, scissors, knife, waxed paper, cornstarch, ruler, tape

Several days in advance: Make feet and wings. Add 1 teaspoon Gum-Tex to 11 oz. fondant. Tint 6 oz. orange, 3 oz. yellow, reserve 2 oz. white. Roll out orange ¼ in. thick. Use pattern to cut 2 feet (flip pattern for 2nd foot); reserve remaining orange fondant for beak. Roll out yellow ⅛ in. thick. Use pattern to cut 2 wings (flip pattern for 2nd wing). Let dry on waxed paper-covered board dusted with cornstarch. Cut plastic dowel rod into 2 pieces 4 in. long. Use melted candy to attach 1 to each foot at 90° angle. Cut 4 Lollipop Sticks to 3 in. long. Use melted candy to attach 2 to back of each wing; allow 2 in. to extend at bottom to insert into cake. Using royal icing, pipe tip 18 pull-out star feathers over wings. Let dry. **Also:** Make hat. Cut 1 in.

off bottom of sugar ice cream cone. Tint 3 oz. green; roll out ⅛ in. thick. Cut a 4 x 2½ in. rectangle; cover cone, trimming as needed. Stand on cornstarch-dusted surface. For fringe, using reserved 2 oz. white, roll out ⅛ in. thick. Cut 2½ x 1 in. wide strips. Use scissors to cut ¾ in. deep slits, ⅛ in. apart, across 1 edge. Roll into tufts; separate cut ends for fluffy look. Use a damp brush to attach around bottom of hat for brim and to top for pompom. Let dry. Tint ½ oz. fondant violet. Roll 1½ in. diameter logs to form number; attach to hat with damp brush. **And:** Prepare bubbles. Use 48 oz. white fondant to roll about 170 bubbles in various sizes from ½ to 1 in. diameter. To pearlize, pour Pearl Dust into a plastic bag. Place several bubbles into bag at once and shake. Remove and brush off excess Pearl Dust. Set on cornstarch-dusted board. Repeat.

Bake and cool 1-layer oval cakes and duck cake using Bear pan and firm-textured batter, such as pound cake. Ice oval cakes smooth and prepare for Stacked Construction (p. 116), inserting dowel rods where duck cake will sit. Position on triple-thick foil-wrapped board (p. 112), cut 1½ in. wider than large oval pan on all sides. For duck cake, cut off ears, muzzle, arms and feet. Position on cake circle. Cover duck with tip 16 stars. Overpipe tip 3 outline eyes. Shape beak from a 1¼ in. ball of reserved orange fondant (p. 128). Insert beak, wings and feet into cake. Position on oval cakes. Pipe tip 5 message. Position bubbles and attach around cakes with dots of icing. Insert 5 in. dowel rod into top of head; attach hat over rod with icing. Serves 44.

▶ The Flock's Afloat

Pans: Standard Muffin, Cookie Sheet, Cooling Grid, p. 159
Tips: 1, 2, p. 136
Colors: Sky Blue, Rose, Violet, Leaf Green, Orange, p. 148
Fondant: White Ready-To-Use Rolled Fondant (5 oz.), p. 149; Sapphire Blue Pearl Dust, Brush Set, p. 151; 9 in. Rolling Pin, Roll & Cut Mat, p. 150
Candy: Yellow, White & Light Cocoa Candy Melts, p.196; Primary Candy Color Set, p. 199; Rubber Ducky Candy Mold, p. 245
Recipes: Buttercream, Royal Icings, Roll-Out Cookies, p. 118
Also: Ducky Baking Cups, p. 243; 23 Count Standard Cupcakes 'N More Dessert Stand, p. 173; 101 Cookie Cutters, p. 203; Parchment Triangles, p. 138; Meringue Powder, p. 145; cotton swabs, mini & large marshmallows, knife, ruler

In advance: Make bubble cookies. Prepare and roll out dough. Using small and medium round cutters from set, cut 13 medium and 13 small cookies. Bake and cool. Outline with tip 3 and full-strength blue royal icing; flow in with thinned white icing. Let dry. Use cotton swab to lightly brush on blue Pearl Dust highlights. Using melted candy, attach large marshmallow to back of medium cookies, mini marshmallow to small; position marshmallows near bottom edge so cookie will stand. Let set. **Also:** Make 23 candy ducks. Tint portion of melted white candy orange. Use piping method (p. 130) to fill in white of eye and orange beak first, then fill with melted yellow candy; chill until firm. Pipe dot pupil using melted cocoa candy in cut parchment bag. Tint fondant: 1 oz. each green, orange, rose, blue and violet. Roll out ⅛ in. thick. Cut triangles for hats, ⅝ in. wide, ¾ in. high. Attach with melted candy.

Bake and cool 23 cupcakes. Ice tops fluffy. Position ducks. Pipe tip 1 zigzag brim and pull-out pompom. Pipe tip 2 bubbles in assorted sizes. Position cupcakes on stand and cookies around base. Each cupcake and each cookie serves 1.

▶ Splashy Smash Cake

Pan: Mini Stand-Up Bear Set, p. 164
Tips: 1, 3, 4, 16, p. 136-137
Colors: Lemon Yellow, Leaf Green, Violet, Orange, Brown, p. 148
Fondant: White Ready-To-Use Rolled Fondant (3 oz.), Gum-Tex, p. 149; White Pearl Dust, Brush Set, p. 151; 9 in. Rolling Pin, Roll & Cut Mat, p. 150
Recipes: Snow-White Buttercream, Royal Icings, p. 118
Also: 2010 Pattern Book (Small Wings, Feet), p. 132; White Candy Melts, p. 196; Cake Boards, Fanci-Foil Wrap, p. 241; Meringue Powder, p. 145; 4 in. Lollipop Sticks, p. 200; knife, waxed paper, cornstarch, ruler

In advance: Make feet and wings. Add ⅛ teaspoon Gum-Tex to 3 oz. fondant. Tint 2 oz. orange, 1 oz. yellow. Roll out ⅛ in. thick. Use pattern to cut 2 feet and 2 wings (flip pattern for 2nd piece); reserve remaining orange fondant for beak. Let dry on waxed paper-covered board dusted with cornstarch. Cut 4 Lollipop Sticks to 3 in. long. Using melted candy, attach to back of wings (extending 1½ in. at bottom to insert into cake) and feet (at 90° angle). Using royal icing, pipe tip 16 pull-out star feathers over wings; overpipe with shorter rows for fullness. Let dry.

Bake and cool cake. Cut off ears, muzzle, arms and feet. Outline and fill in 1 x 2¼ in. wide bib area with tip 3 (smooth with finger dipped in cornstarch). Overpipe outer edge. Cover duck with tip 16 stars. Use tip 3 to pipe dot eyes (flatten slightly) and pupils. Pipe tip 1 dot eye highlight. Shape beak from a ¾ in. ball of reserved orange fondant (p. 128). Insert beak, wings and feet into cake. Pipe tip 4 number on bib. Pipe tip 4 bubbles in various sizes from ¼ to ⅝ in. diameter. Let set, then brush with Pearl Dust. Serves 4.

◀ Cookie Quackers

Cookie: Cookie Sheet, Cooling Grid, p. 159; 4-Pc. Baby Cutter Set, p. 244; 101 Cookie Cutters, p. 203
Tips: 1, 2, 16, 352, p. 136-137
Colors: Sky Blue, Lemon Yellow, Leaf Green, Violet, Orange, p. 148
Recipes: Royal Icing, Roll-Out Cookies, p. 118
Also: Rubber Ducky Party Bags, p. 243; Meringue Powder, p. 145; Parchment Triangles, p. 138; Cake Boards, p. 241; waxed paper, knife

In advance: Make cookies. For each treat, cut 1 circle using medium round from cutters set and 1 bear from Baby Cutter Set. Cut ears off bear, then bake and cool all cookies. **Also:** Decorate ducks. Cover bear cookies with thinned icing (p. 130); let dry overnight. Outline bib and feet with tip 2 and full strength icing; flow in with thinned icing. Let dry overnight. Set cookies on waxed paper-covered board. Pipe tip 16 pull-out wings, tip 2 dot eyes, tip 1 name on bib. For beak, pipe 2 tip 352 leaves; lightly pinch outside corners to blend edges.

Spatula ice round cookies. Attach ducks using extra icing in back for support. Pipe tip 2 dot bubbles on cookies and ducks. Let set and then place in party bag. Each serves 1.

Gather the Animals

It's like a picture book come to life! Tell the story of Noah's Ark with a see-worthy stacked cake—its crew of friendly fondant animals and rows of rolling waves will captivate your little critter. In its wake, serve candy mini arks and 3-D brownie buddies for every guest, plus a dazzling rainbow smash cake for that special some-1!

▲ Ark Adventure

Pans: 3-Pc. Diamond Set (10.25 x 7.4 x 2 in., 15 x 11 x 2 in. used), p. 156

Tips: 1, 2, 8, p. 136

Colors:* Royal Blue, Leaf Green, Violet, Rose, Lemon Yellow, Golden Yellow, Orange, Brown, Black, Ivory, p. 148

Fondant/Gum Paste: White Ready-To-Use Rolled Fondant (107 oz.), Gum-Tex, p. 149; Brush Set, White, Sapphire Blue Pearl Dust, Easy-Glide Fondant Smoother, 10-Pc. Fondant/Gum Paste Tool Set, p. 151; 20 in. Rolling Pin, Roll & Cut Mat, p. 150; Round, Oval, Heart Cut-Outs, p. 153

Recipes: Buttercream Icing, Thinned Fondant Adhesive, p. 118

Also: 2010 Pattern Book (Roof Top, Cabin Side, Small and Large Waves), p. 132;

Candy Melting Plate, p. 199; Piping Gel, p. 145; 4 in. Lollipop Sticks, p. 200; Cake Boards, Fanci-Foil Wrap, p. 241; Dowel Rods, p. 240; 18 x 15 in. plywood or foamcore board (½ in. thick), lemon extract, knife, scissors, tape, cornstarch, ruler, toothpicks, waxed paper

In advance: Make fondant waves. Add 1 teaspoon Gum-Tex to 10 oz. tinted fondant; roll out ⅛ in. thick. Use patterns to cut 20 small waves (four 5½ in. wide, eight each 4 and 3 in. wide in various shapes) and 4 large waves. Let dry on cornstarch-dusted surface. Paint on swirled details using white and blue Pearl Dust mixed with lemon extract (p. 122). **Also:** Make fondant cabin and windows. Tint 4 oz. fondant lime green (reserve 2 oz. green for railings), 2 oz. yellow. Add ½ teaspoon Gum-Tex to each. Roll out ⅛ in. thick. Use

patterns to cut cabin side and roof. Tint 2 oz. fondant dark violet. Roll out ¹⁄₁₆ in. thick. Cut a 1 x 1¾ in. top window, each 1½ x 2 in., and a ¼ x 6¼ in. strip to edge roof. Attach with damp brush. Let dry. Reserve remaining dark violet. Attach roof to wall using Thinned Fondant Adhesive. Attach 2 lollipop sticks to back of wall, allowing 2 in. to extend at bottom to insert into cake. Let dry. **And:** Make fondant animals (p. 128) on waxed paper-covered boards. Attach monkeys to window.

Bake and cool 2-layer cakes. Prepare for Stacked Construction (p. 116) and rolled fondant (p. 119). Tint 51 oz. fondant blue, 24 oz. yellow. Cover cakes and board (p. 119, 123) with rolled fondant. Stack cakes on prepared board. Roll out reserved dark violet fondant ⅛ in. thick. Cut 4 windows 1½ x 2 in.; attach to cake sides with damp brush. Use

toothpicks to mark position for 3 stripes on cake sides; begin ¾ in. down from top edge and mark stripes ¾ in apart. Mark cabin wall for 7 vertical stripes, ½ in. apart. Roll out yellow fondant ⅛ in. thick. Cut ⅛ in. wide strips and attach over marks using damp brush. Attach waves around cakes using fondant adhesive; insert ¼ in. diameter fondant logs as spacers between sections for layered effect. Roll out reserved lime green ⅛ in. thick. Cut two ½ x 13 in. strips with rounded ends for railing; attach around cake using fondant adhesive. Position cabin and insert animals. Serves 32.

*Combine Violet with Rose for violet shown. Combine Lemon Yellow with Golden Yellow for yellow ark. Combine Leaf Green with Lemon Yellow for lime green shown.

▶ Zoo Crew Sets Sail

Candy: White Candy Melts, p. 196; Primary & Garden Candy Color Sets, p. 199; Dessert Shells Candy Mold, p. 197

Tip: 3, p. 136

Colors:* Orange, Violet, Leaf Green, Lemon Yellow, p. 148

Fondant: White Ready-To-Use Rolled Fondant (4 oz.), Gum-Tex, p. 149; Brush Set, p. 151; 9 in. Rolling Pin, Roll & Cut Mat, p. 150

Recipes: Royal Icing, p. 118; favorite crisped rice cereal treats

Also: 2010 Pattern Book (Cabin, Roof, Easel), p. 132; Jungle Pals Fun Pix, p. 175; Meringue Powder, p. 145; Cake Boards, p. 241; cornstarch, craft knife, ruler

In advance: Make fondant cabins. Add ½ teaspoon Gum-Tex to 4 oz. fondant. Tint 1 oz. each orange, violet, yellow and green; roll out ⅛ in. thick. Use patterns to cut cabin, roof and easel in each color. Tint royal icing to match fondant. Use icing to attach roof to different color cabin, allowing ¼ in. overlap; pipe tip 3 e-motion details. Let dry. Attach easel to back; let dry on cornstarch-dusted boards.

Tint portions of melted white candy orange, violet, yellow and green to match. Mold dessert shell boats, following instructions for mold. Chill until firm; unmold and trim edges as needed. Insert shells into outer mold; press in cereal treat mixture to just below top edge. Seal and level top with melted candy. Chill until firm; unmold. Attach cabin to boat with melted candy. Use craft knife to poke small holes through candy where animals will go. Insert Fun Pix, trimming as needed. Each serves 1.

*Combine Leaf Green with Lemon Yellow for green shown.

◀ Animals Arise

Pans: 8-Cavity Silicone Round Brownie Pops Mold, p. 170; Cookie Sheet, Cooling Grid, p. 159

Colors: Black, Lemon Yellow, Golden Yellow, Brown, Red-Red, p. 148

Candy: White, Light Cocoa Candy Melts (3 oz. per treat), p. 196; Primary, Garden Candy Color Sets, Decorator Brush Set, p. 199; Animals Cookie Candy Mold, p. 197

Recipe: Favorite brownie recipe or mix

Also: White Ready-To-Use Rolled Fondant (1 oz. per treat), p. 149

In advance: Make candy heads. Tint portions of melted white candy black, gray, pink, orange and yellow using candy colors. Mold candies ¼ in. thick in mold without cookies, using painting method (p. 130). Chill until firm. Pipe eyes, mouth and inner ears using cut parchment bags. Reserve remaining tinted candy.

Bake and cool brownies in silicone mold supported by cookie sheet. Cover with melted candy (p. 130). Chill until firm; repeat. Tint portions of fondant gray, yellow and brown. Roll a ⅝ in. ball for each leg and arm; shape ¾ in. long legs and arms. Attach with melted candy. Roll a ½ in. fondant ball to support head and attach with melted candy. Each serves 1.

▶ Rainbow Wishes Cake

Pans: 8 x 2 in. Round, p. 157; Cooling Grid, p. 159

Tips: 4, 12, 16, p. 136-137

Colors:* Sky Blue, Rose, Violet, Leaf Green, Lemon Yellow, p. 148

Recipe: Buttercream Icing, p. 118

Also: Cake Board, Fanci-Foil Wrap, p. 241, toothpick

Bake and cool 1-layer cake 1½ in. high. Cut in half, stack halves with icing and position cut side down on foil-wrapped board cut to fit (allow space on ends for clouds). Ice cake smooth; mark ⅜ in. wide divisions for rainbow with toothpick. Cover rainbow sections with tip 16 stars. Print tip 4 name. Pipe tip 12 ball clouds. Serves 10.

*Combine Violet with Rose for violet shown.

A Princess Paradise

For the girl who rules the roost, a magical land of treats is at her command. The Pink Palace cake will delight her as much as the fondant princess on top—with a whirl of sparkling turrets, fondant bunting and flowers. Next, let them eat cupcakes—each topped with a candy face and placed on our colorful Princess Stand. For a storybook finish, serve candy carriages and a rose-topped smash cake she'll have a ball with.

▲ The Pink Palace

Pans: 8 x 3, 16 x 3 in. Round, p. 157

Tips: 1A, 1s, 2A, 10, p. 136-137

Colors: Rose, Black, Kelly Green, Lemon Yellow, Copper (for skin tone shown), p. 148

Fondant: White Ready-To-Use Rolled Fondant (285 oz.), Gum-Tex, p. 149; Square, Flower Cut-Outs, p. 153; Gold Pearl Dust, 10-Pc. Fondant/Gum Paste Tool Set, Fondant Shaping Foam, Flower Forming Cups, Brush Set, Easy-Glide Fondant Smoother, p. 151; 20 in. Rolling Pin, Roll & Cut Mat, p. 150

Recipe: Buttercream Icing, p. 118; Thinned Fondant Adhesive, p. 119

Also: 2010 Pattern Book (Crown, Door, Large & Small Bushes, Balcony Rail Curve, Small, Medium and Large Turret Peaks, Windows), p. 132; Romantic Castle Cake Set, p. 236; 2½ in. Globe Pillar Set, p. 238; Plastic Dowel Rods, p. 240; Heart Plastic Nesting Cutter Set, p. 203; Piping Gel, p. 145; White, Pink Cake Sparkles, p. 146; White Candy Melts, p. 196; Fanci-Foil Wrap, p. 241; 20 in. diameter plywood or foamcore board

(½ in. thick), waxed paper, lemon extract, cornstarch, knife

In advance: Make fondant flowers and accents. Tint 22 oz. fondant light pink, 16 oz. dark pink. For flowers, roll out white and light pink fondant ⅛ in. thick. Using Cut-Outs, cut 15 medium white and 14 each small white and light pink flowers. Cup centers using small ball tool from set on thick foam. Brush medium flowers with damp brush and sprinkle with white Cake Sparkles. Roll small balls for centers and attach with damp brush. Dry medium flowers in small Forming Cups dusted with cornstarch; dry small flowers on waxed paper-covered boards dusted with cornstarch. For top borders and balcony rail, add ½ teaspoon Gum-Tex to remaining light pink fondant and roll out ¼ in. thick. Cut 58 squares using smallest Cut-Out; let dry as above. For balcony rail, cut a ½ x 14 in. long strip; curve and let dry on waxed paper-covered pattern, dusted with cornstarch. For balcony base, add ¼ teaspoon Gum-Tex to 3 oz. dark pink fondant and roll out ¼ in.

thick. Cut 20 squares using smallest Cut-Out and roll ten ¾ in. balls; let dry on board as above. Brush turret peaks lightly with piping gel. Roll out dark pink fondant ⅛ in. thick; use patterns to cut turret peaks and cover 4 large, 1 medium and 2 small peaks. Smooth seam with fingers. Cut ¼ in. wide strips and wrap around peaks in spiral formation, attaching with damp brush. Brush strips with Piping Gel, then sprinkle with pink Cake Sparkles. Using pattern and light pink fondant, cut turret windows; attach with damp brush. Roll and attach ¼ in. diameter logs around windows with damp brush. **Also:** Prepare towers which will be inserted in cake (p. 128). **And:** Make baby topper (p. 128). Tint fondant as follows: 8 oz. light copper, ½ oz. yellow, ½ oz. black.

Bake and cool 2-layer cakes (trim layers to 2½ in. for 5 in. high cakes). Prepare for Stacked Construction (p. 116) and rolled fondant (p. 119). Cover cakes with 176 oz. light pink fondant; smooth with Fondant Smoother. Stack on foil-wrapped cake base, positioning

top cake 2 in. from back edge. Roll out dark pink ⅛ in. thick; cut 2 doors using pattern. Roll out light pink ⅛ in. thick; cut a heart for each door using smallest cutter from set and attach. Roll ⅜ in. logs and attach around each door. Using melted candy, attach a large tower 4 in. from each side of door; attach remaining large towers 12 in. from front towers. Tint 36 oz. fondant dark pink. Make 17 drapes (p. 126) using 5 x 3½ in. strips. Attach around cakes, 4 in. apart, with damp brush. Attach a medium flower at each drape end. Using thinned fondant adhesive, assemble balcony base by attaching a ¾ in. ball between 2 small squares; make 10 groups and attach ¾ in. apart. Attach rail with adhesive. Attach top border squares, ⅝ in. apart. Tint 16 oz. fondant green; roll out ⅛ in. thick. Using patterns, cut large and small bushes; attach around base cake. Attach small flowers to bushes.

At party: Insert medium and small towers in cake. Position turrets on towers. Position baby topper. Serves 97.

► Royal Family

Pan: Standard Muffin, p. 159

Tip: 2, p. 136

Color: Rose, p. 148

Candy: White (2 pks. for 24 treats), Light Cocoa Candy Melts, p. 196; Primary Candy Color Set, Candy Melting Plate, p. 199

Recipe: Buttercream Icing, p. 118

Also: Princess Cupcake Stand Kit, p. 176; Parchment Triangles, p. 138; White Sparkling Sugar, p. 146; Cake Boards, p. 241; waxed paper

In advance: Make candy heads. Use candy color to tint 10 oz. candy light orange (for skin tone shown). Mold 24 heads in candy melting plate. Unmold and set on waxed paper-covered board. Tint candy for a variety of hair colors; tint some candy light red for pink cheeks. Using melted candy in cut parchment bags, pipe curly hair, dot features and outline mouth. Chill until firm.

Bake and cool cupcakes in baking cups from kit. Ice smooth. Sprinkle on sparkling sugar. Using tip 2, pipe light pink scallop outline; add dark pink dots. Attach crown picks from kit to back of candy heads with melted candy; let set.

At party: Assemble stand. Insert heads in cupcakes; position on stand. Each serves 1.

◄ Royal Baby Carriages

Pan: Non-Stick Cookie Sheet, p. 167

Candy: White (1 pk. makes 2 treats), Light Cocoa Candy Melts, p. 196; Primary & Garden Candy Color Sets, p. 199; Fairy Tale Large Lollipop Mold, p. 198; Dessert Accents Candy Mold, p. 197

Also: 101 Cookie Cutters, p. 203; Jumbo Hearts Sprinkles, p. 146; Parchment Triangles, p. 136; knife, ruler

In advance: Make candy base. Set largest round cutter from set on cookie sheet. Fill ½ in. deep with melted candy; chill until firm. **Also:** Pipe candy handle. Tint portion of melted white candy light pink using candy colors. Mold handle using scroll cavity on Dessert Accents mold. Chill until firm. Reserve remaining candy.

For each carriage, use reserved light pink candy and tint additional portions of melted white candy dark pink, orange (for skin tone shown) and yellow. Use piping method (p. 130) to mold carriages. Chill until firm. Using melted candy in cut parchment bags, pipe ⅝ in. round head; let set. Pipe crown, facial features and hair curl. Trim off bottom of scroll accent to fit. Using melted candy, attach handle to back of carriage; attach carriage to base; attach heart sprinkles around base. Let set. Each serves 1.

► Cute Coach

Pans: Mini Ball, p. 165; Cookie Sheet, Cooling Grid, p. 159

Tips: 3, 6, 10, 13, 103, p. 136-137

Color: Rose, p. 148

Recipes: Buttercream Icing, Roll-Out Cookies, p. 118

Also: Round Cut-Outs, p. 153; Flower Nail No. 7, Flower Lifter, p. 140; Cake Dividing Set, p. 138; waxed paper, toothpicks, ruler

In advance: Make wheel cookies. Prepare and roll out dough. For each carriage, cut 4 wheels using medium round Cut-Out. Bake and cool cookies. Ice smooth. Use tip 6 to outline outside edge. For flower, use tip 3 to pipe elongated bead petals and dot center. **Also:** Make tip 103 rose (p. 121) with tip 10 base.

For each carriage, bake and cool 2 Mini Ball cakes. Use toothpicks and Cake Dividing Wheel to divide each cake into 8ths. Use icing to attach cakes to form ball. Mark 2 x 1¼ in. wide oval door; ice top half of door smooth. Decorate bottom half of ball first, then flip and decorate top half. Use tip 3 to outline door and division marks; fill in with tip 13 stars. Add tip 3 dot door handle. Use icing to attach rose to top and cookie wheels to sides. Cake serves 4; each cookie serves 1.

Party, Me Hearties!

What treasures await your pint-size pirate! He'll take to the high seas with a crew of brownie buccaneers on a fondant freighter cake rigged out for fun— they've even raised the mainsail with a special birthday message. Everyone can stake a claim to a flag-topped cupcake or cereal treat, but the treasure chest is for the 1-year-old boy alone. It's just the right size for personal plunder!

▲ Birthday on the Bounty

Pans: Diamond Pan Set (15 x 11 x 2 in. used), p. 156; 8-Cavity Silicone Round Brownie Pops Mold, p. 170; Cookie Sheet, p. 159

Tips: 1A, 1M, 2, 2A, 3, 8, p. 136-137

Colors:* Sky Blue, Royal Blue, Brown, Red-Red, Christmas Red, Kelly Green, Leaf Green, Black, Lemon Yellow, Golden Yellow, Violet, Orange, Copper (for skin tone shown), p. 148

Fondant: White Ready-To-Use Rolled Fondant (140 oz.), Gum-Tex, p. 149; Brush Set, Easy-Glide Fondant Smoother, Flower Former Set, p. 151; Round Cut-Outs, p. 153; 20 in. Rolling Pin, Roll & Cut Mat, p. 150

Recipes: Royal Icing, p. 118; Thinned Fondant Adhesive, p. 119, favorite brownie recipe or mix

Also: 2010 Pattern Book (Large & Small Waves, Small & Large Sails, Pirate Hat, "Happy Birthday"), p. 132; Meringue Powder, Piping Gel, p. 145; White Candy Melts (1 pk.), p. 196; Blue Colored Sugar, p. 146; Wooden, Plastic Dowel Rods, p. 240; Parchment Triangles, p. 138; Cake Boards, Fanci-Foil Wrap, p. 241; 18 x 15 in. plywood or foamcore board (½ in. thick), knife, scissors, tape, waxed paper, ruler, toothpicks, cornstarch, pencil, plastic wrap

In advance: Make waves and cover base board. Tint 48 oz. fondant light blue. Using pan as a guide, cut base board 1¼ in. wider on all sides. Cover with 36 oz. fondant rolled ⅛ in. thick (p. 123). Roll out remaining fondant ⅛ in. thick. Using pattern, cut 4 large and 4 small waves. Working 1 wave at a time, use Piping Gel in cut parchment bag to cover a portion of each wave curl with C-motion lines; sprinkle on blue sugar. Overpipe top

line and add more sugar to darken. Let dry on cornstarch-dusted surface. **Also:** Make pirates, captain and parrot (p. 129). Bake and cool 4 brownies in silicone mold supported by cookie sheet; ice lightly with buttercream. Tint fondant as follows: 15 oz. light copper, 4½ oz. black, 2⅜ oz. red, 2 oz. orange, 2 oz. light green, 2 oz. dark green, 2 oz. dark blue, ¾ oz. violet, 2 oz. yellow, ¼ oz. gray. Roll out ⅛ in. thick as needed. **And:** Make rigging (p. 129). Prepare fondant as follows: Tint 2 oz. brown and mix with ⅛ teaspoon Gum-Tex; mix 1 teaspoon Gum-Tex with 6 oz. white fondant. Tint 1 oz. black and mix with ⅛ teaspoon Gum-Tex.

Bake and cool 2-layer cake, 3 in. high. Prepare for rolled fondant. Tint 36 oz. fondant brown; cover cake and smooth with Fondant Smoother. For planks, use ruler and knife to indent horizontal lines, ½ in. apart, on cake sides. Lightly mark random lines for wood

grain look. Roll out brown and black fondant ⅛ in. thick. Cut 8 black portholes using wide end of tip 1A; attach using damp brush. Cut 8 brown circles using wide end of tip 1A; recut circles using wide end of tip 1M to make porthole rims and attach. Roll two 16½ in. long x ¼ in. diameter brown fondant logs; attach on cake top. Roll four 10 in. long x ⅜ in. diameter logs; attach to cake sides, curling ends for corner details. Using icing, attach cake to prepared board. Attach waves with damp brush, using ¼ in. fondant logs as spacers between waves; trim at corners to fit.

At party: Position pirates. Insert center mast over dowel rods. Attach parrot. Cake serves 20; each brownie serves 1.

*Combine Brown with Red-Red and Black for brown shown. Combine Red-Red with Christmas Red for red shown. Combine Lemon Yellow with Golden Yellow for yellow shown.

▼ Personal Pirate Treats

Cookie: Boy Plastic Cutter, p. 203; Cookie Sheet, Cooling Grid, p. 159
Tips: 1, 2, 3, p. 136
Colors:* Orange, Kelly Green, Copper (for skin tone shown), Red-Red, Lemon Yellow, Violet, Rose, Brown, Black, p. 148
Recipes: Royal Icing, Roll-Out Cookies, p. 118; favorite crisped rice cereal treats
Also: 2010 Pattern Book (Flag), p. 132; 6 in. Lollipop Sticks, p. 200; Meringue Powder, p. 145; spice drops, double-stick tape, waxed paper, cornstarch

Prepare cookie dough; tint light copper. Roll out and cut one boy cookie for each treat. Bake and cool. Outline and pipe in pants and shirt with tip 3 (smooth with finger dipped in cornstarch). Use tip 3 to pipe outline hair and outline and pipe-in bandana (pat smooth); add pull-out ties. Pipe tip 3 rope belt, dot knot. Using tip 2, pipe bandana dots, dot nose and eye, outline mouth and pipe-in eye patch. Add tip 1 dot pupil, string on eye patch and stripes on pants. Pipe tip 2 outline earring. Prepare cereal treats for islands. While treats are still warm shape into 4 x 2 x 1½ in. high mounds; let cool on waxed paper. Copy flag pattern; cut and attach to lollipop stick with tape. Insert flag in treat; insert spice drop on top. Attach cookie with icing. Each serves 1.

*Combine Brown with Red-Red for brown shown. Combine Violet with Rose for violet shown.

▲ Sweet Fleet

Pans: Standard Muffin Pan, Cooling Grid, p. 159
Tips: 1, 2, p. 136
Colors:* Sky Blue, Orange, Red-Red, Leaf Green, Lemon Yellow, Violet, Rose, Black, p. 148
Candy: White, Light Cocoa Candy Melts, p. 196; Primary Candy Color Set, Transportation Candy Mold, p. 199
Recipe: Buttercream Icing, p. 118
Also: Pirates Cupcake Combo Pack, p. 175; small round disk candies, cornstarch

In advance: Make candies. Tint portions of melted white candy blue and red using candy colors. Mold sailboats using piping method (p. 130). Chill until firm.

Bake and cool cupcakes; ice smooth. Attach disk candy faces to sailboats with icing. Pipe tip 1 dot eyes and outline mouth, tip 2 dot bandana (smooth with finger dipped in cornstarch) and pull-out ties. Add tip 1 dot trim. Position sailboats on cupcakes, support with icing in back if needed. Insert pick. Each serves 1.

*Combine Violet with Rose for violet shown.

▶ Treasure Trove

Pan: 9 x 5 in. Loaf, p. 159
Tips: 3, 4, 47, p. 136-137
Colors: Lemon Yellow, Golden Yellow, p. 148
Recipes: Buttercream, Chocolate Buttercream Icings, p. 118
Also: Cake Boards, Fanci-Foil Wrap, p. 241; 11 in. Straight Spatula, p. 140; knife, ruler, cornstarch

Bake and cool cake. Trim to 6 x 3½ in. wide; use pieces to build up a rounded top, 3¼ in. high at the center 2¾ in. high at outer edge. Ice smooth. Use edge of spatula to make horizontal marks for boards, ½ in. apart, across top and sides. Use knife to make random marks for wood grain effect. For banded edges, pipe tip 47 outlines, smooth side up; center band is ½ in. down from top edge. Using tip 4, outline and fill in front lock plate, 1¼ x 2 in. wide (pat smooth with finger dipped in cornstarch. Pipe tip 4 dot rivets at corners and on lock plate; pipe 2 pairs of dots for side handles; flatten with finger. Use edge of spatula to indent line on all sides to indicate separate lid. Use tip 4 to pipe oblong keyhole (flatten slightly), ring keyhole and drop string side handles. Pipe tip 3 name on lid. Serves 6.

*Combine Lemon Yellow with Golden Yellow for yellow shown.

A Great Rookie Year

It's his first season celebration and you're going to hit it out of the park! Topping the lineup, baby's out of uniform and giving high fives all around on a simple star-topped cake. Also taking the field are shortstop pops, colorful brownie benchwarmers with fondant details and a baseball cake that's ready to smash.

▲ Steal Home Cake

Pan: Teddy Bear, p. 163

Tips: 1A, 3, 16, p. 136-137

Colors: Copper (for skin tone shown), Sky Blue, Black, Leaf Green, p. 148

Fondant: White Ready-To-Use Rolled Fondant (8 oz.), Gum-Tex, p. 149; 9 in. Rolling Pin, Roll & Cut Mat, p. 150; Brush Set, p. 151

Recipes: Buttercream Icing, p. 118; Thinned Fondant Adhesive, p. 119

Also: 2010 Pattern Book (Hand, Baseball Cap, Brim), p. 132; Cake Board, Fanci-Foil Wrap, p. 241; Disposable Decorating Bags, p. 138; Baseball Mitt Icing Decorations, p. 179; 4 in. Lollipop Sticks, p. 200; cornstarch, knife

In advance: Make fondant cap. Mix 8 oz. fondant with ¾ teaspoon Gum-Tex; tint half blue; reserve remainder. Roll out blue ⅛ in. thick. Using patterns, cut cap and brim. Curve brim slightly and stand on end to dry on cornstarch-dusted board. Roll a ½ in. diameter ball, flatten slightly and attach to top of cap with damp brush. Let dry. **Also:** Make hands. Tint reserved fondant mixture light copper. Roll out ⅛ in. thick and use pattern to cut right hand; flip pattern and cut left hand. Let dry. **And:** Make toes and ears. Roll 2 balls ¾ in. diameter for big toes, 6 balls ½ in. diameter for middle toes, 2 balls ¼ diameter for small toes. Roll out remaining fondant ⅛ in. thick. Cut ear using wide end of tip 1A; cut in half. Attach 2 lollipop sticks to each hand and 1 to each ear with Thinned Fondant Adhesive, leaving 2½ in. extended.

Bake and cool cake; cut off ears. Ice sides and face area smooth to level. Insert hands and ears in cake. Using tip 3 outline all sections and details. Pipe in eyes (pat smooth with finger dipped in cornstarch). Fill in remaining areas with tip 16 stars; overpipe wrists, feet, and nose for dimension. Attach toes with dots of icing. Pipe tip 3 outline bellybutton and patch number. Add tip 16 pull-out star bottom border. Attach icing decorations. Position cap and attach brim with icing. Serves 12.

▶ High Pop-Ups!

Candy: White (1 pk. makes 10 treats), Red Candy Melts, p. 196; Sports Large Lollipop Mold, p. 198; 8 in. Lollipop Sticks, p. 200

Tips: 1, 1A, 3, 102, p. 136-137

Colors: Copper (for skin tone shown), Leaf Green, Sky Blue, Black, Red-Red, p. 148

Recipe: Royal Icing, p. 118

Also: 2010 Pattern Book (Pennant), p. 132; Cake Board, p. 241; Parchment Triangles, p. 138; Meringue Powder, p. 145; cornstarch, waxed paper, card stock, markers, hole punch

Mold all-white baseball lollipops (p. 130); chill until firm. Add outline stitching using melted red candy in cut parchment bag; chill until firm. Place lollipops on waxed paper-covered cake board. Using royal icing, pipe tip 1A ball heads, tip 3 dot hands and pull-out fingers. Pipe tip 1 dot eyes, nose, ears and outline mouth. Pipe in cap with tip 3 (smooth with finger dipped in cornstarch); add tip 1 dot button. Pipe tip 102 outline brims (shape with finger). Pipe tip 3 numbers; let dry. Using pattern, cut pennants from card stock. Color sections and print names with markers. Punch holes and thread onto lollipop sticks. Each serves 1.

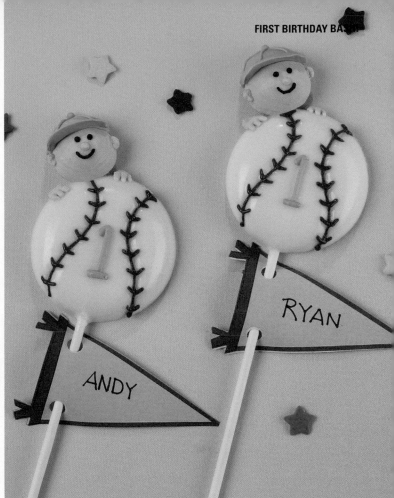

▲ Bonus Baby Brownies

Pans: 8-Cavity Silicone Round Brownie Pops Mold, p. 170; Cookie Sheet, Cooling Grid, p. 159

Colors: Black, Copper (for skin tone shown), p. 148

Fondant: White Ready-To-Use Fondant (24 oz.), Gum-Tex, Primary Colors Fondant Multi Pack, p. 149; Brush Set, p. 151; 9 in. Rolling Pin, Roll & Cut Mat, p. 150

Recipes: Buttercream Icing, p. 118; favorite brownie recipe or mix

Also: toothpicks, knife, ruler

Bake and cool brownies in silicone mold supported by cookie sheet. Ice smooth. Roll out red, green, blue and white fondant 1⁄16 in. thick. Cut pieces and attach with damp brush as follows: For shirts, cut 1½ x 6 in. rectangles and wrap around top of brownies. For white pants, cut ¾ x 6½ in. rectangles and wrap around bottom of brownie. For heads, combine 5 oz. white fondant with ¼ teaspoon Gum-Tex; tint light copper. Roll a 1½ in. ball for each head. Roll ¼ x 1½ in. long logs for each arm; flatten one end and indent fingers with knife. For sleeves, cut ½ x 1¼ in. long strips. Cut ½ x 1½ in. copper triangles for chest area. Cut 1⁄8 in. wide strips for neck trims. Roll ½ in. diameter white baseballs. Roll small copper balls for noses, flat balls for ears. Tint ½ oz. fondant black. Roll small balls for eyes, thin log for mouths; attach. For caps, cut 2 in. circles; attach and smooth. Cut 1 ¾ in. wide x ½ in. deep moon shape from same color fondant for cap brims. Use toothpick to score lines in caps. Roll small ball buttons for top of caps. Shape ¾ x ½ in. ovals for shoes. Roll thin red rope stitching for balls. Each serves 1.

▼ Smash to First!

Pan: Sports Ball Set, p. 165

Tip: 4, p. 136

Color: Red-Red, p. 148

Recipe: Buttercream Icing, p. 118

Also: Cake Board, Fanci-Foil Wrap, p. 241; Disposable Decorating Bags, p. 138

Bake and cool cake in ball pan half. Ice smooth. Pipe tip 4 string and pull-out dot stitching. Serves 6.

Junior Jungle

Mischievous monkeys are ready to welcome your 1-year-old to an unforgettable party safari! Whether they're chasing candy bananas on pretzel trees, wrapping fondant gifts or getting ready to dive into a smash cupcake, these chimps will capture your heart.

▲ Gift-Wrapping Monkey

Pan: Monkey, p. 164

Tips: 3, 4, 6, 16, 21, p. 136-137

Colors:* Lemon Yellow, Violet, Rose, Leaf Green, Royal Blue, Ivory, p. 148

Fondant: White Ready-To-Use Rolled Fondant (12 oz.), Gum-Tex, p. 149; Brush Set, p. 151; 9 in. Rolling Pin, Roll & Cut Mat, p. 150

Recipes: Buttercream, Chocolate

Buttercream Icings, p. 118; Thinned Fondant Adhesive, p. 119

Also: 2010 Pattern Book (Hat), p. 132; Flowerful Medley Sprinkles (confetti), p. 146; 4 in. Lollipop Sticks, p. 200; Cake Boards, Fanci-Foil Wrap, p. 241; large marshmallows, scissors, tape, knife, ruler, waxed paper, cornstarch

In advance: Make birthday hat and gifts (p. 129). Add 1 teaspoon Gum-Tex to 12 oz. fondant. Tint as follows: 3 oz. yellow, 2 oz.

blue, 2 oz. violet, 2 oz. green, 1 oz. pink; reserve 2 oz. white. Roll out ⅛ in. thick unless otherwise specified.

Bake and cool cake; ice sides and background areas smooth. Ice inner ears smooth. Use tip 4 to outline details. Use tip 6 to pipe in eye and muzzle areas (pat smooth with finger dipped in cornstarch). Pipe tip 4 dot pupils and outline nostrils; pipe tip 3 outline mouth. Cover body with tip 16 stars. Position small then large gifts; attach

bows with icing. Attach yellow ribbons. Use tip 4 to outline fingers over ribbon; fill in with tip 16 stars. Use icing dots to attach confetti sprinkles to cake sides. Pipe tip 21 shell bottom border. Insert hat; support with marshmallows if necessary. Serves 12.

*Combine Violet with Rose for violet shown. Combine Leaf Green with Lemon Yellow for green shown.

▶ Happy Habitat

Pans: Cookie Sheet, Cooling Grid, p. 159
Tips: 3, 6, p. 136
Colors:* Lemon Yellow, Leaf Green, Sky Blue, Violet, Rose, Orange, p. 148
Candy: Animals Cookie Candy Mold, p. 197; White, Light Cocoa, Yellow, Orange & Blue Candy Melts, p. 196; Garden Candy Color Set, p. 199; 6 in. & 11¾ in. Lollipop Sticks, p. 200
Recipes: Color Flow Icing, Roll-Out Cookies, p. 118
Also: Flower Forming Cups, p. 151; Square Cut-Outs, p. 153; 9 in. Rolling Pin, p. 150; Parchment Triangles, p. 138; Color Flow Mix, p. 145; 8 in. Cake Circles, Fanci-Foil Wrap, p. 241; 6 x 2 in. craft foam round, small chocolate nougat candies, jelly spearmint leaves, candy-coated chocolates, curling ribbon, knife, scissors, ruler, waxed paper, tape

In advance: Make animal pops. Use candy colors to tint portions of melted white candy black, gray (add a small amount of black to white), pink and green; add white to light cocoa for light brown. Each uses 1 oz. Candy Melts. Using piping method (p. 130), fill in animal head sections of candy mold cavities (let lion face set before adding mane); chill until firm. Fill round backgrounds half full with melted candy in contrasting color; chill until firm. Pipe on facial features using melted candy in cut parchment bag; let set. Attach 6 in. Lollipop Sticks to backs using melted candy; let set. **Also:** Make cookie packages (p. 129). **And:** Make 3 treetops (p. 129).

For base, wrap 6 in. craft foam round in foil. For base board, trim 8 in. Cake Circle to 7½ in.; wrap in foil. Attach base to base board using melted candy. Make tree trunks (p. 129). Attach packages around center using melted candy. Insert trees and animal pops. Curl 18 in. lengths of ribbon. Tie around sticks and scatter over base. Each candy and each cookie serves 1.

*Combine Violet with Rose for violet shown. Combine Leaf Green with Lemon Yellow for green shown.

▶ Baby Chimp's Ready To Chomp!

Pans: Mini Stand-Up Bear Set, p. 164; Standard Muffin, p. 159
Tips: 2, 3, 5, 16, p. 136-137
Colors: Ivory, Leaf Green, p. 148
Fondant: White Ready-To-Use Rolled Fondant (6 oz.), p. 149; Brush Set, p. 151; 9 in. Rolling Pin, Roll & Cut Mat, p. 150
Recipes: Buttercream, Chocolate Buttercream Icings, p. 118
Also: Cake Circles, Fanci-Foil Wrap, p. 241; White Standard Baking Cups, p. 186; vanilla wafers, cornstarch, knife, waxed paper

Bake and cool cupcake and mini cake. Trim ears off mini cake; position on foil-wrapped Cake Circle or serving plate. For ears, trim vanilla wafers to a crescent shape to fit curve of head. For legs, begin with a ½ x 4 in. log of fondant; shape to get a wider thigh tapering to narrow ankle with teardrop-shaped, angled foot. Attach ears and legs with icing. Use tip 5 to outline and fill in inner ears, face and foot pads (smooth with finger dipped in cornstarch). Overpipe muzzle; smooth. Pipe tip 3 dot eyes (flatten slightly) and outline mouth. Pipe tip 2 outline nostrils. Cover body with tip 16 stars. Ice cupcake smooth; position between legs. For arms, roll 2 ½ x 3½ in. logs; shape for bent elbow and slightly flattened hand. Attach with icing, resting hands on cupcake. Lift arm; outline and pipe in palms with tip 5 (pat smooth) and replace on cupcake. Cover arms with tip 16 stars. For tail, shape a fondant rope ¼ x 5½ in. long. Curl and attach to back bottom with icing. Cover with tip 16 stars. Print tip 3 message on cupcake. Serves 4.

◀ Banana Flip!

Pans: 9 x 2 in. Non-Stick Square, Cookie Sheet, Cooling Grid, p. 167
Candy: Light Cocoa, Peanut Butter, White Candy Melts, p. 196; Primary and Garden Candy Color Sets, p. 199; Monkey Large Lollipop Mold, p. 198
Recipe: Favorite crisped rice cereal treats
Also: 9 in. Rolling Pin, p. 150; Parchment Triangles, p. 138; Flower Forming Cups, p. 151; Flowerful Medley Sprinkles, p. 146; Round Comfort-Grip Cutter, p. 202; Cake Board, p. 241; Jungle Pals Party Bags, p. 175; pretzel rods, cellophane tape, jelly spearmint leaves, waxed paper, paring knife, granulated sugar

In advance: Make monkeys. Use candy colors to tint portions of melted white candy black, blue, light and dark yellow. Use piping method (p. 130) to mold candies without sticks, filling mold ⅔ full. Chill until firm. **Also:** Make treetops (p. 129).

Prepare cereal treats and press into greased pan, 1½ in. deep. Cut circles for base using Comfort-Grip cutter. Cover treats with melted candy (p. 130). Chill until firm on waxed paper-covered board. Seal bottom with melted candy; let set. Turn treetop over and cut small opening in center to fit pretzel rod; cut same size opening in base. Trim end of pretzel flat; insert in treetop and secure with melted candy. Attach monkey to pretzel with melted candy; chill until firm. Trim about ½-¾ in. off bottom of pretzel; insert in base and secure with melted candy. Attach confetti sprinkles to base with dots of candy. Place treats in party bags. Each serves 1.

Two are One!

The twins may not have been on the same feeding or changing schedule, but they're ready to share the celebration of their lives! Party caps, colorful balloons and gifts galore are the order of the day. Get your cameras ready to snap 2 smash cake caps, a triple-tiered fondant balloon cake with mini twins on top and quick cupcakes which carry a photo to treasure.

▲ Balloon Buddies

Pans: 6, 8, 10 x 3 in. Round, p. 157

Tips: 1A, 1s, 2A, 10, p. 136

Colors: Royal Blue, Leaf Green, Orange, Lemon Yellow, Violet, Rose, Christmas Red, Copper (for skin tone shown), Black, p. 148

Fondant: White Ready-To-Use Rolled Fondant (110 oz.), Gum-Tex, p. 149; Brush Set, Easy-Glide Fondant Smoother, p. 151; Round Cut-Outs, p. 153; 20 in. Rolling Pin, Roll & Cut Mat, p. 150

Recipe: Buttercream Icing, p. 118

Also: Cakes 'N More 3-Tier Party Stand, p. 236; 101 Cookie Cutters, p. 203; Blue, Light Green Colored Sugar, p. 146; Piping Gel, p. 145; 11¾ in. Lollipop Sticks, p. 200; White Candy Melts, p. 196; 2½ in. Globe Pillar Set, p. 238; Circus Balloons Set, p. 183; Cake Circles, Boards, p. 241; white curling ribbon (18 ft.), waxed paper, cornstarch, knife, ruler, scissors, compass (to draw 5 in. circle), tape

In advance: Make letters. Tint fondant: 4 oz. blue, 2 oz. green. Add ¼ teaspoon Gum-Tex to each; roll out ⅛ in. thick. Cut letters using cutters from set. Brush with Piping Gel and sprinkle on Colored Sugar. Let dry on cornstarch-dusted board. **Also:** Make babies (p. 129). Tint fondant: 16 oz. light copper, 4 oz. blue, 4 oz. green, ½ oz. black.

Bake and cool 1-layer cakes. Prepare and cover with rolled fondant, smooth with Fondant Smoother. Tint fondant: 6 oz. each orange and yellow; 4 oz. each rose, green, blue and violet. Roll out ⅛ in. thick. Cut about 150 circles in assorted sizes and colors using small and medium circle cutters from set and wide end of tips 10, 1A and 2A. Attach to cake sides using damp brush. Use knife and Cake Circle or compass to cut a 6 in. yellow circle; attach to center of 10 in. cake. Cut a 5 in. orange circle and attach to 8 in. cake. Cut 2 pillars to 7 in. long; insert one in each circle. Position babies; insert balloons through hands; secure with melted candy. Attach Lollipop Sticks to back of letters using melted candy; let set. Insert into cake, trimming sticks to vary heights. Use melted candy to attach a 1 ft. length of curled ribbon to each stick. Serves 60.

*Combine Violet with Rose for violet shown. Combine Rose with Christmas Red for rose shown.

▼ Twins Stick Together

Candy: Blue, Lavender, Orange, Yellow, White Candy Melts, p. 196; 10-Pack Candy Mold Set, p. 198; Garden Candy Color Set, p. 199; 6 in. Lollipop Sticks, p. 200
Also: Fanci-Foil Wrap, p. 241; Parchment Triangles, p. 138; cone-shaped corn snacks, curling ribbon, tape, 1 in. thick craft foam block, craft knife, scissors

In advance: Mold candies. Tint portions of melted white candy black using candy color, copper for face using melted orange candy and green using candy color and melted yellow candy. Using piping method (p. 130), mold gifts and faces in candy molds; chill until firm. Using craft knife, carefully trim off raised eye areas on faces. Pipe dot eyes and nose, string mouth. Attach lollipop sticks to back of faces with melted candy. Let set. **Also:** make hats. Cut corn snacks to ¾ in. long; dip in melted candy and let set; repeat as needed.

For base, cut craft foam into 2¼ in. squares; wrap in foil, secure with tape. Insert lollipops, trimming to desired heights. Attach hats with dots of candy. To decorate, add a drop of water to ¼ cup melted candy to thicken. Quickly pipe zigzag trim on hats; let set. Attach gifts around craft blocks with melted candy. Cut 12 in. lengths of curling ribbon and curl. Tie one length to each stick and position additional pieces on base. Each serves 1.

▲ Photo Finish

Pans: Standard Muffin, Cooling Grid, p. 159
Recipe: Buttercream Icing, p. 118
Also: Celebration Standard Baking Cups, p. 177; Flowerful Medley Sprinkles (confetti), p. 146; Add-A-Message Fun Pix, p. 186; photos

Bake and cool cupcakes. Ice smooth; add confetti sprinkles. Insert photos in picks and insert in cupcakes. Each serves 1.

▶ Party Cap Cakes

Pan: Mini Wonder Mold, p. 160
Tips: 5, 16, 18, p. 136-137
Colors: Royal Blue, Leaf Green, Violet, Orange, p. 148
Recipe: Buttercream Icing, p. 118
Also: Cake Circles, Fanci-Foil Wrap, p. 241; knife

Bake and cool cakes. Use knife to trim ¼ in. off sides for straighter hat shape. Use icing to build up point of hat and to seal in crumbs. Use wide end of decorating tip to mark dots. Fill in dots, then background, with tip 16 stars. Pipe tip 18 pull-out star fringe and pom-pom. Pipe tip 5 number. Each serves 1.

◀ Take 1!

Cookie: A-B-C and 1-2-3 (50 Pc.) Cutter Set, p. 203; Cookie Sheet, Cooling Grid, p. 159

Tips: 2, 3, p. 136

Colors:* Sky Blue, Rose, Leaf Green, Lemon Yellow, Golden Yellow, p. 148

Recipes: Buttercream, Color Flow Icings, Roll-Out Cookies, p. 118

Also: Pastel Silicone Baking Cups, p. 174; Color Flow Mix, p. 145; Parchment Triangles, p. 138

In advance: Make cookies. Prepare and roll out cookie dough. Cut using number 1 cutter from set. Bake and cool cookies. Outline cookies with tip 3 and full-strength color flow; let dry. Flow in with thinned color flow to cover; immediately overpipe tip 2 multicolored dots using thinned color flow. Let dry.

Bake and cool cupcakes in silicone cups supported by cookie sheet. Ice smooth with spatula. Insert cookies. Each serves 1.

*Combine Lemon Yellow with Golden Yellow for yellow shown.

▼ The Gifts Stack Up

Pan: 6 x 2 in. Square, p. 157

Tip: 3, p. 136

Colors:* Rose, Leaf Green, Lemon Yellow, Golden Yellow, Royal Blue, p. 148

Fondant: White Ready-To-Use Rolled Fondant (6 oz.), Gum-Tex, p. 149; Brush Set, p. 151; 9 in. Rolling Pin, Roll & Cut Mat, p. 150

Recipe: Buttercream Icing, p. 118

Also: Cake Boards, Fanci-Foil Wrap, p. 241; knife, ruler, cornstarch, waxed paper, scissors

In advance: Make bow loops. Tint 3 oz. fondant pink; add ¼ teaspoon Gum-Tex. Roll out ⅛ in. thick. Cut 5 strips, 1 x 3½ in. Form loops; attach ends with damp brush. Let dry on sides on waxed paper-covered board dusted with cornstarch. Reserve remaining pink fondant.

Bake and cool 2 cakes; trim to form 3 in. and 5 in. squares, 2 in. high. Prepare for Stacked Construction without dowel rods (p. 116). Ice smooth. Tint 3 oz. fondant blue. Roll out ⅛ in. thick. Cut 4 strips, 1 x 3 in.; attach to 5 in. cake. Roll out reserved pink fondant ⅛ in. thick. Cut 4 strips, 1 x 3½ in.; attach to 3 in. cake. Trim ends of bow loops to a V; attach with icing dots. Pipe tip 3 bead bottom borders. Serves 8.

*Combine Lemon Yellow with Golden Yellow for yellow shown.

1 Great Day

Look out for number 1 with a pastel party that puts the focus on fun! Set the tone with a fondant-topped sheet cake embossed with colorful balloons and confetti, or choose a simple bow-wrapped gift cake surrounded by candy, cookies and cupcakes. It all adds up to birthday excitement.

(Projects shown on page 94-95.)

▲ Next Year is Here!

Pans: 11 x 15 x 2 in. Sheet, p. 157; #1, p. 163

Tips: 2, 3, 4, 9, p.136

Colors:* Violet, Rose, Lemon Yellow, Golden Yellow, Leaf Green, Sky Blue, p. 148

Fondant: White Ready-To-Use Rolled Fondant (65 oz.), p. 149; Happy Birthday Fondant Imprint Mat, 20 in. Rolling Pin, Roll & Cut Mat, p. 150

Recipe: Buttercream Icing, p. 118

Also: Cake Board, Fanci-Foil Wrap, p. 241; Dowel Rods, p. 240; 16 x 24 in. plywood or foamcore board (½ in. thick); cornstarch

Bake and cool #1 cake and 2 sheet cakes, 2 in. high. Position #1 cake on same size board and ice smooth. Position sheet cakes on foil-wrapped foamcore board, positioning long sides together; ice together at seam. Prepare for Stacked Construction (p. 116) and rolled fondant (p. 119). Ice cake smooth. Roll out fondant ¼ in. thick; cut a 15 x 22 in. sheet. Following Imprint Mat package directions, imprint pattern and cover top of sheet cake. Using tip 2, outline imprinted messages and designs. Pipe in balloons (pat smooth with finger dipped in cornstarch). Pipe tip 9 ball bottom border, tip 3 bead top border. Position #1 cake on sheet cake. Pipe tip 3 bead top and middle borders, tip 4 bead bottom border. Pipe tip 4 name. Serves 66.

*Combine Violet with Rose for violet shown. Combine Lemon Yellow with Golden Yellow for yellow shown.

◀ One for my Baby

Candy: White Candy Melts (1 pk. makes 20 treats), p. 196; Gift Truffles Candy Mold, p. 197; 10-Pack Candy Mold Set, p. 198; Primary, Garden Candy Color Sets, Decorator Brush Set, p. 199

Also: Flowerful Medley Sprinkles (confetti), p. 146; Parchment Triangles, p. 138; knife

Tint melted white candy yellow, blue, pink, violet and green using Candy Colors. Using painting method (p. 130), fill in bows of Truffles Mold cavities; chill until firm. Fill remainder of cavity using melted white candy. Mold numbers using mold from set; chill until firm. Use warm knife to level bow on package and bottom of number. Attach numbers to bow; chill until firm. Attach confetti sprinkles to sides using melted candy. Each serves 1.

visit the #1 site for *first birthdays:* www.wilton.com!

Wilton knows how to throw a spectacular first birthday bash! Go to www.wilton.com for great ideas and so many ways to celebrate. We make it fun for everyone—baby, siblings, mom & dad, grandma & grandpa, friends, too!

plan the party

Party planning is a Wilton specialty! From cake designs, to party themes, to celebration hints, we'll give you all our incredible ideas!

make an amazing cake

First birthday celebrations start with cake, and a matching cupcake for baby to smash! New to decorating? You'll find step-by-step instructions at www.wilton.com so you can decorate that incredible first birthday cake like a pro!

post your photos & share your memories

Share birthday memories, and those of mom and dad's first birthdays, too, by posting to our website. Take a look at the collection of cakes from years past, and compare them to today's favorite trendy designs.

Plus there's more—you'll see hundreds of new cake, cupcake, cookie and candy ideas; coordinated party themes and how to use them; plus cute and colorful birthday celebration products—all to make it the most memorable first birthday party ever!

Step-By-Step
Decorating Guide

Decorating help starts here! Whatever cake you want to make from this Yearbook, you'll find out how to make it happen on the following pages. Whether you're creating a cake for the first time or need a quick brush-up on a technique, it's easy when you use this handy guide as you decorate.

Want to learn more?

Find Wilton Cake Decorating Classes in your area or register for The Wilton School in Darien, Illinois online at **www.wilton.com**. Our website is also a great place to explore decorating techniques, find recipes and chat with other decorators. Visit us regularly!

Cake Preparation

Think of your cake as the canvas on which you will create beautiful icing decorations. To achieve the masterpiece you want, it is essential that your canvas be smooth and free of crumbs. These steps for preparing and icing your cake will result in the perfect decorating surface essential for your work of art.

BAKING THE CAKE

Follow recipe directions for specific baking instructions and recommended batter amounts for the pan size you choose.

Prepare the pan by generously greasing the inside using a pastry brush or paper towel and solid vegetable shortening. For best results, do not use butter, margarine or liquid vegetable oil. Spread the shortening so that all indentations are covered. Sprinkle about 2 Tablespoons of flour inside the pan and shake so that the flour covers all greased surfaces. Turn pan upside down and tap lightly to remove excess flour. If any uncovered spots remain, touch up with shortening and flour. Or use Bake Easy Non-Stick Spray or Cake Release (p. 154) to coat the pan—no grease or flour needed. Pour batter into pan and place in pre-heated oven.

After cake has baked the specified time, remove it from the oven and let it cool in the pan on a cake rack for 10 minutes. Run a thin knife between the cake and side of the pan. Unmold from pan by placing cooling rack against cake and turning both cooling rack and pan over. Lift pan off carefully. Cool at least one hour and brush off loose crumbs prior to icing.

CUTTING AND WRAPPING A CAKE BOARD

For round and sheet cakes, you don't need to cut a cake board. Simply buy a ready-made board that is 2 in. larger than your cake. (For example, if the cake is 8 in. diameter, buy a 10 in. round board.) For shaped cakes and squares, cut a board to fit. Turn pan upside down and trace outline onto your cake board. Cut board with a craft knife, leaving 1 in. extra around outline.

To wrap, trace your cut board onto Fanci-Foil, making the outline 3-4 in. larger than the board. Cut Fanci-Foil along the outline. Place your board, white side down, on top of your cut foil. Cut deep slits at several points along foil edge, creating tabs of foil to wrap neatly around the board. Secure foil tabs to the board with tape.

LEVELING THE CAKE

After the cake has cooled at least one hour, you'll need to level the top of the cake. This can be done using a serrated knife or the Cake Leveler (p. 154).

Using a Serrated Knife

Place the cake on a cake board, then place the board on a Trim 'N Turn Cake Turntable (p. 141). While slowly rotating the turntable, move the knife back and forth across the top of cake in a sawing motion to remove the crown. Try to keep knife level as you cut.

Using the Wilton Cake Leveler

Position the ends of the cutting wire (or feet on large leveler) into the notches at the desired height. With legs standing on the work surface, cut into the crusted edge using an easy sawing motion, then proceed by gently gliding wire through the cake.

TORTING THE CAKE

Torting adds extra height, drama and taste to the cake when the layers are filled with icing, pudding or fruit filling. A serrated knife or the Cake Leveler may be used to cut a cake into multiple layers.

Using a Serrated Knife

Divide cake sides and mark equal horizontal points with dots of icing or toothpicks all around. Place one hand on top of the cake to hold it steady and rotate the stand. While slowly turning the cake, move the knife back and forth to cut the cake along the measured marks. Repeat for each additional layer.

Using the Cake Leveler

Torting is easily accomplished with the Cake Leveler. Simply follow the same directions as for leveling.

Separating the Layers

Carefully slide the top torted layer onto a cake board to keep it rigid and safe from breakage. Repeat for each additional layer.

FILLING THE LAYERS

Fill a decorating bag with medium consistency icing and use a large round tip, like tip 12. Or simply use the coupler without mounting a tip.

Starting with the bottom layer, leveled side up, create a dam of icing just inside the edge of the cake (about ¾ in. high and ¼ in. from the outside edge). Fill with icing, preserves or pudding. Place next layer on top, level; repeat. Finish with top layer leveled side down.

ICING THE CAKE

For better results, use a revolving turntable like professional decorators do...see our Trim 'N Turn Cake Turntables on p. 141.

Using a Spatula

The trick to keeping crumbs out of your icing is gliding your spatula on the icing—*never allow it to touch the surface of the cake*. Place a large amount of thin consistency icing on the center of the cake.

Spread icing across the top, pushing toward edges. Smooth the top using the edge of the spatula.

Sweep the edge of the spatula from the rim of the cake to its center then lift it off and remove excess icing.

Cover the sides with icing. Smooth sides by holding the spatula upright with the edge against the icing and slowly spinning the turntable without lifting the spatula from the icing surface. Return excess icing to the bowl and repeat until sides are smooth.

Rotate the cake slightly and repeat the procedure, starting from a new point on the rim until you have covered the entire top surface. Smooth the center of the cake by leveling the icing with the edge of your spatula. For easier smoothing, it may help to dip the spatula into hot water, wipe dry and glide it across the entire surface. Set the cake aside and allow the icing to crust over for at least 15 minutes before decorating. At that point you may also lay Non-Stick Parchment Paper (p. 154) on the iced cake top and gently smooth with the palm of your hand.

Using a Decorating Tip

Trim a 16 in. Featherweight bag to fit tip 789. Fill bag half full with icing. Hold bag at 45° angle and lightly press tip against cake. Squeeze a ribbon of icing in a continuous spiral motion to cover cake top, with last ribbon forcing icing over edge of cake top.

To ice the sides, squeeze icing as you turn the cake slowly. Repeat the process until the entire cake side is covered.

Smooth sides and top with spatula, same as above.

Icing Basics

In this section, we've listed general descriptions of icings, their uses, qualities and consistencies. Use this information to determine the right icing for your cake. Refer to our recipes for homemade icings (p. 118) along with color instructions below, to create the look and taste you want.

ICING USAGE GUIDE

Icing Type	Flavor/Description	Consistency	Best Used For…	Coloring	Storage/Freshness	Special Information
Buttercream (Wilton Mix or homemade)	Sweet, buttery flavor. Tastes/looks great for most decorating.	Thin-to-stiff depending on amount of corn syrup or sugar added (sugar stiffens).	Icing cakes smooth. Borders, writing, flowers, decorations.	Yields all colors. Most deepen upon setting. Let set 2-3 hours for deep color. Some may fade in bright light.	Can be refrigerated in airtight container for 2 weeks. Iced cake stores at room temperature for 2-3 days.	Flowers remain soft enough to be cut with a knife.
Snow-White Buttercream (homemade)	Sweet, almond flavor. Ideal for wedding cakes.	Thin-to-stiff depending on amount of corn syrup or sugar added (sugar stiffens).	Icing cakes smooth. Borders, writing, flowers, decorations.	Yields truer colors due to pure white base color. Creates deep colors. Most colors deepen upon setting.	Can be refrigerated in airtight container for 2 weeks. Iced cake stores at room temperature for 2-3 days.	Air-dried flowers have translucent look. Flowers remain soft enough to be cut with knife.
Wilton Ready-To-Use Decorator White (4½ lb. tub)	Sweet, vanilla flavor. Convenient, ready-to-spread icing. Pure white color ideal for tinting.	Thin-to-medium. No need to thin for spreading.	Spreading on cakes right from the can. Piping stars, shells, messages and more.	Yields truer colors due to pure white base color. Creates deep colors. Most colors deepen upon setting.	Leftover icing can be refrigerated for 2 weeks. Iced cake stores at room temperature for 2-3 days.	Available for purchase through Wilton Yearbook, at www.wilton.com or any authorized Wilton retailer.
Wilton Ready-To-Use Decorator White (1 lb. can)	Sweet, vanilla flavor. Convenient, ready-to-spread icing. Pure white color ideal for tinting.	Stiff. Make roses right from the can.	Shells, stars, flowers— use from container. Icing cakes, writing, leaves—thin with milk, water or corn syrup.	Yields truer colors due to pure white base color. Creates deep colors. Most colors deepen upon setting.	Leftover icing can be refrigerated for 2 weeks. Iced cake stores at room temperature for 2-3 days.	Available for purchase through Wilton Yearbook, at www.wilton.com or any authorized Wilton retailer.
Wilton Ready-To-Use Decorator Chocolate (1 lb. can)	Sweet chocolate flavor. Convenient ready-to-spread icing.	Stiff. Make roses right from the can.	Shells, stars, flowers—use from container. Icing cakes, writing, leaves— thin with milk, water or corn syrup.	Recommended when black or brown icing is needed. Add a little black icing color to chocolate for a better tasting black icing.	Leftover icing can be refrigerated for 2 weeks. Iced cake stores at room temperature for 2-3 days.	Available for purchase through Wilton Yearbook, at www.wilton.com or any authorized Wilton retailer.
Royal (made with Wilton Meringue Powder)	Very sweet flavor. Dries candy-hard for lasting decorations.	Thin-to-stiff, depending on the amount of water added.	Flower making, figure piping, making flowers on wires. Decorating cookies and gingerbread houses.	Yields deep colors. Some colors may fade in bright light. Requires more icing color than buttercream to achieve the same intensity.	Icing can be stored in airtight, grease-free container at room temperature for 2 weeks. Air-dried decorations last for months.	Bowls and utensils must be grease-free. Cover icing with damp cloth to prevent crusting.
Rolled Fondant (homemade or Wilton Ready-To-Use Rolled Fondant)	Covers cakes with a perfectly smooth, satiny surface. Easy and fast to use. Knead in flavor of your choice.	Dough-like. Fondant is rolled out before being applied to cake. Stays semi-soft on cake.	Any firm-textured cake, pound cake or fruit cake. Cutting, molding and modeling decorations.	White yields pastels to deep colors. Wilton pre-colored fondant is also available in Multi Packs for fondant decorations in a variety of colors.	Excess can be stored 2 months in an airtight container. Do not refrigerate or freeze. Iced cake stores at room temperature for 3-4 days.	Prior to applying fondant, cake should be lightly covered with a glaze or buttercream icing to seal in freshness and moisture.
Whipped Icing Mix (Wilton Mix)	Light, delicate vanilla flavor. Holds shape like no other mix. **For chocolate icing**, add ½ cup of sifted cocoa powder.	Velvety, perfect for stars, roses, borders, garlands and writing.	Icing cakes. Most decorations. Toppings on pies, puddings, tarts and more.	Yields any color.	Can be refrigerated in airtight container. Iced cake stores at room temperature for 2-3 days.	Exclusive Wilton formula. Available for purchase through Wilton Yearbook, at www.wilton.com or any authorized Wilton retailer.
Stabilized Whipped Cream (homemade)	Creamy, delicate sweetness.	Light, thin-to-medium.	All cakes but especially those decorated with fruits. Borders, large tip work, writing.	Yields pastels only.	Use immediately. Iced cake must be refrigerated.	Texture remains soft on decorated cake.

COLORING ICING

Mixing Colors

Begin with white icing and use concentrated Icing Colors (p. 148) which will not affect your icing consistency. (Using ordinary liquid food colors can thin your icing and affect your ability to pipe certain decorations.) If you are tinting icing dark brown or black, begin with chocolate icing—your icing will not have the aftertaste that large amounts of icing color can produce. If you are tinting a large area red, use No-Taste Red.

Dip a fresh toothpick into the color, then swirl it into the icing. Add color a little at a time until you achieve the shade you desire. Always use a new toothpick each time you add color; you want to avoid getting icing in your jar of color. Blend the icing well with a spatula.

Consider the type of icing you are using when mixing color. Icing colors intensify or darken in buttercream icing about 1-2 hours after mixing. Royal icing requires more color than buttercream icing to achieve the same color intensity.

Always mix enough of each icing color to complete your entire cake. For example, if you are going to decorate a cake with pink flowers and borders, color enough icing for both. It

is difficult to duplicate an exact shade of any color, and you will want to keep your colors consistent on your cake.

Bag Striping Effects

You can easily pipe two-tone decorations just by adding a different color inside the bag before you put in your tinted icing. This is how you pipe flowers with natural light and dark tones or make a rainbow-colored clown suit to brighten up the party.

Brush Striping

Produces more intense multiple colors because it is done with straight icing color brushed into the bag. Apply one or more stripes of icing color with a decorating brush, then fill the bag with white or pastel-colored icing. As the icing is squeezed past the color, your decorations will come out striped.

Spatula Striping

Produces two-tone and realistic pastel tones for flowers and figure piping. It is done with pastel-colored icing, striped inside the decorating bag with a spatula. After striping, fill the bag with white icing or another shade of the same color as the striping. Squeeze out decorations with soft contrasts.

Brush Striping

Spatula Striping

MIXING SKIN SHADES

It's easy to create a wide variety of skin shades using various Wilton Icing Colors. Simply add desired color to white icing with a toothpick. If you wish to reach a shade lighter or darker than what is indicated, add slightly less or more of the icing color. Color listings for projects in this book reflect skin shade shown; feel free to choose your own shade.

1. To reach desired skin tone color, start with enough icing to cover the entire area, as matching shades later may be difficult.
2. Dip the end of a toothpick into the color or colors indicated, and swirl into icing and blend well.
3. Add color a little at a time until you achieve the shade you desire. Always use a new toothpick each time you add color to keep icing out of your jar of color.

Skin Shade Icing Colors

Skin Shade	Icing Colors
	Copper
	Ivory with a touch of Red
	Brown
	Brown with a touch of Red
	More brown, with a touch of Red

Three Essentials of Cake Decorating

Every decoration you make is the result of three things working together: the consistency of your icing, the position of the bag (that is, the way you are holding it) and the amount and type of pressure you apply to the bag. You'll know when you have everything right because you'll get perfect results time after time. This will take practice. The more you concentrate on perfecting these three essentials, the sooner you will achieve perfect results.

ICING CONSISTENCY

If the consistency of your icing is not right, your decorations will not be right either. Just a few drops of liquid can make a great deal of difference in your decorating results. Many factors can affect icing consistency, such as humidity, temperature, ingredients and equipment. You may try using different icing consistencies when decorating to determine what works best for you. As a general guideline, if you are having trouble creating the decorations you want and you feel your icing is too thin, add a little more confectioners' sugar; if you feel your icing is too thick, add a little more liquid. In royal icing recipes, if adding more than ½ cup confectioners' sugar to thicken icing, also add 1-2 additional teaspoons of Meringue Powder (p. 145).

Stiff icing is used for figure piping and stringwork and for decorations like roses, carnations and sweet peas with upright petals. If icing is not stiff enough, flower petals will droop. If icing cracks when piped out, icing is probably too stiff. Add light corn syrup to icing used for stringwork to give strings greater elasticity so they will not break.

Medium icing is used for decorations such as stars, shell borders and flowers with flat petals. If the icing is too stiff or too thin, you will not get the uniformity that characterizes these decorations.

Thin icing is used for decorations such as printing and writing, vines and leaves. Leaves will be pointier, vines will not break and writing will flow easily if you add 1-2 teaspoons light corn syrup to each cup of icing. Thin icing is used to ice cakes smooth. Begin with your prepared icing recipe, then add small amounts of the same liquid used in the recipe (usually milk or water) until the proper spreading consistency is reached.

CORRECT BAG POSITION

The way your decorations curl, point and lie depends not only on icing consistency but also on the way you hold the bag and the way you move it. Bag positions are described in terms of both angle and direction.

Angle

Angle refers to the position of the bag relative to the work surface. There are two basic angle positions, 90° (straight up) and 45° (halfway between vertical and horizontal).

90° angle
or straight up, perpendicular to the surface.

45° angle
or halfway between vertical and horizontal.

Direction

The angle in relation to the work surface is only half the story on bag position. The other half is the direction in which the back of the bag is pointed.

Correct bag direction is easiest to learn when you think of the back of the bag as the hour hand of a clock. When you hold the bag at a

45° angle to the surface, you can sweep out a circle with the back end of the bag by rolling your wrist and holding the end of the tip in the same spot. Pretend the circle you formed in the air is a clock face. The hours on the clock face correspond to the direction you point the back end of the bag.

Back of bag at 6:00   **Back of bag at 3:00**

The technique instructions in this Decorating Guide will list the correct direction for holding the bag. When the bag direction differs for left-handed decorators, that direction will be listed in parentheses. For example, when a bag is to be held at 3:00 for a right-handed decorator, it should be held at 9:00 for a left-handed decorator.

One more thing…since most decorating tip openings are the same shape all the way around, there's no right side and wrong side up when you're squeezing icing out of them. However, some tips, such as petal, ruffle, basketweave and leaf have irregularly shaped openings. For those you must watch your tip position as well as your bag position. If the tip opening must be in a special position, the instructions will tell you.

PRESSURE CONTROL

In addition to having the proper icing consistency and the correct bag position, you'll need to master three types of pressure control: heavy, medium and light. The size and uniformity of your icing designs are affected by the amount of pressure you apply to the bag and the steadiness of that pressure. (In other words, how you squeeze and relax your grip on the decorating bag.) Your goal is to learn to apply pressure so consistently that you can move the bag in a free and easy glide while just the right amount of icing flows through the tip. Practice will help you achieve this control.

Heavy Pressure   **Medium Pressure**   **Light Pressure**

Storing Cakes

Take some final precautions and store your cake the best way possible. After all, your time, effort and creativity have made it very special! Beware of the following factors, which can affect the look of your decorated cake.

Sunlight and fluorescent lighting will alter icing colors. Keep your cake stored in a covered box and out of direct sunlight and fluorescent lighting.

Humidity can soften royal icing, fondant and gum paste decorations. If you live in a climate with high humidity, prepare your royal icing using only pure cane confectioners' sugar (not beet sugar or dextrose), add less liquid and add 1 more teaspoon Meringue Powder (p. 145) to the recipe.

Heat can melt icing and cause decorations to droop. Keep your decorated cake as cool as possible and stabilize buttercream icing by adding 2 teaspoons Meringue Powder per recipe. Protect your cake by placing it in a clean, covered cake box. Avoid using foil or plastic wrap to cover a decorated cake—these materials can stick to icing and crush delicate decorations. The icing that covers your cake determines how it should be stored—in the refrigerator, at cool room temperature, or frozen, if storing for longer than 3 days. If you want to store your iced cake in a different way than noted, make a small test cake.

Icing type determines care. See chart on p. 113 for storage information.

NOTE: Cakes with thoroughly-dried royal icing decorations should be stored according to the type of icing that covers the cake. However, if royal icing decorations are to be put on a cake that will be frozen, it is recommended that these decorations be placed on the cake after thawing so that they don't bleed from condensation or become soft.

Transporting Tiered Cakes

Moving a tiered cake from one location to another does not have to be difficult. It can be quite easy! Following some simple guidelines ensures that your cake will arrive safely—whether you are traveling hundreds of miles or just a few.

Before Moving Cakes

Be certain the cake is constructed on a sturdy base made of three or more thicknesses of corrugated cardboard. Base tiers of very heavy cakes should be placed on a foamcore or plywood base, ½ in. thick. Cakes on pillars must be transported unassembled. Toppers, candles and ornaments should be removed from cakes when they are being moved. For stacked cakes, move the entire assembled cake. Or, for a larger quantity of tiers, transport unassembled and assemble at the reception. Be sure to have with you the equipment and icings you will need to finish any decorating needed after assembly at the reception.

For a cake which combines stacked and 2-plate construction, take tiers apart, keeping stacked tiers as units. Boxing the cake makes transportation easier. Not only does it protect the tiers from damage, but it keeps the tiers clean—free from dirt, dust and bugs. Place the boxes on carpet foam or a non-skid mat on a level surface in the vehicle to prevent shifting. Keep the boxes flat; never place on a car seat. Boxed cakes can also be transported in the trunk of the car, except in hot weather, because air conditioning will not reach the trunk area. It's also important to find out about the reception location before the event. Knowing what to expect when you arrive can make your delivery and setup so much easier. Call the reception hall a few days before the event to get an idea of the conditions you will encounter there. Ask whether the room is located upstairs or downstairs. Find out what is the best location for bringing the cake into the building. That way you can park in the right place the first time and minimize the distance your cake has to travel from your car. Also ask how far in advance the cake can be set up so that you can plan your day and reduce the stress.

At Your Destination

Before you bring in the cake from your car, walk the path you will have to travel to the set-up site. Be alert for any bumps along the way and note any tight spaces you will have to maneuver through. Make sure the cake table is level—it's a good idea to bring a level to check this on setup day. Request a cart on wheels to move the cake into the reception area. This is easier and safer than carrying by hand. Remove the cakes from the boxes on the reception table by cutting the sides of the boxes and sliding the cakes out. Bring along a repair kit, including extra icing, prepared decorating bags and tips, flowers and spatulas, in case it is necessary to make any repairs. Once the cake is assembled, take a picture to establish that the cake was in perfect condition when you left it.

In Pan

Take tiers apart if constructed in Center Column or Push-In Leg method. Leave columns or legs in place. Position the plates on crumpled foil or in shallow pans if they do not sit level. Remove pillars from tier plates; plates stay in position.

In Box

Place the cakes in clean, covered, sturdy boxes that are sized to the base board of each cake. This prevents shifting within the box and possibly crushing the sides of the cake. If the box is too big, roll pieces of masking tape sticky side out and attach to the inside bottom of the box. Position the cake base on top of the tape, securing the base in the box. For taller decorations, prop up box top and sides, secure with masking tape.

On Non-Skid Foam

If tiers cannot be boxed, they can be transported on large pieces of non-skid foam. Place the foam on the floor of the vehicle, then carefully place the tiers centered on each piece of foam. Remove any ornament or fragile decorations before transporting.

Cake Baking and Serving Guides

The charts below are based on baking recommendations from the Wilton Test Kitchen; your results may vary depending on oven performance or altitude in your area. For large cakes, always check for doneness after they have baked for 1 hour.

Serving amounts are based on party-sized portions of 1.5 x 2 in. or smaller wedding-sized portions of approximately 1 x 2 in. Cakes from 3 to 6 in. high, baked in the same size pan, would yield the same number of servings because they follow the same pattern of cutting. Cakes shorter than 3 in. would yield half the number of servings indicated for that pan. Number of servings are intended as a guide only.

Icing amounts are very general and will vary with consistency, thickness applied and tips used. Icing amounts allow for top and bottom borders.

4 IN. HIGH CAKES (using 2 in. high pans)

The figures for 2 in. pans are based on a 2-layer, 4 in. high cake. Fill pans ½ to ⅔ full.

PAN SHAPE	SIZE	NUMBER SERVINGS PARTY	NUMBER SERVINGS WEDDING	CUPS BATTER 1 LAYER, 2 IN.	BAKING TEMP. (F.)	BAKING TIME MINUTES	APPROX. CUPS ICING TO ICE AND DECORATE
Round	6 in.	12	12	2	350°	25-30	3
	8 in.	20	24	3½	350°	30-35	4
	9 in.	24	32	5½	350°	30-35	4½
	10 in.	28	38	6	350°	35-40	5
	12 in.	40	56	7½	350°	35-40	6
	14 in.	63	78	10	325°	50-55	7½
	16 in.	77	100	15	325°	55-60	9
Square	6 in.	12	18	2	350°	25-30	3½
	8 in.	20	32	4	350°	35-40	4½
	10 in.	30	50	6	350°	35-40	6
	12 in.	48	72	10	350°	40-45	7½
	14 in.	63	98	13½	325°	45-50	9½
	16 in.	80	128	15½	325°	50-55	11
Heart	6 in.	8	14	1½	350°	25-30	3½
	8 in.	18	22	3½	350°	30-35	4½
	9 in.	20	28	4	350°	30-35	6
	10 in.	24	38	5	350°	30-35	8½
	12 in.	34	56	8	325°	45-50	9
	14 in.	48	72	10	325°	45-50	10
	15 in.	50	74	11	325°	40-45	11
	16 in.	64	94	12½	325°	40-45	12
Petal	6 in.	6	8	1½	350°	25-30	4
	9 in.	14	18	3½	350°	35-40	6
	12 in.	38	40	7	350°	35-40	9
	15 in.	48	64	12	325°	50-55	11
Hexagon	6 in.	10	12	1¾	350°	30-35	3
	9 in.	20	26	3½	350°	35-40	5
	12 in.	34	40	6	350°	40-45	6
	15 in.	48	70	11	325°	40-45	9
Oval	7.75 x 5.5 in.	9	13	2½	350°	25-30	3
	10.75 x 7.8 in.	20	26	5	350°	25-30	4
	13.5 x 9.8 in.	30	45	8	350°	35-40	5½
	16.5 x 12.4 in.	44	70	11	325°	40-45	7½
Sheet	7 x 11 in.	24	32	5½	350°	30-35	5
	9 x 13 in.	36	50	7	350°	35-40	6
	11 x 15 in.	54	74	11	350°	35-40	8
	12 x 18 in.	72	98	14	325°	45-50	10
Paisley	9 x 6 in.	9	13	3	350°	35-40	5
	12.75 x 9 in.	28	38	7	350°	45-50	6
	17 x 12 in.	40	56	10½	325°	55-60	8
Diamond	10.25 x 7.4	12	18	3¼	350°	20-25	2½
	15 x 11	20	32	7¼	350°	40-45	5
	19.25 x 14.25	42	66	13¼	350°	65-70	8

3 IN. HIGH CAKES (using 3 in. high pans)

The figures for 3 in. pans are based on a 1-layer cake which is torted and filled to reach 3 in. high; fill pans ½ full.

PAN SHAPE	SIZE	NUMBER SERVINGS PARTY	NUMBER SERVINGS WEDDING	CUPS BATTER 1 LAYER, 2 IN.	BAKING TEMP.	BAKING TIME MINUTES	APPROX. CUPS ICING TO ICE AND DECORATE
Round	6 in.	12	12	3	350°	35-40	3
	8 in.	20	24	5	350°	55-60	4
	10 in.	28	38	8	325°	65-75	5
	12 in.	40	56	10½	325°	60-65	6
	14 in.	63	78	15	325°	75-85	8
	16 in.	77	100	18	325°	75-85	9
	18 in. Half, 2 in. layer	110*	146*	9**	325°	60-65	10½
	18 in. Half, 3 in. layer	110*	146*	12**	325°	60-65	10½
Sheet	9 x 13 in.	36	50	11½	325°	70-75	5
	11 x 15 in.	54	74	16	325°	80-85	6½
	12 x 18 in.	72	98	20	325°	85-90	8
Square	8 in.	20	32	6½	350°	60-65	4½
	10 in.	30	50	9	325°	65-75	6
	12 in.	48	72	14	325°	65-75	7½
	14 in.	63	98	19	325°	65-75	9½
Contour	7 in.	6	11	3½	350°	45-50	2
	9 in.	11	17	5½	350°	45-50	2½
	11 in.	16	24	8	325°	80-85	3
	13 in.	22	39	13	325°	75-80	4
	15 in.	32	48	16	325°	75-80	5

For pans 10 in. and larger, we recommend using a heating core (p. 158) to insure even baking. Use 2 cores for 18-in. pans.
*Two half rounds. **For each half round pan.
For additional pan information, check out www.wilton.com

General Cake Cutting Guides

The diagrams below will give you a general plan for cutting the most popular cake shapes. They will help you serve more attractive, uniform pieces while reaching your targeted number of servings. Diagrams show only one size in each shape; you will use the same general technique to cut each size cake in that shape.

WEDDING CAKES—1 x 2 in. slices

The diagrams show how to cut popular shaped wedding tiers into slices approximately 1 x 2 in. and 2 layers high (about 4 in.) For cakes shorter than 3 in. you will need to cut wider slices to serve a proper portion; even if a larger serving size is desired, the order of cutting is still the same. Before cutting the cake, remove the top tier, which is usually saved for the first anniversary and is not included in our serving amounts for wedding cakes in this book. Begin by cutting the 2nd tier, followed by the 3rd, 4th and so on.

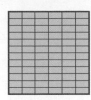

12 in.

Square Tiers:
Move in 2 in. from the outer edge and cut vertically, top to bottom. Slice and serve 1 in. pieces of cake. Now move in another 2 in. and repeat process until the entire tier is cut.

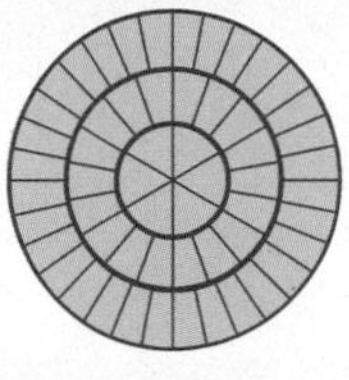

12 in.

Round Tiers:
Move in 2 in. from the tier's outer edge and cut a circle. Slice and serve 1 in. pieces from around the circle. Now move in another 2 in. and cut another circle. Repeat process until the tier is completely cut. The center core of each tier and the small top tier can be cut into 4ths, 6ths, or more, depending on size.

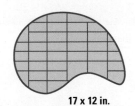

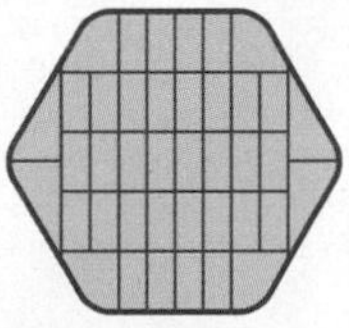

17 x 12 in.

Paisley Tiers:
Move in 2 in. from the outer edge and cut across. Slice and serve 1 in. pieces of cake, similar to oval tiers as diagram shows. Now move in another 2 in., repeat process until the entire tier is cut.

Heart Tiers:
Divide the tiers vertically into 2 in. wide rows. Within rows, slice and serve 1 in. pieces of cake.

12 in.

Hexagon Tiers:
Move in 2 in. from the outer edge and cut across. Slice and serve 1 in. pieces of cake. Now move in another 2 in., repeat process until the entire tier is cut.

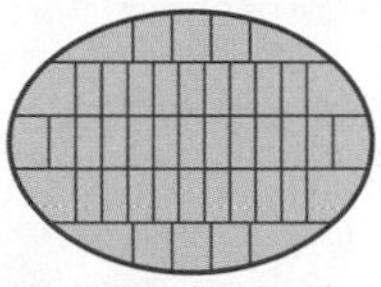

13.5 x 9.8 in.

Oval Tiers:
Move in 2 in. from the outer edge and cut across. Slice and serve 1 in. pieces of cake. Now move in another 2 in., repeat process until the entire tier is cut.

Petal Tiers:
Cut similar to round tiers as diagram shows.

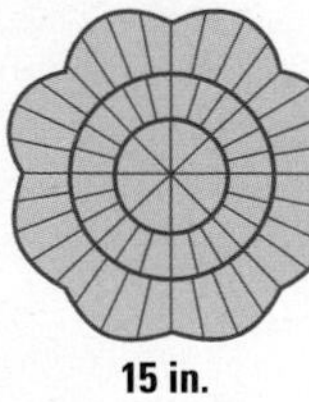

15 in.

Diamond Tiers:
Move in 2 in. from any outer edge and cut across. Slice and serve 1 in. pieces of cake. Now move in another 2 in. and repeat process until the entire tier is cut.

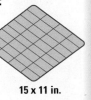

15 x 11 in.

PARTY CAKES— 1.5 x 2 in. slices

Follow the diagrams above to cut party cakes (from 3 to 6 in. high), but adjust for the larger party-size slices. For cakes shorter than 3 in. you will need to cut wider slices to serve a proper portion; even if a larger serving size is desired the order of cutting is still the same.

Rounds:
To cut round cakes, move in 2 in. from the cake's outer edge; cut a circle and then slice approximately 1.5 in. pieces within the circle. Now move in another 2 in. and cut another circle; slice approximately 1.5 in. pieces. Continue until the cake is completely cut. Note: 6 in. diameter cakes should be cut in wedges, without a center circle. Cut petal and hexagon cakes similar to round cakes.

Squares:
To cut square cakes, move in 2 in. from the outer edge and cut top to bottom, then slice approximately 1.5 in. pieces. Now move in another 2 in. and continue until the entire cake is cut.

Sheets:
Cut sheet cakes similar to square cakes.

Tiered Cake Construction

*There are many methods of constructing tiered cakes. Here are some used in this book. Visit **www.wilton.com** for more construction methods.*

TO PREPARE CAKE FOR ASSEMBLY

Place base tier on a sturdy base plate of 3 or more thicknesses of corrugated cardboard. For heavy cakes, use foamcore or plywood ½ in. thick. Base can be covered with Fanci-Foil Wrap and trimmed with Tuk-'N-Ruffle or use Ruffle Boards (p. 241). Each tier of your cake must be on a cake circle or board cut to fit. Place a few strokes of icing on boards to secure cake. Fill and ice layers before assembly.

Adding Dowel Rods to Tiered Cakes

Use the upper tier for size reference when determining dowel rod placement. All the dowel rods must be placed within the area you will mark (see steps below) to provide adequate support.

1. Center a cake board the same size as the tier above it on base tier and press it gently into icing to imprint an outline. Remove. Use this outline to guide the insertion of the dowel rods.

2. Insert one dowel rod into cake straight down to the cake board. Make a knife scratch on the rod to mark the exact height. Pull dowel rod out.

3. Cut the suggested number of rods (see note below) the exact same length, using the mark on the first one as a guide.

4. Insert rods into tier, spacing evenly 1½ inches in from the imprinted outline. Push straight down until each touches the cake board. Repeat this procedure for every stacked or pillared tier on the cake.

NOTE: The larger and more numerous the tiers, the more dowels needed. If the tier above is 10 in. or less, use six ¼ in. wooden dowels. Use 8 dowel rods for 16 in. and 18 in. cakes; on these larger tiers, use ½ in. plastic dowel rods in the base tier. When using white plastic dowel rods that are wider and provide more support, the number needed may be less.

Stacked Construction

Stacking is the most architectural method of tiered cake construction. Tiers are placed directly on top of one another and pillars are not used. Cakes are supported and stabilized by dowel rods and cake boards.

1. Dowel rod all tiers except top tier.

2. Position the middle tier on the base tier, centering exactly.*

3. Repeat with the top tier.

4. To stabilize tiers further, sharpen one end of a long dowel rod and push it through all tiers and cake boards to the base of the bottom tier. To decorate, start at the top and work down.

*Finely shredded coconut or confectioners' sugar, placed in area where cake circles or plastic plates will rest, helps prevent icing on the cake from sticking.

Separator Plate (2-Plate) and Pillar Construction

This most dramatic method features 2, 3 or more single cakes towered together. Use separator plates and pillars (p. 237-239). Check pillars and plates for correct fit before constructing your cake.

1. Set cake tiers on separator plates 2 in. larger in diameter than cakes.

2. Dowel rod cakes and position separator plates on tiers with feet up. (Note: Connect only same size separator plates with pillars.)

3. Position pillars over feet on separator plates.

4. Carefully set cake plate on pillars. Continue adding tiers this way.**

**Assemble cakes when you arrive at the reception or party.

Push-In Pillar Construction

Simple assembly—no dowel rods needed! Use any type of Wilton push-in pillars and plates (p. 237). Check pillars and plates for correct fit before constructing your cake.

1. Mark tier for push-in pillar placement. Use the separator plate for the next tier above, gently pressing it onto the tier, feet down, making sure it is centered. Lift plate away. The feet will leave marks on the icing to guide the position of pillars when you assemble the tier. Repeat this process for each tier, working from largest to smallest tier. The top tier is left unmarked.

2. Place each tier on its separator plate, securing with icing.

3. Position push-in pillars at marks, and insert into tiers. Push straight down until pillars touch the cake plate.

4. To assemble, start with the tier above the base tier. Place the feet of the separator plate on the pillar openings. Continue adding tiers in the same way until the cake is completely assembled.**

Center Column Construction (Tall Tier Stand) (p. 239)

1. Use boards the same size as tiers, or if tiers are shaped, cut boards to fit. Make a waxed paper pattern for each tier except the top tier in order to find the exact center for the columns. Fold the pattern in quarters. Snip the point to make a center hole. Test the hole for size by slipping it over a column, adjust size if necessary. Trace hole pattern on prepared cake board and cut out. Also cut a hole in the top tier board to allow for the column cap nut. Save patterns for marking cake tops later.

2. The base tier of the cake will rest on a 14, 16 or 18 in. plate. (18 in. plate is footed. Do not use a bottom plate smaller than 14 in.) To add legs to bottom plate, turn it upside down; using extra-strength glue designed for plastic, attach the six legs, positioning the legs over each of the ribs on the plate.

3. Prepare and ice tiers and position on prepared cake boards. Make the center holes for the columns in all tiers except the top tier. Mark the top of the cakes with corresponding waxed paper pattern. Cut the hole by pressing a Cake Corer Tube or a Hidden Pillar (p. 237) through the tier right down to the bottom. Hold the corer upright, remove cake corer and push the upper part down to eject the cake center.

4. Screw in a column to the prepared base plate and bottom column bolt from underneath the plate. Slip the next size tier on its plate over the column.

5. Add a second column and position the next size tier on its plate, slipping it over the column. Finally, add on the top plate only, securing the top column nut. Place the top tier on the plate and decorate bottom border.**

Globe Pillar Set Construction

These elegant pearl-look globes (p. 238) are available in separate sets of four 2 in., 2½ in. or 3 in. globes. The 3 in. globes are to be used to support the base cake only. They have a reinforced center channel which eliminates the need for pillars. The 2 and 2½ in. sets should be used with 9 in. "Hidden" Pillars (included in set); do not use these sets to support the base cake. Your cake design may use a base board instead of the 3 in. globes to support the base cake as shown below.

1. Position separator plate holding base cake on 3 in. Globe Base Set or a thick base board. Using the separator plate which will hold the cake above, mark base cake for pillar placement (see Push-In Pillar construction, p. 116). Lift plate away.

2. Insert pillars through cake centered over marked area to rest on its separator plate or base board. Place the correct size globe (2½ in. for cake shown here) over the pillars. Mark pillars where they extend above globes. The cut pillars should be equal to the height of the base cake plus the height of each globe.

3. Trim pillars at markings with craft knife or serrated edge knife.

4. Insert pillars in base cake. Position globes over pillars.

5. Position the tier above on globes.

6. Add additional sets for more tiers.

Tailored Tiers Construction

Our Tailored Tiers Cake Display Set (p. 238) features fabric-wrapped separators which add great texture to your tiered design. The top 2 tiers are decorated on same-size boards, then transported to the reception on larger boards, so that cakes can be easily transferred to the separator plates during assembly. Bottom borders are then added to these tiers. The recommended display for Tailored Tiers separators includes a 14 in. base cake, a 10 in. center cake and a 6 in. top cake.

1. Ice cakes; place 14 in. base cake on 16 in. base board wrapped in foil or 16 in. Silver Cake Base (p. 241). Place 10 in. center and 6 in. top cakes on same size boards. Mark 14 in. and 10 in. cakes for placement of dowel rods. Center the 8 in. plate from the Tailored Tiers set on top of the 14 in. cake and press it gently into icing to imprint an outline. Remove. Use this outline to guide the insertion of dowel rods.

2. Dowel rod 14 in. cake (see page 116). Place the 6 in. plate from set on top of the 10 in. cake and repeat process for marking and inserting dowel rods. Complete decorating on cakes, except bottom borders of 10 in. center and 6 in. top cakes, which will be done at reception. Attach 10 in. and 6 in. cakes to larger boards before transferring to reception.

3. Place the 12 in. plate (spikes up) on table. Center the large (7¼ in.) separator over the plate and press down over the spikes. Position one 8 in. plate (spikes down) on top of the large separator. Place the second 8 in. plate (spikes up) on table. Center the small (4¼ in.) separator over the plate and press down over the spikes. Position the 6 in. plate (spikes down) on top of the small separator.

4. At reception: Position the large separator, with 8 in. plate on bottom and 12 in. plate on top, on the base cake. Remove 10 in. and 6 in. cakes from their larger boards. Position 10 in. cake on large separator.

5. Add bottom border to 10 in. cake. Position the small separator, with 6 in. plate on bottom and 8 in. plate on top, on the 10 in. cake. Position 6 in. cake on small separator. Add bottom border.

To Use Acetate Wrap for Tailored Tiers

1. Insert photos, patterned paper or fabric in pockets of acetate wrap. Trim inserted items as needed to fit.
2. Wrap acetate around separator and fasten hook and loop ends.

Alternate 2-Plate Set-Ups

The Fluted Bowl and Spiral Separator Sets shown below are assembled similar to 2-Plate and Pillar Construction (p. 116)—the separators provide support instead of pillars; each set includes 2 separator plates. Cakes must still use dowel rods to support cakes and secure the separators.

Fluted Bowl Separator Set (p. 238)

Spiral Separator Set (p. 238)

Dowel rod base cake as for 2-Plate & Pillar Construction. Position smaller plate from set on base cake (spikes up). Position Fluted Bowl or Spiral Separator over spikes. Position next tier on larger plate from set. Position plate (spikes down) on separator.

Recipes

The cakes, cookies and other desserts in this Yearbook were made using our favorite kitchen-tested recipes. Follow these instructions for decorated desserts that look and taste their best!

ICING RECIPES

Buttercream Icing (Medium consistency)*

½ cup solid vegetable shortening
½ cup (1 stick) butter or margarine, softened
1 teaspoon Clear Vanilla Extract (p. 145)
4 cups sifted confectioners' sugar (about 1 lb.)
2 tablespoons milk

In large bowl, cream shortening and butter with electric mixer. Add vanilla. Gradually add sugar, one cup at a time, beating well on medium speed. Scrape sides and bottom of bowl often. When all sugar has been mixed in, icing will appear dry. Add milk and beat at medium speed until light and fluffy. Keep bowl covered with a damp cloth until ready to use. For best results, keep icing bowl in refrigerator when not in use. Refrigerated in an airtight container, this icing can be stored 2 weeks. Rewhip before using.

Makes about 3 cups.

For thin (spreading) consistency icing, add 2 tablespoons light corn syrup, water or milk.

For Pure White Icing (stiff consistency), omit butter; substitute an additional ½ cup vegetable shortening for butter and ½ teaspoon No-Color Butter Flavor (p. 145). Add up to 4 tablespoons light corn syrup, water or milk to thin for icing cakes.

Chocolate Buttercream Icing

Add ¾ cup cocoa powder (or three 1 oz. squares unsweetened chocolate, melted) and an additional 1-2 tablespoons milk to buttercream icing. Mix until well blended. For a unique change of pace, substitute ⅛ to ¼ teaspoon Wilton Candy Flavors (p. 199) for vanilla extract.

Chocolate Mocha Icing: Substitute brewed strong coffee for milk in Chocolate Buttercream recipe.

Darker Chocolate Icing: Add an additional ¼ cup cocoa powder (or 1 additional 1 oz. square unsweetened chocolate, melted) and 1 additional tablespoon milk to Chocolate Buttercream Icing.

Snow-White Buttercream* Icing (Stiff consistency)

⅔ cup plus 3 tablespoons water, divided
¼ cup Meringue Powder (p. 145)
12 cups sifted confectioners' sugar (about 3 lbs.), divided
1¼ cups solid vegetable shortening
3 tablespoons light corn syrup
¾ teaspoon salt
¾ teaspoon No-Color Almond Extract (p. 145)
¾ teaspoon Clear Vanilla Extract (p. 145)
½ teaspoon No-Color Butter Flavor (p. 145)

In large bowl, combine ⅔ cup water and meringue powder; whip with electric mixer at high speed until peaks form. Add 4 cups sugar, one cup at a time, beating at low speed after each addition. Add remaining 8 cups sugar and 3 tablespoons water, shortening and corn syrup in 3 additions, blending well after each. Add salt and flavorings; beat at low speed until smooth.

Makes about 7 cups.

For thin (spreading) consistency icing, add up to 4 more tablespoons each water and corn syrup.

NOTE: Recipe may be doubled or halved.

Royal Icing

3 tablespoons Meringue Powder (p. 145)
4 cups sifted confectioners' sugar (about 1 lb.)
6 tablespoons water [1]

Beat all ingredients at low speed for 7-10 minutes (10-12 minutes at high speed for portable mixer) until icing forms peaks. Makes about 3 cups.

[1] When using large countertop mixer or for stiffer icing, use 1 tablespoon less water.

Thinned Royal Icing: To thin for pouring, add 1 teaspoon water per cup of royal icing. Use grease-free spoon or spatula to stir slowly. Add ½ teaspoon water at a time until you reach proper consistency.

Stabilized Whipped Cream Icing

½ pint (1 cup) heavy whipping cream
2 tablespoons confectioners' sugar
2 tablespoons Piping Gel (p. 145)
½ teaspoon Clear Vanilla Extract (p. 145)

Combine whipping cream and sugar in mixing bowl. Whip to soft peak stage. Add Piping Gel and vanilla, then continue to whip until stiff peaks form. Do not overbeat. Makes 1½ to 2 cups.

As an alternative, you can use frozen non-dairy whipped topping or packaged topping mix. Thaw frozen whipped topping in refrigerator before coloring or using for decorating. Use packaged topping mix immediately after preparing. Do not allow either to stay at room temperature, as it becomes too soft for decorating. Store decorated cake in refrigerator until ready to serve.

Heated Wilton Ready-To-Use Decorator Icing (p. 145)

Open icing container, remove foil. Microwave at 30% (Defrost) Power for 20-30 seconds, stirring at least once, until ready to pour. If a microwave is unavailable, icing container can be heated on a warming tray or in a pan of hot water on a stove.

Color Flow Icing Recipe (full-strength for outlining)

¼ cup + 1 teaspoon water
4 cups sifted confectioners' sugar (about 1 lb.)
2 tablespoons Color Flow Mix (p. 145)

With electric mixer, using grease-free utensils, blend all ingredients on low speed for 5 minutes. If using hand mixer, use high speed. Color flow icing "crusts" quickly, so keep bowl covered with a damp cloth while using. Stir in desired icing color. Makes about 2 cups.

Thinned Color Flow: To fill in an outlined area, the recipe above must be thinned with ½ teaspoon of water per ¼ cup of icing (just a few drops at a time as you near proper consistency). Use grease-free spoon or spatula to stir slowly. Color flow is ready for filling in outlines when a small amount dropped into the mixture takes a count of ten to disappear.

NOTE: Color flow designs take a long time to dry, so plan to do your color flow piece up at least 2 or 3 days in advance.

Poured Cookie Icing

This icing dries to a shiny, hard finish. Great to use as icing or to outline and fill in with tip 2 or 3.

1 cup sifted confectioners' sugar
2 teaspoons milk
2 teaspoons light corn syrup

Place sugar and milk in bowl. Stir until thoroughly mixed. Add corn syrup; mix well. For filling in areas, use thinned icing (add small amounts of light corn syrup until desired consistency is reached). Makes about ½ cup.

COOKIE RECIPES

Roll-Out Cookies

1 cup (2 sticks) unsalted butter, softened
1½ cups granulated sugar
1 egg
1½ teaspoons Clear Vanilla Extract (p. 145)
½ teaspoon No-Color Almond Extract (p. 145)
2¾ cups all-purpose flour
2 teaspoons baking powder
1 teaspoon salt

Preheat oven to 400°F. In large bowl, beat butter and sugar with electric mixer until light and fluffy. Add egg and extracts; mix well. Combine flour, baking powder and salt; add to butter mixture 1 cup at a time, mixing after each addition. Do not chill dough. Divide dough into 2 balls. On a floured surface, roll each ball into a circle approximately 12 in. wide and ⅛ in. thick. Dip cookie cutter in flour before each use. Bake cookies on ungreased cookie sheet 6-7 minutes or until cookies are lightly browned.

Makes about 3 dozen cookies. Recipe may be doubled.

Spritz Cookies

1½ cups (3 sticks) butter, softened
1 cup granulated sugar
1 egg
2 tablespoons milk
1 teaspoon Clear Vanilla Extract (p. 145)
½ teaspoon No-Color Almond Extract (p. 145)
3½ cups all-purpose flour
1 teaspoon baking powder

Preheat oven to 375°F. In large bowl, beat butter and sugar with electric mixer until light and fluffy. Add egg, milk, extracts; mix well. Combine flour and baking powder; gradually add to butter mixture, mixing to make a smooth dough. Do not chill. Place dough into cookie press and press cookies onto ungreased cookie sheet. Bake 10-12 minutes or until lightly browned around edges. Remove cookies from cookie sheet; cool on cooling grid. Makes 7-8 dozen cookies.

Grandma's Gingerbread

5 to 5½ cups all-purpose flour
1 teaspoon baking soda
1 teaspoon salt
2 teaspoons ground ginger
2 teaspoons ground cinnamon
1 teaspoon ground nutmeg
1 teaspoon ground cloves
1 cup solid vegetable shortening
1 cup granulated sugar
1¼ cups unsulphured molasses[2]
2 eggs, beaten

Preheat oven to 375°F. Thoroughly mix flour, baking soda, salt and spices. Melt shortening in large saucepan. Cool slightly. Add sugar, molasses and eggs to saucepan; mix well. Add 4 cups dry ingredients and mix well. Turn mixture onto lightly floured surface. Knead in remaining dry ingredients by hand. Add a little more flour, if necessary, to make firm dough. On floured surface, roll out ⅛ to ¼ in. thick for cut-out cookies. Bake on ungreased cookie sheet, small and medium-sized cookies for 6-10 minutes, large cookies for 10-15 minutes. Makes 40 medium-sized cookies.

NOTE: If you're not going to use your gingerbread dough right away, wrap in plastic and refrigerate. Refrigerated dough will keep for a week.

[2] Substitute 1¼ cups light corn syrup for molasses to make Blonde Gingerbread.

SPECIALTY RECIPES

Chocolate Mousse

1 envelope unflavored gelatin
¼ cup liquid (water, liqueur, strong coffee)
1 package (3.4 oz.) regular chocolate pudding mix NOT INSTANT
1½ cups milk
6 ounces bittersweet or semi-sweet chocolate
1 cup heavy whipping cream
¼ cup confectioners' sugar

In small bowl, sprinkle gelatin over liquid; let stand until softened, about 5 minutes. Set aside.

In medium saucepan, whisk together pudding mix and milk. Bring to a boil, stirring constantly; remove from heat. Add chocolate and softened gelatin; stir or whisk until smooth. Transfer to bowl; place bowl in another bowl filled with ice. Whisk until very cool and thick. Whip cream with sugar; fold into pudding mixture. Chill until thickened before piping or ready to serve.

Makes about 4 cups.

For Mocha Mousse:
Use ¼ cup strong coffee for liquid.
Substitute vanilla pudding mix for chocolate.
Reduce chocolate to 3 ounces.
If desired, add 1 teaspoon instant coffee for extra coffee flavor.

Shortbread Cookies

Use with Push 'N Print Cutter Sets (p. 205).

1½ cups (3 sticks) butter, softened
1 cup granulated sugar
½ teaspoon salt
6 egg yolks
2 teaspoons Pure Vanilla Extract
4 cups all-purpose flour

In large bowl, cream butter, sugar and salt with electric mixer until light and fluffy. Add egg yolks one at a time, mixing well after each addition. Add vanilla. Add flour: mix just until combined. (**Note:** Dough can be tinted with Wilton Icing Color. Add small amounts until desired color is reached.) Divide dough in half. Press dough to flatten; wrap with plastic wrap. Refrigerate at least 2 hours or overnight.

Preheat oven to 375°F. Work with one dough disk at a time. Let chilled dough stand at room temperature for 10 minutes. Lightly flour work surface and roll dough ⅛ to ¼ in. thick. Depress imprint disk into flour, then cut and imprint cookies. Gather scraps and roll dough again to make more cookies. For best results, depress disk into flour after each use.

Carefully transfer cookies to an ungreased cookie sheet, leaving 1 in. between cookies. Bake 14-16 minutes or until edges are lightly browned. Remove cookies from cookie sheet and cool completely on cooling grid.

Makes about 2 dozen cookies.

Sugar Cookies (for pan-shaped cookies)

1 cup (2 sticks) butter, softened
1½ cups granulated sugar
1 egg
1½ teaspoons Vanilla Extract (p. 145)
½ teaspoon Almond Extract (optional) (p. 145)
2¾ cups all-purpose flour
1 teaspoon salt

Preheat oven to 350°F. Lightly spray pan or mold cavities with vegetable pan spray.

In large bowl, beat butter and sugar with electric mixer at medium speed until well blended. Beat in egg and extracts; mix well. Combine flour and salt; add to butter mixture. Beat until well blended. Press dough into prepared mold or pan, filling to ¼ in. deep.

Bake 12-15 minutes or until light brown around edges. Cool in pan 10 minutes. Carefully remove cookies. Cool completely on cooling grid. Makes about 3 dozen cookies.

Spooky Popcorn

½ cup granulated sugar
½ cup unpopped popcorn
¼ cup vegetable oil
Leaf Green, Lemon Yellow Icing Colors

Stir all ingredients together in popcorn popper or in heavy pan on stovetop. Pop and serve.

CANDY RECIPE

Basic Ganache and Truffles

14 oz. Candy Melts®* (p. 196)
½ cup heavy whipping cream

Chop candy (you can use a food processor). Heat whipping cream in saucepan just to boiling point. Do not boil. Remove from heat and add chopped candy, stir until smooth and glossy.

Whipped Ganache: Follow recipe above, using 1 cup whipping cream. Allow mixture to set and cool to room temperature (mixture will have the consistency of pudding; this may take 1-2 hours). Whip on high speed with an electric mixer until light and soft peaks form.

Truffles: Add 1 tablespoon liqueur for flavor, if desired. Stir until smooth and creamy. Refrigerate until firm. Roll into 1 in. diameter balls. Can be used as center for dipped candies, served plain or rolled in nuts, coconut or cocoa powder. Store truffles in refrigerator up to 3 weeks. Makes about 2 dozen (1 in.) balls.

Ganache Glaze: If mixture is too thick, add 1 to 2 tablespoons whipping cream. Position cake on wire rack over drip pan. Pour glaze onto center and work out toward edges.

NOTE: Cake may be iced first in buttercream. Let icing set, then pour on ganache glaze. If cake has a perfect surface, no other icing is needed.

*Changes in Wilton's traditional recipes have been made due to Trans Fat Free Shortening replacing Hydrogenated Shortening

ROLLED FONDANT AND GUM PASTE RECIPES

Fondant is rolled out and used as a covering for any firm-textured cake, pound cake or fruit cake, which is traditionally first covered with a layer of marzipan to seal in flavor and moistness of the cake. A light layer of buttercream icing or apricot glaze may also be used. Cakes covered with rolled fondant can be decorated with royal or buttercream icing. Wilton also offers convenient Ready-To-Use Rolled Fondant (p. 149) for easy-to-handle fondant with no mixing.

Rolled Fondant

1 tablespoon plus 2 teaspoons
  unflavored gelatin
¼ cup cold water
½ cup Wilton Glucose (p. 149)
2 tablespoons solid vegetable shortening
1 tablespoon Wilton Glycerin (p. 149)
Icing color and flavoring, as desired
8 cups sifted confectioners' sugar
  (about 2 lbs.)

Combine gelatin and cold water; let stand until thick. Place gelatin mixture in top of double boiler and heat until dissolved. Add glucose, mix well. Stir in shortening and just before completely melted, remove from heat. Add glycerin, flavoring and color. Cool until lukewarm. Next, place 4 cups confectioners' sugar in a bowl and make a well. Pour the lukewarm gelatin mixture into the well and stir with a wooden spoon, mixing in sugar and adding more, a little at a time, until stickiness disappears. Knead in remaining sugar. Knead until the fondant is smooth, pliable and does not stick to your hands. If fondant is too soft, add more sugar; if too stiff, add water (a drop at a time). Use fondant immediately or store in airtight container in a cool, dry place. Do not refrigerate or freeze. When ready to use, knead again until soft. This recipe makes approx. 36 oz., enough to cover a 10 x 4 in. round cake.

Extra-Firm Rolled Fondant

Use this recipe for a fondant with the extra body and pliability ideal for making drapes, swags and elaborate decorations.

1 to 2 teaspoons Gum-Tex (p. 149)
24 oz. Ready-To-Use Rolled Fondant (p. 149)
Knead Gum-Tex into fondant until smooth. Store in an airtight container or tightly wrapped in plastic.

Gum Paste

Clay-like gum paste can be rolled thinner than fondant for finer detail. Gum paste dries hard and is meant for decoration only; remove from cake before serving. For perfectly mixed gum paste whenever you need it, try Wilton Ready-To-Use Gum Paste (p. 149).

1 tablespoon Gum-Tex (p. 149)
3 cups sifted confectioners' sugar
  (about ¾ lb.)
1 heaping tablespoon Glucose (p. 149)
4 tablespoons warm water
1 cup sifted confectioners' sugar
  (save until ready to use)

In a large bowl, mix Gum-Tex into 3 cups confectioners' sugar. Make a well in the center and set aside. Mix water and glucose in a glass measuring cup and blend; heat in microwave on high for about 30 seconds until mixture is clear. Pour into well of 3 cups confectioners' sugar and mix until well blended (mixture will be very soft). Place mixture in a plastic bag and seal tightly; let mixture rest at room temperature for 8 hours or overnight. Knead remaining confectioners' sugar into gum paste when you are ready to use it. As you work it in, gum paste will whiten and soften.

Apricot Glaze

Ideal for preparing a cake for fondant or for crumb-coating cakes before icing.

1 cup apricot preserves

Heat preserves to boiling, strain. Brush on cake while glaze is still hot. Let dry. Glaze will dry to a hard finish in 15 minutes or less. Makes enough to cover a 10 x 4 in. cake.

Thinned Fondant Adhesive

Use this mixture when attaching dried fondant to other fondant decorations or for attaching freshly-cut fondant pieces to lollipop sticks or florist wire.

1 oz. Wilton Ready-To-Use Rolled Fondant (p. 149)
  (1½ in. ball)
¼ teaspoon water

Knead water into fondant until it becomes softened and sticky. To attach a fondant decoration, place mixture in decorating bag fitted with a small round tip, or brush on back of decoration. Recipe may be doubled.

Gum Paste Adhesive

This easy-to-make "glue" will hold your gum paste flowers and other decorations together.

1 tablespoon Wilton Meringue Powder (p. 145)
1 tablespoon water

Mix Meringue Powder and water together; add more water if mixture is too thick. Brush on decorations.

Chocolate Fondant

1 pk. (14 oz.) Dark Cocoa Candy Melts (p. 196)
½ cup light corn syrup
24 oz. White Ready-To-Use Rolled Fondant (p. 149)
Brown or Black Icing Color (p. 148, optional)
Melt Candy Melts following package directions. Add corn syrup; stir to blend. Turn out mixture onto waxed paper; let stand at room temperature to dry and harden several hours. Wrap well and store at room temperature until ready to continue with recipe.

Knead small portions of candy mixture until soft and pliable. Knead softened mixture into fondant until smooth and evenly colored. If darker color is desired, knead in icing color.

Quick-Pour Fondant Icing

6 cups sifted confectioners' sugar (about 1½ lbs.)
½ cup water
2 tablespoons light corn syrup
1 teaspoon No-Color Almond Extract (p. 145)
Wilton Icing Colors (p. 148)

Cakes should be covered with apricot glaze (see recipe above) or a thin coating of buttercream icing. Let set 15 minutes before covering with fondant.

Place sugar in saucepan. Combine water and corn syrup. Add to sugar and stir until well mixed. Place over low heat. Don't allow temperature of fondant to exceed 100°F. Remove from heat, stir in flavor and icing color. To cover, place cake or cookies on cooling grid over a drip pan. Pour fondant into center and work towards edges. Touch up bare spots with spatula. Let set. Excess fondant can be reheated. Makes 2½ cups.

HOW TO COLOR AND FLAVOR FONDANT

You can easily tint our White Ready-To-Use Rolled Fondant (p. 149) or the Rolled Fondant recipe (above) using Wilton Icing Colors (p. 148). Using a toothpick, add icing color, a little at a time, and knead into fondant until color is evenly blended. Wilton Ready-To-Use Rolled Fondant has a mellow flavor which can be enhanced using Wilton No-Color Butter Flavor, Clear Vanilla Extract or No-Color Almond Extract (p. 145). Knead flavor into fondant until well blended.

Using Rolled Fondant

The dough-like consistency of fondant makes it the perfect medium for creating ruffles and braids, stately molded accents, distinctive borders, fun trims and beautiful flowers. Decorators agree that fondant is an icing that is truly easy to work with. It's even easier with Wilton Ready-To-Use Rolled Fondant (p. 149)—no mixing, no mess!

COVERING THE CAKE

Just follow our instructions for the right ways to knead, roll out and lift the fondant, and you'll find that covering a cake is easy. For instructions on covering Square, Petal and other cake shapes, see the *Celebrate With Fondant* book, available on p. 133.

1. Prepare cake by lightly covering with buttercream icing.
2. Before rolling out fondant, knead it until it is a workable consistency. If fondant is sticky, knead in a little confectioners' sugar. Lightly dust your smooth work surface or the Roll & Cut Mat and your rolling pin with confectioners' sugar to prevent sticking. Roll out fondant sized to your cake (see "Fondant Amounts," at right). To keep fondant from sticking, lift and move as you roll. Add more confectioners' sugar if needed.  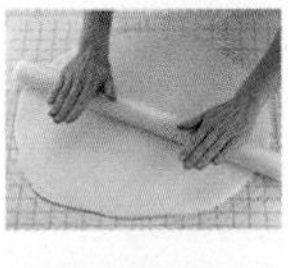
3. Gently lift fondant over rolling pin and position on cake. 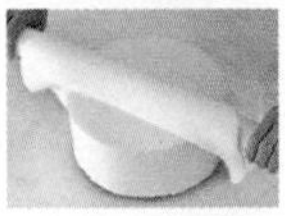
4. Shape fondant to sides of cake with Easy-Glide Smoother. We recommend using the Smoother because the pressure of your hands may leave impressions on the fondant. Use the straight edge of the Smoother to mark fondant at the base of cake. Trim off excess fondant using a spatula or sharp knife. 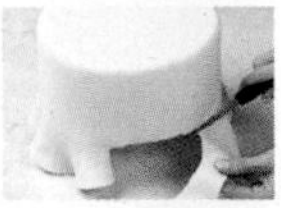 
5. Smooth and shape fondant on cake using Easy-Glide Smoother (p. 14)1. Beginning in the middle of the cake top, move the Smoother outward and down the sides to smooth and shape fondant to the cake and remove air bubbles. If an air bubble appears, insert a pin on an angle, release air and smooth the area again.

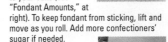

FONDANT AMOUNTS

Use this chart to determine how much Ready-To-Use Rolled Fondant to buy. Wilton Fondant is available in 24 oz. (1 lb., 8 oz.) or 80 oz. (5 lb.) packages. Amounts listed do not include decorations.

Cake Shape	Cake Size	Fondant
Rounds 4 in. high	6 in.	18 oz.
	8 in.	24 oz.
	10 in.	36 oz.
	12 in.	48 oz.
	14 in.	72 oz.
	16 in.	108 oz.
	18 in.	140 oz.
Rounds 3 in. high	6 in.	14 oz.
	8 in.	18 oz.
	10 in.	24 oz.
	12 in.	36 oz.
	14 in.	48 oz.
	16 in.	72 oz.
	18 in.	108 oz.
Sheets 2 in. high	7 x 11 in.	30 oz.
	9 x 13 in.	40 oz.
	11 x 15 in.	60 oz.
	12 x 18 in.	80 oz.
Ovals 4 in. high	7.75 x 5.5 in.	24 oz.
	10.75 x 7.8 in.	36 oz.
	13.5 x 9.8 in.	48 oz.
	16.5 x 12.4 in.	72 oz.
Hearts 4 in. high	6 in.	18 oz.
	8 in.	26 oz.
	9 in.	32 oz.
	10 in.	36 oz.
	12 in.	48 oz.
	14 in.	72 oz.
	16 in.	96 oz.
Petals 4 in. high	6 in.	18 oz.
	9 in.	30 oz.
	12 in.	48 oz.
	15 in.	72 oz.
Squares 4 in. high	6 in.	24 oz.
	8 in.	36 oz.
	10 in.	48 oz.
	12 in.	72 oz.
	14 in.	96 oz.
	16 in.	120 oz.
Hexagons 4 in. high	6 in.	18 oz.
	9 in.	36 oz.
	12 in.	48 oz.
	15 in.	84 oz.
Paisley 4 in. high	9 x 6 in.	20 oz.
	12.75 x 9 in.	48 oz.
	17 x 12 in.	72 oz.
Diamond 4 in. high	10.25 x 7.4 in.	24 oz.
	15 x 11 in.	36 oz.
	19.25 x 14.25 in.	60 oz.

COVERING LARGE CAKES

In most cases, the smaller your cake, the easier it will be to cover with rolled fondant. However, there is an easy way to position and smooth fondant on cakes that are 12 in. diameter or larger. Follow the steps below to lift fondant onto the cake without tearing.

1. Cover cake lightly with buttercream icing. Roll out fondant sized to fit your cake.
2. Slide a large cake circle that has been dusted with confectioners' sugar under the rolled fondant. Lift the circle and the fondant and position over cake. Gently shake the circle to slide the fondant off and into position on the cake. Smooth and trim as described above.

USING FONDANT IMPRINT MATS (p. 150)

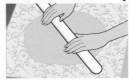

1. Roll out fondant ⅛ in. thick using rolling pin.
2. Lift fondant onto Fondant Imprint Mat using rolling pin. Or, place Fondant Imprint Mat on top of rolled fondant.
3. If fondant is on top of Fondant Imprint Mat, smooth by pressing firmly with Wilton Easy-Glide Fondant Smoother (p. 151) or roll with rolling pin. If fondant is below Fondant Imprint Mat, roll with rolling pin.
4. Lift Fondant Imprint Mat with fondant attached and center imprinted fondant on cake. Peel back mat. Smooth fondant around cake by gently pressing with heel of hand.

Tip Techniques

Your icing turned out great—now you're ready to learn how to pipe beautiful shapes on your cake. Stars, shells, dots, lines and other techniques are the foundation of your decorating knowledge. We'll tell you step-by-step how to pipe each one, including the angle, pressure and movement to use for a uniform look. With practice, you can build on these basics to create many other impressive designs.

ROUND TIPS

Dot

Pipe dots for flower centers, faces, figure piping and border effects. When making large dots, lift the tip as you squeeze to allow icing to fill out completely.

Practice With: Tip 3
Icing Consistency: Medium
Bag Position: 90°
Hold Tip: Slightly above surface

1. Hold the bag straight up with the tip slightly above the surface. Squeeze the bag and keep point of the tip in icing until the dot is the size you want.
2. Stop squeezing the bag completely before you lift the tip from the dot.
3. Lift tip up and pull away from piped dot.

Ball

An important technique to master, the ball shape makes bold borders and is the first step to learn for figure piping. Vary the basic look by adding stars, dots or spirals on the ball shapes.

Practice With: Tip 9
Icing Consistency: Medium
Bag Position: 90°
Hold Tip: Slightly above surface

1. Squeeze the bag, applying steady even pressure. As the icing begins to build up, raise the tip with it, but keep the tip end buried in the icing.
2. Stop squeezing as you bring the end of the tip to the surface.
3. Lift the tip up and pull away from your piped ball. Use the edge of the tip to shave off any point so that your ball is nicely rounded.

Bead

If you can pipe a shell, you can pipe a bead—the movements are similar. To pipe a bead heart, simply pipe one bead, then a second, joining the tails. Smooth together using a decorator brush.

Practice With: Tip 5
Icing Consistency: Medium
Bag Position†: 45° at 3:00 (9:00)
Hold Tip: Slightly above surface

1. Squeeze as you lift tip slightly so that icing fans out.
2. Relax pressure as you draw the tip down and bring the bead to a point.
3. To make a bead border, start the end of your next bead so that the fanned end covers the tail of the preceding bead to form an even chain.

†The technique instructions in this Decorating Guide will list the correct direction for holding the bag. When the bag direction differs for left-handed decorators, that direction will be listed in parentheses. For example, when a bag is to be held at 3:00 for a right-handed decorator, it should be held at 9:00 for a left-handed decorator.

Printing

Practice With: Tip 3 with message press
Icing Consistency: Thin
Bag Position†: 45° at 3:00 (9:00)
Hold Tip: Lightly touching surface

You may pipe letters freehand, pipe over a pattern traced with a toothpick, or pipe after imprinting letters with a message press. If you are using a message press, let icing crust slightly, then imprint the message. With a steady, even pressure, squeeze out a straight line, lifting the tip off the surface to let icing string drop. To prevent tails from forming, be careful to stop squeezing before you touch tip to surface and pull away. Be sure the end of the tip is clean before you go on to another line.

Writing

Practice With: Tip 5
Icing Consistency: Thin
Bag Position†: 45° at 3:00 (6:00)
Hold Tip: Lightly touching surface

You may pipe letters freehand, pipe over a pattern traced with a toothpick, or pipe after imprinting letters with a message press. If you are using a message press, let icing crust slightly, then imprint the message. Steadily squeeze, gliding along the surface in a smooth, continuous motion. Use your arm, not your fingers, to form each line, letter or word. Keep your wrist straight, moving your entire forearm as a single unit. After you begin to master the curves and swings of the letters, lift the tip up slightly as you write. You'll find you have more control if you let the icing draw out slightly over the surface as you write.

Note: Left-handed decorators may have to adjust the bag position to fit their writing style.

Outline

Characters or designs are often outlined first, then piped in with stars or zigzags. Outlines are used for facial features, too. Color flow plaques are also outlined before icing is flowed into the shape.

Practice With: Tip 3
Icing Consistency: Thin
Bag Position†: 45° at 3:00 (9:00)
Hold Tip: Slightly above surface

1. Touch tip to surface. Raise the tip slightly and continue to squeeze.
2. The icing will flow out of the tip while you direct it along the surface.
3. To end, stop squeezing, touch tip to surface and pull away.

To Pipe-In

After outlining, using the same tip, squeeze out rows of lines to fill area. Pat icing down with fingertip dipped in cornstarch or smooth with dampened art brush.

Drop Strings

These flowing strings are a beautiful way to adorn the sides of a cake. The trick to making drop strings is to pull the bag toward you as the string drapes down. If you "draw" the string with the tip, you won't achieve a pretty curve and your strings will tend to break. Pipe at eye level to your cake so that strings line up evenly. The Cake Dividing Set (p. 138) is a great help in accurately dividing and marking your cake for even drop strings.

Single Drop Strings

Practice With: Tip 3
Icing Consistency: Stiff
Bag Position†: Shoulder level at 4:30 (7:30)
Hold Tip: Lightly touching surface to attach

1. With a toothpick, mark horizontal divisions on cake in the width you desire. Touch tip to first mark and squeeze, pausing momentarily so that icing sticks to surface.
2. While squeezing, pull the bag toward you. Continue squeezing to allow the icing to drape naturally into an arc. Icing will drop by itself—do not move the tip down with the string. The end of the tip should be the same distance from the surface as the width from point to point on your cake.
3. Stop pressure before you touch tip to second mark to end string. Repeat, keeping drop strings uniform in length and width.

Multiple Drop Strings

Try a different color for each row of multiple drop strings—put holiday colors together to really dress up your cake.

To add multiple rows of strings, mark the cake for the deepest row and pipe that row. Return to the first drop string point, squeeze the bag, and drop a string with a slightly shorter arc than in the first row. Join the end of this string to the end of the corresponding string in the first row. Repeat the process for a third row of drop strings above the second.

STAR TIPS

Star

Practice With: Tip 16
Icing Consistency: Medium
Bag Position: 90°
Hold Tip: Between ⅛ and ¼ in. above surface

1. Hold the decorating bag straight up, with the tip between ⅛ and ¼ in. above the surface, while using your other hand to hold the tip steady. Squeeze the bag to form a star. Increasing or decreasing the pressure changes the size of the star.
2. Stop squeezing the bag completely before you lift the tip from the star.
3. Lift the tip up and pull away from piped star.

Pull-out stars add even more dimension to your cake. To make them, hold bag at a 45° angle to surface. As you squeeze out icing, pull tip up and away from cake. When your mound is high enough, stop pressure and pull tip away. Work from bottom to top of area to be covered with pull-out stars.

Star Fill In

Because these close-together stars require so much piping from the same bag, it's a good idea to keep replenishing the icing. Replenish icing when it gets soft or stars will be poorly defined.

Practice With: Tip 16
Icing Consistency: Medium
Bag Position: 90°
Hold Tip: ¼ in. above surface

1. Pipe a row of stars evenly and close together, adjusting the tip position slightly each time so that the points of the stars interlock and cover the area without gaps.
2. Pipe a row of stars beneath the first, again adjusting tip position to close any gaps.
3. Continue to fill in entire area.

Zigzag

A quick and popular way to fill in outlined areas, perfect for ribbed sweater and cuff effects. You can use tight zigzags to cover the entire side of your cake—they look great!

Practice With: Tip 16
Icing Consistency: Medium
Bag Position†: 45° at 3:00 (9:00)
Hold Tip: Lightly touching surface

1. Steadily squeeze and move your hand in a tight up and down motion.
2. Continue piping up and down with steady pressure. To end, stop pressure and pull tip away. For more elongated zigzags, move your hand to the desired height while maintaining a steady pressure. For a more relaxed look, just increase the width as you move the bag along.
3. Repeat as you move in a straight line with consistent up/down motion.

Shell

Most popular icing technique of all, the shell is the basis for many borders. Lift tip slightly when piping shells to avoid a bumpy look.

Practice With: Tip 21
Icing Consistency: Medium
Bag Position: 45° at 6:00
Hold Tip: Slightly above surface

1. Hold the bag in the 6:00 position so that you can pull the bag toward you. The tip should be slightly above the surface.
2. Squeeze hard, letting the icing fan out generously as it lifts the tip—do not lift the bag. Gradually relax your pressure as you lower the tip until it touches the surface.
3. Stop pressure and pull the tip away, without lifting it off the surface, to draw the shell to a point.
4. To make a shell border, start the end of your next shell so that the fanned end covers the tail of the preceding shell to form an even chain.

Rope

Finish your piped baskets with pretty edging and handles. Excellent for western or nautical themed cakes. You can make a great-looking rope with star or round tips (or basketweave tips, ridged or smooth side up).

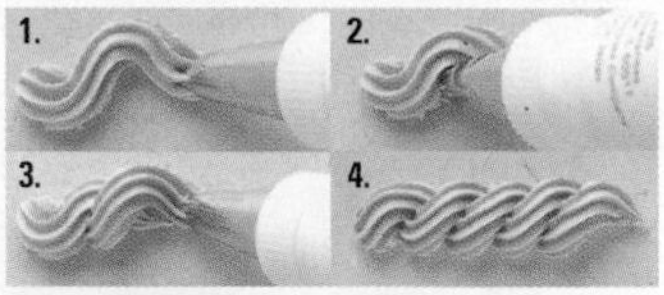

Practice With: Tip 21
Icing Consistency: Medium
Bag Position†: 45° at 4:30 (7:30)
Hold Tip: Lightly touching surface

1. Using a steady, even pressure, move the tip in a gentle sideways "S" curve. Stop pressure and pull tip away.
2. Insert tip under the bottom curve of the "S" shape.
3. Squeeze the bag with steady pressure as you pull down, then lift the tip. Move up and over the tail of the "S" as you continue to squeeze and form a hook.
4. Keep spacing as even as possible and pipe "S" curves uniform in thickness, length and overall size. Be sure to tuck the tip into the bottom curve of the previous "S" before you begin squeezing to insure the clean, continuous look of a rope.

Rosette

Practice With: Tip 16
Icing Consistency: Medium
Bag Position: 90°
Hold Tip: Lightly touching surface

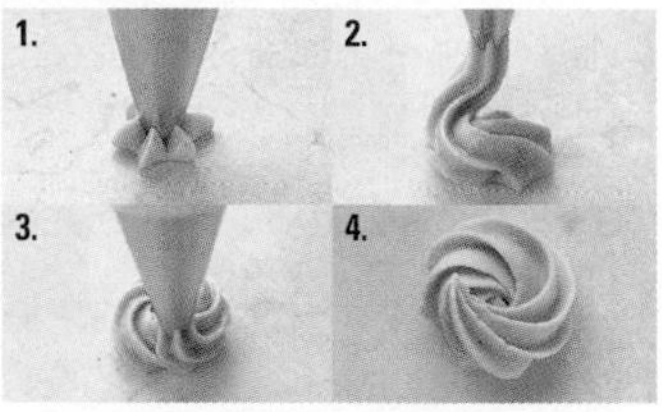

1. Keeping the tip slightly above the surface, squeeze out icing to form a star and, without releasing pressure, move the tip in a tight, complete rotation, starting at 9:00 (3:00), moving to 12:00. . .
2. then to 3:00 (9:00) and 6:00. . .
3. and ending back at 9:00 (3:00).
4. Stop pressure and lift tip away.

BORDER

Fondant Rope Border

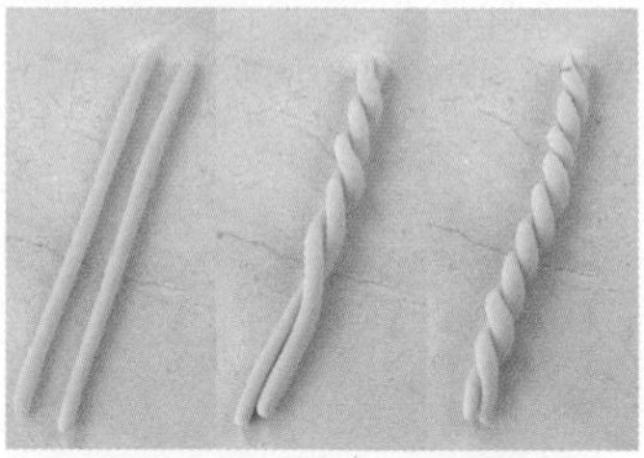

1. Use palms of hands to roll fondant logs, ¼ in. diameter. You will need 4 pieces 36 in. long for cake border; twist 2 ropes together to make each rope section. Lay pieces side by side and gently press together at one end to join.
2. Holding the joined end in a stationary position, twist the other end 2 to 3 complete turns. Continue twisting as needed.
3. Attach rope to bottom border using a damp brush. Moisten cake slightly and position rope, pressing ends lightly to secure.

MULTIPLE TIPS

Swirl Drop Flower

The swirled look adds a nice motion effect to the cake. You must squeeze and turn at the same time.

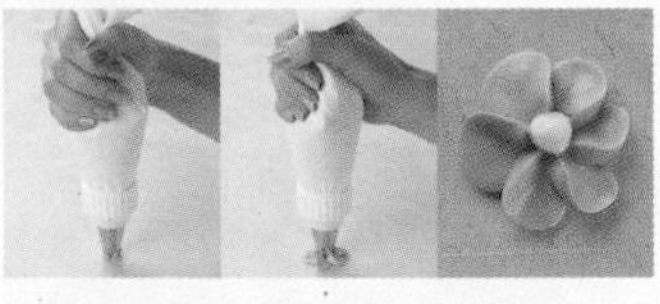

Practice With: Tips 2D, 3; use Large Coupler
Icing Consistency: Use royal icing: medium for flower, thin for center
Bag Position: 90°
Hold Tip: Slightly above surface

1. Turn your wrist in toward you before piping. Hold bag straight up, just touching the surface. You will turn wrist a full twist. Starting with the flat of your knuckles at 9:00 (3:00). As you squeeze out the icing, slowly turn your hand, with knuckles ending at 12:00.
2. Stop squeezing and lift the tip away.
3. Make a tip 3 dot flower center, holding your bag straight up and keeping the tip buried as you squeeze. Stop squeezing, then pull your tip up and away.

Icing Ribbon Roses

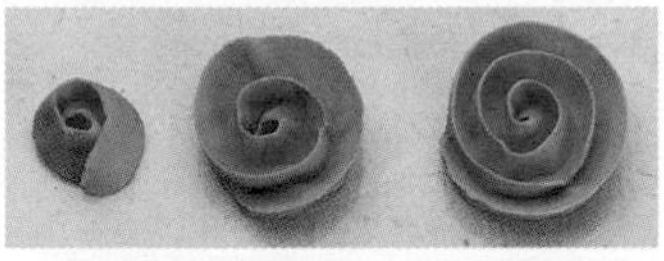

Practice With: Tip 104
Icing Consistency: Use stiff consistency royal icing or Snow White Buttercream Icing
Bag Position: 90° at 3:00 (9:00)
Hold Tip: Wide end touching center of flower nail
Flower Nail: #7

1. Starting at center of flower nail topped with a waxed paper square, turn nail counterclockwise as you squeeze out a ribbon of icing, using even pressure.
2. Continue squeezing, wrapping the ribbon of icing around to form a rose.
3. Slip waxed paper square with ribbon rose from nail and let dry.

PETAL TIPS

Ruffle

Everyone loves a ruffle's graceful motion—ruffles always add interest to your cake. Use them as a top border, to frame a plaque or to trim doll dresses and baby bonnets.

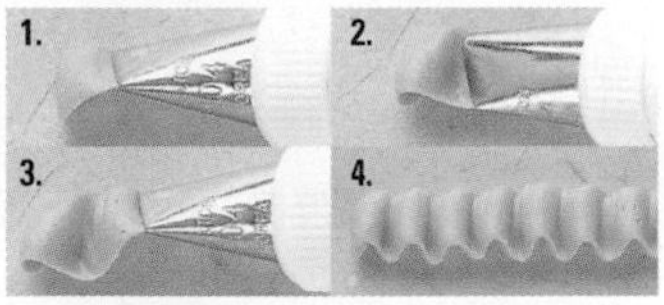

Practice With: Tip 104
Icing Consistency: Medium
Bag Position†: 45° at 3:00 (9:00)
Hold Tip: Wide end lightly touching surface with narrow end facing down and away from surface

1. Keep the wide end of your tip touching the cake with the narrow end down. Move wrist up to pull up icing.
2. Move wrist down to complete one curl of the ruffle.
3. Repeat up and down motion.
4. Raise and lower the narrow end as you move around the cake. Repeat this motion for the entire ruffle.

Flower-Making Techniques

Explore beautiful flowers and leaves, which add lovely color to your cake design. Create the magnificent rose—the most popular icing flower of all. With practice, your flowers will have the just-picked look of real garden flowers.

FLOWER NAIL FLOWERS

Using a Flower Nail

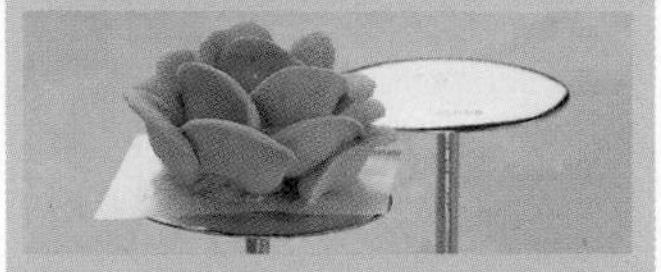

The nail is a revolving platform you hold in your hand to conveniently build roses and other flowers. It allows you to work close up, to turn for easy piping and to remove your completed flowers without damage, to dry.

The key to making the flower on the nail is to coordinate the turning of the nail with the formation of each petal.

Attach a square of waxed paper on the flat surface of the flower nail using a dot of icing. Pipe your flower directly on the waxed paper. Hold the flower nail between the thumb and forefinger of your left (right) hand (use other fingers to support nail) and roll it slowly counterclockwise (clockwise for lefties) as you press out icing with the decorating bag held in the right (left) hand. Your right (left) hand moves in and out, or up and down, as it holds the decorating bag and tip at just the right angle (in most cases 45°) and keeps the icing flowing at an even speed. After piping, slide the waxed paper with flower off the nail to dry.

The Wilton Rose

NOTE: If you are going to be placing your roses on your cake immediately, waxed paper squares are not needed. To remove finished roses, use the Flower Lifter (p. 140). Slide flower from lifter onto cake, using a spatula.

Practice With: Tips 104, 12
Icing Consistency: Royal or stiff buttercream
Bag Position†: Base 90° (straight up); petals 45° at 4:30 (7:30)
Hold Tip: For base, slightly above nail; for petals, wide end touching base
Flower Nail: #7

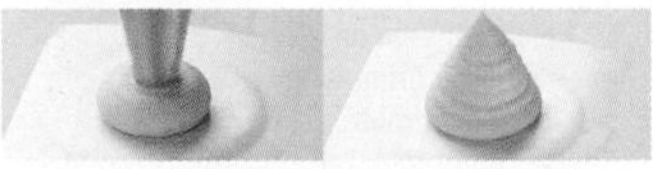

1. Make the rose base, using tip 12 and flower nail #7. Hold the bag straight up, the end of tip 12 slightly above the center of your waxed paper-covered flower nail, which is held in your other hand. Using heavy pressure, build up a base, remembering to keep your tip buried as you squeeze. Start to lift the tip higher, gradually raise the tip, and decrease the pressure.
2. Stop pressure, pull up and lift away. The rose base should be 1½ times as high as the rose tip opening.

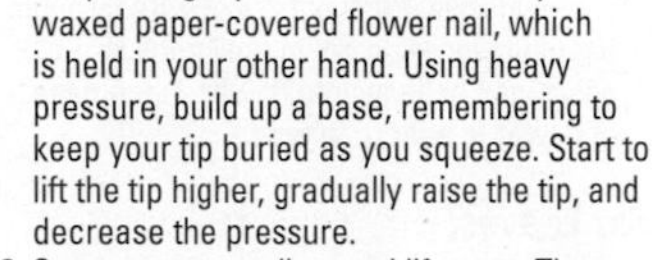

3. Make the center bud, using tip 104. Hold nail containing base in your left (right) hand and bag with rose tip 104 in right (left) hand. Bag should be at a 45° angle to the flat surface of the nail and in the 4:30 (7:30) position. The wide end of the tip should touch the cone of the icing base at or slightly below the midpoint, and the narrow end of the tip should point up and angled in over top of base.
4. Now you must do 3 things at the same time: squeeze the bag, move the tip and rotate the nail. As you squeeze the bag, move the tip up from the base, forming a ribbon of icing. Slowly turn the nail counterclockwise (clockwise for lefties) to bring the ribbon of icing around to overlap at the top of the mound, then back down to starting point. Move your tip straight up and down only; do not loop it around the base.
5. Now you have a finished center bud.

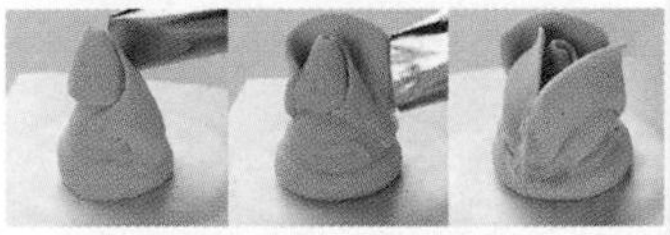

6. Make the top row of 3 petals. Touch the wide end of tip to the midpoint of bud base, narrow end straight up.
7. Turn nail, keeping wide end of tip on base so that petal will attach. Move tip up and back down to the midpoint of mound, forming the first petal.
8. Start again, slightly behind end of first petal, and squeeze out second petal. Repeat for the third petal, ending by overlapping the starting point of the first petal. Rotate the nail ⅓ turn for each petal.

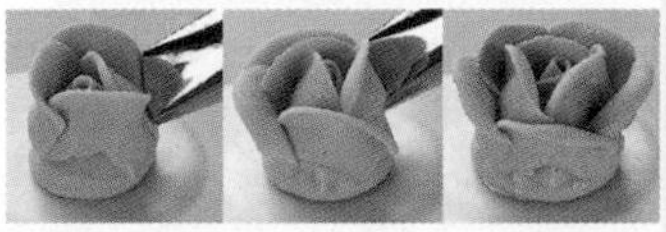

9. Make the middle row of 5 petals. Touch the wide end of tip slightly below center of a petal in the top row. Angle the narrow end of tip out slightly more than you did for the top row of petals. Squeeze bag and turn nail moving tip up, then down, to form first petal.
10. Repeat for a total of 5 petals, rotating the nail ⅕ turn for each petal.
11. The last petal end should overlap the first's starting point.

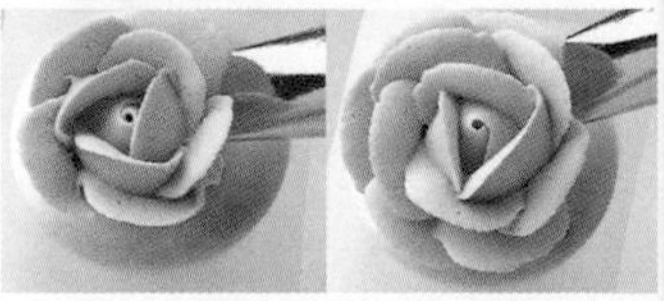

12. Make the bottom row of 7 petals. Touch the wide end of tip below the center of a middle row petal, again angling the narrow end of tip out a little more. Squeeze bag and turn nail to end of fingers, moving tip up, then down to form first petal.
13. Repeat for a total of 7 petals, rotating the nail ⅐ turn for each petal.

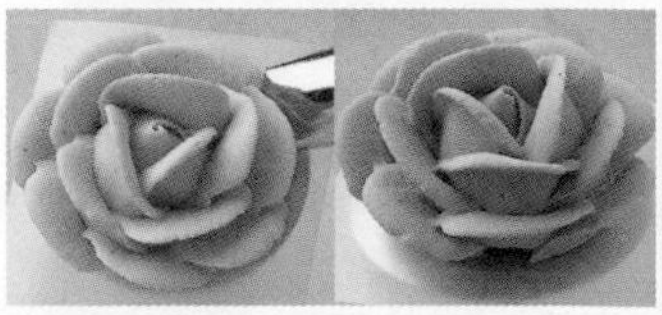

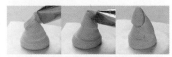

14. The last petal end should overlap the first's starting point.
15. Slip waxed paper and completed rose from nail. This is the completed Wilton Rose.

Flower-Making Techniques (cont.)

Gum Paste Roses and Leaves

(see Floral Frost, p. 77 and Setting the Gold Standard, p. 86)

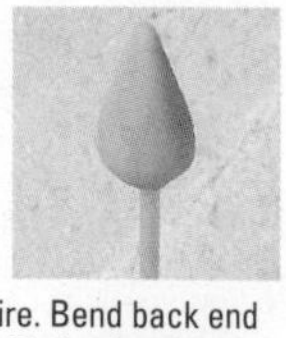

1. In advance: Make the rose center. Roll a ½ in. ball of gum paste and form into a teardrop shape. Projects listed above use 6 in. lengths of 22- or 24-gauge florist wire. Bend back end of wire into a ¼ in. hook. Dip hook end into gum paste adhesive and insert at bottom of rose center, inserting halfway through base. Press bottom of center to shape and smooth against wire. Let dry at least 48 hours.

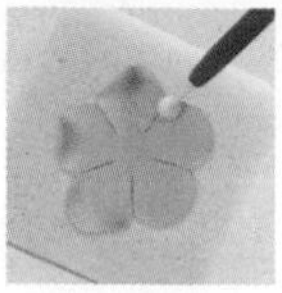

2. Roll out gum paste 1⁄16 in. thick. Using the large rose cutter from the Stepsaving Kit (p. 153), cut blossom shape. Use a knife to make a ½ in. cut between each petal toward middle of blossom. Place on thin foam and use ball tool from 10-Pc. Fondant/Gum Paste Tool Set to soften edges of petals. Move blossom to thick foam and cup center by pressing in middle with ball tool.

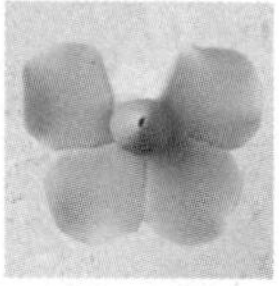

3. Apply gum paste adhesive to rose center. Insert the wire holding the rose center into the middle of the blossom and thread blossom up to the bottom of the rose center. Visualize the 5-petal blossom as a stick figure, with petals corresponding to "head", "arms" and "legs". Wrap the head petal around rose center.

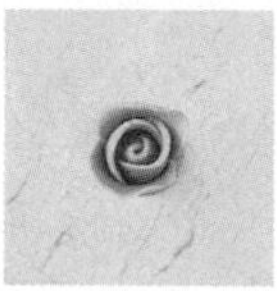

4. Brush bottom half of one "arm" and opposite "leg" with adhesive and wrap around the center bud. Repeat for remaining petals. Gently press bottom to shape. Petals should overlap each other. Pinch off any excess gum paste from bottom. Furl back petal edges of the outer layer of petals.

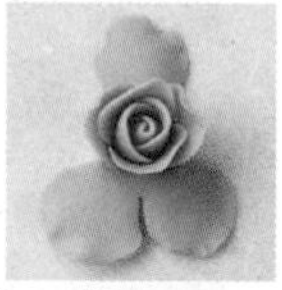

5. Prepare the next blossom; cut slits and soften edges as above. Transfer to thick foam and use ball tool to cup the 2 "arm" petals. Turn over blossom and cup 2 "leg" petals and "head" petal. Turn over blossom again and cup the center. Brush adhesive on bottom of rose center; thread blossom onto wire. Brush the 2 "arm" petals with adhesive and attach, centering over the seams of the previous 2 petals.

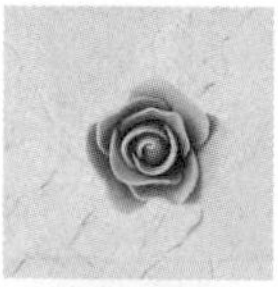

6. Brush bottom half of remaining petals with adhesive and attach, spacing evenly. Press bottom to shape; pinch off excess if needed.

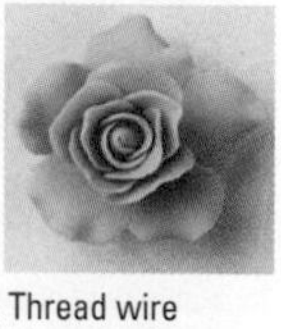

7. Add a third blossom; cut slits and soften edges as in step 2. Transfer to thick foam. Using the ball tool, cup all petals. Turn blossom shape over and cup center. Brush adhesive on bottom of rose center. Thread wire through the center of the blossom shape. Brush adhesive on bottom half of petals as needed.

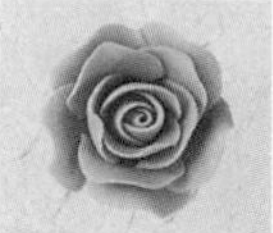

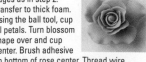

8. Turn rose over and let petals fall naturally into place. Gently press petals against the rose center to attach.

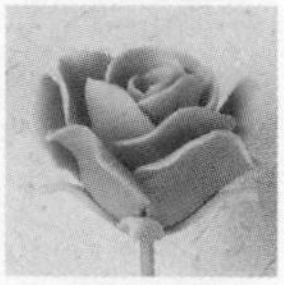

9. Roll out gum paste 1⁄16 in. thick and cut calyx using calyx cutter from the Stepsaving Set. Brush bottom of rose center with adhesive and thread wire through center of calyx. Brush adhesive on bottom half of sepals and press to attach. Bend top half of wire stem down and let rose hang down to dry in craft foam block.

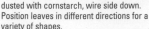

For Stephanotis:

1. Make a ¼ in. hook on end of 6 in. long 24-gauge wire.

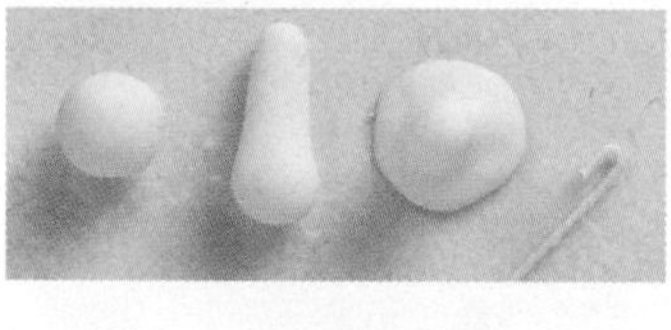

2. Roll a ½ in. ball of gum paste into a teardrop shape. Pinch and flatten wide end into a golf tee shape.

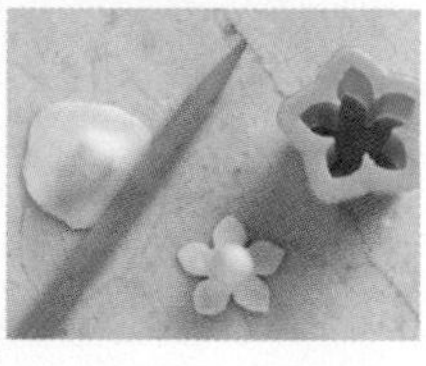

3. Place, tee side down, on smooth surface lightly coated with shortening. Roll out top of tee with modeling stick to the diameter of calyx cutter from Floral Collection Flower Making Set.
4. Center cutter over tee and cut stephanotis. If flower sticks in cutter, push out gently with modeling stick.

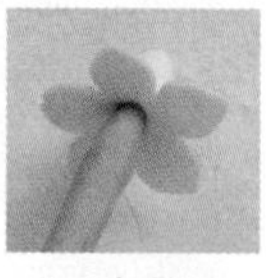

5. Hold stephanotis base between thumb and forefinger. Insert pointed end of modeling stick into center of flower. Rotate stick in a circular motion to widen the center.

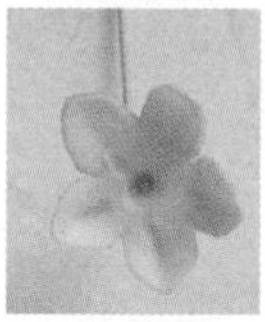

6. Make center vein on each petal, scoring with small veining tool from flower center to petal point.
7. Brush wire, 1 in. down from top hook end with adhesive. Push bottom of wire through top of flower, slide down until hook is positioned halfway into flower. Pinch base of flower to adhere to wire.

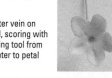

For Leaves:

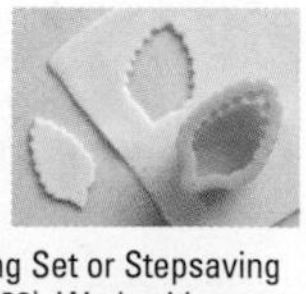

1. Prepare 6 in. piece of 26-gauge wire. Roll out gum paste 1⁄16 in. thick. Cut desired number of leaves using rose leaf cutter from Floral Collection Flower Making Set or Stepsaving Rose Bouquets Set (p. 132). Work with one leaf at a time, keeping other leaves under practice board flap.

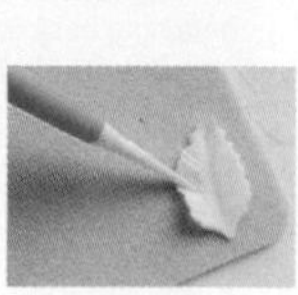

2. Place leaves on thin foam. Use small end of veining tool to draw veins on leaves.

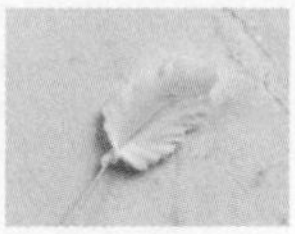

3. Turn leaf over and apply a line of gum paste adhesive, about ⅔ up from bottom in the center of the leaf. Attach wire at moisture line.

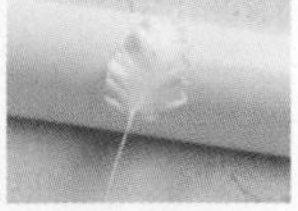

4. Pinch bottom of both sides of leaf slightly toward back of wire stem to attach. Let dry on small flower former dusted with cornstarch, wire side down. Position leaves in different directions for a variety of shapes.

Fondant Ribbon Roses

(see Words Ring True, p. 80)

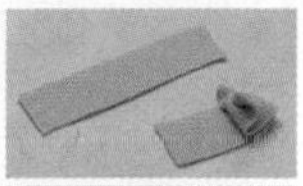

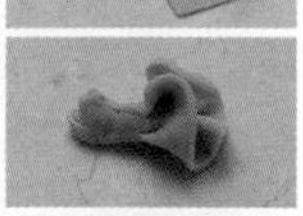

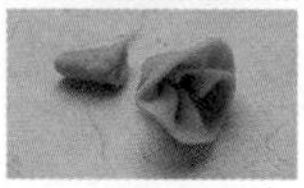

Tint fondant according to project instructions. Roll out 1⁄16 in. thick. Cut a 1 x 6 in. strip for each rose. Brush bottom edge with damp brush; roll and gather, pinching bottom edge to secure. Trim off excess with scissors. Set in candy melting plate dusted with cornstarch; let dry.

Attaching Royal Icing Roses to Wire Stems

(see Contemporary Curves, p. 82)

Follow The Wilton Rose instructions on p. 121. Roses are made using 6 color versions: Creamy Peach with Pink in dark, medium and light, Creamy Peach with Lemon Yellow in dark, medium and light. Make roses as follows: Using tip 124 with tip 12 bases, 3 of each dark shade. Using tip 104 with tip 12 bases, 3 each dark peach/pink and medium peach/yellow. Using tip 103 with tip 10 bases, 3 medium peach/pink and 5 light peach/pink. Using tip 102 with tip 7 bases, 5 each light peach/pink and light peach/yellow. Using tip 101 with tip 5 bases, 6 each light peach/pink and light peach/yellow. On 1 in. waxed paper square, using royal icing, pipe cone-shaped calyx bases. For tip 101, 102 and 103 roses, pipe 30 cone-shaped calyx bases with tip 4. For tip 104 and 124 roses, pipe 12 tip 7 calyx bases. Use 24-gauge florist wire for tip 4 calyxes and 20-gauge florist wire for tip 7 bases. Make ⅛ in. hook on end of florist wire and insert hook into base. With slightly moistened decorator brush, smooth and taper the icing around the wire. Push other end of wire into craft block and let dry. Remove waxed paper and attach pre-made flower with dots of royal icing. Let dry.

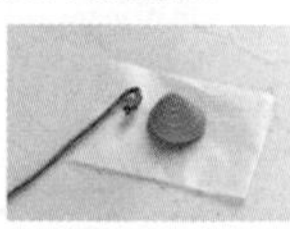

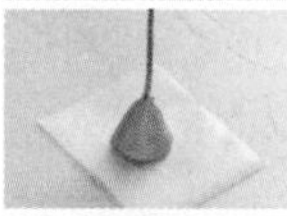

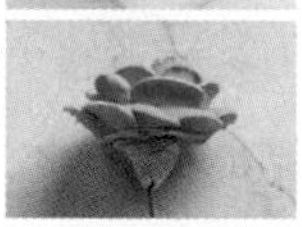

Attaching Royal Icing Leaves to Wire Stems

(see Contemporary Curves, p. 82)

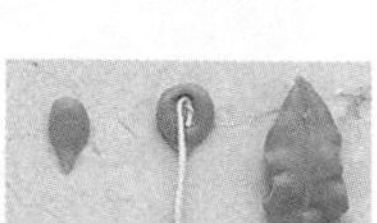

On a 1¼ in. waxed paper square, using royal icing, pipe a dot base with tip 4. Make a ⅛ in. hook on the end of florist wire and insert hook into the dot base. Use tip 352 and pipe leaf directly on top of wire. Push the other end of wire into craft block and let dry. Remove waxed paper square when dry. Make 40 leaves.

FLORAL GREENERY

Leaves

Practice With: Tips 352, 67, 366
Icing Consistency: Buttercream thinned with corn syrup
Bag Position: 45° at 6:00
Hold Tip: Lightly touching surface; wide opening parallel to surface

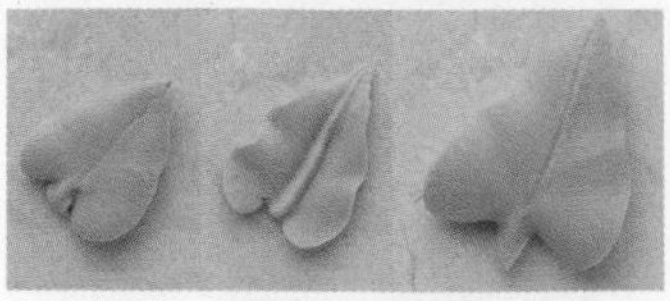

Basic Leaf Tip 352	Veined Leaf Tip 67	Large Leaf Tip 366 Use large coupler

1. Squeeze hard to build up the base and, at the same time, lift the tip slightly.
2. Relax pressure as you pull the tip toward you, drawing the leaf to a point.
3. Stop squeezing and lift away.

Vines

Practice With: Tip 3
Icing Consistency: Thin
Bag Position: 45° at 3:00 (9:00)
Hold Tip: Lightly touching surface

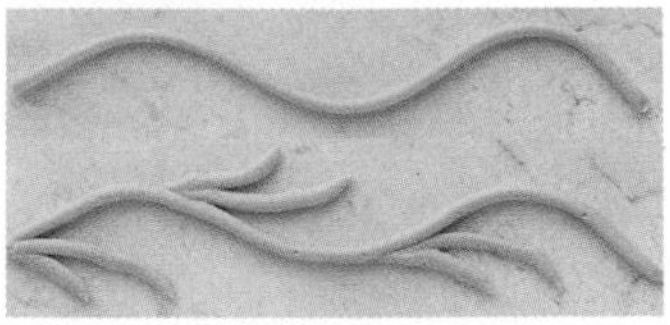

1. Touch your tip lightly to the surface as you start to squeeze, then lift slightly above the surface as you draw out the stem.
2. Move tip gently up and down to form "hills and valleys." To end the line, stop squeezing and pull the tip along the surface.
3. Add secondary curved stems, starting at main stem, stopping pressure as you pull to a point.

Puddle Dots

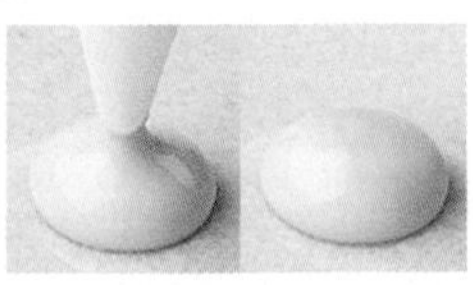

Thin royal icing (or color flow), adding ½ teaspoon water per ¼ cup of icing. Icing is ready for flowing when a small amount dripped back into mixture takes a count of 10 to disappear. On waxed paper, pipe a ball, ¼ to 1¼ in. diameter, depending on project instructions, using thinned icing in a cut parchment bag. Let dry 48 hours. Decorate following project instructions.

BRUSHING DECORATIONS WITH PEARL DUST

It's easy to add a shimmering touch to fondant and candy decorations with Wilton Pearl Dust (p. 151). This **food-safe** powder creates rich, lustrous highlights on flowers, bows, letters and more. To apply, just brush onto your decoration with a soft artist brush. Or, to paint decorations, pour a small amount of clear vanilla, lemon extract or vodka into a Color Tray (p. 157) cavity; stir in a small amount of Pearl Dust and brush onto your decoration.

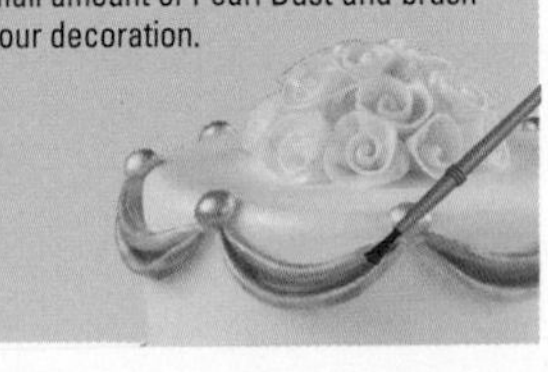

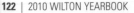

Other Decorating Techniques

Combing

Practice With: Icing Sculptor, Decorating Comb or Triangle (p. 143), Trim 'N Turn Cake Turntable (p. 141)
Icing Consistency: Medium-to-thin buttercream

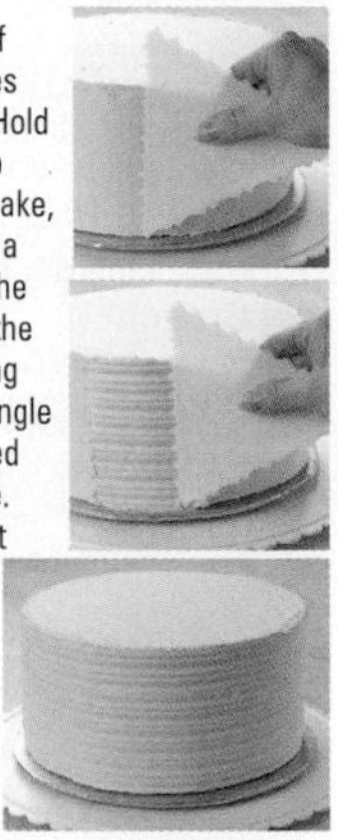

Cover the cake with a slightly thicker coating of icing so the comb's ridges will not touch the cake. Hold comb at 45° angle. Comb immediately after icing cake, while icing is soft. Using a turntable helps to keep the movement smooth. Use the Icing Sculptor, Decorating Comb or Decorating Triangle to add different contoured effects to your iced cake. Choose the type of effect you want—wide or narrow—then run that edge around your cake to form ridges. Ridges will be deep or shallow depending on the Icing Sculptor blade or the side of Decorating Comb or Triangle you use.

Icing Sculptor

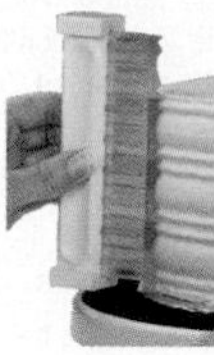

Select the sculpting blades you want and slide into holder. Press sculptor into iced cake as you rotate cake on turntable. Mix and match between the 64 blades to achieve the perfect look for your cake.

Pattern Press

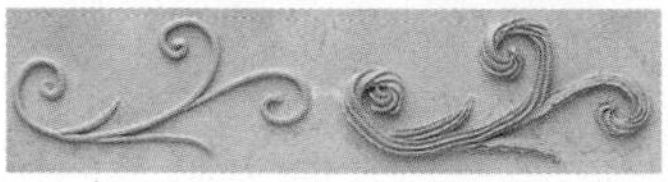

The trick to uniform designs and steady writing and printing is using a pattern press (p. 142). Simply imprint the press on any icing, including fondant.
Practice With: Tips 3, 16
Icing Consistency: Medium
Bag Position: 45° at 3:00
Hold Tip: Slightly above surface

1. Lightly press pattern onto your iced or fondant-covered cake to imprint the design.
2. Outline the imprinted design with icing, using the tip of your choice. Change the tip to change the look of each pattern.

Tinting Shredded Coconut

Place desired amount of coconut in plastic bag, add a little color with a toothpick and knead until color is evenly blended. Dry on waxed paper.

Coating Spaghetti or Lollipop Sticks with Icing

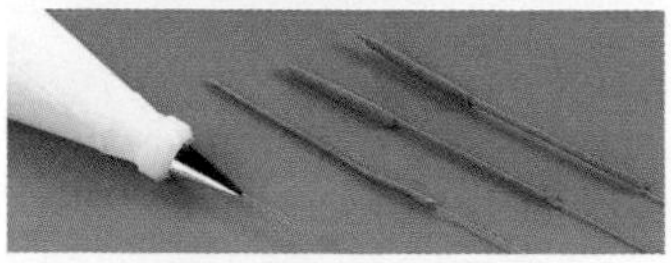

Break pieces of uncooked spaghetti or cut sticks into desired lengths. Use decorating bag with specified tip, and royal or buttercream icing as specified in cake directions. Insert spaghetti or stick into open end of tip, then as you squeeze bag, pull out of tip, coating with icing. Let dry on waxed paper covered boards.

Simple Bow

(See Salute the Students, p. 74 and Ariel's Ocean Hearts, p. 31)

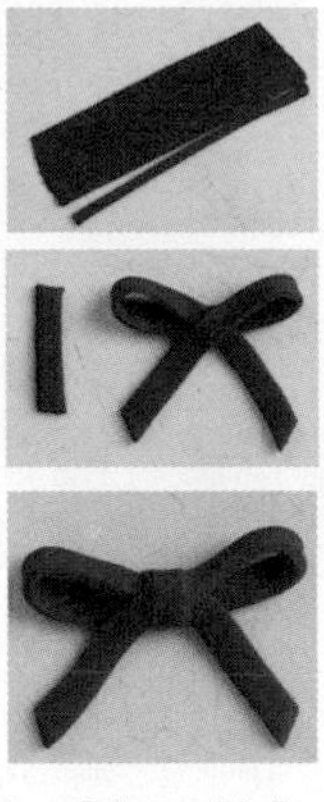

For each bow needed, roll out fondant ⅛ in. thick and cut 1 strip. *For Salute the Students,* cut ¼ x 12 in. red strip. Fold to form loops and streamers. Cut a 4½ x 1 in. strip to wrap around center for knot. Let dry on waxed paper-covered board dusted with cornstarch. Repeat to make 3 more bows. Reserve remaining red fondant. *For Ariel's Ocean Hearts,* cut ¼ x 10 in. rose strip and fold loops and streamers as above. Roll a small ball for center knot and attach with damp brush.

Covering Base Boards with Fondant

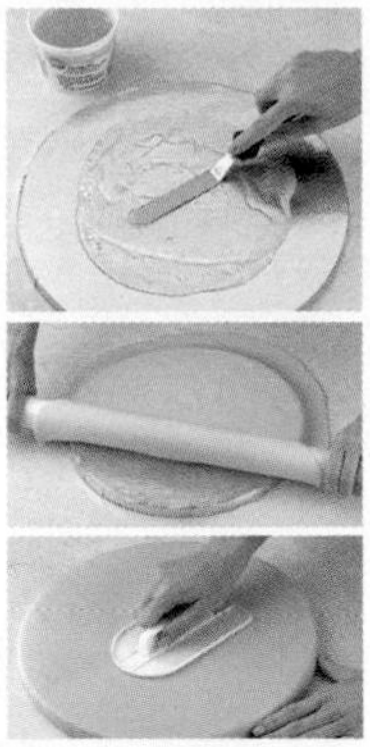

Cut cake boards 2 in. larger in diameter than your cake, unless otherwise directed, then roll out fondant about 1 in. larger than board size. Wrap board with foil.

1. Lightly coat board with piping gel to help the fondant stick to the foil.
2. Roll out fondant to desired size, ⅛ in. thick. Position over board using a rolling pin, draping fondant over edge.
3. Trim excess fondant from edges under bottom of board. Smooth top and sides with Easy-Glide Smoother.

Curliques

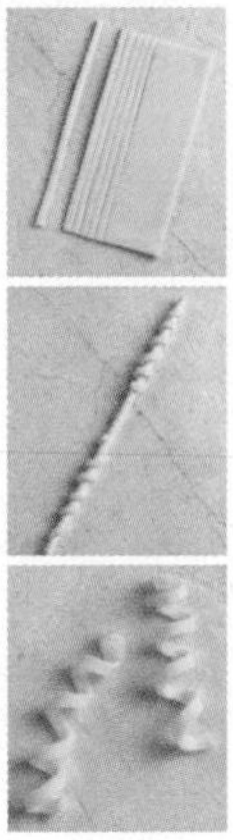

Toothpicks, Lollipop Sticks or dowel rods may be used for various sizes.

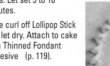

1. Roll out fondant 1⁄16 in. thick on Roll & Cut Mat lightly dusted with cornstarch. Cut into thin strips.
2. Loosely wrap strips around a Lollipop Stick several times to form curls. Let set 5 to 10 minutes.
3. Slide curl off Lollipop Stick and let dry. Attach to cake with Thinned Fondant Adhesive (p. 119).

Marbleizing Fondant

Using Icing Color: Roll fondant into a ball, kneading until it's soft and pliable. Using a toothpick, add dots of icing color in several spots. Knead fondant slightly until color begins to blend in, creating marbleized streaks. Roll out fondant to desired shape.

Using Pre-Tinted Fondant and White Fondant: Roll a log each of tinted and white fondant. Twist one log around the other several times. Knead fondant slightly until color begins to blend in, creating marbleized streaks. Roll out fondant to desired shape.

Decorating Techniques for the 2010 Wilton Yearbook Cakes

We've organized our decorating techniques to make everything easier to find. Special techniques for this book are presented in the same order as our projects, beginning with the Birthday Section projects on page 4 up through our Special Section, ending at page 110.

Fondant Bow Loops, Name, Balloons, Streamers

(see Can't Contain Our Excitement!, p. 4)

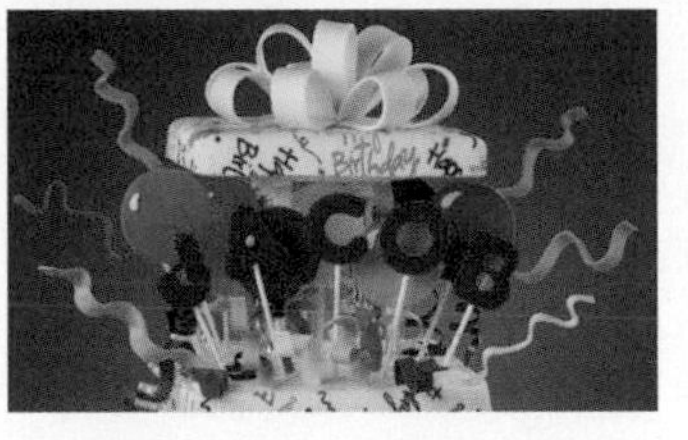

Prepare fondant. Knead 1 tablespoon Gum-Tex into 32 oz. fondant. Divide and tint as follows: 8 oz. yellow, 6 oz. red, 6 oz. blue, 6 oz. green, 2 oz. rose, 4 oz. dark violet. Roll out ⅛ in. thick as needed. **Make bow loops.** Cut 10 yellow strips 1 x 7¾ in. long. Using yellow, blue, red and green, cut 3 strips each 1 x 3½ in. long. Fold strips over to form loops. Brush ends with damp brush; align ends and pinch slightly to secure. Stand loops on sides to dry on cornstarch-dusted surface. **Make fondant name.** Cut letters using cutters from set. Brush with piping gel and sprinkle on red sugar. Let dry then attach to Lollipop Sticks using melted candy. **Make balloons.** Using medium circle cutter from set, cut 1 yellow and 2 each blue, violet and green circles. Let dry then attach to Lollipop Sticks using melted candy. Cut small triangles for balloon knots. Attach to sticks and pipe highlights using melted candy. Curl matching ribbon and tie onto sticks. **Make streamers.** Using Cutter/Embosser Wheel fitted with 2 straight wheels and ¼ in. spacer, cut 25 strips 4 to 8 in. long in assorted colors. Shape into random curved lines; let dry on sides. Cut Lollipop Sticks to 4 in. long. Attach to bottom end of each streamer using melted candy.

Fondant Passengers

(see Flight of Fancy, p. 8 and Water Whirled, p. 9)

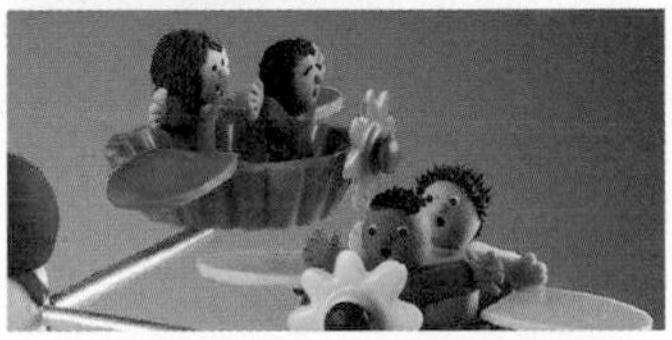

For shirts, roll out Primary and Neon Fondant ½ in. thick. Cut 8 or 16 shirts using People Cut-Out. Bend arms upward and let dry on cornstarch-dusted surface. **For heads and hands,** divide 6 oz. fondant and tint various skin tones. Roll out ⅛ in. thick. Use narrow end of tip 2A to cut circles for hands; use knife to cut and shape fingers. Attach to shirts using damp brush. Roll 1 in. balls for heads. Roll tiny ball noses and flat ⅜ in. circles for necks; attach using damp brush. Using royal icing and tip 1, pipe dot eyes (flatten slightly), dot pupils and outline mouth. Use melted candy to attach shirts to candy shell boats; attach heads. Use royal icing and tip 2 to pipe pull-out dot and C-motion hair.

Spinning Center Support

(see Flight of Fancy, p. 8)

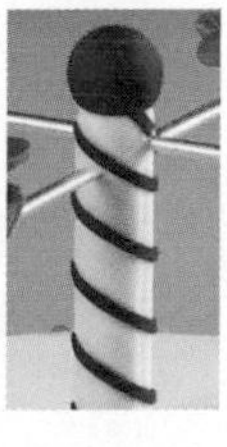

For inner base, cut plastic dowel rod to 9 in. long. Pipe a 1 in. puddle of melted candy on non-stick cookie sheet. Place dowel rod upright in puddle; fill rod with melted candy and chill until firm. For arms, use hot glue to wrap 2 wooden dowel rods with Fanci-Foil. For striped section, use 6 in. Hidden Pillar. Use knife to cut 2 pairs of level holes, ½ in. and 1 in. from top, where wooden dowel rods will pass through pillar. Brush pillar with Piping Gel and cover with white fondant rolled ⅛ in. thick. Use hands to smooth seams; use knife to clear bottom opening and side holes. Roll out some red fondant ⅛ in. thick. Cut a 14 in. x ¼ in. wide strip; brush back with damp brush and attach around pillar in spiral pattern. Slide wrapped dowel rods through pillar; center and secure with hot glue. Roll a 1½ in. diameter ball of red fondant for top; set aside.

Wings, Upper Body and Tiara

(see Working on Your Wishes, p. 11)

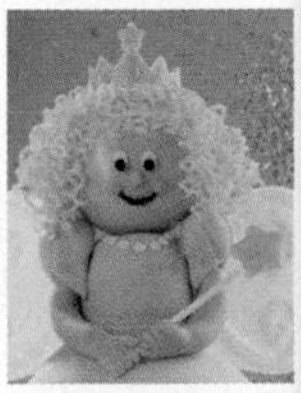

For wings, add ¼ teaspoon Gum-Tex to 4 oz. fondant. Roll out ⅛ in. thick and cut 2 hearts using cutter; let dry on cornstarch-dusted board. Cut two lollipop sticks to 5 in. and attach to back of wings with melted candy for positioning on cake. Tint 30 oz. fondant blue; mix 8 oz. with ½ teaspoon Gum-Tex and reserve remainder. Use 5 oz. to shape upper body, 2½ x 2¼ in. wide. Press top with finger to indent a curve for head to rest. Insert lollipop stick in bottom center; remove. Cut stick to 3¼ in. and insert horizontally, about ¾ in. from top, extending evenly on each side to hold sleeves. For sleeves, shape two 1 in. balls into teardrops. Indent narrow end of sleeve with finger; indent pleat lines with lollipop stick. Insert over sticks on upper body. Let dry on cornstarch-dusted board. Roll out remaining blue fondant mixture ⅛ in. thick. Cut tiara using pattern; shape into a "U" and let dry. Cut star using smallest Cut-Out; for jewels, roll one ¼ in. and four ⅛ in. balls; flatten and let dry.

Fairy Head

(see Working on Your Wishes, p. 11)

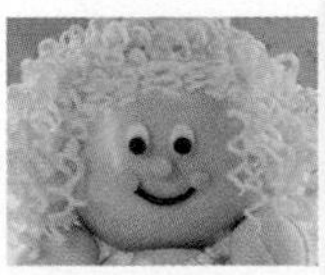

Tint melted candy light orange using candy color. Mold 2 candy shells (p. 130), ⅛ in. thick, in Mini Ball Pan. Attach 2 halves together using melted candy. Warm the end of a sharp knife and create a small hole at bottom seam to fit lollipop stick. Tint 3 oz. fondant copper; mix with ¼ teaspoon Gum-Tex. Tint ½ oz. each black and rose. Roll ¼ in. ball for nose, ⅛ in. ball pupils, flatten and shape oval eyes, roll a thin log for mouth and ¼ in. ball cheeks. Attach all with damp brush. Reserve copper fondant.

Fondant Flowers and Leaves

(see Pegasus Party Cake!, p. 12)

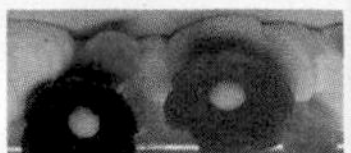

Tint 1½ oz. each: rose, orange, violet and yellow for flowers; tint 1 oz. green for leaves. Roll out ⅛ in. thick. Using medium Cut-Out, cut 7 flowers in each color. Brush tops with damp brush and press into matching Colored Sugar. Roll ¼ in. diameter flattened balls for centers; attach using damp brush. Curve flowers and let dry in Candy Melting Plate dusted with cornstarch. Using smallest Cut-Out, cut 36 leaves. Brush tops with damp brush and press into matching Colored Sugar. Let dry in and on small Flower Formers dusted with cornstarch.

continued on p. 124

Antennae

(see Joy Buzzer, p. 13)

Tint 3 oz. fondant black; mix in ½ teaspoon Gum-Tex. Roll into two 10 x ⅜ in. diameter ropes. Cut in half. Brush 1½ in. of Lollipop Stick with water; push into 1 end of rope; repeat with 2nd rope. Set on waxed paper-covered board dusted with cornstarch. Shape antennas, curling 1 in each direction. Let dry.

Globe Pillar Pirates

(see Buccaneer Tiers, p. 16)

Make 4 small pirates using 2 in. globes. Roll out tinted fondant ⅛ in. thick (unless otherwise specified). Cut a 2 x 7 in. strip to cover each globe using light copper for heads, assorted colors for shirts. Brush globes with piping gel and attach fondant, smoothing with hand. Leave opening for pillars clear of fondant. Cut 1 x 7 in. strips for pants and attach as above using damp brush. For V-neckline, cut away a small triangle of shirt and replace with light copper. Roll 1½ x ½ in. diameter logs for arms. Flatten one end for hand; use knife to cut slits for fingers. For shirt sleeves, roll small amounts of fondant to 1/16 in. thick. Cut ½ x 1½ in. long strips; cut away triangles for torn edge. Attach around arms using damp brush. Attach arms to bodies with melted candy. For shoes, shape 1¼ x ¾ in. ovals; flatten and attach.

Roll out small amount of black and white fondant 1/16 in. thick. Cut eyes using narrow end of tip 12, pupils using tip 9; attach. Add tip 1 white dot highlight. Roll small ball for nose; attach. Cut ¾ x ⅛ in. strip for mouth; attach. For bandanas, cut a 2½ in circle. Attach to head offset to one side; cut away any fondant that blocks hole. Shape 2 teardrops ¾ in. long for ties and small ball for knot; attach with candy. Pipe tip 2 icing dots. For ears, cut circle with tip 2A; cut in half and attach with candy. Roll small log for hoop earring; curve and attach. Let dry on cornstarch-dusted surface.

Make large pirate using 2½ in. globes. Cover top hole of globe for head with tape. Roll out fondant ⅛ in. thick (unless otherwise specified). Cut 2½ x 8 in. strips, light copper for head, red for shirt. Attach as above. Cut a 1¼ x 8 in. strip for pants; attach. Cut a 1 x 1½ in. high rectangle for front shirt panel and 2 small triangles for lapels; attach. Roll out small amount of white very thin; cut a circle using wide end of tip 2A. Fold and curve for rosette neck accent; attach. For arms, roll 1 x ¾ in. diameter logs; attach with candy. Roll and flatten 1 in. ball for hand; cut slits for fingers. Attach with candy. For hook, roll and curve a ¼ in. diameter log. Shape a ¾ in. ball into a tiered base. Attach hook to base and base to arm using candy. For epaulets, cut 2 circles using wide end of tip 1; attach. For shoes, shape 1 x ⅜ in. ovals; flatten and attach.

For facial features, patch, skull and crossbones roll out small amounts of black and white fondant 1/16 in. thick. Cut eye using narrow end of tip 2A, pupil using tip 12; attach. Add tip 1 white dot highlight. Roll small ball for nose; attach. Cut 1 x ⅛ in. strip for mouth; attach. For patch, cut a circle using wide end of tip 2A; cut in half and attach. Cut a ⅛ in. wide strip and attach for strap. For ears, cut a circle using tip 1A; cut in half, indent and attach. Roll small log for hoop earring; attach. Use pattern to cut out hat; fold in half and attach. For skull, cut circle with wide end of tip 2A; shape slightly. Cut out eyes and nose using tip 3; cut slit for mouth. Attach to hat. For bones, cut 2 strips 1 x ⅛ in.; attach. Roll tiny logs and attach to ends of bones. Let dry on cornstarch-dusted surface. Attach to hat.

Golf Course Details

(see Par-Tee on the Green, p. 18)

Golf balls: Roll fondant balls, ¼ in. diameter.

Flags and flagsticks: Use pattern to cut construction paper flags; write number. Tape to lollipop sticks cut to 4½ in. long. Push into ½ in. diameter flattened ball of fondant; let dry.

Putters: Cut lollipop sticks to 3 in. long. Wrap ¼ in. of ends in fondant; push one end into ½ in. long log for club head. Attach to cookie golfers using royal icing.

Loop: Roll out orange fondant ⅛ in. thick; cut a 1 x 10 in. strip. To shape curve, wrap around a 2½ in. diameter cylinder dusted with cornstarch; ends should stay level with ground. Raise cylinder ends on lollipop sticks to prevent from smashing fondant.

Tunnel: Roll out yellow fondant ⅛ in. thick; cut a 2 x 4½ in. strip. Shape tunnel over two 3 in. lengths of plastic dowel rod dusted with cornstarch. Use back of brush handle to imprint diagonal lines, 1 in. apart. Curve tunnel slightly by separating dowel rods to shape and let dry.

Windmill: Use pattern to cut base from cake board. Roll out fondant ⅛ in. thick. Cut out blades and let dry at least 24 hours. Cut wall, roof and door; attach to base using royal icing. Cut circle with wide end of tip 3; attach over center of blades. Roll a 5½ x ¼ in. diameter log; attach around door. Print message with FoodWriter. Using pattern, cut 2 easels from a cake board; attach to windmill back using royal icing; let dry.

Miniature Golf Fairway Ramps

(see Par-Tee on the Green, p. 18)

Tint 13 oz. fondant light brown for bricks. Tint 32 oz. fondant green; roll out ⅛ in. thick. Use patterns to cut small, medium and large fairway ramps from cake boards. Cover with Fanci-Foil Wrap. Brush with piping gel and cover ramps with green fondant; reserve remaining green. Roll out light brown fondant ¼ in. thick. Cut ¼ in. wide strips; attach to sides of ramps using damp brush; leave top and bottom of ramps open. Roll remaining light brown into ¼ in. diameter logs; use piping gel to attach bricks above strips and for random obstacles. Use craft knife to mark brick lines ½ in. apart. Repeat using 10 in. cake circle for bottom green. Reserve remaining green and light brown fondant.

Candy Pail, Shovel Handle, Doorway, Window

(see Sand Castle Mini Cake, p. 21)

For pail, mold 1 solid cordial cup (p. 130); chill until firm and unmold. For shovel handle, doorway and window, tape patterns to cake board and cover with waxed paper. Pipe in shovel with melted yellow, doorway and window with melted Peanut Butter Candy Melts in cut bag. Sprinkle doorway and window with brown sugar; chill until firm.

Large Teapot

(see Tinker Bell's Teapot Townhouse, p. 30)

For teapot, melt 35 oz. white candy. Pour into bottom half of Ball pan. Chill until ¼ in. shell forms; pour out excess candy. Chill until completely set; unmold. Repeat for 2nd half. Attach halves together with melted candy; let set. Roll out 15 oz. white fondant ⅛ in. thick. Cover ball with fondant, smoothing with hands and trimming as needed. **For doorway,** tint 5 oz. dark brown, 5 oz. medium brown, 2 oz. light brown. Roll out light brown ⅛ in. thick. Cut door using medium round from 101 Cutters Set. Use wide end of tip 2A to cut away window. Use knife to mark vertical wood grain lines. Attach door to ball front using damp brush. Using medium brown, roll a ¼ in. diameter log, 10 in. long. Attach around outer edge and across lower portion of door using damp brush; use knife to imprint light wood grain lines. Roll out dark brown ⅛ in. thick. Cut circle window using wide end of tip 2A; insert in door opening and smooth seam. Roll out very thin logs and use damp brush to attach over medium brown sections to look like ropes.

Add ⅛ teaspoon Gum-Tex to 3½ oz. white fondant; roll out ⅛ in. thick. Cut a 9½ x ½ in. strip and use damp brush to attach strip around door. Cut circle using largest round from 101 Cutters Set; cut a 1½ in. section for awning. Use knife to make small V-shaped cuts, about 1 in. apart, around outer edge; attach above doorway with damp brush. Roll a ½ in. diameter ball and attach to top. **For spout,** roll a 2¼ in. long log that tapers from 1¼ to ½ in. diameter. Curve and let dry. **For handle,** roll out fondant ¼ in. thick. Cut a 4 x ¾ in. strip; curve and let dry. Attach spout and handle with melted candy.

Roll 2 small dark brown logs and attach at sides under awning for braces. Roll 2 tiny light brown balls and attach as accents. Reserve remaining dark and medium brown fondant. Use fine tip brush and gold Pearl Dust mixed with lemon extract to paint scroll details around doorway. Use tea strainer to grate ivory chalk; brush over teapot. Attach leaf roof with melted candy.

Flowers, Leaves, Hanging Flower and Branch

(see Tinker Bell's Teapot Treehouse, p. 30)

Tint and prepare fondant as follows: 20 oz. green (add 1 teaspoon Gum-Tex), 2 oz. pink (add ¼ teaspoon Gum-Tex), ½ oz. yellow; ½ oz. white (add ⅛ teaspoon Gum-Tex). Roll out to ⅛ in. thick as needed; cut using cutters from Flower Making set. Using pink, cut 10 pansies and 13 apple blossoms; place on thick foam and cup using ball tool from Tool Set. Use damp brush to attach small yellow fondant ball centers. Using white, cut 10 forget-me-nots; place on thick foam and cup using ball tool. Use damp brush to attach small green ball centers. Let flowers dry on cornstarch-dusted surface. Using green fondant and rose leaf cutters, cut 55 small leaves and 50 large leaves (reserve excess green fondant); imprint veins on thin foam using veining tool from set. Let dry on small Flower Formers dusted with cornstarch. **Make leaf roof** from reserved green fondant. Roll out to ⅛ in. thick. Use patterns to cut 1 large and 3 small leaves. Imprint veins on thin foam using veining tool from set. Shape a 1½ in. ball of green fondant into a flat-bottomed cone, 2 in. high; position on outside top curve of Ball pan. Arrange leaves around cone, using cotton balls to support curves; attach leaves to cone using damp brush. Roll 3 very thin logs of fondant. Wrap loosely around stems. Let dry. **Finish leaves and flowers.** Grate green, yellow and pink artist's chalk into dust using tea strainer. Brush all leaves with various strokes of green and yellow, then brush white Pearl Dust over all. Brush pink onto edges of white forget-me-nots. **Make hanging flower and branch for tree.** For hanging flower, tint 1 in. ball of fondant violet. Indent center; pinch top edge to thin and shape round bottom of flower. Roll out green fondant 1/16 in. thick. Cut calyx using cutter from Flower Making Set; thin edges by rolling with modeling stick from set. Attach to flower with damp brush. Make small hole in center of flower; insert tiny fondant logs for stamens. Make a small hook on one end of wire; dip in water and push ½ in. into bottom of flower Let dry. **For branch,** tint ½ oz. fondant dark brown, ½ oz. medium brown. Add ⅛ teaspoon Gum-Tex; marbleize using the 2 shades of brown (p. 123). Roll and curve into a 5 in. long log, tapering from ⅜ at outer tip to ⅝ in. where branch will attach to tree trunk. Let dry on cornstarch-dusted surface.

Small Teapot

(see Take Tea with Tinker Bell, p. 30)

For teapot, melt 8 oz. white candy. Make two ⅛ in. thick candy shells (p. 130) for each treat in pan cavities. Attach halves together with melted candy; let set. Use warm knife to slowly cut a 1¾ in. diameter round top opening. Roll out 5 oz. white fondant ¼ in. thick. Cover ball with fondant, smoothing with hands and trimming at opening as needed. **For doorway,** tint 6 oz. fondant 3 shades of brown (2 oz. each) by combining brown with red-red; add black for medium and dark shades. Roll out light brown ⅛ in. thick; cut door using smallest round cutter from set. Cut out window using wide end of tip 3. Use knife to mark vertical woodgrain lines. Attach door to ball front using damp brush. Roll medium brown into a ¼ in. diameter log, 8 in. long. Trim to fit and attach 1 section around door and another piece horizontally below window. Roll out dark brown ⅛ in. thick. Cut window with wide end of tip 3; insert in door opening and smooth seam. Roll a ¼ in. diameter log of white fondant, 6 in. long. Attach around door next to brown log.

For awning, roll out white fondant ⅛ in. thick. Cut circle using medium round cutter from set. Cut a 1 in. section and attach above door with melted candy. Roll a ⅜ in. diameter ball and attach to top. Roll 2 small brown logs and attach at sides under awning. **For spout,** roll a 1¼ in. long log that tapers from ¾ to ½ in. diameter. Curve and let dry. **For handle,** roll and flatten a log ½ x 2 in. long, ¼ in. thick. Curve and let dry. Attach spout and handle with candy. Use fine tip brush and gold Pearl Dust mixed with lemon extract to paint scroll details around doorway. Use tea strainer to grate ivory chalk; brush over teapot. Grate and mix green and yellow chalk; brush over leaves and base. Brush white Pearl Dust over leaves and base. Arrange leaves on teapot to form lid; attach leaves to each other with melted candy. Position teapot on base.

Fondant Border Accents

(see Ariel's Cameo Cake, p. 31)

Tint fondant: 6 oz. rose mixed with ½ teaspoon Gum-Tex, 6 oz. aqua mixed with ½ teaspoon Gum-Tex, 3 oz. yellow mixed with ¼ teaspoon Gum-Tex. **For bow:** Roll out rose fondant ⅛ in. thick. **For loops,** cut two 1 x 7 in. long strips; attach ends with damp brush. Align loop ends and pinch together at center to form bow; support at openings with cotton balls. **For knot,** cut a 1 x 2 in. long strip; wrap around center and secure with damp brush. Reserve remaining rose fondant and let bow dry on cornstarch-dusted board. **For snail shell:** Using aqua fondant, roll a 10 in. log, 1 in. wide at one end, tapering to ¼ in. wide. Starting at narrow end, roll into a spiral; indent wide end with large ball tool. Carefully turn over and place in large Flower Forming Cup dusted with cornstarch to dry. **For clam shell:** Using 2 oz. aqua fondant, roll a 2 x 1½ x ¾ in. thick egg shape; roll to thin out 3 sides to make a 3½ x 2½ in. shell. Score lines using modeling stick from tool set. **For star flowers:** Roll out rose, aqua and yellow fondant 1/16 in. thick. Using daffodil petal cutter from Floral Collection Set, cut 1-2 flowers in each color, each with 2 extra petals. Attach extra petals to flower with Fondant Adhesive, adjusting as needed to fit. Curl petal ends over modeling stick. Let dry in Candy Melting Plate cavities dusted with cornstarch. **For centers,** roll 3 yellow balls; attach with damp brush. **For large and medium blossoms:** Use large and medium Flower Cut-Outs to cut 13 blossoms in each size in a variety of colors. Soften edges on thin foam using large ball tool. Let dry on large and small Flower Formers dusted with cornstarch. For centers, roll and attach five ⅛ in. teardrop shapes for large blossoms and one ¼ in. ball for small blossoms. Attach with damp brush.

Fondant Spaceship and Elmo Features

(see Blast Off Elmo, p. 32)

Tint 44 oz. of fondant dark gray; reserve 8 oz.. Prepare cake for rolled fondant (p. 119); cover and smooth with Fondant Smoother. Tint 10 oz. fondant light gray; roll out ¼ in. thick. Cut a 22 x 1 in. strip and attach across spaceship with damp brush. Reserve remaining light gray fondant. **For exhaust pipe,** roll out reserved dark gray fondant 1¼ in. thick; cut using pattern. **For exhaust flames,** tint 8 oz. fondant orange. Roll balls from ¾ to 1 in. diameter and attach to exhaust flames cookie with piping gel. Roll out remaining orange fondant ⅛ in. thick; cover balls with fondant, shaping with hand. **Make hand.** Roll out 16 oz. white fondant ¾ in. thick. Using pattern, cut out hand and fingers. Shape and smooth edges and wrist. Shape 5 oz. of fondant for arm using pattern. **For shoulders,** roll out white fondant 1¼ in. thick. Cut a 7 x 1½ in. strip; taper ends and attach to spaceship cake with damp brush. **For fingers on spaceship,** roll two 2 in. and one 2½ in. logs, 1¼ in. wide; attach with damp brush. **For lights:** Tint 2 oz. fondant yellow. Roll out yellow and reserved light gray ⅛ in. thick. Using patterns, cut four large gray ovals and four medium yellow ovals; attach with damp brush. **For remaining decorations,** tint ½ oz. blue, 4 oz. red. Roll out ⅛ in. thick. **For glove patch,** cut a medium blue oval and a small red oval; attach with damp brush. **For arm,** cut a 3½ x ¼ in. red strip; attach. Cut letters using cutters from set; attach. Brush exhaust flames with water and sprinkle with red sugar.

Sandwich

(see Well Done, SpongeBob, p. 35)

For bun halves, cover soccer ball and 1 round cake with light brown fondant. For burger, ice the 2nd round cake and cut mini marshmallows into ¼ to ½ in. pieces; attach to sides for texture. Cover with dark brown fondant. For cheese, roll out fondant ¼ in thick; cut a 8½ in. square. For lettuce, roll out fondant ⅛ in. thick; use a 10 in. circle as a guide then use knife to cut a wavy edge ½ in. larger than circle. Stack bottom bun, burger, cheese, lettuce and round top on Cake Base. Insert a sharpened 12 in. wooden dowel rod through cakes; the plastic dowel rod from candy plaque will be placed over this.

Boot, Leaves and Vine

(see Growing Up with WALL-E, p. 36)

Tint fondant as follows: 1 oz. brown, ½ oz. green. Add ½ teaspoon Gum-Tex to each. Roll out ⅛ in. thick. Use pattern and craft knife to cut out boot. Let dry on waxed paper-covered board dusted with cornstarch. Cut 2 leaves using smallest Cut-Out; let dry in smallest Flower Former dusted with cornstarch. **For vine,** roll a ¼ in. diameter rope, 3½ in. long. Curve and let dry on cornstarch-dusted surface. Assemble pieces using melted candy. Use icing to pipe tip 3 outlines and tip 1 eyelet details.

Covering Cakes with Blended Fondant

(see Growing Up with WALL-E, p. 36)

Tint fondant as follows: 40 oz. light gray; 4 oz. each blue, red, yellow, black, dark gray; reserve 4 oz. white. **For each cube,** roll out 5 oz. of light gray ⅛ in. thick; pinch off pieces of other colors and press into light gray. Reroll to ⅛ in. thick. Wrap 1 cake cube, smoothing with hand. Repeat until all 8 cubes are covered. Grate black chalk through tea strainer to create a powder. Brush onto cubes for dirty look. Position 6 cubes on base board; center 2 cubes on top. Push sharpened wooden dowel rod through center of each top cube and sink into base board for stability.

Witch Hats and Heads

(see She's Melting!, p. 43)

For hats, using melted candy in cut parchment bag, pipe 1 x 1½ in. oval brims, approx. 1/16 in. thick, on cookie sheet; let set. Cover cone-shaped treats with melted candy; let set. Attach cones to brims with melted candy; chill until firm. **For heads,** tint portions of fondant green, violet, yellow and orange. Roll a 1¼ in. diameter ball for head. Roll small cone for nose; attach using damp brush. Use FoodWriter to draw eyes and mouth. Roll out fondant colors 1/16 in. thick. Cut a 1 x 2½ in. strip for hair. Cut 1/16 in. wide slits, ¾ in. deep. Attach to head. Repeat to add 2nd layer. Cut a ¼ x 2 in. strip for hatband; attach to hat. Cut small fondant buckle; attach. Attach hat to head with melted candy.

Antlers

(see Santa's Deer Friend, p. 48)

For each antler, cut an f-shaped piece from right or left of center of pretzel twist using a sawing motion and a serrated knife held at an angle. Cut a smaller piece from remaining pretzel. Position larger piece on waxed paper, then attach smaller piece on left side with melted candy. Chill until firm.

Skeleton Frame

(see Boneyard Boss, p. 45)

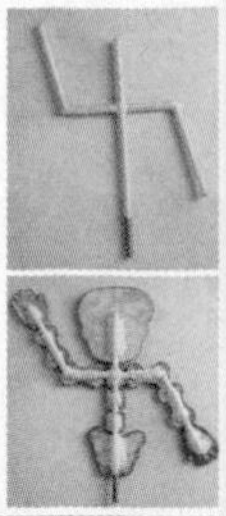

Cut dowel rods as follows: 16½ in. for spine/skull, 4 in. for upper arms (2), 7 in. for lower arms/hands (2). Working on flat, waxed paper-covered surface, use hot glue gun to assemble frame. Attach upper arms 5½ in. down from top to allow room for skull; let set. Attach lower arms to ends of upper arms, holding each rod in angled position until set. When cool, wrap with white ribbon, securing with hot glue as needed; leave bottom 3 in. of spine bare to insert into base. Prepare dowel rods for lower legs and feet: Cut 2 sections, 6 in. each. Wrap with white ribbon, leaving 1½ in. of 2 sections bare to insert into base.

Snowmen

(see Snowman Summit, p. 51)

Knead ½ teaspoon Gum-Tex into 6 oz. white fondant. Roll out ⅛ in. thick. Cut 3 heads using medium Cut-Out, 3 bodies using large Cut-Out and an extra 3 in. circle for top snowman. **For hats,** roll out reserved black fondant ⅛ in. thick. Cut 1 in. square and taper sides slightly; cut a 1¼ x ¼ in. strip for each brim. **For scarf ends,** tint a 1½ in. ball of fondant red; knead in ¼ teaspoon Gum-Tex. Roll out 1/16 in. thick and cut a 4 x ¼ in. strip for each scarf. Fold in half for V-shape; shape slight curves. Cut 1/16 in. wide slits, ⅜ in. deep, in ends for fringe. Let all pieces dry on cornstarch-dusted surface. Reserve remaining red and black fondant. Assemble snowmen on lollipop sticks using fondant adhesive. **For smaller snowmen,** attach heads to sticks, slightly off center, leaving ¾ in. extended at top for hats. Attach bodies, again slightly off center. **For large snowman,** attach 3 in. bottom circle and head; attach center circle, overlapping at waist. Attach hat and brims. Tint a ½ in. ball of fondant green; roll out ⅛ in. thick. Cut a 1 x ¼ in. wide strip and use damp brush to attach at seam for hat band. Roll out reserved red fondant 1/16 in. thick. Cut a 1½ x ¼ in. strip to wrap around neck; attach using damp brush. Attach scarf ends with adhesive. Roll out reserved black fondant ⅛ in. thick. Cut eyes using tip 7 and mouth using tip 6; attach. Tint ½ in. ball of fondant violet and roll out ⅛ in. thick. Cut buttons using tip 8; attach. Tint ½ in. ball of fondant orange. Shape small cones for noses; attach. Brush white areas of snowman with Pearl Dust. Let dry on cornstarch-dusted surface.

Holiday Star, Ornaments, Leaves, Berries

(see Decked Out Tree Tower, p. 53)

For star topper: Roll out prepared fondant ⅛ in. thick. Use patterns to cut large silver and small gold star. Let dry on cornstarch-dusted boards. Using tinted royal icing, decorate with tip 2 and tip 3 lines, dots and swirls. Let dry several hours. Attach Lollipop Stick to center back of large star, allowing 2 in. to extend beyond bottom points of star to insert into cake; let set. Attach small star to front with fondant adhesive. Paint with Pearl Dust/Clear Vanilla mixture (p. 122).

Continued on p. 126.

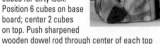

Continued from p. 125

Holiday Star & Ornaments

(see Decked Out Tree Tower, p. 53) cont.

For ornaments: Roll out prepared fondant ⅛ in. thick. Cut 15 silver and 15 gold ornaments using cutters from 3 Pc. Holiday Colored Metal Set. Let dry on cornstarch-dusted surface. Decorate with tinted royal icing using tip 2 and tip 3 lines, dots and swirls. Let dry several hours then paint with Pearl Dust/Clear Vanilla mixture; let dry. Cut ribbon into 5 in. lengths. Attach about 1 in. to back top of each ornament using fondant adhesive. Use Cake Dividing Set to divide 6 in. plate into 8ths, 8 in. plate into 10ths and 10 in. plate into 12ths; mark edges with icing dots. Lay ornaments flat, decorated side up, around plates at marks, about ⅛ in. away from outside edge of plates. Extend ribbons over plate tops and secure using fondant adhesive; let dry. Fold ornaments up onto plate tops for transport.

For leaves: Roll out prepared green fondant ⅛ in. thick. Cut 230 leaves using holly leaf cutter from 6 Pc. Christmas Mini Cutter Set. Place on thin shaping foam and score lines using veining tool from Fondant/Gum Paste Tool Set. Set in various positions on and in small and medium Flower Formers dusted with cornstarch. Let dry then brush with Green Pearl Dust (p. 151).

For berries: Roll white fondant into 70 balls, ⅜ in. diameter. Brush with Piping Gel and roll in red Colored Sugar. Let dry on cornstarch-dusted surface.

Fondant Skis, Ski Poles, Scarf Ends

(see Ski Scene, p. 54)

Knead ½ teaspoon Gum-Tex into 6 oz. white fondant. Divide and tint portions red, green, yellow, blue, pink and black. Roll out ⅛ in. thick. **For each ski,** cut a ⅜ x 3 in. strip. Cut front end to a V; curl over a lollipop stick and let dry on cornstarch-dusted surface. **For each ski pole,** cut a circle using wide end of tip 12. Use lollipop stick to make a center hole. Let dry. Cut lollipop stick to 3 in. long; use thinned fondant adhesive to attach circle with ⅜ in. of stick extended through bottom. Let dry. **For each scarf,** cut a ¼ x 4 in. strip; fold over for V shape. Cut ¼ in. deep slits in ends for fringe. Let dry.

House Assembly and Decoration

(see Let's Raise the Roof!, p. 55)

On foil-wrapped cake circle, using tip 4, attach front, back and side panels with icing; let set. **To support roof,** cut a 2 x 3½ in. long piece of cake board and bend in half. Attach roof panels, centered on each half of support, with icing. Position roof on assembled house. Pipe tip 4 seam on top peak; let set. Remove roof from house and let dry, standing on a side edge. Mark a 1 x 2¼ in. door; outline door and fill in with tip 3 zigzags (smooth with finger dipped in cornstarch). Attach confetti sprinkles from Flowerful Medley (p. 146) assortment on door frame and for doorknob with tip 2 dots of icing. **For windows,** roll out spice drops on surface sprinkled with sugar; cut a ½ in. square for door window. Cut 1 x ½ in rectangle for front window and 1 in. squares for side and back windows. Attach with tip 3. Outline window frames and panes with tip 3; pipe tip 2 icicles. Attach striped candy awnings and jelly rope windowsills, cut to fit, with tip 4. Pipe tip 3 scrolls above front window; attach confetti in center. Using tip 3, attach pinwheel candy above door and spice drop half in center; cut curve off candy canes and attach candy sticks on house corners. Position roof on house (do not attach); ice smooth and cover with jumbo confetti, overlapping from bottom to top. Pipe tip 3 zigzags on peak and position spice drops. Pipe tip 4 icicles on eaves. Attach green spice drops around house for bushes; trim bases as needed for desired height. Ice cake circle fluffy. Position striped candy for front step; let dry.

Feet & Beak

(see Cheep Thrills, p. 58)

Add ¼ teaspoon Gum-Tex to 1½ oz. fondant. Tint 1 oz. brown, ½ oz. orange. Roll out brown ⅛ in. thick. Cut a 2¼ x ½ in. strip. Wrap around end of Lollipop Stick for leg (leave remainder of stick bare to insert into cake); smooth. Repeat. Roll 4 logs, 1½ in. long; match width to leg. Use Thinned Fondant Adhesive to attach to sides for toes. **For beak,** roll ¾ in. ball of fondant into cone 1¼ in. long. Cut lollipop stick to 3 in. Insert into beak, leaving 2½ in. exposed to insert into cake. Let pieces dry overnight on cornstarch-dusted surface.

Ducks

(see Bathtime Buddies, p. 65)

Make small ducks using Rubber Ducky Candy Mold. Dust cavities with cornstarch, press in fondant, then unmold onto cornstarch-dusted surface. Shape a flattened dot for eye and tiny dot for pupil. Attach using damp brush.

Make medium ducks using 2 in. globes. Roll out fondant ⅛ in. thick. Cut a 2 x 7 in. strip to wrap each globe. Brush globes with piping gel and attach fondant, smoothing with hand. Leave opening for pillars clear of fondant. Cut tip 2A eyes and tip 10 pupils using narrow ends of tips; attach using damp brush. Use brush to add White-White dot eye highlight. Shape 2 triangles **for beak**; attach. **Cut wings** using medium leaf Cut-Out; reverse and cut again for a symmetrical wing. Shape and attach. Cut feet using medium leaf Cut-Out. Trim ¾ in. off narrow tip. Use knife to cut and shape webbed feet. Trim bottom of foot using wide end of tip 10, cutting off ¼ in. Let dry on cornstarch-dusted surface.

Make large duck using 2½ in. globes. Cover top hole of globe for head with tape. Roll out fondant ⅛ in. thick. Cut a 2½ x 8 in. strip for each globe. Attach as above. Cut tip 1A eyes and tip 12 pupils; attach. Add White-White dot eye highlight. Shape 2 triangles for beak; attach. Roll out small amount of yellow and orange ¼ in. thick. Cut wings using large leaf cutter from set; trim off point using open end of tip 1A to match body curve. Shape and attach. Use knife to cut small spikes; attach for hair. Cut feet using large leaf Cut-Out; cut and shape webbed feet; attach.

Baby Topper

(see Lunar Lullabyes, p. 69)

Combine 1 teaspoon Gum-Tex with 4 oz. fondant; tint yellow. Roll out ⅛ in. thick. Using a 5 in. diameter bowl or plate as your guide, cut a circle. Move guide over 2 in. and cut again for crescent shape. Let dry on waxed paper-covered board dusted with cornstarch. Tint 1 tablespoon of piping gel with 2-3 drops of White-White. Spread over moon with a spatula. Use a spoon to crush and push Cake Sparkles through strainer and onto moon for an even dusting. Let dry on board.

For baby, combine ½ teaspoon Gum-Tex with 2 oz. fondant; pinch off a ¾ in. ball for diaper and tint remainder light copper. Roll a ¾ in. ball for head, ⅝ in. ball for upper body, ½ in. long log for arm, ⅝ in. long log for leg with foot. With moon still on board, assemble baby, attaching pieces using damp brush. Use tip of knife to indent fingers and mouth. Attach a tiny ball for nose. Use FoodWriter to draw eyes. When completely dry, attach a Lollipop Stick to back using fondant adhesive (or melted candy); allow 4 in. of stick to extend at bottom to insert into cake.

Fondant Daisies

(see Shining in the Spirit, p. 70)

Mix ½ teaspoon Gum-Tex into 6 oz. rolled fondant. Roll out 1⁄16 in. thick. Cut using medium daisy Cut-Out. Place on thin foam and use large veining tool to shape petals, starting at pointed end and working to center. Let dry in large Flower Forming Cups dusted with cornstarch. For center, roll a ¼ in. fondant ball, flatten slightly and attach using damp brush. Brush top with Piping Gel and sprinkle with Sparkling Sugar; brush off excess with dry brush. Let dry.

Stairs, Arches and Railings

(see A Glorious Ascent, p. 71)

Using patterns and gum paste rolled out ⅛ in. thick, cut pieces as follows. **For stairs,** cut 2 side sections; reverse pattern and cut 2 more. Cut 26 regular steps and 2 larger top steps. **For arches,** cut 1 center panel and 2 side panels. Cut 1 each small and large railings. Let all dry 48 hours on cornstarch-dusted surface. Complete stairs, arches and railings using royal icing. Assemble stairs using tip 3; trim if needed to fit and let dry. Pipe tip 2 bead border over outside seams; let dry. Trim arches with a tip 2 outline on edge and ½ in. inside edge. Attach puddle dots (p.122) between edge and outline. Let dry. Attach 2 lollipop sticks (8 in. long) to back of each arch, allowing 3 in. to extend at bottom to insert into cake. Let dry. Outline railings with tip 2; attach puddle dots. Let dry. Paint trim area on arches and railing tops with Clear Vanilla and White Pearl Dust.

Floral Arrangements

(see A Glorious Ascent, p. 71)

Tint 8 oz. fondant rose (or blue); roll out 1⁄16 in. thick. Use forget-me-not cutter from Floral Collection Set to cut 320 flowers (make extras to allow for breakage); reserve remaining fondant for stair runners. Place flowers on thick foam and cup centers using rounded end of modeling stick from set. Let dry, then pipe tip 2 dot centers with white royal icing. Press a ¾ in. ball of fondant or gum paste onto top of Flower Spike (p. 240). Using royal icing and tip 2, attach approx. 35 flowers; add tip 349 leaves. Let dry. Brush with Pearl Dust.

Fondant Swags and Drapes

(see The Quinceañera's Court, p. 72, Fulfilling the Commitment, p. 73 and The Pink Palace, p. 100)

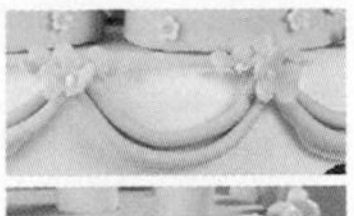

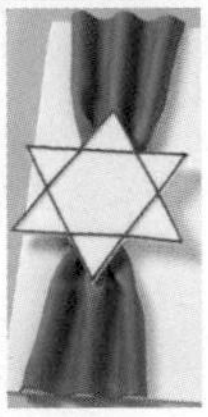

Tint fondant and roll out 1⁄16 in. thick. For *The Quinceañera's Court,* cut 6 x 3 in. strips (22 needed). For *Fulfilling the Commitment and The Pink Palace,* cut 5 x 3½ in. strips (2 needed for *Fulfilling the Commitment* top and bottom halves, 17 needed for *The Pink Palace*). **For looser pleats,** use wooden or plastic dowel rods. **For tighter pleats,** use wooden skewers or lollipop sticks. Form pleats in fondant by placing a dowel rod or stick under bottom edge of fondant strip and one on top, next to the first. Repeat with more rods or sticks to form pleats. Remove dowel rods, gather ends together and brush with water to secure. For *Fulfilling the Commitment,* gather one end only and flatten area approx. 2 in. where star point will rest. Repeat for 2nd half of drape. Let dry on cornstarch-dusted surface.

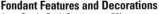

Fondant Features and Decorations

(see Grads Grab Success, p. 75)

Roll 1⅛ in. ball heads, 1¾ x ½ in. logs for arms, ¼ x ⅛ in. ovals for ears, ⅛ in. ball for nose; attach with damp brush. **For hands,** roll ½ in. balls; flatten, cut and score fingers with knife. **For diploma,** roll out white fondant ⅛ in. thick; cut a 1 in. square and roll up. Attach hands and diploma with damp brush. **For hat,** roll a ¾ in. ball; flatten and attach to mortarboard with damp brush. **For hair,** roll out fondant ⅛ in. thick. Cut a ½ x 2 in. strip for boy; cut ⅜ in. strands and attach with damp brush. Repeat for a 2nd row. Cut a 1 x 2 in. strip for girl; cut in thin strips and attach with damp brush. **For tassels,** cut a 1 x ½ in. strip; cut ⅜ in. slits for fringe. Roll up strip. **For strings,** roll a 1¼ x ⅛ in. log. Attach string to cap and tassel to string with damp brush. **For button on cap,** roll a ¼ in. ball, flatten and attach.

Simple Gum Paste Blossoms:

(See Floral Frost, p. 77)
Roll out gum paste 1/16 in. thick. Cut 196 medium blossoms using pansy cutter from Floral Collection Flower Making Set. Place on thick foam and shape flower center using rounded end of modeling stick. Let dry in Candy Melting Plate dusted with cornstarch. Cut 308 small blossoms using apple blossom cutter from Floral Collection Set. Cup centers of flowers on thick foam using rounded end of modeling stick. Let dry on flower formers. Using royal icing, add tip 2 dot centers. Brush all blossoms with Pearl Dust; let set.

Draped Hearts

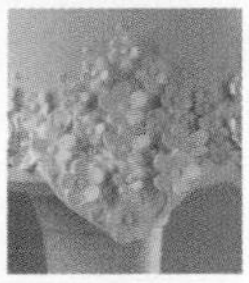

(See Floral Frost, p. 77)
Cover plates from 3-Tier Pillar Cake Stand Set and outside of cake pans with waxed paper. Secure pans to corresponding plates with royal icing dots. Roll 3/8 in. thick fondant logs, long enough to wrap around bottom of each cake pan. Wrap logs in plastic wrap then secure in position with icing dots. Roll out gum paste 1/8 in. thick; cut 28 hearts using 2nd largest cutter from nesting set. Using dots of icing, attach hearts around prepared pans, with heart points hanging about 1½ in. below plates. Position 11 hearts around 12 in. pan, 9 around 10 in. pan. Position 8 hearts around 8 in. pan, trimming 1 heart in back to fit. Using royal icing, decorate hearts with tip 2 scrolls. Attach 3 small and 5 medium blossoms to each heart with tip 4 dots. Let dry for several days. Carefully remove hearts and store on large bubble wrap until reception. Reserve plastic-wrapped fondant logs for assembling cake.

Fondant Heart Plaque

(see Good Answer!, p. 81)
Combine 4 oz. fondant with 1/4 teaspoon Gum-Tex and tint light rose; roll out 1/8 in. thick. Using pattern, cut out heart with knife. Let dry on cake board covered with waxed paper and dusted with cornstarch. **For message,** tape pattern to cake board and cover with waxed paper. Roll a 3/8 x 24½ in. long white fondant rope. Cut a 12½ in. piece for "Y", 8 in. for "es" and 4 in. for exclamation point. Roll small ball for bottom of exclamation point. Form letters over pattern; let dry. Mix Pink Pearl Dust with vanilla; paint message and let dry.

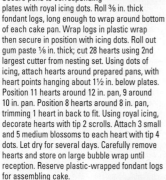

Overlays for Round Cakes

(see Setting the Gold Standard, p. 86)

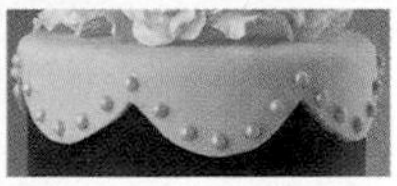

For overlays, tint 48 oz. fondant ivory; roll out 1/8 in. thick. Turn 6 in. pan bottom side up and cover with a cut-to-fit waxed paper circle. Cut a 10 in. fondant circle and gently smooth over waxed paper and down sides of pan. Use pattern to cut scallops. Carefully lift fondant from waxed paper and pan and position overlay on 6 in. tier; smooth. Repeat for 8 in. tier using 12 in. fondant circle. Attach gold dots, about 3/8 in. apart, using dots of icing.

Rounded Gum Paste Blossoms

(see Setting the Gold Standard, p. 86)

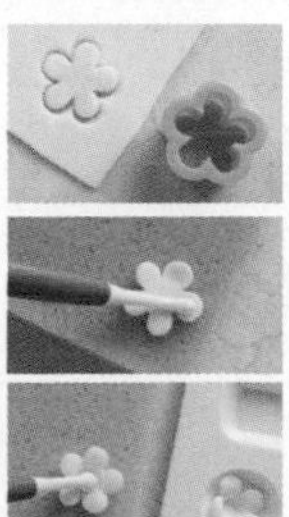

Roll out gum paste 1/16 in. thick. Cut 8 blossoms using Pansy cutter from Floral Collection Flower Making Set. Place on thick foam and cup each petal using large dogbone tool. Turn over flower and cup center with large dogbone tool. Let dry in cavities of Candy Melting Plate dusted with cornstarch.Pipe tip 3 centers using royal icing. Let dry. Paint centers with gold Pearl Dust (p. 151) and lemon extract.

Chocolate Fondant Bow

(see Choc Full of Excitement!, p. 87)
Knead 1 teaspoon Gum-Tex into 8 oz. tinted chocolate fondant. Roll out 1/8 in. thick. Cut about 15 strips, 1 x 7 in. Brush ends with damp brush and pinch together to form loop. Set on cut edge sides on cornstarch-dusted surface; let dry for 2-3 days. Assemble bow on a waxed paper-covered 6 in. cake circle using melted Candy Melts. Position 6-7 loops for base layer (trim pinched ends into a V-shape to fit); add additional loops to fill center.

Top Border Circles and Hanging Plate Circles

(see Crimson Lace, p. 88)
Roll out white fondant 1/8 in. thick. Cut 84 Top Border Circles using medium Cut-Out. Let dry on cornstarch-dusted board. Cut 60 Hanging Plate Circles using large Cut-Out. Mark center of each plate side and position plates on 4 in. high containers. Attach hanging circles with damp brush, positioning so that 1 in. of circle rests on plate. Space circles evenly using 3 per side on 6 in. plate, 5 per side on 10 in. plate, 7 per side on 14 in. plate; let dry. Assemble and decorate using royal icing. Attach prepared red/white teardrops to bottom edge of Hanging Circles; let set. Pipe tip 1 scrolls on all circles. Attach 5 forget-me-nots to each Top Border Circle. Randomly attach additional forget-me-nots and apple blossoms to Hanging Circles; let dry.

Rose Topper

(see Crimson Lace, p. 88)

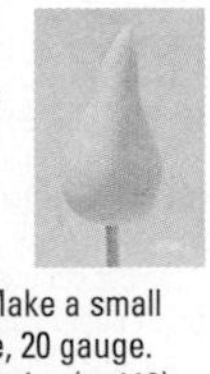

1. You will need 18 roses. (Make extras to allow for breakage.) Tint 16 oz. gum paste red. Make rose bases. Roll a 5/8 in. ball of gum paste into a teardrop shape, 1¼ in. high. Make a small hook at one end of a 5 in. wire, 20 gauge. Dip hook into Gum Paste Adhesive (p. 119) and insert halfway into bottom base. Insert wire in craft block and let dry 48 hours.

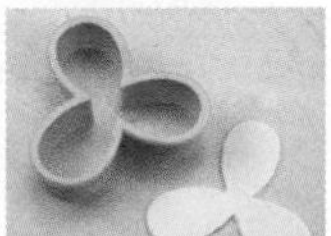

2. Roll out gum paste 1/16 in. thick. For small roses, use tulip petal cutter from Flower Collection Set (p. 153) to cut 1 petal for each rose; cut petal into 3 separate petals.

3. Place petals horizontally on thin foam dusted with cornstarch. Soften top petal edge with large ball tool from Fondant/Gum Paste Tool Set (p. 151).

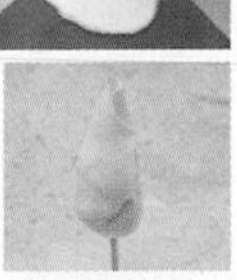

4. Brush back of petals from midpoint down with adhesive. Wrap petals around base to form bud for each rose.

5. Cut another set of 3 petals to add to each base. Slightly widen and elongate each petal using modeling stick. Turn petals so the rounded end is the top of petal and the point is the bottom. Soften top petal edge with ball tool on thin foam. Turn petals over. Add adhesive to bottom half of petals; position and press onto rose base.

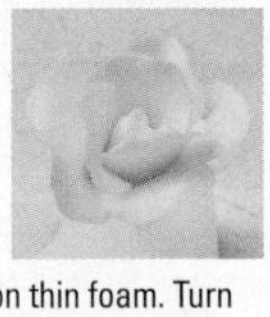

6. Cut and attach a second row of 5 petals. Brush roses with non-toxic red pastel chalk grated through a tea strainer and let dry.

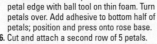

7. For topper base, combine remaining red gum paste with enough fondant to form a 2 in. ball. Shape into a ball half 3 x 1½ in. high. Attach base to 6 in. cake circle covered with waxed paper. Insert roses in base, trimming wires as needed.

Flowers and Leaves

(see Sunbeam Blossoms, p. 91)
For each flower, tint a 1½ in. ball of fondant yellow, peach or rose; add 1/8 teaspoon of Gum-Tex. Roll out 1/16 in. thick; cut 2 daisies for each flower using largest Cut-Out. Place daisies on thin foam dusted with cornstarch. Shape petals with large dogbone tool, lightly pressing with tool from tip to center of petals. Turn daisies over and move to thick foam. Brush center with water. Position second daisy on top of first, positioning so petals are staggered. Cup center with large ball tool. Let dry in Flower Forming Cup dusted with cornstarch. For centers, roll a 3/8 in. ball of yellow fondant; flatten slightly, brush top with water and dip in yellow sugar. Attach inside flower with water. Let dry. For leaves, tint a 1½ in. ball green and mix with 1/8 teaspoon Gum-Tex. Roll out 1/16 in. thick. Cut out 1 leaf for each flower using medium Cut-Out. Place on thin foam. Imprint center vein with small veining tool. Pinch bottom of leaf slightly to shape and place in Flower Forming Cup to dry.

Topiary Stand and Ball

(see Tie-the-Knot Topiary, p. 91)
Insert 19 in. wooden dowel rod 4 in. deep into craft foam rectangle. Attach bottom of craft foam rectangle to inside bottom center of pail with hot glue. Slide plastic dowel rod over wooden rod, pressing into craft foam 2 in. Fill pail to top with fondant. Insert extending portion of wooden rod into bottom of craft foam ball to make hole and remove ball. Ice ball with a thin coat of royal icing; immediately wrap ball with self-sealing plastic wrap. Reposition ball on wooden rod and secure with melted candy.

Rose Refinement Petits Fours

(see Tie-the-Knot Topiary, p. 91)
Pans: 9 x 13 x 2 in. Sheet, p. 157; Cookie Sheet, Cooling Grid, p. 159; **Tips:** 7, 102, p. 136-137
Colors: Kelly Green, Rose, p. 148; **Recipes:** Royal Icing, p. 118; Quick-Pour Fondant, p. 119; **Also:** Round Cut-Outs, p. 153; Meringue Powder, p. 145: Flower Nail No. 7, p. 140; waxed paper, knife.

In advance: Make flowers. For each treat, using royal icing, make a tip 102 rose with tip 7 base. Make extras to allow for breakage and let dry. Bake and cool 1-layer sheet cake; trim cake to 1¼ in. high. Cut circles using largest Cut-Out. Cover cakes with Quick-Pour Fondant Icing (p. 119); let set. Attach rose with dots of royal icing. Each serves 1.

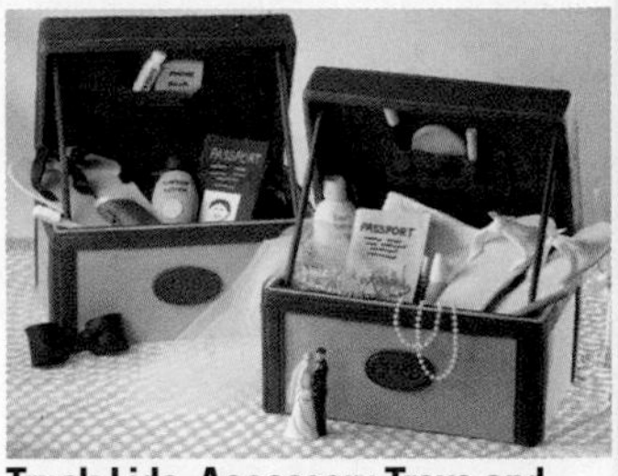

Trunk Lids, Accessory Trays and Accessories

(see Beach Bound, p. 92)

For trunk lids and trays: Mold 4 candy plaques (p. 130) in 9 x 13 in. Cake Pan using 2 packs of melted Light Cocoa Candy Melts for each plaque. These will be used for top and bottom sections. Chill until firm; unmold onto waxed paper-covered cake boards to return to room temperature.
For side panels, mold 4 candy plaques (p. 130) in medium Non-Stick Cookie Pan using 2 packs of melted Light Cocoa Candy Melts for each plaque. Chill completely then unmold onto waxed paper-covered cake boards to return to room temperature. Cut two strips 2 x 8½ in. and two strips 2 x 12 ¾ in. for sides of each lid or tray. Attach strips to 9 x 13 in. candy plaques using melted candy; let set. Level edges using warming tray or knife. Prepare 2 recipes (1 for each trunk) of Chocolate Fondant (p. 119). Brush outside of lid with damp brush. Roll out Chocolate Fondant 1/8 in. thick and cover outside of lid. Use ridged wheel of Cutter/Embosser to imprint stitching along edges. Let dry. Knead ½ teaspoon Gum-Tex into a 2½ in. ball of fondant. Roll out 1/8 in. thick. Cut 2 strips 6½ x 3 in. for pockets inside lids. Imprint stitching along edges. Place on waxed paper-covered board. Use cotton balls dusted with cornstarch to shape indentations for accessories. Let dry at least 48 hours. For lid supports, roll out remaining fondant 1/16 in. thick. Cut 4 strips 12 x 1½ in. Brush backs with damp brush and wrap around 4 wooden dowel rods. Smooth and trim as needed. Let dry. Reserve remaining fondant.
Prepare fondant for accessories: Add 12 oz. white fondant and 1½ teaspoons Gum-Tex to ½ of reserved Chocolate Fondant (reserve other ½ for trunk trims); tint black. Add 1 tablespoon Gum-Tex to 36 oz. white fondant and tint as follows. For light pink, add a 2 in. ball of pink Neon to 14 oz. of white. For gray, add a 1½ in. ball of black to 3 oz. of white. Tint 10 oz. of white light blue. Reserve remaining white.

Flip-Flops: Roll out 10 oz. light pink fondant ¼ in. thick. Use pattern to cut 1 flip-flop; reverse and cut mate. Repeat using blue fondant. **For straps,** roll out white 1/8 in. thick. Cut 3 strips 4 x 5/8 in. Imprint stitching marks on 2 using ridged wheel of Cutter/Embosser. Set a large Flower Former on 2 dowel rods to create open space under the bottom; dust with cornstarch. Brush ends of 2 imprinted strips with damp brush; pinch to join at an angle. Position toward end of Flower Former. Curve remaining strip evenly over and around joint; pinch loose ends together, allowing toe section to hang down off front end. Fold long ends of straps slightly and tuck under Flower Former. Repeat for 2nd white strap and for 2 black straps. Let dry at least 48 hours. Cut 2 white flowers using medium Cut-Out. Place on foam and cup petals using dog bone tool from set; turn over and cup center. Let dry in Candy Melting Plate dusted with cornstarch. Pipe tip 5 dot centers in royal icing; let dry. Brush flowers with white Pearl Dust. Attach straps to flip-flops and flowers to white strap using fondant adhesive (p. 119).

Continued on p. 128.

Continued from p. 127

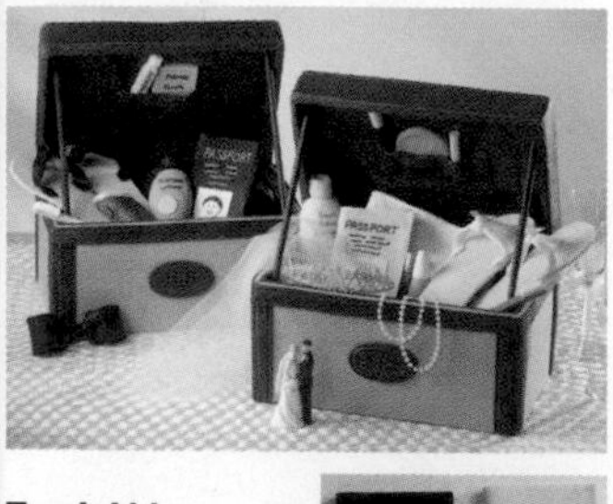

Trunk Lids, Accessory Trays and Accessories

(see Beach Bound p. 92) cont.

Passports: Roll out 4 oz. light pink fondant ⅛ in. thick. Cut a 6 x 8 in. rectangle. Roll out a small amount of white fondant ⅛ in. thick; cut a 5 ¾ x 7½ in. rectangle for inside pages. Center white pages on pink cover and position a brush vertically in center. Fold pages and cover in half over handle; remove brush. Let dry. Repeat using black fondant. Roll out white fondant 1/16 in. thick; cut a 2 x 1⅞ in. rectangle for photo area. Attach with damp brush. Using royal icing, pipe tip 5 heads; flatten and smooth with finger dipped in cornstarch. Pipe tip 2 dot eyes and nose, outline neck and ears, e-motion woman's hair and fill-in blouse and shirt. Pipe tip 1 dot pupils, outline mouth, pull-out man's hair, PASSPORT and lettering lines.

Comb: Roll out black fondant ⅛ in. thick. Cut a 1 x 4 in. strip; round corners. Use a craft knife to cut ¾ in. deep slits, 1/16 in. apart for teeth.

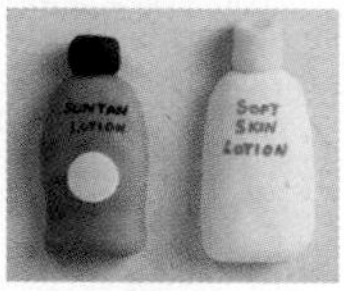

Lotion Bottles: Cut 2 blocks 2 x 4 in. from prepared cereal treats. Shape and round edges. Knead together a 1½ in. ball of white and a 2 in. ball of yellow or purple Neon fondant. Roll out ⅛ in. thick and cover bottle shape. Shape caps from ¾ in. fondant balls; attach using damp brush. Score lines using smooth wheel of Cutter/Embosser. Roll out some Neon yellow 1/16 in. thick. Use wide end of tip 1A to cut circle for suntan lotion; attach using damp brush. Let dry. Print labels using FoodWriters.

Shaver: Cut a block 1¾ x 3½ in. from prepared crisped rice cereal treats. Shape and round edges. Cover with dark gray fondant rolled ⅛ in. thick. Roll out some light gray ¼ in. thick. Cut a 1 x 1¼ in. rectangle for blades; attach using damp brush. Imprint lines using edge of small spatula. Shape ⅜ x 1 in. on/off switch and attach to side.

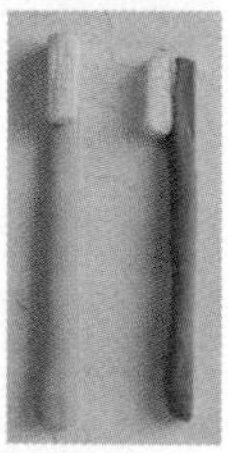

Toothbrushes: Roll a ½ x 5 in. long fondant log from pink Neon fondant. Insert lollipop stick trimmed to 5¼ in. long. Reshape for handle. Roll a ½ x 1¼ in. white fondant log. Flatten and shape for bristles. Imprint lines using smooth wheel of Cutter/Embosser. Attach to handle with damp brush. Repeat in blue.

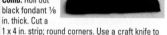

Toothpaste: Tint a 1½ in. white ball golden yellow. Roll a 4 x ½ in. diameter log. Flatten sides and pinch end for tube shape. Shape cap from ½ in. fondant ball; attach using damp brush. Score lines using smooth wheel of Cutter/Embosser; let dry. Print letters with FoodWriter.

Phone Book: Roll out gray fondant ⅛ in. thick. Cut a 4½ x 3 in. rectangle. Fold in half; let dry. Print letters with FoodWriter.

Bow Tie: Roll out black fondant ⅛ in. thick. Cut 2 strips 2 x 5 in. long. Brush ends with damp brush; fold over and pinch together ends to form loops. Insert cotton balls to shape. For knot, roll out fondant 1/16 in. thick; cut a 1½ x 2¼ in. strip. Brush back with damp brush; wrap and smooth over center.. Let dry before removing cotton balls.

Shaving Bag: Cut and stack prepared crisped rice cereal treats to form a 6¼ x 2 x 3 in. high block. Roll out black fondant ⅛ in. thick; cut a 10 in. square. Position treat on square; fold ends to meet at top and extending down sides, trimming to shape. Roll a ¼ in. log and flatten slightly for zipper; attach using damp brush. Imprint teeth using wavy wheel of Cutter/Embosser.

Make-Up Bag: Roll out 12 oz. white fondant ⅛ in. thick. Imprint design using Graceful Vines mat. Cut an 8 x 10 in. rectangle. Fold, smooth side in, to form bag. Brush side edges with damp brush and pinch to seal. Use 2 crumpled paper towels to fill center and shape bag. Brush top edges with damp brush and pinch together. Roll a ¼ in. log and flatten slightly for zipper; attach using damp brush. Imprint teeth using wavy wheel of Cutter/Embosser (p. 152). **For tassel,** roll out fondant 1/16 in. thick. Cut a 1½ in. square. Cut 1 in. slits, ⅛ in. apart. Roll and pinch end; attach using damp brush. Let dry then brush entire bag with white Pearl Dust.

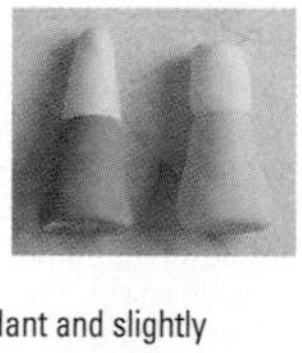

Nail Polish: Shape a 1½ in. ball of pink Neon fondant into tapered base about 1¼ in. wide at the bottom and 1½ in. high. Shape tapered cap from a 1 in. ball of white fondant. Attach using damp brush. Repeat using light pink fondant and slightly different cap shape.

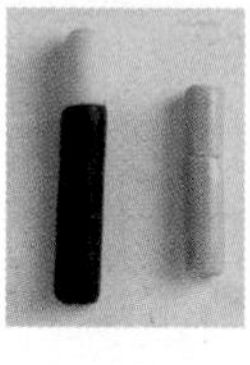

Lipstick & Mascara: Roll a 3 x ½ in. diameter light gray fondant log for lipstick; imprint cap line using edge of spatula. When dry, brush with silver Pearl Dust. Roll a 3 x ½ in. diameter black fondant log for mascara; use damp brush to attach a 1 x ½ in. diameter yellow Neon log to top.

Compact: Roll out pink Neon fondant ¼ in. thick. Cut circle using medium round cutter from 101 Pc. Cutter Set. Use edge of spatula to make indentation around outside edge.

Fondant Couple

(see Headed for a Honeymoon!, p. 93)

Add ¼ teaspoon Gum-Tex to 4 oz. fondant. Tint 2 oz. light copper, ½ oz. each yellow and light blue and a ⅝ in. ball brown. Reserve remaining white mixture. Roll out all colors ⅛ in. thick. Cut copper bride and groom using boy and girl cookie cutters; position on cornstarch-dusted board. Cut groom's hair and clothes using cutters as a guide. Cut shirt collar, bride's dress, veil and tiara using patterns. Score pleats on dress using veining tool. Attach with damp brush. Cut ¼ x 1 in. strip for cuffs on shorts; attach. **For groom's hair,** score lines with veining tool; attach. **For bride's hair,** cut ⅛ x 1½ in. strips; wrap around toothpick to curl and attach. Draw eyes and mouths with black FoodWriter. Pipe tip 1 dots for pearls. Roll and attach small ball for nose. Attach crown to veil and let dry on cornstarch-dusted board. For bouquet streamers, cut two 1 x ¼ in. strips; cut v-shaped bottom and attach to hand.

Duck Beak

(see Ducky Debut, p. 97 and Happy Bath Day, p. 96)

Roll fondant into ball as specified in instructions. Use fingers and thumb to pinch sides to shape corners of mouth. Shape top of beak. Use knife to cut slit for mouth; adjust opening. Curve slightly to follow shape of cake. Insert two 3 in. long Lollipop Sticks in back to push into cake.

Noah's Animals

(see Ark Adventure, p. 98)

Mix 2 teaspoons Gum-Tex into 16 oz. fondant to make 2 of each animal. **For monkeys,** tint a 1½ in. ball brown, a ⅝ in. ball ivory, a ⅜ in. ball rose. **For elephants,** tint: 4 in. ball light blue, 1 in. ball medium blue. **For lions,** tint: 1 in. ball dark orange, 1½ in. ball light orange, ½ in. ball medium orange, ¼ in. ball brown; reserve ½ ball white. **For giraffes,** tint: 3 in. ball yellow, 1 in. ball violet, ½ in. ball rose. **For sheep,** tint: 1½ in. ball yellow, ¼ in. ball rose; reserve a 1 in. ball white. You will also need a small amount of icing tinted black to pipe fine details. Assemble pieces in order described using damp brush.

Monkeys: Using brown, shape a ½ in. diameter ball and flatten to a ¾ in. circle for head; shape ¼ in. diameter flattened circles for ears. Roll out ivory ⅛ in. thick. Cut face using smallest heart Cut-Out; cut a ½ in. oval for muzzle. Roll out white and black 1/16 in. thick; cut eyes using narrow end of tip 8. Cut black pupils using narrow end of tip 2. Using pink, roll 2 small balls and indent with rounded end of thin modeling stick for inside ears; roll tiny ball for nose. Use knife to cut slit for mouth. Roll out some brown ⅛ in. thick. Cut a ½ x 1 in. triangle for body; attach to roof window. Shape 2 hands from ¼ in. ovals; use knife to cut slits for fingers. Attach heads.

Elephants: Using lighter blue, shape a 1 in. ball and flatten to 1½ in. diameter for head. Shape a tapered ½ x 1½ in. long log for trunk. Curve trunk; draw lines with modeling stick and indent trunk with rounded end of thin modeling stick. Roll out some light and some dark blue 1/16 in. thick. Cut outer and inner ears using medium heart Cut-Out. Press edges of outer ear to make it about ⅛ in. larger; attach inner ear then trim ½ in. off bottom point. Cut out a ½ in. oval; cut slits and curl up for his hair. Indent eye sockets with small ball tool. Use icing to pipe tip 1 outline eyebrows, tip 2 dot eyes and outline and fill-in mouth. Attach to lollipop sticks, leaving 3 in. extended at bottom.

Lions: Roll out dark orange ⅛ in. thick. Cut mane using largest round Cut-Out; use knife to cut wavy edge. Using light orange, shape a 1 in. ball and flatten to 1¼ in. diameter for head. Flatten ¼ in. balls for ears and ½ in. long pyramid shaped nose. Indent ears and eye sockets using rounded end of thin modeling stick. Roll ⅛ in. balls in medium orange; flatten and attach for inside of ears; indent with ball tool. Roll out some white and brown 1/16 in. thick. Cut white muzzle using smallest oval Cut-Out; cut ⅜ in. brown triangle for nose tip. Use icing to pipe tip 2 dot and outline features. Attach to lollipop sticks, leaving 3 in. extended at bottom.

Giraffes: Roll a ½ x 4 in. diameter log; flatten back for ¾ in. wide neck. Roll a 1 in. ball for head, ¾ in. ball for snout; flatten backs. Roll ½ in. high cone-shaped ears. Indent ears and nostrils with rounded end of thin modeling stick. Cut slit and shape open mouth. Using rose, shape ⅜ in. long ovals for inner ears and tongue; indent with rounded end of thin modeling stick. Roll and flatten violet balls for spots. Shape ⅛ in. wide x ⅜ in. long logs for horns; attach ¼ in. balls to tips. Pipe tip 2 dot eyes with icing. Attach to lollipop sticks, leaving 2 in. extended at bottom.

Sheep: Roll out some white ⅛ in. thick; cut a 1¼ in. disk with a wavy edge for head/neck base. Using yellow, shape teardrops 1⅛ in. long x ¾ in. wide for head and ⅜ x ⅝ in. long for ears. Indent ears, nostrils and eye sockets using rounded end of thin modeling stick. Cut slit for open mouth. Shape pink oval for tongue; indent with ball tool. Shape 1 in. wide oval for hair; indent and shape with modeling stick. Pipe tip 2 dot eyes with icing. Cut lollipop sticks to 3 in. Attach stick to back of head at a 90° angle with Thinned Fondant Adhesive; let set.

Turret Towers in Cake

(see The Pink Palace, p. 100)

To make towers which will be inserted into cakes more stable, cut Plastic Dowel Rods to 4 in. Attach to bottom of 1 medium and 2 small towers as follows: Stand towers upside down; attach cut dowel rod to base with melted candy. Chill until firm.

Baby Topper

(see The Pink Palace, p. 100)

Tint fondant as stated in instructions. Roll out ⅛ in. thick as needed; cut and attach all pieces with damp brush. **For head,** tape top hole of 1 globe closed. Cut a 2½ x 8 in. light copper strip to wrap around globe head and body. Brush globe with piping gel and attach fondant; smooth with hands. Leave openings for pillar clear. **For white diaper and shirt,** cut 1½ x 8 in. strips. Attach diaper and place shirt on thin Shaping Foam. Ruffle bottom edge of shirt with large ball tool; attach. Cut a pillar into 2 sections, 4 in. long. Slide globe over pillars. **For arms,** begin with ⅜ x 1½ in. logs; flatten end and shape hand, cutting slits for fingers. Attach to body with melted candy; let set. For feet, begin with 1 x 1¾ in. flattened ovals. Roll tiny balls for toes; attach with melted candy. Cut eyes using tip 10; use knife to cut mouth. Cut cheeks using tip 2A; roll tiny ball for nose. Cut 2 tip 1A circles, trim off ⅛ in. then shape ears. Attach features. Cut crown using pattern and attach ends together in back. paint with gold Pearl Dust mixed with lemon extract. Cut one ⅝ x ⅞ in. high and two ⅜ x ½ in. high diamonds; attach to crown then attach to head. Roll 1/16 in. yellow logs for hair; attach. Pipe tip 1s message.

Pirate Ship Rigging

(see Birthday on the Bounty, p. 102)

For sails: Roll out white fondant ⅛ in. thick. Cut 2 sails using patterns. Curve over medium Flower Formers dusted with cornstarch; let dry. Use toothpicks and pattern to mark "Happy Birthday!" on sails; outline and pipe in using tip 2 and royal icing. Let dry. For pirate flag: Roll out small amount of black ⅛ in. thick. Cut a 1½ x 2 in. wide rectangle. Roll out white fondant 1/16 in. thick. For skull, cut circle using wide end of tip 2A; shape slightly with fingers. Cut out eyes and nose using narrow end of tip 3; use knife to cut slit for mouth. Attach to flag using damp brush. Roll ⅛ x ¼ in. long logs for bones; attach. Roll tiny logs for bone ends; attach to each bone. Lay flag over crumpled plastic wrap to shape; let dry.

For masts: Paint top 4 in. of an 8½ in. wooden dowel rod with brown icing color for top of center mast; wipe off excess with damp paper towel and let dry. For horizontal booms, roll brown fondant into two ¼ in. diameter logs, 4½ and 7½ in. long; let dry. To assemble: Center top sail over plastic dowel rod, about ¼ in. from top; mark 2 places where sail hits rod. Center bottom sail about ½ in. below lower mark; mark where sail hits rod. Use knife to cut ¼ in. wide slits at marks. Insert sails and secure with melted white candy; let set. Attach horizontal booms to sail points and mast with Fondant Adhesive. Attach flag to top of mast with melted candy. Push 1 in. ball of fondant into top of plastic dowel rod; insert wooden mast in center. Cut 4 dowel rods to 7 in.; tape together on top end for mast support. Mark mast position on cake using plastic dowel rod. Insert mast support into marked circle on cake. Slide main mast over support. Use melted candy or royal icing to attach parrot after assembling cake.

Brownie Pop Pirates, Captain & Parrot

(see Birthday on the Bounty, p. 102)

Make 3 pirates. Roll out tinted fondant ⅛ in. thick (unless otherwise specified). Cut a 6 x 1½ in. strip for each shirt in assorted colors; wrap around brownies and smooth. Cut 6 x 1 in. strips in different colors for pants; attach using damp brush. **For V-neckline,** cut away a small triangle of shirt and replace with light copper. Cut thin strips in shirt colors and attach for edging. Roll 1¼ x ½ in. diameter logs for arms. Flatten one end for hand; use knife to cut slits for fingers. For shirt sleeves, roll out small amounts of fondant 1/16 in. thick. Cut ½ x ½ in. squares; cut away triangles for torn edge. Attach around arms using damp brush. For shoes, shape ⅝ x 1 in. ovals; flatten. Attach arms and shoes to bodies with melted candy.

For heads, roll 1 ¾ oz. fondant balls. Cut slits for mouth. Indent eye sockets using brush handle; roll tiny black balls for eyes and attach. Roll ¼ in. balls for noses; attach. For bandanas, cut circles using largest round Cut-Out, use knife to cut 2 tear drops ½ in. long for ties, use tip 8 to

cut dots; attach using damp brush. For ears, cut circle with tip 2A; cut in half, shape and attach with candy. For hair, cut various C or V shapes; attach. Attach heads to bodies using melted candy. Let dry on cornstarch-dusted surface.

Make 1 captain. Roll out tinted fondant ⅛ in. thick (unless otherwise specified). Cut a 1¾ x 6 in. red strip for shirt; wrap around brownie, smooth. Cut a 6 x 1 in. black strip for pants; attach. Cut a 1 x ¾ in. rectangle for shirt front, ½ in. wide triangles for lapels; attach. Roll tiny ball buttons; attach. Cut a white ¼ x 1 in. strip; pinch and roll for ascot, attach. Roll red 1 x ½ in. diameter logs for sleeves. Roll and flatten a ¾ in. ball for hand; use knife to cut fingers. For gray hook, roll a thin log ¾ in. long; curve. Shape a ½ in. diameter disk for base. Use melted candy to attach hook to base, base and hand to sleeves and sleeves to body. For shoes, shape 1 x ¾ in. ovals; flatten and attach.

For head, roll a 1 ¾ in. ball. Cut slit for mouth. Indent 1 eye socket using brush handle; roll tiny black ball for eye and attach. Cut a ¼ in. diameter circle for patch and 1/16 in. wide strips for string; attach. Roll a ¼ in. ball for nose; attach. Use pattern to cut hat. Cut skull shape ⅝ x ¾ in. high. Use tip 3 to cut out eyes and nose; use knife to cut mouth. Attach to hat. Roll thin ¼ in. long logs for bones; attach. Use tip 3 to cut tiny circles for bone tips; attach 2 to end of each bone. Pinch hat to shape and attach to head with damp brush. For ears, cut circle with tip 2A; cut in half, shape and attach with candy. Roll small log for hoop earring; curve and attach. Attach head to body using melted candy. Let dry on cornstarch-dusted surface.

Make parrot. Use light green fondant for body and wings; use light blue for tail. Shape 1½ in. long body tapering from ½ in. diameter head to ⅝ in. diameter tummy. Attach 2 flattened, teardrop-shaped wings, 1¼ in. long. Attach a flattened ½ x 1¼ in. rectangle to back for tail. Cut a ⅞ in. long yellow oval and attach to tummy. Shape small triangle beak and tiny ball eyes; attach.

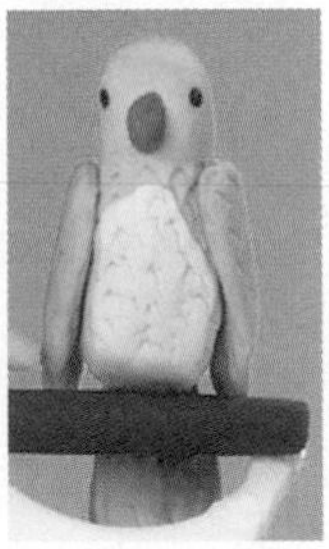

Birthday Gifts

(see Gift-Wrapping Monkey, p. 106)

For gifts, cut one 3½ x 5 in. wide rectangle

and two 3 x 3 in. squares. Set on waxed paper-covered board dusted with cornstarch. **For large gift ribbon,** cut a 1 x 3½ in. long strip; attach to center using damp brush. **For square gift ribbons,** cut 3 in. long strips, ½ or ⅜ in. wide; attach to centers. **For long yellow ribbon being tied,** cut 2 strips, 1 x 5 in. long and 1 x 8 in. long. Cut V into 1 end; lightly pinch opposite end. Drape in position over back of cake pan dusted with cornstarch; let dry. **For bows,** cut ½ and ⅜ in. wide strips to match center ribbons. Cut 3 in. long strips for loops; curve and pinch ends together. Cut 1½ in. long strips for straight ribbons; cut V into end. Cut 1 in. long strip for knot; roll ¼ in. diameter flattened ball for button. Use fondant adhesive to assemble bows on waxed paper-covered board dusted with cornstarch. Let dry.

Birthday Hat

(see Gift-Wrapping Monkey, p. 106)

Roll out yellow fondant ⅛ in. thick. Use pattern to cut hat. Set on waxed paper-covered board dusted with cornstarch. Roll out small amount of violet 1/16 in. thick. Cut out number; attach to hat using damp brush. Roll out white 1/16 in. thick. Cut 6-8 strips ¾ x 5 in. long. Use scissors to cut ½ in. deep slits, ⅛ in. apart, across 1 edge. Brush uncut edge with damp brush and roll to form fringed tufts. Attach 1-2 for top pompom and 5-7 for bottom fringe. Let dry 48 hours. Attach 2 Lollipop Sticks to back using fondant adhesive; allow 2½ in. of sticks to extend at bottom to insert into cake. Let dry.

Treetops

(See Banana Flip and Happy Habitat, p. 106-107)

For each treetop, roll out 4 spearmint leaves on waxed paper to flatten and lengthen to 2-2½ in. Tape over center hole of Flower Forming Cups. Pipe a 1 in. circle of melted candy in center of cup; position 4 leaves in candy, trimming ends to a V for a snug fit. Pipe a large dot of candy over leaves to secure. Chill until set.

Tree Trunks

(see Happy Habitat, p. 107)

For each tree trunk, thread 5 or 6 nougat candies onto 11¾ in. Lollipop Stick, leaving ⅛ in. exposed at the top. Trim exposed bottom to just 2 in. Use knife tip to make a small hole in the candy center of each treetop bottom; insert exposed tip of tree trunk. Secure with melted candy; let set. Attach candy-coated chocolates around trunk with melted candy; let set.

Cookie Packages

(see Happy Habitat, p. 107)

Prepare and roll out dough. Cut 10 squares using largest Cut-Out; cut ½ in. off 1 side to make 2 in. wide rectangles. Bake and cool cookies. Outline cookies using tip 3 and full-strength color flow; fill in with thinned color flow; let dry 24 hours. Set on waxed paper-covered board. Use full-strength color flow and tip 5 to outline and pipe in ribbon and bow; let set then add dot knot. Let dry completely.

Twin Babies

(see Balloon Buddies, p. 108)

Tint fondant as stated in instructions. Roll out ⅛ in. thick as needed. For heads, tape top hole of 2 globes closed. Cut a 2½ x 8 in. light copper strip to wrap around each globe head and body. Brush globes with piping gel and attach fondant; smooth with hand. Leave openings for pillar clear. Roll out white for diapers, cut 9 x 1½ in. strips; attach using damp brush. For blue and green shirts, cut 9 x 1½ in. strips and attach. Cut a pillar into 2 sections, 4 in. long. Slide globes over pillars. For arms, begin with ⅜ x 1½ in. logs; flatten end and shape hand, cutting slits for fingers. Attach to bodies with melted candy; let set. Curl fingers over lollipop stick. Slide out stick and let fingers dry in curled position. For sleeves, cut ¼ x 2½ in. strips and attach around arms. For feet, begin with 1 x 1¾ in. flattened ovals. Roll tiny balls for toes; attach with melted candy. Roll out black fondant. Cut eyes using tip 10; use knife to cut mouth or smile. Cut cheeks using tip 2A; roll tiny ball for nose. Cut 2 tip 1A circles, then cut in half for ears. Attach features using damp brush. For hats, shape a 1½ in. ball of fondant into a 1¾ in. high cone. For fringe, cut a ½ x 3 in. strip; cut ¼ in. deep slits, ⅛ in. apart. Cut a 2 in. section and roll for pompom. Separate slits for feathered look. Attach to top and bottom using damp brush. Cut thin fondant strips and shape number; attach to hat. Use tip 1s to pipe names on shirts.

Candy Making Techniques

USING CANDY MELTS

Fast-melting confectionery coating wafers are the key to easy candy making. Smooth texture and great taste make Candy Melts your most convenient option for molding. Check out all the great colors on p. 196.

To Melt

Chocolate Pro Electric Melting Pot (p. 196): The most convenient way to melt—no microwave or double boiler needed! Melts large amounts of Candy Melts in minutes.

Double boiler method: Fill lower pan with water to below level of top pan. Bring water to simmer, then remove from heat. Put Candy Melts in top pan and set in position on lower pan. Stir constantly, without beating, until smooth and completely melted.

Microwave method: In microwave-safe container, microwave 1 package Candy Melts at 50% power or defrost setting for 1 minute. Stir thoroughly. Continue to microwave and stir at 30 second intervals until smooth and completely melted. Candy Melts may also be melted in Candy Decorating Bags (p. 196). Melt as described above, squeezing bag between heating intervals to blend Candy Melts together. When completely melted, snip off end of bag and squeeze melted Candy Melts into molds. Throw away bag when empty.

NOTE: Confectionery coating will lose its pouring and dipping consistency if overheated, or if water or other liquid is added. If coating is overheated, add 2 teaspoons hydrogenated vegetable shortening per 14 oz. Candy Melts.

To Mold (1 color candies)

Pour melted candy into clean, dry mold; tap lightly to remove air bubbles. Place mold on level surface in refrigerator until bottom of mold appears frosty or until candy is firm. Pop out candy. For lollipops, fill molds, tap to remove air bubbles, then position sticks in mold. Rotate sticks to thoroughly cover with candy so they remain securely in place. Chill to set then unmold.

To Color

Add Candy Colors (p. 199) to melted Candy Melts a little at a time. Mix thoroughly before adding more color. Colors tend to deepen as they're mixed. Pastel colored candies are most appetizing, so keep this in mind.

To Flavor

The creamy, rich taste of Candy Melts can be enhanced by adding approx. ¼ teaspoon oil-based Candy Flavor (p. 199) to 14 oz. (one pack) of melted Candy Melts. Never use water based flavorings; they will cause candies to harden.

Multi-colored candy

"Painting" Method: Before filling mold cavity, use a decorator brush dipped in melted Candy Melts to paint features or desired details; let set. Fill mold and chill until firm as described above.

Piping Method: Use a parchment or Candy Decorating Bag filled halfway with melted candy. Cut small hole in tip of bag and gently squeeze to add candy detail to mold; let set. Fill mold and Chill until firm as described above.

Marbleizing Method

Separately melt 2 different colors of Candy Melts. Stir colors together, using a lollipop stick to draw lines in mixture. Do not overmix. Quickly spoon or place into molds while mixture is still soft. Tap. Chill until firm; unmold.

Layering Method

Pour melted Candy Melts into dry molds to desired height. Chill until partially set. Pour melted contrasting color to desired height. Chill until partially set. Repeat until desired number of layers are formed; chill until firm and unmold.

SPECIALTY TECHNIQUES

Candy Shells

Fill pan cavity to the top edge with melted candy. Tap on counter to remove air bubbles. Let chill for 8 to 10 minutes or until a ⅛ to ¼ in. shell has formed. Pour out excess candy then return shell to refrigerator to chill completely. Carefully unmold shells (if you have difficulty removing shells, place pan in freezer for 2-3 minutes, then unmold). Smooth top edges by sliding across warmed cookie sheet or warming plate. Excess candy can be reheated and reused.

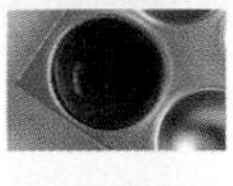

Candy Shells in Baking Cups

Spoon or pipe 1 to 2 tablespoons of melted candy into the bottom of a standard baking cup. Brush candy up sides, to desired height, forming an even edge. Chill 5 to 8 minutes. Repeat process if a thicker shell is needed. Chill until firm. Carefully peel baking cup off candy shell.

Covering Cakes and Cookies with Candy Melts or Poured Icings

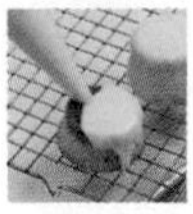

For Candy Melts, melt following package directions. For icing recipes, follow recipe directions to reach pouring consistency. For canned icing, heat in microwave at Defrost setting (30% power) for 20-30 seconds; stir. Repeat until consistency of icing will pour. Place cooled cakes or cookies on cooling grid positioned over cookie sheet or pan. Pour or pipe candy or icing on center of item, continue covering top so that candy or icing drips down and covers sides. Let dry.

COLOR FLOW

Working With Color Flow

1. Trace your design pattern onto parchment paper, then tape paper onto a cake circle or the back of a cookie pan. Cover with waxed paper; smooth and tape. Using tip 2 and parchment bag half-filled with full-strength color flow, squeeze, pull and drop icing string following pattern outline. Stop, touch tip to surface and pull away. If you will be using the same color to fill in, let outline dry a few minutes until it "crusts." To prevent bleeding of different colors, let outline dry 1-2 hours before filling in.

2. Thin color flow mixture with water. Cut opening in parchment bag to the size of tip 2. Fill in design with thinned color flow.

3. Let decorations air dry thoroughly, at least 48 hours. To remove, cut away waxed paper from board, then turn over and peel waxed paper off the color flow piece.

Hint: For curved decorations, dry pieces on flower formers. To easily remove dried color flow, pull waxed paper backing over the edge of a table with one hand, while holding decoration with other hand. Waxed paper will pull off naturally. Or, with dried color flow resting on cookie sheet, place cardboard sheet over color flow, lift and turn over so that top of decoration rests on cardboard. Lift off waxed paper.

Since any moist icing will break down color flow, either position color flow decorations on cake shortly before serving or place on sugar cubes, attaching with full-strength Color Flow.

CANDY PLAQUES

You can use pans as candy molds to make solid decorative plaques. If your pan has detail, it may be painted or filled in desired colors as you would for any candy mold.

Pour melted candy into center of pan cavity. Tap pan gently on counter to eliminate bubbles. Candy should be ¼ to ¾ in. thick, depending on project instructions. Place pan in refrigerator for about 30-40 minutes until firm (check occasionally; if candy becomes too chilled, it may crack). Unmold onto hand or soft towel (tap gently if necessary).

Pegasus Candy Plaque

(see Pegasus Party Cake, p. 12)

Use tape or foil to block off rockers of Rocking Horse Pan. Melt candy and pour into pan; tap to eliminate bubbles. Chill 30-40 minutes until firm; unmold. Position plaque on foil-wrapped board, cut to fit. In royal icing, pipe tip 18 pull-out star mane and tail. Pipe tip 3 dot nose, outline eye and mouth. Outline and pipe in hooves (pat smooth with finger dipped in cornstarch).

SpongeBob Candy Plaque

(see Well Done, SpongeBob!, p. 35)

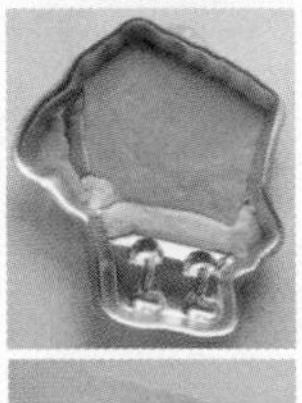

Pipe details into *SpongeBob* pan using melted candy in cut parchment bags. Tint candy as follows: 2 oz. lime green (combine green and yellow candy colors), 1 oz. each blue, red, pink (combine pink and orange candy colors) and black (brown fondant pants are added later); reserve melted white. Pipe in black pupils and inside of mouth; pipe in lime spots and red tie. Chill to set. Pipe in blue of eyes and pink tongue; chill. Pipe in whites of eyes, teeth, shirt, pant area and sleeves; chill. Melt 2 bags yellow Candy Melts; pour into pan for arms and head, filling pan only up to background areas. Chill until completely set; unmold. Using melted candy in cut parchment bags, pipe black lashes, red cheeks, freckles and lip. Overpipe back of arms for support. Let set. Attach plastic dowel rod to back of plaque with melted candy, allowing 3½ in. of dowel rod to extend at bottom to insert into cake.

Disney/Pixar *WALL•E* Candy Plaque

(see Growing Up with WALL•E, p. 36)

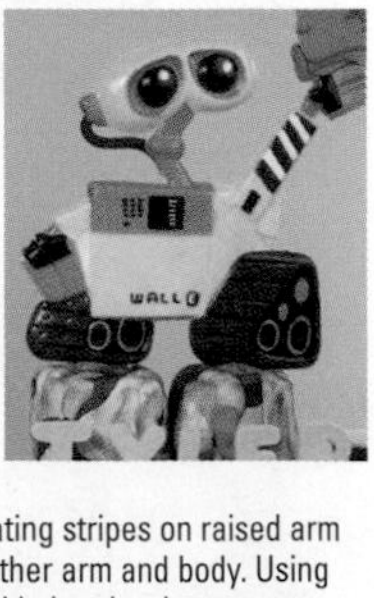

Tint melted white candy as follows: 5 oz. dark gray, 4 oz. light gray, 3 oz. black, 1 oz. red; reserve 1 oz. white. Use melted candy in cut parchment bags to pipe in details of *WALL-E* cake pan; chill to set candy between each step. Using white, fill in eye highlights, alternating stripes on raised arm and space between other arm and body. Using black, fill in pupils, inside hands, chest square and connector on raised arm. Using light gray, pipe in outer eyes, ear, neck, hands and gears inside tires; pipe a 1¼ x 3¼ in. rectangle across upper chest. Using red, pipe in remaining stripes and square where "E" will go. Using black, pipe in inside of tires and gears. Using dark gray, pipe in outside of tires (treads are added later). Melt yellow candy. Use disposable decorating bag to fill in remaining design areas and to back all other colors. Attach lollipop stick supports behind neck, raised arm and hand with melted candy. Chill 30-40 minutes, then unmold onto soft towel and set on waxed paper-covered board.

Tint 1 oz. fondant black; add ¼ teaspoon Gum-Tex. Roll a ¼ diameter rope, 3½ in. long, for connector. Curve and let dry: attach to back of plaque from ear to neck with melted candy. Cut 2 plastic dowel rods to 5 in. long. Attach to back of plaque using melted candy, positioning rods 1 in. from inside edge of each tire tread with 3 in. extended at bottom; chill to set completely. Turn plaque over and pipe on details using melted candy in cut parchment bags. Pipe white "E," yellow vents in square, red "WALL•" and chest button, black tire treads and controls; overpipe around pupils with dark gray. Using melted candy, attach a Lollipop Stick to back of raised hand; attach stem of plant to boot; let set. Attach boot to hand; let set. Position at party by sliding plastic dowel rods over wooden dowel rods you've inserted in your cakes.

Disney/Pixar Cars Candy Plaque

(see Once Around the Oval, p. 36-37)

Using candy colors, tint 14 oz. dark cocoa Candy Melts black. Using white candy, tint 3 oz. each yellow, orange and gray; tint 1 oz. blue. Reserve 3 oz. white. Pipe melted candy into cake pan using cut parchment bags; chill until set after each color. Pipe: blue ring irises, gray windows, muffler, small lightning bolt, yellow lightning bolt, orange number and bold, red wheel centers, black tires, pupil and center of number, white dots on hood, mouth, headlights and windshield. Chill until firm. Fill pan with 35 oz. melted red candy. Chill 30-40 minutes or until set; unmold. Using melted candy in cut parchment bags, outline number with white candy; overpipe details and pipe in tongue with black candy. Chill until firm. Cut 2 dowel rods to 6 in. long. Attach to back at wheels using melted candy, allowing 2 in. to extend at bottom to insert into cake.

Candy Sleigh, Reindeer, Santa

(see Hoofs on the Roofs, p.. 49)

For Sleigh: Position sleigh cutter from set on non-stick pan, pour in melted green candy ⅛ in. thick; Chill until firm. Repeat to make opposite side of sleigh. Fold a sheet of aluminum foil into a 4 x 3 in. dam; fill with melted green candy ⅛ in. thick. Chill until firm; unmold. Bring to room temperature before cutting. Using ruler and knife, cut a 1 x 1 in. front and two 1 x 1½ in. pieces for bottom and back of sleigh. Assemble sleigh on waxed paper using melted candy in a cut parchment bag. Tint portion of white candy gray using black color. Pipe gray runners and white snow along top. Chill until firm.

For Reindeer: Tint portion of melted white candy black. Add a small amount of light cocoa candy to white for antlers. Using piping method, mold 6 reindeer filling only body area of Santa & Reindeer Pretzel Mold. Chill until firm; overpipe to reinforce body. Chill until firm; unmold. Attach lollipop stick to back legs at an angle using melted candy. Let set.

For Santa: Tint portion of melted white candy with a small amount of red candy for face. Mold Santa without pretzel using piping method.

2010 PRODUCT SHOPS

FIND IT FAST... ORDER WITH EASE!

Welcome to the most complete selection of cake decorating products anywhere! Here you'll find all the great Wilton tools, ingredients, accents and more you need to create every design in this Yearbook.

Go ahead and browse! Our shops are conveniently organized to help you find what you need fast. Whether you're decorating a batch of holiday cookies or creating a 3-tiered wedding cake, it's easy to find everything on your list.

When you're ready to buy, we make it a breeze! Charge your order 4 easy ways at your convenience:

PHONE TOLL-FREE
800-794-5866
8:00 am-4:30 pm, Monday-Friday CST
(RETAIL CUSTOMERS ONLY)

FAX TOLL-FREE
888-824-9520
24 HOURS A DAY/7 DAYS A WEEK

ORDER ON-LINE
www.wilton.com
24 HOURS A DAY/7 DAYS A WEEK

MAIL YOUR ORDER
Use the convenient retail order form in this book.

Se Habla Español!
Para mas informacion, marque 800-436-5778

Wilton Instructional

Find inspiration with Wilton how-to books and videos. There's something perfect for your next celebration, from kids' birthday cakes to multi-tiered wedding designs.

Specialty Publications

Brownie Fun!

NEW!

It's the book that proves brownies can be as colorful and fun as your favorite party treats! In *Brownie Fun!*, the fudgy treats everyone loves take on amazing new shapes and dazzling colors that will be the talk of your next celebration. *Brownie Fun!* is packed with over 140 easy-to-make designs and delicious recipes for brownies and mini treats. You'll find fun shapes like flowers, footballs, burgers, volcanos and space aliens that are perfect for kids' birthday parties. Create perfect brownies for every holiday, too, dressed up in festive seasonal colors. From stand-up Easter eggs and Halloween witches' brooms to candy-topped Christmas ornaments and shaped snowflakes, you can enjoy Brownie Fun all year long. You'll even find brownies elegant enough to serve at weddings, showers and other special occasions, with candy monograms, fondant flowers and more. We'll also show you how to mix, bake and decorate the perfect brownies using the complete line of Wilton brownie products. With the *Brownie Fun!* book and our unique pans, cutters and toppings, it's easy to make brownies everyone will remember! Soft cover, 112 pages.
902-V-1105 $14.99

Cupcake Fun!

Wilton presents today's hottest party dessert like you've never seen it before. This all-new collection features over 150 exciting cupcake and treat ideas for all occasions, with complete baking and decorating instructions to make them easy. Discover captivating new shapes from coffee cups to flying saucers, plus a great recipe section with delicious surprises like Key Lime Cupcakes, Mocha Icing and more. Great baking and decorating products, too! *Cupcake Fun!* is the book you need to create the ultimate cupcake celebration. Look for many more great cupcake ideas and recipes at www.cupcakefun.com. Soft cover, 128 pages.
902-V-795 $12.99

Gifts from the Kitchen

Wrap up your homemade food gifts with pizzazz! *Wilton Gifts from the Kitchen* shows you dozens of great ways to package and present a food gift that is as welcoming and tasteful as the good things inside. This book makes it easy, using supplies you may already have on hand, along with convenient Wilton accents. *Wilton Gifts from the Kitchen* is also a great recipe book, with over 50 easy-to-prepare foods—you'll find delicious tastes for every season, fancy dipped treats, special occasion desserts, fun food gifts for kids and more. With *Wilton Gifts from the Kitchen,* you'll find the perfect food to please the eye and warm the heart. Soft cover, 96 pages.
902-V-1225 $12.99

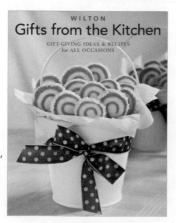

2010 Yearbook of Cake Decorating

NEW!

A great cake makes any celebration more fun! There's no better place to find that unforgettable decorated cake or dessert than this new edition of the *Wilton Yearbook*. It's our biggest Yearbook ever, with more than 220 designs for cakes, cookies, candies and more. You'll find a look perfect for your event, from exciting theme birthday cakes and colorful holiday treats to dramatic tiered wedding designs that capture the moment beautifully. In our First Birthday Bash special section we'll help you make the day a smashing success with the ideal theme ideas. Discover an amazing Noah's Ark cake with captivating animals, delightful 3-D rubber ducky tiers and a rollicking pirate ship with fun fondant details from stem to stern. It's all here, along with step-by-step instructions, technique resource guide, complete product section and a website link to more great designs. Soft cover; 248 pages.
English 1701-V-2045 $11.99
Spanish 1701-V-2046 $11.99

2009 Pattern Book

Duplicate many of the beautiful cake designs featured in the *2010 Yearbook* and on the Wilton website. Includes over 160 decorating outlines to transfer to your cake. Easy-to-follow instructions. Soft cover; 30 pages of patterns.
408-V-2010 $8.99

NEW!

Cake Decorating Beginner's Guide

- How to bake and ice perfect cakes
- How to mix any color icing with ease
- 15 fantastic cake ideas to decorate in 6 steps or less
- Step-by-step decorating instructions for stars, rosettes, drop flowers and more

Wilton, the #1 name in cake decorating, shows beginners everything they need to know, step-by-step. The *Beginner's Guide* makes decorating easy to learn and fun to do for everyone! Soft cover, 40 pages.
902-V-1232 $3.99

Candy Making Beginner's Guide

- 20 incredible candy ideas—all made in a few easy steps
- Easy ways to melt perfectly every time
- Painting color details in candy
- How to make classic creme-filled and dipped candies
- Great candy gift and favor ideas

You'll be amazed at the fantastic candies you can make using this book. The possibilities are endless, using the great selection of Wilton Candy Melts and Candy Molds. The *Beginner's Guide* shows you how, step-by-step, so you will make great-looking candies your very first time. The *Beginner's Guide* has the information you need to start making candy like a pro. Soft cover, 40 pages.
902-V-1231 $3.99

Wilton Wedding Style

NEW!

You've pictured your dream wedding day all your life. Wilton Wedding Style will help you color in every detail. From the experts in cake decorating, this is the book that shows you the full spectrum of wedding color possibilities from white to bright. In each color-themed section, you'll see how to incorporate your signature color into every part of the day—including exciting invitations, cakes that capture the moment and favors your guests will always remember.
Wilton Wedding Style gives you:
• 100-plus ideas for invitations, favors, tabletop décor and more
• 18 dream cakes plus petits fours, cupcakes and edible favors
• Step-by-step project instructions with materials checklists
• Hundreds of decorating ideas for ceremonies and receptions
Soft cover, 124 pages.
902-V-1101 $14.99

Celebrate! With Fondant

It's the first book to feature fondant done the Wilton way—using our exciting cake designs, step-by-step instructions and convenient fondant products. More than 40 terrific cakes, along with alternate ways to decorate every design. Soft cover, 120 pages.
902-V-911 $14.99

Wilton Tiered Cakes

The most contemporary looks in reception cakes! In *Wilton Tiered Cakes,* you'll see how to mix colors on a wedding cake using textured fondant or floral accents. Discover our cute teddy bear tower with fondant baby blocks used as separators. It's all here—38 amazing cake designs—along with complete instructions, techniques, construction and cutting guides, plus great Wilton products. Soft cover, 128 pages.
902-V-1108 $14.99

Wilton Wedding Cakes—A Romantic Portfolio

A Romantic Portfolio sets the bride's imagination free, with 38 exquisite cakes, along with coordinating ornament, favor suggestions and tiered cake accessories. With step-by-step instructions, a comprehensive construction guide, patterns, techniques and recipes, *A Romantic Portfolio* has everything decorators need to recreate each cake to perfection. Soft cover, 144 pages.
902-V-907 $16.99

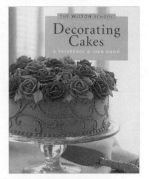

The Wilton School— Decorating Cakes

This book presents what Wilton has learned in 80 years of teaching cake decorating, including
• 30 exciting cakes with complete instructions and product listings
• 103 techniques with instructions
• Helpful recipes, plus in-depth sections on baking cakes, preparing icing, and more
• Complete product guide
Soft cover, 116 pages.
902-V-904 $14.99

Instructional Videos

Winner of 2 Telly Awards

BAKE DECORATE CELEBRATE!
Seasons 1-3 on DVD!

It's the ultimate introduction to cake and dessert decorating on video! Each boxed set includes a complete 13-episode season of the popular Telly Award-winning Public Television series, which makes it easy for anyone to create something great to serve. In every episode, hosts Nancy Siler and Melanie Glasscock focus on a specific theme, such as Kids' Birthdays, Shaped Pans or Whimsical Cupcakes. They'll decorate specialty projects based on that theme and give you related decorating ideas to make the celebration complete. Special segments in each episode include Decorating Basics, featuring essential techniques, and Decorating Tips, with a variety of designs made using one specific tip. Each set includes 4 DVDs, approx. 6 hours total.

Season 1
Garden Party Desserts, Chocolate Treats, Fruits, Easy Flowers and more.
DVD 901-V-121 Set/4 $39.99

Season 2
Roses, Tarts, Pool & Beach, Patriotic and more.
Closed captioned.
DVD 901-V-131 Set/4 $39.99

Season 3
Apples, Apples, Apples, Tropical & Tasty, Critters You Can Eat, Quick Change Cakes and more.
Closed captioned.
DVD 901-V-132 Set/4 $39.99

Cake Decorating Basics

See and learn the essentials of creating amazing cakes and desserts, step by step! Everything from tools to icings, baking perfect cakes, decorating stars, shells, flowers and more, is covered in this 60-minute program.
DVD 901-V-120 $19.99

How to Make Icing Flowers

Learn how to make roses, Easter lilies, violets, pansies, daisies, poinsettias and more! Five cake designs incorporate all the flowers included in this 60-minute video.
DVD 901-V-258 $19.99

How to Make Wedding Cakes

Invaluable lessons on how to design and assemble tiered cakes for weddings, showers, anniversaries and other special occasions. Hints for transporting and serving are also included in this 60-minute video.
DVD 901-V-256 $19.99

Uses of Decorating Tips

Valuable quick reference and idea book for any decorator. Features five of the most popular decorating tip families and explains what each does. Shows the versatility of many tips by presenting varied cake designs. Soft cover, 48 pages.
902-V-1375 $9.99

Cake Decorating

Wilton products are designed by decorators for decorators. We've been helping people make amazing cakes since 1929—and we continue to create the innovative products you need to succeed. From ready-to-use icing that's the ideal consistency to our exclusively formulated bags and tips, Wilton quality makes a difference in the cakes you serve.

Tool Caddies

Every decorator knows that keeping organized saves time and makes cakes easier to complete. With Wilton Tool Caddies, all your supplies will be easy to find and easy to carry. No more searching for the tip or color you need—these neatly arranged caddies keep your essentials in easy reach!

Ultimate Tool Caddy

It's the storage solution designed specifically for cake decorators! Perfect for keeping your decorating space neat—or take it with you for touching up your cake at the event. The Ultimate Tool Caddy features 3 levels of organization to help you find your tools and accessories with ease. Patent Pending.
409-V-623 $59.99

Top level:
Tip & Accessory Organizer Compartments
36 pegs hold virtually any size tip including wired drop flower tips, and let you stack to hold more! Tip organizer compartments allow for stacking of tips, which increases holding capacity. Two tip accessory compartments hold couplers, brushes and more.

Middle level: Flip-top and Icing Color Drawers
Two slide-out drawers feature 3 compartments with snap-open tops. The perfect space for Fondant Cut-Outs, stamens, flower nails, decorating bags, candles and more. Icing color drawer holds up to 24 - ½ oz. jars or 10 each 1 oz. and ½ oz. jars.

Bottom level: Oversized Drawer
Large pull-out drawer is ideal for oversized items. Create customized spaces with 3 dividers! Use the recessed lid to hold cake leveler.

Plus:
Spatula slots on both sides for straight and angled spatulas.

Classic Tool Caddy

Lift out tray keeps 48 tips and 12 color jars within reach (tips and colors not included). Stores colors upright to prevent spilling. Plastic.
409-V-860 $26.29

Supplies not included.

Tip Sets

Be ready for virtually any decorating need with these generous sets. Each includes a great variety of nickel-plated brass tips in the most popular families—round, petal, drop flower, leaf, open star and more—stored upright in a convenient locking case.

Deluxe

Includes: 26 metal decorating tips (2, 4, 7, 13, 16, 17, 18, 30, 42, 46, 47, 61, 65, 66, 67, 74, 78, 97, 98, 101, 102, 103, 104, 106, 107 and 199); 1¼ in. flower nail No. 9; tip coupler; plastic tipsaver case.
2104-V-6666 Set/28 $28.59

Master

Includes: 52 metal decorating tips: (1, 2, 3, 4, 6, 7, 12, 13, 16, 17, 18, 22, 24, 27, 30, 31, 32, 42, 45, 46, 47, 48, 54, 59, 61, 65, 66, 67, 68, 69, 70, 73, 74, 78, 96, 97, 98, 101, 102, 103, 104, 106, 108, 109, 123, 124, 129, 134, 136, 195, 199 and 2C); two standard tip couplers; two 1¼ in. flower nails No. 9; plastic tipsaver case.
2104-V-7778 Set/56 $49.49

ORDER TOLL FREE: 800-794-5866

Decorating Sets

Convenient sets of decorating essentials give you instant versatility! From the perfect assortment of tips and bags for decorating your first cakes to comprehensive collections of tools and supplies in easy-to-carry caddies, Wilton has a set that's right for you. Each features Wilton nickel-plated brass tips for achieving many of the most popular techniques.

101 Piece Tool Caddy Collection

This convenient caddy contains our most complete collection of tools, colors and flavors for the cake decorator. It's a great way to organize, carry and store the essentials—tips, couplers, colors, spatulas and more. Lift-out tray holds tips, couplers, brushes and colors securely. Upright storage prevents spills and makes it easy to find what you need. Generous storage area keeps books, spatulas, bags and other large supplies neatly organized.

2109-V-861 Set/101 $144.99

Save over $40 Compared to individual prices

Includes These Tools:
- Eight .5 oz. Icing Colors: Golden Yellow, No-Taste Red, Brown, Violet, Pink, Royal Blue, Black, Kelly Green
- 3 Couplers (2 standard, 1 large)
- 2 Tip/Coupler Dishwasher and Storage Bags
- Tip Cleaning Brush
- 24 Disposable 12 in. Decorating Bags
- 3 Professional Reusable Decorating Bags (8, 10 and 16 in.)
- 4 Tip Covers
- Tip Saver
- 1½ in. Flower Nail No. 7
- Flower Lifter

- 3 Spatulas (8 and 13 in. Angled,   8 in. Tapered)
- Garland Marker
- *Decorating Cakes* Book
- 20 All-Purpose Disposable Decorating Gloves
- Practice Board with Patterns
- 2 Bake-Even Strips
- 8 oz. Clear Vanilla and No-Color Butter Flavors
- Cake Leveler
- Quick Ease Roller
- Easy-Glide Fondant Smoother
- Decorating Brush

Plus 18 Tips:
- Round: 1, 2, 2A, 3, 12
- Star: 16, 18, 21, 32
- Basketweave: 48
- Leaf: 67, 352
- Petal: 102, 103, 104, 125
- Drop Flower: 2D
- Cake Icer: 789

50 Piece Tool Caddy Decorating Set

We've put together the perfect set for both beginning and advanced decorators. The generous selection of tips, colors and tools gives you the flexibility to decorate virtually any kind of cake. There's also plenty of room to add new items and keep everything organized to save you time. Set includes all tools specified as needed in our Course I class.

2109-V-859 Set/50 $61.99

Includes These Tools:
- Tip Brush
- Decorating Brush
- 1½ in. Flower Nail No. 7
- 2 Standard Couplers
- 18 Disposable 12 in. Bags
- One 10 in. Professional Bag

- 8 in. Angled Spatula
- Four .5 oz. Icing Colors: Lemon Yellow, Christmas Red, Royal Blue, Leaf Green
- Practice Board with Stand
- *Cake Decorating Beginner's Guide*

Save $26 Compared to individual prices

Plus 19 Tips:
- Round: 2, 3, 5, 7, 12
- Leaf: 67, 352
- Drop Flower: 225
- Closed Star: 133
- Basketweave: 47
- Open Star: 16, 18, 21, 32
- Petal: 101, 103, 104
- Large Drop Flower: 2004 (2D)
- Multi-Opening: 233

53 Piece Cake Decorating Set

The works! Decorate many advanced wedding, floral and basketweave cakes as well as basic cakes. Set includes: metal decorating tips 2, 3, 5, 7, 12, 16, 18, 21, 32, 48, 67, 101, 103, 104, 129, 225, 349 and 352; 24 disposable 12 in. decorating bags, two tip couplers; 5 icing colors (.5 oz. each: Golden Yellow, Moss Green, Rose Petal Pink, Cornflower Blue, Violet); one 1¼ in. flower nail No. 9; 8 in. angled spatula; storage tray; and 40-page *Cake Decorating Beginner's Guide*.

2104-V-2546 Set/53 $32.99

25 Piece Cake Decorating Set

A solid foundation set for decorating. Set includes: metal decorating tips 3, 16, 32, 104 and 352; 12 disposable 12 in. decorating bags; two tip couplers; 4 icing colors (.5 oz. each: Lemon Yellow, Pink, Sky Blue, Violet, Leaf Green); 1¼ in. flower nail No. 9; instruction booklet.

2104-V-2536 Set/25 $12.99

18 Piece Cake Decorating Set

Perfect for Wilton character cakes! Set includes: metal decorating tips 4, 12, 18 and 103; 6 disposable 12 in. decorating bags; 2 tip couplers; 5 liquid color packets (.067 fl. oz. each: Yellow, Red, Green, Orange, Blue); instruction booklet.

2104-V-2530 Set/18 $7.99

12 Piece Cupcake Decorating Set

Create all kinds of fun cupcake designs perfect for celebrations or everyday treats! Includes star tips 1M (rosettes, stars, drop flowers), star tip 22 (zigzags, pull-out stars), round tip 12 (outlines, dots, messages) and Bismarck tip 230 for exciting filled cupcakes, plus 8 disposable bags, instruction booklet.

2104-V-6667 Set/12 $8.39

Decorating Tips

Presenting the best quality tips on the market, used by decorators throughout the world. Wilton tips are made from durable nickel-plated brass to hold their shape and create precise decorations year after year. Rust-proof and dishwasher safe tips are tested for consistent performance in the Wilton Test Kitchen. All tips work with standard bags and couplers, unless otherwise indicated.

ROUND TIPS

Outline, lettering, dots, balls, beads, stringwork, lattice, lacework.

#1
402-V-1 $0.99

#1L
402-V-901** $1.89

#1s
402-V-1009 $1.59

#2
402-V-2 $0.99

#3
402-V-3 $0.99

#4
402-V-4 $0.99

#5
402-V-5 $0.99

#6
402-V-6 $0.99

#7
402-V-7 $0.99

#8
402-V-8 $0.99

#9
402-V-9 $0.99

#10
402-V-10 $0.99

#11
402-V-11 $0.99

#12
402-V-12 $0.99

#2A
Smaller version of 1A.
402-V-2001* $1.69

#1A
Bold borders, figure piping.
402-V-1001* $1.89

#230
Fill eclairs and bismarcks.
402-V-230** $2.19

#55
402-V-55 $0.99

#57
402-V-57 $0.99

#301
For flat lettering.
402-V-301 $0.99

PETAL TIPS

Realistic flower petals, dramatic ruffles, drapes, swags and bows.

#59s/59
402-V-594 $0.99

#59
402-V-59 $0.99

#60
402-V-60 $0.99

#61
402-V-61 $0.99

#62
402-V-62 $0.99

#64
402-V-64 $0.99

#97
402-V-97 $0.99

#101s
402-V-1019 $1.59

#101
402-V-101 $0.99

#102
402-V-102 $0.99

#103
402-V-103 $0.99

#104
402-V-104 $0.99

#150
402-V-150 $1.69

#116
402-V-116* $1.69

#121
402-V-121* $1.69

#123
402-V-123* $1.69

#124
402-V-124* $1.69

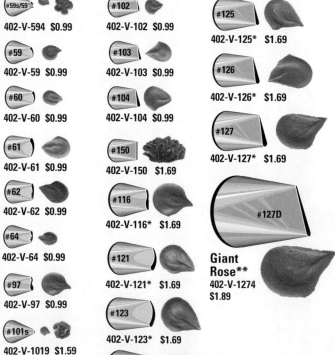

#125
402-V-125* $1.69

#126
402-V-126* $1.69

#127
402-V-127* $1.69

#127D
Giant Rose**
402-V-1274 $1.89

DROP FLOWER TIPS

Small (106-225); medium (131-194); large (2C-1G, great for cookie dough).

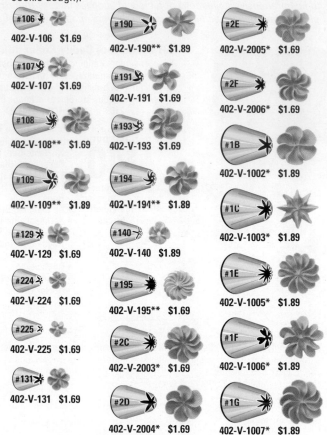

#106
402-V-106 $1.69

#107
402-V-107 $1.69

#108
402-V-108** $1.69

#109
402-V-109** $1.89

#129
402-V-129 $1.69

#224
402-V-224 $1.69

#225
402-V-225 $1.69

#131
402-V-131 $1.69

#190
402-V-190** $1.89

#191
402-V-191 $1.69

#193
402-V-193 $1.69

#194
402-V-194** $1.89

#140
402-V-140 $1.89

#195
402-V-195** $1.69

#2C
402-V-2003* $1.69

#2D
402-V-2004* $1.69

#2E
402-V-2005* $1.69

#2F
402-V-2006* $1.69

#1B
402-V-1002* $1.89

#1C
402-V-1003* $1.89

#1E
402-V-1005* $1.89

#1F
402-V-1006* $1.89

#1G
402-V-1007* $1.89

BASKETWEAVE TIPS

Tips 44, 45 make only smooth stripes; rest of basketweave tips and Cake Icer make both smooth and ribbed stripes.

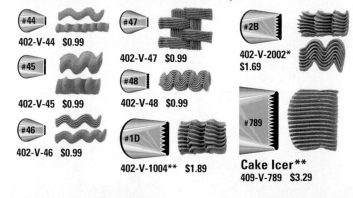

#44
402-V-44 $0.99

#45
402-V-45 $0.99

#46
402-V-46 $0.99

#47
402-V-47 $0.99

#48
402-V-48 $0.99

#1D
402-V-1004** $1.89

#2B
402-V-2002* $1.69

#789
Cake Icer**
409-V-789 $3.29

MULTI-OPENING TIPS

Rows and clusters of strings, beads, stars, (Use 233 for grass).

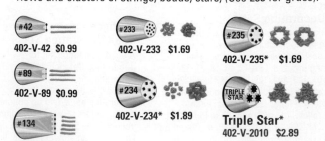

#42
402-V-42 $0.99

#89
402-V-89 $0.99

#134
402-V-134** $1.89

#233
402-V-233 $1.69

#234
402-V-234* $1.89

#235
402-V-235* $1.69

TRIPLE STAR
Triple Star*
402-V-2010 $2.89

OPEN STAR TIPS

Star techniques, drop flowers; the finely cut teeth of 199 through 364 create decorations with many ridges; use 6B and 8B with pastry dough too.

 #13 402-V-13 $0.99

#14 402-V-14 $0.99

#15 402-V-15 $0.99

#16 402-V-16 $0.99

#17 402-V-17 $0.99

#18 402-V-18 $0.99

#19 402-V-19 $0.99

#20 402-V-20 $0.99

#21 402-V-21 $0.99

#22 402-V-22 $0.99

#32 402-V-32 $0.99

#199 402-V-199 $1.69

#362 402-V-362 $1.69

#363 402-V-363 $1.69

#364 402-V-364 $1.69

 #172 402-V-172** $1.69

 #1M (2110) 402-V-2110* $1.69

 #4B 402-V-4400** $1.69

 #6B 402-V-6600** $1.69

#8B 402-V-8800** $1.89

SPECIALTY TIPS

Shells, ropes, hearts, Christmas trees, ring candle holders!

#98 402-V-98 $0.99

#347 402-V-347 $1.69

#136 402-V-136 $1.89

#77 402-V-77 $0.99

#78 402-V-78 $0.99

#83 402-V-83 $0.99

#96 402-V-96 $0.99

#79 402-V-79 $0.99

#105 402-V-105 $0.99

#80 402-V-80 $0.99

#81 402-V-81 $0.99

#250 402-V-250* $1.89

#252 402-V-252* $1.89

#95 402-V-95 $0.99

CLOSED STAR TIPS

Create deeply grooved shells, stars and fleurs de lis.

#24 402-V-24 $0.99

#26 402-V-26 $0.99

#27 402-V-27 $0.99

#28 402-V-28 $0.99

#29 402-V-29 $0.99

#30 402-V-30 $0.99

#31 402-V-31 $0.99

#33 402-V-33 $0.99

#35 402-V-35 $0.99

#133 402-V-133 $0.99

#54 402-V-54 $0.99

LEFT-HANDED TIP SETS

Now left-handers can achieve the same beautiful flowers as right-handed decorators! Nickel-plated brass tips fit standard bags and couplers.

LEFT-HAND

#106L

#107L

#59°L

#97L

116L

Drop Flower Set
Includes Left tips 106 and 107 for making small swirled flowers.
418-V-613† Set/2 $3.29

Petal Set
Includes Left tip 59° for violets, Left tip 97 for Victorian roses and Left tip 116** for large Wilton roses.
418-V-612† Set/3 $3.29

LEAF TIPS

So realistic! Ideal for shell-motion borders too.

#65s 402-V-659 $1.59

#66 402-V-66 $0.99

#68 402-V-68 $0.99

#73 402-V-73 $0.99

#75 402-V-75 $0.99

#352 402-V-352 $1.59

#70 402-V-70 $0.99

#65 402-V-65 $0.99

#67 402-V-67 $0.99

#69 402-V-69 $0.99

#74 402-V-74 $0.99

#349/352s 402-V-349 $1.59

#326 402-V-326 $1.59

#112 402-V-112** $1.69

#113 402-V-113* $1.69

#115 402-V-115* $1.69

#366 402-V-366* $1.89

Makes leaves for larger flowers.

RUFFLE TIPS

Plain, fluted, shell-border, special effects.

#86 402-V-86 $0.99

#87 402-V-87† $0.99

#88 402-V-88† $0.99

#100 402-V-100 $0.99

#353 402-V-353 $1.59

#340 402-V-340 $1.59

#401 402-V-401 $1.59

#402 402-V-402* $1.69

#406 402-V-406* $1.89

#403 402-V-403** $1.89

†For left-handers. *Fits large coupler.

Decorating Bags

All decorating bags are not the same! Wilton bags are tested to be the best. They simply feel better in your hand—soft and strong to provide decorating performance you can count on. From pure parchment triangles to our convenient Disposable or premium reusable Featherweight styles, Wilton bags are made to our strict specifications for consistent quality.

Featherweight Decorating Bags

The best quality bags for decorating, with strong resilient seams to help them last for years! Featherweight bags feel soft and comfortable in the hand—the polyester material becomes softer the more the bags are used. Lightweight, strong and flexible, they'll never get stiff. Coated to prevent grease from seeping through. Each batch is tested in the Wilton Test Kitchen to meet our exacting standards. Dishwasher safe. Instructions included; sold singly.

8 in.
404-V-5087 $3.19
10 in.
404-V-5109 $4.79
12 in.
404-V-5125 $5.79
14 in.
404-V-5140 $6.79
16 in.
404-V-5168 $8.39
18 in.
404-V-5184 $9.49

15 in. Parchment Triangles

Authentic parchment paper is the professional's choice for convenience and quick bag preparation. Make use-and-toss decorating bags ideal for small amounts of icing or brush striping. Excellent wet strength for candy or a variety of icings. Also great for smoothing iced cakes and transferring patterns.
2104-V-1508
Pk./100 $6.99

12 in. Disposable Decorating Bags

Wilton's strict testing standards ensure the highest quality disposable bags you can buy. Our proprietary blend of materials helps Wilton bags feel more comfortable and outperform competitive bags. They can be used with or without a coupler and work great for microwave-melting and piping of Candy Melts. Fits standard tips and couplers. Just use, then toss! Instructions included.
2104-V-358 Pk./12 $4.19
2104-V-1358 Pk./24 $6.79

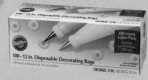

Dispenser Boxes

Convenient Value Packs make it easy to pull out one bag at a time, so you can keep your decorating space uncluttered. Instructions included.
2104-V-1273 Pk./50 $13.19
2104-V-1249 Pk./100 $20.99

16 in. Disposable Decorating Bags

Larger size lets you decorate longer without refilling the bag—great for piping borders on large cakes. It's the only size bag to use with Cake Icer Tip 789, for covering cakes fast. Just use, then toss. Strong flexible plastic; fits standard tips and couplers. Also perfect for microwave-melting and piping of Candy Melts. Instructions included.
2104-V-1357
Pk./12 $5.29

Practice Board with Patterns Set

Includes stand and 20 full-size patterns. 9 x 6 in.
406-V-9464 $7.99

Cake Dividing Set

Measures equal sections of your cake for precise placement of garlands, stringwork and other designs. Cake Dividing Wheel marks up to 16 divisions on cakes up to 20 in. diameter. Garland Marker adjusts to 7 widths. Instructions included.
409-V-806 Set/2 $9.99

Decorating Bag Holder

Keep your icing bags close at hand and organize your decorating space with this convenient stand. Great for Wilton Featherweight, Disposable or Parchment Bags! The 2 large and 6 small spaces hold bags upright so they'll be easy to grab. Use the smallest openings to hold flower and cupcake nails. To prevent air from drying out icing, we suggest using Wilton Silicone Decorating Tip Covers below or placing a damp towel that touches tip ends under the Bag Holder. 11.5 x 7.25 x 4.5 in. Patent pending.
417-V-115 $9.99

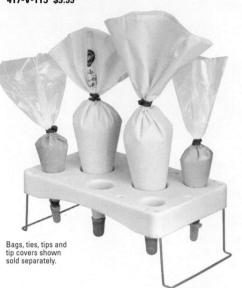

Bags, ties, tips and tip covers shown sold separately.

Saves decorating space and time!

NEW!

Decorating Nail Set

A great selection of sizes for creating virtually any size nail flower! Includes a cupcake nail, with a recessed platform for finishing a standard cupcake with a perfectly-swirled top. Hand-held nails provide the perfect turntable for close-up decorating—just turn as you pipe. Includes 1.5, 2, 2.5 in. Flower Nails and 2.25 x 2.5 in. Cupcake Nail. Stems insert easily in nails to create a secure platform. Top rack dishwasher safe.
417-V-107 Pk./4 $6.99

NEW!

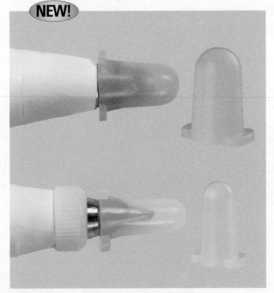

Silicone Decorating Tip Cover Set

With convenient silicone covers, icing won't dry out in your bag between uses. They fit snugly over all standard and most large tips to keep air out. Top rack dishwasher safe.
414-V-916 Pk./6 $5.99

Icing Bag Ties

Convenient bands wrap around the twist of your decorating bag, then lock to prevent icing from oozing out of the top. As you squeeze out icing, slide the tie down to maintain the pressure.
417-V-173 Pk./12 $4.49

CAKE DECORATING

Decorating Tools & Accessories

NEW!

Pre-Cut Icing Flower Squares
No more cutting! Perfectly sized waxed paper squares attach to your flower nail with a dot of icing for easy piping and transfer of flowers. Save work and get a fresh flat surface every time.
414-V-920 Pk./50 $1.99

Flower Lifter
Easily transfers buttercream flowers from nail to cake without damage. Angled design keeps your hands from touching the cake. Detachable blades for easy cleaning. Plastic. 5¼ in. long.
417-V-1199 $3.29

Flower Nail No. 7
For basic flower making. Provides the control you need when piping icing flowers. Just rotate the nail between your thumb and fingers as you pipe a flower on the head. Stainless steel. 1½ in. wide.
402-V-3007 $1.19

Lily Nail Set
Essential for making cup flowers. Includes ½, 1¼, 1⅝ and 2½ in. diameter cups.
403-V-9444 Sct/8 $2.19

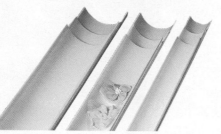

Flower Former Set
Dry icing leaves and flowers in a convex or concave shape. Three each of 1½, 2 and 2½ in. wide holders, all 11 in. long.
417-V-9500 Set/9 $6.29

Flower Stamen Assortment
Finish your royal icing or gum paste flowers with these 3 lovely stamen styles. Cut stamens to desired size and insert in flower center. Includes 60 each Pearl, Glitter and Fluffy. May be tinted (except Pearl) with Wilton Icing Colors added to vanilla. 2.5 in. long.
1005-V-410 Pk./180 $3.19

Tip/Coupler Dishwasher and Storage Bag
Place nylon mesh bag in dishwasher silverware rack for easy tip and coupler cleaning. Tips not included. 5¾ x 6 in.
417-V-1640 Pk./2 $3.29

Decorating Couplers
Couplers make it easy to change decorating tips on the same icing bag.

Standard
Fits all decorating bags and standard tips.
411-V-1987 $0.69

Large
Use with large decorating tips and 14 to 18 in. Featherweight Bags.
411-V-1006 $1.69

Tipsaver Cases
Small case holds 26 tips; large case holds 52 tips Tips not included.
Small 405-V-8773 $6.99
Large 405-V-7777 $8.49

Tip Saver
Restores bent tips to their proper shape; opens clogged tips. Place tip over pointed or cone-shaped end, put on cover and twist back and forth to reshape. Heavy-duty plastic.
414-V-909 $3.09

Tip Brush
Great for cleaning small tip openings. Plastic bristles. ¼ x 4 in. long.
418-V-1123 $1.59

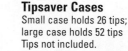

Spatulas

Wilton gives decorators more choice—a variety of spatula styles and sizes to fit every need. All have stainless steel blades for strength and flexibility. Keep a variety on hand for icing and filling cakes of every size, bag striping and more.

ROSEWOOD HANDLES
Quality rosewood handle spatulas have been favorites for years. They have strong, flexible stainless steel blades and sturdy riveted handles.

Straight Blade
11 in.; 6 in. blade.
409-V-7695
$5.29
8 in.; 4¼ in. blade.
409-V-6044
$3.19

Angled Blade
12 in.; 6¼ in. blade.
409-V-135
$6.29
8 in.; 4½ in. blade.
409-V-739
$3.19

Tapered Blade
8 in.; 4 in. blade.
409-V-518
$3.19

CONTOURED HANDLES
Decorate with greater comfort, more control and less fatigue, thanks to contoured handle with finger pad. Flexible stainless steel blade is perfect thickness for gliding over icing.

Straight Blade
15 in.; 10⅛ in. blade.
409-V-6030 $10.49
11 in.; 6 in. blade.
409-V-6018 $6.29
9 in.; 4½ in. blade.
409-V-6006
$4.19

Angled Blade
15 in.; 9⅞ in. blade.
409-V-6036 $10.49
13 in.; 7¾ in. blade.
409-V-6024 $6.79
9 in.; 4½ in. blade.
409-V-6012
$4.79

Tapered Blade
9 in.; 4 in. blade.
409-V-6003
$4.19

ORDER TOLL FREE: 800-794-5866

Cake Decorating Turntables

A quality cake turntable is a must for easy decorating. Turntables lift your cake off the work surface so you can create borders conveniently. And they rotate, allowing you to decorate all the way around the cake without straining.

Trim 'N Turn ULTRA Cake Turntable

Experience the ultimate in turntable control. The Trim 'N Turn ULTRA combines an extra-high smooth-turning platform with non-slip detail for secure performance. The easy-locking platform keeps your cake steady as you create delicate flowers and writing. Platform turns in either direction for easy icing, borders, combing and leveling. Great for left-hand or right-hand users.

- Non-slip design with soft-grip ring molded into platform to keep cake in place
- 3 in. raised base with arched sides for easy grip
- Hidden ball bearing track for smooth turning
- Lock platform with ease using the pull-out tab
- 12 in. platform removes from base for easy cleaning
- Holds cakes up to 11 in. with platform visible—holds larger cakes if needed

307-V-301 $20.99

Trim 'N Turn PLUS Cake Turntable

Decorate with more convenience and control with the Trim 'N Turn PLUS. Its smooth-turning performance puts your cake in the ideal position for decorating beautiful borders and icing sides perfectly smooth.

- Non-slip base is raised for better control.
- Arched sides for easy lifting
- Removable 12 in. platform for easy cleaning
- Hidden ball-bearing track for smooth turning
- Holds cakes up to 11 in. with platform visible—holds larger cakes if needed

307-V-303 $13.69

Tilting Cake Turntable

It tilts! Decorate any part of your cake conveniently!

The Tilting Cake Turntable moves to 3 preset angles (12°, 24°, and level) and locks in place, making every decorating technique easier! 6 in. high turntable smoothly rotates in any of the angled positions for effortless decorating of top borders, stringwork, lettering on top and sides of cake, more. Includes lock to prevent rotation. Non-slip bottom, 12 in. diameter.
307-V-894 $69.99

Professional Turntable

Extra strength and effortless turning for decorating tiered wedding cakes. Heavy-duty aluminum stand is 4½ in. high with 12 in. diameter plate. Holds cakes up to 16 in. diameter.
307-V-2501 $69.99

Trim 'N Turn Cake Stand

Turns smoothly on hidden ball bearings for easy decorating and serving. Flute-edged 12 in. plate is white molded plastic. Holds cakes up to 10 in. diameter.
2103-V-2518 $8.39

Spatulas

Decorate with more control and less fatigue. The ergonomic handle features a finger pad, which tapers to the flexible stainless steel blade for better control.

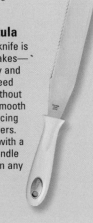

Straight
Great for spreading and smoothing fillings, all-around kitchen use.
9 in.
409-V-6045
$7.99
11 in.
409-V-6046
$9.99
15 in.
409-V-6047
$13.99

Angled
Ideal angle for smoothing cake sides and spreading fillings.
9 in.
409-V-6040
$7.99
13 in.
409-V-6041
$9.99
15 in.
409-V-6042
$13.99

Tapered
Easily ices hard-to-reach spots on your cake.
9 in.
409-V-6057
$7.99

Cake Knife/Spatula
This stainless steel knife is perfect for torting cakes—it cuts layers cleanly and has the width you need to transfer layers without breakage. Use the smooth edge for spreading icing or filling on cake layers. It's easy to control, with a lightweight nylon handle that is comfortable in any hand. 15 in. long
409-V-6048 $9.99

Press Sets

Block Message Press Set
Includes Best, Happy, Wishes, Anniversary, Birthday and Congratulations. Message holder. Word height ⅞ in.
2104-V-2077 Set/6 $4.09

Make-Any-Message Letter Press Set
Imprint the perfect sentiment! Press words up to 10½ in. wide, letters ¾ in. high. Includes letter holder.
2104-V-10 Set/56 $8.99

Italic Make-Any-Message Press Set
Pretty and sophisticated letters for a custom message. Press words up to 10½ in. wide, letters ¾ in. high. Includes letter holder.
2104-V-2277 Set/58 $8.99

Decorator Favorites Pattern Press Set
Includes: fleur-de-lis; double heart; medallion; open heart; closed scroll; heart; large, medium and small C-scrolls; crest; double scroll; vine.
2104-V-3160 Set/12 $6.99

Designer Pattern Press Set
Imprints elegant designs for easy overpiping. Includes: symmetrical swirl; small and large fleurs de lis; corner flourish; flower; heart bow; scroll; curlicues.
2104-V-3112 Set/8 $6.99

Script Message Press Set
Combine the words Best, Happy, Wishes, Birthday, Anniversary, and Congratulations. Word height ⅞ in.
2104-V-2061 Set/6 $4.09

CAKE STENCILS VARIETY PACK
Our collection of 4 stencil designs gives you several ways to make birthday and everyday cakes more festive. It's so easy —just place on your iced cake, then sprinkle with Wilton Cake Sparkles, add exciting Wilton Sugars in a rainbow of colors or use Color Mist Food Color Spray. Try them with Wilton Dusting Sugars on brownies and sheet cakes—powdered sugar in exciting pastel colors. Also works beautifully with Wilton Rolled Fondant—fill in designs with sugars or decorate with FoodWriter Markers. Includes Happy Birthday, Flower, Swirl and Heart designs.
417-V-148 Pk./4 $7.99

ORDER TOLL FREE: 800-794-5866

Decorating Tools

Icing Sculptor
Now your cakes can have an elegant sculpted finish that will give them a beautiful professional look. It's easy with the Icing Sculptor. Just insert any combination of the 64 design blades—mix and match between the 14 sculpting edges to create your favorite customized effects. Then glide the comb over the iced cake sides to create attractive ridges that will beautifully frame your design. Create hundreds of pattern combinations—wide or narrow ridges, dramatic swirls and vertical designs too. Also includes sculptor handle and complete instructions. This versatile tool has a Patent No. D489,582.
2104-V-12 Set/66 $13.69

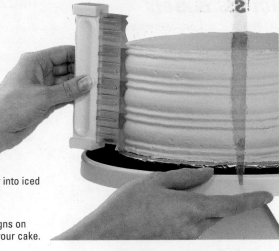

CAKE DECORATING

Includes 8 of each 2-Sided Design Blade

So Easy!
Select the sculpting blades you want and slide into handle. Press sculptor into iced cake as you rotate cake on turntable.

So Versatile!
Mix and match between the 14 edge designs on 64 blades to achieve the perfect look for your cake.

Garland Marker
Adjusts to 7 preset widths and varying depths to easily mark perfectly uniform garlands on cake sides. Instructions included.
409-V-812 $4.49

Decorating Triangle
Each side adds a different contoured effect to iced cakes. Easy to hold. Plastic, 5 x 5 in.
417-V-162 $1.19

Basic Dessert Decorator
Give your cakes and pastries a beautiful finishing touch in seconds. The easy-to-control lever helps you fill and decorate all kinds of desserts. The 4 decorating nozzles included let you pipe stars, rosettes, shells and many other accents. Works great with Wilton Icing Mixes (p. 145).
415-V-825 $11.59

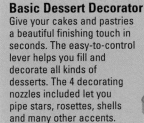

Decorating Comb
Run edge across your iced cake to form perfect ridges. Plastic, 12 x 1½ in.
417-V-156 $1.69

It's easy to add beautiful decorations to any dessert or appetizer in minutes! Designed for comfortable one-hand decorating and effortless tip positioning, this is the most convenient dessert tool you'll ever use. Create beautiful decorations—shells, stars, rosettes, leaves. The recipe book included is filled with fabulous ideas to tempt your family and friends. Decorate desserts with elegant whipped cream or icing designs. Dress up pastry shells with dramatic swirls of mousse. With Dessert Decorator Pro, you can do it all!
415-V-850 $31.49

Dessert decorator Pro™

Rotating Cylinder
Just turn to place the tip in the correct position for any decoration.

Ergonomic Design
Easy, comfortable grip for right or left hand. Outer sleeve fits your fingers like a glove.

Stainless Steel Cylinder
Preferred by pastry chefs because stainless won't transfer flavors and it maintains temperature of fillings.

Fits Virtually Any Tip/Coupler
Use with the tips included or with most other Wilton tips.

Pull-Out Plunger
Inner ring pushes filling smoothly through cylinder.

Convenient Thumb Lever
The ideal distance from cylinder for comfortable one-handed decorating.

Durable Construction
Cylinder and plunger are housed in an impact-resistant sleeve for years of great decorating performance.

Easy To Fill and Clean
Most parts detach with ease; wash in warm, soapy water.

Dessert Decorator Pro includes all this:

Tip 366 Leaf Tip 4B Star Tip 125 Petal Tip 21 Star Tip 1M Star Tip 230 Bismarck

Two Tip Couplers
Two sizes to hold standard (small) and large tips.

Six Durable Nickel-Plated Tips
Quality metal tips produce perfectly-shaped decorations every time.

Tips in bag for size reference only. Tips included are shown at left.

Tip/Coupler Dishwasher and Storage Bag
Just place nylon mesh bag with tips and couplers in your dishwasher silverware rack for easy tip and coupler cleaning.

Recipes and Instructions
Includes delicious recipes and easy decorating instructions for elegant desserts and appetizers.

Icings & Gels

All Wilton icings are formulated for easy decorating as well as great taste. Our convenient ready-to-use icings are the perfect medium consistency for decorating, so you don't need to worry about mixing or measuring.

TUBE ICINGS, GELS

Tube Decorating Icings

The same high quality as our Ready-To-Use Decorator Icing, in a convenient tube. Create flowers, borders and more. Ideal for small areas of color on character cakes. Use with the Tip Set or Coupler Ring Set (below) and any standard-size Wilton metal tip (not included). Colors match Wilton Icing Colors (p. 148). 4.25 oz. Certified Kosher. **$1.99**

Red 704-V-218	**Royal Blue** 704-V-248
Violet 704-V-242	**Leaf Green** 704-V-224
Lemon Yellow 704-V-236	**Kelly Green** 704-V-227
Orange 704-V-212	**Chocolate** 704-V-254
Pink 704-V-230	**White** 704-V-200

Black 704-V-206

Coupler Ring Set

Attach Wilton standard size metal decorating tips onto Wilton tube icings to create any technique.
418-V-47306 Set/4 **$2.19**

Tip Set

Tips easily twist onto Wilton tube icings to create many decorating techniques. Includes Star, Round, Leaf and Petal Tips.
418-V-621 Set/4 **$2.19**

Tube Decorating Gels

Add shimmering accents and colorful highlights to your decorating with these transparent gels. Create a beautiful stained-glass effect and add distinctive writing and printing. Great for cakes and cookies. Colors match Wilton Icing Colors (p. 148). .75 oz. Certified Kosher. **$1.49**

Red 704-V-318	**Orange** 704-V-312	
Pink 704-V-330	**Royal Blue** 704-V-348	
Violet 704-V-342	**Leaf Green** 704-V-324	**White** 704-V-302
Lemon Yellow 704-V-336	**Brown** 704-V-354	**Black** 704-V-306

Lemon Yellow	Orange	Red	Pink
Violet	Royal Blue	Leaf Green	† Kelly Green
† Chocolate	Brown	White	Black

†Not available in gel.

DRIZZLE ICING

Just heat and squeeze over brownies and other treats to add a ribbon of flavor. Use with Brownie Fudge Icing (p. 145) for exciting marbleized designs. 10 oz. bottle. Certified Kosher. **$4.99**

NEW!

Mint 704-V-152

Peanut Butter 704-V-150

Vanilla Crème 704-V-151

SPARKLE GEL

Make your cake decorations more dynamic! Squeeze on sparkling color effects with our ready-to-use gel. Great for dots, messages, water effects and fondant accents. Try it on cookies, cupcakes, ice cream and more! Resealable 3.5 oz. tubes. Certified Kosher. **$2.99**

NEW! **NEW!** **NEW!**

Black 704-V-1061	**White** 704-V-107	**Gold** 704-V-1060	**Red** 704-V-112
Blue 704-V-110	**Yellow** 704-V-108	**Green** 704-V-111	**Pink** 704-V-356

Ready-To-Decorate Icing

Add an exciting finishing touch to treats, without mixing or mess. Just slip one of the four free tips over the nozzle and start the fun. Colors match Wilton Icing Colors (p. 148). 6.4 oz. Certified Kosher. **$4.29**

Red 710-V-4400	**Green** 710-V-4401	**White** 710-V-4402	**Black** 710-V-4404
Pink 710-V-4406	**Blue** 710-V-4407	**Violet** 710-V-4408	**Yellow** 710-V-4409	**Orange** 710-V-4410

Four FREE decorating tips included:

Small Round Tip
For dots and outlining

Leaf Tip
For basic and ruffled leaves

Large Round Tip
For writing and printing

Star Tip
For stars, swirls and pretty borders

White Cookie Icing

Quick-setting microwavable icing covers cookies with a shiny finish—perfect for decorating with colorful Wilton Icing Writer accents or FoodWriter markers! Easy to use—just heat and squeeze onto cookies using the convenient cap. Sets smooth in just 45 minutes. 10 oz. bottle covers approx. 12 cookies, 3 in. each; 20 oz. covers approx. 24. Certified Kosher.
10 oz. Bottle 704-V-481 **$4.49**
20 oz. Bottle 704-V-492 **$7.99**

Icing Writer

Squeeze colorful accents onto fondant and Wilton Cookie Icing with this ready-to-use icing! It's easy to control, just squeeze the bottle and icing flows smoothly from the built-in round tip. Dries to a smooth, satin finish. 3 oz. bottle. Certified Kosher. **$2.49**

Red 710-V-2225	**Yellow** 710-V-2226	**Pink** 710-V-2230
White 710-V-2228	**Green** 710-V-2229	**Violet** 710-V-2231	**Blue** 710-V-2227

ORDER TOLL FREE: 800-794-5866

Bakers Make Wilton Bakeware #1!

Once you've baked with a Wilton pan, you'll know
why it's the best. Wilton bakeware is built with more
features to bake the best-looking cakes every time.
Now let our customers tell you why
they bake with Wilton.

*"I have been baking for years and nothing compares!
It is thicker than your everyday bakeware which makes for
an even heat distribution and a perfectly baked item every time.
Thank you Wilton for making me look so good!"*
Patti T. Elkhorn, WI

*"Not only are there so many character pans to choose from,
the best wedding cake results come from Wilton Bakeware.
We are not willing to risk our cake results on inferior pans."*
Nicole V. Franklin, IN

*"With all the time and work that goes into decorating
a wedding cake, I wouldn't use anything else.
You can tell just by holding the round and oblong pans,
that they are thicker and a higher, superior quality."*
Jane K. Littleton, CO

*"The basic round, square and rectangular pans give my cakes
sharp edges and corners which make covering with fondant a breeze."*
Mariana P. Mexico City, Mexico

*"I had other more expensive brands, but Wilton rivaled them!
Now I prefer Wilton Bakeware over any other."*
Jessica B. Vienna, WV

Shop the complete selection of Wilton Bakeware on pages 156-168.

Retail Order Form

...eight Bags ...ressure!

...ngest-lasting bags you can buy.
...ar after year; our exclusive
...more you use them.
...o our customers:

*...lightweight
...ue in cake
...ars of use."*
...IN

12 in.
Featherweight™
Decorating Bag

10 in.
Featherweight™
Decorating Bag

8 in.
Featherweight™
Decorating Bag

*...They wash beautifully and are ready
...go again. The bags are so soft which
makes them easy to handle."*
Sharon C. Bayou La Batre, AL

*"I never had one break at the
seam and they wash up nicely to
use over and over again."*
Debbie B. Bloomer, WI

...ght Decorating Bags on page 138.

READY-TO-USE DECORATOR ICINGS

Wilton makes the only ready-to-use icing that is the perfect consistency for decorating. The pure white color is best for creating true vivid colors using Wilton Icing Colors. Rich and creamy, with a delicious homemade taste.

NEW!

4.5 Lb. Tub
Ideal thin-to-medium consistency for use in Wilton Method Cake Decorating Classes in a convenient easy-carry tub. Great for icing cakes, making borders, messages and more. Contains 9 cups—enough to decorate ten 8 or 9 in. round cake layers. Certified Kosher.
White 704-V-680 $14.99

1 Lb. Can
Ideal stiff consistency for making roses and flowers with upright petals. One 16 oz. can covers two 8 or 9 in. layers or one 9 x 13 in. cake.
White 710-V-118 $3.29
Chocolate 710-V-119 $3.29

Brownie Fudge Icing
Rich fudge flavor and velvety texture makes this the perfect icing for spreading on brownies. Heat it in the microwave for an easy glaze; use with Wilton Drizzle Icing (p. 144) to create delicious designs.
1 Lb. can.
710-V-9700 $3.29

"In the 29 years that I have been decorating cakes, I have not been able to make nor have I bought any icing that is as good as Wilton Ready-to-Use Tub Icing! The icing covers well, tastes delicious, colors well, and even works well when used in my decorator bags! Thank you, Wilton."

Pamela R.
Hope Mills, North Carolina

Vanilla Whipped Icing Mix
Our light, whipped icing provides the ideal texture for decorating in an easy-to-make, delicious mix. Just add ice water and it whips up velvety-smooth for icing or decorating. Light and delicate flavor. Makes 5 cups. Certified Kosher Dairy.
710-V-1241 $4.99

Creamy White Buttercream Icing Mix
Our convenient mix has the delicious taste and creamy texture of homemade buttercream icing. Use just as you would your favorite buttercream recipe. Makes 1½ to 2 cups. Enough to ice a 2-layer 8 in. cake. Certified Kosher Dairy.
710-V-112 $2.99

Meringue Powder
Primary ingredient for royal icing. Stabilizes buttercream, adds body to boiled icing and meringue. Replaces egg whites in many recipes. Resealable top opens for easy measuring. 4 oz. can makes 5 recipes of royal icing; 8 oz. can makes 10 recipes. 16 oz. can makes 20 recipes. Certified Kosher.
4 oz. 702-V-6007 $5.29
8 oz. 702-V-6015 $8.49
16 oz. 702-V-6004 $16.99

Color Flow Mix
Create dimensional flow-in designs for your cake. Just add water and confectioners' sugar. 4 oz. can makes ten 1½ cup batches. Certified Kosher.
701-V-47 $7.49

Piping Gel
Pipe messages and designs or glaze cakes before icing. Use clear or tint with icing color. 10 oz. Certified Kosher.
704-V-105 $3.99

Flavorings

Decorators trust Wilton flavorings for great taste that won't change icing consistency. Wilton flavors are concentrated—only a drop or two adds delicious taste to icings, cakes, beverages and other recipes.

Pure Vanilla Extract
The world's finest vanilla is from Madagascar. Unmatched flavor and aroma enhances cakes, puddings, pie fillings, custards and more. 4 fl. oz. Certified Kosher.
604-V-2270 $7.99

No-Color Flavorings
Recommended and used in Wilton Method Classes, these delicious flavors won't change your icing color. Essential for making pure white icings for wedding cakes and maintaining vibrant colors in all your decorating. Certified Kosher.

Clear Vanilla Extract
2 fl. oz.
604-V-2237 $1.99
8 fl. oz.
604-V-2269 $4.99

No-Color Butter Flavor
2 fl. oz.
604-V-2040 $1.99
8 fl. oz.
604-V-2067 $4.99

No-Color Almond Extract
2 fl. oz.
604-V-2126 $1.99

Sprinkles & Sugars

NEW!

DUSTING SUGAR

Colorful powdered sugar adds a dash of excitement to your plain brownies. Use with our Sugar Shaker (p. 170) and Brownie Stencil Set (p. 169) or Cake Stencils (p. 142) for a quick and easy decorating touch. 3 oz. pouch. **$1.99**

Blue
710-V-2558

Green
710-V-2560

Pink
710-V-2559

JUMBO SPRINKLES

Give your cupcakes a big finish! Top them with our new Jumbo Sprinkles in exciting shapes and colors. These big and bold decorations are perfect for cupcakes, mini cakes, jumbo and king-size cupcakes, brownies and cookies. Innovative shapes for birthday, holiday or any celebration. Certified Kosher. **$4.09**

Jumbo Hearts
3.25 oz.
710-V-032

Heart Drops
5.25 oz.
710-V-035

Jumbo Stars
3.25 oz.
710-V-026

Jumbo Confetti
3.25 oz.
710-V-029

Jumbo Diamonds
3.5 oz.
710-V-027

Jumbo Rainbow Nonpareils
4.8 oz. 710-V-033

Jumbo Daisies
3.25 oz.
710-V-028

SPRINKLES

Pour on the fun! Great shapes and colors add a dash of excitement to cakes, cupcakes, ice cream and more. Certified Kosher. **$2.29**

Chocolate Hearts
2.5 oz. Naturally and artificially flavored.
710-V-622

Cinnamon Drops
3 oz.
710-V-769

White Nonpareils
3 oz.
710-V-773

Rainbow Nonpareils
3 oz.
710-V-772

Chocolate Flavored Jimmies
2.5 oz. 710-V-774
6.25 oz.
710-V-168 **$4.49**

Rainbow Jimmies
2.5 oz. 710-V-776
6.25 oz.
710-V-994 **$4.49**

SPARKLING SUGARS

Put extra dazzle in your decorating! These easy-pour sugars have a coarse texture and a brilliant sparkle that makes cupcakes, cookies and cakes really shine. 5.25 oz. bottle. Certified Kosher. **$3.99**

Yellow
710-V-036

Blue
710-V-039

Lavender
710-V-037

Pink
710-V-038

8 oz. bottle. Certified Kosher. **$4.49**

White
710-V-992

Lavender/White
710-V-993

Rainbow
710-V-991

Colored Sugars

Wilton sugar is excellent for filling in brightly colored designs on cakes, cupcakes and cookies. 3.25 oz. bottle. Certified Kosher. **$2.29**

Blue
710-V-750

Yellow
710-V-754

Orange
710-V-759

Pink
710-V-756

Red
710-V-766

Lavender
710-V-758

Light Green
710-V-752

Dark Green
710-V-764

Black
710-V-762

Cake Sparkles

Add shimmering color to cakes, cupcakes, cookies and ice cream! Brilliant edible glitter in a great variety of colors, great for stencilling, highlighting messages, snow scenes. .25 oz. Certified Kosher. **$3.19**

Silver
703-V-1285

White
703-V-1290

Yellow
703-V-1272

Purple
703-V-1266

Blue
703-V-1314

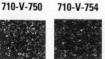
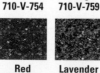

Red
703-V-1284

Green
703-V-1278

Pink
703-V-1260

Orange
703-V-1308

Black
703-V-1302

6-Mix Assortments

They're so convenient! Assorted fun shapes in an easy-pour flip-top bottle. Top cupcakes, ice cream and other goodies. Certified Kosher. **$4.99**

Flowerful Medley
Includes Confetti, Colorful Leaves, Daisies, Pastel Hearts, Wild Flowers, Butterflies. 2.23 oz. total.
710-V-4122

Animals and Stars
Includes Cows, Stars, Dinosaurs, Stars and Moons, Bears, Dolphins. 2.1 oz. total. 710-V-4123

Nonpareils
Includes Pink, Orange, Green, Red, Yellow, Purple. 3 oz. total.
710-V-4125

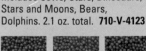

Jimmies
Includes Pink, Orange, Green, Red, Yellow, Blue. 2.52 oz. total.
710-V-4127

4-Mix Assortments

They're so convenient! Assorted sugars in an easy-pour flip-top bottle. Top cupcakes, ice cream and other goodies. 4.4 oz. total. Certified Kosher. **$4.99**

Bright Sugars
Includes Yellow, Light Green, Lavender, Pink. 710-V-651

Primary Sugars
Includes Red, Dark Green, Blue, Yellow. 710-V-650

Toppings

You've never had more exciting ways to top your treats! Wilton makes decorating quick, easy and colorful with a great variety of toppings to give your iced cakes, cupcakes and cookies the perfect finishing touch. From glistening pearlized sugars and flavorful crunches to beautifully-detailed icing flowers and edible Dessert Designs that melt a pretty accent into your icing, Wilton has a dazzling decoration for every occasion.

PEARLIZED SPRINKLES **NEW!**

Add a shimmering look with these softly-shaded pearlized toppings. Your cakes and cupcakes will shine with new jewel-tone colored sugars, plus jimmies and sugar pearls. **$4.49**

Sugar Pearls
5 oz.
710-V-044

Pearlized Sugar
5.25 oz.
710-V-043

Gold Pearlized Sugar
5.25 oz.
710-V-041

Silver Pearlized Sugar
5.25 oz.
710-V-042

Sapphire Pearlized Sugar
5.25 oz.
710-V-047

Emerald Pearlized Sugar
5.25 oz.
710-V-048

Ruby Pearlized Sugar
5.25 oz.
710-V-046

Pearlized Jimmies
4.5 oz.
710-V-045

CRUNCHES

Add delicious flavor and a colossal crunch! Sprinkle over iced cupcakes. Certified Kosher.

NEW!

Mint
5 oz.
710-V-9701 $4.99

NEW!

Cookies 'N Cream
5 oz.
710-V-9702 $4.99

NEW!

Turtle
5 oz.
710-V-9703 $4.99

NEW!

Rainbow Chip
Certified Kosher Dairy.
5.25 oz.
710-V-9704 $4.99

Toffee
3.5 oz. Naturally and artificially flavored.
710-V-023 $3.99

Chocolate
3.5 oz.
710-V-025 $3.99

Almond
3.5 oz. Artificially flavored. **710-V-024 $3.99**

DESSERT DESIGNS **NEW!**

Just peel. . .

Give iced cakes, cookies and cupcakes a fun hand-decorated look with ease! Dessert Designs are made from an edible paper that melts into your freshly iced treats, leaving the image on the surface. It's so easy! Just plan where to place your Dessert Design, ice the treat, peel the design away from backing and position the design. Choose from 4 great styles, each with more than 12 designs—it's the easy way to add color and excitement to any occasion. **$5.99**

. . .and place!

Celebrate
710-V-1331

Happy Birthday
710-V-1332

Baroque
710-V-1330

Garden
710-V-1329

ICING FLOWERS

Add breathtaking color and detail to your special cakes! Wilton Icing Flowers are the ideal time-saver, with beautifully-shaped petals that rival the best hand-piped flowers. They're the perfect way to dress up brownies, cupcakes and other treats for parties and gifts. With Wilton Icing Flowers, it's easy to create an impressive caketop bouquet in a variety of styles and colors. **$5.99**

White Roses

NEW!

Small
.75 in.
710-V-7155
Pk./12

Medium
1.25 in.
710-V-7154
Pk./8

Large
1.75 in.
710-V-7153
Pk./6

Daisy
4 large, 1.125 in.;
6 small, .75 in.
710-V-7157
Pk./10

Pink Posy
4 large, 1.125 in.;
6 small, .75 in.
710-V-7158
Pk./10

Pansy
4 large, 1.25 in.;
6 small, .75 in.
710-V-7156
Pk./10

Red Roses

Small
.75 in.
710-V-7152
Pk./12

Medium
1.25 in.
710-V-7151
Pk./8

Large
1.75 in.
710-V-7150
Pk./6

All sizes are approximate.

Icing Colors

Produce deep, rich color with just a small amount using this fast-mixing gel. The Wilton exclusive concentrated gel formula was developed to help decorators achieve the exact shade desired without changing icing consistency. An unmatched color selection makes it easy for you to achieve virtually any shade.

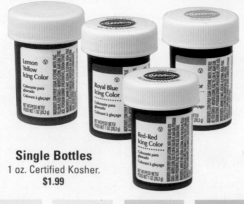

Single Bottles
1 oz. Certified Kosher.
$1.99

*Note: Large amounts of these colors may affect icing taste.

Use No-Taste Red for large areas of red on a cake. When using Black, start with chocolate icing to limit the amount of color needed.

‡Daffodil Yellow is an all-natural color. It does not contain Yellow #5. The color remains very pale.

Ivory 610-V-208	Daffodil Yellow‡ 610-V-175	Buttercup Yellow 610-V-216	Golden Yellow 610-V-159	Lemon Yellow 610-V-108	Copper 610-V-450	Creamy Peach 610-V-210	Rose Petal Pink 610-V-410

Terra Cotta 610-V-206	Orange 610-V-205	Red-Red* 610-V-906	Christmas Red* 610-V-302	Red (no-taste) 610-V-998	Rose 610-V-401	Burgundy 610-V-698	Pink 610-V-256	Violet 610-V-604	Delphinium Blue 610-V-228

Cornflower Blue 610-V-710	Royal Blue 610-V-655	Sky Blue 610-V-700	Teal 610-V-207	Kelly Green 610-V-752	Leaf Green 610-V-809	Moss Green 610-V-851	Juniper Green 610-V-234	Brown 610-V-507	Black* 610-V-981

Primary 4-Icing Colors Set
Lemon Yellow, Sky Blue, Christmas Red, Brown in .5 oz. jars. Certified Kosher.
601-V-5127 Set/4 $4.99

8-Icing Colors Set
Lemon Yellow, Orange, Pink, Christmas Red, Violet, Sky Blue, Leaf Green and Brown in .5 oz. jars. Certified Kosher.
601-V-5577 Set/8 $9.99

12-Icing Colors Set
Our most popular collection creates the spectrum of primary colors plus light and dark skin tones, teal and burgundy. Lemon Yellow, Golden Yellow, Pink, No-Taste Red, Burgundy, Violet, Royal Blue, Teal, Kelly Green, Copper, Brown, Black in .5 oz. jars. Certified Kosher.
601-V-5580 Set/12 $13.99

Pastel 4-Icing Colors Set
Creamy Peach, Rose Petal Pink, Willow Green, Cornflower Blue in .5 oz. jars. Certified Kosher.
601-V-25588 Set/4 $4.99

Garden Tone 4-Icing Colors Set
Buttercup Yellow, Delphinium Blue, Aster Mauve, Juniper Green in .5 oz. jars. Certified Kosher.
601-V-4240 Set/4 $4.99

White-White Icing Color
Stir in to whiten icing made with butter or margarine. Perfect for wedding cakes. 2 fl. oz. Certified Kosher.
603-V-1236 $2.99

Glycerine
Stir into dried out icing color, fondant or gum paste to restore consistency. 2 fl. oz. Certified Kosher.
708-V-14 $1.99

COLOR MIST FOOD COLOR SPRAY
This easy-to-use spray gives decorators the versatility and dazzling effects of an airbrush in a convenient can! Creates a rainbow of excitement on so many desserts. Use it to transform a plain iced cake with sensational color, add splashes of holiday color to iced cookies and cupcakes. Great for party desserts—highlighting whipped topping or ice cream with color. No mess, taste-free formula; add a little color or a lot. Colors match Wilton Icing Colors above. 1.5 oz. Certified Kosher. **$3.29**

Red 710-V-5500	Blue 710-V-5501
Yellow 710-V-5502	Green 710-V-5503
Violet 710-V-5504	Pink 710-V-5505
Black 710-V-5506	Orange 710-V-5507

ORDER TOLL FREE: 800-794-5866

Rolled Fondant

White Ready-To-Use Rolled Fondant

Fondant has never been more convenient and easy to use for decorating! With Wilton Ready-To-Use Rolled Fondant, there's no mess, no guesswork. The 24 oz. (1.5 Lb.) package covers an 8 in. 2-layer cake plus decorations; the 80 oz. (5 Lb.) package covers a 2-layer 6 in., 8 in. and 10 in. round tiered cake plus decorations. Pure white. Certified Kosher.

24 oz. (1.5 Lb.) Pk.
710-V-2076 **$6.79**

80 oz. (5 Lb.) Pk.
710-V-2180 **$22.99**

1. Roll out.   **2. Layer over cake.**   **3. Trim and decorate.**

Color Fondant Multi Packs

Convenient four-pouch assortments are perfect for multicolored flowers and borders. Each 17.6 oz. package contains four 4.4 oz. packs. Certified Kosher. **$10.49**

Primary Colors
Green, Red, Yellow, Blue
710-V-445

Neon Colors
Purple, Orange, Yellow, Pink
710-V-446

Pastel Colors
Blue, Yellow, Pink, Green
710-V-447

Natural Colors
Light Brown, Dark Brown, Pink, Black
710-V-448

FoodWriter Edible Color Markers

Use like ink markers to add fun and dazzling color to countless foods. Kids love 'em! Decorate on fondant, color flow, Wilton Cookie Icing, royal icing, even directly on cookies. Brighten everyday foods like toaster pastries, cheese, fruit slices, bread and more. Each set includes five .07 oz. FoodWriter markers. Certified Kosher.

Primary Colors Sets

Yellow	Green	Red	Blue	Black

Fine Tip 609-V-100 Set/5 **$8.39**
Bold Tip 609-V-115 Set/5 **$8.39**

Neon Colors Set

Purple	Orange	Pink	Light Green	Black

Fine Tip 609-V-116 Set/5 **$8.39**

FINE TIP
BOLD TIP

Gum Paste and Ingredients

Ready-To-Use Gum Paste
Create beautiful handmolded flowers right from the package.

Now you can have gum paste on hand whenever you need it! With Ready-To-Use Gum Paste, there's no mixing, no mess—just tint, roll out and cut to create incredible floral bouquets for your cakes. Follow the easy instructions included and use with Wilton Gum Paste Decorating Sets to make roses, daisies, apple blossoms, tulips and many more beautiful blooms. 1 Lb. Certified Kosher.
707-V-130 **$9.99**

Gum Paste Mix
Just add water and knead. Workable, pliable dough-like mixture molds beautiful flowers and figures. 1 Lb. Certified Kosher.
707-V-124 **$5.99**

Gum-Tex
Makes fondant and gum paste pliable, elastic, easy to shape. Plastic resealable lid. 6 oz. Certified Kosher.
707-V-117 **$7.99**

Glucose
Essential ingredient for making fondant and gum paste from scratch. Use with Wilton Gum-Tex. 12 oz. Certified Kosher.
707-V-107 **$3.99**

Glycerine
Stir into dried out fondant, gum paste or icing color to restore consistency. 2 fl. oz. Certified Kosher.
708-V-14 **$1.99**

Fondant Mats and Rolling Pins

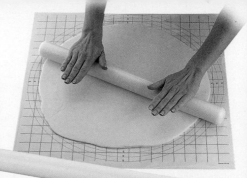

FONDANT IMPRINT MATS

Imprint a beautiful recessed pattern to cover your cake! Just smooth your rolled fondant over the mat, place on your cake and peel back the mat. The recessed design imprinted in the fondant adds beautiful definition, so even white cakes stand out. Also great for textured fondant ribbons and edging. *20 x 20 in.* **$19.99**

NEW!

Star Power
409-V-416

NEW!

Happy Birthday
409-V-417

Floral Fantasy
409-V-415

Graceful Vines
409-V-414

Using Fondant Imprint Mats

1. Roll out fondant ⅛ in. thick using rolling pin.
2. Lift fondant onto Fondant Imprint Mat using rolling pin. Or, place Fondant Imprint Mat on top of rolled fondant.

3. If fondant is on top of Fondant Imprint Mat, smooth by pressing firmly with Wilton Easy-Glide Fondant Smoother (p. 151) or roll with rolling pin. If fondant is below Fondant Imprint Mat, roll with rolling pin.

4. Lift Fondant Imprint Mat with fondant attached and center imprinted fondant on cake. Peel back mat. Smooth fondant around cake by gently pressing with heel of hand.

20 in. Rolling Pin

Its extra-wide, smooth design is perfect for covering cakes with rolled fondant. The non-stick surface makes handling large pieces of fondant easy—just dust the surface with confectioners' sugar and roll out fondant to the size you need, then use the Rolling Pin to lift the fondant from your work surface to the cake. Great for rolling out pastry dough and pie crusts too. 20 x 1.5 in. diameter. (Mat sold below.)
1907-V-1210 $21.99

20 in. Rolling Pin Guide Rings

Slip these easy-to-use guide rings onto the ends of your 20 in. rolling pin to achieve the perfect thickness every time. Includes ¹⁄₁₆ in. (blue) for flower petals and leaves, ³⁄₁₆ in. (gold) for letters, numbers and appliqué shapes, ⅛ in. (orange) for shapes cut with Wilton Cut-Outs or cookie cutters and for covering cakes with fondant.
1907-V-1010 Set/3 $4.49

9 in. Rolling Pin

Roll out fondant evenly, in the perfect thickness for easy cutting and shaping, with this 3-piece non-stick roller. Roll to the perfect ⅛ or ¹⁄₁₆ in. height used for cutting many fondant decorations, using the slide-on guide rings. Easy to handle—just the right size for preparing small amounts of fondant to place on your cake. Perfect for use with Fondant Multi Packs and Cut-Outs. 9 x 1 in. diameter. Includes ⅛ and ¹⁄₁₆ in. rings.
1907-V-1205 $6.99

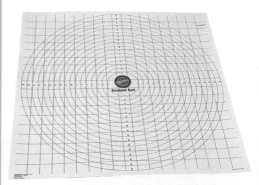

Roll & Cut Mat

For precise measuring, rolling and cutting of fondant or dough. Pre-marked circles for exact sizing. Square grid helps you cut precise strips. Non-stick surface for easy release. 20 in. square with circles from 3 in. to 19 in. diam.
409-V-412 $9.49

ORDER TOLL FREE: 800-794-5866

Fondant Tools and Accessories

No one has more ways to decorate with rolled fondant than Wilton! We've developed a complete line of tools that make fondant easier than ever to shape, cut and imprint. Finish your decorations with a dazzling accent—brush on Pearl Dust to create colorful highlights for flowers, bows and swags.

10-Pc. Fondant/Gum Paste Tool Set

Here are the tools every decorator needs to create breathtaking gum paste and fondant flowers, leaves and accents. Precise modeling tools feature comfortable grips for easy handling. Colored grips and numbered tip designs make tools easy to identify. Convenient case keeps the collection organized and handy. Includes large/small veining tool, shell tool/knife, large/small dogbone tool, serrated quilting/cutting wheel, umbrella tool with 5 and 6 divisions, scriber/cone tool, large/small ball tool, palette knife and modeling sticks #1 and #2.

1907-V-1107 Set/10 $29.99

Easy-Glide Fondant Smoother

Essential tool for shaping and smoothing rolled fondant on your cake. Works great on top, edges and sides! Shapes fondant to sides of cake so that no puffed areas appear. Trim off excess with a sharp knife. 6.25 x 3.35 in. wide.

1907-V-1200 $5.49

Fondant Shaping Foam

Thick and thin squares are the ideal soft surface for shaping flowers, leaves and other fondant or gum paste cutouts. Use the thin square for thinning petal edges with a ball tool, carving vein lines on leaves and making ruffled fondant strips. Use the thick square for cupping flower centers. Thin: 4 x 4 x .2 in. Thick: 4 x 4 x 1 in.

1907-V-9704 Set/2 $3.29

Flower Stamen Assortment

Finish your royal icing or gum paste flowers with these 3 lovely stamen styles. Cut stamens to desired size and insert in flower center. Includes 60 each Pearl, Glitter and Fluffy. May be tinted (except Pearl) with Wilton Icing Colors added to vanilla. 2.5 in. long.

1005-V-410 Pk./180 $3.19

Flower Forming Cups

Curved round shape is ideal for drying gum paste, fondant and royal icing flowers and leaves. Openings in bottom center make it easy to pull wires through and adjust for the perfect drying position. Includes 2.5 and 3 in. diameter cups for drying everything from simple blossoms and briar roses to large daisies.

1907-V-118 Set/6 $5.49

Flower Former Set

Dry fondant or icing leaves and flowers in a convex or concave shape. Three each of 1.5, 2 and 2.5 in. wide holders, all 11 in. long.

417-V-9500 Set/9 $6.29

Quick Ease Roller

Makes it easy to prepare small pieces of fondant and gum paste for cutting flowers and designs. Wooden roller fits comfortably in palm of hand. 4.2 in. wide.

1907-V-1202 $5.49

Dusting Pouches

Essential for rolling out gum paste or fondant! Fabric pouch dusts surfaces with a cornstarch/confectioners' sugar mixture to prevent your rolling pin from sticking. Gathering cord closes bag securely—just tap lightly on the pouch to sprinkle. 7 in. diameter.

417-V-106 Pk./4 $3.29

PEARL DUST

Give your fondant, gum paste, royal icing and molded Candy Melts decorations a beautiful, glittering finish! Wilton Pearl Dust creates rich, lustrous highlights on flowers, bows, letters and more. Easy to use, just brush onto your decoration with a soft artist brush. Or, to paint decorations, pour a small amount of lemon extract into a a Color Tray cavity; stir in Pearl Dust and brush onto your decoration. Edible; Certified Kosher (except Orchid Pink and Lilac Purple). .05 oz. bottle. **$3.99**

Leaf Green 703-V-215	**Lilac Purple** 703-V-221	**Sapphire Blue** 703-V-222	**Ruby Red** 703-V-223	**Gold** 703-V-216
Yellow 703-V-213	**Bronze** 703-V-214	**Orchid Pink** 703-V-217	**Silver** 703-V-218	**White** 703-V-219

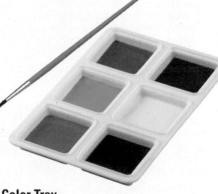

Color Tray

Become a true fondant artist with this convenient tray! Pour in Icing Writer (p. 144) and use with the Brush Set to add vivid designs to your fondant cakes.

1907-V-1208 $3.29

Brush Set

Fine-bristle brushes in three tip designs (round, square and bevel) help you achieve different painted effects. Use with Icing Writer (p. 144); or attach fondant decorations with water or adhesive.

1907-V-1207 Set/3 $3.29

Fondant Tools and Accessories

Look at the fondant shapes you can add to your cakes! Fantasy flowers, floral bouquets, textured bows and geometric designs—they're all so easy to cut and shape with Wilton tools.

FONDANT CUT & PRESS SETS

Give your cake the perfect finish! Create a beautifully-textured fondant and/or gum paste design in seconds with the Fondant Cut & Press. It's easy—just roll out fondant, gum paste or a 50/50 mixture, cut with the rectangular cutting edge, then place on inside of press bottom, cover with top and press to imprint design. Includes 2 piece cutter/press, instructions.

Button Flower
1907-V-1306 $6.99

Rose Leaf
1907-V-1300 $6.99

Just roll to cut and emboss textured fondant strips

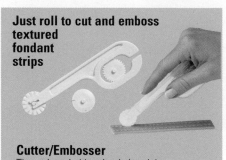

Cutter/Embosser
Three detachable wheels (straight, wavy and ridged) for cutting and for embossing patterns on fondant. Light, easy-rolling design cuts at the perfect angle. Comfortable handle also stores wheels.
1907-V-1206 $4.49

FONDANT CUT & PRESS SET INSTRUCTIONS

- Roll out fondant/gum paste mixture 1/8 in. thick on Roll & Cut Mat. Use cutting side of white tray included in set to cut four 4 in. x 6 in. rectangles.

- Lift a 4 in. x 6 in. rectangle of fondant/gum paste mixture off mat (cover remaining rectangles on mat with plastic wrap to keep pliable) and place directly on top of press bottom with indentations. Make sure that side that was face down on mat (with shortening) is face down on press.

- Apply pressure to imprint and cut designs.

- Open press and use tool or fingers to remove excess fondant/gum paste mixture from around cutters.

DO NOT REMOVE FONDANT/ GUM PASTE MIXTURE FROM INSIDE INDIVIDUAL DESIGNS.

- Reopen press and use Veining Tool from Gum Paste Tool Set, Modeling Tool or Tapered Blade Spatula to carefully remove shapes from press starting at one end.

- Position flowers and leaves on Flower Forming Cups or on the Flower Former Set to achieve concave or convex shapes.

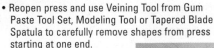

Fondant Decorative Punch Set
Punch out fondant accents with elegant openwork shapes. As you punch, the disk imprints a detailed design that adds a pretty touch of texture. The comfortable angled handle holds 8 design disks. Disks turn to lock into place.
1907-V-1204 Set/9 $9.99

Add exciting 3-dimensional decorations in fondant

| Large Tulip with Leaves | Dutch Blossom | Paisley with Dots | Wide Diamond with Scrolls | Small Tulip with Leaves | Snapdragon with Leaves | 4-Leaf Clover with Dots | Narrow Diamond with Scrolls |

Fondant Ribbon Cutter/ Embosser Set
Just choose the cutting and embossing wheel designs you want, slide the washer, core, wheels and spacers on the roller handle, and roll on fondant. Produces ribbon widths from ¼ in. to 3¾ in. when combining spacers. Complete set includes: 8 embossing wheels; 9 spacers; 9 cutting wheels; roller handle with detachable core; assembly hardware.
1907-V-1203 Set/26 $16.49

Add beautiful textured fondant ribbons, stripes and bows to your cake!

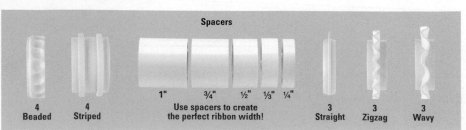

Spacers

| 4 Beaded | 4 Striped | 1" | ¾" | ½" | ⅓" | ¼" | 3 Straight | 3 Zigzag | 3 Wavy |

Use spacers to create the perfect ribbon width!

Stepsaving Rose Bouquets Flower Cutter Set

Create gorgeous fondant and gum paste roses and forget-me-nots using book and cutters in this set. Cutters include large and small rose, rose leaf, calyx and forget-me-not.
1907-V-1003 Set/6 $8.99

Floral Garland Cutter/Ejector Set

Quickly and easily cuts and positions fondant or gum paste flowers on cakes. Includes ejector, 5 cutters and instructions.
1907-V-1001 Set/7 $10.99

Floral Collection Flower Making Set

Make incredibly lifelike gum paste flowers. Full-color how-to book includes many arranging ideas and step-by-step instructions. Kit includes 24 plastic cutters, 1 leaf mold, 3 wood modeling tools, protector flap, 40-page instruction book and 2 foam squares for modeling.
1907-V-117 Set/32 $21.99
Book only 907-V-117 $9.99

Letters & Numbers Gum Paste & Fondant Mold Set

With this set, it's easy to put the finishing touches on your cakes with a beautiful 3-dimensional message or monogram. Just fill molds with a 50/50 gum paste and fondant blend, press and smooth with tool included and release. Great for 2-tone letters and numbers, a perfect way to personalize cake and cupcakes. Includes 11 mold sheets with 52 alphabet molds (upper and lower case A-Z), 3 punctuation marks and 10 numeral molds, stainless steel smoothing/releasing tool, molding instructions.
2104-V-3070 Set/13 $21.99

CUT-OUTS

- Fast, fun way to brighten any fondant cake!
- Great assortment of shapes for any occasion.

With Cut-Outs, it's easy to make fun 3-D shapes for your fondant cakes and cupcakes. Just roll out fondant, press down with Cut-Out and lift away. Remove shapes with a small spatula. Stainless steel (except for plastic Daisy) shapes range from .6 in. to 2.5 in.

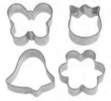

Crinkle Shapes
Circle, Square, Triangle, Heart
417-V-444 Set/4 $3.19

Fancy Shapes
Flower, Leaf, Oval, Heart
417-V-445 Set/4 $3.19

Garden Shapes
Butterfly, Tulip, Bell, Flower
417-V-443 Set/4 $3.19

Daisy
Durable plastic.
417-V-439 Set/3 $2.59

Oval
417-V-438
Set/3 $2.59

Round
417-V-432
Set/3 $2.59

Square
417-V-431
Set/3 $2.59

People
417-V-441
Set/6 $4.19

Heart
417-V-434
Set/3 $2.59

Star
417-V-433
Set/3 $2.59

Flower
417-V-435
Set/3 $2.59

Funny Flower
417-V-436
Set/3 $2.59

Leaf
417-V-437
Set/3 $2.59

Alphabet/Number
417-V-442 Set/37 $15.79

Baking Accessories

Bake Easy! Non-Stick Spray

For cakes that turn out beautifully every time, start by spraying pans with Bake Easy. This convenient non-stick spray helps your cakes release perfectly with fewer crumbs for easier icing and a flawless look for decorating. Just a light, even coating does the job. Use for all mixes and recipes, versatile for all types of baking and cooking. 6 oz.
702-V-6018 $3.29

Cake Release

Another step-saving Wilton idea! No need to grease and flour your baking pan—Cake Release coats in one step. Simply spread Cake Release lightly on pan bottom and sides with a pastry brush and add batter. Cakes release perfectly every time without crumbs, giving you the ideal surface for decorating. In convenient dispensing bottle. 8 oz. Certified Kosher.
702-V-6016 $3.49

Bake-Even Strips

A Wilton innovation! Cakes bake perfectly level and moist, without cracking, when you wrap these strips around the outside of the pan before baking. Oven-safe, instructions and clips included.

Small Set
Two 1½ in. high strips, 30 in. long. Enough for two 8 or 9 in. round pans.
415-V-260 Set/2 $8.99

Large Set
Four 1½ in. high strips, 36, 43, 49 and 56 in. long. Enough for one each: 10, 12, 14, 16 in. round pans.
415-V-262 Set/4 $18.99

Non-Stick Parchment Paper

Use Wilton silicone-treated non-stick parchment to line baking pans and cookie sheets—a non-fat alternative that saves cleanup time. Roll out cookie dough between 2 sheets, dough won't stick and will easily transfer to your cookie sheet. You can even reuse it for the next batch. Oven-safe to 400°F, great for conventional ovens, microwaves and the freezer. Double roll is 41 square feet, 15 in. wide. Certified Kosher.
415-V-680 $5.29

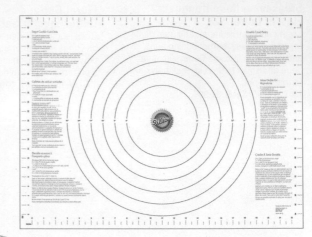

Pastry Mat

Non-stick mat with pre-marked measurements for easy rolling and precise cutting! Includes circles for pie, tart and pizza crusts from 6 to 16 in. diameter, pre-marked inches and centimeters for exact cutting of lattice strips. Delicious cookie and pie crust recipes are printed on the mat. Non-stick surface for easy release. 18 x 24 in.
409-V-413 $9.49

Cake Leveler

Make your cake top perfectly level for precise decorating—just place adjustable wire in notches to desired height up to 2 in. and glide through the cake. Makes torting easy, too! For cakes up to 10 in. wide.
415-V-815 $3.19

Large Cake Leveler

Blade easily levels and tortes cakes up to 18 in. wide. Adjusts up to 3 in. high—just twist feet to lock into notch at desired height then glide the stainless steel blade through your cake.
417-V-1198 $23.09

6-Piece Covered Mixing Bowl Set

Perfect for preparing decorating icings—clear lids snap on tight to keep icing the right texture. Includes one each 1, 2 and 3 quart nesting bowls with easy-grip handles and easy-pour spouts for better control. Rubberized base keeps bowls from sliding on countertops. Measurements clearly marked for precise mixing. Dishwasher safe.
417-V-469 Set/6 $13.69

Cake Carriers

Cake Caddy

The 6 in. high see-through plastic dome has 3 locking latches that hold the base securely in place wherever you go. Convenient handle gives you a firm grip. The elegant base is approximately 13 in. diameter and holds and stores up to 10 in. round cake or pie, cupcakes, cookies and more.
2105-V-9952 $14.99

THE ULTIMATE 3-IN-1 CADDY

The versatile and safe way to carry cakes and desserts.

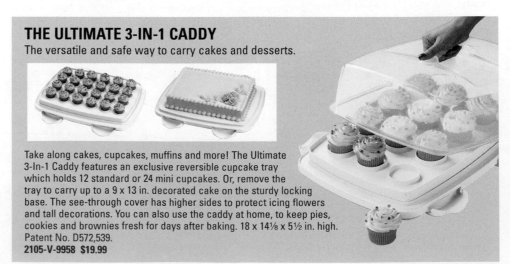

Take along cakes, cupcakes, muffins and more! The Ultimate 3-In-1 Caddy features an exclusive reversible cupcake tray which holds 12 standard or 24 mini cupcakes. Or, remove the tray to carry up to a 9 x 13 in. decorated cake on the sturdy locking base. The see-through cover has higher sides to protect icing flowers and tall decorations. You can also use the caddy at home, to keep pies, cookies and brownies fresh for days after baking. 18 x 14⅛ x 5½ in. high. Patent No. D572,539.
2105-V-9958 $19.99

Better Baking Tools

Essential tools designed to do more! Wilton Better Baking Tools are designed with exclusive features that make baking easier:

- The patented Twist 'N Measure has a rotating dial to create 6 different measurements in 1
- The unique patented clip slides along the wires of the Baker's Pastry Blender to remove butter and dough
- The Cyclone Whisk has an innovative center spiral that incorporates more air into batters
- The Rolling Pin has removable handles making it fully submersible and dishwasher safe

Twist 'N Measure Cup
2103-V-321 $7.99

Scoop It Measuring Spoons
2103-V-325
Set/5 $5.99

Scoop It Measuring Cups
2103-V-324
Set/4 $7.99

2 Cup Liquid Measure
Patent Pending.
2103-V-334 $7.99

4 Cup Liquid Measure
Patent Pending.
2103-V-335 $9.99

Cake Lifter
2103-V-307
$9.99

Baker's Blade
Patent No. D587,538.
2103-V-310
$7.99

Silicone Spoon Scraper
Patent No. D584,927.
2103-V-328 $6.99

Silicone Stand Mixer Scraper
Patent No. D587,537.
2103-V-329 $6.99

Silicone Universal Scraper
Patent No. D586,630.
2103-V-327 $6.99

Cyclone Whisk
Patent No. D582,223.
2103-V-317 $9.99

Baker's Pastry Blender
2103-V-313
$6.99

Tilt 'n Mix 3-Pc. Bowl Set
2103-V-306
$29.99

Rolling Pin
2103-V-301 $24.99

Kitchen Tools

Make decorating and kitchen tasks easier! Lightweight, comfortable tools with contoured handles and quality blades of stainless steel and silicone heads suited for the task.

Pastry Wheel
Create crisp straight or graceful scalloped edges with this smooth-rolling pastry wheel. Comfortable handle with finger/thumb guard. 6.5 in. long.
2103-V-315 $8.99

Pastry Brush
Flexible silicone bristles are great for brushing on Cake Release, shortening or hot glazes. More durable than nylon bristles. Comfortable ergonomic handle. 8.5 in. long.
409-V-6056 $5.99

Cookie Spatula
Angled stainless steel blade moves cookies from pan to plate with ease. Slides easily under cookies—great for serving brownies and bar cookies too. Comfortable ergonomic handle with thumb rest. 9 in. long.
409-V-6054 $6.99

Cake and Pie Server
Slice and serve with greater control. The comfortable ergonomic handle with thumb rest and angled blade makes lifting every slice easier. Serrated stainless steel blade cuts even the first slice cleanly. 9 in. long.
409-V-6058 $6.99

All-Purpose Spatulas
Blend and mix with greater comfort, more control and less fatigue, thanks to the contoured Comfort Grip handle. Flexible silicone blade is ideal for blending and removing icing from bowls or containers—great for all-around kitchen use. Stain and odor resistant.
9 in. 409-V-6050 $7.99
12 in. 409-V-6052 $8.99

Bakeware

Wilton is the #1 bakeware brand in America. From fun novelty shapes for birthday cakes to dramatic cast aluminum styles for elegant desserts, count on Wilton for the best results.

Performance Pan Sets

Create a classic tiered cake with confidence when you start with Wilton even-baking aluminum pan sets. For generations, decorators have counted on Wilton quality pans to bake the light golden-brown surface essential for beautiful tiers. The precise lines and seamless baking surface of each pan helps you achieve a perfect cake for decorating. In addition to traditional tiered shapes such as rounds, squares and ovals, you'll find exciting new diamond and paisley shapes to help you create cakes that set any special occasion apart. Each pan is 2 inches deep, except where noted. Aluminum.

NEW!

3-Pc. Diamond Set
A dazzling shape for dramatic tiered cakes. Create a contemporary look for weddings, showers, anniversaries and more—the unique diamond design is ideal for rolled fondant cakes. Includes 10.25 x 7.4; 15 x 11 in. and 19.25 x 14.25 in. pans.
2105-V-4204 Set/3 $47.99

4-Pc. Oval Set
An elegant shape ideal for cascading arrangements. The large 16.5 in. pan also works well as a base for round tiers, giving you added space for floral arrangements or large decorations. Includes 7.75 x 5.5 in; 10.75 x 7.8 in.; 13.5 x 9.8 in. and 16.5 x 12.38 in. pans.*
2105-V-2130 Set/4 $41.99

4-Pc. Round Set
Our most popular collection offers the versatility of constructing classic wedding tiers or creating individual round party cakes in exactly the size you want. Includes 6, 8, 10, 12 in. pans.*
2105-V-2101 Set/4 $35.49

4-Pc. 3 in. Deep Round Set
Extra-tall design helps you create impressive 2-layer wedding tiers, 5 in. high. Includes 8, 10, 12, 14 in. pans.*
2105-V-2932 Set/4 $47.99

3-Pc. Square Set
A favorite graduated grouping, highlighted by a 16 in. pan for a dramatic base tier. Includes 8, 12, 16 in. pans.*
2105-V-2132 Set/3 $47.99

*Heating Core (p. 158) is recommended for pans which are 10 in. diameter or larger.

3-Pc. Paisley Set
Create a beautiful tiered cake with graceful curves unlike any other. Ideal for cascading floral arrangements—perfect for weddings, showers and more. Includes 9 x 6 in., 12.75 x 9 in. and 17 x 12 in. pans.
2105-V-4039 Set/3 $47.99

4-Pc. Petal Set
The lively curves of this best-selling tiered set tie in perfectly with floral-themed weddings and showers. Or, use one petal tier in combination with other shapes—the petal sections are a great way to add texture to your design. Includes 6, 9, 12, 15 in. pans.*
2105-V-2134 Set/4 $41.99

4-Pc. Hexagon Set
A great choice for fondant-covered designs. The sharp lines of our hexagon pans create a strong presence for weddings, religious occasions, graduations and more. Includes 6, 9, 12, 15 in. pans.*
2105-V-3572 Set/4 $41.99

ORDER TOLL FREE: 800-794-5866

Performance Pans

The classic aluminum pans—durable, even-heating and built to hold their shape through years of use. We named them Performance Pans because they perform beautifully. These are great all-purpose pans you'll use for casseroles, entrees, baked desserts and more. Wilton has sold millions of Performance Pans because decorators and bakers know they can depend on them.

Rounds

A great selection of sizes for the most popular cake shape of all. Put together your own set to create classic tiers or bake an individual round cake your guests will love. Even-heating aluminum for the best baking results.

6 x 2 in.
2105-V-2185 $7.99

8 x 2 in.
2105-V-2193 $8.99

10 x 2 in.
2105-V-2207 $9.99

12 x 2 in.
2105-V-2215 $12.99

14 x 2 in.
2105-V-3947 $16.49

16 x 2 in.
2105-V-3963 $19.99

2-Pan Round Set
9 x 2 in. deep
2105-V-7908 $14.49

Sheets
9 x 13 x 2 in. deep
2105-V-1308 $12.99

11 x 15 x 2 in. deep
2105-V-158 $17.99

12 x 18 x 2 in. deep
2105-V-182 $19.99

Covered Baking Pan
Clear, durable cover makes it easy to transport desserts and keep them fresh at home. 11 x 15 x 2 in.
2105-V-3849 $22.99

Squares

You'll call on this shape constantly for cakes, brownies and entrees—fortunately, our quality aluminum pans are built for years of great baking results. Find the right size for a single cake or a tiered masterpiece.

6 x 2 in.
507-V-2180 $7.99

8 x 2 in.
2105-V-8191 $9.99

10 x 2 in.
2105-V-8205 $11.99

12 x 2 in.
2105-V-8213 $16.49

14 x 2 in.
2105-V-8220 $20.99

16 x 2 in.
2105-V-8231 $22.99

SweetHeart
A gently curving shape gives the classic heart a more romantic flair. Whether you accent it with pretty icing flowers or pair it with bold fondant decorations, this cake will charm guests for birthdays, Mother's Day, Valentine's Day, showers and more. Takes 1 standard mix. 10.25 x 11 x 2 in.
2105-V-1197 $12.99

Specialty Pans

Classic Angel Food
If you're looking for a healthy dessert, you can't do better than angel food! It's delicious with a simple fresh fruit topping. Removable inner core sleeve, cooling legs. Aluminum.

7 x 4.5 in. deep.
Takes ½ standard mix.
2105-V-9311 $15.49

10 x 4 in. deep.
Takes 1 standard mix.
2105-V-2525 $18.99

Fancy Ring Mold
Beautiful sculpted pan, ideal for pound cakes, mousse and more! Takes 1 standard mix. 10 in. diameter x 3 in. Aluminum.
2105-V-5008 $12.99

Springform Pans

When shopping for a springform pan, you want strong construction and an easy-release design that will let you remove a perfect cheesecake every time. Wilton springform pans are built tough, with strong springlocks that hold up year after year. The removable waffle-textured bottom design keeps crusts from sticking while distributing heat evenly. Springlock releases sides. Aluminum.

6 x 3 in.
2105-V-4437 $12.99

8 x 3 in.
2105-V-8464 $14.49

9 x 3 in.
2105-V-5354 $15.49

10 x 3 in.
2105-V-8465 $15.49

Decorator Preferred®

Professional Aluminum Bakeware

Built with the most features to help decorators bake their best! Compare these benefits to any brand:

STRAIGHT SIDES

Bake perfect 90° corners for the precise look wedding cakes require.

GRIP LIP EDGES

Extra-wide rims make heavy filled pans easy to handle.

PURE ALUMINUM

The best material for baking cakes—creates a light, golden brown cake surface, beautiful for decorating.

SUPERIOR THICKNESS

Thicker than ordinary bakeware, built to distribute heat evenly for more consistent baking.

HANDCRAFTED CONSTRUCTION

Sheets and squares are handwelded for excellent detail and durability.

LIFETIME WARRANTY

Superior construction and performance designed and guaranteed to last a lifetime.

OUR MOST POPULAR BAKEWARE!

Squares

Perfect 90° corners give you the flawless look necessary for wedding tiers.

8 x 2 in.
2105-V-6142 $11.99

12 x 2 in.
2105-V-6144 $19.99

10 x 2 in.
2105-V-6143 $16.49

Sheets

Extra-thick aluminum distributes heat efficiently on these large pans.

9 x 13 x 2 in.
2105-V-6146 $18.99

12 x 18 x 2 in.
2105-V-6148 $25.49

11 x 15 x 2 in.
2105-V-6147 $20.99

Rounds

What a selection of sizes —including the hard-to find 18 in. Half Round, which lets you bake and ice two halves to create one 18 in. round cake.

6 x 2 in.
2105-V-6122 $7.99

8 x 2 in.
2105-V-6136 $8.99

9 x 2 in.
2105-V-6137 $9.99

10 x 2 in.
2105-V-6138 $11.99

12 x 2 in.
2105-V-6139 $14.49

14 x 2 in.
2105-V-6140 $19.99

16 x 2 in.
2105-V-6141 $21.99

6 x 3 in.
2105-V-6106 $9.99

8 x 3 in.
2105-V-6105 $10.99

10 x 3 in.
2105-V-6104 $12.99

12 x 3 in.
2105-V-6103 $16.49

14 x 3 in.
2105-V-6102 $19.99

16 x 3 in.
2105-V-6101 $22.99

18 x 3 in. Half Round
2105-V-6100 $26.99

3-Pc. Round Set

6, 10 and 14 in. diameter x 3 in. deep.
2105-V-6114 Set/3 $40.99

Contour

Create cakes with an elegant, rounded top edge. This is the perfect shape for positioning rolled fondant. 9 x 3 in. deep.
2105-V-6121 $14.49

Heating Core

Distributes heat to bake large cakes evenly. Recommended for pans 10 in. diameter or larger. Releases easily from cake. 3.5 x 3.5 x 4 in. diameter.
417-V-6100 $8.49

Hearts

Ultimate heart cake is beautiful for showers, weddings, more!

6 x 2 in.
2105-V-600 $7.49

8 x 2 in.
2105-V-601 $8.49

10 x 2 in.
2105-V-602 $10.99

12 x 2 in.
2105-V-607 $12.99

14 x 2 in.
2105-V-604 $15.49

16 x 2 in.
2105-V-605 $17.99

4-Pc. Heart Set

Now redesigned for a perfect fit when used with our Decorator Preferred Heart Separator Plates shown on page 237. Includes 6, 10, 12 and 14 in. pans. Aluminum.
2105-V-606 Set/4 $41.99

ORDER TOLL FREE: 800-794-5866

Cookie Sheets and Pans

A warped sheet can ruin a batch of cookies. With Wilton Cookie Sheets, you won't worry about warping. The extra-thick aluminum heats evenly for perfectly browned bottoms. Versatile sheets are great for baking appetizers, turnovers and more.

Aluminum Sheet
Extra-thick construction heats evenly for perfectly browned bottoms.

Jumbo 14 x 20 in.
2105-V-6213
$19.99

Insulated Aluminum Sheet
Two quality aluminum layers sandwich an insulating layer of air for perfect browning without burning.

14 x 16 in.
2105-V-2644
$20.99

Jelly Roll and Cookie Pans
Wilton pans are 1 in. deep for fuller-looking desserts.

10.5 x 15.5 x 1 in.
2105-V-1269 $14.49

12 x 18 x 1 in.
2105-V-4854 $16.49

Muffin Pans

With so many great Wilton muffin pans to choose from, you'll be making muffins and cupcakes more often. You'll love our mini pans for the perfect brunch muffins and the jumbo size pan for bakery-style muffins and cupcakes.

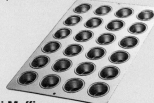

Standard Muffin
Most popular size for morning muffins, after-school cupcakes and desserts. Twelve cups, each 3 in. diameter x 1 in. Aluminum.
2105-V-9310 $18.99

White Standard Baking Cups (shown on p. 183)
Microwave-safe paper. 2 in. diameter.
415-V-2505 Pk./75 $1.59

Mini Muffin
Great for mini cheesecakes, brunches, large gatherings. Cups are 2 in. x .75 in. Aluminum.
12 Cup 2105-V-2125 $12.99
24 Cup 2105-V-9313 $19.99

White Mini Baking Cups (shown on p. 183)
Microwave-safe paper. 1.25 in. diameter.
415-V-2507 Pk./100 $1.59

Jumbo Muffin
Make super-size cupcakes and muffins. Six cups, each 4 x 2 in. Aluminum.
2105-V-1820 $18.99

White Jumbo Baking Cups (shown on p. 183)
Microwave-safe paper. 2.25 in. diameter.
415-V-2503 Pk./50 $1.59

Loaf Pans

It's all in the crust. Wilton Loaf Pans bake bread with hearty, crisp crusts and soft, springy centers. Our superior anodized aluminum promotes better browning, resulting in the perfect texture for all your breads.

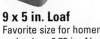

Petite Loaf
Great for single-size dessert cakes, frozen bread dough. Nine cavities, each 2.5 x 3.38 x 1.5 in. Aluminum.
2105-V-8466 $11.99

Mini Loaf
Everyone loves personal-sized nut breads or cakes. Six cavities are 4.5 x 2.5 x 1.5 in. Aluminum.
2105-V-9791 $11.99

9 x 5 in. Loaf
Favorite size for homemade breads and cakes. 2.75 in. Aluminum.
2105-V-3688 $8.49

Long Loaf
Legs provide support for cooling angel food cakes, breads or classic cakes. 16 x 4 x 4.5 in. deep. Aluminum.
2105-V-1588 $15.49

Chrome-Plated Cooling Grids

Sturdy design will never rust. Great selection of popular sizes.

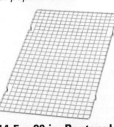

13 in. Round
2305-V-130 $8.99

10 x 16 in. Rectangle
2305-V-128 $6.99

14.5 x 20 in. Rectangle
2305-V-129 $9.99

3-Tier Stackable
Use singly or stack to save space while cooling three cake layers, pies and tarts or batches of cookies at the same time. Individual grids are 13.5 x 9.75 x 3 in. high; stacked grids are 9.75 in. high.
2305-V-151 $14.49

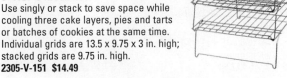

BAKEWARE

Mini Shaped Pans

One cake mix makes 12-14 mini cakes. Aluminum.

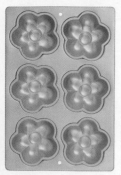

Mini Daisy
Six cavity pan is 12.25 x 8.2 x 1.5 in.; individual cavities are 3 x 3.25 x 1.5 in. deep.
2105-V-1239 $14.49

Mini Tulip
Six cavity pan is 12.25 x 8.2 x 1.75 in.; individual cavities are 3.5 x 2.5 x 1.75 in. deep.
2105-V-1233 $14.49

Mini Fluted Mold
Six cavity pan is 14.75 x 9.75 in.; individual cavities are 4 x 1.25 in. deep.
2105-V-2097 $20.99

Mini Star
Six cavity pan is 14.5 x 11 in.; individual cavities are 4.75 x 1.25 in. deep.
2105-V-1235 $14.49

Wonder Mold Pans

Mini Wonder Mold
Use with Mini Doll Picks for a quartet of party treats. Great with the Wilton Classic Wonder Mold (at right) for a color-coordinated bridal party centerpiece. One cake mix makes 4 to 6 cakes. Pan is 10 x 10 x 3 in. deep. Individual cakes are 3.5 x 3 in. Aluminum.
2105-V-3020 $12.99

Mini Doll Picks

4¼ in. high with pick.
1511-V-1019
Pk./4 $6.29

Classic Wonder Mold
Creates an elegant 3-D shape for decorating fabulous dress designs. Use with our Teen Doll Pick to make the doll of your dreams. Pan is 8 in. diameter and 5 in. deep; takes 5–6 cups of firm-textured batter. Heat-conducting rod assures even baking. Kit contains pan, rod, stand, 7 in. brunette doll pick and instructions. Aluminum/plastic.
2105-V-565 $19.99

Teen Doll Picks

Her hair and face are prettier than ever to give your Wonder Mold cakes a realism and sophistication unlike anything you've seen. 7¼ in. high with pick.
$3.19
Brunette 2815-V-101
Blond 2815-V-102

Ethnic Doll Pick

Beautiful face for realistic doll cakes. 7¾ in. high with pick.
2815-V-103
$3.19

Novelty Shaped Pans

Two-Mix Book
Serves up to 30. 15 x 11.5 x 2.75 in. deep. Aluminum.
2105-V-2521 $17.99

Stand-Up House
A delightful "welcome home". Haunted houses, Easter hutches, Christmas cottages, school houses and dog houses are a few ideas for this pan. Cakes can stand up or lay flat. One-mix pan is 9 x 3 x 8.75 in. high. Aluminum.
2105-V-2070 $15.49

ORDER TOLL FREE: 800-794-5866

Novelty Shaped Pans

NEW!

NEW!

Party Pony
This proud pony will spur you on to create the perfect party cake. He's a sure bet for birthdays, race day parties and school celebrations. One-mix pan is 13.75 x 10.5 x 2 in. deep. Aluminum.
2105-V-1011 $12.99

Ballerina Bear
She moves gracefully from dance recital parties to luaus to game day pep rallies! Decorate her to match your own little ballerina or cheerleader as a reward for a great performance! One-mix pan is 14.5 x 10 x 2 in. deep. Aluminum.
2105-V-1028 $12.99

Crown
Treat your little princess (or prince) like royalty at their next celebration! This majestic crown cake is a fun way to honor both kids and adults alike—perfect for birthdays, school parties, Mother's and Father's Day, more! One-mix pan is 14.25 x 10.5 x 2 in. deep. Aluminum.
2105-V-1015 $12.99

Princess Carriage
Create a birthday celebration fit for a princess! Give it the royal treatment with dazzling windows and wheels decorated in her favorite colors. Or, decorate a classic carriage cake for the bridal shower, with flowers and accents to match your colors. One-mix pan is 13.75 x 12 x 2 in. deep. Aluminum.
2105-V-1027 $12.99

Enchanted Castle
Royal treat for little girls' birthdays or any event. Wonderful for molded sugar or ice cream. One-mix pan is 11.5 x 11.75 x 2 in. deep. Aluminum.
2105-V-2031 $12.99

Purse
Fun is in the bag with a cake that carries excitement galore for birthday parties, showers and school celebrations. Accessorize for the event with custom colors and designs. One-mix pan is 10.5 x 8 x 2 in. deep. Aluminum.
2105-V-1192 $12.99

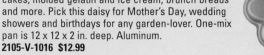

Dancing Daisy
One perfect flower makes bunches of great desserts! It's a big, bouncy blossom that's the perfect shape for cakes, molded gelatin and ice cream, brunch breads and more. Pick this daisy for Mother's Day, wedding showers and birthdays for any garden-lover. One-mix pan is 12 x 12 x 2 in. deep. Aluminum.
2105-V-1016 $12.99

Sunflower
There's no better way to spread sunshine at the celebration! Ideal for cakes, mousse, gelatin and salad molds. Center can be filled with fruit and whipped topping. One-mix pan is 10 in. round x 2 in. deep. Aluminum.
2105-V-1019 $12.99

BAKEWARE

Novelty Shaped Pans

Pirate Ship
Your ship has come in with this favorite kids' shape and its cargo of great decorating ideas on the label! Birthdays, movie parties and school celebrations provide a bounty of decorating opportunities. One-mix pan is 13.2 x 11.25 x 2 in. deep. Aluminum.
2105-V-1021 $12.99

3-D Cruiser
Bake exciting 3-D cakes, ready to customize for all occasions. One-mix pan is 11 x 6.75 x 4 in. deep. Aluminum.
2105-V-2043 $12.99

Train
Load with delicious cargo! One-mix pan is 14 x 7.25 x 2 in. deep. Aluminum.
2105-V-2076 $12.99

Tractor
Down on the farm has never been so much fun. One-mix pan is 13.5 x 9.5 x 2 in. deep. Aluminum.
2105-V-2063 $12.99

Choo-Choo Train Set
Two-piece pan snaps together to create a cake 10 x 4 x 6 in. high. Takes 6 cups batter. Aluminum.
2105-V-2861 Set/2 $14.49

Firetruck
When the occasion calls for a five-alarm celebration. One-mix pan is 15.5 x 8.5 x 2 in. deep. Aluminum.
2105-V-2061 $12.99

Topsy Turvy
Our topsy turvy "tiered" cake is just the right look for wacky birthdays, wild parties or special occasions. One-mix pan is 10.25 x 12 x 2 in. deep. Aluminum.
2105-V-4946 $12.99

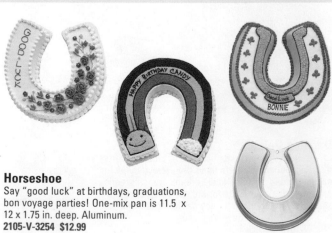

Horseshoe
Say "good luck" at birthdays, graduations, bon voyage parties! One-mix pan is 11.5 x 12 x 1.75 in. deep. Aluminum.
2105-V-3254 $12.99

Novelty Shaped Pans

NEW!

Rocking Horse
This happy hobby horse sets the pace for a birthday that rocks! It's a favorite kids shape that's also ideal for showers and playgroup parties. One-mix pan is 11 x 12.75 x 2 in. deep. Aluminum.
2105-V-2009 $12.99

Baby Bottle
Here's the formula for a great shower or baby naming celebration—serve a delightful dessert made in this adorable Baby Bottle Pan! Its outstanding detail creates exciting cakes along with molded mousse, gelatin and ice cream. One-mix pan is 13.75 x 7.25 x 2.5 in. deep. Aluminum.
2105-V-1026 $12.99

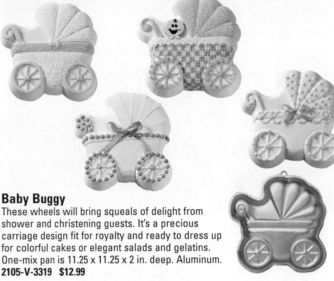

Baby Buggy
These wheels will bring squeals of delight from shower and christening guests. It's a precious carriage design fit for royalty and ready to dress up for colorful cakes or elegant salads and gelatins. One-mix pan is 11.25 x 11.25 x 2 in. deep. Aluminum.
2105-V-3319 $12.99

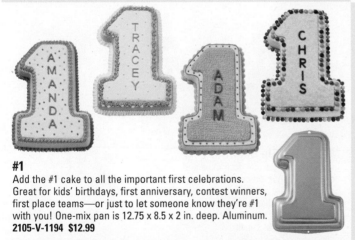

#1
Add the #1 cake to all the important first celebrations. Great for kids' birthdays, first anniversary, contest winners, first place teams—or just to let someone know they're #1 with you! One-mix pan is 12.75 x 8.5 x 2 in. deep. Aluminum.
2105-V-1194 $12.99

3-D Rubber Ducky
This bathtime favorite will make the biggest splash for birthdays, baby showers and school celebrations. Five adorable designs included. Two-piece pan takes 5½ cups batter, 9 x 5 x 7 in. high. Aluminum.
2105-V-2094 $16.49

Cupcake
Here's a "cupcake" cake that's big enough for the whole crowd to eat. Bake and decorate it to look like your favorite party cupcake—only bigger! Create endless color and flavor combinations, including the luscious Chocolate Supreme design on the label. One-mix pan is 9.75 x 9.5 x 2 in. deep. Aluminum.
2105-V-3318 $12.99

Teddy Bear
Everybody just loves teddy bears. This cutie will be busy all year 'round with birthdays, school parties and baby showers. No time for hibernating with all these fun events on the agenda. One-mix pan is 13.5 12.25 x 2 in deep. Aluminum.
2105-V-1193 $12.99

BAKEWARE

Novelty Shaped Pans

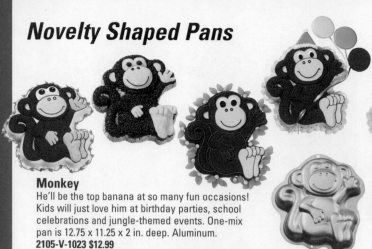

Monkey

He'll be the top banana at so many fun occasions! Kids will just love him at birthday parties, school celebrations and jungle-themed events. One-mix pan is 12.75 x 11.25 x 2 in. deep. Aluminum.
2105-V-1023 $12.99

Dinosaur

Our prehistoric party pal has a fun-loving look that's just right for kids birthdays, school functions and animal-themed celebrations. One-mix pan is 12.75 x 11 x 2 in. deep. Aluminum.
2105-V-1022 $12.99

Butterfly

A butterfly cake or molded salad is the perfect way to captivate! Go wild with fun colors. One-mix pan is 11 x 8.5 x 2 in. deep. Aluminum.
2105-V-2079 $12.99

Animal Crackers

Make a zoo full of fun animals with this versatile pan! Pick your favorite from the menagerie of critters on the box—pig, cat, giraffe or panda bear—or create a furry face of your own. One-mix pan is 10.75 x 9.25 x 2 in. deep. Aluminum.
2105-V-4945 $12.99

Lady Bug

These critters are so cute, you'll want them dropping in at all your celebrations. It's a pan that adapts to any environment—try it as a birthday bee, a Valentine love bug or even a friendly fly for that special gardener in your life. One-mix pan is 12 x 10 x 2 in. deep. Aluminum.
2105-V-3316 $12.99

Mini Stand-Up Bear Set

Includes baking stand, four clips and instructions. Two-piece pan takes 1 cup of batter; standard pound cake mix makes about 4 cakes. Assembled cakes are 4 x 3.25 x 4.75 in. high. Aluminum.
2105-V-489 Set/8 $14.49

Tropical Fish

Everyone at the party will be hooked by this fish! Catch it at kids' celebrations and school events—it's a great cake for that special fisherman's birthday. One-mix pan is 12.5 x 11.5 x 2 in. deep. Aluminum.
2105-V-1014 $12.99

Stand-Up Cuddly Bear Set

Five decorating ideas on the box! Two-piece pan takes 6.75 cups of firm textured batter. Includes 6 clips, heat-conducting core and instructions. Pan is 9 x 6.75 x 8.5 in. high. Aluminum.
2105-V-603 Set/10 $26.99

Novelty Shaped Pans

NEW!

Helmet
Take one for the team! With this pan, it's easy to create the ideal victory celebration cake, with school colors, stats or the final score as part of the design. Great for tailgate parties, homecoming rallies or to honor the performer that makes your family proud. One-mix pan is 12.75 x 10.5 x 2 in. deep. Aluminum.
2105-V-1029 **$12.99**

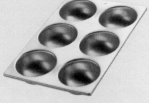

Mini Ball
Ice two mini balls and push together for a 3-D effect. One cake mix makes 10–12 mini balls. Six cavities, each 3.5 x 3.5 x 1.5 in. deep. Aluminum.
2105-V-1760 **$12.99**

First and Ten Football
Touching down at Super Bowl parties, homecomings, award dinners and much more. One-mix pan is 12 x 7.75 x 3 in. deep. Aluminum.
2105-V-6504 **$12.99**

Sports Ball Set
Use this four-piece set to create a perfect sports cake centerpiece. Includes two 6 in. diameter half-ball pans and two metal baking stands. Each pan half takes 2.5 cups batter. Aluminum.
2105-V-6506 **Set/4 $12.99**

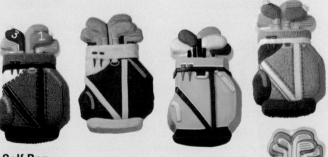

Soccer Ball
A great way to reward a season or a game well done! One-mix pan is 8.75 x 8.75 x 3.5 in. deep. Aluminum.
2105-V-2044 **$12.99**

Golf Bag
A stroke of genius for your favorite golfer's birthday, group golf outings, awards dinners and more. Whether decorated for men or women, it always shows perfect form. One-mix pan is 13.25 x 8.25 x 2 in. deep. Aluminum.
2105-V-1024 **$12.99**

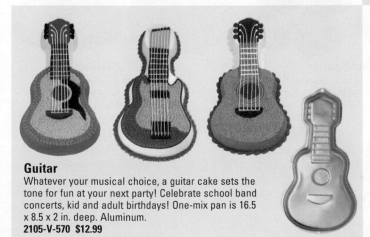

Guitar
Whatever your musical choice, a guitar cake sets the tone for fun at your next party! Celebrate school band concerts, kid and adult birthdays! One-mix pan is 16.5 x 8.5 x 2 in. deep. Aluminum.
2105-V-570 **$12.99**

Star
Brighten birthdays, opening nights, even law enforcement occasions. One-mix pan is 12.75 x 12.75 x 1.8 in. deep. Aluminum.
2105-V-2512 **$12.99**

ORDER TOLL FREE: 800-794-5866

Non-Stick Bakeware

Our premium non-stick bakeware combines superior non-stick performance, serving convenience and elegant design, to provide the highest level of baking satisfaction.

- Oversized handles for safe lifting of the pan
- Pan dimensions permanently stamped into handles
- Heavy-duty steel construction prevents warping
- Durable, reinforced non-stick coating offers superior release and easy cleanup
- 10-Year Warranty

CHECKERBOARD CAKE SET

With this unique baking set, you'll create cakes with an exciting multicolored pattern—there's style in every slice! Just place the Dividing Ring in one of the three 9 x 1.5 in. pans in the set and follow instructions for adding dark and light colors of batter in the divisions. Enjoy two tastes in one cake—try the Golden Yellow/Chocolate recipe on the package. Great for colorful holiday cakes too! Three pans feature oversized handles for safe lifting from the oven; each takes 5½ cups batter. Non-stick steel pans; plastic Dividing Ring.
2105-V-9961 Set/4 $15.99

Cake and Pie Pans

9 x 1.5 in. Round Cake
2105-V-408 $9.99

9 x 9 x 2 in. Square Cake
2105-V-407 $10.99

11 x 7 x 1.5 in. Biscuit/Brownie
2105-V-443 $11.99

2105-V-408

13 x 9 x 2 in. Oblong Cake
2105-V-411 $14.99

13 x 9 x 2 in. Oblong Cake w/Plastic Cover
2105-V-423 $19.99

2105-V-411

9 x 1.5 in. Pie w/Fluted Edges
2105-V-438 $9.99

Muffin and Loaf Pans

6 Cup Regular Muffin
2105-V-405 $11.99

12 Cup Mini Muffin
2105-V-403 $8.99

2105-V-405

12 Cup Regular Muffin
2105-V-406 $16.99

Large Loaf
9.25 x 5.25 x 2.75 in.
2105-V-402 $9.99

4 Cavity Mini Loaf
5.75 x 3 x 2.2 in.
2105-V-444 $21.49

2105-V-402

Cookie Pans and Sheets

Small Cookie
13.25 x 9.25 x .5 in.
2105-V-436 $13.99

Medium Cookie
15.25 x 10.25 x .75 in.
2105-V-412 $14.99

2105-V-412

Large Cookie/ Jelly Roll
17.25 x 11.5 x 1 in.
2105-V-413 $16.99

Jumbo Air Insulated Sheet
18 x 14 in.
2105-V-422 $23.99

2105-V-422

Specialty Pans

Fluted Tube
9.75 x 3.4 in.
2105-V-416 $16.99

6 Cavity Mini Fluted Tube 4.2 x 2 in.
2105-V-445 $21.49

2105-V-445

Angel Food 9.4 x 4.25 in.
2105-V-415 $19.99

14 in. Pizza Crisper
14 x .5 in.
2105-V-420 $16.99

2105-V-420

Springform Pans

4 x 1.75 in. Round
2105-V-453 $6.99

6 x 2.75 in. Round
2105-V-447 $11.99

9 x 2.75 in. Round
2105-V-414 $16.99

2105-V-435

10 x 2.75 in. Round
2105-V-435 $17.99

4 x 1.75 in. Heart
2105-V-457 $9.99

9 x 2.75 in. Heart
2105-V-419 $21.49

2105-V-419

Tart/Quiche Pans

9 x 1.2 in. Round
2105-V-442 $11.99

11 x 1.2 in. Round
2105-V-450 $13.99

Round 3-Pc. Set
8 x 1.2 in., 9 x 1.2 in., and 10 x 1.2 in.
2105-V-451 Set/3 $26.99

2105-V-450

4 in. Tart 4-Pc. Set
4 x .75 in. with removable bottom.
2105-V-466 $11.99

4 in. Tart/Quiche 6-Pc. Set 4 x .75 in. with removable bottom.
2105-V-441 $17.99

Cooling Grids

10 x 16 in. Rectangle
2305-V-228 $9.99

2305-V-228

14.5 x 20 in. Rectangle
2305-V-229 $14.49

13 in. Round
2305-V-230 $10.49

2305-V-230

3-Tier Stackable
15.8 x 9.8 in.
2105-V-459 $11.99

Filled Cake Pan Sets

Serve delicious filling in every slice! Create filled cakes and entrees with incredible flavor combinations using these convenient non-stick pans. The patented recessed design creates a contour you can fill with ice cream, fruit, mousse and more—just bake, fill, flip and frost! The premium non-stick coating provides easy release so cakes unmold perfectly from the pan. Also great for pasta and potato entrees, molded salads and appetizers.

Fanci-Fill

Set includes two 8.75 x 2 in. non-stick pans, bonus recipe booklet with 12 delicious ideas and complete instructions. Non-stick steel.
2105-V-150 Set/2 $17.99

Mini Tasty-Fill

Set includes four 4 x 1.25 in. non-stick pans, bonus recipe booklet with 12 delicious ideas and complete instructions. Non-stick steel.
2105-V-155 Set/4 $11.99

Heart Tasty-Fill

It's easy to create delicious cakes with a heart-shaped filled center! Set includes two 8.5 x 2.75 in. non-stick pans, bonus recipe book with delicious recipe ideas and complete instructions. Non-stick steel.
2105-V-157 Set/2 $17.99

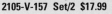

Silicone Molds

Make treats in favorite party shapes using these colorful, easy-release molds! Great for baking mini cakes and brownies, molding ice cream, gelatin and more.* Individual cavities are 2.5 x 2.5 x 1.25 in. deep.

Silicone Mini Stars
2105-V-4819 $9.99

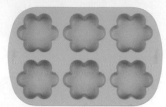

Silicone Mini Rounds
2105-V-4832 $9.99

Silicone Mini Hearts
2105-V-4824 $9.99

Silicone Mini Flowers
2105-V-4825 $9.99

*One cake mix makes 20 to 24 cakes.

BROWNIE MOLDS

Shaped brownies on a stick are the perfect fun-to-eat treat for parties and favors! Just bake, cool, pop in a stick and decorate.

Blossom Brownie
One 8 x 8 in. size brownie mix makes 6 brownies.
2105-V-4924 $9.99

Round Brownie Pops
One 8 x 8 in. size brownie mix makes 24 brownies. Individual cavities are 1.75 x 1.75 x 1.75 in. deep.
2105-V-4925 $9.99

Bite-Size Brownie Squares
Little brownie bites— just the right size for parties and snacks. One 8 x 8 in. size brownie mix makes 40 to 42 brownies. Individual cavities are 1.5 x 1.5 x .75 in. deep.
2105-V-4923 $9.99

Wilton
EASY-Flex
SILICONE BAKEWARE

Flexible pans and tools for great baking performance

Silicone Bakeware

Discover the convenience and easy release of flexible silicone bakeware!

• Exceptional baking performance for your favorite recipes
• Freezer, refrigerator, oven, microwave and dishwasher safe**
• Resists stains and odors
• Oven safe to 500ºF
• Easy and convenient storage
• Limited lifetime warranty

9 in. Round
2105-V-4800 $9.99

9 x 5 in. Loaf
2105-V-4804 $9.99

6-Cup Muffin
2105-V-4802 $9.99

12-Cup Mini Muffin
2105-V-4829 $9.99

Baking Mat
Line cookie sheets—protects against burned bottoms and cleans up with ease! Or, use as a pastry mat.
10 x 15 in. **2105-V-4808** $9.99
11 x 17 in. **2105-V-4809** $12.99

Standard Baking Cups
2 in. diameter. Convenient fill line.
415-V-9400 Pk./12 $9.99

**Always place silicone bakeware on a cookie sheet for easy removal from oven.

Non-Stick Oven Liner
Never Scrub Your Oven Again!

• **EASY TO CLEAN**
  Spills or burned-on foods wipe away with a soft, damp cloth.
• **CUT TO FIT**
  Use as is or trim with scissors to custom fit ovens.
• **OVEN-SAFE UP TO 500°F**
  Withstands high baking temperatures while maintaining non-stick performance.

Oven Liner
23 x 16.25 in.
2102-V-1021
$14.99

ORDER TOLL FREE: 800-794-5866

 # Brownie Fun!

Wilton is raising the bar for brownies, with a complete line of products that will help you create the best-looking, most delicious brownies ever!

Brownie Fun!

It's the book that proves brownies can be as colorful and fun as your favorite party treats! In *Brownie Fun!*, the fudgy treats everyone loves take on amazing new shapes and dazzling colors that will be the talk of your next celebration. *Brownie Fun!* is packed with over 140 easy-to-make designs and delicious recipes for brownies and mini treats. We'll also show you how to mix, bake and decorate the perfect brownies using the complete line of Wilton brownie products. Soft cover, 112 pages.
902-V-1105 $14.99

12 Piece Brownie Decorating Set

The ideal set for discovering the fun of cake and brownie decorating! Create most of the fun icing techniques in the *Brownie Fun!* book with the tips included—rosettes, stars, drop flowers, messages and more. Includes tips 5, 21, 352 and 2D, standard coupler, decorating triangle, 6 disposable decorating bags and instruction sheet.
2104-V-2533 $8.99

CRUNCHES

Add delicious flavor and a colossal crunch! **$4.99**

Mint
Certified Kosher. 5 oz. **710-V-9701**

Cookies 'N Cream
Certified Kosher. 5 oz. **710-V-9702**

Turtle
Certified Kosher. 5 oz. **710-V-9703**

Rainbow Chip
Certified Kosher Dairy. 5.25 oz.
710-V-9704

DUSTING SUGAR

Colorful powdered sugar adds a dash of excitement to your plain brownies. Use with our Sugar Shaker (p. 170) and Brownie Stencil Set (below) for a quick and easy decorating touch. 3 oz. pouch. **$1.99**

Blue	Green	Pink
710-V-2558	710-V-2560	710-V-2559

Brownie Stencil Set

With 6 fun designs, it's easy to make homemade brownies look great for the party or for giving. Decorate small, large pans or single brownies.
417-V-1312 $7.99

DRIZZLE ICING

Just heat and squeeze over brownies to add a ribbon of flavor. Use with Brownie Fudge Icing (at right) for exciting marbleized designs. 10 oz. bottle. Certified Kosher. **$4.99**

Mint	Peanut Butter	Vanilla Crème
704-V-152	704-V-150	704-V-151

Brownie Fudge Icing

Rich fudge flavor and velvety texture make this the perfect icing for spreading on brownies. Heat it in the microwave for an easy glaze; use with Wilton Drizzle Icing (at left) to create delicious designs. 1 Lb. can.
710-V-9700 $3.29

BROWNIE FUN!

Brownie Tools

Easy-to-handle Brownie Tools from Wilton make mixing, cutting and serving brownies a breeze!

Brownie & Treat Cutter
Cut brownies and treats at a fun new angle! The zigzag blade cuts clean decorative edges. Great for crispy treats, pizza and sandwiches, too! 4.9 x 3.75 in.
2308-V-1480 $7.99

Perfect Cut Brownie Marker
No more messy edges! Just insert the stainless steel tines into a pan of warm brownies to score. When completely cool, cut with a knife for a perfect, clean edge. 4.9 x 3.75 in. Patent Pending.
570-V-1159 $7.99

Brownie Lifter
Move your brownies from pan to plate looking great! Its tapered nylon blade is set at the perfect angle for getting under brownies without breakage. 9 in. long.
570-V-1160 $6.99

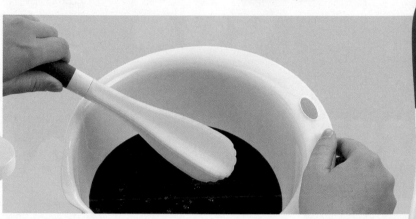

Sugar Shaker
Shake up your brownies with color using our Dusting Sugar (p. 169) and this easy-to-fill Sugar Shaker! Easy-to-fill, easy-to-handle shaker is also great for dusting brownies and cakes with cocoa. Fine mesh strainer with color grip and fitted lid for easy use and storage. 10 oz. capacity.
2103-V-388 $8.99

Batter Blender
Mix thick brownie batter faster and with less effort. Silicone head is great for stirring, scraping and spreading batter. Scalloped tip breaks up clumps. 11 in. long. Patent Pending.
570-V-1158 $7.99

Bakeware

NON-STICK BAKEWARE

Our premium non-stick bakeware combines superior non-stick performance, serving convenience and elegant design, to provide the highest level of baking satisfaction.

SILICONE BAKEWARE

Flexible silicone is ideal for releasing moist-textured brownies —they pop right out. Wilton silicone bakeware creates the perfect single servings in fun new shapes!

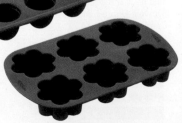

9 in. Square Covered Brownie Pan
Perfect for taking homemade brownies to the party! Ideal size for most standard brownie mixes. 9 x 9 x 2 in.
2105-V-9199 $7.99

6-Cavity Dessert Shell Pan
Bakes edible individual dessert shells, great for brownie bowls, sponge cakes and more. One 8 x 8 in. size brownie mix makes 6 brownies. Individual cavities are 3.5 in. diameter x 1.5 in. deep.
2105-V-8600 $8.99

Bite-Size Brownie Squares 24-Cavity Silicone Mold
Little brownie bites—just the right size for parties and snacks. One 8 x 8 in. size brownie mix makes 40 to 42 brownies. Individual cavities are 1.5 x 1.5 x .75 in. deep.
2105-V-4923 $9.99

Round Brownie Pops 8-Cavity Silicone Mold
One 8 x 8 in. size brownie mix makes 24 brownies. Individual cavities are 1.75 x 1.75 x 1.75 in. deep.
2105-V-4925 $9.99

12 in. Brownie Sticks
For fun brownie pops.
1912-V-1003 Pk./20 $3.99

Blossom Brownie 6-Cavity Silicone Mold
One 8 x 8 in. size brownie mix makes 6 brownies. Individual cavities are 2.25 x 2.25 x 1 in. deep.
2105-V-4924 $9.99

Cutters

COMBO CUTTERS

Make multiple shapes with just one cut. Stainless steel Combo Cutters are divided into a neat space-saving square, which maximizes the number of treats you get from one pan.

Each cutter approx. 4 x 2.5 x 2.75 in. deep.
$3.99

Triangles
Patent Pending.
2308-V-1473

Hearts
Patent Pending.
2308-V-1471

Mini
Patent Pending.
2308-V-1474

PUSH 'N POP! BROWNIE & TREAT CUTTER

Cut a sensational heart-shaped treat with the stainless steel cutter and pop it out with the built-in plunger. 4.5 x 3 x 3 in. deep.
2308-V-4074 $7.99

Brownie Presentation

BROWNIE GIFT BOX KITS

Colorful window boxes, tissues and accents are the ideal way to present your gift of homemade brownies.

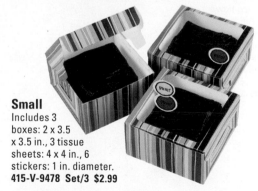

Small
Includes 3 boxes: 2 x 3.5 x 3.5 in., 3 tissue sheets: 4 x 4 in., 6 stickers: 1 in. diameter.
415-V-9478 Set/3 $2.99

Medium
Includes 3 boxes: 2 x 6.25 x 6.25 in., 3 bands: 1.5 ft. long, 3 tissue sheets: 10 x 10 in., 3 inserts, 1 sticker sheet.
415-V-9477 Set/3 $5.99

MINI TREAT BASKETS

Showcase brownies, cookies or other treats for the party or a great-looking gift. Dress them up with your favorite tissue squares, ribbons and gift bags for the perfect presentation.

Square
3.5 x 3.5 x 1.5 in. high.
415-V-9474 Set/6 $4.99

Round
3.5 in. diam. x 1.5 in. high.
415-V-9475 Set/6 $4.99

Brownie Envelope Kit

Create a fun brownie gift with envelopes, lace-look doilies and colorful seals. Just lay envelope flat and place doily and brownie in center; fold flaps toward center and secure with seals. Includes 6 envelopes: 4.5 x 4.5 in, 6 doilies: 4.5 in. diameter, 6 seals: 1.5 in. diameter.
1912-V-1297 Set/6 $3.99

Brownie Gift Bag Kit

Showcase your gift of homemade brownies in patterned bags that show off the tempting treats inside. Ribbons and tags included for a fun finishing touch. Includes 6 bags: 18 x 5 x 4 in., 6 tags: 2 x 2 in. and ribbon: 1 ft. 5 in.
1912-V-1298 Set/6 $3.19

Cupcake Fun!

What makes Wilton cupcakes more fun? It's our exciting products, which make baking, decorating and serving one-of-a-kind cupcakes a pleasure! See www.cupcakefun.com, for more great products and ideas!

Cupcake Fun!

Wilton presents today's hottest party dessert like you've never seen it before. This all-new collection features over 150 exciting cupcake and treat ideas for all occasions, with complete baking and decorating instructions to make them easy. Discover captivating shapes from coffee cups to flying saucers, plus a great recipe section with delicious surprises like Key Lime Cupcakes, Mocha Icing and more. Great baking and decorating products, too. *Cupcake Fun!* is the book you need to create the ultimate cupcake celebration. Soft cover, 128 pages.
902-V-795 $12.99

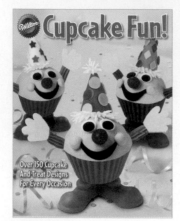

12-Piece Cupcake Decorating Set

Wait until you see how much fun cupcakes can be using the decorating tips in this set! You'll create all kinds of fun designs perfect for celebrations or everyday treats! Includes star tip 1M (rosettes, stars, drop flowers), star tip 22 (zigzags, pull-out stars), round tip 12 (outlines, dots, messages) and Bismarck tip 230 for exciting filled cupcakes; 8 disposable bags, instruction booklet.
2104-V-6667 Set/12 $8.39

6-Cup King-Size Muffin Pan

Create extra-tall treats! Great for cupcakes, ice cream, molded gelatin, mini angel food cakes, and mousse. Heavy-gauge premium non-stick for quick release and easy clean-up. Use with King-Size Baking Cups, p. 174.
2105-V-9921 $9.99

Jumbo Muffin Pan

Make super-size cupcakes and muffins. Six cups, each 4 x 2 in. Heavy-gauge premium non-stick for quick release and easy clean-up.
2105-V-955 $6.99

Cupcake Pedestals

Perfectly display cupcakes, muffins, party favors and more —or turn the pedestal over for the perfect ice cream cone holder! 5.2 in. high.
307-V-839 Pk./4 $7.99

The Ultimate 3-In-1 Caddy

It's the most convenient way to take along cakes, cupcakes, muffins and more! The Ultimate 3-In-1 Caddy features an exclusive reversible cupcake tray which holds 12 standard or 24 mini cupcakes. Or, remove the tray to carry up to a 9 x 13 in. decorated cake on the sturdy locking base. The see-through cover has higher sides to protect icing flowers and tall decorations. You can also use the caddy at home, to keep pies, cookies and brownies fresh for days after baking. 18 x 14 x 6.75 in. high. Patent No. D572,539.
2105-V-9958 $19.99

SILICONE BUILD-A-CAKE SETS

Arrange the shaped silicone cups on a baking pan, fill and bake, then decorate and serve. Decorating Puzzle Cakes! is easy! Check the instructions inside for 3 fun designs you can create using simple icing techniques and colorful candies. Or, use your imagination and create more fun shapes of your own. **Set/24 $14.99**

Transportation
415-V-9453

Animal
415-V-9452

Enjoy the fun of a party cake with the convenience of cupcakes!

CUPCAKES 'N MORE DESSERT STANDS

The look is fresh and fun, featuring bold silver-finished wire spirals to securely hold each cupcake. The twisting, towering design is perfect for any setting—showers, kids' birthdays, weddings, holidays and more.

13 Count Standard
9.25 in. high x 9 in. wide.
Holds 13 standard cupcakes.*
307-V-831 **$13.69**

24 Count Mini
10.5 in. high x 9 in. wide.
Holds 24 mini cupcakes.*
307-V-250 **$15.79**

19 Count Standard
18 in. high x 12 in. wide.
Holds 19 standard cupcakes.
307-V-666 **$20.99**

23 Count Standard
12 in. high x 13 in. wide.
Holds 23 standard cupcakes.*†
307-V-826 **$31.49**

*Pat. No. 7,387,283. †Pat. No. D516,385.

38 Count Standard
15 in. high x 18 in. wide.
Holds 38 standard cupcakes.*
307-V-651 **$41.99**

Collapsible for easy storage

4-Tier Stacked Dessert Tower
Great way to display cupcakes, appetizers, brownies and other party treats! Four plastic stacking sections with angled tiers for the best view of decorated desserts. Sections easily disassemble and nest for storage; assembled tower is 16.25 in. high x 12 in. wide. Holds 36 standard cupcakes.
Pat. No. D560,974.
307-V-856 **$19.99**

JUMBO SPRINKLES

Give your cupcakes a big finish! Top them with Jumbo Sprinkles in exciting shapes and colors. These big and bold decorations are perfect for cupcakes, mini cakes, jumbo and king-size cupcakes, brownies and cookies. Innovative shapes for holiday, birthday or any celebration. Certified Kosher.
$4.09

Jumbo Stars
3.25 oz. **710-V-026**

Jumbo Confetti
3.25 oz. **710-V-029**

Jumbo Diamonds
3.5 oz. **710-V-027**

Jumbo Daisies
3.25 oz. **710-V-028**

Jumbo Hearts
3.25 oz. **710-V-032**

Jumbo Rainbow Nonpareils
4.8 oz. **710-V-033**

Heart Drops
5.25 oz. **710-V-035**

CUPCAKE CRUNCHES

Add delicious flavor and a colossal crunch to your cupcakes! Sprinkle over iced cupcakes. Certified Kosher.
$3.99

Chocolate
3.5 oz. **710-V-025**

Almond
3.5 oz. Artificially flavored. **710-V-024**

Toffee
3.5 oz. Naturally and artificially flavored. **710-V-023**

CUPCAKE FUN!

SILICONE BAKING CUPS

Discover the convenience and easy release of flexible silicone! Reusable oven-safe cups in fun colors and exciting shapes are perfect for baking and serving. All have convenient batter fill line.

Silly-Critters!
Brown, Pink, Blue, Yellow. Cups are 2 in. diameter. 2.3 in. high with feet.
415-V-9451 Pk./4 $9.99
Patent Pending.

Bear Fun Cups
6 Brown, 6 Tan. 2 in. wide.
415-V-9449 Pk./12 $9.99

Silly-Feet!
Orange, Yellow, Blue, Purple. Cups are 2 in. diameter. 2.3 in. high with feet.
415-V-9428 Pk./4 $9.99
Patent Pending.

Flower Fun Cups
6 Pink, 6 Yellow. 2 in. wide.
415-V-9450 Pk./12 $9.99

Pastel Round
3 each pink, yellow, green, blue. 2 in. diameter.
415-V-9410 Pk./12 $9.99

Triangle
6 Pink, 6 Purple. 2.4 in. wide.
415-V-9423 Pk./12 $9.99

Diamond
6 Yellow, 6 Red. 3 in. wide.
415-V-9419 Pk./12 $9.99

Square
6 Blue, 6 Green. 2 in. wide.
415-V-9424 Pk./12 $9.99

Heart
6 Pink, 6 Red. 2 in. wide.
415-V-9409 Pk./12 $9.99

BAKING CUPS

Microwave-safe paper. Standard size, 2 in. dia., Mini size, 1.25 in. dia., King size (3 in. high) and Jumbo size (2 in. high) are 2.25 in. dia.

Be My Cupcake
$2.09
Standard
415-V-127 Pk./75
Mini
415-V-128 Pk./100

Bubble Stripes
$2.09
Standard
415-V-114 Pk./75
Mini
415-V-115 Pk./100

Cupcake Heaven
$2.09
Standard
415-V-422 Pk./75
Mini
415-V-426 Pk./100

Snappy Stripes
$2.09
Standard
415-V-5381 Pk./75
Mini
415-V-5380 Pk./100

White
King-Size $2.09
415-V-2118 Pk./24
Jumbo $2.09
415-V-427 Pk/75
Standard $1.59
415-V-2505 Pk./75
Mini $1.59
415-V-2507 Pk./100

Add-A-Message Fun Pix
Clip on messages, pictures and more with these colorful plastic picks! Great for place markers, announcing awards at banquets and favorite sayings. Four fun colors to go with your favorite baking cups. 3 in. high.
2113-V-7611 Pk./12 $2.09

CUPCAKE BOXES

Brightly-patterned window boxes are the perfect way to hold and display your cupcakes! Each box includes an insert with recessed space to hold standard size cupcakes safely in place. Easy folding assembly; great for gifts and favors! Choose single, 4-cupcake size or 6-cupcake size.

Be My Cupcake
Holds 6 standard cupcakes.
415-V-129 Pk./2 $5.29

Bubble Stripes
Holds 1 standard cupcake.
415-V-116 Pk./3 $3.19

Cupcake Heaven
Holds 1 standard cupcake.
415-V-289 Pk./3 $3.19

Holds 6 standard cupcakes.
415-V-1207 Pk./2 $5.29

Holds 4 standard cupcakes.
415-V-1206 Pk./3 $5.29

Snappy Stripes
Holds 6 standard cupcakes.
415-V-1209 Pk./2 $5.29

Holds 1 standard cupcake.
415-V-1205 Pk./3 $3.19

ORDER TOLL FREE: 800-794-5866

Party

You've written the guest list—now start your decorating list here! From baking cups to candles, cake toppers to treat bags, Wilton has the exciting and colorful party designs you want.

Theme Party Products

Give your party personality! See how easy it is to pull your look together with the great selection of Wilton theme party products. You'll discover favorite subjects including jungle animals, colorful flowers, over-the-hill tombstones and sports for every season. Find candles, party bags, baking cups, candy molds, cake pans and more—all with the Wilton touch of fun design and detail.

PIRATES
Give kids a party to treasure with cakes and cupcakes that carry high seas excitement.

NEW!

Cupcake Combo Pack
Quick and colorful way to serve cupcakes that set the tone for your celebration. Contains 24 each 2 in. diameter baking cups and 3 in. high paper party picks.
415-V-1015 Pk./24 $2.09

Pirate Ship
Your ship has come in with this favorite kids' shape and its cargo of great decorating ideas on the label! Birthdays, movie parties and school celebrations provide a bounty of decorating opportunities. One-mix pan is 13.2 x 11.25 x 2 in. deep. Aluminum.
2105-V-1021 $12.99

JUNGLE PALS
Kids will just love these adorable creatures for birthdays, school parties and special events.

Animals Cookie Candy Molds
With Cookie Candy Molds and easy-melting Wilton Candy Melts®, it's a breeze to add a great tasting and colorful candy design to your favorite cookies. Great for sandwich cream cookies or any round cookie 2 in. diameter or less. 4 designs, 8 cavities.
2115-V-1354 $1.99

NEW!

Monkey Large Lollipop Mold
3 designs, 3 cavities.
2115-V-2100 $1.99

Monkey Pan
He'll be the top banana at so many fun occasions! Kids will just love him at birthday parties, school celebrations and jungle-themed events. One-mix pan is 12.75 x 11.25 x 2 in. deep. Aluminum.
2105-V-1023 $12.99

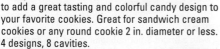

Baking Cups
Standard size 2 in. diameter.
415-V-1012 Pk./50 $1.59

Party Bags
20 plastic bags, 20 ties included. 4 x 9.5 in.
1912-V-1012 Pk./20 $2.09

Fun Pix
Approx. 3¼ in. high.
2113-V-1012 Set/24 $2.09

Jungle Animals Topper Set
1¾ to 3 in. high.
2113-V-2095 Set/4 $4.19

Candle Picks
Approx. 2 in. high.
2811-V-1012 Set/4 $3.89

Theme Party Products

PRINCESS

The royal treatment for any birthday girl begins here, with colorful treats and cakes that rule!

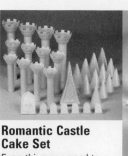

Romantic Castle Cake Set

Everything you need to transform your tiered cake into a fantasy castle is included: three sizes of detailed turret towers with removable peak pieces, lattice windows, a paneled door and roof pieces. Complete assembly and decorating ideas included. For design ideas visit www.wilton.com!
301-V-910 Set/32 $20.99

Princess Carriage Pan

Create a birthday celebration fit for a princess! Give it dazzling windows and wheels decorated in her favorite colors. Or, decorate a classic carriage cake for the bridal shower, with flowers and accents to match your colors. One-mix pan is 12.25 x 9.5 x 2 in. deep. Aluminum.
2105-V-1027 $12.99

NEW!

Candles

Approx. 2¼ in. high.
2811-V-1001 Set/4 $3.89

Fairy Tale Lollipop Mold

3 designs, 3 cavities.
2115-V-1033 $1.99

Cupcake Combo Pack

Quick and colorful way to serve cupcakes that set the tone for your celebration. Contains 24 each 2 in. diameter baking cups and 3 in. high paper party picks.
415-V-1313 Pk./24 $2.09

Princess Cupcake Stand Kit

It's an instant princess party, with a bright 3-tier cupcake stand, fun decorative topper, colorful baking cups and Fun Pix! Includes 12 x 15 in. high stand, 24 - 2 in. diameter cups and 24 - 3 in. high picks. Holds up to 24 cupcakes.
1510-V-1008 $9.99

ICE CREAM

A refreshing look for any celebration, from birthdays to backyard barbecues.

Candles

Approx. 2¼ in. high.
2811-V-9349 Set/4 $3.89

Baking Cups

Standard size 2 in. diameter.
415-V-121 Pk./50 $1.59

Party Bags

20 plastic bags, 20 ties included. 4 x 9.5 in.
1912-V-3106 Pk./20 $2.09

PARTY TIME

What a great way to cap off any celebration, from birthdays to that New Year's Eve bash!

Party/Birthday Large Lollipop Mold
4 designs, 4 cavities.
2115-V-4434 $1.99

NEW!

Party Icing Decorations
Certified Kosher.
710-V-461 Pk./9 $2.29

Baking Cups
Microwave- safe paper.
Standard size, 2 in. diameter.

NEW!

Celebration
415-V-986
Pk./75 $2.09

Topsy Turvy Pan
Our topsy turvy "tiered" cake is just the right look for wacky birthdays, wild parties or special occasions. One-mix pan is 10.25 x 12 x 2 in. deep. Aluminum.
2105-V-4946 $12.99

Candles
Approx. 1½ in. high.
2811-V-860
Set/4 $3.89

DANCING DAISY FLOWER

Pick this daisy for Mother's Day, wedding showers and birthdays for any garden-lover.

Flowers Cookie Candy Molds
With Cookie Candy Molds and easy-melting Wilton Candy Melts, it's a breeze to add a great tasting and colorful candy design to your favorite cookies. Great for sandwich cream cookies or any round cookie 2 in. diameter or less. 4 designs, 8 cavities.
2115-V-1351 $1.99

Icing Decorations
Certified Kosher.
710-V-353 Pk./12 $2.29

Pan
One perfect flower makes bunches of great cakes and desserts! One-mix pan is 12 x 12 x 2 in. deep. Aluminum.
2105-V-1016
$12.99

Lollipop Mold
1 design, 9 cavities.
2115-V-1430 $1.99

Party Bags
20 plastic bags, 20 ties included. 4 x 9.5 in.
1912-V-7813 Pk./20 $2.09

Baking Cups
Microwave-safe paper.
Standard size, 2 in. diameter; Mini size, 1.25 in. diameter.
Standard 415-V-7812
Pk./50 $1.59
Mini 415-V-1088
Pk./100 $2.09

Daisy Comfort-Grip
Easy-grip stainless steel cutter with extra-deep sides approximately 4 x 4 x 1.75 in. Recipe included.
2310-V-619 $3.19

Candle Picks
Approx. 2 in. high.
2811-V-217
Set/6
$3.89

Theme Party Products

SMILEY FACE

Have a nice party! This friendly face has a way of making everyone happy at birthdays, housewarmings and welcome home parties.

Pretzel Mold
Easy to mold;
1 design,
6 cavities.
2115-V-4437
$1.99

Lollipop Mold
1 design, 10 cavities.
2115-V-1715 $1.99

Baking Cups
Standard size,
2 in. diameter.
415-V-261
Pk./50 $1.59

Candles
1½ in. high.
2811-V-9351 Set/6 $3.89

Chunky Candles
Thicker candles to energize any cake! They feature bold textured spirals and a fun hand-carved shape on top.
3¼ in. high.
Pk./4 $3.89

Smiley Stars
2811-V-6325

Smiley Flames
2811-V-6326

Party Bags
20 plastic bags, 20 ties included. 4 x 9.5 in.
1912-V-2361
Pk./20 $2.09

Candle Picks
2½ in. high.
2811-V-6327
Set/4 $3.89

RUBBER DUCKY

This bathtime favorite will make the biggest splash for birthdays and baby showers.

Candles
1½ in. high.
2811-V-9337
Set/6 $3.89

3-D Cake Pan
Five adorable designs included. Two-piece pan takes 5½ cups batter. Aluminum.
2105-V-2094 $16.49

Candy Mold
1 design, 6 cavities.
2115-V-1565 $1.99

Baking Cups
Microwave- safe paper. Standard size, 2 in. diameter. mini size, 1.25 in. diameter.

Party Bags
20 plastic bags, 20 ties included. 4 x 9.5 in.
1912-V-1275 Pk./20 $2.09

Rubber Ducky Standard
415-V-378
Pk./50 $1.59

Ducky Standard
415-V-1016 Pk./75 $2.09
Mini
415-V-1017 Pk./100 $2.09

ORDER TOLL FREE: 800-794-5866

SPORTS

Here's the perfect game plan for your next party, whatever sport you favor: Action-packed, colorful ways to serve cakes, cupcakes or treats.

Sports Ball Pan Set
Includes two 6 in. diameter half-ball pans and two metal baking stands. Each pan half takes 2½ cups batter. Aluminum.
2105-V-6506 Set/4 $12.99

Mini Ball Pan
Ice two mini balls and push together for a 3-D effect. One cake mix makes 10–12 mini balls. Six cavities, each 3.5 x 3.5 x 1.5 in. deep. Aluminum.
2105-V-1760 $12.99

Sports Lollipop Mold
Makes favorite sports balls from every season. 4 designs, 4 cavities.
2115-V-4432 $1.99

Sports Cupcake Stand Kit
It's an instant sports celebration, with a bright 3-tier cupcake stand, fun decorative topper, colorful baking cups and Fun Pix! Includes 12 x 15 in. high stand, 24 - 2 in. diameter cups and 24 - 3 in. high picks. Holds up to 24 cupcakes.
1510-V-1009 $9.99

Sports Cookie Candy Mold
With Cookie Candy Molds and easy-melting Wilton Candy Melts, it's a breeze to add a great tasting and colorful candy design to your favorite cookies. Great for sandwich cream cookies or any round cookie 2 in. diameter or less. 4 designs, 8 cavities.
2115-V-1353 $1.99

Cupcake Combo Pack
Quick and colorful way to serve cupcakes that set the tone for your celebration. Contains 24 each 2 in. diameter baking cups and 3 in. high paper party picks.
415-V-1314 Pk./24 $2.09

BASEBALL/SOFTBALL

From Little League to World Series celebrations, cover the bases with 3-D cakes and hit candles and toppers.

Take Me Out To The Ballgame Candles
Approx. 2 in. high.
2811-V-9341 Set/4 $3.89

Topper Set with Decals
Includes 1 topper, 6 candleholders, 6 -2 in. high candles, 1 sheet of decals.
2811-V-8425 Set/14 $5.49

Soccer Ball Pan
One-mix pan is 8.75 x 8.75 x 3.5 in. deep. Aluminum.
2105-V-2044 $12.99

Baking Cups
Standard size, 2 in. diameter.
415-V-298 Pk./50 $1.59

Icing Decorations
Certified Kosher.
710-V-475 Pk./9 $2.29

Baseball Topper Set*
Batter, catcher, three fielders and pitcher, 2.1 to 2.75 in. high.
2113-V-2155 Set/6 $3.19

PARTY

Theme Party Products

FOOTBALL

Touching down at Super Bowl parties, homecomings, award dinners and much more.

NEW!

Baking Cups
Standard
2 in. diameter.
415-V-5152
Pk./75 **$2.09**

Mini
1.25 in. diameter.
415-V-5154
Pk./100 **$2.09**

Icing Decorations
Certified Kosher.
710-V-478
Pk./9 **$2.29**

Colored Metal Cutter Set
Built to last, they cut cleanly and release easily. Recipe included. Each approx. 3 in. Pennant, football, jersey, and helmet.
2308-V-1263 **Set/4 $4.79**

First and Ten Football Pan
One-mix pan is 12 x 7.75 x 3 in. deep. Aluminum.
2105-V-6504
$12.99

Topper Set with Decals
Includes 1 topper, 6 candleholders, 6 - 2 in. high candles, 1 sheet of decals.
2811-V-8424
Set/14 $5.49

Football Topper Set*
Eight players and two goal posts, 1½ to 4½ in. high.
2113-V-2236 **Set/10 $3.19**

SOCCER

A great way to reward a season or a game well played!

Topper Set with Decals
Includes 1 topper, 6 candleholders, 6 - 2 in. high candles, 1 sheet of decals.
2811-V-8421 **Set/14 $5.49**

Baking Cups
Standard size, 2 in. diameter.
415-V-296 **Pk./50 $1.59**

Soccer Topper Set*
Seven players and two nets, 1¾ to 2 in. high.
2113-V-9002
Set/9 $3.19

Soccer Ball Pan
One-mix pan is 8.75 x 8.75 x 3.5 in. deep. Aluminum.
2105-V-2044 **$12.99**

Icing Decorations
Certified Kosher.
710-V-477
Pk./9 **$2.29**

HOCKEY

Topper Set With Decals
Includes 1 topper, 6 candleholders, 6 - 2 in. high candles, 1 sheet of decals.
2811-V-8422 **Set/14 $5.49**

⚠ ***WARNING: CHOKING HAZARD**
Small parts. Not for children under 3 years.

ORDER TOLL FREE: 800-794-5866

BASKETBALL
Slam dunk winners! Create thrilling cakes and candies.

Topper Set with Decals
Includes 1 topper,
6 candleholders,
6 - 2 in. high candles.
1 sheet of decals.
2811-V-8423 Set/14 $5.49

Basketball Topper Set*
Includes
1 forward,
2 centers,
3 guards and
1 hoop, 2¼ to
4 in. high.
2113-V-2237
Set/7 $3.19

Soccer Ball Pan
One-mix pan is 8.75
x 8.75 x 3.5 in. deep.
Aluminum.
2105-V-2044 $12.99

GOLF
Great ways to top cakes with perfect form.

Topper Set with Decals
Includes 1 topper,
6 candleholders, 6 - 2 in. high
candles. 1 sheet of decals.
2811-V-8420 Set/14 $5.49

Golf Topper Set*
Includes 4½ in. high golfer plus three each: 2½ in. wide greens, 4 in. high flags,
5 in. clubs and golf balls.
1306-V-7274 Set/13 $3.19

Golf Bag Pan
A stroke of genius for your
favorite golfer's birthday, group
golf outings, awards dinners and
more. One-mix pan is 13.25 x 8.25
x 2 in. deep. Aluminum.
2105-V-1024 $12.99

 *WARNING: CHOKING HAZARD
Small parts. Not for children under 3 years.

FISHING

Land the perfect cake for your angler, with bright candles and toppers.

Frustrated Fisherman Topper*
4½ in. high.
2113-V-2384 $3.69

Tropical Fish Candles
Approx. 1½ in. high.
2811-V-9333 Set/4 $3.89

Metal Cutter
Cuts cleanly and releases with ease. Approximately 3 in.
2308-V-1017 $0.69

Tropical Fish Pan
Everyone will be hooked by this fish—it's a keeper! One-mix pan is 11.5 x 12.5 x 2 in. deep. Aluminum.
2105-V-1014 $12.99

CAMOUFLAGE

NEW!

Attention! That's what your cakes and cupcakes will get when you outfit them in our camouflage-pattern accents. Perfect for birthdays and coming-home celebrations.

Cupcake Combo Pack
Quick and colorful way to serve cupcakes that set the tone for your celebration. Contains 24 each 2 in. diameter baking cups and 3 in. high paper party picks.
415-V-1082 Pk./24 $2.09

Chunky Candles
Thicker candles to energize any cake! They feature a fun hand-carved shape on top. 2¼ in. high.
2811-V-1009
Pk./4 $3.89

OVER THE HILL

The secret of aging is keeping your sense of humor! These Wilton products help anyone face those big birthdays with a smile!

Icon Candles
Candles that feature a fun hand-carved tombstone. Instant fun, great size for cupcakes too! 2½ in. high.
2811-V-8417
Pk./10 $2.19

Cupcake Combo Pack
Quick and colorful way to serve cupcakes that set the tone for your celebration. Contains 24 each 2 in. diameter baking cups and 3 in. high paper party picks.
415-V-1315 Pk./24 $2.09

Candle
2¼ in. high.
2811-V-553
$2.19

Candle Picks
1¾ in. high.
2811-V-786
Set/13 $2.19

Cake Toppers and Stands

With Wilton toppers, a decorated cake is just minutes away! The excellent detail you expect from Wilton is evident in every design.

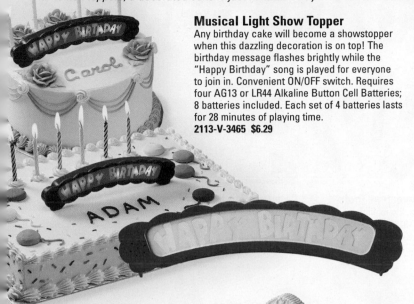

Musical Light Show Topper

Any birthday cake will become a showstopper when this dazzling decoration is on top! The birthday message flashes brightly while the "Happy Birthday" song is played for everyone to join in. Convenient ON/OFF switch. Requires four AG13 or LR44 Alkaline Button Cell Batteries; 8 batteries included. Each set of 4 batteries lasts for 28 minutes of playing time.
2113-V-3465 $6.29

DOLL PICKS

Teen Doll Pick

Her hair and face are prettier than ever—she'll give your Wonder Mold cakes a realism and sophistication unlike anything you've seen. 7¾ in. high with pick.
$3.19

Brunette	Blond	Ethnic
2815-V-101	2815-V-102	2815-V-103

Mini Doll Pick Set

4¼ in. high with pick.
1511-V-1019
Set/4 $6.29

RELIGIOUS

Inspiring decorations add a beautiful touch to spiritual events —Christening, Communion, Confirmation and more!

Inspirational Cross

Polished resin with finely sculpted scroll and bead highlighting. 5½ in. high.
202-V-398 $14.99

Communion Boy†

3½ in. high.
2113-V-7886
$3.69

Communion Girl†

3½ in. high.
2113-V-7878
$3.69

† Designed by Ellen Williams

Silly-Feet! Cake Stand

Watch your friends make tracks to your treats! Just insert the plate onto the foot support, add your decorated cake, cupcakes or other desserts. Take the fun a step further—bake and serve cupcakes in Silly-Feet! Silicone Baking Cups (p. 173). 10 in. cake plate holds an 8 in. or 9 in. round cake.
307-V-878 $14.99

Small Derby Clowns Set*

2 in. high with pick.
2113-V-2759
Set/6 $2.09

Circus Balloons Set

12 in a bunch, 3 bunches per set, 6.5 in. high.
2113-V-2366 Set/36 $3.19

⚠ *WARNING: CHOKING HAZARD Small parts. Not for children under 3 years.

Classic Candles

Pearlized

Watch them shimmer from the moment you light them! 2½ in. high.
Pk./10 $2.19
White
2811-V-3658
Multicolor
2811-V-3665

Glitter

2½ in. high.
Pk./10 $1.09
White
2811-V-248
Pink 2811-V-244
Blue 2811-V-246
Black
2811-V-247

Celebration

2½ in. high.
Pk./24 $0.79
White 2811-V-207
Pink 2811-V-213
Red 2811-V-209
Blue 2811-V-210
Black 2811-V-224

Assorted Celebration

Classic spirals in attractive two-tones. 2½ in. high.
2811-V-215
Pk./24 $0.79

"Trick"

Blow 'em out —they relight! 2½ in. high. Assorted: White, Yellow, Pink, Blue.
2811-V-220
Pk./10 $1.09

Silver and Gold

2¼ in. high.
Pk./10
$1.69
Silver
2811-V-9123
Gold
2811-V-9122

Numerals

Festive way to mark age or year. Edged in green unless specified. 3 in. high. **$0.89**

#1	Pink #1	Blue #1
2811-V-9101	2811-V-240	2811-V-241

#2	2811-V-9102	#7	2811-V-9107
#3	2811-V-9103	#8	2811-V-9108
#4	2811-V-9104	#9	2811-V-9109
#5	2811-V-9105	#0	2811-V-9100
#6	2811-V-9106	?	2811-V-9110

PARTY

Candles

CANDLE SETS

Wilton gives you more choices! Top your cake with candles in the perfect colors—and check out our exciting designs.

Farm
Approx. 1⅝ in. high.
2811-V-9347
Set/4 $3.89

Firefighting
Approx. 1½ in. high.
2811-V-9339
Set/4 $3.89

Baby Things
Approx. 2 in. high.
2811-V-855 Set/4 $3.89

Fiesta
Approx. 1¾ in. high.
2811-V-9345 Set/4 $3.89

Home Improvement Tools
Approx. 2¼ in. high.
2811-V-9136 Set/5 $3.89

Construction Vehicles
Approx. 1¾ in. long.
2811-V-858 Set/4 $3.89

Race Cars
Approx. 1¾ in. high.
2811-V-9135 Set/4 $3.89

Beach Sandals
⅜ in. high,
⅞ in. long.
2811-V-9352
Set/6 $3.89

Margaritas
1¼ in. high.
2811-V-9343
Set/6 $3.89

Champagne Bottles
2 in. high.
2811-V-163 Set/6 $3.89

Beer Cans
1¾ in. high.
2811-V-9326
Set/6 $3.89

NOVELTY

Glow-in-the-Dark

They light up the room even before you light them! These luminous candles will lend an extra touch of fun to any celebration. Assorted colors: white, yellow, green, blue. 2½ in. high.
2811-V-165
Pk./10 $2.19

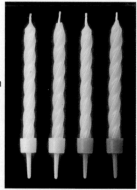

Glow Candle Set

Turn out the lights and get ready to serve your cake in a thrilling glow of color. Set of 4 light stick candle holders with candles gives cakes an aura of excitement that lasts up to 6 hours. No batteries needed—the glow starts when you bend the light sticks. Includes 4 each light sticks, connectors and candles. 6½ in. high.
2811-V-6215
Set/4 $5.59

PICK SETS

Put your celebration message in lights! These bright candle picks are a unique and easy way to pick up the party theme on your cake top. Fun colors are just right for the occasion.

Happy Birthday
1¾ in. high.
2811-V-785
Set/15 $2.19

Congratulations
1¾ in. high.
2811-V-787 Set/15 $2.19

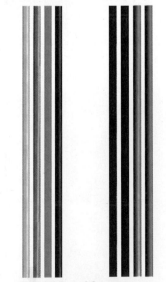

Longs
Sized right for larger cakes or for making a bold statement on any cake. 5⅞ in. high. **Pk./12 $2.19**

White
2811-V-773

Multicolor
2811-V-777

Slenders
6½ in. high.
2811-V-1188
Pk./24 $0.89

"Trick" Sparklers
Blow 'em out—they relight!
6½ in. high. **Pk./18 $1.09**

Assorted
2811-V-1230

Red and Blue
2811-V-704

ORDER TOLL FREE: 800-794-5866

RAINBOW COLORS

Curly
Twisting,
turning fun.
3 in. high.
2811-V-9127
Pk./12 $1.69

COLOR FLAME CANDLES
Candle and flame are colored the same!

NEW!

Color Flame
Candles give
your cake that
extra dash of
excitement and
fun. Includes 4
vivid colors—
blue, red, orange
and green. They
make a plain
iced cake a
party treat to
remember.
2 in. high.
2811-V-1011
Pk./12 $2.99

PARTY

Shimmer
2½ in. high.
2811-V-3663
Pk./10 $2.19

Lattice
2½ in. high.
2811-V-3656
Pk./10 $2.19

Tricolor
2½ in. high.
2811-V-779
Pk./10 $2.19

Crayons
3¼ in. high. $1.69
2811-V-226 Pk./8
2½ in. high. $1.69
2811-V-227 Pk./10

**Triangle
"Trick"
Sparklers**
2½ in. high.
2811-V-278
Pk./9 $1.09

**Wavy
"Trick"
Sparklers**
2½ in. high.
2811-V-272
Pk./10 $2.19

Rounds
2½ in. high.
2811-V-284
Pk./24
$0.79

**Party
Thins**
8 in. high.
2811-V-239
Pk./20
$1.09

HOT COLORS

Shimmer
2½ in. high.
2811-V-3662
Pk./10 $2.19

Lattice
2½ in. high.
2811-V-3655
Pk./10 $2.19

Twist
2½ in. high.
2811-V-3659
Pk./8 $2.79

Rounds
2½ in. high.
2811-V-225
Pk./24 $0.79

SOFT COLORS

Shimmer
2½ in. high.
2811-V-3664
Pk./10 $2.19

Tricolor
2½ in. high.
2811-V-782
Pk./10 $2.19

Rounds
2½ in. high.
2811-V-291
Pk./24 $0.79

Tricolor
2½ in. high.
2811-V-781
Pk./10
$2.19

Crayons
3¼ in. high.
2811-V-282
Pk./8 $1.69

**Triangle
"Trick"
Sparklers**
2½ in. high.
2811-V-276
Pk./9 $1.09

**Wavy
"Trick"
Sparklers**
2½ in. high.
2811-V-270
Pk./10 $2.19

**Party
Thins**
8 in. high.
2811-V-237
Pk./20
$1.09

**Wavy
"Trick"
Sparklers**
2½ in. high.
2811-V-289
Pk./10 $2.19

**Triangle
"Trick"
Sparklers**
2½ in. high.
2811-V-288
Pk./9 $1.09

**Party
Thins**
8 in. high.
2811-V-255
Pk./20
$1.09

Musical Candle
Plays "Happy
Birthday To You".
4¾ in. high.
2811-V-1231 $4.09

Baking Cups

The easiest way to dress up a cupcake! Ideal for holding candy and nuts, too.

Made of microwave-safe paper unless otherwise noted. Jumbo cups are 2.25 in. diameter, standard cups are 2 in. diameter, mini cups are 1.25 in. diameter, candy cups are 1 in. diameter.

NEW!

Lilac Polka Dots $2.09
Mini
120-V-168
Pk./100

Pink Polka Dots $2.09
Standard
120-V-169
Pk./75

Dazzling Dots $1.59
Standard
415-V-582
Pk./50
Mini
415-V-1141
Pk./75

Snappy Stripes $2.09
Standard
415-V-5381
Pk./75
Mini
415-V-5380
Pk./100

Assorted Primary $2.09
Assorted red, yellow, blue.
Standard
415-V-987 Pk./75
Mini
415-V-1110 Pk./100

Assorted Pastel $1.59
Assorted pink, yellow, blue-green.
Standard
415-V-394 Pk./75
Mini
415-V-2123
Pk./100

NEW!

Pastel Silicone Baking Cups
No muffin pan needed! Bake and serve in reusable oven-safe cups in pretty pastels. 3 each pink, yellow, green, blue. Standard size, 2 in. diameter.
415-V-9110 Pk./12 $9.99

White $1.59
Jumbo 415-V-2503 Pk/50
Standard 415-V-2505 Pk./75
Mini 415-V-2507 Pk./100

Gold Foil $1.59
Wax-laminated paper on foil.
Standard 415-V-206 Pk./24
Candy 415-V-306 Pk./75

Silver Foil $1.59
Wax-laminated paper on foil.
Standard 415-V-207 Pk./24
Candy 415-V-307 Pk./75

Petite Loaf Cups*
Microwave-safe paper.
White 415-V-450 Pk./50 $1.59
*Petite Loaf Cups are 3¼ x 2 in. and fit Petite Loaf Pan p. 159.

Nut and Party Cups
Mini 1.25 oz.
415-V-500 Pk./36 $1.79
Standard 3.25 oz.
415-V-400 Pk./24 $1.79

Party Bags

Wrap up cookies, candies, favors and more with color and fun!
Contains 20, 4 x 9.5 in. bags and 20 twist ties, unless otherwise noted. **Pk./20 $2.09**

  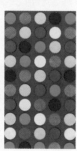  

Yellow
1912-V-2359

Red
1912-V-2357

Dazzling Dots
1912-V-1090

Snappy Stripes
1912-V-1089

Colorful Stars
1912-V-2362

Clear Party Bags
4 x 9.5 in. Each pack contains 25 bags and 25 ties.
1912-V-1240
Pk./25 $2.09
50 Ct. Megapack
1912-V-1239 $3.19
100 Ct. Megapack
1912-V-1294 $4.19

Clear Shaped Party Bags
4.5 x 7.25 in. Each pack contains 100 bags and 100 ties.
1912-V-1112 Pk./100 $4.19

Icing Decorations

Wilton Icing Decorations are perfect for topping cupcakes, cookies and ice cream. Mint-flavored edible shapes are Certified Kosher.

HAPPY BIRTHDAY
Alphabet/Numerals
710-V-494 Pk./70 $2.29

HAPPY BIRTHDAY
Script Alphabet
710-V-546 Pk./62 $2.29

Happy Birthday with Balloons
710-V-547 Pk./21 $2.29

Add-A-Message Fun Pix
Serve party cupcakes in an exciting new way —clip on messages, pictures and more with these colorful plastic picks! Great for place markers, announcing awards at banquets and favorite sayings. Four fun colors to go with your favorite baking cups. 3 in. high.
2113-V-7611 Pk./12 $2.09

ORDER TOLL FREE: 800-794-5866

Gifts from the Kitchen

Your homemade treats are even more welcome when packaged in our boxes, bags and accessories. We make it easy to present your delicious foods with pride!

GIFT-GIVING CONTAINERS

Create a custom food gift with our crisp white containers! Add color and flair with your own gift wrap, ribbon, tissue and tags.

Treat Boxes
Create the perfect gift with window boxes. Great for candies or 3.5 in. cookies. Includes seals/sticker sheet. 4.5 x 4.5 x 1.5 in.
415-V-102 Pk./3 $3.19

Treat Basket
Roomy handled basket is ideal for your gifts. Great for muffins, mini loaves and more. 6.5 x 6.5 x 3 in.
415-V-104 Pk./2 $5.29

Popcorn Treat Boxes
Classic shape stands up tall to hold popcorn, nuts and other snacks. 3.75 x 2.25 x 5.25 in. high.
1904-V-1141 Pk./4 $3.19

CLEAR TREAT BAGS
Find the perfect size to wrap up any treats.

Hexagon Treat Boxes
Self-closing top forms a pretty petal box top. Great for cookies, candy and favors. 4 x 6.25 in. high.
415-V-105 Pk./4 $5.29

10 x 16 in. Treat Bags
Wrap up bread loaves, smaller bowls and plates of treats. Includes 4 - 10 x 16 in. bags; 4 - 18 in. ribbons, 4 gift tags.
1912-V-1142 $3.19

16 x 20 in. Treat Bags
Ideal size for Treat Baskets filled with muffins. Great for a cookie platter, pie, scones and more. Includes 3 - 16 x 20 in. bags; 3 - 18 in. ribbons, 3 gift tags.
1912-V-1143 $4.19

Entertaining

Every big event needs a main attraction—the Wilton Chocolate Pro Fountain will be the most popular stop at the party!

CHOCOLATE PRO CHOCOLATE FOUNTAIN
- Holds 4 lbs. of melted chocolate
- Tiers come apart for easy cleaning
- Three adjustable feet, plus bubble level, allow perfect leveling from all angles

Bring the excitement of chocolate dipping to your next party! The Chocolate Pro Chocolate Fountain makes it easy to enjoy delicious hand-dipped desserts any time! The graceful canopy style creates an elegant flow from all 3 levels; the bowl is designed to keep chocolate melted and flowing.

With the Chocolate Pro, any celebration becomes more special. Let your guests dip cake and cookies for a flavorful finishing touch. Great for fruit, or try a sweet and salty combination by dipping potato chips and pretzels. 120V; UL listed.
2104-V-9008 $109.99

CHOCOLATE PRO FOUNTAIN AND FONDUE CHOCOLATE

The best real melting chocolate for fountains and fondues is here! Made from premium ingredients for superior melting and a delicious chocolate taste. Ideal texture and rich flavor for making dipped desserts. No tempering needed! 2 Lbs.
2104-V-2618 $17.99

Famous Favorites

Wilton helps you make kids feel like stars! We have a great cast of today's favorite faces and themes on fun party products for cakes, cookies and more.

NEW!

Cake Pan
Where *Hannah Montana* goes, a party is soon to follow! She's an average teenager by day and a pop star by night! You'll be a star too, when you decorate a rocking *Hannah Montana* cake for the birthday party. Includes plastic *Hannah Montana/Star* to position on cake. One-mix pan is 13 x 13 x 2 in. deep. Aluminum.
2105-V-4060 $14.49

Party Toppers
Let *Hannah Montana* put the star spotlight on your party treats. Lenticular image; food-safe plastic is great on cupcakes, brownies, cakes and more. 1¾ in. high.
2113-V-4060 Set/6 $4.19

Candle
Handpainted, clean-burning with fun details. 2¾ in. high.
2811-V-4060 $4.39

Icing Decorations
Edible sugar shapes to decorate cupcakes, cookies, ice cream and cake. Certified Kosher.
710-V-4060 Pk./12 $2.49

Icing Color Set
Includes four .5 oz. jars: Purple, Blue, Pink and Bright Pink. Certified Kosher.
601-V-4060 Set/4 $4.99

Baking Cups
Standard size, microwave-safe paper. 2 in. diameter.
415-V-4060 Pk./50 $1.79

Treat Bags
Fill with candy, cookies and other goodies; great for gifts and surprises, too! Includes sixteen 4 x 9.5 in. bags with closures.
1912-V-4060 Pk./16 $2.09

©Disney
Visit the Disney Website at www.DisneyChannel.com

ORDER TOLL FREE: 800-794-5866

NEW!

Cake Pan
Optimus Prime transforms any birthday party into an action-packed celebration! The Transformers have been a smash everywhere they go and now they're here on an energy-charged cake pan kids will love. One-mix pan is 9 x 12 x 2 in. deep. Aluminum.
2105-V-5060 $14.49

Party Toppers

These robotic aliens capture all the thrills and excitement you'll want at the party. Lenticular image; food-safe plastic is great on cupcakes, brownies, cakes and more. 1½ in. high.
2113-V-5060 Set/6 $4.19

Icing Decorations
Edible sugar shapes to decorate cupcakes, cookies, ice cream and cake. Certified Kosher.
710-V-5060 Pk./9 $2.49

Baking Cups
Standard size, microwave-safe paper. 2 in. diameter.
415-V-5060 Pk./50 $1.79

Cake Decoration

Handpainted with fun details. 2¾ in. high.
2811-V-5060 $4.39

Icing Color Set
Includes four .5 oz. jars: Blue, Dark Blue, Gray and Black. Certified Kosher.
601-V-5060 Set/4 $4.99

Treat Bags

Fill with candy, cookies and other goodies; great for gifts and surprises too! Includes sixteen 4 x 9.5 in. bags with closures.
1912-V-5060 Pk./16 $2.09

FAMOUS FAVORITES

THE AMAZING SPIDER-MAN ®

NEW!

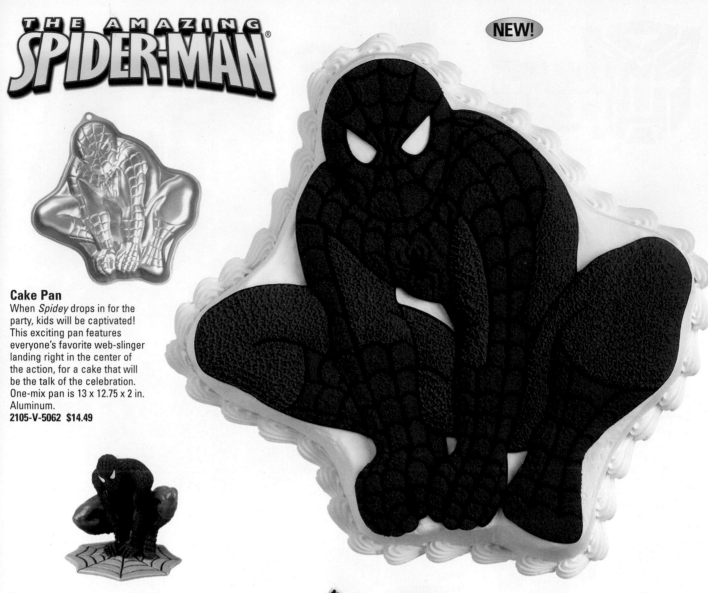

Cake Pan
When *Spidey* drops in for the party, kids will be captivated! This exciting pan features everyone's favorite web-slinger landing right in the center of the action, for a cake that will be the talk of the celebration. One-mix pan is 13 x 12.75 x 2 in. Aluminum.
2105-V-5062 $14.49

Party Toppers
Spider-Man finishes on top again—and he'll complete your treats with excitement! Handpainted, food-safe plastic is great on cupcakes, brownies, cakes and more. 1⅝ in. high.
2113-V-5062 Set/6 $4.19

Candle
Handpainted, clean-burning with exciting details. 3 in. high.
2811-V-5062 $4.39

Icing Decorations
Edible sugar shapes to decorate cupcakes, cookies, ice cream and cake. Certified Kosher.
710-V-5062 Pk./11 $2.49

Icing Color Set
Includes four .5 oz. jars: Blue, Black and 2 Red. Certified Kosher.
601-V-5062 Set/4 $4.99

Baking Cups
Standard size, microwave-safe paper. 2 in. diameter.
415-V-5062 Pk./50 $1.79

Treat Bags
Fill with candy, cookies and other goodies; great for gifts and surprises too! Includes sixteen 4 x 9.5 in. bags with twist ties.
1912-V-5062 Pk./16 $2.09

ORDER TOLL FREE: 800-794-5866

Cake Pan

Everyone's favorite seafaring star will make a big splash at the party. One-mix pan is 13.5 x 11.75 x 2 in. deep. Aluminum.
2105-V-5130 $14.49

Party Toppers

He's surfing your party goodies on these cool handpainted toppers. Food-safe plastic to use on cupcakes, brownies, cakes and other treats. 2 in. high.
2113-V-5130 Set/6 $4.19

Candle

SpongeBob is swimming in loot—giving you a cake to treasure! Handpainted, clean-burning with colorful details. 3½ in. high.
2811-V-5130 $4.39

Cupcake Stand Kit

It's an instant *SpongeBob SquarePants* party, with a bright 3-tier cupcake stand, fun decorative topper, colorful baking cups and Fun Pix! Includes 12 x 15 in. high stand, and 24 each 2 in. diameter cups and 3.5 in. high picks. Holds up to 24 cupcakes.
1510-V-1005 $9.99

Icing Color Set

Includes four .5 oz. jars: Yellow, Red, Blue and Brown. Certified Kosher.
601-V-5130 Set/4 $4.99

Icing Decorations

Edible sugar shapes to decorate cupcakes, cookies, ice cream and cake. Certified Kosher.
710-V-5130 Pk./9 $2.49

Baking Cups

Standard size, microwave-safe paper. 2 in. diameter.
415-V-5130 Pk./50 $1.79

Treat Bags

Fill with candy, cookies and other goodies; great for gifts and surprises too! Includes sixteen 4 x 9.5 in. bags with twist ties.
1912-V-5130 Pk./16 $2.09

ORDER ONLINE: WWW.WILTON.COM

Cake Pan
WALL•E brings the excitement and fun of his hit movie to your celebration. This fun shaped pan is programmed to make a kid's birthday unforgettable! One-mix pan is 10 x 11 x 2 in. deep. Aluminum.
2105-V-9999 $14.49

Party Toppers
WALL•E is no wallflower! He greets your guests with a friendly wave that invites everyone to join in the fun. Handpainted, food-safe plastic is great on cupcakes, brownies, cakes and more. 2 in. high.
2113-V-9999 Set/6 $4.19

© Disney/Pixar

Candle
Handpainted, clean-burning with fun details. 2¾ in. high.
2811-V-9999 $4.39

Icing Color Set
Includes four .5 oz. jars: Red, Black and two Yellow. Certified Kosher.
601-V-9999 Set/4 $4.99

Icing Decorations
Edible sugar shapes to decorate cupcakes, cookies, ice cream and cake. Certified Kosher.
710-V-9999 Pk./9 $2.49

Baking Cups
Standard size, microwave-safe paper. 2 in. diameter.
415-V-9999 Pk./50 $1.79

Treat Bags
Fill with candy, cookies and other goodies; great for gifts and surprises too! Includes sixteen 4 x 9.5 in. bags with twist ties.
1912-V-9999 Pk./16 $2.09

Cake Pan
Any party is a joy ride when you serve a cake starring *Lightning McQueen*! All the fun details you love on the big screen are here. One-mix pan is 13.75 x 6.25 x 2.75 in. Aluminum.
2105-V-6400 $14.49

Party Toppers
Rev up the fun with treats topped with your favorites from *Disney/Pixar Cars*! Handpainted, food-safe plastic is great on cupcakes, brownies, cakes and other treats. 1¼ in. high.
2113-V-6400 Set/6 $4.19

©Disney/Pixar

Icing Decorations
Edible sugar shapes to decorate cupcakes, cookies, ice cream and cake. Certified Kosher.
710-V-6400 Pk./9 $2.49

Candle
Handpainted, clean-burning with fun details. 3½ in. high.
2811-V-6400 $4.39

Icing Color Set
Includes four .5 oz. jars: Red, Blue, Yellow, Black. Certified Kosher.
601-V-6400 Set/4 $4.99

The World of Cars

Baking Cups
Standard size, microwave-safe paper. 2 in. diameter.
415-V-6400 Pk./50 $1.79

Treat Bags
Fill with candy, cookies and other goodies; great for gifts and surprises too! Includes sixteen 4 x 9.5 in. bags with twist ties.
1912-V-6400 Pk./16 $2.09

ORDER TOLL FREE: 800-794-5866

Cupcake Stand Kit
It's an instant *Disney Fairies* party, with a bright 3-tier cupcake stand, fun decorative topper, colorful baking cups and Fun Pix. Includes 12 x 15 in. high stand, 24 each 2 in. diameter cups and 3.5 in. high picks. Holds up to 24 cupcakes.
1510-V-1003 $9.99

Cake Pan
Tinker Bell makes birthday wishes come true! She brings fun to the celebration on a cake that captures the twinkle in her eye and the magic in her smile. One-mix pan is 10.5 x 12 x 2 in. Aluminum.
2105-V-5110 $14.49

Party Toppers
Top your treats with *Tinker Bell* and create enchantment! Handpainted, food-safe plastic is great on cupcakes, brownies, cakes and other treats. 2¼ in. high.
2113-V-5110 Set/6 $4.19

© Disney
Please visit Disney Fairies at DisneyFairies.com

Icing Decorations
Edible sugar shapes to decorate cupcakes, cookies, ice cream and cake. Certified Kosher.
710-V-5110 Pk./9 $2.49

Candle
Handpainted, clean-burning with colorful details. 3 in. high.
2811-V-5110 $4.39

Icing Color Set
Includes four .5 oz. jars: Blue, Yellow, Red, *Tinker Bell* Skin Tone. Certified Kosher.
601-V-5110 Set/4 $4.99

Baking Cups
Standard size, microwave-safe paper. 2 in. diameter.
415-V-5110 Pk./50 $1.79

Treat Bags
Fill with candy, cookies and other goodies; great for gifts and surprises too! Includes sixteen 4 x 9.5 in. bags with twist ties.
1912-V-5110 Pk./16 $2.09

Cake Pan
Enter *Ariel's* world of enchantment under the sea! Her sweet look will captivate kids and bring all the thrills of *The Little Mermaid* story to your celebration. One-mix pan is 10.5 x 11.75 x 2 in. Aluminum.
2105-V-4355 $14.49

Party Toppers
When *Ariel* surfaces on party desserts, there's a new wave of birthday excitement! Handpainted, food-safe plastic is great on cupcakes, brownies, cakes and other treats. 1¾ in. high.
2113-V-4355 Set/6 $4.19

© Disney

Icing Decorations
Edible sugar shapes to decorate cupcakes, cookies, ice cream and cake. Certified Kosher.
710-V-4355 Pk./9 $2.49

Candle
Handpainted, clean-burning with fun details. 3 in. high.
2811-V-4355 $4.39

Baking Cups
Standard size, microwave-safe paper. 2 in. diameter.
415-V-4355 Pk./50 $1.79

Icing Color Set
Includes four .5 oz. jars: *Ariel* Skin Tone, Teal and 2 Red. Certified Kosher.
601-V-4355 Set/4 $4.99

Candle
Handpainted, clean-burning with colorful details. 3¼ in. high.
2811-V-4250
$4.39

Cake Pan
Kids will follow *Diego* everywhere—they've watched him race to the rescue on TV, and now he's ready to save the party with the perfect birthday cake! The fun detailed design really captures his adventurous attitude. One-mix pan is 16 x 10 x 2 in. Aluminum.
2105-V-4250 $14.49

Icing Decorations
Edible sugar shapes to decorate cupcakes, cookies, ice cream and cake. Certified Kosher.
710-V-4250 Pk./9 $2.49

Baking Cups
Standard size, microwave-safe paper. 2 in. diameter.
415-V-4250
Pk./50 $1.79

Party Toppers
Diego scopes out all the party fun on these colorful toppers. They're easy ways to complete your treats! Handpainted, food-safe plastic is great on cupcakes, brownies, cakes and more. 2 in. high.
2113-V-4250 Set/6 $4.19

Icing Color Set
Includes four .5 oz. jars: *Diego* Skin Tone, Brown, Blue and Black. Certified Kosher.
601-V-4250
Set/4 $4.99

Treat Bags
Fill with candy, cookies and other goodies; great for gifts and surprises too! Includes sixteen 4 x 9.5 in. bags with twist ties.
1912-V-4250
Pk./16 $2.09

NickJr.com

Candle
Handpainted, clean-burning with colorful details. 3¼ in. high.
2811-V-6300
$4.39

Cake Pan
Wherever *Dora* goes, it's always "una fiesta"! Discover a world of party excitement with this great pan. One-mix pan is 13.75 x 10 x 2 in. deep. Aluminum.
2105-V-6300 $14.49

Icing Decorations
Edible sugar shapes to decorate cupcakes, cookies, ice cream and cake. Certified Kosher.
710-V-6300 Pk./8 $2.49

Baking Cups
Standard size, microwave-safe paper. 2 in. diameter.
415-V-6300
Pk./50 $1.79

Party Toppers
Dora is ready to top your delightful party treats! Handpainted, food-safe plastic is great on cupcakes, brownies, cakes and other treats. 2¼ in. high.
2113-V-6300 Set/6 $4.19

Icing Color Set
Includes four .5 oz. jars: Red, Pink, Brown and *Dora* Skin Tone. Certified Kosher.
601-V-6300
Set/4 $4.99

Treat Bags
Fill with candy, cookies and other goodies; great for gifts and surprises too! Includes sixteen 4 x 9.5 in. bags with twist ties.
1912-V-6300
Pk./16 $2.09

ORDER TOLL FREE: 800-794-5866

Elmo Face Cake Pan

He's sweet, lovable and popular with kids of all ages. One-mix pan is 13.5 x 10.5 x 2 in. Aluminum.
2105-V-3461 $14.49

Icing Decorations
Edible sugar shapes to decorate cupcakes, cookies, ice cream and cakes. Certified Kosher.
710-V-3460 Pk./9 $2.49

Baking Cups
Standard size, microwave-safe paper. 2 in. diameter.
415-V-3461 Pk./50 $1.79

Elmo with Crayons Candle
Elmo brings smiles to the party. Handpainted, clean-burning with colorful details. 3½ in. high.
2811-V-3463 $4.39

Treat Bags
Fill with candy, cookies and other goodies; great for gifts and surprises too! Includes sixteen 4 x 9.5 in. bags with closures.
1912-V-3461 Pk./16 $2.09

Cake Pan
Kids everywhere have fallen for *Abby Cadabby*! This 3-year-old fairy-in-training has moved to Sesame Street and is winning new friends every day. She's here on a cake pan that captures all her magic and fun. One-mix pan is 9.5 x 11.75 x 2 in. deep. Aluminum.
2105-V-4444 $14.49

Icing Decorations
Edible sugar shapes to decorate cupcakes, cookies, ice cream and cake. Certified Kosher.
710-V-4444 Pk./9 $2.49

Baking Cups
Standard size, microwave-safe paper. 2 in. diameter.
415-V-4444 Pk./50 $1.79

Candle
Handpainted, clean-burning with fun details. 2¾ in. high.
2811-V-4444 $4.39

Icing Color Set
Includes four .5 oz. jars: Pink, Purple, Blue and Yellow. Certified Kosher.
601-V-4444 Set/4 $4.99

Treat Bags
Fill with candy, cookies and other goodies; great for gifts and surprises, too! Includes sixteen 4 x 9.5 in. bags with closures.
1912-V-4444 Pk./16 $2.09

Candy Making

Let Wilton show you how much fun candy making can be! Use our Candy Melts and molds for beautiful candy in 3 easy steps—just melt, mold and serve!

Candy Melts

Delicious, creamy, easy-to-melt wafers are ideal for all your candy making—molding, dipping or drizzling. Make tempting custom candies using the Candy Flavoring Set (p. 199).

14 oz. bag. Certified Kosher Dairy. **$2.99**

Dark Cocoa
1911-V-358

Light Cocoa
1911-V-544

NEW!

Colorburst Brights Candy Melts

Capture a rainbow of color in every candy you mold with new Colorburst Candy Melts! Brilliant flecks of color are blended into each easy-melting wafer, for candies that will look great for showers, receptions, holidays and more. 10 oz. bag. Certified Kosher Dairy.
1911-V-491 $2.99

Dark Cocoa Mint
1911-V-1920

Peanut Butter
1911-V-481

Green
1911-V-405

Blue
1911-V-448

Yellow
1911-V-463

Orange
1911-V-1631

Red
1911-V-499

Pink
1911-V-447

Lavender
1911-V-403

White
1911-V-498

Candy Melting Accessories

CHOCOLATE PRO ELECTRIC MELTING POT

The fast and easy way to melt chocolate and Candy Melts!
• Melting base stays cool to the touch
• Removeable non-stick Melting Pot holds 2½ cups
• Easy-pour spout
• Non-skid feet keep Chocolate Pro steady
It's the fast and fun way to mold candies like a pro. With the Chocolate Pro, you'll be able to mold lollipops and fancy dipped-center candies. Serve elegant dipped desserts like fruit, cake, cookies and fondue. Add the great taste of chocolate to potato chips and pretzels. Create flavored chocolate sauces for ice cream or silky ganache glaze to pour over cakes. 120 volts. CUL Listed.
2104-V-9004 $32.99

STAY-WARM CERAMIC CANDY MELTING CUPS & BOWLS

Ceramic keeps candy melted longer for easier candy-making because microwave-safe ceramic retains heat. Great for heating and pouring dessert toppings too.

Candy Melting Cups
Cups are great for melting colors separately. Use them like an art palette for painting colors. Holds heat up to ½ hour. Includes 6 cups (2 x 1.5 in. deep) and 6 decorating brushes.
1904-V-1067 Set/12 $10.49

Candy Melting Bowls
Ideal for filling all types of Wilton molds. Take them to the table for easy dipping. Holds heat up to 1 hour. Two, 4 x 3.5 in. deep.
1904-V-1076 Set/2 $10.49

Candy Decorating Pen Set

Give your homemade candies a delicious touch of color with these easy-melting candy pens. Just melt in hot water and squeeze into detailed areas of candy mold. The snip-off tip makes it easy to control the flow and add great-looking details. Includes 1.6 oz. tubes of Red, Yellow, Blue and White.
1914-V-1285 Set/4 $9.49

Candy Decorating Bags

The convenient way to melt small amounts of Candy Melts and pipe color detail in your molds! Flexible 12 in. plastic bags—just use, then toss.
2104-V-4825
Pk./12 $4.19

ORDER TOLL FREE: 800-794-5866

Pretzel Molds

Easy to mold: add your favorite melted Candy Melts, position pretzel rod and chill to set. **$1.99**

Race Car
2 designs,
6 cavities.
2115-V-1034

NEW!

Baby
2 designs, 6 cavities.
2115-V-2101

Butterfly
2 designs, 6 cavities.
2115-V-1032

Smiley Face
1 design, 6 cavities.
2115-V-4437

Flowers
1 design, 6 cavities.
2115-V-4436

Presents
1 design, 6 cavities.
2115-V-4442

Cookie Candy Molds

Turn store-bought cookies into candy-coated treats! With Cookie Candy Molds and easy-melting Wilton Candy Melts, it's a breeze to add a great tasting and colorful candy design to your favorite cookies. Just brush colored candy details in the mold, let set, then add more melted candy and position your cookie in the mold. Great for sandwich cream cookies or any round cookie 2 in. diameter or less. Hearts and Flowers molds have 2 designs, 8 cavities, Sports and Animals molds have 4 designs, 8 cavities. **$1.99**

Animals
2115-V-1354

Sports
2115-V-1353

Flowers
2115-V-1351

Hearts
2115-V-1352

Classic Candy Molds

Wilton has a great selection of traditional shapes to create elegant gift assortments and party trays.

Dessert Accents
Finish your signature dessert with flair—top it with a dramatic candy shape using this exciting mold. Swirls, scrolls, zigzags, triangles and leaves add 5-star style. 5 designs, 10 cavities.
2115-V-2102 **$1.99**

NEW!

Truffles
1 design, 14 cavities.
2115-V-1521 **$1.99**

Peanut Butter Cups
1 design, 11 cavities.
2115-V-1522 **$1.99**

Deep Heart Truffles
1 design, 8 cavities.
2117-V-100 **$1.99**

Mint Discs
1 design, 18 cavities.
2115-V-1739 **$1.99**

Gift Truffles
1 design, 13 cavities.
2115-V-1728 **$1.99**

Dessert Shells
2-piece mold. 1 design, 3 cavities.
2115-V-1035 **$2.99**

Add-A-Message Candy Bar
Create a sweet memory for your guests . . . a candy bar featuring your special message. Present them beautifully in Candy Bar Boxes (p. 200). Each candy bar measures 3.75 x 1.75 x .25 in. deep. Mold has 1 design, 4 cavities.
2115-V-1356 **$1.99**

Candy Bar
1 design, three 4-block cavities measure 4 x 2 x .25 in. deep.
2115-V-4431 **$1.99**

Cordial Cups
Mold a candy "glass" for dessert liqueurs, or fill with whipped cream and float in cocoa or coffee. 1 design, 6 cavities.
2115-V-1535 **$1.99**

Candy Molds

More fun shapes and greater detail make Wilton Candy Molds the perfect way to create candy. Look at the variety! You can do it all, from exciting kids' party treats to elegant wedding and shower favors. Molding and coloring couldn't be easier when you use Candy Melts. Look for terrific design ideas and molding instructions on every mold package. For specific Holiday designs, see our Seasonal Section, p. 206-227.

LARGE LOLLIPOP MOLDS

NEW!

Monkey
3 designs, 3 cavities.
2115-V-2100 $1.99

Fairy Tale
3 designs, 3 cavities.
2115-V-1033 $1.99

Sports
4 designs, 4 cavities.
2115-V-4432 $1.99

Party/Birthday
4 designs, 4 cavities.
2115-V-4434 $1.99

Double Heart
2 designs, 4 cavities.
2115-V-4440 $1.99

Pinwheel
2 designs, 3 cavities.
2115-V-4443 $1.99

Cross/Bible
4 designs, 6 cavities
(2 lollipop, 4 candy).
2115-V-4435 $1.99

2-PACK CANDY MOLD SETS

Girl Power
10 designs, 10 cavities.
2115-V-1604 Pk./2 $2.99

Baby
10 designs, 10 cavities.
2115-V-1605 Pk./2 $2.99

Pets
10 designs, 11 cavities.
2115-V-1606 Pk./2 $2.99

Garden Goodies Lollipop
10 designs, 10 cavities.
2115-V-1607 Pk./2 $2.99

Summer Fun Lollipop
10 designs, 10 cavities.
2115-V-1608 Pk./2 $2.99

10-PACK CANDY MOLD SET

Be ready for any celebration with this great variety of theme molds! Includes 72 total shapes and 114 total cavities for fun candy messages, sports treats, flowers and more.
2115-V-1724 Pk./10 $9.99

Alphabet
26 designs, 26 cavities

Numbers
10 designs, 10 cavities

Transportation
6 designs, 7 cavities

Sports Champ
7 designs, 7 cavities

Celebration
5 designs, 10 cavities

Hearts
1 design, 15 cavities

Peanut Butter Cups
1 design, 11 cavities

Snack Time
6 designs, 12 cavities

Fruit Lollipop
5 designs, 5 cavities

Garden Flowers
5 designs, 11 cavities

ORDER TOLL FREE: 800-794-5866

CANDY & LOLLIPOP MOLDS

Stars
1 design, 12 cavities,
2115-V-1554 **$1.99**

Dancing Daisies Lollipop
1 design, 9 cavities.
2115-V-1430 **$1.99**

Transportation
5 designs, 5 cavities.
2115-V-1413 **$1.99**

Summer Fun
5 designs, 11 cavities.
2115-V-1741 **$1.99**

Wedding Favor
3 designs, 6 cavities.
2115-V-4446 **$1.99**

Roses in Bloom
1 design, 10 cavities.
2115-V-1738 **$1.99**

Smiley Face Lollipop
1 design, 10 cavities.
2115-V-1715 **$1.99**

Sea Creatures Lollipop
5 designs, 5 cavities.
2115-V-1414 **$1.99**

Seashells
5 designs, 11 cavities.
2115-V-1561 **$1.99**

Wedding Shower Lollipop
5 designs, 10 cavities.
(4 lollipop, 6 candy).
2115-V-1711 **$1.99**

Rubber Ducky
1 design, 6 cavities.
2115-V-1565 **$1.99**

Roses & Buds Lollipop
3 designs, 9 cavities.
(4 lollipop, 5 candy).
2115-V-1708 **$1.99**

Springtime Treats Lollipop
8 designs, 9 cavities.
2115-V-1716 **$1.99**

Baby Treats
5 designs, 5 cavities.
2115-V-4447 **$1.99**

Candy Making Tools

Candy Thermometer
Precise measurement essential for preparing hard candy, nougat, more.
1904-V-1200 **$14.99**

Candy Dipping Set
Easy-handling spoon and fork, each 7.75 in. long.
1904-V-3230 **Set/2** **$3.19**

Metal Dipping Set
Professional-quality stainless steel with wooden handles. 8.75 in. long.
1904-V-925 **Set/2** **$10.49**

Easy-Pour Funnel
Push-button controls flow of candy. 5 x 4 in. diameter, nylon.
1904-V-552 **$4.19**

Squeeze Bottles
Melt candy with ease, then fill your mold without mess! Our convenient bottles are available in 3 sizes so you can melt just the amount of Candy Melts you need, right in the bottle. Great way to store and reheat leftover candy.

Mini
6 oz.
1904-V-1166 Pk./2 $1.99

Regular
12 oz.
1904-V-1189 $1.69

Candy Melting Plate
Microwave-melt up to 11 Candy Melts colors at one time with less mess! Plastic with non-slip grip edge. Includes decorating brush.
1904-V-8016 **$3.19**

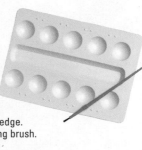

Decorator Brush Set
Plastic, durable bristles, easy-to-hold handle.
2104-V-9355
Set/3 **$1.69**

CANDY MAKING

Candy Color and Flavoring Sets

Primary Candy Color Set
Concentrated oil-based colors blend easily with Candy Melts. Includes Yellow, Orange, Red and Blue in .25 oz. jars. Certified Kosher.
1913-V-1299 **Set/4** **$3.99**

Garden Candy Color Set
Create pretty pastel colors! Concentrated oil-based colors blend easily with Candy Melts. Includes Pink, Green, Violet and Black in .25 oz. jars. Certified Kosher.
1913-V-1298 **Set/4** **$3.99**

Candy Flavoring Set
Includes Peppermint, Cherry, Cinnamon and Creme de Menthe in .25 oz. bottles. Certified Kosher.
1913-V-1029 **Set/4** **$5.49**

Candy Wraps and Boxes

Your homemade candy deserves a beautiful presentation. Wilton has everything you need to wrap and package your candy gifts like a pro.

Pretzel Candy Gift Boxes NEW!
Your tempting pretzel pop gifts show through the front window. Tented design holds pretzels upright to protect against breakage. 3 x 2 x 9.5 in. high. White.
1904-V-2000 Pk./3 $2.99

Tented Candy Gift Boxes
Stand-up design with front window will give your homemade candy gift the ideal showcase. 3.25 x 1.6 x 5.75 in. high. White.
1904-V-1087 Pk./3 $2.09

Candy Box Liners
Padded paper liners cushion candy and prevent breakage. Fits ½ Lb. Candy Gift Boxes.
1904-V-1191 Pk./4 $1.59

Gold Elastic Ties
Pre-tied with a bow. Use with Candy Gift Boxes.
1904-V-1186 Pk./5 $1.59

Candy Gift Boxes
For attractive gift giving.
1 Lb. White Candy Boxes
1904-V-1172 Pk./3 $2.59
½ Lb. Candy Boxes Pk./3 $2.09
White **1904-V-1150** Red **1904-V-1152**

Love Chocolate Candy Gift Boxes
Bright, fun pattern makes your gift even sweeter!
½ Lb. Candy Boxes **1904-V-4242 Pk./3 $2.09**

"Home Made" Box Seals
Let everyone know the care you put into your candy gift with these embossed seals. Add this "homemade" touch whenever you give baked goods too!
1904-V-8936 Pk./24 $1.09

Candy Bar Boxes
Designed to hold candies made in our Candy Bar Molds (p. 197), the window displays your special message.
White 1904-V-1157 Pk./10 $4.19

Truffle Boxes
An elegant look, with a lock-close top that forms a perfect "bow." Holds 2-3 pieces of candy.
Pk./4 $2.09
White **1904-V-1154**
Gold **1904-V-1156**

Glassine Candy Cups
Crisply-pleated, just like professionals use. White glassine-coated paper. **$1.59**
1.25 in. Diameter.
1912-V-1245 Pk./75
1 in. Diameter.
1912-V-1243 Pk./100

Foil Wrappers
Bright, shiny coverings for candy and lollipops! 4 x 4 in. squares.
Pk./50 $1.99
Gold **1904-V-1197**
Silver **1904-V-1196**
Red **1904-V-1198**

Foil Candy Cups
Crisply-pleated, just like professionals use. Wax-laminated paper on foil.
Pk./75 $1.59
Red **415-V-314**
Blue **415-V-313**
Pink **415-V-315**
Gold **415-V-306**
Silver **415-V-307**

LOLLIPOP AND TREAT STAND

Show off your fun lollipops and other treats! This lively looping metal stand neatly serves up to 18 treats for the ideal celebration centerpiece. Great for marshmallows, jelly candies and caramels too—just insert 4 in. sticks. Use the top slot to add a fun message! Assembled size 6 x 14 in. high.
1904-V-1068 $10.99

Accessories

Create the perfect pop with sticks in every size. Clear wrappers and tags make giving easy.

Lollipop Tags
Write a name or a message, then slide the tag onto your lollipop stick. Perfect for party lollipops, cookie pops and more.
Pk./12 $2.09
Star **1904-V-1089**
Flower **1904-V-1071**

Drawstring Lollipop Bags
Fill with your favorite candies, then pull the drawstring to close—a fun way to give your goodies. Clear bags are also great for cookies, nuts and other treats. 4.5 x 5.5 in.
1912-V-9469 Pk./15 $2.09

Lollipop Wrapping Kit
Cover your candy lollipops and special treats for gift-giving! Contains 18 sticks, (4 in.) 18 bags, 18 twist ties.
1904-V-1193 $2.09

Clear Treat Bags Only
3 x 4 in. **1912-V-2347**
Pk./50 $2.89

Pretzel Bags
See-through bags are ideal for showing off your candy-coated pretzels—great for favors and gifts. 20 plastic bags, 20 twist ties. 2.25 x 9.75 in.
1912-V-5911 Pk./20 $2.09

Lollipop Sticks
Sturdy paper sticks in 4 sizes. Not for oven use.
4 in.
1912-V-1006 Pk./50 $1.99
6 in.
1912-V-1007 Pk./35 $1.99
8 in.
1912-V-9320 Pk./25 $1.99
11¾ in.
1912-V-1212 Pk./20 $3.99

Cookie Making

Wilton has just what you need to make cookies fun! Easy-to-use presses, colossal cutter sets, fun stencils, colorful icings and unique toppings sure to create unforgettable cookies!

Cookie Presses

Wilton has the best selection of feature-packed presses anywhere! From our Comfort Grip Press, designed for easy handling and filling, to our powerful cordless Cookie Master Plus, spritz cookie-making has never been easier!

Cookie Pro™ ULTRA II

Making traditional spritz cookies has never been so easy! Cookie Pro Ultra II is designed to be the easiest to fill, most comfortable press you've ever used. And, with 12 terrific shapes, plus 4 fun mini cookie designs, your holiday cookie baskets will be more festive than ever! Includes complete instructions and delicious recipes.
2104-V-4018 Set/17 $24.99

Twelve Disks in Festive Shapes

Plus 4 BONUS Disks For Mini Cookies!

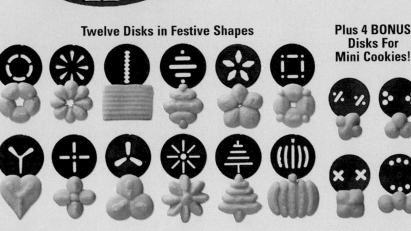

COOKIE MASTER® Plus
Cordless Cookie Press

Our cordless cookie press is so powerful and easy to operate, you'll use it all year to create cookies, appetizers, desserts and more. Exclusive patented reverse action means there's no need to take press apart for refilling. Ergonomic design is shaped to fit in your hand for excellent comfort.

Includes 12 aluminum disks in classic and seasonal shapes, 4 accent tips for decorating and filling and 2 bonus recipe booklets—sweet and savory. Uses 4 AA batteries, not included. Patent Nos. D484,755; 6,701,828.
2104-V-4008 Set/19 $39.99

4 Accent Tips

12 Disk Designs

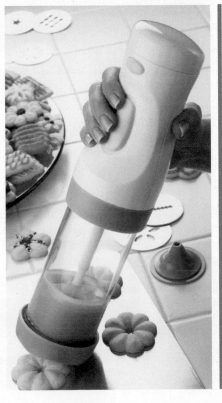

COMFORT GRIP™
Cookie Press

Experience a classic press that is truly comfortable. Its ergonomic handle feels great in your hand and the easy-squeeze action releases perfectly shaped dough. Clear barrel takes the guesswork out of refilling. Fluted bottom raises press off the cookie sheet for better-defined shapes. Includes 12 cookie disks in a variety of shapes and our classic spritz recipe.
2104-V-4011 Set/13 $12.99

12 Disk Designs

Comfort-Grip Cutters

Easy-grip stainless steel cutters with extra-deep sides are perfect for cutting so many favorite foods into spectacular shapes. Ideal for brownies, biscuits, sandwiches, sheet cakes, cheese, crispy rice treats, fudge and much more. The cushion grip gives you comfortable control even when cutting into thick desserts. Each approximately 4 x 4 x 1.75 in. Recipe included.
Each $3.19

Heart
2310-V-616

Round
2310-V-608

Flower
2310-V-613

Teddy Bear
2310-V-609

Double Heart
2310-V-647

Daisy
2310-V-619

Butterfly
2310-V-614

Star
2310-V-605

"I love the Comfort-Grip cookie cutters. When we make roll-out cookies, we make 3-6 dozen at a time and the gripper saves your hands from discomfort. Once you try one, you'll fall in love with it!"

Nila P.
Bismarck, North Dakota

Cookie Decorating Accents

Add that extra touch that makes cookies more exciting. With Wilton products it's easy! Squeeze on the fun with Wilton Cookie Icing and Icing Writer, for colorful decorations with a satin finish. Or let kids draw designs and messages in cool colors with FoodWriter Edible Color Markers.

FOODWRITER EDIBLE COLOR MARKERS

Use edible markers to add fun and dazzling color to countless foods. Kids love 'em! Decorate on Wilton Cookie Icing, fondant, color flow and royal icing designs. Brighten everyday foods like toaster pastries, cheese, fruit slices, bread, more. Each set includes five .07 oz. FoodWriter pens. Certified Kosher.

Primary Colors Sets

Yellow	Green	Red	Blue	Black

Bold Tip 609-V-115 Set/5 $8.39
Fine Tip 609-V-100 Set/5 $8.39

Neon Colors Set

Purple	Orange	Pink	Light Green	Black

Fine Tip 609-V-116 Set/5 $8.39

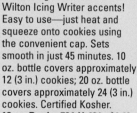

FINE TIP

BOLD TIP

WHITE COOKIE ICING

Use this quick-setting microwavable icing to cover your cookies with a shiny finish—perfect for decorating with colorful Wilton Icing Writer accents! Easy to use—just heat and squeeze onto cookies using the convenient cap. Sets smooth in just 45 minutes. 10 oz. bottle covers approximately 12 (3 in.) cookies; 20 oz. bottle covers approximately 24 (3 in.) cookies. Certified Kosher.
10 oz. Bottle 704-V-481 $4.49
20 oz. Bottle 704-V-492 $7.99

ICING WRITER

Squeeze colorful accents onto fondant and Wilton Cookie Icing with this ready-to-use icing! It's easy to control, just squeeze the bottle and icing flows smoothly from the built-in round tip. Dries to a smooth, satin finish. 3 oz. bottle. Certified Kosher. **$2.49**

Yellow **710-V-2226**	**Pink** **710-V-2230**
Red **710-V-2225**	**White** **710-V-2228**
Green **710-V-2229**	**Violet** **710-V-2231**

Blue
710-V-2227

Cookie Sprinkles & Sugars

6-MIX COLORED SPRINKLE ASSORTMENTS

They're so convenient! Assorted fun shapes in an easy-pour flip-top bottle. Top cupcakes, ice cream and other goodies. Certified Kosher. **$4.99**

Nonpareils
Includes Pink, Orange, Green, Red, Yellow, Purple. 3 oz. total.
710-V-4125

Jimmies
Includes Pink, Orange, Green, Red, Yellow, Blue. 2.52 oz. total.
710-V-4127

4-MIX COLORED SUGAR ASSORTMENTS

Brighten up plain cookies fast with our colorful decorating sugars. Just sprinkle these extra-fine sugars on cookies before baking. Certified Kosher. **$4.99**

Brights 4-Mix
Contains Pink, Yellow, Light Green, Lavender. 4.4 oz. total.
710-V-651

Primary 4-Mix
Contains Red, Dark Green, Blue, Yellow. 4.4 oz. total.
710-V-650

ORDER TOLL FREE: 800-794-5866

Cookie Cutters

Wilton has the cutter shapes and styles you need to set your cookies apart! Check out our variety—from cutter collections and theme sets that cover any occasion to Stackable sets that cut unique 3-D cookie designs, Wilton is your most complete source for cookie fun!

PLASTIC CUTTER SETS

101 Cookie Cutters

With this set, you're covered! Make cookies featuring popular holiday and theme shapes like sports, flowers, animals and more. Or use the complete alphabet and numeral collections included to create the perfect cookie message. Great for cutting all kinds of food into fun shapes—perfect for crafting, too. Average cutter size approx. 3.5 x 3.5 in. Recipe included.
2304-V-1050 Set/101 $14.99

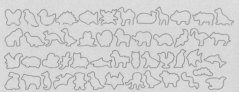

Animal Pals 50-Piece Cutter Set

Everyone will go wild for cookies, foods and crafts made with this menagerie of favorite animal shapes. Shapes include fish, dog, cat, birds, butterflies, reptiles and more. Average cutter size approx. 3.5 x 3.5 in. Recipe included.
2304-V-1055 Set/50 $8.99

A-B-C and 1-2-3 50-Piece Cutter Set

Complete alphabet and numeral collection, great for cookies, brownies, gelatin treats, learning games, crafts and more. Average cutter size approx. 3.5 x 3.5 in. Recipe included.
2304-V-1054 Set/50 $8.99

Plastic Cutters

With our large variety of brightly-colored cutter shapes, the making is as much fun as the eating! Child-safe design means kids can help. Each approx. 3 x 4 in. **Each $0.69**

Fish	Dinosaur	Teddy Bear	Butterfly	Puppy	Dog Bone
2303-V-128	2303-V-112	2303-V-133	2303-V-116	2303-V-137	2303-V-123

Star	Hand	Foot	Girl	Boy	Airplane	Flower
2303-V-135	2303-V-147	2303-V-113	2303-V-120	2303-V-124	2303-V-101	2303-V-117

Locomotive Engine	Heart	Cat	Duck	Four-Leaf Clover	Cross
2303-V-139	2303-V-100	2303-V-118	2303-V-148	2303-V-134	2303-V-141

Plastic Nesting Cutter Sets

Your favorites in child-safe, graduated shapes. Discover all the fun ways to use our cutters—for bread shapes, stencils, sun catchers and so much more.

Blossom
1.2 to 4.5 in.
2304-V-116 Set/6 $2.99

Heart
1.5 to 4.2 in.
2304-V-115 Set/6 $2.99

Star
1.6 to 4.6 in.
2304-V-111 Set/6 $2.99

Cookie Cutters

STACKABLE! COOKIE CUTTER SETS

Use these fun shaped cutters to create a sensational, stackable 3-D cookie design! Just cut and bake the cookies using your favorite roll-out recipe, decorate with icing and stack them to make a terrific treat. Let the kids help—they'll love to create their own cookie bears or flowers. Stackable cookies are perfect for parties, favors and gift baskets. Other cutters just don't stack up! Cutters measure approx. 5, 2.5 and 1.5 in.
Set/3 $3.99

Teddy Bear
2308-V-1287

Flower
2308-V-1288

COLORED METAL CUTTER SETS

NEW!

4-piece sets add variety. Built to last, they cut cleanly and release easily. Recipe included. Each approx. 3 in.

Football
Pennant, football, jersey, and helmet.
2308-V-1263 Set/4 $4.79

Baby
Carriage, rocking horse, teddy bear, and onesie.
2308-V-1067 Set/4 $4.79

Wedding
Cake, dress, bells and double heart.
2308-V-1071 Set/4 $4.79

METAL CUTTER SETS

Multi-piece sets add variety. Built to last, they cut cleanly and release easily. Recipe included.

Mini Romantic
Butterfly, heart, bell, crinkled heart, tulip, and blossom.
Each approx. 1.5 in.
2308-V-1225
Set/6 $3.19

Mini Noah's Ark
Horse, ark, elephant, bear, giraffe and lion.
Each approx. 1.5 in.
2308-V-1206
Set/6 $3.19

Mini Geometric Crinkle
Square, circle, heart, diamond, oval and triangle. Each approx. 1.5 in.
2308-V-1205
Set/6 $3.19

Classic
Geometric, crinkle diamond, heart, half moon, star and flower. Each approx. 3 in.
2308-V-1235
Set/6 $5.29

Animals
Horse, dove, lion, duck, pig and cat. Each approx. 3 in.
2308-V-1236
Set/6 $5.29

Hearts
Seven different heart cutter designs from stylized to traditional. Sizes range from 1.5 to 3 in.
2308-V-1237
Set/7 $5.29

Bug Buddies
Caterpillar, dragonfly, spider, butterfly, bee and ladybug. Each approx. 3 in.
2308-V-1245
Set/6 $5.29

Nesting From The Heart
Two crinkled, two smooth. Largest is approx. 5 in.
2308-V-1203
Set/4 $4.79

Nesting Stars
For holidays and more! Largest is approx. 5 in.
2308-V-1215
Set/4 $4.79

Nesting Blossoms
Flowers in four sizes. Largest is approx. 5 in.
2308-V-1204
Set/4 $4.79

METAL CUTTERS

Metal cutters from Wilton are built to last through years of cookie making; they cut cleanly and release with ease. Each shape is approximately 3 in.
Each $0.69

Star
2308-V-1008

Daisy
2308-V-1007

Butterfly
2308-V-1015

Chick
2308-V-1000

Heart
2308-V-1003

Fish
2308-V-1017

Shamrock
2308-V-1011

Oak Leaf
2308-V-1013

Gingerbread Boy
2308-V-1002

Bear
2308-V-1009

Bell
2308-V-1006

Circle
2308-V-1010

Cross
2308-V-1018

ORDER TOLL FREE: 800-794-5866

Push 'N Print Cutter Set

Use Push 'N Print Cutters to emboss a fun message before baking! It's so easy! Load one of the 3 cutter disk designs in the press, cut the cookie, then press the plunger with disk in place to imprint the design. Bake, cool and serve a treat that's perfect for celebrations and cookie gift baskets. Great for embossed fondant decorations, too! Disks are 3 in. diameter. Recipe included.
2308-V-4004 Set/4 $7.99

Cookie Bakeware and Accessories

Cookie Treat Pans

Cookie treats on a stick are so easy! Just press cookie dough into pan, insert a cookie stick, then bake, cool and decorate. Create your own cookie blossoms for that special someone; also great for rice cereal treats and candy. Recipe included. Each pan makes 6 individual treats, 3.5 in. x .25 in. deep. Aluminum.
Each $9.99

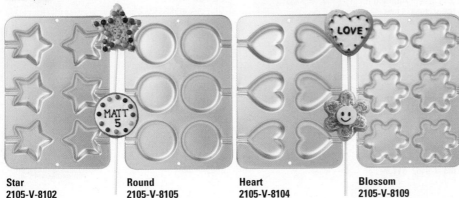

Star
2105-V-8102

Round
2105-V-8105

Heart
2105-V-8104

Blossom
2105-V-8109

Cookie Treat Sticks

For fun cookie pops.
6 in. **1912-V-9319**
Pk./20 $1.99
8 in. **1912-V-9318**
Pk./20 $2.99

Clear Party Bags

4 x 9.5 in. Each pack contains 25 bags and 25 ties.
1912-V-1240
Pk./25 $2.09

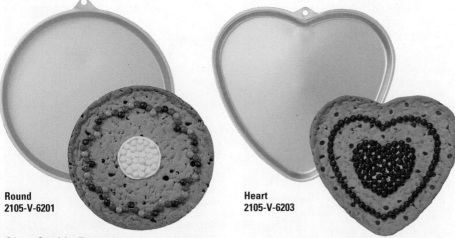

Round
2105-V-6201

Heart
2105-V-6203

Giant Cookie Pans

Our Giant Cookie Pans help you create a jumbo pan cookie in a shape that will be a big hit for any occasion. Specially designed for one package of refrigerated dough, they are also great for brownies and pizza! Each shape is approximately .75 in. deep and can be used with recipes that call for a standard 13 x 9 in. pan. Aluminum. **Each $7.49**

Cookie Sheets

Wilton Cookie Sheets are extra thick aluminum to heat evenly for perfect browning.

Aluminum
Extra-thick construction.
Jumbo 14 x 20 in.
2105-V-6213 $19.99

Insulated Aluminum
Two quality aluminum layers sandwich an insulating layer of air for perfect browning without burning.
16 x 14 in.
2105-V-2644 $20.99

Cooling Grids

Chrome
Sturdy design will never rust.
13 in. Round
2305-V-130 $8.99
10 x 16 in.
2305-V-128 $6.99
14.5 x 20 in.
2305-V-129 $9.99

Non-Stick
Cookies and cakes won't stick with our slick non-stick coating.
13 in. Round
2305-V-230 $10.49
10 x 16 in.
2305-V-228 $9.99
14.5 x 20 in.
2305-V-229 $14.49

3-Pc. Stackable Chrome-Plated
Use singly or stack to save space while cooling three batches of cookies at the same time. Individual grids are 13.5 x 9.75 x 3 in. high; stacked grids are 9.75 in. high.
2305-V-151 $14.49

See p. 156-168 for the full line of Wilton Bakeware.

Non-Stick Parchment Paper

Use Wilton silicone-treated non-stick parchment to line baking pans and cookie sheets—a non-fat alternative that saves cleanup time. Oven-safe to 400°F, great for conventional ovens, microwaves and the freezer. Double roll is 41 square feet, 15 in. wide. Certified Kosher.
415-V-680 $5.29

Cookie Spatula

Angled stainless steel blade moves cookies from pan to plate with ease. Slides easily under cookies—great for serving brownies and bar cookies too. Comfortable ergonomic handle with thumb rest. 9 in. long.
409-V-6054 $6.99

Jumbo Cookie Spatula

Generously-sized spatula is great for handling multiple or oversized cookies, brownies, pastries and large treat bars. The easy-grip handle helps balance large cookies and desserts. Stainless steel; dishwasher safe. 11 in. long.
570-V-2018 $6.99

Seasonal

Wilton makes every time of year worth celebrating! With so many fun ways to serve cakes, cookies and other treats, it's easy to let everyone taste the excitement of each season.

Bakeware

Non-Stick Jack-O-Lantern Mini Cakes Pan
Bake fun single-size cakes, brownies and more. Non-stick steel releases treats easily. One mix makes 24 - 28 jack-o-lanterns, each 3.75 x 1.25 in. deep.
2105-V-1541
$11.99

Mini Ghost Pan
Create gobs of goblins at one time! One mix makes 9-15 ghosts ready for decorating. 6 cavities, each 4 x 4.9 x 1.4 in. deep. Aluminum.
2105-V-3845 $12.99

Iridescents! Jack-O-Lantern Pan
This bright, colorful shape is as much fun for serving party treats as it is for baking! Designed for quick, easy cake decorating. Also ideal for crisped rice cereal treats, molded gelatin, bread dough and more. One-mix pan is 11.75 x 11.2 x 2 in. deep. Aluminum.
2105-V-2059 $7.49

Petite Jack-O-Lantern Pan
Make personal petite smiling pumpkins. One mix makes 9-13 dozen jack-o-lanterns. 12 cavities, each 2 x 1.2 in. deep. Aluminum.
2105-V-8462 $11.99

SILICONE MOLDS
NEW!
Discover the convenience and easy release of flexible silicone bakeware! Freezer, refrigerator, microwave and dishwasher safe—oven safe to 500°F. $9.99

Mini Jack-O-Lantern Faces Mold
One mix makes 20-24 jack-o-lanterns. 6 cavities, each 2.5 x 1.5 in. deep.
2105-V-4939

Mini Spiders & Webs Mold
One mix makes 20-24 spiders and webs. 6 cavities, each 2.5 x 1.5 in. deep.
2105-V-4904

Icings
See Color Guide at right.

Striped Icing
Double the color, double the decorating excitement! Create fun 2-color decorations in colors perfect for the season. Tubes can be used with our Tip and Nail Set or Coupler Ring Set (p. 144) and any standard size Wilton metal tip. 4.25 oz. Certified Kosher.
Green/Black 704-V-201 $2.49
Orange/Black 704-V-202 $2.49

Tube Decorating Icing
Tubes can be used with our Tip and Nail Set or Coupler Ring Set (p. 144) and any standard size Wilton metal tip. Colors match Wilton Icing Colors (p. 148). 4.25 oz. Certified Kosher. $1.99
Orange 704-V-212
Black 704-V-206
Violet 704-V-242
White 704-V-200

Tube Decorating Gel
Transparent gels are great for writing messages and decorating cakes and cookies. Colors match Wilton Icing Colors (p. 148). .75 oz. Certified Kosher. $1.49
Orange 704-V-312
Black 704-V-306
Violet 704-V-342
White 704-V-302

NEW!

Sparkle Gel
Squeeze on sparkling color effects with our ready-to-use gel. Great for dots, messages and fondant accents. Resealable 3.5 oz. tube. Certified Kosher. $2.99
Orange 704-V-109
Black 704-V-1061
White 704-V-107

NEW!

Cookie Icing
Easy to use—just heat and squeeze onto cookies using the convenient cap. Sets smooth in just 45 minutes. 10 oz. bottle covers approximately 12 cookies, 3 in. each; 20 oz. bottle covers approx. 24. Certified Kosher.
10 oz. White 704-V-481 $4.49
20 oz. White 704-V-492 $7.99
10 oz. Orange 704-V-496 $4.49

Ready-to-Decorate Icing
Anyone can decorate with Wilton Ready-to-Decorate Icing! Our brilliant colors and 4 decorating tips make it a breeze to add an exciting finishing touch to treats—without mixing or mess. 6.4 oz. Certified Kosher. $4.29
Orange 710-V-4410
Black 710-V-4404
Violet 710-V-4408
White 710-V-4402

Colors

HALLOWEEN COLOR GUIDE

Orange	Black	Violet	White

Halloween Icing Colors Set
.5 oz. jars of Black and Orange. Certified Kosher.
601-V-3010 Set/2 $2.99

FoodWriter Edible Ink Markers
Add fun, dazzling color to foods. Decorate on fondant, color flow, royal icing designs and cookie icing. Includes Black and Orange markers (.07 oz. each). Certified Kosher.
609-V-101 Set/2 $4.19

Color Mist Food Color Spray
Gives decorators the versatility and dazzling effects of an airbrush in a convenient can! Use it to add sensational color to iced cookies and cupcakes. No mess, taste-free formula. 1.5 oz. Certified Kosher. $3.29
Orange 710-V-5507
Black 710-V-5506
Violet 710-V-5504

ORDER TOLL FREE: 800-794-5866

Party

Baking Cups
Microwave-safe paper. Standard size, 2 in. diameter; Mini size, 1.25 in. diameter.
**Standard Pk./75
Mini Pk./100
$2.09**

NEW!

**Haunted Manor
Standard 415-V-1114
Mini 415-V-1116**

**Boo! Scary!
Standard 415-V-1709
Mini 415-V-1710**

**Happy Haunters
Standard 415-V-961
Mini 415-V-962**

Boo! Scary!
Plastic.
2113-V-1307 Pk./12

Happy Haunters
Paper.
2113-V-9216 Pk./12

Party Bags
Colorful Halloween designs for candy and cookie treats. Unless otherwise noted, 20 plastic bags, 20 ties included. 4 x 9.5 in.
Pk./20 $2.09

NEW!

Fun Pix
Add a spooky touch to cakes, cupcakes, ice cream and more. Approx. 3½ in. high.
$2.09

NEW!

Haunted Manor Shaped Bags with Ties
Large bags are 6 x 9 in.
1912-V-1031 Pk./15 $2.09

**Haunted Manor
1912-V-1028**

**Boo! Scary!
1912-V-1225**

**Happy Haunters
1912-V-2389**

Icing Decorations
Perfect for topping cakes, cupcakes and cookies. Certified Kosher. **$2.29**

**Smiling Pumpkins
710-V-7200 Pk./12**

**Spiders & Bats
710-V-187 Pk./10**

Halloween Cupcake and Cookie Stencils
Just place one of the fun designs over your iced treat, then sprinkle with Wilton Cake Sparkles or Colored Sugars (p. 209) or spray with Color Mist Food Color Spray (p. 206). 8 designs.
417-V-499 $2.19

Happy Haunters Cupcake Boxes
Brightly-patterned window boxes are the perfect way to hold and display your cupcakes! Each box includes an insert with recessed space to hold standard cupcakes safely in place. Easy to fold assembly; great for gifts and favors! Holds 4 standard cupcakes. 6.25 x 6.25 x 3 in.
415-V-3220 Pk./3 $5.29

COOKIE TREAT PAN

Silicone Baking Cups
No muffin pan needed! Bake and serve in these reusable oven-safe cups. 6 violet, 6 orange.
Standard 415-V-9408 Pk./12 $9.99

Halloween Cupcakes 'N More Dessert Stand
Cupcakes are the perfect way to add a personal touch to your Halloween party! Great for caramel apples and party favor bags, too! 9.25 in. high x 9 in. wide. Holds 13 standard cupcakes. Patent No. 7,387,283.
307-V-828 $13.69

Jack-O-Lantern
Create cookie blossoms, rice cereal treats and candy pops. Recipe included. Six-cavity pan, each cavity measures 3.25 x .25 in. deep. Aluminum.
2105-V-8100 $9.99

Cookie Treat Sticks
**6 in. 1912-V-9319
Pk./20 $1.99
8 in. 1912-V-9318
Pk./20 $2.99**

SEASONAL

Candy

**Witch Fingers
Pretzel Mold**
2 designs, 6 cavities.
2115-V-1616 $1.99

**Mummies
Pretzel Mold**
1 design, 6 cavities.
2115-V-1783 $1.99

**Haunted Halloween
Pretzel Mold**
2 designs, 6 cavities.
2115-V-1417 $1.99

**Creepy Tombstone
Candy Mold**
Makes 3 creepy tombstones
with interchangeable bases.
2115-V-1415 $1.99

**Smiling Pumpkins
Lollipop Mold**
1 design, 7 cavities.
2115-V-1750 $1.99

Halloween Candy Kit for Pretzels

NEW!

Transform store-bought pretzels into candy-coated treats! It's Halloween fun for everyone with lots of spooky shapes and colorful Candy Melts. Everything you need is here—just add pretzels! Includes 3 molds: Mummy/Jack-O-Lantern (2 designs, 6 cavities), Witch Fingers (2 designs, 6 cavities), Spiders/Bats (2 designs, 6 cavities); 16 oz. Candy Melts (4 oz. each Light Cocoa, Orange, White and Green); 4 disposable decorating bags; decorating brush and 20 pretzels bags/ties. Certified Kosher Dairy.
2104-V-3236 $9.99

Halloween Candy Kit MEGA PACK

NEW!

Everything you need to have a howling good time making dozens of Halloween lollipops and candies. Spooky shaped molds and a great assortment of Candy Melts colors help you create the coolest treats in town. Kit includes: 3 molds: Monsters Large Lollipop (4 designs, 4 cavities), Spiders and Bats Candy (2 designs, 8 cavities, Ghost and Jack-O-Lantern Lollipop (2 designs, 6 cavities); 16 oz. Candy Melts (4 oz. each Light Cocoa, Orange, White and Green); 20 lollipop sticks (6 in.); 4 disposable decorating bags; decorating brush and 20 party bags/ties. Certified Kosher Dairy.
2104-V-3235 $9.99

Candy Melts

Ideal for molding, dipping or coating. Artificially vanilla flavored unless otherwise indicated. 14 oz. bag. Certified Kosher Dairy. **$2.99**

Orange	1911-V-1631
Yellow	1911-V-463
Dark Green	1911-V-405
Dark Cocoa	1911-V-358
Light Cocoa	1911-V-544
Dark Cocoa Mint	1911-V-1920
White	1911-V-498
Lavender	1911-V-403

NEW!

**Spooky Green
1911-V-488**

**Midnight Black
1911-V-489**

Halloween Candy Melts

Two creepy new colors make your homemade Halloween candies cooler than ever! Create ghoulish green or bonechilling black highlights on your favorite molded shapes. Artificially vanilla flavored. 10 oz. bag. Certified Kosher Dairy. **$2.99**

Halloween Candy Necklace Kit*

It's the perfect party activity—kit makes 8 tasty necklaces! Give each kid their own candy necklace pack and watch them have a ball stringing their own treats to wear and share. They'll love the cool colors and great flavors—and stringing the candy beads and charm is a breeze. Includes 8 necklace packs; each pack contains over 50 candy beads, 1 candy pumpkin charm and 17.5 in. elastic string.
2104-V-1274 $3.99

See pages 196-200 for more Wilton candy items.

⚠ *WARNING: CHOKING HAZARD
Small parts. Not for children under 3 years.

ORDER TOLL FREE: 800-794-5866

Sprinkles
INDIVIDUAL BOTTLES

Shake up your Halloween treats with fun colors and designs. Add a dash of dazzling color with Wilton Sugars and Cake Sparkles or pour on the texture with Wilton Sprinkle Mixes, a medley of festive seasonal shapes and colors. Plastic bottles for convenient pouring and storing. Certified Kosher.

Spider Mix
2.5 oz. bottle.
710-V-186 $2.29

Jumbo Ghost
3 oz. bottle.
710-V-567 $4.09

Hallow Pumpkin Mix
2.5 oz. bottle.
710-V-182 $2.29

Halloween Nonpareils
3 oz. bottle.
710-V-584 $2.29
5.25 oz. bottle.
710-V-183 $3.29

Orange Sugar
3.25 oz. bottle.
710-V-759
$2.29

Black Sugar
3.25 oz. bottle.
710-V-762
$2.29

Lavender Sugar
3.25 oz. bottle.
710-V-758
$2.29

Cake Sparkles

Edible glitter, .25 oz. bottle. Certified Kosher. **$3.19**

Orange
703-V-1308

Black
703-V-1302

Purple
703-V-1266

White
703-V-1290

6-Mix Halloween Pumpkin

Includes Black and Orange Nonpareils, Halloween Confetti, Hallow Pumpkin Mix, Black, Orange and Purple Sugars. 7.1 oz. Certified Kosher.
710-V-185 $5.99

Cookie Cutters
COMFORT-GRIP CUTTERS

These easy-grip cutters with extra-deep sides are perfect for cutting so many favorite foods into spectacular shapes. The cushion grip gives you comfortable control even when cutting thick desserts. Recipe included. Stainless steel sides, 4.5 x 4.5 x 1.5 in. deep. **$3.19**

Bat
2310-V-661

Pumpkin
2310-V-600

Ghost
2310-V-607

Witch's Hat
2310-V-630

4 PC. GRIPPY CUTTER SET

Safe, easy cutting, with a comfortable grip and deep plastic sides. Four shapes include cat, ghost, pumpkin and bat, approx. 3.5 in.
2311-V-257 Set/4 $4.49

Halloween Stackable! Cookie Cutter Set

NEW!

Use these fun shaped cutters to create a sensational, stackable 3-D cookie design! Just cut and bake the cookies using your favorite roll-out recipe, decorate with icing and stack them to make a terrific treat. Let the kids help— they'll love to create their own spooky spiders, bats and pumpkins. Stackable cookies are perfect for parties, favors and gift baskets. Other cutters just don't stack up!
2308-V-1296 Set/9 $9.99

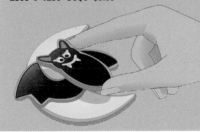 

Pre-Baked Cookie Kits

No baking, just fun! Everything you need is included to make great haunted designs.

Pre-Baked and Pre-Assembled Halloween Cookie House Kit

It's perfect for home, school or office celebrations—so easy and fun to make. Includes pre-baked, pre-assembled cookie house (measures 7 x 4 x 8 in. high), orange and black decorating icing mixes, colorful candy (Halloween mini round candies, orange, yellow and black jelly beans, purple round candies), 1 ghost icing decoration, 2 round decorating tips, 2 disposable decorating bags, cardboard base and complete decorating instructions.
2104-V-4319 $16.49

Pre-Baked Halloween Cookie House Kit

Easy to assemble and fun to decorate—it's the ideal family activity for Halloween. Includes 10 pre-baked gingerbread house pieces (assembled house measures 7 x 4 x 8 in. high), orange and black decorating icing mixes, 1 ghost icing decoration, colorful candy (Halloween mini round candies, jelly beans and candy corn), 2 decorating tips, 2 disposable decorating bags, cardboard base, complete assembly and decorating instructions.
2104-V-4318 $16.49

SEASONAL

Cookie

NEW!

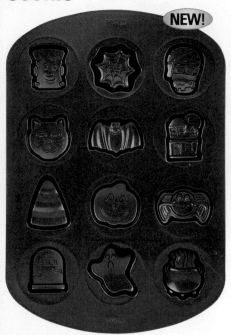

Halloween Cookie Shapes Non-Stick Pan

Includes 12 classic shapes for your Halloween cookies and single-serving molded desserts. 12 cavities, each approximately 2.75 x 2.25 x .25 in. deep.
2105-V-8131 $11.99

Halloween Push 'N Print Cutter Set

Serve cookies that make a great impression—use Push 'N Print Cutters to emboss a fun design before baking! It's so easy! Load one of the 3 imprint disks in the cutter, cut the cookie, then press the plunger with disk still in place to imprint the design. Bake, cool and serve a treat that's perfect for celebrations and cookie gift baskets. Great for embossed fondant decorations too! Disks are 2.9 in. diameter. Recipe included.
2308-V-4002 Set/4 $7.99

METAL CUTTERS

Put variety in your cookie making with fun Halloween multi-shape sets. There are styles to please everyone. Recipe included.

18 Pc. Halloween Cutter Set

Set of 18 includes witch, pumpkin, cat, coffin, maple leaf, house, apple, witch's broom, tombstone, moon, candy corn, bat, ghost, spider, spider web, Frankenstein, oak leaf and cauldron, each approx. 3 in.
2308-V-1131 Set/18 $10.49

3 Pc. Halloween Cutter Set

Set of 3 includes pumpkin, ghost and cat. Each approx. 3 in. Coated metal.
2308-V-1265 Set/3 $3.69

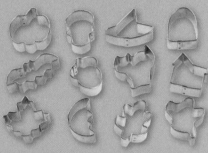

12 Pc. Halloween Mini Cutter Set

Set includes pumpkin, skull, witch's hat, tombstone, bat, acorn, cat, house, maple leaf, moon, oak leaf and ghost, each approx. 1.5 to 2.25 in.
2308-V-1246 Set/12 $5.29

6 Pc. Halloween Mini Cutter Set

Set includes cat, pumpkin, bat, skull, ghost and moon, each approx. 1.5 in.
2308-V-1211 Set/6 $3.19

9 Pc. Halloween Cutter Set

Set includes bat, ghost, cat, witch, moon, witch's broom, tombstone, house and pumpkin, each approx. 3 to 3.75 in. Colored aluminum.
2308-V-2501 Set/9 $10.49

4 Pc. Spooky Shapes Cutter Set

Set includes moon, pumpkin, witch and ghost, each approx. 3 in. Coated metal.
2308-V-1200 Set/4 $4.79

4 Pc. Nesting Cutter Sets

Create boo-tiful Halloween treats in 4 sizes. Each cuts neatly and is easy to handle. Sizes from 2.25 to 4.5 in.
Set/4 $4.79

Ghosts
2308-V-1238

Pumpkins
2308-V-1210

Bakeware

Silicone Mini Leaf and Pumpkin Mold
Freezer, refrigerator, microwave and dishwasher safe; oven safe to 500°F. One mix makes 20-24 cakes. 6 cavities, each 2.6 x 2.5 x 1.5 in. deep.
2105-V-4874 **$9.99**

Pumpkin Pie Pan
Holds one 15 oz. can of pumpkin pie filling. Use for apple, peach and cherry pies, too! Ideal for ready-to-bake pie crusts. 9 x 1.5 in. deep. Aluminum.
2105-V-3970 **$8.49**

DIMENSIONS DECORATIVE BAKEWARE

With Dimensions Non-Stick Cast Aluminum Bakeware, anyone can create desserts with elegant shapes and spectacular detail. Heavyweight cast aluminum conducts heat extremely evenly. Premium non-stick surface for easy release and cleanup. Aluminum.

Multi-Cavity Pumpkin
Finished cakes 3.4 x 3.4 in. 5 cup total capacity.
2105-V-1183 **$30.99**

Party

Baking Cups
Microwave-safe paper. Standard size, 2 in. diameter; Mini size, 1.25 in. diameter.
Standard Pk./75
Mini Pk./100
$2.09

Autumn Leaves
Standard
415-V-431
Mini
415-V-433

Harvest
Standard
415-V-2160
Mini
415-V-417

Party Bags
Colorful Autumn designs for candy and cookie treats. 20 plastic bags, 20 ties included. 4 x 9.5 in.
Pk./20 **$2.09**

Autumn Leaves
1912-V-1430

Harvest
1912-V-1288

Icing Decorations
Wilton Icing Decorations are perfect for topping cakes, cupcakes and cookies. Certified Kosher.
$2.29

Petite Leaves
710-V-230
Pk./12

Mini Pumpkins
710-V-538
Pk./18

Candy

Scarecrows Lollipop Mold
2 designs, 4 cavities.
2115-V-1613 **$1.99**

Pumpkin Harvest Pretzel Mold
2 designs, 6 cavities.
2115-V-1420 **$1.99**

Candy Melts
Ideal for all your candy making—molding, dipping or coating. Artificially vanilla flavored unless otherwise indicated. 14 oz. bag. Certified Kosher Dairy. **$2.99**

Red	1911-V-499	Dark Cocoa	1911-V-358
Light Cocoa	1911-V-544	Dark Cocoa	
Orange	1911-V-1631	Mint	1911-V-1920
Yellow	1911-V-463	White	1911-V-498
Dark Green	1911-V-405	Peanut Butter	1911-V-481

See pages 196-200 for more Wilton candy items.

Sprinkles

Individual Bottles
Plastic bottles for convenient pouring and storing. Certified Kosher.

Autumn Pumpkin Mix
2.5 oz. bottle.
710-V-7206 **$2.29**

Jumbo Leaves Mix
3.25 oz. bottle.
710-V-565 **$4.09**

Leaves Mix
2.5 oz. bottle.
710-V-787
$2.29

Red Sugar
3.25 oz. bottle.
710-V-766
$2.29

Dark Green Sugar
3.25 oz. bottle.
710-V-764 **$2.29**

Cake Sparkles
Edible glitter in .25 oz. bottle. Certified Kosher. **$3.19**

Red
703-V-1284

Dark Green
703-V-1278

Orange
703-V-1308

Yellow
703-V-1272

6-Mix Assortment
Includes Yellow, Red, Orange and Light Green Sugar, Leaves Mix and Chocolate Jimmies. 7.2 oz. Certified Kosher.
710-V-751 **$5.99**

Cookie

Comfort-Grip Cutters
Cushion grip cutters have extra-deep stainless steel sides. Great for cutting, cushion grip gives comfortable control. Recipe included. Approx. 4.5 x 1.5 in. deep.
$3.19

Maple Leaf
2310-V-632

Oak Leaf
2310-V-633

Autumn Cupcake & Cookie Stencils
Just place one of the fun designs over your baked treat, then sprinkle with Wilton Cake Sparkles or Colored Sugars (shown at left) or spray with Color Mist Food Color Spray (p. 148). 8 designs.
417-V-495 **$2.19**

METAL CUTTERS

Sure-to-please shapes. Recipe included.

3 Pc. Harvest Cutter Set
Includes turkey, pumpkin and leaf, each approx. 3 to 3.5 in. Coated metal.
2308-V-1264
Set/3 **$3.69**

9 Pc. Leaves and Acorns Nesting Cutter Set
Graduated acorns, oak and maple leaves, (3 each). 1.75 to 3.75 in.
2308-V-2000 Set/9 **$6.29**

6 Pc. Harvest Mini Cutter Set
Oak leaf, maple leaf, apple, pumpkin, elm leaf and acorn, approx. 1.5 in.
2308-V-1217 Set/6 **$3.19**

SEASONAL

Bakeware

Iridescents! Tree Pan

This bright, colorful shape is as much fun for serving party treats as it is for baking! Designed for quick, easy decorating. Also ideal for crisped rice cereal treats, molded gelatin, bread dough and more. One-mix pan is 14 x 10 x 2 in. deep. Aluminum.
2105-V-2081 **$7.49**

Mini Snowman Pan

Bake a blizzard of snowmen! One mix makes 12-18 snowmen. 6 cavities, each 2.9 x 4.6 x 1.9 in. deep. Aluminum.
2105-V-472 **$12.99**

Bite-Size Gingerbread Boy Pan

Bake plenty of fun little guys for everyone. One mix makes 24-36 boys. 9 cavities, each 2.75 x 3.4 x .75 in. deep. Aluminum.
2105-V-926 **$12.99**

DIMENSIONS DECORATIVE BAKEWARE

Heavyweight cast aluminum conducts heat extremely evenly. Premium non-stick surface for easy release and cleanup.

4-Cavity Mini Snowflakes

Finished cakes 5 x 2.25 in.; 7 cup total capacity.
2105-V-5028 **$30.99**

Mini Snowman/ Stocking Pan

NEW!

Two favorite seasonal shapes create delightful holiday cakes and treats. One mix makes 12-18. 6 cavities, each approximately 4 x 1.25 in. deep. Aluminum.
2105-V-4897 **$14.49**

SILICONE MOLDS

Discover the convenience and easy release of flexible silicone bakeware! Freezer, refrigerator, microwave and dishwasher safe—oven safe to 500°F.

Petite Snowflake Mold

NEW!

One mix makes 40-48 snowflakes. 12 cavities, each 2.25 x 1 in. deep.
2105-V-4920 **$9.99**

Mini Snowflake Mold

One mix makes 20-24 snowflakes. 6 cavities, each 2.5 x 1.5 in. deep.
2105-V-4831 **$9.99**

Petite Tree Mold

One mix makes 40-48 trees. 12 cavities, each 2 x 1 in. deep.
2105-V-4898 **$9.99**

Mini Tree Mold

One mix makes 20-24 trees. 6 cavities, each 2.5 x 1 in. deep.
2105-V-4830 **$9.99**

Gingerbread Boys and Trees Non-Stick Mini Cakes Pan

Non-stick steel releases treats easily and delivers great detail. One mix makes 16 gingerbread boys and trees. 6 cavities, each approximately 2.8 x 3.7 x 1.3 in. deep.
2105-V-1515 **$11.99**

Mini Stocking/ Gingerbread Boy/Tree Mold

NEW!

One mix makes 20-24 stockings/gingerbread boys and trees, each approximately 2.5 x 1.5 in. deep.
2105-V-4893 **$9.99**

Cookie

Holiday Cookie Shapes Pan

Includes 12 classic shapes for your single-serving holiday cookies and molded desserts. 12 cavities, each approximately 2.75 x 2.25 x .25 in. deep.
2105-V-8122 **$11.99**

Icings

NEW!

See Color Guide at right.

Striped Icing

Double the color, double the decorating excitement! Create fun 2-color decorations in colors perfect for the season. Tubes can be used with our Tip and Nail Set or Coupler Ring Set (p. 144) and any standard size Wilton metal tip. Colors match Wilton Icing Colors (p. 148). 4.25 oz. Certified Kosher.
Green/Red 704-V-204 **$2.49**
Red/White 704-V-203 **$2.49**

Ready-to-Decorate Icing

Anyone can decorate with Wilton Ready-to-Decorate Icing! Our brilliant colors and four decorating tips make it a breeze to add an exciting finishing touch to treats—without mixing or mess. 6.4 oz. Certified Kosher. **$4.29**
Green 710-V-4401
Red 710-V-4400
White 710-V-4402

Tube Decorating Icing

Can be used with our Tip and Nail Set or Coupler Ring Set (p. 144) and any standard size Wilton metal tip. Colors match Wilton Icing Colors (p. 148). 4.25 oz. Certified Kosher. **$1.99**
Kelly Green 704-V-227
Red 704-V-218
Leaf Green 704-V-224
White 704-V-200

Cookie Icing

Easy to use—just heat and squeeze onto cookies using the convenient cap. Sets smooth in just 45 minutes. 10 oz. bottle covers approximately 12 cookies, 3 in. each; 20 oz. bottle covers approx. 24. Certified Kosher.
10 oz. Green 704-V-493 **$4.49**
10 oz. White 704-V-481 **$4.49**
20 oz. White 704-V-492 **$7.99**
10 oz. Red 704-V-488 **$4.49**

Sparkle Gel

Squeeze on sparkling color effects with our ready-to-use gel. Great for dots, messages and fondant accents. Resealable 3.5 oz. tube. Certified Kosher. **$2.99**
Green 704-V-111
Red 704-V-112
White 704-V-107
Gold 704-V-1060 **NEW!**

Tube Decorating Gel

Transparent gels are great for writing messages and decorating cakes and cookies. Colors match Wilton Icing Colors (p. 148). .75 oz. Certified Kosher. **$1.49**
Leaf Green 704-V-324
Red 704-V-318
White 704-V-302

Party

Baking Cups

Microwave- safe paper. Standard size, 2 in. diameter; Mini size, 1.25 in. diameter.
Standard
Pk./75
Mini
Pk./100
$2.09

NEW!

Snowflake Wishes Standard
415-V-1245
Mini 415-V-1246
Patent Pending.

Shiver Me Snowman Standard
415-V-5766
Mini 415-V-5765

Santa Standard
415-V-5295
Mini 415-V-5405

NEW!

Shiver Me Snowman Treat Box Kit

With these holiday treat boxes, the party begins! Fill the colorful boxes with candy, cookies or other small treats, then add a fun to/from gift sticker. Includes 3 boxes 4.5 x 4.5 x 1.5 in. deep, 1 sticker sheet.
415-V-9472 Set/3 $3.19

Party Bags

NEW!

Colorful Christmas designs for candy and cookie treats. 20 plastic bags, 20 ties included.
4 x 9.5 in.
Pk./20 $2.09

Snowflake Wishes
1912-V-1309

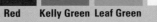

Shiver Me Snowman
1912-V-9140

Santa
1912-V-1325

NEW!

Icing Decorations

Perfect for topping cakes, cupcakes and cookies
Certified Kosher.
$2.29

Petite Winter Splendor
710-V-543 Pk./12

Snowman
710-V-349 Pk./9

Shiver Me Snowman Cookie Box Kit

What a welcome gift—your homemade cookies presented in our merry holiday boxes! The windowbox design lets your beautiful cookies show through, while colorful stickers let friends know you made them yourself! Includes 3 boxes 6.75 x 6.25 x 3 in. deep, 1 sticker sheet.
415-V-1301 Set/3 $5.29

Snowflake Wishes Shaped Bags with Ties

NEW!

Large bags are 6 x 9 in.
1912-V-1310
Pk./15 $2.09

Red/Green Mini Cups

Mixed, glassine paper.
1 in.
1912-V-1247 Pk./72 $1.59

Petite Loaf Baking Cups

For gift breads. White paper. Fits Petite Loaf Pan (p.159).
415-V-450 Pk./50 $1.59

Christmas Cookie Gift Bag Set

Wrap up a festive holiday cookie gift with colorful bags, ribbons and tags. Includes 3 each 16 x 20 inch bags, tags and 18 in. ribbon.
415-V-1302
Set/3 $4.19

Candy Cups

Perfect for holiday sweets! 1 in. dia.
Pk./75 $1.59
Red Foil 415-V-314
Silver Foil 415-V-307
Gold Foil 415-V-306

Christmas Cupcake and Cookie Stencils

Turn plain treats into holiday visions. Just place 1 of the 8 fun designs over your iced treat, then sprinkle with Wilton Cake Sparkles or Colored Sugars (p. 214) or use FoodWriter Edible Ink Markers or Color Mist Food Color Spray (below). 8 designs.
417-V-510 $2.19

Colors

CHRISTMAS COLOR GUIDE

Red	**Kelly Green**	**Leaf Green**	**White**

Holiday Icing Colors Set

Red-Red and Kelly Green in .5 oz. jars.
Certified Kosher.
601-V-3011 Set/2
$2.99

FoodWriter Edible Color Markers

Add fun, dazzling color to countless foods. Kids love 'em! Decorate on fondant, color flow, royal icing designs and cookie icing. Includes Green and Red markers (.07 oz. each). Certified Kosher.
609-V-102 Set/2 $4.19

Color Mist Food Color Spray

The dazzling effects of an airbrush in a convenient can! Use it to add sensational color to iced cakes, cookies and cupcakes. No mess, taste-free formula. 1.5 oz. Certified Kosher. **$3.29**
Green   710-V-5503
Red   710-V-5500

SEASONAL

Candy

Pretzel Molds

Easy to mold, fun to eat. Position pretzel rod, spoon in your favorite melted Candy Melts and refrigerate to set. Use with lollipop sticks, too.

NEW!

Santa/Reindeer Pretzel Mold
2 designs, 6 cavities.
2115-V-1572 **$1.99**

Santa Pretzel Mold
1 design, 6 cavities.
2115-V-1501 **$1.99**

Christmas Trees Pretzel Mold
1 design, 6 cavities.
2115-V-1747 **$1.99**

Candy Cane Molds

NEW!

Add a new twist to store-bought candy canes by molding a fun candy character on them! Fill mold cavities with your favorite melted Candy Melts, position candy cane and refrigerate to set.

Santa Claus Candy Cane Mold
2 designs, 2 cavities.
2115-V-1575 **$1.99**

Frosty Friends Candy Cane Mold
2 designs, 2 cavities.
2115-V-1573 **$1.99**

NEW!

Snowflake Large Lollipop Mold
3 designs, 3 cavities.
2115-V-1571 **$1.99**

Santa Lollipop Mold
1 design, 9 cavities.
2115-V-1706 **$1.99**

Christmas Candy Kit for Pretzels

NEW!

Transform store-bought pretzels into candy-coated treats! It's holiday fun for everyone with lots of merry designs and colorful Candy Melts. Everything you need is here—just add pretzels! Includes 3 molds: Presents (1 design, 6 cavities), Snowman & Snowflake (2 designs, 6 cavities), Santa (1 design, 6 cavities); 16 oz. Candy Melts (4 oz. each Light Cocoa, White, Red and Green); 4 disposable decorating bags; decorating brush and 20 pretzel bags/ties.
2104-V-3238 **$9.99**

Christmas Candy Kit MEGA PACK

NEW!

Everything you need to have a jolly time making dozens of Christmas lollipops and candies. Festive shaped molds and a great assortment of Candy Melts colors help you create the coolest treats in town. Kit includes: 3 molds: Christmas Characters Lollipop (3 designs, 6 cavities), Snowflake Lollipop (1 design, 9 cavities), Decorated Trees Large Lollipop (3 designs, 3 cavities); 16 oz. Candy Melts (4 oz. each Light Cocoa, Orange, White and Green); 20 lollipop sticks (6 in.); 4 disposable decorating bags; decorating brush and 20 party bags/ties.
2104-V-3237 **$9.99**

Candy Melts

Ideal for molding, dipping or coating. Artificially vanilla flavored unless otherwise indicated. 14 oz. bag. Certified Kosher Dairy. **$2.99**

Red	1911-V-499	Dark Cocoa	1911-V-358
White	1911-V-498	Dark Cocoa Mint	1911-V-1920
Dark Green	1911-V-405	Yellow	1911-V-463
Light Cocoa	1911-V-544		

See pages 196-200 for more Wilton candy items.

Sprinkles

Jumbo Sprinkles

Try our Jumbo Sprinkles—big bold toppers perfect for cookies, brownies and more. Plastic bottles for convenient pouring and storing. Certified Kosher. **$4.09**

Trees
2.8 oz. bottle.
710-V-568

Snowflakes
2.6 oz. bottle.
710-V-569

Gingerbread Boys
2.75 oz. bottle.
710-V-586

Individual Bottles

Shake up your holiday treats with fun colors and designs. Plastic bottles for convenient pouring and storing. Certified Kosher.

Twinkling Trees Mix
2.5 oz. bottle.
710-V-696 **$2.29**

Christmas Confetti
2 oz. bottle.
710-V-172 **$2.29**

Snowflake Mix
2.5 oz. bottle.
710-V-797 **$2.29**

Christmas Nonpareils
3 oz. 710-V-585 **$2.29**
5.25 oz. 710-V-173 **$3.29**

Cinnamon Drops
3 oz. bottle.
710-V-769 **$2.29**

Chocolate Jimmies
2.5 oz. bottle.
710-V-774 **$2.29**

Red Sugar
3.25 oz. bottle.
710-V-766 **$2.29**

Dark Green Sugar
3.25 oz. bottle.
710-V-764 **$2.29**

Sparkling Sugars

Easy-pour sugars have a coarse texture and brilliant sparkle. 8 oz. bottle. Certified Kosher. **$4.49**

Holiday Mix
710-V-308

Red/White
710-V-998

Green/White
710-V-997

Cake Sparkles

Edible glitter in .25 oz. bottle. Certified Kosher. **$3.19**

Red
703-V-1284

Green
703-V-1278

White
703-V-1290

6-Mix Assortment

Includes Christmas Nonpareils, Confetti, Twinkling Trees Mix, Green and Red Sugar and Christmas Jimmies. 6.8 oz. Certified Kosher.
710-V-755 **$5.99**

Christmas Cookie Tree Cutter Kit

Create a beautiful Yule tree as a perfect holiday centerpiece. . . it's easy and fun! Just bake, stack and decorate. Kit includes 10 plastic star cookie cutters in graduated sizes, 3 disposable decorating bags, round decorating tip, cookie and icing recipes, baking and decorating instructions for 4 great designs. Tree measures approx. 8 x 11 in. high when assembled.
2104-V-1555 **$7.99**

ORDER TOLL FREE: 800-794-5866

Gingerbread Kits

NEW!

Pre-Baked Gingerbread House Kit

Includes pre-baked gingerbread pieces, icing mix, assorted candies, decorating bag and tip, cardboard base, complete instructions and decorating ideas. House measures 8 x 7 x 6.5 in. high.
2104-V-1509 $16.49

Pre-Baked/ Pre-Assembled Gingerbread House Kit

Includes assembled house with cardboard base, icing mix, candies, decorating bag and tip, complete instructions and decorating ideas. House measures 5.5 x 5.5 x 4.5 in. high.
2104-V-1516 $16.49

Pre-Baked Giant Gingerbread House Kit

A big, big house with more candy for more fun! Enough goodies for everyone to join in the excitement of building and decorating! Everything you need is inside—6 pre-baked house pieces and 2 pre-baked gingerbread kids, 3 packets of icing mix, 3 decorating bags and 2 tips, loads of candy for decorating and complete instructions for assembling and decorating. House measures 8.25 in. high x 9 in. wide x 8.5 in. deep.
2104-V-4689 $39.99

Pre-Baked Gingerbread House Kit

Includes pre-baked house pieces, icing mix, assorted candies, decorating bag and tip, cardboard base, complete instructions and decorating ideas. House measures 5.25 x 5.5 x 4.75 in. high.
2104-V-1537 $12.99

Pre-Baked Gingerbread Boy Cookie Decorating Kit

Decorate 8 fun cookies! Great for gifts or special treats. Includes cookies, icing mix, colorful candies, decorating bag, tip and complete instructions.
2104-V-1090 $12.99

Pre-Baked Gingerbread Tree Kit

Just stack pre-baked star cookies, decorate with icing and candy and add the star icing decoration tree top! Includes cookies, white and green icing mix, icing decorations, candies, 2 decorating tips, 2 decorating bags and complete instructions. Tree measures 5.5 x 8.25 in. high.
2104-V-2621 $12.99

Gingerbread Accessories

NEW!

Time for some home improvement! We have the perfect add-ons for your gingerbread projects— easy-mix icing to complete construction and decorate, fun candies to brighten the look and a convenient stand to display your design.

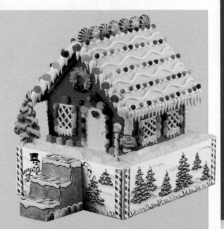

Frosty White Icing Mix

Mixes to the perfect texture for assembling and decorating gingerbread! Sets up and dries quickly for great results. Excellent for lattice, garland, icicle and scallop details on houses; great for decorating details on cookies. 14 oz.
2104-V-6001 $4.49

Handmade Icing Decorations

Delightful details add the charm that makes your gingerbread house a home! Nine fun shapes include: snowman, girl, boy, wreath, Santa, reindeer, gingerbread boy, tree and bear.
2104-V-6025 Pk./9 $6.49

Holiday Candies Assortment

Light up your gingerbread home or dress up gingerbread boy cookies with candies in dazzling holiday colors! Four bright shapes include mini tree and star candies, mini gum drops and green leaves; 3 oz. of each candy. Decorating instructions included on package.
2104-V-6002 $6.49

Gingerbread House Stand Kit

Display your house with pride and create the ideal holiday centerpiece—complete with fun accents to give your design even more seasonal spirit! Kit includes easy-to-assemble centerpiece stand, stairs, personalized sign and tree. Complete instruction sheet included. Assembled stand is 3 x 9.25 x 8 in. Fits house with baseboard no larger than 6.5 in. x 8.5 in.
1509-V-6004 $5.99

SEASONAL

CHRISTMAS
Cookie Cutters

Christmas Push 'N Print Cutter Set

Serve cookies that make a great impression—use Push 'N Print Cutters to emboss a fun design before baking! It's so easy! Load one of the 3 imprint disks in the cutter, cut the cookie, then press the plunger with disk still in place to imprint the design. Bake, cool and serve a treat that's perfect for celebrations and cookie gift baskets. Great for embossed fondant decorations too! Disks are 2.9 in. diameter. Recipe included.
2308-V-4003 Set/4 $7.99

COMFORT-GRIP CUTTERS

These easy-grip cutters with extra-deep sides are perfect for cutting so many favorite foods into spectacular shapes. The cushion grip gives you comfortable control even when cutting thick desserts. Recipe included. Stainless steel sides, 4.5 x 4.5 x 1.5 in. deep. $3.19

NEW!

Gingerbread House
2310-V-662

Candy Cane
2310-V-644

Santa Hat
2310-V-640

Christmas Tree
2310-V-604

Gingerbread Boy
2310-V-602

Mitten
2310-V-639

Snowman
2310-V-634

Star
2310-V-631

4-PC. GRIPPY CUTTER SET

Safe, easy cutting, with a comfortable grip and deep plastic sides. Four shapes include stocking, tree, star and gingerbread boy, each approx. 3.5 in.
2311-V-260
Set/4 $4.49

Holiday Red Cookie Scoop

Festive color and convenient design make holiday baking more fun! Scoops and releases approx. 1 tablespoon of dough with ease. Dishwasher safe plastic.
417-V-320 $2.79

Plastic Cutters

Great shapes for end-of-year celebrations! 3 x 4 in. high. $0.69

5-Pt. Star
2303-V-135

Christmas Tree
2303-V-132

METAL CUTTERS

Put variety in your cookie-making with fun Christmas multi-shape sets. There are styles to please everyone. Recipe included.

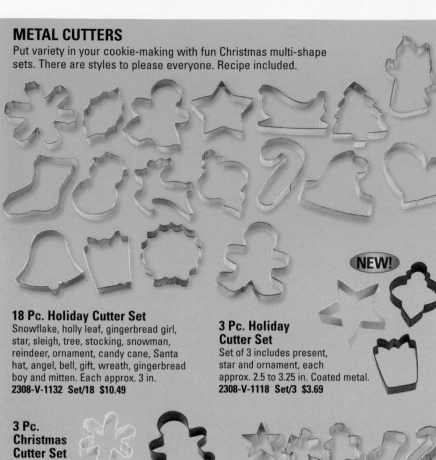

NEW!

18 Pc. Holiday Cutter Set

Snowflake, holly leaf, gingerbread girl, star, sleigh, tree, stocking, snowman, reindeer, ornament, candy cane, Santa hat, angel, bell, gift, wreath, gingerbread boy and mitten. Each approx. 3 in.
2308-V-1132 Set/18 $10.49

3 Pc. Holiday Cutter Set

Set of 3 includes present, star and ornament, each approx. 2.5 to 3.25 in. Coated metal.
2308-V-1118 Set/3 $3.69

3 Pc. Christmas Cutter Set

Set of 3 includes snowflake, gingerbread boy and tree, each approx. 3 to 3.75 in. Coated metal.
2308-V-1266 Set/3 $3.69

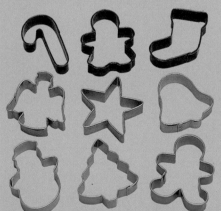

12 Pc. Holiday Mini Cutter Set

Star, angel, gingerbread girl, stocking, candy cane, teddy bear, bell, holly leaf, tree, gingerbread boy, ornament, and sleigh. Each approx. 1.5 in.
2308-V-1250 Set/12 $5.29

6 Pc. Holiday Mini Cutter Set

Bell, gingerbread boy, holly leaf, tree, candy cane and angel, each approx. 1.5 in.
2308-V-1214
Set/6 $3.19

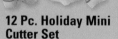

9 Pc. Holiday Cutter Set

Candy cane, gingerbread girl, stocking, angel, star, bell, snowman, tree and gingerbread boy, each approx. 3 to 3.75 in. Colored aluminum.
2308-V-2500 Set/9 $10.49

4 Pc. Nesting Cutter Sets

Bake your favorite holiday shapes in four fun sizes! Quality metal cuts neatly and is easy to handle. Sizes from 5 to 2.5 in.
Set/4 $4.79

Snowflakes
2308-V-1244

Gingerbread Boys
2308-V-1239

4 Pc. Jolly Shapes Cutter Set

Stocking, star, tree and candy cane, each approx. 3 in. Coated metal.
2308-V-1201 Set/4 $4.79

Cookie Presses

Making traditional spritz cookies has never been so easy! Cookie Pro Ultra II is designed to be the easiest to fill, most comfortable press you've ever used. And, with 12 terrific shapes, plus 4 fun mini cookie designs, your holiday cookie baskets will be more festive than ever! Includes complete instructions and delicious recipes.
2104-V-4018 Set/17 $24.99

Twelve Disks in Festive Shapes

Plus 4 BONUS Disks For Mini Cookies!

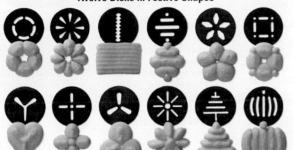

COOKIE MASTER™ Plus

Cordless Cookie Press

Our cordless cookie press is so powerful and easy to operate, you'll use it all year to create cookies, appetizers, desserts and more. Exclusive patented reverse action means there's no need to take press apart for refilling. Ergonomic design is shaped to fit in your hand for excellent comfort.

Includes 12 aluminum disks in classic and seasonal shapes, 4 accent tips for decorating and filling and 2 bonus recipe booklets—sweet and savory. Uses 4 AA batteries, not included. Patent Nos. D484,755, 6,701,828.
2104-V-4008 Set/19 $39.99

12 Disk Designs

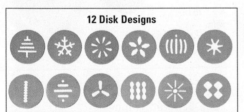

4 Accent Tips

Cookie Press

Experience a classic press that is truly comfortable. Its ergonomic handle feels great in your hand and the easy-squeeze action releases perfectly shaped dough. Clear barrel takes the guesswork out of refilling. Fluted bottom raises press off the cookie sheet for better-defined shapes. Includes 12 cookie disks in a variety of shapes and our classic spritz recipe.
2104-V-4011 Set/13 $12.99

12 Disk Designs

Bakeware

Recipe Right Non-Stick

Built with all the right qualities for better baking results. Pan dimensions are embossed on handles for easy reference. Heavy-gauge construction means pans spread heat evenly and won't warp. Non-stick coating provides exceptionally quick release and easy cleanup. 5-year warranty. Aluminum.

Non-Stick Parchment Paper
Use Wilton silicone-treated non-stick parchment to line baking pans and cookie sheets—a non-fat alternative that saves cleanup time. Double roll is 41 square feet, 15 in. wide. Certified Kosher.
415-V-680 $5.29

15 x 10 in. Cookie Sheet
2105-V-967 $5.49

12 Cup Muffin Pan
2105-V-954 $6.99

24 Cup Mini Muffin Pan
2105-V-914 $10.99

Bake Easy! Non-Stick Spray

This convenient non-stick spray helps your baked goods release perfectly. Just a light, even coating does the job. Use Bake Easy! for all mixes and recipes —cookies, muffins, cupcakes, brownies, breads and more. Versatile for all types of baking and cooking. 6 oz.
702-V-6018 $3.29

SEASONAL

Bakeware
DIMENSIONS DECORATIVE BAKEWARE

With Dimensions Non-Stick Cast Aluminum Bakeware everyone can create Valentine desserts with elegant shapes and spectacular detail. Heavyweight cast aluminum conducts heat evenly. Premium non-stick surface for easy release and cleanup.

Mini Heart
Each heart is 4 x 2 in. deep. Six 1 cup cavities.
Pat. No. D487,211.
2105-V-5012 $30.99

Queen Of Hearts
9 x 3.25 in. deep.
10 cup total capacity.
Pat. No. D478,466.
2105-V-5001 $30.99

SweetHeart Pan
Its gently curving shape gives the classic heart a more romantic flair. One-mix pan is 10.25 x 2 in. deep. Aluminum.
2105-V-1197 $12.99

Silicone Heart Molds
Discover the convenience and easy release of flexible silicone bakeware! Freezer, refrigerator, microwave and dishwasher safe—oven safe to 500°F. One mix makes 40-48 petite hearts; 20-24 mini hearts. Petite hearts each 1.5 x 1.5 x 1 in. deep. Mini hearts each 2.6 x 2.5 x 1.5 in. deep.

Ruffled Mini Heart Mold
2105-V-4861 $9.99

Mini Heart Mold
2105-V-4012 $9.99

Petite Heart Mold
2105-V-4860 $9.99

9 in. Non-Stick Heart Pan
Your classic heart cake will release perfectly. Cleanup is easy too. 9 x 2.25 in. deep. Non-stick steel.
2105-V-410 $13.99

Heart Pans
For graceful expressions of love on Valentine's Day or anytime, in just the size you need. 2 in. deep. Aluminum.
6 in. 2105-V-600 $7.49
9 in. 2105-V-5176 $8.99
12 in. 2105-V-607 $12.99

Non-Stick Mini Heart Pan
Perfect size for party petits fours, molded salads and more. Non-stick steel releases treats easily. One mix makes 20-24 hearts; 6 cavities, each 2.25 x 2.4 x 1.25 in. deep.
2105-V-1539 $8.99

Mini Heart Pan
Great size for petits fours, individual brownies and more. One mix makes 12-18 hearts. 6 cavities, each 3.5 x 1 in. deep. Aluminum.
2105-V-11044 $12.99

Petite Heart Pan
Bite-size muffins, brownies and cookies will win hearts. One mix makes 10-15 dozen hearts. 12 cavities, each 1.75 x 1.6 x .5 in. deep. Aluminum.
2105-V-2432 $11.99

Heart Springform Pans
Create elegant Valentine cheesecakes with these easy-releasing non-stick pans. Springlock sides, removable bottom for easy serving. Non-stick steel.

9 x 2.75 in.
Standard
2105-V-419
$21.49

4 x 1.75 in.
Mini
2105-V-457 $9.99

Icings

VALENTINE COLOR GUIDE

Red	Pink	Violet	White

Ready-to-Decorate Icing
Includes 4 decorating tips! Anyone can decorate with Wilton Ready-to-Decorate Icing. Add an exciting finishing touch to treats without mixing or mess. 6.4 oz. Certified Kosher.
$4.29
Red	710-V-4400
Pink	710-V-4406
Violet	710-V-4408
White	710-V-4402

Cookie Icing
Just heat and squeeze onto cookies using the convenient cap. Sets smooth in just 45 minutes. 10 oz. bottle covers approximately 12 cookies, 3 in. each; 20 oz. bottle covers approx. 24. Certified Kosher.
10 oz. White
704-V-481 $4.49
20 oz. White 704-V-492 $7.99
10 oz. Red 704-V-488 $4.49
10 oz. Pink 704-V-486 $4.49

Sparkle Gel
Squeeze on sparkling color effects with our ready-to-use gel. Great for dots, messages, water effects and fondant accents. Resealable 3.5 oz. tubes. Certified Kosher. **$2.99**
Red 704-V-112
Pink 704-V-356
White 704-V-107

NEW!

Tube Decorating Icing
Tubes can be used with our Tip and Nail Set or Coupler Ring Set (p. 144) and any standard size Wilton metal tip. Colors match Wilton Icing Colors (p. 148). 4.25 oz. Certified Kosher.
$1.99
Red	704-V-218
Pink	704-V-230
Violet	704-V-242
White	704-V-200

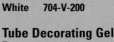

Tube Decorating Gel
Transparent gels are great for writing messages and decorating cakes and cookies. Colors match Wilton Icing Colors (p. 148). .75 oz. Certified Kosher.
$1.49
Red	704-V-318
Pink	704-V-330
Violet	704-V-342
White	704-V-302

Party

Baking Cups
Microwave-safe paper. Standard size, 2 in. diameter, Mini size, 1.25 in. diameter.
Standard Pk/75 $2.09
Mini Pk/100 $2.09

Sweetheart Bandana
Standard 415-V-1223
Mini 415-V-1224

Hearts
Standard 415-V-517
Mini 415-V-414

Party Bags
Colorful solid red and Valentine designs for candy and cookie treats. 20 plastic bags, 20 ties included. 4 x 9.5 in.
Pk./20 $2.09

Red Party Bags
(not shown.)
1912-V-2357

Sweetheart Bandana
1912-V-1084

Hearts
1912-V-1269

Heart Silicone Baking Cups
No muffin pan needed! Bake and serve in these reusable oven-safe cups. 6 red, 6 pink.
Standard 415-V-9409 Pk./12 $9.99
Mini 415-V-9425 Pk./12 $7.99

Candy Cups
Wax-laminated paper on red foil. 1 in. diameter
415-V-314 Pk./75 $1.59

Hearts Remembered Icing Decorations
Perfect for topping cakes, cupcakes and cookies. Certified Kosher.
710-V-824 Pk./18 $2.29

Sprinkles

Individual Bottles
Shake up your Valentine treats with fun colors and designs. Plastic bottles for convenient pouring and storing. Certified Kosher.

Hearts Mix
2.5 oz. bottle.
710-V-854 $2.29

Jumbo Hearts
3.25 oz. bottle.
710-V-032 $4.09

Valentine Nonpareils
3 oz. bottle.
710-V-625 $2.29
5.25 oz. bottle.
710-V-558 $3.29

Chocolate Hearts Mix
Naturally and artificially flavored.
2.5 oz. bottle.
710-V-622 $2.29
3.75 oz. bottle.
710-V-6315 $3.29

Sugars
3.25 oz. bottle. Certified Kosher. **$2.29**

Red
710-V-766

Pink
710-V-756

Lavender
710-V-758

Cake Sparkles
Edible glitter, .25 oz. bottle. Certified Kosher. **$3.19**

Red
703-V-1284

Pink
703-V-1260

Purple
703-V-1266

6-Mix Assortment
Includes 2 Heart Mixes, Sweetheart Nonpareils, Pink, Red and Lavender Sugars. 7.2 oz. Certified Kosher.
710-V-738 $5.99

Candy

NEW!

Rose Heart Pretzel Mold
1 design, 6 cavities.
2115-V-1494 $1.99

Love Pretzel Mold
2 designs, 6 cavities.
2115-V-1451 $1.99

Heart Pretzel Mold
1 design, 6 cavities.
2115-V-3025 $1.99

Kissy Lips Candy Mold
1 design, 8 cavities.
2115-V-1450 $1.99

Double Heart Large Lollipop Mold
2 designs, 4 cavities.
2115-V-4440 $1.99

Roses and Buds Lollipop Mold
3 designs, 9 cavities.
2115-V-1708 $1.99

Hearts Candy Mold
1 design, 15 cavities.
2115-V-1712 $1.99

Heart Candy Necklace Kit
NEW!

It's the perfect party activity—kit makes 8 tasty necklaces! Give each kid their own candy necklace pack and watch them have a ball stringing their own treats to wear and share. They'll love the cool colors and great flavors—and stringing the candy beads and charm is a breeze. Includes 8 necklace packs; each pack contains over 50 candy beads (artificial strawberry, blue raspberry and fruit punch flavors), 1 heart shaped charm (artificial strawberry flavor) and 17.5 in elastic string.
2104-V-1058 $2.99

Candy Melts
Ideal for molding, dipping or coating. Artificially vanilla flavored unless otherwise indicated. 14 oz. bag. Certified Kosher Dairy. **$2.99**

Red	**1911-V-499**
Pink	**1911-V-447**
White	**1911-V-498**
Light Cocoa	**1911-V-544**
Dark Cocoa	**1911-V-358**

Valentine Candy Making MEGA PACK
Lots of fun shapes and colorful Candy Melts! Kit includes: Bearing Love Large Lollipop Mold (3 designs, 3 cavities), Valentine Lollipop Mold (3 designs, 6 cavities), Hugs & Kisses Candy Mold (3 designs, 10 cavities); 16 oz. Candy Melts brand confectionery coating (4 oz. each light cocoa, white, red and pink); 20 lollipop sticks (6 in.); 4 disposable decorating brush and 20 party bags/ties. Certified Kosher Dairy.
2104-V-1651 $9.99

See pages 196-200 for more Wilton candy items.

Color Mist Food Color Spray
Gives decorators the versatility and dazzling effects of an airbrush in a convenient can! Use it to add sensational color to cakes, iced cookies and cupcakes. No mess, taste-free formula. 1.5 oz. Certified Kosher. **$3.29**

Red	**710-V-5500**
Pink	**710-V-5505**
Violet	**710-V-5504**

See Color Guide p. 218.

SEASONAL

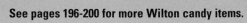

Cookie

Heart Giant Cookie Pan

Create a giant-sized pan cookie or brownie in a heart shape. Ideal for refrigerated dough and brownie mix. Recipe included. Pan is 11.5 x 10.5 x .5 in. deep. Aluminum.
2105-V-6203 $7.49

Heart Cookie Treat Pan

Just press cookie dough into pan, insert a cookie stick, then bake, cool and decorate. Also great for adding fun shapes to other goodies like rice cereal treats and candy pops. Each treat is 3.5 in. x .25 in. deep. Aluminum.
2105-V-8104 $9.99

Cookie Treat Sticks

6 in. 1912-V-9319 Pk./20 $1.99
8 in. 1912-V-9318 Pk./20 $2.99

6 Pc. Nesting Hearts Cutter Set

Great for cookies, imprinting patterns in icing, cutting bread shapes and more. Plastic in sizes from 2.25 to 4.2 in.
2304-V-115 Set/6 $2.99

Sweetheart Cupcake and Cookie Stencils

Just place one of the 8 fun designs over your baked or iced treat, then sprinkle with Wilton Cake Sparkles or Colored Sugars or spray with Color Mist Food Color Spray (p. 219).
417-V-494 $2.19

Valentine Push 'N Print Cutter Set

Emboss a fun design in cookies before baking! Load one of the 3 imprint disks in the cutter, cut the cookie, then press the plunger with disk still in place to imprint the design. Disks are 2.9 in. wide. Recipe included.
2308-V-4000 Set/4 $7.99

Comfort-Grip Cutters

Cushion-grip cutters with extra-deep stainless steel sides. The cushion grip gives you comfortable control even when cutting into thick desserts. Recipe included. 4.5 x 4.5 x 1.5 in. deep.
$3.19

**Heart
2310-V-616**

**Lips
2310-V-646**

**Double Heart
2310-V-647**

METAL CUTTERS

Put variety in your cookie-making with fun Valentine multi-shape sets. Recipe included.

9 Pc. Valentine Cutter Collection

Great variety of hearts, hugs and kisses designs from 1 to 5 in. Colored aluminum.
2308-V-2502 Set/9 $10.49

4 Pc. From The Heart Nesting Cutter Set

Includes 2 crinkled shapes. Largest cutter is approx. 5 in. Metal and coated metal.
2308-V-1203 Set/4 $4.79

Heart Cutters

Cuts neatly and is easy to handle. 3 in. wide.
**Red Metal
2308-V-1322 $0.79
Metal
2308-V-1003 $0.69**

7 Pc. Hearts Cutter Set

7 different heart cutter designs from stylized to traditional. Sizes range from 1.5 to 3 in.
2308-V-1237 Set/7 $5.29

6 Pc. Valentine Mini Cutter Set

Double heart, crinkle heart, heart with arrow, heart, O and X, each approx. 1.5 in.
2308-V-1255 Set/6 $3.19

Easter Icings

See Color Guide p. 221.

Ready-to-Decorate Icing

Includes 4 decorating tips! Anyone can decorate with Wilton Ready-to-Decorate Icing. Add an exciting finishing touch to treats without mixing or mess. 6.4 oz. Certified Kosher. **$4.29**
Pink 710-V-4406
White 710-V-4402
Violet 710-V-4408
Yellow 710-V-4409
Green 710-V-4401

Cookie Icing

Just heat and squeeze onto cookies using the convenient cap. Sets smooth in just 45 minutes. 10 oz. bottle covers approximately 12 cookies, 3 in. each; 20 oz. bottle covers approx. 24. Certified Kosher.
10 oz. White   704-V-481 $4.49
20 oz. White   704-V-492 $7.99
10 oz. Pink   704-V-486 $4.49
10 oz. Yellow   704-V-487 $4.49

Sparkle Gel

Squeeze on sparkling color effects with our ready-to-use gel. Great for dots, messages, water effects and fondant accents. Resealable 3.5 oz. tubes. Certified Kosher.
$2.99
Pink   704-V-356
Green   704-V-111
Yellow 704-V-108
White   704-V-107

 NEW!

Tube Decorating Icing

Tubes can be used with our Tip and Nail Set or Coupler Ring Set (p. 144) and any standard size Wilton metal tip. Colors match Wilton Icing Colors (p. 148). 4.25 oz. Certified Kosher. **$1.99**
Pink 704-V-230   Yellow 704-V-236
Violet 704-V-242   White 704-V-200
Leaf Green 704-V-224

Tube Decorating Gel

Great for writing messages and decorating cakes and cookies. Colors match Wilton Icing Colors (p. 148). .75 oz. Certified Kosher. **$1.49**
Pink   704-V-330   Green 704-V-324
Violet 704-V-342   White 704-V-302
Yellow 704-V-336

ORDER TOLL FREE: 800-794-5866

Bakeware

Step-By-Step Bunny Pan
Get springtime celebrations hopping—just bake, ice and decorate! He's also perfect for molding gelatin, ice cream, salads and more. One-mix pan is 9.75 x 14 x 2 in. deep. Aluminum.
2105-V-2074 $7.49

3-D Bunny Pan
Instructions for 5 different decorating ideas included. Two-piece pan bakes bunny approx. 7.25 x 4.75 x 7 in. high. Pan takes 4½ cups of pound cake batter. No heating core needed. Aluminum.
**2105-V-2042
Set/2 $14.49**

Stand-Up Lamb Pan
This 3-D lamb will charm everyone at your Easter table. Two-piece pan makes lamb 10 x 4.5 x 7 in. high; takes 6 cups of pound cake batter. Instructions included. Aluminum.
**2105-V-2010
Set/2 $14.49**

3-D Egg Pan
Hatch a great Easter centerpiece! Two-piece pan takes just one cake mix. Includes 2 ring bases for level baking of each half. Each half is 9 x 6 x 2.75 in. Aluminum.
**2105-V-4793
Set/4 $14.49**

EASTER COLOR GUIDE

Pink	Violet	Yellow	Green/Leaf Green	White

Color Mist Food Color Spray
Gives decorators the versatility and dazzling effects of an airbrush in a convenient can! Use it to add sensational color to cakes, iced cookies and cupcakes. No mess, taste-free formula. 1.5 oz. Certified Kosher. **$3.29**
Pink   710-V-5505
Violet   710-V-5504
Yellow 710-V-5502
Green   710-V-5503

6-Cavity Non-Stick Mini Cake Pans
Mini cakes are fun to serve at Easter brunch or wrap them up and add to baskets. Easy-release, easy-clean non-stick steel bakes cakes with great detail. Also excellent for brownies, ice cream molds, muffins and more.

Flower
Each cavity 4 x 4 x 1.5 in. deep. One mix makes about 14 cakes.
2105-V-5490 $11.99

Decorated Egg
Each cavity 4.2 x 2.9 x 1.5 in. deep. One mix makes about 14 cakes.
2105-V-1550 $11.99

Bunny
Each cavity 4 x 2.6 x 1.2 in. deep. One mix makes about 18 cakes.
2105-V-1551 $11.99

Cross Pan
Truly inspiring for holidays, Christenings and other religious occasions. Bevel design is excellent with rolled fondant. One-mix pan is 14.5 x 11.2 x 2 in. deep. Instructions included. Aluminum.
2105-V-2509 $9.99

Cookie

Easter Push 'N Print Cutter Set
Emboss a fun design before baking! It's so easy! Load one of the 3 imprint disks in the cutter, cut the cookie, then press the plunger with disk still in place to imprint the design. Disks are 2.9 in. wide. Recipe included.
2308-V-4001 Set/4 $7.99

Silicone Molds
Discover the convenience and easy release of flexible silicone bakeware! Freezer, refrigerator, microwave and dishwasher safe; oven safe to 500°F.

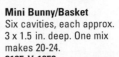

Mini Bunny/Basket
Six cavities, each approx. 3 x 1.5 in. deep. One mix makes 20-24.
**2105-V-1052
$9.99**

 **NEW!**

Mini Decorated Egg
Six cavities, each 3.5 x 1.5 in. deep. One mix makes 20-24 eggs.
**2105-V-4847
$9.99**

Petite Easter Egg
Twelve cavities, each 1.75 x 1.5 in. deep. One mix makes 40-48 eggs.
**2105-V-4864
$9.99**

Cookie Pans

Easter Cookie Shapes Non-Stick Pan
NEW!
Includes 12 classic shapes for your holiday cookies and single-serving molded desserts. 12 cavities, each approximately 2.75 x 2.25 x .25 in. deep.
**2105-V-8129
$11.99**

Bunny Cookie Treat Pan
Just press cookie dough into pan, insert a cookie stick, then bake, cool and decorate. Each treat is 3.5 x 2.75 x .25 in. deep. Aluminum.
2105-V-8106 $9.99

Cookie Treat Sticks
6 in. 1912-V-9319 Pk./20 $1.99
8 in. 1912-V-9318 Pk./20 $2.99

SEASONAL

Party

Baking Cups
Microwave-safe paper. Standard size, 2 in. diameter; Mini size, 1.25 in. diameter.
Standard
Pk./75 $2.09
Mini
Pk./100 $2.09

Spring Party
Standard 415-V-4761
Mini 415-V-4762

Fuzzy Bunny
Standard 415-V-163
Mini 415-V-164

Party Bags
Colorful Easter designs for candy and cookie treats. 20 plastic bags, 20 ties included. 4 x 9.5 in.
Pk./20 $2.09

Spring Party
1912-V-1204

Fuzzy Bunny
1912-V-9168

Fuzzy Bunny Fun Pix
Add a fun touch to cakes, cupcakes, ice cream and more. Approx. 3.5 in. high. Plastic.
2113-V-1499 Pk./12 $2.09

Sprinkles

Individual Bottles
Shake up your Easter treats! Plastic bottles for convenient pouring and storing. Certified Kosher.

Bunny Mix
2.5 oz. bottle.
710-V-1014 $2.29

Spring Confetti
2 oz. bottle.
710-V-1278 $2.29
3 oz. bottle.
710-V-970 $3.29

Colorful Egg Mix
2.5 oz. bottle.
710-V-7486 $2.29
3.75 oz. bottle.
710-V-716 $3.29

6-Mix Assortment
Includes Bunny Sprinkle Mix, Colorful Egg Mix, Spring Confetti, Lavender, Pink and Yellow Sugars. 6.8 oz. Certified Kosher.
710-V-1017 $5.99

Candy

NEW!

Hoppy Easter Pretzel Mold
2 designs, 6 cavities.
2115-V-1419 $1.99

Hatching Chick Pretzel Mold
2 designs, 6 cavities.
2115-V-1495 $1.99

Bunny Basket Lollipop Mold
1 design, 2 cavities.
2115-V-1416 $1.99

Fuzzy Bunny Lollipop Mold
4 designs, 4 cavities.
2115-V-1496 $1.99

Hoppy Easter Lollipop Mold
8 designs, 9 cavities.
2115-V-1718 $1.99

Decorated Eggs Lollipop Mold
3 designs, 3 cavities.
2115-V-1497 $1.99

Easter Candy Making MEGA PACK
It's easy and fun, with lots of favorite Easter shapes! Kit includes: Spring Flowers Large Lollipop Mold (3 designs, 3 cavities), Easter Treats Lollipop Mold (6 designs, 12 cavities), Just Hatched Candy Mold (1 design, 8 cavities); 16 oz. Candy Melts (4 oz. each light cocoa, white, pink and yellow); 20 lollipop sticks (6 in.); 4 disposable decorating bags; decorating brush and 20 party bags/ties. Certified Kosher Dairy.
2104-V-1652 $9.99

Candy Melts
Ideal for molding, dipping or coating. Artificially vanilla flavored unless otherwise indicated. 14 oz. bag. Certified Kosher Dairy. **$2.99**

Pink	1911-V-447	White	1911-V-498
Lavender	1911-V-403	Dark Cocoa Mint	1911-V-1920
Yellow	1911-V-463	Light Cocoa	1911-V-544
Blue	1911-V-448	Dark Cocoa	1911-V-358

See pages 196-200 for more Wilton candy items.

NEW!

Decorated Egg & Treat Stand
It's the colorful centerpiece that will get your Easter celebration hopping! The ideal way to display eggs after coloring, with a frisky fuzzy bunny topper that sets the tone for springtime fun. Sturdy, easy-to-assemble stand with locking tabs that keep plates in place. Holds 16 eggs, mini cupcakes, cereal treats or other small goodies. Stand measures 10 x 10.25 in. high. Instructions included.
307-V-130 $4.99

Cookie

Easter Cupcake & Cookie Stencils
Just place one of the 8 fun designs over your baked or iced treat, then sprinkle with Wilton Cake Sparkles or Colored Sugars or spray with Color Mist Food Color Spray (p. 221).
417-V-496 Set/8 $2.19

ORDER TOLL FREE: 800-794-5866

Cookie

METAL CUTTERS
Put variety in your cookie-making with fun Easter multi-shape sets. There are styles to please everyone. Recipe included.

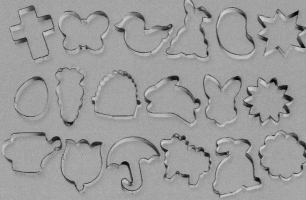

18 Pc. Easter Cutter Collection
Cross, butterfly, chick, bunny, jelly bean, sun, egg, carrot, basket, leaping bunny, bunny face, daisy, sprinkling can, tulip, umbrella, lamb, rabbit and flower cutters are approx. 3 in.
2308-V-1134
Set/18 $10.49

12 Pc. Easter Mini Cutter Collection
Bunny face, egg, cross, flower, tulip, sun, carrot, chick, butterfly, sprinkling can, umbrella and bunny cutters are approx. 1.5 in.
2308-V-1254
Set/12 $5.29

6 Pc. Easter Mini Cutter Set
Butterfly, daisy, tulip, bunny face, chick and bunny, each approx. 1.5 in.
2308-V-1209 Set/6 $3.19

Colorful Cutter Sets
Our metal cutters look great with their bright colors and fun shapes. Perfect for hanging until your next cookie-baking bash.

3 Pc. Easter Cutter Set
Set of 3 includes bunny, tulip and butterfly, each approx. 3 to 3.5 in. Coated metal.
2308-V-1216 Set/3 $3.69

4 Pc. Hoppy Easter Cutter Set
Springtime favorites in pastels of the season. Tulip, egg, butterfly and bunny. Coated metal. Each approx. 3.5 in.
2308-V-1207 Set/4 $4.79

9 Pc. Easter Cutter Collection
Lamb, tulip, flower, bunny, chick, egg, butterfly, bunny face, and carrot cutters are approx. 3 in. Colored aluminum.
2308-V-2503
Set/9 $10.49

Pre-Baked and Pre-Assembled Bunny Hutch Cookie House Kit
Everything is included: a pre-baked, pre-built hutch, yellow and pink decorating icing mixes, candies, icing decorations, 2 cookie bunny ears, 2 decorating bags and tips, cardboard base and complete instructions. Hutch 5.25 x 5.25 x 6 in. high.
2104-V-1594 $16.49

COMFORT-GRIP CUTTERS
Cushion-grip cutters with extra-deep stainless steel sides. Recipe included. Approx. 4.5 x 1.5 in. deep. **$3.19**

Bunny
2310-V-659

Chick
2310-V-625

Egg
2310-V-649

Bunny Face
2310-V-626

4 PC. GRIPPY CUTTER SET
Includes bunny, flower, egg, and butterfly, approx. 3.5 in.
2311-V-258 Set/4 $4.49

PLASTIC CUTTERS
Child-safe design means kids can have a great time helping. And remember all the fun ways to use our cutters—for bread shapes, stencils, sun catchers and so much more.

10 Pc. Easter Egg Canister Cutter Set
A fun and convenient egg canister holds 10 cutters, each approx. 3.5 in.
2304-V-95 Set/10
$5.99

Individual Cutters
Each approx. 3 x 4 in.
$0.69

Cross
2303-V-141

Duck
2303-V-148

Egg
2303-V-119

SEASONAL

COMMUNION

Cross Pan
Beveled design is excellent with rolled fondant. One-mix pan is 14.5 x 11.2 x 2 in. deep. Instructions included. Aluminum.
2105-V-2509 $9.99

TOPPERS

Inspirational Cross
Beautifully designed in sculpted resin. 5½ in. high.
202-V-398 $14.99

Communion Girl†
3½ in. high.
2113-V-7878 $3.69

Communion Boy†
3½ in. high.
2113-V-7886 $3.69

†Designed by Ellen Williams.

Faith Cross Stationery
Beautifully designed in white 80 lb. card stock with white pearlized trim. Professionally print at home at **www.wiltonprint.com**.

Invitations
Border and cross accent. Invitation: 5.5 x 8.5 in.; envelope: 5.75 x 8.75 in.
1008-V-775 Pk./12 $4.99

Cross Seals
Self adhesive, silver tone, 1 in. diameter.
1008-V-2337 Pk./50 $2.99

ST. PATRICK'S DAY

Shamrock Pan
Celebrate St. Patrick's Day with this fun symbol of joy and celebration. Also great for school parties, birthdays, sports celebrations and much more. One-mix pan is 11.75 x 2 in. deep. Aluminum.
2105-V-185 $9.99

Cookie Icing **NEW!**
Just heat and squeeze onto cookies using the convenient cap. Sets smooth in just 45 minutes. 10 oz. bottle covers approx. 12 cookies 3 in. each; 20 oz. bottle covers approximately 24. Certified Kosher.

10 oz. White	704-V-481	$4.49
20 oz. White	704-V-492	$7.99
10 oz. Green	704-V-493	$4.49

Shamrock Baking Cups
Microwave-safe paper. Standard size, 2 in. diameter; Mini size, 1.25 in. diameter. $2.09
Standard 415-V-1410 Pk./75
Mini 415-V-1411 Pk./100

Shamrock Comfort-Grip Cutter
Cushion-grip with extra-deep stainless steel sides gives you comfortable control even when cutting into thick desserts. Recipe included. 4.5 x 1.5 in. deep.
2310-V-648 $3.19

Sparkle Gel
Squeeze on sparkling color effects with our ready-to-use gel. Great for dots, messages, water effects and fondant accents. Resealable 3.5 oz. tubes. Certified Kosher. $2.99
Green 704-V-111
White 704-V-107

NEW!

Shamrock Sprinkle Mix
Shake up your St. Patrick's Day treats! Plastic 2.5 oz. bottle for convenient pouring and storing. Certified Kosher.
710-V-7485 $2.29

Shamrock Foil Fun Pix
Add a shimmering, lucky touch to cakes, cupcakes, ice cream and more. Approx. 3½ in. high.
2113-V-1347 Pk./12 $2.09

Shamrock Pretzel Mold
2 designs, 6 cavities.
2115-V-1499 $1.99

Shamrock Lollipop Mold
1 design, 5 cavities.
2115-V-1545 $1.99

Shamrock Party Bags
20 plastic bags, 20 ties included. 4 x 9.5 in.
1912-V-2233 Pk./20 $2.09

Shamrock Icing Decorations
Sugar-flavored. Certified Kosher.
710-V-286 Pk./9 $2.29

Shamrock Green Metal Cookie Cutter
Quality metal cuts neatly. Approx. 3 in.
2308-V-1320 $0.79

4-Leaf Clover Cookie Cutter
Cut cookies, sandwiches and use in crafts. Plastic; 3 in. wide.
2303-V-134 $0.69

ORDER TOLL FREE: 800-794-5866

Bakeware

Stars and Stripes Pan
Decorate a grand old flag cake perfect for that July 4th cookout. Accent Old Glory with Piping Gel and fresh summer fruit. One-mix pan is 13 x 9 x 2 in. Aluminum.
2105-V-183 $9.99

Star Pan
Your colorful star cake will set off sparks on the 4th and brighten parties all year long. One-mix pan is 12.75 x 1.9 in. deep. Aluminum.
2105-V-2512 $12.99

Mini Star Pan
One mix makes 12-16 stars. 6 cavities, 4.75 x 1 in. deep. Aluminum.
2105-V-1235 $14.49

Silicone Mini Star Mold
Microwave, freezer, refrigerator, and dishwasher safe; oven safe to 500°F. One mix makes 20-24 stars. 6 cavities, each 2.6 x 2.5 x 1.5 in. deep.
2105-V-4819 $9.99

Cookie

3 Pc. Red, White and Blue Cutter Set
Bake a star-studded salute to the USA with colorful cutters in sizes from 3.25 to 5 in. Coated metal.
2308-V-1240 Set/3 $4.19

Star Metal Cookie Cutter
Quality metal is clean-cutting and easy to handle. 3 in.
2308-V-1008 $0.69

Comfort-Grip Cutters
Cushion-grip cutters with extra-deep stainless steel sides perfect for cutting so many favorite foods into patriotic shapes. The cushion grip gives you comfortable control even when cutting into thick desserts. Recipe included. 4.5 x 1.5 in. deep. **$3.19**

Flag 2310-V-651

Star 2310-V-605

Patriotic Cupcake & Cookie Stencils
Just place one of the 8 fun designs over your baked or iced treat, then sprinkle with Wilton Cake Sparkles or Colored Sugars or spray with Color Mist Food Color Spray (p. 226).
417-V-498 $2.19

4 Pc. Patriotic Cutter Set
Bold colors add to the fun! Set of 4 favorite shapes includes star, USA, flag and shooting star. Sizes from 3 to 3.5 in. Coated metal.
2308-V-1257 Set/4 $4.79

4 Pc. Nesting Stars Metal Cutter Set
A parade of small to large stars to create fun cookies for the 4th or all year long Sizes from 5 to 2.5 in.
2308-V-1215 Set/4 $4.79

6 Pc. Nesting Stars Cutter Set
Plastic. 1.6 to 4.6 in.
2304-V-704 Set/6 $2.99

Star Cookie Treat Pan
Press cookie dough into pan, insert a cookie stick, then bake, cool and decorate. Makes 6 individual treats, 3.5 x .25 in. deep. Aluminum.
2105-V-8102 $9.99

Cookie Treat Sticks
6 in. 1912-V-9319 Pk./20 $1.99
8 in. 1912-V-9318 Pk./20 $2.99

Icings

PATRIOTIC COLOR GUIDE

Red	White	Blue

Ready-to-Decorate Icing
Includes 4 decorating tips! Anyone can decorate with Wilton Ready-to-Decorate Icing! Our brilliant colors add an exciting finishing touch to treats without mixing or mess. 6.4 oz. Certified Kosher. **$4.29**
Red 710-V-4400
White 710-V-4402
Blue 710-V-4407

Cookie Icing
Just heat and squeeze onto cookies using the convenient cap. Sets smooth in just 45 minutes. 10 oz. bottle covers approx. 12 cookies 3 in. each; 20 oz. bottle covers approximately 24. Certified Kosher.
10 oz. White 704-V-481 $4.49
20 oz. White 704-V-492 $7.99
10 oz. Red 704-V-488 $4.49

Sparkle Gel
Squeeze on sparkling color effects with our ready-to-use gel. Great for dots, messages, water effects and fondant accents. Resealable 3.5 oz. tubes. Certified Kosher. **$2.99**
Red 704-V-112
Blue 704-V-110
White 704-V-107

Tube Decorating Icing
Tubes can be used with our Tip and Nail Set or Coupler Ring Set (p. 144) and any standard size Wilton metal tip. Colors match Wilton Icing Colors (p. 148). 4.25 oz. Certified Kosher. **$1.99**
Red 704-V-218
White 704-V-200
Royal Blue 704-V-248

Tube Decorating Gel
Transparent gels are great for writing messages and decorating cakes and cookies. Colors match Wilton Icing Colors (p. 148). .75 oz. Certified Kosher. **$1.49**
Red 704-V-318
White 704-V-302
Royal Blue 704-V-348

NEW!

SEASONAL

Party

Baking Cups
Microwave-safe paper. Standard size, 2 in. diameter.
Pk./75 $2.09

Old Glory
415-V-2236

Patriotic Stars
415-V-2235

Party Bags
Colorful Patriotic designs for candy and cookie treats. 20 plastic bags, 20 ties included.
4 x 9.5 in.
Pk./20 $2.09

Old Glory
1912-V-3056

Patriotic Stars
1912-V-1254

Icing Decorations
Perfect for topping cakes, cupcakes, cookies. Certified Kosher. $2.29

Patriotic Flags
710-V-726 Pk./9

Stars and Stripes Party Picks
3 in. high mini flags. Paper.
2113-V-704 Pk./40 $1.49

Patriotic Foil Pix
Looks like a dazzling fireworks display on your holiday treats! Great for cakes, cupcakes. 4 in. high.
2113-V-712 Pk./12 $2.09

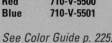
CANDLES

Patriotic
Feature bold textured spirals and a fun handcarved star on top. 3¼ in. high.
2811-V-1122 Pk./4 $3.89

Beer Cans
1¾ in. high.
2811-V-9326 Set/6 $3.89

Red and Blue Sparklers
6½ in. high.
2811-V-704 Pk./18 $1.09

Cupcakes 'N More Dessert Stands
Individually decorated cupcakes are the perfect way to add a personal touch to celebrations. Now, with Cupcakes 'N More, you have the perfect way to serve them, featuring wire spirals to securely hold each cupcake.

38 Count Standard
15 x 18 in. wide. Holds 38 cupcakes.*
307-V-651 $41.99

23 Count Standard
12 x 13 in. wide. Holds 23 standard cupcakes.*†
307-V-826 $31.49

13 Count Standard (shown)
9.25 x 9 in. wide. Holds 13 standard cupcakes.*
307-V-831 $13.69

24 Count Mini
10.5 x 9 in. wide. Holds 24 mini cupcakes.*
307-V-250 $15.79

*Pat. No. 7,387,283. †Pat. No. D516,385.

Sprinkles

Individual Bottles
Plastic bottles for easy pouring and storing. Certified Kosher. $2.29

Patriotic Mix
2.5 oz. bottle.
710-V-786

Patriotic Nonpareils
3 oz. bottle.
710-V-1123

Red Sugar
3.25 oz. bottle.
710-V-766

Blue Sugar
3.25 oz. bottle.
710-V-760

Cake Sparkles
Edible glitter, .25 oz. bottle. Certified Kosher. $3.19

Red
703-V-1284

Blue
703-V-1314

6-Mix Assortment
Includes Red and Blue Jimmies, Patriotic Mix, Red and Blue Sugar and Red, White and Blue Confetti. 6.45 oz. Certified Kosher.
710-V-656 $5.99

Candy

Patriotic Pretzel Mold
3 designs, 6 cavities.
2115-V-4439 $1.99

Stars Candy Mold
1 design, 12 cavities,
2115-V-1554 $1.99

Candy Melts
Ideal for molding, dipping or coating. Artificially vanilla flavored unless otherwise indicated. 14 oz. bag. Certified Kosher Dairy. $2.99

Red	1911-V-499	Dark Cocoa Mint	1911-V-1920
White	1911-V-498	Light Cocoa	1911-V-544
Blue	1911-V-448	Dark Cocoa	1911-V-358

See pages 196-200 for more Wilton candy items.

Silicone Mini Mortarboard Mold
Microwave, freezer, refrigerator, and dishwasher safe; oven safe to 500°F. One mix makes 20-24 caps. 6 cavities, each 2.7 x 2.7 x 1.25 in. deep.
2105-V-4907 $9.99

Topping Off Success Pan
Decorate in your grad's school colors. One-mix pan is 14.75 x 11.75 x 2 in. deep. Aluminum.
2105-V-2038 $9.99

Two-Mix Book Pan
Detail any of life's important chapters, including graduation. 11.5 x 15 x 2.75 in. deep. Serves up to 30. Aluminum.
2105-V-2521 $17.99

Party

Baking Cups
Microwave-safe paper. Standard size, 2 in. diameter.
Pk./75 $2.09

Congrats
415-V-1349

Smiley Grad
415-V-4592

Party Bags
Colorful grad designs for candy and cookie treats. 20 plastic bags, 20 ties included. 4 x 9.5 in.
Pk./20 $2.09

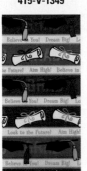
Congrats
1912-V-1349

Smiley Grad
1912-V-1130

Icing Decorations
Perfect on cakes, cupcakes, cookies. Mint-flavored. Certified Kosher.
$2.29

Graduation
710-V-1125 Pk./12

Petite Smiley Grad
710-V-503
Pk./12

Fun Pix
Add a fun touch to cakes, cupcakes, ice cream and more. Approx. 3½ in. high. Paper.
$2.09

 NEW!

Congrats
2113-V-1350 Pk./24

Grad
2113-V-717 Pk./24

Graduation Cupcake Stand
NEW!
Greet the grad with cupcakes and treats served on this fun centerpiece stand. In minutes, you can create a bright and colorful 3-tiered cupcake stand with a graduation cap topper. Your cupcakes will look perfect for the party. Stand measures 1 ft. wide x 1.2 ft. high. Instructions included.
1510-V-1046 $5.99

NEW!

3 Pc. Graduation Cutter Set
Set of 3 includes diploma, graduation cap and star ribbon, each approx. 3 to 3.5 in. Coated metal.
2308-V-1491 Set/3 $3.69

Graduation Cap Black Metal Cookie Cutter
Quality metal cuts neatly and is easy to handle. Coated metal. Approx. 3.5 in.
509-V-319 $0.79

Candle Set
3 caps, 3 diplomas, ½ to 2 in. high.
2811-V-1800
Set/6 $3.89

Champagne Bottle Candles
2 in. high.
2811-V-163
Set/6 $3.89

Candy

Graduation Pretzel Mold
3 designs, 6 cavities.
2115-V-1445
$1.99

Graduation Lollipop Mold
6 designs, 8 cavities.
2115-V-1729
$1.99

See pages 196-200 for more Wilton candy items.

Candy Melts
Ideal for all your candy molding, dipping or coating. Artificially vanilla flavored unless otherwise indicated. 14 oz. bag. Certified Kosher Dairy. $2.99

Yellow	1911-V-463
White	1911-V-498
Blue	1911-V-448
Dark Cocoa Mint	1911-V-1920
Light Cocoa	1911-V-544
Dark Cocoa	1911-V-358

SEASONAL

Wedding Style

Wilton has a beautiful selection of products for today's bride. From invitations to toasting glasses to favors, we'll help you design the wedding day of your dreams!

Wedding Ensembles

Fulfill your wedding day dreams with the finest coordinated wedding accessories. A complete collection makes a beautiful gift. Or choose individual accessories that personalize and accessorize the wedding day perfectly!

IVORY **NEW!**

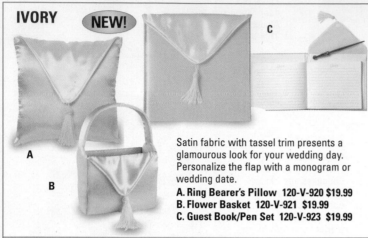

Satin fabric with tassel trim presents a glamourous look for your wedding day. Personalize the flap with a monogram or wedding date.
A. Ring Bearer's Pillow 120-V-920 **$19.99**
B. Flower Basket 120-V-921 **$19.99**
C. Guest Book/Pen Set 120-V-923 **$19.99**

PRINCESS **NEW!**

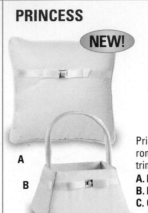
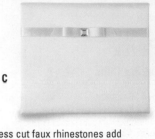

Princess cut faux rhinestones add romantic shimmer. Accessories are trimmed with organza and satin ribbons.
A. Ring Bearer's Pillow 120-V-109 **$19.99**
B. Flower Basket 120-V-200 **$19.99**
C. Guest Book/Pen Set 120-V-198 **$29.99**

GRACEFUL

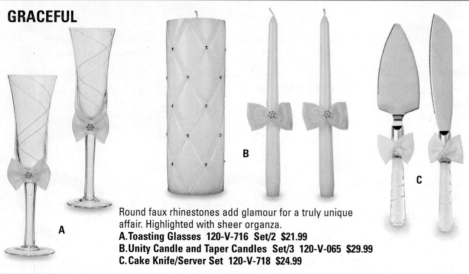

Round faux rhinestones add glamour for a truly unique affair. Highlighted with sheer organza.
A.Toasting Glasses 120-V-716 **Set/2 $21.99**
B.Unity Candle and Taper Candles Set/3 120-V-065 **$29.99**
C.Cake Knife/Server Set 120-V-718 **$24.99**

TRADITIONAL

Guest book with attached pen creates a beautiful display at the reception table. Crafted in pearlized paper.
Guest Book & Pen
120-V-082 **$14.99**

TIMELESS

A lovely, opulent look with sophisticated detailing.
Cake Knife/Server Set
120-V-4004 **$29.99**

HEART SILVER

Heart Silver Toasting Glasses and Serving Ensemble
Bring the ultimate look of romance to your celebration.
Silver-plated. 120-V-232 **Set/4 $49.99**

TOASTING GLASSES

Fluted
Fluted glasses toast the bride and groom on their special day.
120-V-784 **Set/2 $21.99**

Print Your Own Stationery

Create your own distinctive invitations and more with professional results right at home. It's easy to do—simply go to www.wiltonprint.com and see how. All stationery includes test sheets for perfect printing!

POCKET INVITATIONS

Today's trend in wedding stationery—the invitation is displayed on one side and the accessory cards are tucked into the pocket on the opposite side.

NEW!

Chocolate Daisy
Ivory with Brown Accents.
Set of 25 Includes:
• 25 Invitations and Mailing Envelopes
• 25 Reply Cards, 25 Envelopes
• 25 Backer Cards
• 25 Adhesives, 25 Ribbons
1008-V-168 Set/25 $24.99

String of Pearls
White with Pearlized trim.
Set of 25 Includes:
• 25 Invitations
• 25 Pocket Folders
• 50 All-Purpose Cards
• 25 Mailing Envelopes
• 25 Reply Cards & Envelopes
• 25 Printable Seals
1008-V-177 Set/25 $34.99

Vintage Ivy
Ivory and Brown.
Set of 25 Includes:
• 25 Invitations
• 25 Pocket Folders
• 50 All-Purpose Cards
• 25 Mailing Envelopes
• 25 Reply Cards & Envelopes
• 25 Adhesives, Ribbons & Pre-Tied Bows
1008-V-178 Set/25 $34.99

Black & White Elegance
White with Black Trim.
Set of 25 Includes:
• 25 Invitations and Mailing Envelopes
• 25 Reply Cards, 25 Envelopes
• 50 All-Purpose Cards
• 25 Pockets
• 75 Foam Adhesives
• 25 White Organza Ribbons & Bows
1008-V-186 Set/25 $34.99

Monogram Ribbon Kit
White with White Organza Ribbon Trim.
Set of 25 Includes:
• 25 Invitations and Mailing Envelopes
• 25 Reply Cards, 25 Envelopes
• 25 Adhesives, 25 ribbons
1008-V-169 Set/25 $24.99

Royal Lining Kit
Ivory with Gold Trim.
Set of 25 Includes:
• 25 Invitations and Mailing Envelopes
• 25 Reply Cards, 25 Envelopes
1008-V-179 Set/25 $24.99

Chocolate Brown Thank You
Ivory with Gold Trim and Brown Envelopes.
Set of 50 Includes:
• 50 Thank You Cards
• 50 Mailing Envelopes
1008-V-166 Set/50 $14.99

Flirty Fleur
White.
Set of 50 Includes:
• 50 Invitations and Mailing Envelopes
• 50 Reply Cards and Envelopes
1008-V-525 Set/50 $24.99

Glitz and Glamour
White/Pearlized White/Glittered Vellum Wrap.
Set of 25 Includes:
• 25 Invitations and Mailing Envelopes
• 25 Reply Cards and Envelopes
• 25 Vellum Wraps
• 25 Ribbon and Flower Embellishments, Adhesives
1008-V-314 Set/25 $24.99

Pressed Floral
Ivory with Natural Paper Wrap.
Set of 50 Includes:
• 50 Invitations and Mailing Envelopes
• 50 Reply Cards and Envelopes
• 50 Ribbon and Pre-Tied Bows, Adhesives
1008-V-662 Set/50 $34.99

Happy Day
White with White/Glittered Vellum Pocket.
Set of 25 Includes:
• 25 Invitations and Mailing Envelopes
• 25 Reply Cards and Envelopes
• 25 Pre-Tied Bows with Faux Rhinestone Trim, Adhesives
1008-V-711 Set/25 $24.99

Scroll Bi-Fold Program
Ivory with Gold Trim.
Includes:
• 50 Programs
1008-V-1555 Pk./50 $14.99

Bended Knee
Pink with Black Silhouettes.
Set of 12 Includes:
• 12 Invitations
• 12 Mailing Envelopes
1008-V-334 Set/12 $5.99

Pink Gerber Daisy
Blue with Shades of Pink, Green.
Set of 12 Includes:
• 12 Invitations
• 12 Mailing Envelopes
1008-V-160 Set/12 $4.99

Bride
White/Blue.
Set of 12 Includes:
• 12 Invitations and Mailing Envelopes
• 12 Tulle and Pre-Tied Bow Embellishments, Adhesives
1008-V-789 Set/12 $9.99

Wedding Day Accessories

French Rose Wedding Bouquet
Perfect, beautiful blooms to keep or to use during the bouquet toss. Hand-crafted, fine faux flowers. Bouquet measures approx. 9.5 in. diameter x 7.5 in.
120-V-1013 $24.99

Flower-Shaped Petals
Fill the flower girl's basket, scatter on the cake table, decorate favors. Lifelike 2.5 in. diameter flower petals. Approx. 300 petals. **$9.99**

 NEW!

Multi-Colored Stephanotis
1006-V-953

 NEW!

White Stephanotis
1006-V-952

 NEW!

Heart Petals
120-V-126

Red Rose
1006-V-695

Wedding Day Décor

Aisle Runner
Decorate the wedding aisle with a floral runner that adds a touch of elegance to the wedding ceremony. Aisle Runner also ensures that the bride's dress stays clean on the walk down the aisle! With pull cord for even unrolling; runner measures 100 ft. long x 36 in. wide.
1006-V-996 $29.99

BRIDAL GARLANDS
You'll find so many uses for the ceremony and reception. Drape on pews and line the aisles, place along table edges and around the cake, wrap around pillars.

Lighted White Rose
Romantic garland adds a soft glow to your wedding ambiance! Uses 2 D Batteries, not included. 6 Ft. Length.
1006-V-350 $23.99

Rose Garland
Life-like roses strung together by organza ribbon. 6 foot length. Non-lighting.
1006-V-917 $9.99

Flameless Votives
Add the romantic glow of candlelight with safe, no flame candles. Includes: 8 flameless votives (with 8 replaceable CR2032 batteries included), 8 holders. Average battery life: 24 hours.
1006-V-7137 Set/8 $15.99

RECEPTION GIFT CARD HOLDERS
Attractively keep the wedding gift cards together at the reception. Tulle, ribbon, flowers and cards not included.

Gift Shape
Whimsical gift box design of sturdy metal construction with faux gem trim. Extra long slot for envelopes, box opens from the top, heart-shaped lock and key. 10.75 in. high x 8 in. long x 8 in. deep
120-V-220 $24.99

Mailbox
Personalize the flag with a photo or saying at www.wiltonprint.com. Includes easy to assemble mailbox, 2 printable labels, 1 test sheet. White printed corrugated cardboard. 12 in. high x 15.25 in. wide x 10.25 in. deep.
1006-V-396 $14.99

Wishing Well
A charming display for any shower, wedding, or anniversary celebration. White printed corrugated cardboard, easy to assemble. 30.5 in. high x 16 in. wide x 14 in. deep.
1006-V-395 $14.99

Celebration Tree
Use it as a party decoration, on the gift table, and as a centerpiece. Easy to assemble. Metal construction. Assembled tree approx. 14 in. high x 11 in. wide. (Favors and decorations shown not included.)
1006-V-571 $9.99

ORDER TOLL FREE: 800-794-5866

Send-Off Favors

Wedding Style

Newest wedding book from Wilton features color-themed ideas for invitations, favors, decorations. Includes step-by-step instructions and materials checklists. Wilton Wedding Style gives you:
- 100-plus ideas for invitations, favors, tabletop décor and more
- 18 dream cakes plus petits fours, cupcakes and edible favors
- Step-by-step project instructions with materials checklists
- Hundreds of decorating ideas for ceremonies and receptions

Soft cover, 124 pages.
902-V-1101 $14.99

Fan Kit

Create a distinctive favor for your special day! Wedding fans not only keep guests comfortable, but let guests wave their approval of the bride and groom! Personalize the fan front and back with photos, special messages, and wedding day details online at www.wiltonprint.com, then print at home. Assembled fan measures approximately 10 in. long. Includes 24 fans, 24 ribbon bows, 24 fan handles, 24 adhesive strips.
120-V-516 Pkg./24 $9.99

Ribbon Wands

Celebrate the bride and groom with a wave of these ribbon wands. Adds a festive flair to the celebration and great photo opportunities at send-off! Can be personalized with your wedding colors.
1006-V-9099 Pk./24 $19.99

Wedding Banner

Beautiful fabric banner announces the bride's arrival. Reverse side displays the just married message. Banner can be personalized with bride and groom's names or wedding date. Messages are embroidered on 100% polyester. 20 in. wide x 24 in. high.
1006-V-9100 $19.99

Pop Out Streamers

Great for weddings, graduations, birthdays, New Year's celebrations, surprise parties. Just aim and press lever. Each contains ten silver foil streamers that stay attached to tube for easy disposal. Streamers are over 10 feet long. Spring loaded, the streamers do not contain gunpowder or other explosives.
1006-V-932 Pkg./14 $24.99

Love Knot Bubble Wands

Use after the ceremony or at the reception. 36 wands are packed in a convenient tray for reception table use. Each wand contains .16 fl. oz. bubble solution. Ribbon not included. Pat. Nos. D485,584 and D536,395.
1007-V-8017 Pk./36 $9.99

Silver-Tone Celebration Bells

Ring for a special kiss after the ceremony and at the reception. Hand to guests exiting the church, and place one at each setting at the reception. Contains 24 metal bells, poem tags and ties. Bell measures 1.25 in. tall.
1007-V-8012 Pk./24 $6.49

Car Decorating Kit

Eye-catching decorations trim the bride and groom's getaway vehicle with style! Includes: magnetic "Just Married" sign, window clings, pre-fluffed pom-poms, streamers, balloons. Crafted of weather-resistant materials, reusable (except balloons).
1006-V-483 $15.79

Favor-Making Kits

Fun and festive kits make it easy to personalize your favors online, at www.wiltonprint.com. Just download the template and print out the tags or labels. Each kit includes instructions and 2 test sheets. Candy not included.

Goblet Favor Kit
Raise the goblet favors and toast the bride and groom! Add a tulle circle, fill with your favorite candy, add a personalized tag and place one at each guest's place setting. Goblets measure 2.75 in. high. Includes 24 each favor containers, satin ribbons, tulle circles, printable tags.
1006-V-923 Pk./24 $24.99

Love Potion Favor Kit
Fill to match your celebration theme and surprise your guests. Bottles measure 2.75 in. high. Kit includes 24 glass bottles with slotted corks. 24 (12 in.) satin ribbon lengths, funnel for easy filling, 24 printable labels.
1006-V-1009 Pk./24 $24.99

Martini Glass Favor Kit
Create a favor that toasts your guests with a treat and a personalized message. Martini glasses measure 3.5 in. high. Includes 24 each favor containers, satin ribbons, tulle circles, printable tags.
120-V-518 Pk./24 $24.99

Champagne Bottle Favor Kit
Create a shower or reception favor that toasts your guests with a treat and a personalized message. Bottles measure 4 in. high. Includes 24 each favor containers, satin ribbons, printable labels.
120-V-519 Pk./24 $24.99

Favor Tin Kit
Create personalized favor tins for your celebration using your computer, or hand design. Includes 25 tins, 25 adhesive labels and strips. Tins measure 2 in. diameter.
1006-V-8038 Pk./25 $19.99

Umbrella Favor Kit
Shower your guests with a favor that carries a personalized message. Use as a place card, add an announcement or a thank you. Umbrellas measure 4 in. high. Includes 24 each favor containers, satin ribbons, printable tags.
120-V-520 Pk./24 $24.99

Silver-Tone Bell Favor Kit
Set a bell at each place setting, guests will ring for the newlyweds to kiss. Bells measure 2.25 in. high. Includes 20 metal favor bells, 20 (12 in.) satin ribbon lengths, 20 printable place cards.
1006-V-1136 Pk./20 $24.99

Heart Favor Kit
Fill with your favorite candy, wrap in the tulle, add a personalized tag to make beautiful favors for bridal shower and wedding reception. Hearts measure 2.5 in. wide x 1 in. deep. Includes 24 each favor containers, satin ribbons, tulle circles, printable tags.
1006-V-924 Pk./24 $24.99

Favor Accents

Romantic accents add sparkling beauty and elegance to favors, table decorations!

Thank You Tags
Send a message of gratitude —tie to favor boxes or bags. Stamped tin. Measures 1.75 in. diameter.
1006-V-987 Pk./12 $1.99

Sweetheart Charms
Shows the sweet, sentimental sign of love. Stamped tin. Measures 1.25 x .75 in.
1006-V-411 Pk./12 $1.99

Engagement Rings
Add sparkle to favors, table decorations, centerpieces. "Diamond" measures .25 in. diameter. Metal.
1006-V-115 Pk./12 $1.99

White Pearl Beading
Molded on one continuous 5-yard strand. Plastic.
Large (6 mm)
211-V-1990 $3.99

ORDER TOLL FREE: 800-794-5866

Favor Containers

These beautiful containers hold favors for shower, wedding and anniversary celebrations. Perfect for mints, almonds, potpourri and small gifts.

Flirty Fleur Favor Boxes
2.25 in. high x 2.25 in. wide. Paper.
1006-V-936 Pk./10 $4.99

Sweet Heart Ribbon Favor Bags
6 in. high x 3.25 wide x 1.75 in. deep. Includes sheer white ribbon. Paper.
1006-V-940 Pk./10 $4.99

Flirty Fleur Ribbon Favor Bags
6 in. high x 3.25 wide x 1.75 in. deep. Includes sheer white ribbon. Paper.
1006-V-941 Pk./10 $4.99

Candy Bar Molds

Create a sweet memory for your guests, a candy bar featuring a special message.

Molding is easy using Wilton Candy Melts (p. 196). Present them beautifully in Candy Bar Boxes. Each bar measures 3.25 in. wide x 1.75 in. tall x .25 in. deep. 1 design, 4 cavities.
Add-A-Message
2115-V-1356 $1.99

Candy Bar Boxes
The window displays your special message. Paper.
1904-V-1157 Pk./10 $4.19

Cake Slice Boxes
Bakery style boxes measure 5 in. square x 3.5 in. high.
415-V-955 Pk./5 $3.89

Cookie Cutters

Bride's favorite cutter shapes are perfect for cookie making or as favors for guests at the shower and reception.

4 Pc. Wedding Cutter Set
Shapes include wedding bells, tiered cake, wedding dress, joined hearts. Recipe included. Each approx. 3 in. Coated metal.
2308-V-1071 Set/4 $4.79

NEW!

Favor Candy

Trendy and traditional candies make great fillers for favors and candy dishes at showers, weddings, and celebrations!

Bling Rings
30 pieces per package. Sweet/tart fruit flavored. Each measures 1.12 in. high x 1 wide.
1006-V-6173 $4.19

NEW! **NEW!**

White Gum Drops
Nonpareil-covered. Fruit flavored. 12 oz. bag.
1006-V-9048 $6.29

Love Mix
Sweet/tart flavored. 12 oz. bag.
1006-V-9041 $6.29

Classic Doves
Sweet/tart flavored. 12 oz. bag.
1006-V-9052 $6.29

Pastel Jelly Beans
Fruit flavored. 12 oz. bag.
1006-V-9050 $4.19

Hearts
Sweet/tart strawberry flavored. 12 oz. bag.
1006-V-9053 $6.29

Pastel Pearls
Fruit flavored. 10 oz. bag. Certified Kosher.
1006-V-904 $4.19

Wedding Bells
Sweet/tart flavored. 12 oz. bag.
1006-V-1140 $6.29

Mint Drops
Pastel. Certified Kosher. 14 oz. bag.
1006-V-788 $6.29

NEW! 32 oz. bag.
1006-V-3710 $13.99

Peppermint Pearls
10 oz. bag. Certified Kosher.
1006-V-9401 $4.19

Pillow Mints
10 oz. bag. Pastel.
1006-V-858 $4.19
48 oz. bag. Pastel.
1006-V-379 $20.99

NEW! 48 oz. bag. White.
1006-V-3711 $20.99

Jordan Almonds
Certified Kosher.
16 oz. bag. Pastel.
1006-V-779 $7.99
16 oz. bag. White.
1006-V-778 $7.99
44 oz. bag. Pastel.
1006-V-1133 $21.99
44 oz. bag. White.
1006-V-1134 $21.99

Wedding Cakes

The beautiful cake designs Wilton is famous for are just the beginning of your dream wedding presentation. Richly detailed Wilton cake toppers, accents, stands and separators complement your design to capture the moment forever.

Wedding Toppers

Discover the unmatched detail that has made Wilton figurines the perfect finishing touch for generations. The rich, sculpted crafting, realistic detailing and romantic designs make these figurines perfect wedding day keepsakes.

First Kiss
Height: 6.75 in.
Base: 3 in. diameter. Bonded marble.
202-V-258 $24.99

Sweet Couple
Sits on the edge of the cake.
Height: 4.25 in.
Base: 1.75 in. Resin.
1006-V-7145 $14.99

Clear Bianca
Height: 5.5 in. Base: 3.75 x 3.5 in. Acrylic.
202-V-424 $24.99

Threshold of Happiness
Height: 5 in.
Base: 3.25 x 2 in. Resin.
202-V-202 $24.99

Reflections
Porcelain couple. Height: 8 in. Base: 4.75 in. diameter. Plastic, fabric flowers, tulle.
117-V-268 $25.99

Our Day
Height: 4.75 in.
Base: 2 x 1.75 in. Poly resin. Blonde/White Gown.
202-V-409 $6.99

Lasting Love
Height: 4.5 in.
Base: 2.25 x 1.75 in. Poly resin.
202-V-302 $6.99

Two Rings
Height: 5.5 in. Base: 3.75 in. diameter. Plastic, resin.
1006-V-1121 $34.99

Simple Joys
Height: 8 in.
Base: 4.5 in. diameter. Plastic, fabric flowers, fabric.
103-V-150 $24.99

Petite Spring Song
Height: 7 in.
Base: 3.25 in. diameter. Plastic, fabric flowers.
106-V-159 $12.99

HUMOROUS WEDDING FIGURINES

Add a lighthearted touch to the celebration. Great for pre-wedding events such as showers, these figurines are sure to bring a smile to the face of anyone who has ever planned a wedding!

Oh No You Don't
Height: 4.25 in. Base: 6 x 3 in. Resin.
115-V-102 $19.99 Ethnic **115-V-104 $19.99**

Now I Have You
Height: 4.25 in. Base: 4.25 x 3.75 in. Resin.
115-V-101 $19.99

Ball and Chain
Height: 2.25 in. Base: 3.5 in. Resin.
1006-V-7143 $19.99

ORDER TOLL FREE: 800-794-5866

CAKE PICKS

The new look—stunning picks draw attention to your celebration—perfect for cake tops, floral arrangements, bouquets and centerpieces. Beautifully appointed with rhinestones, crafted of painted resin.

NEW!

Decorative
Perfect for wedding and anniversary celebrations.

I Do
3.5 in. high, 7 in. wide.
120-V-928 $14.99

Double Hearts
5 in. high, 4.5 in. wide.
1006-V-985 $14.99

Anniversary
Delicately detailed picks with the look of silver or gold create a cake to remember.

Silver 25th
5 in. high, 4 in. wide.
1008-V-758 $14.99

Gold 50th
5.25 in. high, 4.25 in. wide.
1008-V-762 $14.99

Cake Displays

Stunning Wilton Cake Displays are the perfect way to show off your special wedding cake. Take a look—there's one perfectly suited to your wedding cake size and design.

NEW!

Fancy Scrolls Cake Stand
The perfect way to display your party cakes or fancy desserts. Slide the two scrolled base pieces together to form the base and place the 12 in. plate on top for a secure cake presentation. After the party, the base pieces easily disassemble and lock into the plate for compact storage.
307-V-854 $14.99

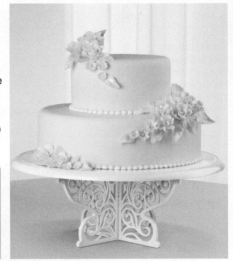

Graceful Tiers Cake Stand
Ideal for garden-themed wedding cakes, but also perfect to display cupcakes, muffins, candies, fruit and more. The three-tiered, scrollwork stand features crystal-clear plates which nest securely in each section. Set includes cream-colored powder-coated metal stand, 14.5 in. wide x 29.5 in. high; 3 clear separator plates, 8, 10 and 12 in. diameter; 1 wrench, all hardware; assembly instructions.
307-V-841 $54.99

Replacement Plate Set
302-V-7925 $10.49

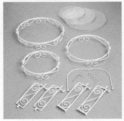

3 Tier Pillar Cake Stand
A distinctive display, featuring locking pillars in a secure base, providing dramatic tier heights and stable support. Its unique design and clean construction complements any setting—great for cakes, mini cakes, appetizers and more. Set includes 15.75 in. off-white plastic base; 3 pillars—5.75 in., 12.75 in. and 19.5 in. high; 3 plate supports and plates (10 in., 12 in. and 14 in. plates hold 10 in., 12 in. and 14 in. round cakes).
307-V-350 $59.99

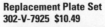

Cake Displays

FLOATING TIERS CAKE STANDS
The beautiful illusion of floating tiers makes a grand display for your cakes.

Round (Collapsible)
Includes tier support rings, ring support bars, connector bar, 8, 12, and 16 in. separator plates. Assembly required. Instructions and all hardware included. Disassembles for easy storage.
307-V-710 $77.99

Heart (Stationary)
Includes 17 in. high enamel coated white metal stand, 8, 12, and 16 in. Decorator Preferred Heart Separator Plates and instructions. This is a stationary stand and does not disassemble.
307-V-872 $77.99

Replacement plates are available at www.wilton.com

Cakes 'N More 3-Tier Party Stand
Contemporary stairstep stand with crystal-clear plates puts the focus where it belongs—on your stunning cake and desserts! Constructed in metal with chrome-plated finish, stand holds 3 different size cake plates—8, 10 and 12 in. (included).
307-V-859 $31.49
Replacement Plates 302-V-7925 Set/3 $10.49

Candlelight Cake Stand
Elegant scrollwork and soft candlelight show off your cake design. Flameless votives are convenient and safe. Stand supports 40 Lbs., use with 14 in. smooth or scallop edge separator plate (not included). Set includes 21.5 in. diameter x 5 in. high stand, 4 flameless votives (with 4 replaceable CR2032 batteries included), 4 glass holders. Average battery life: 24 hours.
307-V-351 $44.99

CUPCAKES 'N MORE DESSERT STANDS
Individually decorated cupcakes are the perfect way to add a personal touch to celebrations. Now, with Cupcakes 'N More, you have the perfect way to serve them, featuring wire spirals to securely hold each cupcake.

38 Count Standard
15 in. high x 18 in. wide. Holds 38 cupcakes.*
(shown). 307-V-651 $41.99
23 Count Standard
12 in. high x 13 in. wide. Holds 23 cupcakes.*†
307-V-826 $31.49
13 Count Standard
9.25 in. high x 9 in. wide. Holds 13 cupcakes.*
307-V-831 $13.69
24 Count Mini
10.5 in. high x 9 in. wide. Holds 24 mini cupcakes.*
307-V-250 $15.79
*Pat. No. 7,387,283. †Pat. No. D516,385.

Romantic Castle Cake Set
Create a fairy tale for your wedding. Everything you need to transform your tiered cake into a fantasy castle is included: three sizes of detailed turret towers with removable peak pieces, lattice windows, a paneled door and roof pieces. Complete assembly and decorating ideas included. For design ideas visit www.wilton.com!
301-V-910 Set/32 $20.99

ORDER TOLL FREE: 800-794-5866

Separator Plates and Pillars

Decorator Preferred Smooth Edge Plates

Built for unmatched stability, with patented Circles of Strength design.

6 in.	302-V-4101	$2.39	14 in.	302-V-4105	$6.29
8 in.	302-V-4102	$3.19	16 in.	302-V-4106	$9.49
10 in.	302-V-4103	$4.19	18 in.	302-V-4107	$12.59
12 in.	302-V-4104	$5.29			

Decorator Preferred Scalloped Plates

Built for unmatched stability, with patented Circles of Strength design.

6 in.	302-V-6	$2.39	12 in.	302-V-12	$5.29
7 in.	302-V-7	$2.59	13 in.	302-V-13	$5.79
8 in.	302-V-8	$3.19	14 in.	302-V-14	$6.29
9 in.	302-V-9	$3.69	15 in.	302-V-15	$7.39
10 in.	302-V-10	$4.19	16 in.	302-V-16	$9.49
11 in.	302-V-11	$4.79	18 in.	302-V-18	$12.59

Decorator Preferred Heart Plates

Perfectly sized to fit Wilton heart pans, for a stunning tiered heart creation.

8 in.	302-V-60	$3.19	14 in.	302-V-63	$6.29
10 in.	302-V-61	$4.19	16 in.	302-V-64	$9.49
12 in.	302-V-62	$5.29	18 in.	302-V-65	$12.59

Decorator Preferred Square Plates

Clean lines, smooth edges, unmatched strength. Features patented Circles of Strength design.

6 in.	302-V-1801	$3.19
8 in.	302-V-1802	$4.19
10 in.	302-V-1803	$5.29
12 in.	302-V-1804	$6.29
14 in.	302-V-1805	$7.39
16 in.	302-V-1806	$10.49
18 in.	302-V-1807	$13.69

Crystal-Look Plates

Wilton Crystal-Look plates have an elegance like no other, with ridged sides that look like cut crystal. Use with Crystal-Look pillars (sold below).

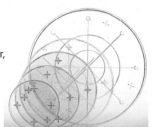

7 in.	302-V-2013	$4.19	13 in.	302-V-2078	$8.39
9 in.	302-V-2035	$5.29	* 17 in.	302-V-1810	$15.79
11 in.	302-V-2051	$6.29			

*Use only with 13.75 in. Crystal-Look pillars (sold below).

17 in. Crystal-Look Plate and Pillar Set

Contains four 13.75 in. pillars and two 17 in. plates. (not shown)
301-V-1387 **$48.29**

FILLABLE PILLARS

Fill pillars with colorful gems, ribbon or decorative stones to personalize your cake design! A great way to add reception colors or themes to a classic wedding cake design. Pillars are designed to be used with Wilton Decorator Preferred Separator Plates in a variety of sizes and shapes. Sets include 4 pillars, 8 pedestals. Not recommended to be filled with any type of liquid. Plastic.

NEW!

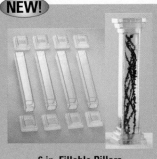

4 in. Fillable Pillars
303-V-801 Pk./12 $7.99

6 in. Fillable Pillars
303-V-802 Pk./12 $9.99

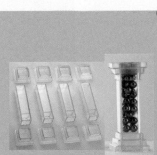

"Hidden" Pillars

Separate cake tiers and create a floating illusion. Pushed into tiers as dowel rods, they fit onto all Decorator Preferred separator plates. Trimmable, hollow plastic. 6 in. high.
303-V-8 Pk./4 $3.19

Crystal-Look Pillars

Contemporary cut crystal look.

3 in.	303-V-2171	Pk./4	$3.69
5 in.	303-V-2196	Pk./4	$4.79
7 in.	303-V-2197	Pk./4	$5.29
*13.75 in. (not shown)			
	303-V-2242		$4.19

*Sold singly. Use only with 17 in. Crystal-Look plate (sold above).

Grecian Pillars

Elegantly scrolled and ribbed.

3 in.	303-V-3606	
5 in.	303-V-3703	
Pk./4	$4.19	
7 in.	303-V-3705	
Pk./4	$5.29	

Crystal-Look Spiked Pillars

For single plate cake construction.

7 in.	303-V-2322	
Pk./4	$4.79	
9 in.	303-V-2324	
Pk./4	$5.79	

Grecian Spiked Pillars

For single plate cake construction. Wide base increases stability.

5 in.	303-V-3708	
Pk./4	$2.59	
7 in.	303-V-3710	
Pk./4	$3.69	
9 in.	303-V-3712	
Pk./4	$4.79	

Baker's Best Disposable Pillars with Rings

For single plate cake construction.

7 in.	303-V-4000	
Pk./4	$3.19	
9 in.	303-V-4001	
Pk./4	$3.69	

Roman Columns

Handsome pillars may be used with 16 and 18 in. plates.
10.25 in.
303-V-8136
Pk./2 $6.29
13.75 in.
303-V-2130
Pk./2 $7.39

Cake Assembly Sets

Fluted Bowl Separator Set

Simply fill it with fresh or silk flowers, tulle or patterned fabric, or use it on its own. Setup could not be simpler—spiked separator plates fit inside the top and bottom openings of the bowl for a secure presentation. Set includes 4 in. high fluted bowl and 2 smooth-edge separator plates (6 and 10 in. diameter).
303-V-823 Set/3 $20.99

Globe Pillar and Base Sets

The 2 and 2.5 in. Pillar Sets are positioned between tiers, as globes fit over hidden pillars to provide strong support. The 3 in. Base Set features a reinforced center channel which fits over separator plate feet to hold your base cake. Sets include four globes and four 9 in. pillars. Globe Base Set includes 4 pillar globe bases.

2 in. Globe Pillar Set
303-V-822 Set/8 $8.39
2.5 in. Globe Pillar Set
303-V-824 Set/8 $10.49
3 in. Globe Base Set
303-V-825 Set/4 $10.49
9 in. Replacement Pillars Set
303-V-4005 Set/4 $4.19

Tailored Tiers Cake Display Set

The elegant patterned fabric complements most wedding, shower and anniversary designs. As an added bonus, use the included acetate photo wraps to customize the separators with treasured family photos, wrapping paper or an alternate fabric. Set includes 2 satin brocade wrapped craft foam separators (4.25 and 7.25 in. diameter x 2 in. high), 4 smooth-edge spiked separator plates (one 6 in., two 8 in., one 12 in. diameter) and 2 acetate photo wraps.
304-V-8174 Set/8 $31.49

Spiral Separator Sets

Add an elegant touch to your special occasion cakes with these beautifully scrolled separators. Setup could not be simpler—the smooth-edge plates are spiked to fit inside the top and bottom rings for a secure presentation.

10 in. Set
Includes 7 x 4.25 in. high wire separator ring, 2 smooth-edge separator plates, 8 and 10 in. diameter.
303-V-8176 Set/3 $20.99

14 in. Set
Includes 10.5 x 4.25 in. high wire separator ring, 2 smooth-edge separator plates, 10 and 14 in. diameter.
303-V-8175 Set/3 $31.49

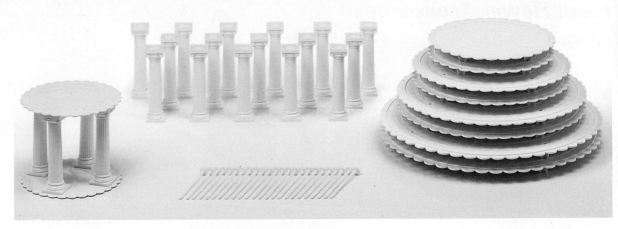

Grecian Pillar and Plate Set

A deluxe money-saving collection for the serious cake decorator. Decorator Preferred scalloped-edge separator plates and 5 in. pillars. Includes 54 pieces: two each 6 in., 8 in., 10 in., 12 in. and 14 in. plates; 20 Grecian pillars and 24 pegs.
301-V-8380
Set/54 $52.49

Roman Column Tier Set

Stately Roman pillars and scalloped-edge plates create beautiful settings for all tiered cakes. Includes 8 pieces: six 13.75 in. Roman columns and two 18 in. round Decorator Preferred separator plates.
301-V-1981
Set/8 $41.99

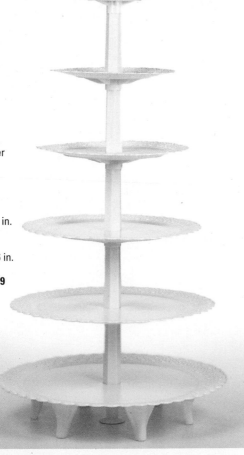

Tall Tier Cake Stand

Display your multi-tiered cakes up to 6 tiers high with this majestic stand. Lace-look plates enhance every cake design and hold tiers from 6 to 16 in. diameter. The twist-together center columns and strong, interchangeable plates provide stability.

Basic Set

Includes: 5 columns, 6.5 in. high; top nut and bottom bolt; 18 in. footed base plate; 8, 10, 12, 14 and 16 in. separator plates.
304-V-7915 Set/13 $49.99

Crystal-Clear Cake Divider Set

Sparkling twist legs push through the cake, rest on plate below and beautifully accent your cake design. (Dowel rods not needed). Includes 6, 8, 10, 12, 14 and 16 in. separator plates, and 24 7.5 in. twist legs.
301-V-9450
Set/30 $52.49

Additional Plates
6 in.
302-V-9730 $3.19
8 in.
302-V-9749 $4.19
10 in.
302-V-9757 $5.29
12 in.
302-V-9765 $7.39
14 in.
302-V-9773 $9.49
16 in.
302-V-9780 $11.59

7.5 in. Twist Legs
303-V-9794
Pk./4 $4.19

9 in. Twist Legs
303-V-977 Pk./4 $5.29

Fresh Flower Accessories

NEW!

NEW!

Flower Display Cups
Blossom-shaped display cups are a creative way to add the beauty of fresh flowers to cake designs. Flower Cups help with the arrangement of flowers by keeping them in place while displayed on the cake surface. Bottom spike holds cup in place on fondant or buttercream icing; top spike can hold a ball of fondant for easy insertion of stems. Plastic.
205-V-8504 Pk./3 $6.99

Fresh Flower Cake Spikes
The perfect way to display fresh flowers on cakes. Spike is topped by a silicone cap to prevent spills and hold flowers in place. Also ideal holders for wired icing flowers and artificial flower displays. Plastic.
205-V-8501 Pk./6 $6.99

Flower Holder Ring
Use at the base of Fanci Fountain. 12.5 in. diameter x 2 in. high. 1.75 in. wide opening; inside ring diameter is 8.5 in. Plastic.
305-V-435 $5.49

Crystal-Look Bowl
4.5 in. diameter.
1.5 in. deep.
205-V-1404 $3.29

Cake Fountain

Fanci Fountain
Add the drama of flowing water to your wedding cake design. The crystal-clear design enhances any tiered cake. Adjustable, smooth water flow. Use with 16 or 18 in. scalloped edge plates; or 18 in. smooth edge plate (p. 237). Set-up instructions included. Height: 12 in. Diameter: 10 in.
306-V-2000 $73.49

Replacement Parts for Fanci Fountain are available at www.wilton.com.

Stairways and Bridges

Bridge the gap between lavish tiers.

Crystal Bridge and Graceful Stairway Set
Includes two stairways (16.75 in. long) and one platform (4.75 x 5 in.). Plastic.
205-V-2311 Set/3 $16.49

Filigree Bridge and Stairway Set
Includes two stairways (16.25 in. long) and one platform (4.75 x 5 in.). Plastic.
205-V-2109 Set/3 $12.99

Dowel Rods and Pegs

Wooden Dowel Rods
Cut and sharpen with strong shears or serrated knife. Length: 12 in. Diam.: .25 in.
399-V-1009 Pk./12 $3.19

Plastic Dowel Rods
Heavy-duty hollow plastic provides strong, stable support. Cut with serrated knife or strong shears to desired length. Length: 12.75 in. Diam.: .75 in.
399-V-801 Pk./4 $2.59

Plastic Pegs
Insure that cake layers and separator plates atop cakes stay in place. Pegs do not add support; dowel rod cake properly before using. Length: 4 in.
399-V-762 Pk./12 $1.49

ORDER TOLL FREE: 800-794-5866

Cake Boards and Accents

Your cake will look its best when presented with quality Wilton boards, doilies and ruffled trims.

Cake Boards
Shaped cakes look best on boards cut to fit! Strong corrugated cardboard, generously-sized in rectangular shapes. Perfect for sheet and square cakes. For shaped cakes, use the pan as a pattern and cut out board to fit cake.

10 x 14 in.	2104-V-554	Pk./6	$5.29
13 x 19 in.	2104-V-552	Pk./6	$5.89

Cake Circles
Corrugated cardboard for strength and stability.

6 in. diameter	2104-V-64	Pk./10	$3.59
8 in. diameter	2104-V-80	Pk./12	$4.69
10 in. diameter	2104-V-102	Pk./12	$5.89
12 in. diameter	2104-V-129	Pk./8	$5.89
14 in. diameter	2104-V-145	Pk./6	$6.29
16 in. diameter	2104-V-160	Pk./6	$6.89

Silver Cake Bases
Convenient .5 in. thick silver foil-covered bases are grease-resistant, food-safe and reusable. Strong to hold heavy decorated cakes without an additional serving plate. Perfect for all types of cakes and craft creations.

10 in. Round	2104-V-1187	Pk./2	$7.99
12 in. Round	2104-V-1188	Pk./2	$8.99
14 in. Round	2104-V-1189	Pk./2	$10.99
16 in. Round	2104-V-1190	Pk./2	$12.99

Show 'N Serve Cake Boards
Scalloped edge has the look of intricate lace. Food-safe, grease-resistant coating.

10 in. diameter	2104-V-1168	Pk./10	$4.99
12 in. diameter	2104-V-1176	Pk./8	$5.49
14 in. diameter	2104-V-1184	Pk./6	$5.99
14 x 20 in. Rectangle	2104-V-1230	Pk./6	$6.99

Ruffle Boards
Ready-to-use cake board and ruffle in one. Bleached white board and all-white ruffling complement any cake.

8 in. (for 6 in. round cake)	415-V-950	$2.79
10 in. (for 8 in. round cake)	415-V-960	$3.29
12 in. (for 10 in. round cake)	415-V-970	$4.49
14 in. (for 12 in. round cake)	415-V-980	$4.99
16 in. (for 14 in. round cake)	415-V-990	$5.99
18 in. (for 16 in. round cake)	415-V-1000	$8.49

Tuk-'N-Ruffle
A pretty touch that attaches to edge of your serving tray or board with royal icing or tape. White.

60 ft. bolt per box.
802-V-1008 $16.49

6 ft. pkg.
802-V-1991 $3.29

Fanci-Foil Wrap
Serving side has a non-toxic grease-resistant surface. Continuous roll: 20 in. x 15 ft.

White
804-V-191 $8.99
Gold
804-V-183 $8.99
Silver
804-V-167 $8.99

Cake Doilies

Add instant elegance to cake plates, dessert trays, entrée and sandwich servings. Use under table centerpieces and plants, for decorations and crafts, too.

Silver Foil
4 in. Round
2104-V-90404 Pk./12 $2.49
6 in. Round
2104-V-90116 Pk./18 $2.49
8 in. Round
2104-V-90006 Pk./12 $2.49
10 in. Round
2104-V-90007 Pk./6 $2.49
12 in. Round
2104-V-90412 Pk./4 $2.49

Gold Foil
4 in. Round
2104-V-90304 Pk./12 $2.49
6 in. Round
2104-V-90306 Pk./18 $2.49
8 in. Round
2104-V-90308 Pk./12 $2.49
10 in. Round
2104-V-90310 Pk./6 $2.49
12 in. Round
2104-V-90312 Pk./4 $2.49

Grease-Proof White

4 in. Round	2104-V-90204	Pk./30	$1.99
6 in. Round	2104-V-90206	Pk./20	$1.99
8 in. Round	2104-V-90208	Pk./16	$1.99
10 in. Round	2104-V-90210	Pk./10	$1.99
12 in. Round	2104-V-90212	Pk./6	$1.99
14 in. Round	2104-V-90214	Pk./4	$1.99
10 x 14 in. Rectangle	2104-V-90224	Pk./6	$1.99

Cake Accents
Romantic accents add a sparkling beauty and elegance to cakes.

White Pearl Beading
Molded on one continuous 5-yard strand. Remove before cutting and serving cake. 6 mm beads.
211-V-1990 $3.99

Baby

Start planning the party! From pink to blue, and themes in between, this dazzling array of Wilton products will inspire you to make the cutest things for your baby celebration.

Shower Accessories

Decorate, entertain and celebrate the new baby with a selection of clever shower accessories!

NEW!

Mommy-to-Be Sash
Honorary sash lets the Mommy–to-Be know she is special. Polyester. 8 ft. long.
1003-V-1007 $4.99

NEW!

Tummy Belt Baby Shower Game
Good-natured game lets guests guess mom-to-be's tummy size by cutting off a length of sash. Sash measures 150 ft. long.
1003-V-1041 $3.99

Decorate-A-Bib Shower Game
Fun shower activity entertains guests as they create personalized bibs for the new baby. Includes 6 bibs (6.25 x 5.75 in.) and 6 permanent color markers.
1003-V-1072 Pk./6 $9.99

NEW!

NEW! ECO-OCCASIONS BABY SHOWER DECORATIONS
Show your love for baby and the earth! Crafted in recycled paper, soy-based ink, cotton ribbon or twine.

Garland
6 ft. long.
1004-V-3100
$4.99

Centerpiece
8.5 x 9.25 in.
1004-V-3101
$4.99

Mobile
10.5 in. wide x 2.2 ft. long.
1004-V-3102
$4.99

Trivia Coasters
Fun baby shower game—20 clever baby-related trivia questions printed on drink coasters. Play the game and see which guest table has the most correct answers.
1003-V-2501 Pk./20 $5.99

Autograph Mat
Holds a 5 x 7 in. photo, with room for autographs and good wishes from friends and family. Few gifts touch so many like this one! For use in an 11 x 14 in. frame. Pen included.
1009-V-1106 $5.99

Celebrate the New Baby with Special Stationery!

Announce the birth, and invite guests to baby's first milestone events.

Baby Feet Invitations
Beautifully designed in white 80 lb. card stock with pastel and white pearlized baby feet embossed trim. Professionally print at home at www.wiltonprint.com. 5.5 x 8.5 in. invitations; 5.75 x 8.75 in. envelopes.
1008-V-8135 Pk./12 $4.99

Faith Cross Stationery
Inspiring design adds a beautiful touch to spiritual events. Beautifully crafted in white 80 lb. card stock with white pearlized trim. Professionally print at home at www.wiltonprint.com.

Invitations
White with white border and cross accent. Invitation: 5.5 x 8.5 in.; envelope: 5.75 x 8.75 in.
1008-V-775 Pk./12 $4.99

Cross Seals
Self adhesive, silvertone, 1 in. diameter.
1008-V-2337 Pk./50 $2.99

Eco-Occasions Bear Fill In Stationery
Crafted in recycled paper. You write in the information on this cute die cut design. Invitation: 5.5 x 8.5 in.; envelope: 5.75 x 8.75 in.
1008-V-120 Pk./8 $4.99

Thank You Cards
1008-V-121 Pk./8 $4.99

NEW!

Favor Boxes, Bags & Baking Cups

Fun finishing touches add flair to baby's celebration.

NEW!

Eco-Occasions Favor Boxes
Crafted in recycled paper, soy- based ink, cotton ribbon. 2 x 2 x 2 in. Plate not included.
1004-V-3105 Pk./6 $5.99

Favor Boxes
Each box has 2 acetate windows. 2 in. x 2 in. x 2 in. square paper boxes are easy to assemble. Candy not included.
1003-V-1017 Pk./12 $5.99

Favor Tote Bags
Fill with your favorite baby shower candy or a small gift. Paper bags measure 3 x 2.25 x 5.5 in. Candy not included.
1003-V-1055 Pk./12 $5.99

Ribbon Favor Bags
Paper bags hold treats and small gifts. Thread the ribbon through the holes at top of bag to close. 2.75 x 4.5 x 1.4 in. Includes 12 ribbon lengths. Candy, plate and curling ribbon not included.
1003-V-1053 Pk./12 $5.99

Party Bags

Fill with candy, cookies and other goodies; great for gifts and surprises, too! 20 plastic bags, 20 ties included. 4 x 9.5 in.
Pk./20 $2.09

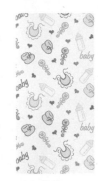

Baby Feet	Rubber Ducky	Baby
1912-V-1100	**1912-V-1275**	**1912-V-2365**

Baking Cups

Microwave-safe paper. Standard size, 2 in. diameter, pack 75; mini size, 1.25 in. diameter, pack 100. **$2.09**

Baby Feet Standard	Rubber Ducky Standard	Ducky Standard
415-V-113	**415-V-378**	**415-V-1016**
Mini 415-V-112	**Pk./50 $1.59**	**Mini 415-V-1017**

BABY

Favor-Making Kits

Oh-so-cute baby shower favors add so much to the celebration. Conveniently packaged in larger quantities to complete your favor making in no time at all. Personalize the tags at www.wiltonprint.com; it's easy to do, just download the template and print! Use as a place card, add an announcement or a thank you note. Add your favorite candy (not included), and your favors are ready for the party!

Pacifier Favor Kit
Perfect for fun baby celebrations! Pacifiers measure 2.5 in. long. Multicolor pastel assortment includes: 20 favor containers, 20 ribbons, 20 print-your-own tags, 2 test sheets.
1003-V-1062 Pk./20 $24.99

Rattle Favor Kit
Baby rattles look so sweet at each place setting. Rattles measure 4 in. long. Multicolor pastel assortment includes: 20 favor containers, 20 ribbons, 20 print-your-own tags, 2 test sheets.
1006-V-572 Pk./20 $24.99

Pail Favor Kit
Perfect for the baby celebration. Pails measure 2 in. high with 1.25 in. high handle and are all white. Includes: 18 favor containers, 18 ribbons, 18 print-your-own tags, 2 test sheets. Tulle and safety pin accent not included.
1006-V-916 Pk./18 $24.99
Pail Only 1006-V-915 $1.29 each

Baby Bottle Favor Kit
Mom-to-be will love these adorable favor containers. Bottles measure 4 in. high. Multicolor pastel assortment includes: 24 favor containers, 24 ribbons, 24 print-your-own tags, 2 test sheets. Bear accent not included.
1006-V-577 Pk./24 $24.99
Bottles Only 1006-V-696 Pk./6 $5.99

Baby Block Favor Kit
Favorite baby icon celebrates the big occasion. Blocks measure 1.75 in. square. Multicolor pastel assortment includes: 20 favor containers, 20 ribbons, 20 print-your-own tags, 2 test sheets. Tulle not included.
1006-V-284 Pk./20 $24.99

Favor Accents

Add special touches to your baby favors, gift tie-ons and table decorations.

Baby Bracelets*
Pink, blue, yellow, mint green. 1.25 in. high.
1103-V-56 Pk./6 $2.29

Mini Clothes Pins*
Pink, lavender, blue, yellow, mint green.
1.3 in. high.
1103-V-27 Pk./20 $1.99

Shower Rattles*
Pink, lavender, blue, yellow, mint green.
3.75 in. high.
1103-V-29 Pk./6 $2.99

⚠ *WARNING: CHOKING HAZARD
Small parts. Not for children under 3 years.

Newborn Baby Figurines*
1 in. high.
1103-V-62 Pk./6 $1.99

Mini Baby Bottles*
Pink, lavender, blue, yellow, mint green.
1.25 in. high.
1103-V-16 Pk./20 $1.99

Pacifiers*
Pink, lavender,
blue, yellow,
mint green.
.75 in. high.
**1003-V-1086
Pk./20 $2.99**

Safety Pins*
1.5 in. long.
Pk./20 $1.99

Pink 1103-V-21
Blue 1103-V-26

Cookie Cutters

NEW!

4-Pc. Baby Cutter Set
Carriage, rocking horse, bear, onesie, each
approximately 3 in. Coated metal.
2308-V-1067 Set/4 $4.79

Candles

Wilton gives you more choices! Top your cake
with candles in the perfect colors. Check out
our handpainted details and clean-burning,
matching designs.

Rubber Ducky
1.5 in. high.
2811-V-9337 Set/6 $3.89

Baby Things
Approx. 2 in. high.
2811-V-855 Set/4 $3.89

Shimmer
2½ in. high.
**2811-V-3664
Pk./10
$2.19**

Tricolor
2½ in. high.
**2811-V-782
Pk./10 $2.19**

Favor Candy

Fun shapes, beautiful colors, great flavors!
Wilton candy makes the perfect filler for
favors, treat bags, candy dishes.

Baby Talk
Fruit flavored.
10 oz. bag.
1006-V-1115 $4.19

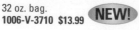

Mint Drops
Pastel. Certified
Kosher. 14 oz. bag.
1006-V-788 $6.29

32 oz. bag.
1006-V-3710 $13.99 **NEW!**

NEW!

White Gum Drops
Fruit flavored.
12 oz. bag.
1006-V-9048 $6.29

Pastel Pearls
Fruit flavored. 10 oz.
bag.Certified Kosher.
1006-V-904 $4.19

NEW!

Baby Feet
Sweet/tart fruit
flavored. 12 oz. bag.
1006-V-9047 $6.29

Pastel Jelly Beans
Fruit flavored.
12 oz. bag.
1006-V-9050 $4.19

Mini Pacifiers
Sweet/tart fruit
flavored. 12 oz. bag.
1006-V-540 $6.29

Pillow Mints
10 oz. bag. Pastel. **1006-V-858 $4.19**
48 oz. bag. Pastel. **1006-V-379 $20.99**

48 oz. bag. White.
1006-V-3711 $20.99 **NEW!**

**Jordan
Almonds**
Certified Kosher.
16 oz. bag. Pastel.
1006-V-779 $7.99
16 oz. bag. White.
1006-V-778 $7.99
44 oz. bag. Pastel.
1006-V-1133 $21.99
44 oz. bag. White.
1006-V-1134 $21.99

ORDER TOLL FREE: 800-794-5866

Bakeware

NEW!

Rocking Horse
This happy hobby horse sets the pace for a birthday that rocks! It's a favorite kids shape that's also ideal for showers and playgroup parties. One-mix pan is 11 x 12.75 x 2 in. deep. Aluminum.
2105-V-2009 $12.99

#1
Add the #1 cake to all the important first celebrations. One-mix pan is 12.75 x 8.5 x 2 in. deep. Aluminum.
2105-V-1194 $12.99

Baby Buggy
It's a precious carriage design for shower and christening, for cakes or elegant salads and gelatins. One-mix pan is 11.25 x 11.25 x 2 in. deep. Aluminum.
2105-V-3319 $12.99

3-D Duck
This bathtime favorite will make a big splash at baby showers. Five adorable designs included. Two-piece pan takes 5½ cups batter. 9 x 5 x 7 in. high. Aluminum.
2105-V-2094 $16.49

Baby Bottle
Here's the formula for a great shower or baby naming celebration—serve a delightful dessert made in this adorable Baby Bottle Pan! Its outstanding detail creates exciting cakes along with molded mousse, gelatin and ice cream. One-mix pan is 13.75 x 7.25 x 2.5 in. deep. Aluminum.
2105-V-1026 $12.99

Teddy Bear
Everybody just loves teddy bears. This cutie will be busy all year 'round with birthdays, school parties and baby showers. No time for hibernating with all these fun events on the agenda. One-mix pan is 13.5 x 12.25 x 2 in deep. Aluminum.
2105-V-1193 $12.99

Cake Server
Whimsical stacked blocks spell out B-A-B-Y on the handle. Crafted in plastic with serrated edge. 10 in. long.
1006-V-1312 $5.99

Candy Molds

Fun-shaped, reusable molds celebrate baby over and over again. Making candy is easy to do, complete directions are included! Use with Wilton Candy Melts brand confectionery coating. **$1.99**

NEW!

Baby Pretzel Mold
Position pretzel rod and refrigerate to set. 2 designs, 6 cavities.
2115-V-2101

Baby Treats
5 designs, 5 cavities.
2115-V-4447

Baby Bottles Lollipop
1 design, 6 cavities.
2115-V-1560

Baby Shower
4 designs, 11 cavities.
2115-V-1710

Mini Baby Icons
5 designs, 20 cavities.
2115-V-1537

Rubber Ducky
1 design, 6 cavities.
2115-V-1565

Candy Melts
Ideal for molding, dipping or coating. Artificially vanilla flavored unless otherwise indicated. 14 oz. bag. Certified Kosher Dairy. **$2.99**

Orange 1911-V-1631	**Pink** 1911-V-447
Yellow 1911-V-463	**Blue** 1911-V-448
Dark Cocoa 1911-V-358	**Lavender** 1911-V-403
Light Cocoa 1911-V-544	**White** 1911-V-498
Dark Cocoa Mint 1911-V-1920	

See pages 196-200 for more Wilton candy items.

BABY

The *Wilton*® School

of Cake Decorating & Confectionery Art

in Darien, Illinois

Learn cake decorating from the experts—attend a course at The Wilton School! From the first class in a Chicago kitchen in 1929, The Wilton School has provided professionals and hobbyists with the world's most complete cake decorating education. Students have come from 90 countries and all 50 states to receive one-on-one guidance from world-class instructors. Register now!

THE MASTER COURSE

Join students from around the world at the most comprehensive decorating course! In 2 exciting weeks, students learn the skills to become a pro—20 borders, 15 flowers including The Wilton Rose. Learn color flow, piping gel and figure piping. All of these lead to the design, assembly and decoration of a 3-tiered wedding cake. Virtually all materials included.

SUPPLEMENTARY CLASSES

(available during the Master Course)
Expand your skills with individual specialty courses in rolled fondant, figure piping, fondant modeling, candy making, sugar art and Isomalt design! Each session will make you a more versatile decorator.

EXPLORE OTHER GREAT CLASSES!

Real Tiered Cakes, Lambeth, Advanced Sugar Artistry, Chocolate Inspirations, Advanced Gum Paste & Fondant.

1-DAY WORKSHOPS

Baking, Art of Sweet Tables, Artistic Gelatin, Petits Fours and Mini Cakes, Cupcakes Galore and more!

CHECK OUT OUR WEEKEND AND BILINGUAL CLASSES!

For class schedules, details and enrollment, visit **www.school.wilton.com** or call 630-810-2888 or 800-772-7111, ext. 2888.

Certificate of Approval to operate issued by the Illinois State Board of Education, 100 N. First Street, Springfield, IL 62777.

INDEX

BE SURE TO SEE...
You'll find dozens of new products and designs in the 2010 Wilton Yearbook. Here are a few we think you'll find particularly exciting!

Discover the

You can decorate the perfect party cake! Let a friendly Wilton Method Instructor show you how, step-by-step, in our fun 4-lesson classes. In Wilton Method Classes, we've introduced thousands of people to the fun and excitement of cake decorating. Our trained instructors guide you as you create perfectly-formed flowers, borders and accents that make cakes unforgettable. It's a great chance to have fun, make new friends and learn a skill that will make family celebrations more exciting. You can do it!

Course 1
Discover Cake Decorating

Start here and learn the essentials you need to create amazing cakes! In no time, you'll be decorating stars, shells and messages for a sensational birthday cake. From baking the perfect cake to mastering the beautiful Wilton Rose, your friendly Instructor will guide you through every step.

Course 2
Flowers and Borders

Build on your skills from Course 1 with a garden of amazing icing flowers! Rosebuds, lilies, daffodils, mums and more—we cover them all, along with elegant borders like reverse shells and rosettes. Finish with an impressive flower basket cake accented with your beautiful blooms!

Course 3
Fondant and Tiered Cakes

Discover the beauty of decorating with rolled fondant—for covering cakes, shaping fun figures and hand-molding elegant flowers. Create dazzling holiday flowers like poinsettias, along with beautiful fondant accents like embroidery, ruffles and lace. For a Grand Finale, you'll decorate a towering tiered cake with fondant embellishments.

Sign up today for a class near you!

In U.S.A. call 800-942-8881 or visit www.wilton.com
In Canada, call (416) 679-0790 x200 or E-mail classprograms@wilton.ca
In Mexico, visit www.wiltonenespanol.com